WITHDRAWN

John Dewey

The Later Works, 1925–1953

Volume 2: 1925–1927

EDITED BY JO ANN BOYDSTON

TEXTUAL EDITOR, BRIDGET A. WALSH

With an Introduction by James Gouinlock

Carbondale and Edwardsville

Southern Illinois University Press

Copyright © 1984 by the Board of Trustees,
Southern Illinois University
All rights reserved
Manufactured in the United States of America
Designed by Richard Hendel

CENTER FOR
SCHOLARLY EDITIONS
AN APPROVED TEXT
MODERN LANGUAGE
ASSOCIATION OF AMERICA

®

Editorial expenses for this edition have been met in part by grants from the
National Endowment for the Humanities. Publishing expenses have been met in
part by grants from the John Dewey Foundation and from Mr. Corliss Lamont.

Library of Congress Cataloging in Publication Data

Dewey, John, 1859–1952.
  The later works, 1925–1953.

  Vol. 2 has introd. by James Gouinlock.
  Continues The middle works, 1899–1924.
  Includes indexes.

  CONTENTS: v. 1. 1925.—v. 2. 1925–1927.—v. 3. 1927–1928.
  1. Philosophy—Collected works. I. Boydston, Jo Ann, 1924–.
B945.D41 1981   191   80-27285
ISBN 0-8093-1131-3 (V. 2)

Contents

Introduction by James Gouinlock   ix

ESSAYS   1

The Development of American Pragmatism   3

Corporate Personality   22

A Naturalistic Theory of Sense-Perception   44

Individuality and Experience   55

Events and the Future   62

The Meaning of Value   69

Value, Objective Reference and Criticism   78

The Ethics of Animal Experimentation   98

Affective Thought   104

Art in Education—and Education in Art   111

What Is the Matter with Teaching?   116

The "Socratic Dialogues" of Plato   124

Substance, Power and Quality in Locke   141

William James in Nineteen Twenty-Six   158

Bishop Brown: A Fundamental Modernist   163

America's Responsibility   167

America and the Far East   173

Highly Colored White Lies   176

Is China a Nation or a Market?   181

We Should Deal with China as Nation to   185
Nation

The Problem of Turkey   189

Church and State in Mexico   194

Mexico's Educational Renaissance   199

From a Mexican Notebook   206

REVIEWS   211

Practical Democracy. Review of Walter   213
Lippmann's *The Phantom Public*

The Changing Intellectual Climate. Review of   221
Alfred North Whitehead's *Science and the
Modern World*

A Key to the New World. Review of Bertrand   226
Russell's *Education and the Good Life*

Review of Graham Wallas's *The Art of*   231
Thought

The Public and Its Problems   235

    1. Search for the Public   238

    2. Discovery of the State   259

    3. The Democratic State   282

    4. The Eclipse of the Public   304

    5. Search for the Great Community   325

    6. The Problem of Method   351

MISCELLANY   373

1946 Introduction to *The Public and Its*   375
Problems

Dedication Address of the Barnes Foundation   382

Literature or Mathematics? Comment on   386
Raymond Weeks's *Boys' Own Arithmetic*

Foreword to William James Durant's *The Story*   387
of Philosophy

An International Symposium on Scholasticism   388

APPENDIX   391

Value and Thought-Process by David Wight   393
Prall

NOTES   403

TEXTUAL APPARATUS   405

Textual Principles and Procedures by Fredson   407
Bowers

Textual Notes   419

Textual Commentary   421

Emendations List   434

Alterations in Typescripts   451

Line-end Hyphenation   471

Substantive Variants in Quotations   473

Checklist of Dewey's References   482

INDEX   489

Introduction
By James Gouinlock

John Dewey was not the sort of philosopher who confines himself to technical and abstruse subjects. He wrote on a much wider variety of topics than most philosophers. He wrote essentially to educate—not by means of prescription, but by making the meanings of life experience as luminous as possible. When he did engage in technical analysis (and many of his writings are of this sort), he did so in order to provide the assumptions of thought and action that would be most effective in the conduct of life. Accordingly, even the technical subjects are treated not only with extraordinary rigor and learning but with insight, imagination, and humanity as well.

The writings contained in the present volume are typically diverse. In the period from 1925 to 1927 he wrote, for example, on conditions in China, Turkey, and Mexico, drawing on his first-hand experience in those nations. He analyzed Locke's theory of knowledge, engaged in controversy concerning value theory, assessed the meaning of American pragmatism, maintained his fundamental concern with education, analyzed aesthetic experience, and in *The Public and Its Problems* (the only book in this volume) produced a systematic treatment of the problems of politics in modern industrial society. He even advanced a method for interpreting the Socratic dialogues of Plato.

In this heterogeneity we also find a remarkable uniformity. Most of the works of 1925–27, like so many of Dewey's other writings, are unified by the theme of the function of ideas in human conduct. Realization of the good life depends, in Dewey's view, on the exercise of intelligence. Indeed, his instrumentalism when fully explicated is a theory concerning the nature of intelligent conduct. Instrumentalism is conspicuously in evidence throughout the following pages. In this uniformity we have evidence of the efficacy of a coherent philosophic point of view in analyzing the plural forms of human experience. The Introduction cannot refer to all the pieces included in this volume, nor can it include an examination of all the issues to which Dewey attended. However, a great deal of what Dewey wrote in this period can be illuminated by reference to his conception of intelligent conduct which is therefore selected as the most suitable theme to develop. Before turning to the texts themselves, it is appropriate to provide a brief summary of the nature of Dewey's instrumentalism.

This eminently practical philosophy begins with a technical analysis of meaning and truth. The meaning of a concept is determined by the effects that are presumed to occur to the conceived entity when it functions in relation to other entities. The meaning of "glass," for example, is all of the functions of the material we call glass: it will shatter if dropped, will not be permeated by water but will be by light, will come into existence as the consequence of certain operations, and so on. Likewise, the meaning of a proposition is the consequences presumed to follow from the conditions specified in the proposition. The meaning of "this is a tree" is the sum of the tree's functions with its environment: it has roots, it grew from a seed, it can be cut with a saw, it is a shelter from sun and rain, etc. Meanings, then, are not something antecedently given and intuited, but are determined by experimental operations. To find the meaning of "glass," or of "tree," one must perform various operations with the things so denominated.

The truth of a proposition is determined by performing the requisite operations and observing whether the results are in fact those entailed by the meaning of the proposition. "This is a tree" is verified by tests—usually very simple ones. Perhaps, however, the alleged tree is really made of plastic. Hence certain predicted experiences will not in fact occur. The acquisition of new knowledge, as distinguished from what others have already recorded, is always a matter of engaging in some kind of conduct, simple or complex, deliberate or accidental, in relation to the matter being investigated.

Knowledge, then, is inseparable from action. In controlled inquiry, action is directed by a hypothesis. One might hypothesize, for example, that certain seeds when planted, fertilized, and cultivated in a prescribed manner would provide a certain yield of grain per acre. The hypothesis specifies conditions to be introduced in order to produce a certain result. The inquirer must then perform definite operations—planting, fertilizing, cultivating, etc.—in order to test the hypothesis. When the operations are performed as prescribed, the inquirer can discover whether the hypothesis is in fact correct. Thus ideas direct conduct. It should be stressed that hypotheses conceived in this way are creative; they are proposals for reconstructing present conditions in order to produce a future result. The processes of nature may be deliberately reordered according to a plan, with the purpose of establishing more favorable outcomes. These plans, or hypotheses, may be extremely inventive, prescribing reconstructions hitherto unexampled.

Finally, it must be noted that inquiry always takes place, according to instrumentalism, in response to what Dewey calls a problematic situation: there is something wrong—something lacking, obstructing, or unmanageable in ongoing experience. Inquiry takes place in order to remedy these deficiencies. It aims at establishing a unified and determinate situation in lieu of what is problematic. The researcher looks for a greater yield of food grains. The traveler lost in the woods looks for a way out. The situation prompting inquiry will become unified when yields per acre are increased or when a way is found out of the forest. The relevant hypotheses are verified when the specified actions have the predicted result. Normally, there is personal satisfaction attending the successful transformation of the situation, but it is not such satisfaction that verifies the hypotheses at issue.

In the process of inquiry, events in the situation acquire added meaning. The lost traveler considers, for example, that the vague sounds in the distance are those of axes cutting into tree trunks. The sounds are no longer mere sounds; they are significant. They imply the presence of other events—events that mean a return to safety. Or certain constituents in a grain of wheat, say, are no longer opaque in meaning; they are found to aid in the multiplication of grains on the stalk. As we learn how various conditions function in relation to each other, they become more meaningful. At the same time, they become more valuable, for we know how to act with them in order deliberately to transform situations causing distress into situations causing satisfaction.

The instrumentalist theory is in contrast to both rationalism and classical empiricism. The rationalist supposes that knowledge is the direct intuition of essences; the empiricist supposes that it is a summary of antecedently given sense data. In both cases knowing is passive; it does not imply action. Due to the inaction, moreover, the "knowledge" gained would not be of the functional relations between events in nature. In the case of both rationalism and empiricism, ideas are not conceived as anticipations of the future but as mirrors of what is given. Accordingly, neither the rationalist nor the empiricist arrives at the notion that ideas may be used creatively to give specific direction to action. Rather than be passively accepted as mental replicas of the *status quo*, ideas can be used aggressively in the service of an enriched experience. Instrumentalism teaches the organic unity of thought, action, and the values of experience. This teaching pervades Dewey's writings on a multitude of subjects, as we shall see at once.

Appropriately, the first essay in the volume is "The Development of American Pragmatism." In this article Dewey is principally concerned to set forth the main ideas in the pragmatism of Charles Sanders Peirce and William James. Peirce, Dewey notes, adopted the term "pragmatism" because it denotes methods of thought and inquiry addressed to the solution of definite practical problems. It is inquiry for a specific purpose in response to encountered problems, whether in the laboratory or daily life. Inquiry, in other words, occurs in the context of activity, and its ends are given by that context.

Peirce's pragmatism, Dewey holds, was focused above all on a theory of meaning, and he quotes (this volume, pp. 4–5) Peirce's statement that the meaning of a term lies in its conceivable bearing on practice. Peirce is clear, however, as Dewey shows, that pragmatism does not glorify action for its own sake. Action is not the end, but the intermediary. One can determine the actual import of a conception only by undertaking action, and only by that action which is indicated by the concept. Dewey notes with appreciation that for Peirce a concept gives a "rule of action," and that is its great value. By knowing the meaning of "glass," for example, we know how to behave with glass. Dewey observes that Peirce's realism consists in the latter's contention that concepts provide universal rules of action.

Peirce, according to Dewey, wrote as a logician, while James wrote as a humanist and educator. It is to these differences in intent that Dewey ascribes the differences in their respective versions of pragmatism. James was more interested in the unique and the individual; so he is more the nominalist: the meaning of a concept is in the experiences that persons actually have, rather than in the experiences that conceivably could follow from a concept. Dewey sees the pragmatic method used with particular effect by James in the way that he spells out the consequences of holding particular ideas. In being either a monist or a pluralist, for example, one is in effect committed to certain kinds of evaluation and behavior. Monism (patterned after absolute idealism) regards the nature and history of the world as forever fixed according to a pattern of antecedently determined necessity. A true monist, then, cannot regard human action as introducing genuine alternatives and novelties into the course of events. The monist regards the human agent as no more than an actor playing a part written for him from eternity. A pluralist, on the other hand, believes that human endeavor really does introduce change and novelty. The future is not "foredoomed," as James put it. Accordingly, the monist resigns himself to necessity, while the pluralist throws himself into life with vigor and zest, confident that his exertions on their own account will make a difference. The world is still incomplete, and events can take different directions, depending on human participation in their movement.[1]

Dewey gives great praise to what he calls the "biological psychology" in James's *The Principles of Psychology* (1890). Inspired by Darwin, James discovered the real nature of thought. Ideas, including scientific ideas, function in life experience to direct us from present to future experiences. Science, or reasoning, is not an imposition on biological life but is the most functional constituent of it. When intelligence is construed in this way, we see that human nature is most functional when it is most intelligent. Pragmatism, in other words, puts intelligence and reflection in the most prominent role in life activity.

1. In the essay "Events and the Future" (pp. 62–68), Dewey criticizes an argument by C. D. Broad because Broad conceives of objects as "ultimate and eternal." Dewey shows that such a conception dictates precisely the consequence of monism: the future is closed to real alternatives.

The differences between Peirce and James are of a minor sort, Dewey believes. What they hold in common is of the greatest importance:

> Pragmatism . . . does not insist upon antecedent phenomena but upon consequent phenomena; not upon the precedents but upon the possibilities of action. And this change in point of view is almost revolutionary in its consequences. An empiricism which is content with repeating facts already past has no place for possibility and for liberty. It cannot find room for general conceptions or ideas, at least no more than to consider them as summaries or records. But when we take the point of view of pragmatism we see that general ideas have a very different role to play than that of reporting and registering past experiences. They are the bases for organizing future observations and experiences.[2]

Instrumentalism as a development of pragmatism has its distinctive nature, Dewey says, in carrying out in more detail the essential insights of Peirce and James. A complete logic would distinguish all propositional forms in terms of their respective functions and interrelations in the actual processes of experimental inquiry. (Dewey's most systematic undertaking of this task was published later, in 1938: *Logic: The Theory of Inquiry*.) Dewey regards pragmatism to be in some ways a distinctively American philosophy in its origins. Conceived more broadly, however, pragmatism stands in the great tradition of the British and French Enlightenment, for it perpetuates and develops the ideal of making intelligence the possession of each and all, and making intelligence operative in the conduct of life.

The second article, "Corporate Personality," is a model of pragmatic analysis. In response to the long-standing legal/philosophic problem of how a legal or corporate entity can be regarded as a responsible agent, Dewey insists that we abjure forever the attempt to find in such entities an antecedently existing essence that qualifies them to be treated as personalities. Dewey's analysis proceeds by inquiring what such entities *do*. They are defined functionally. When persons or groups are invested, say, with rights and responsibilities, their subsequent behavior is different.

2. P. 12.

At issue are the powers and limitations of corporate bodies. What do we want their behavior to be? Depending on how that question is answered, such bodies are permitted and/or required to behave in certain ways. To be a bearer of rights, for example, would mean simply and only that certain kinds of behavior would be legally protected and certain other kinds required. There is no mysterious essence that needs to be invoked to determine the meaning of corporate agency.

The next article, "A Naturalistic Theory of Sense-Perception," is largely a refutation of a certain approach to theory of knowledge. This approach Dewey calls epistemological, in contrast to his own view, which he calls naturalistic. The subject matter of this essay is not pragmatism or instrumentalism, but in a profound sense its method is. Accordingly, it is fitting to present some of Dewey's discussion and to show in what sense it exemplifies instrumentalism.

The reigning theory of sense perception—whether from the British or Continental tradition—is the so-called epistemological view. It typically holds that perceptual images are subjective; they occur *within* the alleged mind-substance. These images are thought to resemble external physical objects. Indeed, these objects are thought to be the cause of the images. As this theory has it, then, what is experienced is not the external object at all, but the image of it. Accordingly, we have no access to the outer world; its existence can at best only be inferred. Human experience, as such, exists in the mind alone, and the human agent is entirely isolated by the very nature of his own experience. This subjectivism had bedevilled philosophy for more than two centuries, and Dewey must be credited with making some of the most devastating analyses of it.

He finds some fatal difficulties in the epistemological position. One of them is that the argument is given plausibility only by systematically confusing the *causes* of a perception with the *constituents* of a perception. One of the causes of the occurrence of a perception is, indeed, sense organs; but, Dewey says, the perception itself does not determine the nature of the qualities perceived. One simply perceives qualities, and the qualities, whatever their causes, are what they are perceived to be. Sense organs, of course, affect the properties perceived, but to acknowledge that much is not to say that what is perceived does not have these qualities. The object has these properties, however they may be produced.

The epistemologists have made the mistake of concluding that the properties perceived are properties *of* perception; they assume that perception itself constitutes these qualities. According to this argument, the qualities perceived are not characteristics of real events in the world. They are relegated to an existence within the mind, where, as images, they (conceivably) represent an external world. The epistemologists have made the error of (1) assuming that the cause of the properties perceived is perception itself and (2) absorbing the properties of things into their causes. To show the illogic of this argument, Dewey likens it to an analysis of brush painting. In studying brush painting, we learn about brushes and paintings and how brushes affect paintings; but paintings don't disappear into the brushes as a consequence of the analysis. In failing to distinguish perception from the means of perception, epistemologists have put the painting in the brush.

Dewey notes that epistemologists are fond of supporting the subjectivistic hypothesis by referring to such phenomena as the straight stick that looks bent when it is half submerged in water or seeing double when the eye is pressed with the finger. Surely, the epistemologists argue, such phenomena prove that the perceptions are within the mind, for the stick itself is really straight, while what we perceive is bent; and there is only one tree out there, but we have an image of two of them. In reply Dewey says that what we perceive is a function of an inclusive field (or situation, as he calls it in most other discussions). It is the constituents of this field that cause perceptions. In a field where light is refracted through media of two different densities (air and water), the straight stick appears bent. But it is *the stick* that is perceived and it is *the stick* that so appears. To say that a perception is not veridical is not to say that it is subjective. There is nothing in the analysis that constrains us to put the appearance within the mind. A similar analysis could be made for the two trees and the countless ingenious examples presented by epistemologists.

Not only does Dewey's naturalistic analysis accommodate all these phenomena, but the epistemologist, Dewey observes, conducts his argument by first taking for granted that such objects as eyes, fingers, trees, water, sticks (sticks somehow determined to be straight, at that!), etc., really exist. The existence imputed to these things is then used in an argument to prove that we really have no experience of them at all!

Dewey's analysis illustrates the fundamental character of his instrumentalism. While the epistemologists have advanced ideas that make our ordinary experience something essentially mysterious, Dewey's naturalistic approach restores the world to us and us to the world. Innocent of epistemological dialectics, we believe we function in a real world with real properties. We believe the events of this world exhibit a multitude of qualities; we actively seek out those that we especially appreciate, and we try to eliminate or avoid those that are hurtful. We believe we can acquire knowledge of the world and can discover how its array of properties comes into existence. The epistemologist declares that none of this is as it seems. We only mistakenly impute these traits to the world. The whole arena of existence is, they say, in the mind. With an instrumentalist analysis, on the other hand, our experience is once again evidential of reality. In other words, Dewey's theories are those which enlighten and clarify experience, helping us to function in the world, rather than making it opaque to us and making philosophy an exotic irrelevance.

Another brilliant article bearing on epistemology is "Substance, Power and Quality in Locke" (pp. 141–57). Locke's *Essay concerning Human Understanding* has been taken as one of the most influential sources of the sort of epistemology just examined. While admitting that Locke has some responsibility for views of this sort, Dewey points out in a fully documented analysis that Locke did not in fact succumb to all these errors. An analysis of the Locke article would be too much removed from the theme of this Introduction, but the reader of the article will learn that Locke himself was sensitive to the very distinctions that Dewey insists on in his naturalistic theory. Had Locke not, after all, persisted in holding the notion of atomistic substances with inherent essences, he logically would have been impelled to conclude that knowledge is of the relations between objectively experienced events.

"Individuality and Experience" (pp. 55–61) is one of the many writings in which Dewey argues that an instrumentalist use of ideas would be of enormous value in education. Educational theory and practice oscillate between demands for expression of individuality on the one hand and the imposition of rigid and uniform requirements on the other. The former arrangement leads to the failure to acquire the discipline needed for learning, while the latter ignores the variations in interest and ability that distinguish different students. Reiterating one of his most familiar themes, Dewey insists that the growth of students requires that they engage in intrinsically satisfying activity. The teacher must identify such activities for each pupil and show how they are guided by ideas as well as by practical technique. For the pupil, to have a full conception of such an activity is to have a conception of the plans and methods instrumental to it. It is to have a conception of intelligent conduct. Thus students will learn the value of intelligence as the means to an enriched experience and will more willingly embrace its methods. To acquire the techniques of intelligence is, moreover, to assume discipline voluntarily rather than have it imposed from without. Then students will have discipline and growth at once.

Dewey had a lifelong interest in value theory. The nature of value has to be understood in order to facilitate the actual processes of identifying, criticizing, constructing, and possessing values. Dewey's most fundamental thought in this regard is found in one of the great philosophic works of the modern era, *Experience and Nature*.[3] In the two articles on value theory in the present volume, the instrumentalist analysis of value is the central concern. Dewey exhibits in each case how values must be conceived as organic to thought and action. Some background can provide a full sense of the meaning of these articles.

The process of evaluation occurs in actual problematic situations. Something has gone wrong, is somehow unsatisfactory, and the agent or agents try to remedy the situation, resolving its problematic status and restoring integrated activity. In such situations, several possibilities for action might present themselves; these possibilities might, upon examination, turn out to be faulty in some way. Prior to investigation, then, all these possibilities must be regarded as problematic.

Consider the example of the man lost in the woods. In this

---

3. *The Later Works of John Dewey, 1925–1953*, ed. Jo Ann Boydston, vol. 1 (Carbondale: Southern Illinois University Press, 1981).

predicament he might study several alternatives. It might occur to him to climb a tall tree to get a better view; but on giving thought to the matter, he concludes that the trees are too difficult to climb and that he would risk serious injury in the attempt. Then he hears what appears to be the sound of axes striking timber. He considers heading in the direction where the sound seems to come from. There being, let us suppose, no evident drawback to this plan, the man proceeds to follow it. When he actually succeeds in finding the woodcutters, he will have achieved what Dewey calls value: a reunified situation. As this example illustrates, both thought and action are necessary for value. If we do not take thought, the chances for failure are much greater; and we cannot produce an integrated situation without taking action.

It was pointed out earlier that events in situations acquire additional meaning when their relations to other events are determined. Thus the sounds in the woods become meaningful when they are thought to be made by axes. The prospect of climbing a tree becomes more meaningful when it is thought to portend injury. Typically, some kind of inquiry is needed in order to take events out of their immediacy and determine their meaning. Values, then, are more meaningful than problematic goods; and they cannot as values be achieved without action directed by thought.

The first of the two articles to be considered against this background is "The Meaning of Value." It was written in response to an article by David Wight Prall in which Prall criticized Dewey's views and set forth a theory of his own. (Prall's article, "Value and Thought-Process," is republished as the Appendix to the present volume.) The crucial issue between Dewey and Prall is whether values are in any way constituted by thought. The burden of Prall's argument is that values are constituted simply by liking, and Dewey, of course, finds this view unacceptable. More specifically, Dewey criticizes Prall for declaring that "value" denotes a fixed essence, which is: to be constituted by liking. Dewey asks, "In the situations having value-quality, is liking the sole and exclusive ingredient from the side of the subject, or is thought also involved? . . . I state as explicitly as possible that I regard liking as an indispensable ingredient or constituent in those situations which have value quality, but not as a *sufficient* ingredient or constituent."[4] The dispute between Prall and Dewey is not verbal. Attainments consequent upon intelligently directed action must be distinguished from events in their immediacy. The difference between meaningless and meaningful events is all-important, yet Prall fails to recognize this distinction. Hence his analysis of value fails to provide the knowledge that is crucial to the conduct of life.

The second article, "Value, Objective Reference and Criticism," pursues the same themes, but with somewhat less reference to Prall. Dewey again insists on the ideational component in the constitution of value, and he likewise points out the role of deliberate action in constructing values. In this essay he gives attention to the affectional state that is a necessary condition of value. He finds ordinary language too vague and ambiguous to be of help in identifying this state. Explicitly following Ralph Barton Perry, he stresses that the liking, wanting, or whatever, is of a sort implying movement towards a specific object. Thus "value" has an objective reference and implies a fulfillment or consummation due to active exertion. Value implies a movement from one condition to another. Predictably, then, Dewey goes on to say that this movement implies an ideational function. If the object is to be deliberately sought, there has to be at least some idea of how that object will function in one's activity. In addition, there has to be at least a rudimentary conception of means, some plan in accordance with which the movement towards the object will proceed. These initial beliefs can be checked and corrected by further reflection and investigation, and consequently the inquirer may determine more reliably whether his intended object will function as anticipated. As such beliefs are revised, the very meaning of the object undergoes change, and hence also its value. Only by recognizing these ideational components of value do we have intellectual instruments at our disposal for effective action.[5]

---

4. See this volume, p. 73.
5. In his insistence on the ideational factors in the determination of value, Dewey goes beyond the position of Perry, who failed to identify the operative presence of ideas in movement toward an end. Dewey specifically acknowledges that his own position on these issues is the same as that of Santayana in *The Life of Reason*, vol. 5, *Reason in Science* (1906).

Instrumentalist chords are struck again in two more papers, "Affective Thought" and "Art in Education—and Education in Art." Here Dewey points out the continuities in the nature of art and science. Both are a function of practice. In each, the beginning of activity is occasioned by a problem in the relation between the human organism and its environment. Both the artist and the scientific inquirer in their respective activities are engaged in reconstructing their situation, and imaginative plans are required in each instance. They must select, manipulate, and reorder elements in the situation; and they aim for a new integration of the constituent elements. As so often elsewhere, Dewey wants to emphasize that inquiry is an activity. It is not a mere beholding, a passive contemplation, of alleged sense data or rational essences. And art, likewise, is not creation *de novo*, springing fully fledged from the mind. It is not an externalizing of artistic intuitions completed in the soul of the artist; but art, too, is a business carried on by the individual in and with his characteristic environment.

It is not a mere curiosity that art and science have common characteristics. What is shared by both is that they are forms of intelligent conduct. To recognize this fundamental similarity is to gain an understanding of the continuities of thought and experience. Art is a deliberate reordering of qualitative events to produce an aesthetic outcome. It is perfectly intelligible in Dewey's terms to say that art is a form of experimental inquiry. (Dewey, indeed, prefers to say that inquiry is a form of art.) When knowledge is thought to have nothing to do with the events of immediate experience, however, we cannot conceive how ideas can be used instrumentally to produce a qualitatively enriched situation. Inquiry and aesthetic experience are thought to be wholly discontinuous with each other. Hence science is regarded as something remote and aloof from experience; and aesthetic experience is thought to occur only in highly specialized environments, such as the art gallery or the concert hall. The split between the cognitive and the aesthetic plagues not just theory, but practice as well. We have a conception of neither art nor intelligence such that intelligence can be used to enrich experience, and this failure is felt in our daily life. It has become characteristic of our culture that sharp separations are made between activities that are aesthetic, practical, and intellectual. Aesthetic traits are systematically segregated from other dimensions of activity and experience—for example, from education and work. In these essays Dewey urges that we learn habits of artistic/intelligent behavior that will enable us to find the aesthetic in all experience.[6]

The survey of the presence of instrumentalism in this volume would be incomplete without some reference to the nine short articles running from page 167 to 210, which address such questions as American foreign policy; domestic issues (especially education) in China, Turkey, and Mexico; the outlawry of war; and international trade relations. What is conspicuous in them is Dewey's insistence that historical change of all sorts be governed by ideas appropriate to the respective cultures. As in any problematic circumstance, plans should not be imposed *a priori* and from without. Neither should they be a mere following of custom and precedent. Rather, plans should be formulated with regard to the special limitations and resources of the situation. Necessarily, the formulation of such plans must somehow take into account the traditions, beliefs, needs, abilities, and aspirations of the persons implicated in change. In this way, ideas can function successfully to mediate and direct change. In Dewey's reports of this period, he sometimes sees signs of change being conducted in this way. His exuberance on these occasions is almost unbounded.

Four book reviews were published in the period 1925–27. Dewey was an excellent reviewer, and the reader will find his comments extremely informative and stimulating. Three of the works reviewed, however, are mostly at a tangent to the theme of instrumentalism; so they will not be discussed. (One of the three, Graham Wallas's *The Art of Thought*, would appear at first to be eminently eligible for analysis. Dewey reports that he came to this work with keen anticipation but left it with great disappointment; for, if Wallas really knew anything about the art of thought, he didn't divulge it in this book.) The fourth review is of Walter Lippmann's *The Phantom Public* (1925). It will be in-

---

6. In the second of these articles, Dewey finds an ally in Alfred North Whitehead, and he makes extremely laudatory comments about Whitehead's *Science and the Modern World* (1925). Many of the themes of these articles are pursued in the dedication address delivered by Dewey at the inauguration of the Barnes Foundation, this volume, pp. 382–85.

structive to see what Dewey said about Lippmann's study, because *The Phantom Public* inspired Dewey to write *The Public and Its Problems*, which will receive sustained attention later.

The gravamen of Lippmann's analysis is that the public is not and cannot be equal to the tasks expected of it in democratic theory. Theory postulates an "omnicompetent citizen," who possesses in common with other citizens a universal moral code, keen and impartial public spirit, and command of all the facts necessary to make public policy decisions. According to theory, democracy is literally self-government: the public rules itself through its representatives.[7] Lippmann demolishes these assumptions. Even he, Walter Lippmann, a close and zealous student of public affairs, is insufficiently informed on most issues. What, then, of the ordinary citizen? He suffers from ignorance, apathy, and bias; and for these ills there is no remedy, Lippmann declares. We must reconstruct our conception of democracy. Governing is done by officials—"insiders," as Lippmann calls them—and it cannot be done otherwise. The proper role of the public is to recognize the occurrence of crises and then, by voting, to intervene on behalf of one set of insiders as opposed to another. The public cannot be expected to judge the issues on their merits. The most that it can do is judge that one party is seeking to do something which that party judges to be in the public interest, while another party is not.

Dewey's review acknowledges the justice in most of Lippmann's arguments. He agrees that the notion of the omnicompetent voter is a myth. He doubts, indeed, whether anyone ever really believed in such a being; but in any case a reconstruction in democratic theory is sorely needed. In this review, Dewey appears to have no essential quarrel with Lippmann but regards *The Phantom Public* as a beginning to the rethinking of democracy. Dewey immediately set to work at the task. His review was published in December of 1925. In January of 1926 he gave a series of lectures on these issues at Kenyon College. They were published in 1927 as *The Public and Its Problems*.

There is a sense in which *The Public and Its Problems* and not

---

7. A notable omission in Lippmann's book and Dewey's review is a specification of the authors of the reigning democratic theory. The conceptions to which Lippmann and Dewey refer, however, can be traced to Locke and Rousseau, among others.

Logic: The Theory of Inquiry is the culmination of Dewey's instrumentalism. The latter book, to be sure, systematizes functional logic; but *The Public and Its Problems* is a proposal for the actual realization of intelligent conduct in practical life. It is indeed a reconstruction of political—particularly democratic—theory. While Dewey himself is perhaps the greatest critic of the Enlightenment's concept of reason, he does not despair of intelligent political life, so long as the nature of intelligence is properly understood. He will by no means succumb to despair for democracy nor acknowledge that human beings are irreparably irrational. As we shall see, he will find it realistic to demand much more of the democratic citizen than Lippmann thought possible.

Dewey commences *The Public and Its Problems* with the complaint that the issue of the nature of the state has not yet been approached scientifically. Instead, mythical accounts of the state have been offered. From the time of Aristotle, these have taken the form of postulating inherent "state forming forces." When Aristotle says that man is by nature an animal that lives in a state, this to Dewey means no more than there is something about human nature such that men live in states. This is not profound; it is uninformative. Of course we know that men live in states, but such knowledge tells us nothing about how actual states come into existence, nor does it give us the first idea of why the state takes now one form and now another. Likewise, the idealists tell us that the state exists as the expression of an antecedently given will and reason. That is, again, there is postulated an inherent nisus towards the formation of the state; and with this account none of the specific characteristics and variations in the state can be explained. Or—as in the contract theory of classical liberalism—a definite and fixed pre-social human nature is posited, and from this conception the state with all its functions is deduced. In all such positions, Dewey remarks, the theorist has in fact merely observed the outcome of a given social process and has postulated the outcome as the cause. Logically, this procedure is no different from saying that opium makes you sleep because of its sleep inducing powers.

Dewey undertakes a scientific analysis of the state. To this end he distinguishes private and public forms of association. The conduct in private associations has consequences for the members. These Dewey calls direct consequences. But the activities of such groups often have consequences for persons who are not within the group. These Dewey calls indirect consequences. Sometimes indirect consequences are serious, persistent, and widespread. The persons affected by consequences of this sort Dewey denominates a public. A public comes into existence as the result of the behavior of private associations. Insofar as they produce this sort of indirect consequence, the activities of the private association have to be brought under some kind of management—the consequences have to be controlled or regulated. When the persons constituting a public perceive these indirect consequences, and when they communicate to each other an interest in taking action to regulate them, the state comes into being. Officials are selected with the duty of controlling these consequences in a manner responsible to the public. The officials are a government. The government and the public together constitute the state. The state is the politically organized public.

The analysis so far is worthy of some observation. On the negative side, it can be noted that the distinction between private and public is not as clear or as serviceable as it appears. Why should private associations be immune to interference? The family would seem to be preeminently a private association, yet members of this group are sometimes so abused by other members that we think it necessary to intervene on their behalf. In so doing, we regulate *direct* consequences. Does a contract between labor and management create a private association? In one sense it would seem so, yet we also think it appropriate for government authority to be used occasionally to constrain one or the other or both groups. Must we conclude that the association is not really private? How then do we distinguish private and public after all? Perhaps Dewey would have done well merely to speak of the problem of regulating the adverse consequences that arise out of social behavior *per se*, when these consequences are enduring, severe, and widespread. Additionally, his formulation of the origin and nature of the state gives special emphasis to the function of regulating unwelcome consequences. While this interpretation would be applauded by all those who prefer the state as it is conceived in classical liberalism, it is not in fact what Dewey himself intends. As virtually all of his relevant writings declare, the state should not be confined exclusively to preventing harm, but it should actively promote welfare, too, when necessary. (Dewey himself suggests as much in other passages of *The Public and Its Problems*.) There seems to be no inherent reason why the notion of a public could not be modified to incorporate groups enduring significant deprivation not inflicted on them by others. A more curious difficulty in Dewey's analysis is that, in one important sense, it is not scientific. Dewey purports to be describing the state; but surely, as he himself would insist, what we have is not *the* state, but states, which have come into existence in all manner of different ways—not least by conquest and exploitation, rather than through a public articulating itself politically. What Dewey has in fact done is to offer a proposal of what the state *ought* to be. It is, indeed, a rudimentary definition of the democratic state, with the implied assumption that this is the most desirable state.

Granting (readily) the normative assumptions, Dewey's analysis is most suggestive. He has attempted to provide a functional—that is, instrumentalist—definition of the public and the state. Rather than resort to ready-made and fixed social classifications, Dewey urges us to identify the groupings that actually emerge as a consequence of real behavior. Thus a public comes into existence, for example, as a consequence of one group exploiting another, or—on a lesser scale—of industries polluting the air and water. A public comes into being as a result of the existence of weapons of mass destruction. Another is formed due to the ambitions of a bureaucracy, and so forth. The same person will belong to different publics, depending on the different ways he is subjected to adverse effects from various sources. Some publics will be large, some small; some will be limited by geography, others will not. No two publics will have precisely the same membership (the group suffering from bureaucracy is not identical to that threatened with mass destruction); and any given public will have members from other publics. Insofar as new problems develop, change, and pass out of existence, publics will do likewise. As different historical situations occur, different publics are created and others vanish.

The state, accordingly, is an agency to meet the needs of a specific group with specific problems in a specific place and time. The form of governing institutions would not be conceived as eternal and immutable, but would change in order to perform particular functions in particular circumstances. Thus the state under some conditions might have much to do, and under others rather little. The state is not an all-inclusive entity (as it is according to Hegelians), incorporating the entire life of the community. The state is only one of the associations in which one participates. A person is a member of many associations, and in most instances these associations do not have consequences requiring regulation. "Thus it happens that the state, instead of being all absorbing and inclusive, is under some circumstances the most idle and empty of social arrangements."[8] Under many conditions, indeed, "the state is an impertinence."[9]

Publics are brought into existence and they pass away. Moreover, it is always an experimental and in some measure controversial question what conduct should be regulated and how it should be done. Thus the state is always in a process of formation and change. It always has to be rediscovered, Dewey says. "By its very nature, a state is ever something to be scrutinized, investigated, searched for."[10] Rigid adherence to given conceptions of what form the state should take and what it should do implies failure to acknowledge the fact of change and failure to contend with variations in historical conditions. In any case, according to Dewey's proposal for the state, all variations introduced for the sake of adapting institutions to social problems could take place only by using ideas instrumentally. Political action, like all action, would be guided by experimental ideas.

After elaborating these conceptions in the first two chapters, Dewey turns to a brief analysis of the events and ideas that led to the actual emergence of the democratic state. This emergence, he says, was marked by the liberation of the individual in theory and by his submergence in fact. The vast forces spawned by the industrial revolution have led to a regimentation of the ordinary individual. Human association is increasingly impersonal, and its forms are dictated by the demands of industrial production for private profit. Modern industrial life, that is, has had a profoundly damaging effect on the local, face-to-face community. Traditional communities have been largely disintegrated, and new forms of personal association have not emerged to replace

8. *The Public and Its Problems.* See this volume, p. 253.
9. Ibid., p. 261.
10. Ibid., p. 255.

them. Government is not used as the means to an "inclusive and fraternally associated public,"[11] but functions primarily to preserve the capitalist way of life. Any improvement must await the formation of a democratic public.

In Chapter 4, "The Eclipse of the Public," Dewey characterizes as realistically as anyone the failures of actual democratic practice. He rivals Lippmann in itemizing voter ignorance and apathy and the corruptions of democratic intent by powerful private interests. Dewey, however, is not resigned to these deficiencies. The problem in democratic politics is that the public is too bewildered to identify itself as a public. The social forces in industrial society are so many and so intricately intertwined that the public literally does not know what is happening to it and hence cannot recognize itself as a public. Until it does, it can take no effective action.

> The local face-to-face community has been invaded by forces so vast, so remote in initiation, so far-reaching in scope and so complexly indirect in operation, that they are, from the standpoint of the members of local social units, unknown.[12]

Once the public—or, more accurately, publics—are identified and organized as such, we may at least hope for improvement in political institutions and practices. The first condition for this transformation is effective communication. Through the media of communication, the public must acquire knowledge of those conditions that have created it and of how these conditions affect the values of associated life. Yet, Dewey says, we live in a Babel of communications. In the succeeding chapter he addresses himself to the creation of the democratic public. He calls it "Search for the Great Community."

The chapter begins with a characterization of the democratic community as a norm or ideal limit of human association. In democratic life each individual shares in forming and directing group activity, and each shares in the values created in associated life. By his interactions in social life, each person is engaged in a process of growth. His powers are liberated and formed in harmony with the interests of the groups in which he participates. Ideally, each group interacts flexibly and accommodatingly with

11. Ibid., p. 303.
12. Ibid., p. 316.

others. With these complementary and reinforcing relations between groups, the individual personality develops fully and harmoniously. Dewey characterizes individuality, liberty, equality, and fraternity in this context. E.g., "Liberty is that secure release and fulfillment of personal potentialities which take place only in rich and manifold association with others: the power to be an individualized self making a distinctive contribution and enjoying in its own way the fruits of association."[13] His point is to characterize traditional values such as liberty and individuality as modes of social behavior, rather than treating them—as in classical liberalism—as properties of the individual contradistinguished from society.

Dewey declines to state what political institutions such a community might create. To do so would be for him to abandon his contextualism and to seem to prescribe what it is for the democratic community itself to decide. In any case, the method of forming policies and guiding conduct would be thoroughly democratic and experimental. The method is consultative, of course, and the ideas that are presented for consideration would be examined as instruments for conduct. Their bearings on the life of the entire community would be studied; and when ideas are adopted as policies, they would take the form of specifying conditions to be introduced in order to reconstruct the problematic situations of the community.

Dewey is confident that human nature is capable of being democratic. People are not essentially anti-social and irrational. On the contrary, cooperative and experimental behavior can be learned and can be habitual. All habits, Dewey believes, are acquired. Human beings learn the modes of behavior already established in the activities in which they participate. If the individual functions in an environment where action as a matter of course embodies the appropriate habits, then intelligent and democratic behavior would be readily learned and massively reinforced. Dewey pursues the issue of the potentialities of human nature at greater length in his final chapter. At this point he remarks that our environment is highly deficient as a medium of democratic learning. While conceding that there is a large measure of freedom of inquiry and communication in the United

13. Ibid., p. 329.

States, he insists that we lack the means to utilize such freedom effectively. The social sciences remain primitive, and very few individuals possess experimental habits of thought. Hence freedom of thought and communication are lacking in efficacy, because they are insufficiently informed with knowledge and method. We have advertising and the brief, episodic, sensational news item as the principal media of communication. We have the means of education, inquiry, and communication as never before, but we haven't begun to use them adequately. He concludes this chapter by noting that communication of scientifically determined knowledge needn't be dry and unappealing. It might well be so, he says, were it not for the potency of art; and he suggests that the powers of artists be used in transmitting social knowledge.

The concluding chapter of *The Public and Its Problems* addresses two main issues: the nature and function of social inquiry, and the conditions under which the public could utilize the results of such inquiry. As a prelude to the first point, Dewey notes a principal obstacle to social inquiry: the persistent assumption that the question to be resolved is the proper relation of the individual to society, when "individual" and "society" are conceived as antithetical to each other. He declares that we still postulate a "ready-made and complete" individual existing independently of society. Then the fundamental social problem is conceived as the determination of a rule that prescribes the sphere of activity for this atomistic individual that shall be protected from social interference. The complement of this individualism is the notion of society as a single undifferentiated aggregate of these self-complete beings.

The trouble with this theory is that the atomistic individual is sheer myth. Likewise it is myth that society is a single mass. Individual human nature is not a fixed and original condition. It is a product, an outcome, of the interaction of the organism and the environment.[14] As the environment, above all the social environment, varies, so too does human nature. Society, for its part, is not a single entity. It is composed of a great plurality of groups.

14. For the most complete statement of Dewey's social psychology, see *Human Nature and Conduct, The Middle Works of John Dewey, 1899–1924*, ed. Jo Ann Boydston, vol. 14 (Carbondale: Southern Illinois University Press, 1983).

Individuals are not related to society as a whole. They are related to a variety of groups, and groups have diverse interrelations. On Dewey's assumptions, it is impossible to regard the individual as inherently antithetical to a social existence. There are conflicts, of course, but participation in associated life is a necessary condition of any growth for the individual. The individualistic position, moreover, seems to be oblivious to the values of shared experience. Conflicts occur, Dewey holds in this chapter, because of an antagonism between the role the individual has in one group and the role he has in another. According to this more sophisticated analysis, social problems are not about the relation of *the* individual to society at large. When correctly identified, they are about the relations between individuals and groups and between one group and another. Adjustments between contending parties cannot be determined by an *a priori* formula. Adjustment is always contextual and always experimental.

> One reason for the comparative sterility of discussion of social matters is because so much intellectual energy has gone into the supposititious problem of the relations of individualism and collectivism at large, wholesale, and because the image of the antithesis infects so many specific questions. Thereby thought is diverted from the only fruitful questions, those of investigation into factual subject-matter, and becomes a discussion of concepts. The "problem" of the relation of the concept of authority to that of freedom, of personal rights to social obligations, with only a subsumptive illustrative reference to empirical facts, has been substituted for inquiry into the *consequences* of some particular distribution, under given conditions, of specific freedoms and authorities, and for inquiry into what altered distribution would yield more desirable consequences.[15]

A functional social science, Dewey argues, would address itself to two matters. It would constantly refine its methods of inquiry and it would direct this inquiry to specific social problems. He is emphatic that social scientists in a democratic community would not prescribe solutions to these problems. Scientists would have no such authority whatever. Instead, they would de-

15. See this volume, pp. 355–56.

vote themselves to determining how the complex and powerful forces in society actually function. The interrelations and effects of different kinds of groups, institutions, practices, laws, technologies, industries, diplomacies, communications, and so on, would be investigated. In this way the knowledge needed by the public would be provided. To a significant extent, then, the omnicompetence of the citizen would be unnecessary. The voter need not be a professional inquirer.

Is it plausible, however, that the public could learn to use this knowledge? It is possible, Dewey insists, for the citizen to know how to utilize the information provided by social scientists. His principal argument is that *effective* intelligence is not an innate possession of the individual. It was a fundamental error in the thought of the Enlightenment to assume that reason is a faculty both innate and fixed. Effective intelligence is an acquired power; experimental habits of thought can be learned. Dewey acknowledges that there are significant differences in native capacities; but whatever one's native capacities, the habits by which they are utilized are acquired in social practice. The intellectual powers of the isolated individual, whatever they may be, will never be realized; and virtually any person can attain the needed level of rationality if he develops in a community where intelligence is exhibited in the habits of social action. Unite the intellectual powers of individuals in the appropriate social process, and each participant can learn and achieve in vastly greater measure than if excluded from intelligent social life. Dewey writes,

> The level of action fixed by *embodied* intelligence is always the important thing. . . . A mechanic can discourse of ohms and amperes as Sir Isaac Newton could not in his day. Many a man who has tinkered with radios can judge of things which Faraday did not dream of. It is aside from the point to say that if Newton and Faraday were now here, the amateur and mechanic would be infants beside them. The retort only brings out the point: the difference made by different objects to think of and by different meanings in circulation. A more intelligent state of social affairs, one more informed with knowledge, more directed by intelligence, would not improve original endowments one whit, but it would raise the level

upon which the intelligence of all operates. The height of this level is much more important for judgment of public concerns than are differences in intelligence quotients.[16]

Accordingly, one could have high native intelligence but be short on habits of intelligent thought. On the other hand, one could have a modest native endowment and still learn much of the art of intelligent inquiry. Notice the crucial difference between the Enlightenment conception of reason and Dewey's conception of active intelligence. If we accept the Enlightenment doctrine of a fixed and given reason, and if we also conclude that most individuals have rather little of it, then we must also accept the conclusion that persons are irremediably in that condition. Dewey's position relieves us of this unhappy burden.

Insofar as Dewey is correct, we could assume that individuals could learn to utilize the information provided by the professional scientist. They could identify the diversity of social forces and recognize their effects. More particularly, they could understand how these forces affect various forms of associated life, and they could learn how reconstructions of existing conditions might introduce welcome change. Presumably, once in possession of this knowledge, groups would advocate policies for social action. Policies would be formulated as hypotheses that predicted desired outcomes conditional upon a specified reconstruction of existing circumstances. At this juncture, social scientists would again contribute, making informed estimates of how such policies would actually work. Finally, the policies would be tried out—tested—and adjusted as the tests warrant. On the basis of this procedure, the democratic process would yield the policies most in the public interest.

Even if the voter had the training to appropriate the relevant scientific knowledge, would he actually do so? Would he overcome the apathy that has distinguished him hitherto? Again, Dewey believes it is possible. The means of communicating such information would have to be greatly improved, of course, as Dewey has already remarked. Even more important is that this information be presented to the appropriate audience and be addressed to its most vital interests. The most precious experi-

16. Ibid., pp. 366–67.

ence is found in the local, or face-to-face, community. (See esp. pp. 368–69.) It is this experience that has been ravaged in modern life. Social knowledge, as Dewey conceives it, is not abstract theory. It is information about what is invading the life of the local community and how this invasion is taking place. It is also information about how this life can be restored, revitalized, and enriched. Thus it is of the utmost and most immediate practical importance. When it is transmitted to and through the neighborly community, and when its bearing on the life of the group is discussed and shared within it, then democracy might reach its full potential. Dewey concludes,

> There is no limit to the liberal expansion and confirmation of limited personal intellectual endowment which may proceed from the flow of social intelligence when that circulates by word of mouth from one to another in the communications of the local community. That and that only gives reality to public opinion. We lie, as Emerson said, in the lap of an immense intelligence. But that intelligence is dormant and its communications are broken, inarticulate and faint until it possesses the local community as its medium.[17]

The Public and Its Problems is rich in content and, like so many of Dewey's writings, extremely fertile in ideas. One may quarrel with various of his analyses—historical, social, conceptual, or normative. (Dewey frequently says that science has yielded almost no social knowledge, yet much of the time he writes as if he has a lot of it.) One can also point out that his treatment is incomplete: many issues in democratic theory are untouched. There is a further difficulty attending Dewey's theory, but the fault is not with the theory itself: even today the social sciences have not attained the competence to provide the knowledge Dewey demanded of them. Nevertheless, there is a compelling thrust to the book. The reconstruction of political life that he calls for is more fundamental than, say, the issues of capitalism and socialism. It is more fundamental than any particular issue of public policy. It is a radical call for democracy to be both the final arbiter of social issues and the consummation of human growth and shared experience. We must remember that democracy means both community and the method of ex-

17. Ibid., pp. 371–72.

perimental intelligence. Thus it is far more than the counting of heads and far more than accepting at face value the ravings of groups or individuals bent on power and domination. At the same time it is humbler and more effective than the various absolutisms, with their inherently irreconcilable claims.

As noted, Dewey's notion of intellience is not burdened with eighteenth-century assumptions. By regarding the development and active exercise of experimental habits as organic to the values of shared experience, Dewey sees the way to making intelligence a prized possession. If science can be suitably addressed to the local community, the apathy attending social knowledge and action may be diminished. His conception of ideas, moreover, affords far more insight into the nature of intelligent conduct than any philosophy antecedent to pragmatism.

The idea of the state is particularly fertile. It is a deliberate attempt to define it in a way that facilitates the matching of institutions to problems. In its very conception, the state implies a continuous and experimental adaptation to change. This is a much more serviceable approach than that of the ahistorical liberals, and it avoids the stultifying all-inclusive state conceived by Hegel. At the same time, Dewey's idea of society avoids both the atomism of classical liberalism and the stifling monism of Rousseau and the idealists. It could be argued as well that Dewey's conceptions of the public, the state, and intelligence are far more sophisticated than the corresponding analyses of Marx, who never quite mastered the experimental point of view.

The Public and Its Problems appeared just before a tide of ideological theorizing swept over the United States in the 1930s. Inspired by Marx, the intellectuals' devotion to rigid political dogmas was apparently stronger than Dewey's plea for experimentalism. Dewey, of course, was the sworn foe of all forms of rationalistic and absolutistic philosophizing. Remarkably, after a period of dormancy, just these traits are reappearing in contemporary moral thought. The most conspicuous example is *A Theory of Justice*,[18] by Rawls. This text aspires to a rational deduction of eternally valid principles of justice. The book called forth another, *Anarchy, State, and Utopia*,[19] by his colleague, Robert Nozick, who provided his own deduction. Rawls derives his

18. John Rawls, *A Theory of Justice* (Cambridge: Harvard University Press, 1971).
19. Robert Nozick, *Anarchy, State, and Utopia* (New York: Basic Books, 1974).

principles from the decisions of nameless, faceless denizens of a changeless world. Nozick derives his from a postulated state of nature, replete with absolute rights. In addition to their rationalistic method, what the two authors have in common is a disregard for the actual moral convictions of the persons inhabiting the real world. The conditions from which their principles are derived bear no resemblance to actual human circumstances; and whenever the principles "demonstrated" in either of these works clash with those of actual historical beings, the latter are sacrificed without qualm. (There is no other way to preserve the logic of absolutistic moral theories.) Democratic intelligence counts for nothing in either of these systems, which have an abundance of ingenuity but are lacking in wisdom. What is also particularly notable about these books is that their respective principles of justice are radically incompatible with *each other*—quite an embarrassment for such "rational" constructions. Given the repeated embarrassments suffered by absolutistic philosophies (of which that of Rawls and Nozick is only the most recent), we should by now be extremely wary of non-experimental thought and action. It is to be hoped that Dewey's influence will be reasserted.

The democratic public, in the way that Dewey conceives it, would seem to be a promising medium for contending with social problems. Nevertheless, as Dewey himself would insist, it could never be regarded as a method that is not liable to degrees of conflict and uncertainty, controversial decisions, and failed hopes. A perfect system (whatever that might mean) is beyond human competence; and philosophy no more than human nature should be blamed for failing to solve all our problems. Yet democracy, in Dewey's conception, is creative and experimental; it has a greater capacity for self-correction and growth than other human arrangements. Its practice, moreover, would enlist the intelligence of citizens as absolutistic systems cannot. This is at once a genial and heroic idea of democracy, yet perhaps its realization is beyond human capacity. Like any theory, its adequacy can be determined only by putting it to the test of practice. At this stage in our history, it would be premature to resign ourselves to lesser ambitions.

Essays

The Development of
American Pragmatism

The purpose of this article is to define the principal theories of the philosophical movements known under the names of Pragmatism, Instrumentalism, or Experimentalism. To do this we must trace their historical development; for this method seems to present the simplest way of comprehending these movements and at the same time avoiding certain current misunderstandings of their doctrines and their aims.

The origin of Pragmatism goes back to Charles Sanders Peirce, the son of one of the most celebrated mathematicians of the United States, and himself very proficient in the science of mathematics; he is one of the founders of the modern symbolic logic of relations. Unfortunately Peirce was not at all a systematic writer and never expounded his ideas in a single system. The pragmatic method which he developed applies only to a very narrow and limited universe of discourse. After William James had extended the scope of the method, Peirce wrote an exposition of the origin of pragmatism as he had first conceived it; it is from this exposition that we take the following passages.

The term "pragmatic," contrary to the opinion of those who regard pragmatism as an exclusively American conception, was suggested to him by the study of Kant. In the *Metaphysic of Morals* Kant established a distinction between *pragmatic* and *practical*. The latter term applies to moral laws which Kant regards as *a priori*, whereas the former term applies to the rules of art and technique which are based on experience and are applicable to experience. Peirce, who was an empiricist, with the habits of mind, as he put it, of the laboratory, consequently refused to call his system "practicalism," as some of his friends suggested. As a logician he was interested in the art and tech-

[First published in *Studies in the History of Ideas*, ed. Department of Philosophy, Columbia University (New York: Columbia University Press, 1925), 2:353–77.]

nique of real thinking, and especially interested, as far as pragmatic method is concerned, in the art of making concepts clear, or of construing adequate and effective definitions in accord with the spirit of scientific method.

Following his own words, for a person "who still thought in Kantian terms most readily, '*praktisch*' and '*pragmatisch*' were as far apart as the two poles; the former belonging in a region of thought where no mind of the experimental type can ever make sure of solid ground under his feet, the latter expressing relation to some definite human purpose. Now quite the most striking feature of the new theory was its recognition of an inseparable connection between rational cognition and rational purpose."[1]

In alluding to the experimental type of mind, we are brought to the exact meaning given by Peirce to the word "pragmatic." In speaking of an experimentalist as a man whose intelligence is formed in the laboratory, he said: "Whatever assertion you may make to him, he will either understand as meaning that if a given prescription for an experiment ever can be and ever is carried out in act, an experience of a given description will result, or else he will see no sense at all in what you say." And thus Peirce developed the theory that "the rational purport of a word or other expression, lies exclusively in its conceivable bearing upon the conduct of life; so that, since obviously nothing that might not result from experiment can have any direct bearing upon conduct, if one can define accurately all the conceivable experimental phenomena which the affirmation or denial of a concept could imply, one will have therein a complete definition of the concept."[2]

The essay in which Peirce developed his theory bears the title: "How to Make Our Ideas Clear."[3] There is a remarkable similarity here to Kant's doctrine. Peirce's effort was to interpret the universality of concepts in the domain of *experience* in the same way in which Kant established the law of practical reason in the domain of the *a priori*. "The rational meaning of every proposition lies in the future. . . . But of the myriads of forms into which a proposition may be translated, what is that one which is to be called its very meaning? It is, according to the pragmatist,

1. *Monist*, vol. 15, p. 163.
2. *Monist*, vol. 15, p. 162.
3. *Popular Science Monthly*, 1878.

that form in which the proposition becomes applicable to human conduct, not in these or those special circumstances, nor when one entertains this or that special design, but that form which is most directly applicable to self-control under every situation, and to every purpose."[4] So also, "the pragmatist does not make the *summum bonum* to consist in action, but makes it to consist in that process of evolution whereby the existent comes more and more to embody generals . . ."[5]—in other words—the process whereby the existent becomes, with the aid of action, a body of rational tendencies or of habits generalized as much as possible. These statements of Peirce are quite conclusive with respect to two errors which are commonly committed in regard to the ideas of the founder of pragmatism. It is often said of pragmatism that it makes action the end of life. It is also said of pragmatism that it subordinates thought and rational activity to particular ends of interest and profit. It is true that the theory according to Peirce's conception implies essentially a certain relation to action, to human conduct. But the role of action is that of an intermediary. In order to be able to attribute a meaning to concepts, one must be able to apply them to existence. Now it is by means of action that this application is made possible. And the modification of existence which results from this application constitutes the true meaning of concepts. Pragmatism is, therefore, far from being that glorification of action for its own sake which is regarded as the peculiar characteristic of American life.

It is also to be noted that there is a scale of possible applications of concepts to existence, and hence a diversity of meanings. The greater the extension of the concepts, the more they are freed from the restrictions which limit them to particular cases, the more is it possible for us to attribute the greatest generality of meaning to a term. Thus the theory of Peirce is opposed to every restriction of the meaning of a concept to the achievement of a particular end, and still more to a personal aim. It is still more strongly opposed to the idea that reason or thought should be reduced to being a servant of any interest which is pecuniary or narrow. This theory was American in its origin in so far as it insisted on the necessity of human conduct and the fulfillment of

4. *Monist*, vol. 15, pp. 173–74.
5. *Monist*, vol. 15, p. 178.

some aim in order to clarify thought. But at the same time, it disapproves of those aspects of American life which make action an end in itself, and which conceive ends too narrowly and too "practically." In considering a system of philosophy in its relation to national factors it is necessary to keep in mind not only the aspects of life which are incorporated in the system, but also the aspects against which the system is a protest. There never was a philosopher who has merited the name for the simple reason that he glorified the tendencies and characteristics of his social environment; just as it is also true that there never has been a philosopher who has not seized upon certain aspects of the life of his time and idealized them.

The work commenced by Peirce was continued by William James. In one sense James narrowed the application of Peirce's pragmatic method, but at the same time he extended it. The articles which Peirce wrote in 1878 commanded almost no attention from philosophical circles, which were then under the dominating influence of the neo-Kantian idealism of Green, of Caird, and of the Oxford School, excepting those circles in which the Scottish philosophy of common sense maintained its supremacy. In 1898 James inaugurated the new pragmatic movement in an address entitled, "Philosophical Conceptions and Practical Results," later reprinted in the volume, *Collected Essays and Reviews*. Even in this early study one can easily notice the presence of those two tendencies to restrict and at the same time to extend early pragmatism. After having quoted the psychological remark of Peirce that "beliefs are really rules for action, and the whole function of thinking is but one step in the production of habits of action," and that every idea which we frame for ourselves of an object is really an idea of the possible effects of that object, he expressed the opinion that all these principles could be expressed more broadly than Peirce expressed them. "The ultimate test for us of what a truth means is indeed the conduct it dictates or inspires. But it inspires that conduct because it first foretells some particular turn to our experience which shall call for just that conduct from us. And I should prefer to express Peirce's principle by saying that the effective meaning of any philosophic proposition can always be brought down to some particular consequence, in our future practical experience, whether active or passive; the point lying rather in the fact that the experience must be particular, than in the fact that it must be active." [6] In an essay written in 1908 James repeats this statement and states that whenever he employs the term "the practical," he means by it, "the distinctively concrete, the individual, the particular and effective as opposed to the abstract, general and inert— 'Pragmata' are things in their plurality—particular consequences can perfectly well be of a theoretic nature." [7]

William James alluded to the development which he gave to Peirce's expression of the principle. In one sense one can say that he enlarged the bearing of the principle by the substitution of particular consequences for the general rule or method applicable to future experience. But in another sense this substitution limited the application of the principle since it destroyed the importance attached by Peirce to the greatest possible application of the rule, or the habit of conduct—its extension to universality. That is to say, William James was much more of a nominalist than Peirce.

One can notice an extension of pragmatism in the above passage. James there alludes to the use of a method of determining the meaning of truth. Since truth is a term and has consequently a meaning, this extension is a legitimate application of pragmatic method. But it should be remarked that here this method serves only to make clear the meaning of the term "truth," and has nothing to do with the truth of a particular judgment. The principal reason which led James to give a new color to pragmatic method was that he was preoccupied with applying the method to determine the meaning of philosophical problems and questions and that moreover, he chose to submit to examination phil-

6. *Collected Essays and Reviews*, p. 412.
7. *The Meaning of Truth*, pp. 209–211. In a footnote James gave an example of the errors which are committed in connection with the term "Practical," quoting M. Bourdeau who had written that "Pragmatism is an Anglo-Saxon reaction against the intellectualism and rationalism of the Latin mind. . . . It is a philosophy without words, a philosophy of gestures and of acts, which abandons what is general and holds only to what is particular." In his lecture at California, James brought out the idea that his pragmatism was inspired to a considerable extent by the thought of the British philosophers, Locke, Berkeley, Hume, Mill, Bain, and Shadworth Hodgson. But he contrasted this method with German transcendentalism, and particularly with that of Kant. It is especially interesting to notice this difference between Peirce and James: the former attempted to give an experimental, not an *a priori* interpretation of Kant, whereas James tried to develop the point of view of the British thinkers.

osophical notions of a theological or religious nature. He wished to establish a criterion which would enable one to determine whether a given philosophical question has an authentic and vital meaning or whether, on the contrary, it is trivial and purely verbal; and in the former case, what interests are at stake, when one accepts and affirms one or the other of two theses in dispute. Peirce was above all a logician; whereas James was an educator and humanist and wished to force the general public to realize that certain problems, certain philosophical debates have a real importance for mankind, because the beliefs which they bring into play lead to very different modes of conduct. If this important distinction is not grasped, it is impossible to understand the majority of the ambiguities and errors which belong to the later period of the pragmatic movement.

James took as an example the controversy between theism and materialism. It follows from this principle that if the course of the world is considered as completed, it is equally legitimate to assert that God or matter is its cause. Whether one way or the other, the facts are what they are, and it is they which determine whatever meaning is to be given to their cause. Consequently the name which we can give to this cause is entirely arbitrary. It is entirely different if we take the future into account. God then has the meaning of a power concerned with assuring the final triumph of ideal and spiritual values, and matter becomes a power indifferent to the triumph or defeat of these values. And our life takes a different direction according as we adopt one or the other of these alternatives. In the lectures on pragmatism published in 1907, he applies the same criticism to the philosophical problem of the One and the Many, that is to say of Monism and Pluralism, as well as to other questions. Thus he shows that Monism is equivalent to a rigid universe where everything is fixed and immutably united to others, where indetermination, free choice, novelty, and the unforeseen in experience have no place; a universe which demands the sacrifice of the concrete and complex diversity of things to the simplicity and nobility of an architectural structure. In what concerns our beliefs, Monism demands a rationalistic temperament leading to a fixed and dogmatic attitude. Pluralism, on the other hand, leaves room for contingence, liberty, novelty, and gives complete liberty of action to the empirical method, which can be indefinitely extended. It accepts unity where it finds it, but it does not attempt to force the vast diversity of events and things into a single rational mold.

From the point of view of an educator or of a student or, if you will, of those who are thoroughly interested in these problems, in philosophical discussions and controversies, there is no reason for contesting the value of this application of pragmatic method, but it is no less important to determine the nature of this application. It affords a means of discovering the implications for human life of philosophical conceptions which are often treated as of no importance and of a purely dialectical nature. It furnishes a criterion for determining the vital implications of beliefs which present themselves as alternatives in any theory. Thus as he himself said, "the whole function of philosophy ought to be to find the characteristic influences which you and I would undergo at a determinate moment of our lives, if one or the other formula of the universe were true." However, in saying that the whole function of philosophy has this aim, it seems that he is referring rather to the teaching than to the construction of philosophy. For such a statement implies that the world formulas have already all been made, and that the necessary work of producing them has already been finished, so that there remains only to define the consequences which are reflected in life by the acceptance of one or the other of these formulas as true.

From the point of view of Peirce, the object of philosophy would be rather to give a fixed meaning to the universe by formulas which correspond to our attitudes or our most general habits of response to the environment; and this generality depends on the extension of the applicability of these formulas to specific future events. The *meaning* of concepts of "matter" and of "God" must be fixed before we can even attempt to reach an understanding concerning the *value* of our belief in these concepts. Materialism would signify that the world demands on our part a single kind of constant and general habits; and God would signify the demand for another type of habits; the difference between materialism and theism would be tantamount to the difference in the habits required to face all the detailed facts of the universe. The world would be one in so far as it would be possible for us to form a single habit of action which would take account of all future existences and would be applicable to them. It would be many in so far as it is necessary for us to form several habits, differing from each other and irreducible to each other, in order to be able to meet the events in the world and control them. In short, Peirce wrote as a logician and James as a humanist.

William James accomplished a new advance in Pragmatism by his theory of the will to believe, or as he himself later called it, the right to believe. The discovery of the fundamental consequences of one or another belief has without fail a certain influence on that belief itself. If a man cherishes novelty, risk, opportunity and a variegated esthetic reality, he will certainly reject any belief in Monism, when he clearly perceives the import of this system. But if, from the very start, he is attracted by esthetic harmony, classic proportions, fixity even to the extent of absolute security and logical coherence, it is quite natural that he should put faith in Monism. Thus William James took into account those motives of instinctive sympathy which play a greater role in our choice of a philosophic system than do formal reasonings; and he thought that we should be rendering a service to the cause of philosophical sincerity if we would openly recognize the motives which inspire us. He also maintained the thesis that the greater part of philosophic problems and especially those which touch on religious fields are of such a nature that they are not susceptible of decisive evidence one way or the other. Consequently he claimed the right of a man to choose his beliefs not only in the presence of proofs or conclusive facts, but also in the absence of all such proof. Above all when he is forced to choose between one meaning or another, or when by refusing to choose he has a right to assume the risks of faith, his refusal is itself equivalent to a choice. The theory of the will to believe gives rise to misunderstandings and even to ridicule; and therefore it is necessary to understand clearly in what way James used it. We are always obliged to act in any case; our actions and with them their consequences actually change according to the beliefs which we have chosen. Moreover it may be that, in order to discover the proofs which will ultimately be the intellectual justification of certain beliefs—the belief in freedom, for example, or the belief in God—it is necessary to begin to act in accordance with this belief.

In his lectures on Pragmatism, and in his volume of essays bearing the title *The Meaning of Truth*, which appeared in 1909, James extended the use of the pragmatic method to the problem of the nature of truth. So far we have considered the pragmatic method as an instrument in determining the meaning of words and the vital importance of philosophic beliefs. Now and then we have made allusion to the future consequences which are implied. James showed, among other things, that in certain philosophic conceptions, the affirmation of certain beliefs could be justified by means of the nature of their consequences, or by the differences which these beliefs make in existence. But then why not push the argument to the point of maintaining that the meaning of truth in general is determined by its consequences? We must not forget here that James was an empiricist before he was a pragmatist, and repeatedly stated that pragmatism is merely empiricism pushed to its legitimate conclusions. From a general point of view, the pragmatic attitude consists in "looking away from first things, principles, 'categories,' supposed necessities; and of looking towards last things, fruits, consequences, facts." It is only one step further to apply the pragmatic method to the problem of truth. In the natural sciences there is a tendency to identify truth in any particular case with a verification. The verification of a theory, or of a concept, is carried on by the observation of particular facts. Even the most scientific and harmonious physical theory is merely an hypothesis until its implications, deduced by mathematical reasoning or by any other kind of inference, are verified by observed facts. What direction therefore, must an empirical philosopher take who wishes to arrive at a definition of truth by means of an empirical method? He must, if he wants to apply this method, and without bringing in for the present the pragmatic formula, first find particular cases from which he then generalizes. It is therefore in submitting conceptions to the control of experience, in the process of verifying them, that one finds examples of what is called truth. Therefore any philosopher who applies this empirical method, without the least prejudice in favor of pragmatic doctrine, can be led to conclude that truth "means" verification, or if one prefers, that verification either actual or possible, is the definition of truth.

In combining this conception of empirical method with the theory of pragmatism, we come upon other important philosophical results. The classic theories of truth in terms of the coherence or compatibility of terms, and of the correspondence of an idea with a thing, hereby receive a new interpretation. A merely mental coherence without experimental verification does not enable us to get beyond the realm of hypothesis. If a notion or a theory makes pretense of corresponding to reality or to the facts, this pretense cannot be put to the test and confirmed or refuted except by causing it to pass over into the realm of action and by noting the results which it yields in the form of the concrete observable facts to which this notion or theory leads. If, in acting upon this notion, we are brought to the fact which it implies or which it demands, then this notion is true. A theory corresponds to the facts when it leads to the facts which are its consequences, by the intermediary of experience. And from this consideration the pragmatic generalization is drawn that all knowledge is prospective in its results, except in the case where notions and theories after having been first prospective in their application, have already been tried out and verified. Theoretically, however, even such verifications or truths could not be absolute. They would be based upon practical or moral certainty, but they are always subject to being corrected by unforeseen future consequences or by observed facts which had been disregarded. Every proposition concerning truths is really in the last analysis hypothetical and provisional, although a large number of these propositions have been so frequently verified without failure that we are justified in using them as if they were absolutely true. But logically absolute truth is an ideal which cannot be realized, at least not until all the facts have been registered, or as James says "bagged," and until it is no longer possible to make other observations and other experiences.

Pragmatism, thus, presents itself as an extension of historical empiricism, but with this fundamental difference, that it does not insist upon antecedent phenomena but upon consequent phenomena; not upon the precedents but upon the possibilities of action. And this change in point of view is almost revolutionary in its consequences. An empiricism which is content with repeating facts already past has no place for possibility and for liberty. It cannot find room for general conceptions or ideas, at least no more than to consider them as summaries or records. But when we take the point of view of pragmatism we see that general ideas have a very different role to play than that of reporting and registering past experiences. They are the bases for organizing future observations and experiences. Whereas, for empiricism, in a world already constructed and determined, reason or general thought has no other meaning than that of summing up particular cases, in a world where the future is not a mere word, where theories, general notions, rational ideas have consequences for action, reason necessarily has a constructive function. Nevertheless the conceptions of reasoning have only a secondary interest in comparison with the reality of facts, since they must be confronted with concrete observations.[8]

Pragmatism thus has a metaphysical implication. The doctrine of the value of consequences leads us to take the future into consideration. And this taking into consideration of the future takes us to the conception of a universe whose evolution is not finished, of a universe which is still, in James' term, "in the making," "in the process of becoming," of a universe up to a certain point still plastic.

Consequently reason, or thought, in its more general sense, has a real, though limited function, a creative, constructive function. If we form general ideas and if we put them in action, consequences are produced which could not be produced otherwise. Under these conditions the world will be different from what it would have been if thought had not intervened. This consideration confirms the human and moral importance of thought and of its reflective operation in experience. It is therefore not true to say that James treated reason, thought and knowledge with contempt, or that he regarded them as mere means of gaining personal or even social profits. For him reason has a creative function, limited because specific, which helps to make the world other than it would have been without it. It makes the world really more reasonable; it gives to it an intrinsic value. One will understand the philosophy of James better if one considers it in its totality as a revision of English empiricism, a revision which replaces the value of past experience, of what is already given, by the future, by that which is as yet mere possibility.

These considerations naturally bring us to the movement

8. William James said in a happy metaphor, that they must be "cashed in," by producing specific consequences. This expression means that they must be able to lead to concrete facts. But for those who are not familiar with American idioms, James' formula was taken to mean that the consequences themselves of our rational conceptions must be narrowly limited by their pecuniary value. Thus Mr. Bertrand Russell wrote recently that pragmatism is merely a manifestation of American commercialism.

called instrumentalism. The survey which we have just made of James' philosophy shows that he regarded conceptions and theories purely as instruments which can serve to constitute future facts in a specific manner. But James devoted himself primarily to the moral aspects of this theory, to the support which it gave to "meliorism" and moral idealism, and to the consequences which followed from it concerning the sentimental value and the bearing of various philosophical systems, particularly to its destructive implications for monistic rationalism and for absolutism in all its forms. He never attempted to develop a complete theory of the forms or "structures" and of the logical operations which are founded on this conception. Instrumentalism is an attempt to establish a precise logical theory of concepts, of judgments and inferences in their various forms, by considering primarily how thought functions in the experimental determinations of future consequences. That is to say, it attempts to establish universally recognized distinctions and rules of logic by deriving them from the reconstructive or mediative function ascribed to reason. It aims to constitute a theory of the general forms of conception and reasoning, and not of this or that particular judgment or concept related to its own content, or to its particular implications.

As far as the historical antecedents of instrumentalism are concerned, two factors are particularly important, over and above this matter of experimental verification which we have already mentioned in connection with James. The first of these two factors is psychological, and the second is a critique of the theory of knowledge and of logic which has resulted from the theory proposed by neo-Kantian idealism and expounded in the logical writings of such philosophers as Lotze, Bosanquet, and F. H. Bradley. As we have already said, neo-Kantian influence was very marked in the United States during the last decade of the nineteenth century. I myself, and those who have collaborated with me in the exposition of instrumentalism, began by being neo-Kantians, in the same way that Peirce's point of departure was Kantianism and that of James was the empiricism of the British School.

The psychological tendencies which have exerted an influence on instrumentalism are of a biological rather than a physiological nature. They are, more or less, closely related to the important movement whose promoter in psychology has been Doctor John Watson and to which he has given the name of Behaviourism. Briefly, the point of departure of this theory is the conception of the brain as an organ for the coordination of sense stimuli (to which one should add modifications caused by habit, unconscious memory, or what are called today "conditioned reflexes") for the purpose of effecting appropriate motor responses. On the basis of the theory of organic evolution it is maintained that the analysis of intelligence and of its operations should be compatible with the order of known biological facts, concerning the intermediate position occupied by the central nervous system in making possible responses to the environment adequate to the needs of the living organism. It is particularly interesting to note that in the *Studies in Logical Theory* (1903), which was their first declaration, the instrumentalists recognized how much they owed to William James for having forged the instruments which they used, while at the same time, in the course of the studies, the authors constantly declared their belief in a close union of the "normative" principles of logic and the real processes of thought, in so far as these are determined by an objective or biological psychology and not by an introspective psychology of states of consciousness. But it is curious to note that the "instruments" to which allusion is made, are not the considerations which were of the greatest service to James. They precede his pragmatism and it is among some of the pages of his *Principles of Psychology* that one must look for them. This important work (1890) really developed two distinct theses.

The one is a re-interpretation of introspective psychology, in which James denies that sensations, images and ideas are discrete and in which he replaces them by a continuous stream which he calls "the stream of consciousness." This conception necessitates a consideration of relations as an immediate part of the field of consciousness, having the same status as qualities. And throughout his *Psychology* James gives a philosophical tinge to this conception by using it in criticising the atomism of Locke and of Hume as well as the *a-priorism* of the synthesis of rational principles by Kant and his successors, among whom should be mentioned in England, Thomas Hill Green, who was then at the height of his influence.

The other aspect of his *Principles of Psychology* is of a biological nature. It shows itself in its full force in the criterion which James established for discovering the existence of mind. "The pursuance of future ends and the choice of means for their attainment are thus the mark and criterion of the presence of mentality in a phenomenon."[9] The force of this criterion is plainly shown in the chapter on Attention, and its relation to Interest considered as the force which controls it, and its teleological function of selection and integration; in the chapter on Discrimination and Comparison (Analysis and Abstraction), where he discusses the way in which ends to be attained and the means for attaining them evoke and control intellectual analysis; and in the chapter on Conception, where he shows that a general idea is a mode of signifying particular things and not merely an abstraction from particular cases or a super-empirical function,—that it is a teleological instrument. James then develops this idea in the chapter on reasoning where he says that "the only meaning of essence is teleological, and that classification and conception are purely teleological weapons of mind."

One might complete this brief enumeration by mentioning also the chapter of James' book in which he discusses the Nature of Necessary Truths and the Effects of Experience, and affirms in opposition to Herbert Spencer, that many of our most important modes of perception and conception of the world of sensible objects are not the cumulative products of particular experience, but rather original biological sports, spontaneous variations which are maintained because of their applicability to concrete experiences after once having been created. Number, space, time, resemblance and other important "categories" could have been brought into existence, he says, as a consequence of some particular cerebral instability, but they could by no means, have been registered on the mind by outside influence. Many significant and useless concepts also arise in the same manner. But the fundamental categories have been cumulatively extended and reinforced because of their value when applied to concrete instances and things of experience. It is therefore not the origin of a concept, it is its application which becomes the criterion of its value; and here we have the whole of pragmatism in embryo. A phrase of James' very well summarizes its import: "the popular

9. *Psychology*, vol. 1, p. 8.

notion that 'Science' is forced on the mind *ab extra*, and that our interests have nothing to do with its constructions, is utterly absurd."

Given the point of view which we have just specified, and the interest attaching to a logical theory of conception and judgment, and there results a theory of the following description. The adaptations made by inferior organisms, for example their effective and coordinated responses to stimuli, become teleological in man and therefore give occasion to thought. Reflection is an indirect response to the environment, and the element of indirection can itself become great and very complicated. But it has its origin in biological adaptive behaviour and the ultimate function of its cognitive aspect is a prospective control of the conditions of the environment. The function of intelligence is therefore not that of copying the objects of the environment, but rather of taking account of the way in which more effective and more profitable relations with these objects may be established in the future.

How this point of view has been applied to the theory of judgment is too long a story to be told here. We shall confine ourselves here to saying that, in general, the "subject" of a judgment represents that portion of the environment to which a reaction must be made; the predicate represents the possible response or habit or manner in which one should behave towards the environment; the copula represents the organic and concrete act by which the connection is made between the fact and its signification; and finally the conclusion, or the definitive object of judgment, is simply the original situation transformed, a situation which implies a change as well in the original subject (including its mind) as in the environment itself. The new and harmonious unity thus attained verifies the bearing of the data which were at first chosen to serve as subject and of the concepts introduced into the situation during the process as teleological instruments for its elaboration. Until this final unification is attained the perceptual data and the conceptual principles, theories, are merely hypotheses from a logical point of view. Moreover, affirmation and negation are intrinsically a-logical: they are acts.

Such a summary survey can hardly pretend to be either convincing or suggestive. However, in noting the points of resemblance and difference between this phase of pragmatism and the logic of neo-Hegelian idealism, we are bringing out a point of great importance. According to the latter logic, thought constitutes in the last analysis its object and even the universe. It is necessary to affirm the existence of a series of forms of judgment, because our first judgments, which are nearest to sense, succeed in constituting objects in only a partial and fragmentary fashion, even to the extent of involving in their nature an element of contradiction. There results a dialectic which permits each inferior and partial type of judgment to pass into a more complete form until we finally arrive at the total judgment where the thought which comprehends the entire object or the universe is an organic whole of interrelated mental distinctions. It is evident that this theory magnifies the role of thought beyond all proportion. It is an objective and rational idealism which is opposed to and distinct from the subjective and perceptual idealism of Berkeley's school. Instrumentalism, however, assigns a positive function to thought, that of *re*constituting the present stage of things instead of merely knowing it. As a consequence, there cannot be intrinsic degrees, or a hierarchy of forms of judgments. Each type has its own end, and its validity is entirely determined by its efficacy in the pursuit of its end. A limited perceptual judgment, adapted to the situation which has given it birth, is as true in its place as is the most complete and significant philosophic or scientific judgment. Logic, therefore, leads to a realistic metaphysics in so far as it accepts things and events for what they are independently of thought, and to an idealistic metaphysics in so far as it contends that thought gives birth to distinctive acts which modify future facts and events in such a way as to render them more reasonable, that is to say, more adequate to the ends which we propose for ourselves. This ideal element is more and more accentuated by the inclusion progressively of social factors in human environment over and above natural factors; so that the needs which are fulfilled, the ends which are attained are no longer of a merely biological or particular character, but include also the ends and activities of other members of society.

It is natural that continental thinkers should be interested in American philosophy as it reflects, in a certain sense, American life. Thus it should be clear after this rapid survey of the history of pragmatism that American thought continues European thought. We have imported our language, our laws, our institutions, our morals, and our religion from Europe, and we have adapted them to the new conditions of our life. The same is true of our ideas. For long years our philosophical thought was merely an echo of European thought. The pragmatic movement which we have traced in the present essay as well as neo-realism, behaviourism, the absolute idealism of Royce, the naturalistic idealism of Santayana, are all attempts at re-adaptation; but they are not creations *de novo*. They have their roots in British and European thought. Since these systems are re-adaptations they take into consideration the distinctive traits of the environment of American life. But as has already been said, they are not limited to reproducing what is worn and imperfect in this environment. They do not aim to glorify the energy and the love of action which the new conditions of American life exaggerated. They do not reflect the excessive mercantilism of American life. Without doubt all these traits of the environment have not been without a certain influence on American philosophical thought; our philosophy would not be national or spontaneous if it were not subject to this influence. But the fundamental idea which the movements of which we have just spoken, have attempted to express, is the idea that action and opportunity justify themselves only to the degree in which they render life more reasonable and increase its value. Instrumentalism maintains in opposition to many contrary tendencies in the American environment, that action should be intelligent and reflective, and that thought should occupy a central position in life. That is the reason for our insistence on the teleological phase of thought and knowledge. If it must be teleological in particular and not merely true in the abstract, that is probably due to the practical element which is found in all the phases of American life. However that may be, what we insist upon above all else is that intelligence be regarded as the only source and sole guarantee of a desirable and happy future. It is beyond doubt that the progressive and unstable character of American life and civilization has facilitated the birth of a philosophy which regards the world as being in continuous formation, where there is still place for indeterminism, for the new and for a real future. But this idea is not exclusively American, although the conditions of American life have aided this idea in becoming self-conscious. It is also true that Americans tend to underestimate the value of tradition and of rationality considered as an achievement of the past. But the world has also given proof of irrationality in the past and this irrationality is incorporated in our beliefs and our institutions. There are bad traditions as there are good ones: it is always important to distinguish. Our neglect of the traditions of the past, with whatever this negligence implies in the way of spiritual impoverishment of our life, has its compensation in the idea that the world is recommencing and being re-made under our eyes. The future as well as the past can be a source of interest and consolation and give meaning to the present. Pragmatism and instrumental experimentalism bring into prominence the importance of the individual. It is he who is the carrier of creative thought, the author of action, and of its application. Subjectivism is an old story in philosophy; a story which began in Europe and not in America. But American philosophy, in the systems which we have expounded, has given to the subject, to the individual mind, a practical rather than an epistemological function. The individual mind is important because only the individual mind is the organ of modifications in traditions and institutions, the vehicle of experimental creation. One-sided and egoistic individualism in American life has left its imprint on our practices. For better or for worse, depending on the point of view, it has transformed the esthetic and fixed individualism of the old European culture into an active individualism. But the idea of a society of individuals is not foreign to American thought; it penetrates even our current individualism which is unreflective and brutal. And the individual which American thought idealises is not an individual *per se*, an individual fixed in isolation and set up for himself, but an individual who evolves and develops in a natural and human environment, an individual who can be educated.

If I were asked to give an historical parallel to this movement in American thought I would remind my reader of the French philosophy of the enlightenment. Every one knows that the thinkers who made that movement illustrious were inspired by Bacon, Locke, and Newton; what interested them was the application of scientific method and the conclusions of an experimental theory of knowledge to human affairs, the critique and reconstruction of beliefs and institutions. As Höffding writes, they were animated by "a fervent faith in intelligence, progress, and humanity." And certainly they are not accused today, just because of their educational and social significance, of having sought to subordinate intelligence and science to ordinary utilitarian aims. They merely sought to free intelligence from its impurities and to render it sovereign. One can scarcely say that those who glorify intelligence and reason in the abstract, because of their value for those who find personal satisfaction in their possession, estimate intelligence more truly than those who wish to make it the indispensable guide of intellectual and social life. When an American critic says of instrumentalism that it regards ideas as mere servants which make for success in life, he only reacts, without reflection, to the ordinary verbal associations of the word "instrumental," as many others have reacted in the same manner to the use of the word "practical." Similarly a recent Italian writer after having said that pragmatism and instrumentalism are characteristic products of American thought, adds that these systems "regard intelligence as a mere mechanism of belief, and consequently attempt to re-establish the dignity of reason by making of it a machine for the production of beliefs useful to morals and society." This criticism does not hold. It is by no means the production of beliefs useful to morals and society which these systems pursue. It is the formation of a faith in intelligence, as the one and indispensable belief necessary to moral and social life. The more one appreciates the intrinsic esthetic, immediate value of thought and of science, the more one takes into account what intelligence itself adds to the joy and dignity of life, the more one should feel grieved at a situation in which the exercise and joy of reason are limited to a narrow, closed and technical social group and the more one should ask how it is possible to make all men participators in this inestimable wealth.

Corporate Personality

The survey which is undertaken in this paper points to the conclusion that for the purposes of law the conception of "person" is a legal conception; put roughly, "person" signifies what law makes it signify. If this conclusion had not been disputed, if it were even now generally accepted, if even when it is accepted in substance it were not complicated by the use of non-legal concepts employed to justify certain reasonings and conclusions, this paper would have no particular excuse for being written. For in that case, being a legal concept, it would be one to be discussed by lawyers rather than by a layman. Accordingly, the justification for a layman venturing into the field is precisely the fact that discussions and theories which have influenced legal practice have, with respect to the concept of "person," introduced and depended upon a mass of non-legal considerations: considerations popular, historical, political, moral, philosophical, metaphysical and, in connection with the latter, theological.[1] So many of these extraneous influences have received a formulation in philosophy and from thence have proceeded to affect legal doctrines that a student of philosophy does not have to travel far beyond his own field to discuss them.

1. Thus Geldart, an upholder of the doctrine of "real personality," says: "The question is at bottom not one on which law and legal conceptions have the only or the final voice: it is one which law shares with other sciences, political science, ethics, psychology, and metaphysics." Geldart, *Legal Personality* (1911) 27 L. QUART. REV. 90, at 94. On the next page he goes on to assert that "To say that all legal personality—whether of so-called natural or so-called juristic persons—is equally real because in fact the law gives it an existence, and equally artificial or fictitious because it is *only* the law which gives it an existence, is really to confound personality with capacity." But he makes no attempt to show the difference between them, nor to state what harm would result in law if the two were "confounded." That "artificial" is not synonymous with "fictitious" is shown by Machen, *Corporate Personality* (1910) 24 HARV. L. REV. 253, at 257: "That which is artificial is real, and not imagi-

[First published in *Yale Law Journal* 35 (April 1926): 655–73.]

As a starting point we may take the following statement from Maitland, who has done so much to bring the question of the nature of corporate legal personality to the attention of English readers: "The corporation is (forgive this compound adjective) a right-and-duty-bearing unit. Not all the legal propositions that are true of a man will be true of a corporation. For example, it can neither marry nor be given in marriage; but in a vast number of cases you can make a legal statement about x and y which will hold good whether these symbols stand for two men or for two corporations, or for a corporation and a man."[2] In saying that "person" might legally mean whatever the law makes it mean, I am trying to say that "person" might be used simply as a synonym for a right-and-duty-bearing unit. Any such unit would be a person; such a statement would be truistic, tautological. Hence it would convey no implications, except that the unit has those rights and duties which the courts find it to have. What "person" signifies in popular speech, or in psychology, or in philosophy or morals, would be as irrelevant, to employ an exaggerated simile, as it would be to argue that because a wine is called "dry," it has the properties of dry solids; or that, because it does not have those properties, wine cannot possibly be "dry." Obviously, "dry" as applied to a particular wine has the kind of meaning, and only the kind of meaning, which it has when applied to the class of beverages in general. Why should not the same sort of thing hold of the use of "person" in law?

To take an illustration nearer to our theme, when the common law refused to recognize any paternity for an illegitimate son, and said he was *filius nullius*, it was not understood to deny the fact of physiological begetting; it was asserting that such a one

---

nary; an artificial lake is not an imaginary lake." Again he says: "A corporation cannot be at the same time 'created by the state' and fictitious. If a corporation is 'created' it is real, and therefore cannot be a purely fictitious body having no existence except in the legal imagination." Much the same points were made by Pollock. He says, that "artificial" means "in accordance with rules of art, lawyerlike, juridical," and that "fiction" should be derived from *fingere* in the sense of creating or making, not feigning. *Has the Common Law Received the Fiction Theory of Corporations?* (1911) 27 L. QUART. REV. 219, 220, reprinted in *Essays in the Law* (1922) 153. Geldart's introduction of the word "only" in the phrase "because it is *only* the law" is like saying of a locomotive that "only" man gives it existence.

2. Maitland, 3 *Collected Papers* (1911) 307. Throughout this paper, "corporate" is used in its broad sense, of which a business corporation is but a species and which includes bodies not technically incorporated.

did not possess the specific rights which belong to one who was *filius*, implying wedlock as a legal institution. That *filius* signifies a certain kind of heir, one implying a prior union of man and woman authorized by law, is an example of a term signifying what the system of rights and duties makes it signify. To take another illustration still nearer our topic, suppose that a number of married women, who, under common law suffered from disability to contract, had formed a corporation. It may be doubted whether even the most ardent disciple of the theory that the association is nothing but the sum of its individual members would infer that the corporation could not contract—although of course it might have been denied that the women could form a corporation. Admitting, however, the existence of the corporation, the right to contract would have been limited to the new relationship; because of it, the members of the corporation would possess a right *sui generis*. In a similar way, even if it were true, as it is not, that "natural person" is a wholly unambiguous term, to term a "natural" person a person in the legal sense is to confer upon him a new, additive and distinctive meaning; a meaning *sui generis*, as far as "natural person" is concerned.

If in justification of a particular decision in some particular and difficult controversy, a court supports itself by appealing to some prior properties of the antecedent non-legal "natural person," the appeal may help out the particular decision; but it either involves dependence upon non-legal theory, or else it extends the legal concept of "natural person," or it does both. This statement cuts in two ways. On the one hand, it indicates that much of the difficulty attending the recent discussion of the real personality of corporate bodies is due to going outside the strictly legal sphere so that legal issues have got complicated with other theories, and with former states of scientific knowledge; and on the other hand it suggests that law, at critical times and in dealing with critical issues, has found it difficult to grow in any other way than by taking over contemporary non-jural conceptions and doctrines. Just as the law has grown by taking unto itself *practices* of antecedent non-legal status, so it has grown by taking unto itself from psychology or philosophy or whatnot extraneous *dogmas* and *ideas*. But just as continued growth with respect to the former requires that law be again changed with great changes in further practices, just as, to be specific, the adoption of the law-merchant will not provide law adequate for the complex industrial relations of today, so it is even more markedly true that old non-legal doctrines which once served to advance rules of law may be obstructive today. We often go on discussing problems in terms of old ideas when the solution of the problem depends upon getting rid of the old ideas, and putting in their place concepts more in accord with the present state of ideas and knowledge. The root difficulty in present controversies about "natural" and associated bodies may be that while we oppose one to the other, or try to find some combining union of the two, what we really need to do is to overhaul the doctrine of personality which underlies both of them.

The purpose of the article is, in other words, to point out some of the non-legal factors which have found their way into the discussion of the personality of so-called natural and artificial persons, and to indicate the original conditions which gave these extraneous factors their efficacy. The postulate, which has unconsciously led to the merging of popular and philosophical notions of the person with the legal notion, is the conception that before anything can be a jural person it must intrinsically possess certain properties, the existence of which is necessary to constitute anything a person. If the conception as to the nature of these inherent and essential attributes had remained constant perhaps no harm would have resulted from shoving such a notion under the legal idea; the legal doctrine would at least have remained as constant as that of the nature of the seat of personality. But the history of western culture shows a chameleon-like change in the latter notion; this change has never, moreover, effected complete replacement of an earlier by a later idea. Almost all concepts have persisted side by side in a confused intermixture. Hence their influence upon legal doctrine has necessarily been to generate confusion and conflict.

We may illustrate by recourse to Maitland. The quotation above made, taken apart from its context, would appear to use "person" in a neutral sense, as signifying simply a right-and-duty-bearing unit. But actually his discussion depends upon an assumption that there are properties which any unit must antecedently and inherently have in order to be a right-and-duty-bearing unit. They are stated in his summary of Gierke's position, although the statement is found in another book. A "*universitas* [or corporate body] . . . is a living organism and a real person, with body and members and a will of its own. Itself can will, itself can act . . . it is a group-person, and its will is a group-will."[3] I do not intend to imply that Maitland or Gierke ever adopted into his corporate unit all the extreme analogies with an "organism," but a "will" he certainly thinks is presupposed for being a legal person. In short, some generic or philosophic concept of personality, that is, some concept expressing the intrinsic character of personality *ueberhaupt*, is implied. And here is room for questions of general theory and for the writing of many books to show that legal units do or do not have the properties required by the concept, and that "will" means this or that or the other thing.

Another example may make the implication more explicit. Michoud says: "For legal science, the notion of person is and should remain a purely juridical notion. The word signifies simply a *subject of rights-duties* [*sujet de droit*], a being capable of having the subjective rights properly belonging to him."[4] This sounds very much like saying "person" means what the law makes it mean in real distribution of rights and duties—although the word "subjective" prefixed to rights might make wary one who was acquainted with philosophical literature. But Michoud at once goes on to say: "To know if certain beings correspond to this definition, it is not necessary to ask if these beings constitute persons in the philosophical sense of the word. It is enough to ask if they are of such a *nature* that subjective rights may be attributed to them." Considerations extraneous to law are here nominally excluded, but they are actually taken in under the guise of the necessity of inquiring into the nature of the subjects, independently of and prior to the attribution of duty-rights. The word "subject" *might* have been used in legal theory simply as a descriptive term, denoting whatever is a right-and-duty-bearing unit. But in fact it has not been so used; it has been thought necessary—especially in German theory which has spread—first to define what makes anything properly a subject, as a *precondition* of having right-duties. And the German theory

3. Maitland, Introduction to *Political Theories of the Middle Age*, by Gierke (1900) xxvi.
4. Michoud, *La Notion de personnalité morale* (1899) 11 REVUE DU DROIT PUBLIC, 5, at 8.

of "subjectivity" is itself a theme for volumes. This something-or-other must then be the same in whatever has rights and duties. The readiest starting point is a singular man; hence there is imposed the necessity of finding some nature or essence which belongs both to men in the singular and to corporate bodies. If one denies that he can find such a common essence he holds that "person" as applied to corporate bodies denotes only a fiction. But if he denies the fictitious character of a corporate entity, then some personality identical in essence, or with respect to "subjectivity," must be discovered for all right-and-duty-bearing units, from the singular man on one side (including infants, born and unborn, insane, etc.) to the state on the other, together with all kinds of intervening corporate bodies such as "foundations," "associations" and corporations in the economic sense.[5] Clearly, this is not an easy task; it is so difficult of accomplishment that it accounts in the main for the voluminous continental literature concerning juridical personality, or as French writers generally say, "*Les Personnes Morales*." But this is not the whole story. "Subject" and "subjectivity" occupy in modern German philosophy (which directly and through writings on jurisprudence has had an enormous influence in Latin countries and considerable in England) the place taken in ancient metaphysics by "substance" and also by "subject" of a judgment in a logical sense. Thus the search for the common essence has been so affected by philosophical theories regarding "the subject" that it is extremely difficult to get the full force of the various solutions proffered for the problem without knowledge of German technical philosophy, that of Kant in particular.

It may be objected, however, that aside from all such philosophical theories regarding an "essence" or "nature" and regarding a "subject," it is only common sense that whatever is a right-and-duty-bearing unit should have a character of its own in virtue of which it may possess rights—obligations; there *must* be a subject to which these legal relations belong or in which they inhere or to which, at all events, they are imputed. Other-

5. The first of these terms have their doctrinal significance in Continental rather than in Anglo-American law, the institution of trusteeship in the latter covering much of the ground. The theory of "associations" derived much of its point in the past from controversies regarding the legal status of religious congregations, to which is now added that of trade-unions.

wise why are not molecules, or trees or tables just as fit candidates for legal attributes as singular men and corporate bodies? The objection seems serious. But consider first an argument *ad hominem*, or rather *ad hoc*. There is no general agreement regarding the nature *in se* of the jural subject; courts and legislators do their work without such agreement, sometimes without any conception or theory at all regarding its nature; it can be shown that recourse to some theory has more than once operated to hinder rather than facilitate the adjudication of a special question of right or obligation. Moreover, English jurisprudence has accomplished by means of "trust" much that Continental law has accomplished by other means. One might then be justified in adopting a position of legal agnosticism, holding that even if there be such an ulterior subject *per se*, it is no concern of law, since courts can do their work without respect to its nature, much more without having to settle it.

It would, however, be retorted that such an attitude does not become jurisprudence, that some theory is *implied* in the procedure of courts, and that the business of the theory of law is to make explicit what is implied, particularly as false theories have done practical harm, while the lack of intelligent consensus of ideas has encouraged judicial empiricism, and thereby wrought confusion, conflict and uncertainty in specific decisions. This retort brings us to a deeper level. There are two radically different types of definitions; first, the type inherited from Greek logic reflecting a definite metaphysical conception regarding the nature of things. This definition proceeds in terms of an essential and universal inhering nature. There is another mode of definition which proceeds in terms of *consequences*. In brief, for the latter a thing is—is defined as—what it does, "what–it–does" being stated in terms of specific effects *extrinsically* wrought in other things. This logical method was first stated by Charles S. Peirce as the pragmatistic rule: "Consider what effects, which might conceivably have practical bearings, we conceive the object of our conception to have. Then, our conception of these effects is the whole of our conception of the object."[6] The mode of definition, however, has no inherent dependence upon pragmatism as

6. *Chance, Love, and Logic* (1923) 45, edited by Morris R. Cohen. The original article was printed in the *Popular Science Monthly* for January, 1878.

a philosophy. It has been stated and adopted on the basis of analysis of mathematics and physics by writers who would be horrified to be called pragmatists. Thus stated, it is the principle known as "extensive abstraction," and assumes this form: ". . . what really matters to science is not the inner nature of objects but their mutual relations, and that any set of terms with the right mutual relations will answer all scientific purposes as well as any other set with the same sort of relations."[7]

From this point of view, the right-and-duty-bearing unit, or subject, signifies whatever has consequences of a specified kind. The reason that molecules or trees are not juridical "subjects" is then clear; they do not display the specified consequences. The definition of a legal subject is thus a legitimate, and quite conceivably a practically important matter. But it is a matter of analysis of facts, not of search for an inhering essence. The facts in question are whatever specific consequences flow from being right-and-duty-bearing units. This analysis is a matter to be conducted by one competent in law, and not by the layman. But even a layman can point out the field within which the search falls. The consequences must be social in character, and they must be *such* social consequences as are controlled and modified by being the bearing of rights and obligations, privileges and immunities. Molecules and trees certainly have social consequences; but these consequences are what they are irrespective of their having rights and duties. Molecules and trees would continue to behave exactly as they do whether or not rights and duties were ascribed to them; their consequences would be what they are anyway. But there are some things, bodies singular and corporate, which clearly act differently, and produce different consequences, depending upon whether or not they possess rights and duties, and according to what specific rights they possess and what obligations are placed upon them. If the logical principle be granted, it is a factual matter to decide what bodies have the specifiable consequences and what these consequences are; while it is a verbal matter whether we call them all "persons," or

7. Broad, *Scientific Thought* (1923) 39. The idea and the name are taken, however, by him from A. N. Whitehead. This is a more general statement than Peirce's, because it applies to mathematical concepts, such as "point," whose "consequences" are not physical effects. In concrete matters, the "mutual relations" which count are, however, of the nature of effects.

whether we call some of them persons and not others—or whether we abandon the use of the word entirely.[8]

The general statement as to the type of definition demanded may be made more specific by reference to Michoud. He finds what he is in search of primarily in "interests." Now while he had asserted the necessity of determining whether the beings who are "persons" "are of such a nature that subjective rights may be attributed to them," his conclusion that "interests" are primary shifts the logical ground. For "interests," whatever else they are or are not, fall within the region of consequences, not of "beings." Certain interests are protected by the rights and duties of charitable foundations; but these interests are those of recipients, who have no rights in the matter. Beings possessed of will, administrators, are necessary as the organs of the interest. His secondary mark or criterion may be said then to introduce an inherent factor, that of "will." But our former logical question recurs: Is "will" conceived or defined in terms of something intrinsic, or in terms of specifiable consequences? If the former, then we are at once involved in all the controversies regarding the nature of will found in psychology and philosophy:—there is no question upon which there is less consensus than upon the nature of will.[9] If the man of "common sense" retorts, "Away with these metaphysical subtleties; everybody knows well

8. English statutory law comes, in some respects, close to doing the latter by its very generalization of the term "person." In (1833) 3 & 4 Wm. IV, c. 74, it is said: "The Word 'Person' shall extend to a Body Politic, Corporate, or Collegiate, as well as an Individual." In the Interpretation Act of 1889, 52 & 53 Vict. c. 63, sec. 19, it is stated: "In this Act and in every Act passed after the commencement of this Act the expression 'person' shall, unless the contrary intention appears, include any body of persons corporate or unincorporate."

   I owe the reference to Maitland, *op. cit. supra* note 2, at 401. He explains that the inclusion of "incorporate bodies" is probably due to the desire to include some organs of local government, such as boards of health, under their relevant legal rules. He adds: "It is not inconceivable that the above cited section of the Act of 1889 may do some work hereafter; but I have not heard of its having done any work as yet." This statement indicates what is meant by the assertion that a generalization of the term "person" may be equivalent to an abandonment of the term, the work being done by specific statutes and by judicial decisions bearing upon specific matters.

9. One illustration, trivial in itself, but significant in what it stands for, is the necessity the adherents of the "will" theory find themselves under, of distinguishing *volitions* from *volonté*. Volitions may proceed from the singular members of an association; *volonté* belongs to the association as such. Saleilles, *De la personnalité juridique* (1910) 565.

enough the difference between a being with will and one without one," his retort may be true for most cases; but it involves more than "common sense" is usually willing to acknowledge: namely, that "will" denotes certain empirically detectable and specifiable consequences, and not a force or entity, psychological or metaphysical. In other words, we determine the absence or presence of "intent," and the kind of "intent," by discrimination among concrete consequences, precisely as we determine "neglect," which by definition is not a peculiar kind of inhering agency. Neglect may, of course, be made into a positive and intrinsic force or agency by hypostatization, but this is parallel to the procedure of school-teachers who make a positive existential entity out of "inattention." If we recur to the logical method of conception by "extensive abstraction," "will," like "interests," denotes a *function*, not an intrinsic force or structure.[10]

II

The foregoing section does not attempt to define what it is to be a "person" in the sense of a right-and-duty-bearing unit. Its purpose is to show the logical method by which such a definition should be arrived at; and, secondly, to show that the question has been enormously complicated by the employment of a wrong logical method, and by the introduction of irrelevant conceptions, imported into legal discussion (and often into legal

10. It would require an article longer than this one merely to list and describe various theories about will which, as held at one time or another, have influenced legal doctrines. One reference must suffice. Professor Pound has repeatedly shown how the conception of "will" was central in the Roman law idea of legal transactions and how it affected the nineteenth century theory of contracts and related subjects. The entire post-Kantian German concept of real personality is affected by Kant's theory of will. Practically, the movement fell in with another, quite different in character, which made "liberty" of will the central thing in order to find a universal basis of political liberty—as with Rousseau. Subsequently, the German and French ideas flowed together, and the conflux was affected by the notion of economic liberty, which readily rationalized itself by getting under the cover of the reigning theory of will. That the idea assisted in promoting movements which were socially useful there can be no doubt. To give one instance, Henderson has suggested its utility in liberalizing the treatment of foreign corporations, which upon the "concession" theory find the going very difficult. See Henderson, *Position of Foreign Corporations in American Constitutional Law* (1918) 5.

practice) from uncritical popular beliefs, from psychology, and from a metaphysics ultimately derived from theology. It is not intended, however, to imply that these extraneous considerations have not been historically significant, nor that the causes of their emergence into law is not of importance for legal history. The reverse is the case. To the student, and not merely the historical student, of human culture, they afford a fascinating, if intricate, field of inquiry; and the history and present status of legal institutions are involved in this study of human culture. The sources, career and effects of the conceptions of "intent" and of "malicious" intent would alone lay bare an instructive cross-section of the whole history of religion, morals and psychology. Of more direct significance for our special theme is the fact that the underlying controversies and their introduction into legal theory and actual legal relations, express struggles and movements of immense social import, economic and political. Such a formal or logical analysis as we have been engaged in is in fact but preliminary. What is back of these factors which are logically extraneous? What vital issues have led to their getting so thoroughly mixed up with questions of legal definition? To answer this question is to engage in a survey of the conflict of church and empire in the Middle Ages; the conflict of rising national states with the medieval Roman empire; the struggle between dynastic and popular representative forms of government; the conflict of feudal institutions, ecclesiastic and agrarian, with the economic needs produced by the industrial revolution and the development of national territorial states; the conflict of the "proletariat" with the employing and capitalist class; the struggle between nationalism and internationalism, or trans-national relations, to mention only a few outstanding movements.[11] These

---

My colleague, Professor H. W. Schneider, has called my attention to the important influence exercised upon theories of the "real" legal personality of corporate groups by the traditional association of the ideas of "agency," "responsibility" and "guilt" with will. I have omitted discussion of this point because its importance would demand an entire paper, at least, for adequate treatment. I would only suggest that the grouping of these ideas together is at present a matter of *historic* interest, but is unnecessary from the standpoint of contemporary thought.

11. Since the last-named topic will not concern us further, one illustration may be mentioned. A potent recent motive for the insistence upon the real "personality" of social groups, or corporate bodies, independent of the state, is op-

conflicts are primarily political and economic in nature. But there is not one of them which has not left its profound impress upon the law, including particularly upon the doctrines of the nature and seat of juridical personality. Discussions and concepts may have been in form intellectual, using a full arsenal of dialectical weapons; they have been in fact, where they have any importance, "rationalizations" of the positions and claims of some party to a struggle. It is this fact which gives such extraordinary interest to the history of doctrines of juridical personality. Add to this fact that the intellectual and scientific history of western Europe is reflected in the changing fortunes of the meanings of "person" and "personality," a history which has both affected and been affected by the social struggles, and the interest and complexity of the doctrines about juridical personality are sufficiently obvious.

For example, the "fiction" theory of the personality of corporate bodies, or *universitates*, was promulgated if not originated, by Pope Innocent IV (1243–1254. St. Thomas Aquinas died in 1274). It is hardly a coincidence that Pope Innocent was one of the strongest upholders of the supremacy of the spiritual over the temporal power, and that he was Pope immediately after the time of the greatest political power of the Papal Empire.[12] In outward form the doctrine that corporate bodies are *personae fictae* was directed at ecclesiastic bodies. The doctrine was stated as the reason why an ecclesiastic *collegium* or *universitas*, or *capitu-*

position to the claim that the state is the sole or even supreme Person. The latter notion reflects the increase of importance of the national territorial state. Opposition from the side we are alluding to, is due to the fact that the doctrine of the ultimate personality of these states finds fitting expression in war. Moreover, war confers upon the states too unrestricted power over their citizens, and also unfavorably affects the complex economic interdependences wrought by modern methods of industry and commerce. In an article written before the war, Lindsay rightly cites Norman Angell as a factor "in the newest political gospel" which "makes open and declared war against the doctrine that the State is a personality." This attack is inspired "not by a belief in the isolation of individuals, but by a perception that the co-operation of individuals and their common dependence on one another extends beyond the bounds of the State." Lindsay, *The State in Recent Political Theory* (1914) 1 POLITICAL QUARTERLY, 128, at 130 and 132.

12. Of a not far remote predecessor, it is said that "The fully rounded ecclesiastic theory, at the climax of actual ecclesiastic power, is to be found in the writings of Pope Innocent III (pontificate 1198–1216)." Dunning, *A History of Political Theories, Ancient and Mediaeval* (1902) 162, 163.

lum could not be excommunicated, or be guilty of a delict. For *nomina sunt juris et non personarum*; they have neither a body nor a will. A chapter was but a name and an incorporeal *res*. Other canonists declared that corporate bodies could not be punished or excommunicated because they had neither a soul nor a body, and carried their nominalism so far as to say that they had being only *in abstracto*, like "man" in respect to men. The doctrine did not imply, however, that excommunication was of no effect; on the contrary, it signified that, in order that a decree of punishment or excommunication should not lack effect, it was to be applied to all, *omnes singulos*. Even if Pope Innocent had not included *populus et gens et hujus modi* along with ecclesiastical groups (we cannot call them bodies on his theory), we may be sure that what applied to religious organizations applied *a fortiori* to civil. A chapter or a *populus* regarded as an entity would not suffer especially from excommunication; it was wholly different when the ban fell upon "*omnes singulos.*"[13] The intellectual factor in the doctrine takes us to the fact that being a "person" was denied to these groups because of the dominant conception of person. The current idea is expressed in the definition of St. Thomas Aquinas, *vera persona est rei rationabilis individua substantia*. In this definition every one of the three last words has a technical meaning that goes back to the metaphysical discussions of Aristotle; the problem of the nature of the "individual" being, indeed, for the Middle Age philosophers, even more of a problem than that of "substance," which had been decided once for all by Aristotle.[14] The consequences of including "rational individuated substance" in the conception of "person" endured long after the metaphysics and theology which gave it

13. I have relied upon Gierke for the references (3 *Das deutsche Genossenschaftsrecht*, 279–85). Gierke says that Pope Innocent IV "was the father of the dogma of the purely fictitious and intellectual character of juridical persons which still rules." Even if this statement were not literally correct the reference would be of great importance because of the currency Maitland gave to the discussion and to Gierke, and because of the influence of Maitland upon Laski, one of the chief modern propounders of the doctrine that organized groups have personality independent of, and in many cases prior to, state action.

14. We are far away from the Latin *persona* which when applied to a man in the concrete hardly meant more than a separate physical body. The change in meaning was undoubtedly of theological origin, the term "*persona*" having been applied by the fathers (first I believe by Tertullian) to the hypostases of the Trinity.

birth were obscured if not forgotten; and they account for much of the difficulty in even recent discussion in attributing "person" to corporate as well as to single units.

The "concession" theory of juridical persons, while often confused with the "fiction" theory, had a different origin, and testifies to quite a different situation of conflict of interests. It is essentially a product of the rise of the national state, with its centralizing tendencies and its objection to *imperia in imperio* at a time when religious congregations and organizations of feudal origin (*communes* and guilds) were rivals of the claim of the national state to complete sovereignty. The shortest cut to making good this claim was to treat all minor organizations as "conjurations" and conspiracies, except as they derived all their powers from an express grant of a supreme power, the State. Certain classes were as much interested in magnifying the government and regulation by statute law as Pope Innocent III was in magnifying the authority and power of the Papacy. The choice of the word "concession" was probably influenced by Roman law.[15]

In lieu of an extended discussion of the practical motivation of the basic ideas of the concession theory, I shall give one quotation. "In its various forms of ecclesiastical bodies and foundations, gilds, municipalities, trading companies, or business organizations, the corporation has always presented the same problem of how to check the tendency of group action to undermine the liberty of the individual or to rival the political power of the state. The somewhat vague theory of the later Middle Ages that communal organization not sanctioned by prescription or royal license was illegal was at least from the fifteenth century on supplemented by the technical doctrine, developed under canonist influences, that there is no capacity to act as a body corporate without positive authorization. To grant this authority has remained in England an attribute of the royal pre-

---

15. Gaius, Digest, III, 4, 1. In all events, it is suggestive that the statements of Gaius were made at a time (161 A.D.) when the Empire was in full centralizing course. It should be noted, however, that Gaius is not referring explicitly to anything he calls persons. His point is that being a *universitas* or *collegium* is something dependent upon statutes, *sensatus consulta* and imperial constitutions. It is interesting, moreover, to note in connection with the efforts to bring Roman ideas into the whole controversy that Maitland expressly says that "The admission must be made that there is no text which directly calls the *universitas* a *persona*, and still less any that calls it *persona ficta*." Gierke (with preface by Maitland), *op. cit. supra* note 3, at xviii.

rogative. . . . It is hardly possible to overestimate the theory that corporate existence depends on positive sanction as a factor in public and legislative policy. It is natural that the charter or incorporation law should be made the vehicle of restraints or regulations which might not be readily imposed upon natural persons acting on their own initiative, and the course of legislative history bears this out." [16]

It is clear that there is nothing essentially in common between the fiction and concession theories, although they both aimed toward the same general consequence, that of limitation of the power of corporate bodies. The fiction theory is ultimately a philosophical theory that the corporate body is but a name, a thing of the intellect; the concession theory may be indifferent as to the question of the reality of a corporate body; what it *must* insist upon is that its *legal power* is derived. In some respects, the concession theory is the more favorable to expanded power of corporations; a charter of broad powers might be granted and the courts might construe its terms liberally. Its promoted assimilation to the singular person, even when a corporation is called "artificial," might even enlarge its rights, privileges and immunities. In an "individualistic" period—that is, an era chiefly concerned with rights of private property and contract—it is pretty sure to do so. Consider, for example, the court decisions that a business corporation is a "person" in the sense covered by the Fourteenth Amendment, and the effects of this decision. On the other hand, the fiction theory that a corporation having no soul cannot be guilty of delict gives a corporation considerable room in which to manoeuvre. Thus we cannot say, without qualifica-

16. Freund, *Standards of American Legislation* (1917) 39. The quotation continues by indicating the restraints imposed on banking and insurance corporations, railways and express companies. Historically, the restrictive attitude towards at least business corporations finds its explanation and justification in the fact that they were few and exceptional, being usually huge trading companies, actually and often nominally, monopolies, whose "rights" were privileges and immunities. As so often happened, words, with associated ideas and temper of mind, persisted after corporations had become commonplace and, indeed, the usual means of carrying on business. Henderson, in the work already referred to, has shown the effect of possession of extraordinary privileges by early corporations in creating fear of them and the extent to which this fear influenced court decisions, as for example, that in the case of *The Bank of the United States v. Deveaux, op. cit. supra* note 10, at 19, 55, 56.

tion in respect of time and conditions, that either theory works out in the direction of limitation of corporate power.[17]

In spite of their historical and logical divergence, the two theories flowed together. Their conflux and its result is exhibited in many decisions of American judges. The practical key to the union, in which the feigned theory on the whole got the better of the concession theory, resides in the allusion just made to an "individualistic" age. When it is difficult to lay hands on the single persons who are said to be the only "real" persons, it is very convenient to do business on a fiction. With respect to its property, the fictitious entity has a clear title as an entity; with respect to its liabilities and burdens outside of property and contract, its position is not so clear; its fictitious character may be cited to relieve it of some obligations usually regarded as moral, and yet legally enforceable as regards single persons. Pope Innocent IV was under no such difficulty. Excommunication could reach down to every part of the aggregate whole; it is not so easy to reach the fluctuating "real" persons who form that "merely collective aggregate," the share-holders in a joint-stock company, especially if they are "widows and orphans." To a considerable extent, the corporation has "had it both ways" when it was regarded as nothing but a name for an aggregate or collection of real persons. Adequately to develop this fact and the reasons for it would require an excursion into the change which took place in the eighteenth and nineteenth centuries in the concept of the "singular person," now become the full-fledged individual in his own right. The excursion cannot be undertaken. Suffice it to say that the single person, as the "real person," is no longer either a physical body or a rational substance. These two meanings persist, but they are covered up with vestments derived from the theory of natural rights inhering in individual persons as such.

17. Imaginary beings or fictions may not only gain privileges because of the absence of souls, but because of the unlimited elasticity of fictions. As Machen says, "If the corporate personality is imaginary, there is no limit to the characteristics and capacities which may be attributed to that personality. . . . If you can imagine a corporate entity is a person, you can also imagine that this person has a mind." Machen, *op. cit. supra* note 1, at 347, 348. The "fiction theory," if it had been separated wholly from the "concession theory," might have lent itself to liberalizing the theory of foreign corporations. Difficulties regarding "residence" and "migration" might easily have been got over; for imaginary creatures are notoriously nimble.

The contrast of "natural" and "artificial" persons got its point from the fact that "natural" connoted possession of inherent and inviolable rights. The dialectic of the courts, under the pressure of social facts, was equal to declaring that corporations, while artificial and fictitious, nevertheless had all the natural rights of an individual person, since after all they were legal persons.

Perhaps a reader may infer that the foregoing amounts to a plea for the "real" personality of corporate bodies. Recurrence to the introductory remarks should, however, dissipate this impression. As far as the historical survey implies a plea for anything, it is a plea for disengaging specific issues and disputes from entanglement with *any* concept of personality which is other than a restatement that such and such rights and duties, benefits and burdens, accrue and are to be maintained and distributed in such and such ways, and in such and such situations.

III

The fact of the case is that there is no clear-cut unity, logical or practical, throughout the different theories which have been advanced and which are still advanced in behalf of the "real" personality of either "natural" or associated persons. Each theory has been used to serve the same ends, and each has been used to serve opposing ends. The doctrine of the personality of the state has been advanced to place the state above legal responsibility on the ground that such a person has no superior person—save God—to whom to answer; and in behalf of a doctrine of the responsibility of the state and its officers to law, since to be a person is to have legal powers and duties. The personality of the state has been opposed to both the personality of "natural" singular persons and to the personality of groups. In the latter connection it has been employed both to make the state the supreme and culminating personality in a hierarchy, to make it but *primus inter paros*, and to reduce it to merely one among many, sometimes more important than others and sometimes less so. These are political rather than legal considerations, but they have affected law. In legal doctrines proper, all theories have been upheld for the same purpose, and each for opposed ends. Corporate groups less than the state have had real personality ascribed to them, both in order to make them more amenable to liability, as in the case of trade-unions, and to exalt their dignity and vital power against external control. Their personality has been denied for like reasons; they have been pulverized into mere aggregates of separate persons in order to protect other laborers from them, to make more difficult their unified action in trade disputes, as in collective bargaining, and to enable union property to escape liability, the associated individuals in their severalty having no property to levy upon. The group personality theory has been asserted both as a check upon what was regarded as anarchic and dissolving individualism, to set up something more abiding and worthful than a single human being, and to increase the power and dignity of the single being as over against the state. Even the doctrine that true personality resides only in the "natural" person has been worked in opposed directions. It was first used to give church or state a short and direct road of approach which would lessen the power of the singular being over against the collective being, while lately, through being affected by "natural" in the sense of natural rights, it has been employed to exalt private, at the expense of public, interests.

Unfortunately, the human mind tends toward fusion rather than discrimination, and the result is confusion. I quote at length from a recent writer: "A position intermediate between the biological and the psychological theories of the state is held by Gierke and Maitland, whose point of view is shared by such writers as Figgis, Laski and Duguit. The founder of this position was the German jurist, Johannes Althusius. . . . His theory of the state as a hierarchy of constituent groups was broadened out by his modern interpreter, Otto Gierke, in his *Genossenschafts-lehre*, which was sponsored and clarified by the eminent English historian and jurist, F. W. Maitland. Briefly, the doctrine is that the state is not a collection of individuals but an aggregation of groups. These groups, in turn, are not merely a plural number of individuals, but an organization of individuals designed to achieve a definite purpose. As purposive groups they are psychic organisms, possessing not a fictitious but a real psychic personality. . . . The exponents of this doctrine of the reality and significance of the group range in their interpretation of the place and significance of the state all the way from the position of such writers as Ernest Barker, who supports an Aristotelian-Hegelian adulation of the state, to the extreme pluralists and the Syndicalists, who would eliminate the state altogether." [18]

The author is writing from the political point of view, not the legal; and the last sentence makes allowance for divergence of views as to the place of the state. But the passage gives the impression of a single school, coherent in its premises if not in its political conclusions. Analysis of the account, therefore, is not just for the sake of convicting Mr. Barnes of error, but for the sake of revealing the fate of any conception that, by ignoring context and purpose, tries to introduce unity into a conception where the facts show utmost divergence. There is a forced assemblage of persons. Laski, like Althusius, has a political interest; but the political interest of Althusius was to afford a basis for popular government, while that of Laski was to moralize the idea of the state, to attack the idea of irresponsible sovereignty, and, under the influence of the pluralistic philosophy of James, to utilize the importance of the group, assumed currently in the sociology of the period, so as to dwell upon the vitality and autonomy of group interests. Althusius, on the other hand, held that the latter, in contracting themselves into the state, lost their autonomous standing with respect to it. [19] The interest of Figgis in group-personality appears to be wholly conditioned upon his

18. Barnes, *Sociology and Political Theory* (1924) 29–30.

19. His (Laski's) article on *Personality of Associations* closes with a section introduced by these words: "If what we have here been urging is true, it reacts most forcibly upon our theory of the state. Thus far, for the most part, we have sought its unification. We have made it intolerant of associations within itself—associations that to Hobbes will appear comparable only to 'worms within the entrails of a natural man'. As a result we have made our state absorptive in a mystic, Hegelian fashion. It is all-sovereign and unchallengeable. . . . But sovereign your state no longer is if the groups within itself are thus self-governing. Nor can we doubt this polyarchism. Everywhere we find groups within the state which challenge its supremacy. They are, it may be, in relations with the state, a part of it; but one with it they are not. They refuse the reduction to unity. We find the state, in James' phrase, to be distributive and not collective." *Foundations of Sovereignty* (1921) 168–169, originally printed in (1916) 29 HARV. L. REV. 404. The statements about the relation of groups and the state may be true, historically, sociologically and ethically. But they are an argument for the volitional personality of these associations only on the theory that the state is also a personal unified will. It was not the Hobbesian theory, or any similar theory, which produced the magnification of the state; the centralizing tendencies of the new national state produced the theory. Similarly, the rising social, economic and political importance of associations is producing, *in analogy with the concept of the older theory of*

desire to preserve the autonomy of ecclesiastic organizations, especially that of the Church of England.[20]

Gierke's interest was primarily legal; he wrote at a time when no German writer of influence would have thought of depreciating the personality of the state; that was taken for granted. The practical issue was found in the quarrel between Romanists and Germanists; Savigny the great Romanist had come out for the *persona ficta* theory of corporate bodies. Gierke wrote as a Germanist to oppose him, and the quarrel found its practical bearing in the fact that the German Civil Code was being drawn. Maitland writes primarily as a historian of legal institutions, although his political interest is sufficient to make him remark that "the State's possession of a real will is insecure if no other groups may have wills of their own." [21] While he leans toward the real personality theory, it is safe to say that he is much more interested in a comparison of German and English theories and practices than he is in any theory; and any one interested in denying the theory can find much material in the rich store Maitland provides.[22] Duguit writes as a lawyer, and his political interest is in making the "state," all officers of government legally liable. He

---

the state, a theory of *their* metaphysical personality. One can get the same practical results with a theory like Duguit's, which denies not only the personality of both state and groups but also of the natural individual, as a substratum of rights-duties. "Public law has become objective just as private law is no longer based on individual right or the autonomy of a private will, but upon the idea of a social function imposed on every person." Duguit, *Law in the Modern State* (1919, translated by Laski) 49. Again, "In private law the autonomy of the human will is in process of disappearance; the individual will is powerless by itself to create a legal situation." Duguit, *supra* at 243.

20. It is interesting to note, as an instance of the particular and "pragmatic" origin of much of the English theorizing, the large part played by the case of the *Free Church of Scotland v. Overtoun* [1904] A. C. 515, and of the trades unions decisions in the *Taff Vale* case [1901] A. C. 426 and the *Osborne* case [1910] A. C. 87. For the former see Vinogradoff, *Juridical Persons* (1924) 24 COL. L. REV. 594, at 597–599. Laski, *op. cit. supra* note 19, at 165–166 has a few comments on the latter two cases. There is a strange logic implied in the reasonings of the "real group personality" school that, since unwise decisions have been reached in a number of cases under cover of the "fictitious person" theory, the "real personality" view must be necessary to reach a correct decision. There is surely more than one alternative possibility omitted.

21. Gierke (with preface by Maitland), *op. cit. supra* note 3, at xlii.

22. Thus his whole discussion of trusts shows how much has been accomplished, avoiding some of the attending difficulties of German law, "without troubling the State to concede or deny the mysterious boon of personality." 3 *Collected Papers* 283. His remark that "it's often struck me that morally

denies will and personality to both the state *and* all other groups. "Nor is it [fault] imputable to the collectivity since the latter outside the imagination of lawyers has no personal existence."[23] As for Ernest Barker, he is indeed strong for the personality of the state, but his purpose is identical with that of Duguit, who denies precisely what Barker asserts: "What is needed is, in the first place, the conception of the State or the Public as a legally responsible person; and, in the second place, the application to this person of the idea of agency in such sort that it shall admit responsibility for the acts of its servants done in its service."[24] Specifically he wants some kind of administrative and law courts, in which the state through its agents, can be rendered liable, although not administrative law of the French type. Finally, the reference to "psychic organisms" is either gratuitous or highly misleading. It is not psychic personality which these writers—as far as they do hold to the personality of the state—are concerned with, but a moral personality, that is unity of organized action involving "will." The idea of psychic personality is read in from writers on social psychology and sociology.

I do not make this examination for the sake of indicating that Mr. Barnes sins above others. As already stated, the collection of commissions and omissions is the sort of thing which is bound to happen when one assumes that there is in existence some single and coherent theory of personality and will, singular or associated. Nothing accurate or intelligible can be said except by specifying the interest and purpose of a writer, and his historical context of problems and issues. Thus we end where we began: with the statement that the entire discussion of personality, whether of single or corporate personality, is needlessly encumbered with a mass of traditional doctrines and remnants of old issues. Almost every English writer, beginning with Maitland, who has written in behalf of the doctrine of the "real personality" of

---

there is most personality where legally there is least" certainly cuts both ways. The fact that the family, which is the most intimate emotional and volitional unity, is not a jural personality, has given the adherents of the real personality theory much difficulty.

23. Duguit, *Law in the Modern State* (1919) 205–6.
24. Barker, *The "Rule of Law"* (May, 1914) THE POLITICAL QUARTERLY, 117, at 123. For a full discussion of this matter see Borchard, *Government Liability in Tort* (1924–1925) 34 YALE LAW JOURNAL, 1, 129, 229.

corporate bodies, has felt obliged to quote the following from Dicey: "When a body of twenty or two thousand or two hundred thousand men bind themselves together to act in a particular way for some common purpose, they create a body which by no fiction of law but by the very nature of things, differs from the individuals of whom it is composed." Assuredly; but why should such a fact be thought to have any bearing at all upon the problem of personality? Only because the doctrine of "fictitious" personality had been employed, under the influence of the "individualistic" philosophy already referred to, to deny that there is any social reality at all back of or in corporate action. Hence the assertion of the simple fact that there is some social reality involved got bound up with the notion of a real, as distinct from fictitious personality. The example, it seems to me, is sufficiently striking to enforce the value of eliminating the *idea* of personality until the concrete facts and relations involved have been faced and stated on their own account: retaining the *word* will then do no great harm.

A Naturalistic Theory of
Sense-Perception

In its primary and unsophisticated use, sense-perception signifies observation and recognition of objects by means of bodily organs, eyes, ears, hands, nose, *etc*. As a term, it is like pen-writing, brush-painting, hammer-pounding, steel-engraving. It tells nothing about the nature of perceiving, but conveys information about the means by which the act of perceiving occurs, just as the other phrases specify tools through which acts take place. However in each case the act and its characteristic consequences are modified by the traits of the organs and means which are involved. Thus questions arise: In what way do the employed instrumentalities affect the act and thereby its results? In carrying on such inquiries, investigators are led to discoveries far outside the scope of the first question. In connection with acts performed by the use of tools, not only are their specific effects learned, but principles of friction, mechanical equivalents of heat, the correlation of energies are ascertained. Similarly, in connection with the use of the eyes, ears, *etc*., in the act of perceiving, not only are the particular functions of different organic structures learned, but such things as the effects of color blindness, astigmatism, muscular adjustments, refraction by the lens. In short, we learn how nerve-elements interact with external physical changes in bringing about the occurrence of certain perceived qualities. But all this concerns the things perceived. It does not affect the act of perceiving. Hence such problems as present themselves are of the same order as those hit upon in any naturalistic inquiry. They do not concern the nature of perception, awareness, or knowledge. There is nothing peculiar, nothing unique about them.

The adjectives "sense" and "sensory" are prefixed to qualities

[First published in *Journal of Philosophy* 22 (22 October 1925): 596–605.]

as well as to the act of perceiving. Colors, sounds, odors, rough, smooth, *etc.*, are named "sense-qualities." Here the term "sense" is prefixed by a figure of speech. The qualities themselves are not sensory; "sensory" designates an important condition of their occurrence, not a constituent in their nature. By precisely a similar usage of speech, a house, factory, barn is called a building, meaning that which is the outcome of the operation of building; no one is misled by the word into transferring the properties of the act of building into the house or factory. So a picture is named a painting or an oil-color or a water-color. In each case the name is given because of the consequences of the means employed upon the object produced, yet its traits, uses, and career when produced are independent of the act of generation. We might also call "sense" qualities vibration qualities, or cerebral qualities, or by the name of any other factor which conditions their occurrence. In short, perception does not affect or infect the nature of the qualities perceived, although sense-*organs*, and their structural connections which are the means of perceiving, do affect the properties of the thing produced. But there is nothing unique or peculiar about this fact. The same thing happens in any natural sequence when traits of a consequence are correlated with traits of interacting antecedents.

The significance of the point of view thus briefly indicated lies in its contrast with the epistemological theory of sense-perception; in contrast with that theory, the one set forth may be termed naturalistic. By the epistemological theory, sense-perception means a unique kind of perception, and sense quality means a kind of quality so distinctive that it may be called psychical or mental. Upon the naturalistic theory, all perception is one and the same, and prefixed adjectives, like sensory, refer to its means or organs; the difference between an object perceived by means of the senses and an object recalled by means of some other organic structure is comparable to the difference between any two concrete things, say between a cat and dog, land and water. The difference is in one factual subject-matter, "sense-presentation" having for its subject-matter a thing in some *present* space-relation, memory-presentation that thing in a specified past temporal relation. But upon the other theory, perception is made unique and heterogeneous because of its "sense" nature, and hence the objects of the two modes of presentation are so different in kind that a problem is constituted. And the same thing occurs in the case of contrast of things presented as "conceptual" (or reflectively determined) objects in distinction from "sense" objects. In one theory the difference between colors and, say, electro-magnetic disturbances is a difference in specified facts in one and the same world of objects, comparable again to the difference between land and water as objects of perception; on the other theory, there is a gulf in kind between them, and we have to decide which is "the reality," or else find some method of "reconciling" the reality of the one kind of object with that of the other kind of object.

There is, therefore, a question of fact behind the epistemological question. Until this question of fact has been decided the epistemological problem may possibly be a wholly artificial question due to assuming as a fact something which is not a fact. Is the prefixing of "sense" or "sensory" to "perception" metaphorical, transferring by an intrinsically harmless and common figure of speech traits of the tools and effects of an act to the act itself? Is it properly analogous to water-color painting and oil-painting, to etching and engraving, as names for pictures?[1] Or does it properly denote a distinctive and unique kind of presentation, "sensory" affecting and qualifying throughout the intrinsic nature of the being aware, and thereby determining that of which we are aware to be a distinctive and unique kind of thing?

This question is primarily, as indicated, a question of fact. The factual reasons assigned for accepting the second alternative have to do with various "abnormalities" in connection with perception by means of sense-organs. There is an almost endless list of such occurrences so that only a few samples need be given. They are such affairs as double images when the object remains one; the changes which take place in an image while the object remains unaltered—as seeing a thing dance when the eye-ball is

1. The implication of the question is not that reference to mode of production is an illegitimate way of distinguishing different specific qualities from one another. The nature of the difference between an engraving and an etching, a wood-engraving and a steel-engraving, may be more exactly and surely determined if we know the different ways in which they are produced. But this is an *added* knowledge about pictures; it does not create a problem as to the nature of pictorial representation *ueberhaupt*. Similarly the effect of sensory and other organic conditions upon the particular things which we perceive does not create a problem as to the nature of perception as such.

pushed; a stick seemingly bent in water; the change in the visual form of things seen in different perspectives and angles; the change in apparent pitch of sound with velocity of approach or removal; converging railway tracks *etc.*, to say nothing of outright illusions. In the words of a contemporary epistemological writer: "The point is, that all these cases can easily be described in terms of actual and potential *sensations*, while a description in terms of *objects* leads to grave difficulties."[2] The contrast drawn by the italicized words, "sensations" and "objects," is equivalent to the difference between statements in terms of specified subject-matters on one hand, and a unique peculiarity of perception on the other, "sensations" meaning, as here used, a peculiar kind of existence called psychical.

Discussion of facts is however bound up with difficulties arising from implications of terminology and from diverse theories inherited from previous philosophizing. This paper is given to an effort to clear away some of the underbrush which obscures vision.

In the first place, traditional ideas have had an effect because of language which persisted after the beliefs that had given it significance and pertinence had disappeared. "Sense qualities" is, historically, a survival of *sensible* qualities: but while "sense" prefixed to qualities has no import save that of causal reference, "sensible" was, given the metaphysical creed which once obtained, a genuine characterization of some qualities in distinction from others, namely, "intelligible" qualities. Nature was divided, cosmically, into kinds of objects, or at least of objects with two kinds of properties. One set was permanent; the other was of nature in movement or change; one was of things as actualized, the other of things *qua* potential. Since the properties of natural change were actualized in animals, including man, through sense organs, these qualities were fittingly called sensible. The "ible" clearly implies potentiality, requiring sense for their actualization into sense-forms or sensory essences. Intellig*ible* forms, on the other hand, were actualized through the intellect. Thus the term "sensible qualities" had a characteristic and, given the premises, legitimate meaning. When modern physi-

2. Durant Drake, in an article entitled "What Kind of Realism?" in the *Journal of Philosophy*, Vol. 9, p. 150, italics mine.

cal science asserted the homogeneity of all things in the physical world and abandoned the category of potentiality and actuality for that of physical contact and motion ("efficient causality"), the term "sensible qualities" still continued in use. It was "rationalized" by interpreting it to mean qualities due to perception in distinction from qualities belonging to things themselves.[3]

Secondly, epistemological arguments that make qualities in the generation of which sense organs play a part to be of a different order from things, are pervasively infected with an ambiguity. This consists in treating empirical things (trees, stones, stars, candle-flames, *etc.*, all the things designated by ordinary common nouns) now as the causes of qualities, and now as correlated groups of the qualities. Thus we are told that a *tree* affects the *optic nerve*—(or the light reflected from a tree), giving rise to "sensations" of light and color; that a *stick*, partly in the *air* and partly in the *water*, through interaction with *sense-organs* and *brain*, occasions "sensations" which in turn give rise to a perception of a bent stick. Now it is clear that all the italicized words, whether naming things within or without the organism, designate empirical objects, not the objects of distinctively physical science. They are all, so to speak, in the same boat with colors and figures. The same is true, of course, when the finger pressing upon the eye-balls is said to cause the perception of double images, *etc.*, *etc.* Now a moment's reflection shows that tree, stick, water, air, finger, and all such objects as figure in these arguments can not be opposed as real or as physical objects to sensations as mental. For these things, by the logic of the epistemologists, are themselves groups or combinations of "sensations," or of their equivalent mental "images." They are, in Locke's language, themselves complex modes, and can be distinguished from the sensation or sense quality only as the compound from the simple. They are of the same order, not of a dif-

---

3. Locke, for example, does not use the expression "sense" or "sensory" qualities, but retains the older terminology, "sensible qualities," although repudiating the science and metaphysics which gave it significance. But it should also be noted that Locke uses "sensation" not to denote an existence, but an *operation* of mind. It is the act of mind which takes place when the mind perceives an idea upon occasion of changes in sense organs, themselves due to changes of objects which affect the sense-organs. We get the idea of sensation, therefore, not from sensation, but, as in the case of all ideas of operations of the mind, from "reflection." See Book II of the *Essay*, Chaps. 9 and 19.

ferent order. And if we do not use the language of epistemology, but of common sense, we are dealing with things and *their* qualities.

The thing which is to be distinguished from a quality as its cause is not tree, finger, water *etc.*, but certain molecular disturbances. The latter are contrasted with the empirical thing, the finger, as well as with the immediate color quality. The bearing of this fact upon our present topic may be seen by taking the well-worn illustration of a penny seen now as a round flat disc, now as an ellipse with various degrees of distortion, and now, seen edgewise, as a curved line—or from a distance as a straight line. Unless there is a passage from one genus, from one universe of discourse, to another the facts must be stated in one or other of the two following ways. (1) Certain molecular disturbances in interaction with another set of molecular arrangements— empirically identified as the human organism—*cause* various phenomena of shape to appear. The round, flat form is no more the "real" (physical) object than are the ellipses and lines; the latter are not appearances of it, but they and it alike are "appearances" due to physical, or physical and physico-chemical changes. "Appearance" here has no other meaning than *effects*, effects used, as effects are everywhere used in scientific inquiry, to make inferences regarding their cause. In this case, the problems involved are similar to those found in any scientific inquiry where certain facts serve as evidence from which to infer something else, externally of quite a different sort. Thus a form in a rock is used to tell of the presence and traits of an animal which lived in some by-gone age. It is thus an "appearance" of that animal: that is, it is an effect which gets its full meaning only when placed in connection with something else of which it serves as sign or evidence.

(2) The other mode of statement is concerned simply with empirical relations between what is empirically perceived. The relations with which it deals are those of whole and part, or of a thing and its "belongings," not those of inference from what is perceived to some hypothetical or inferred cause. Thus an object when placed in a certain position with reference to the body presents a flat, round form, while when otherwise placed, it presents an elliptical form, or that of a curved edge. Or, suppose we begin with a form like that of a narrow curved band; we find that

it can be placed in a serial order of other forms, some elliptical and some round and that a single formula can be found for the entire serial order, just as some numbers which first present themselves at random, or as a jumble, are finally arranged in a series having a principle of connection. There is no question of cause and effect, of "reality" and "appearance" even in the logical, non-epistemological sense, found in our previous case. There is simply and only a question of the correlation according to a constant formula of various qualities, the total correlated series constituting the object, say a penny. "It," the penny, has or is a series of phases, and physical conditions are such that the phases can not occur simultaneously but only serially—just as there is a series of phases by a determinable formula of gas, liquid, and solid. We may ask which most frequently occurs, and we may take, if we please, the frequency mode, for *practical* purposes, as the standard. But there is no sense in regarding one of them exclusively as the real and the others as its appearances. Every conceivable form or phase may, by the formula of the series, be taken as real in turn and the others as its appearances. But the fact denoted by this language is simply the existence of a series of a determined type.

There are thus two universes of discourse. In one we deal with the physical, existential relation of causal connection, as between colors, sounds, *etc.*, and their conditions such as vibrations of a physical medium. In the other, we deal with the integrations of various perceptual objects into a whole. The problem is not one of causation, but neither is it one of the connection of a perceived object with an inferred object. It is like the problem of, say, getting the meaning of a sentence by integrating the meaning of words, or, *vice-versa*, of defining the meaning of a word otherwise unknown by considering its contextual connections. A problem different from the problems of physical science and from those of ordinary empirical interpretation arises only if we mix and confuse terms taken from the two different universes of discourse.

Let "real object" be taken at one juncture in the discussion to signify the cause of certain qualitative and immediate effects, and at another juncture as the correlation of these effects into a single whole, and the confusion will generate the epistemological problem of perception as that is ordinarily stated. The confusion is increased by the ambiguities of the word "appear." Sometimes it signifies "be the effect of," as color is the effect of physical rays, or a fossil stone is the "appearance" of a once living animal; sometimes it signifies "be evident, apparent, immediately open to perception" like something before me in contrast with something in the next room, or the edge of a coin in contrast with the entire coin, or a particular role of an actor in contrast with the whole set of roles which define the actor. Then the confused mixture of the two senses generates the idea of "appearance" as distinct from the "real," and hence the problem of the relation of the perceived object as, metaphysically, an appearance in contrast with the unperceived but real object.

In the third place, there is the persistent notion, taken over from Locke by psychological doctrine, that the first qualities perceived are simple and independent: that "red" is sensed before blood or a dress is perceived; blue before the sky, sweet before sugar, orange color and a peculiar odor before *an* orange, *etc*. This is pure superstition. Yet if it is surrendered, the whole current distinction between sensation and perception as modes of "consciousness" or of knowing objects disappears. The so-called "sensation" signifies simply a perception of a *discriminated* quality; the limit of perceptual discrimination by means of a given organ. Red is not *a* sensation; it is a quality which we perceive, differing only from the perception of sunset in its relative simplicity and isolation, a difference which is not in any sense original and primitive, but which is the product of discerning analysis purposefully undertaken, as much so as the chemical determination of hydrogen as simple and different from water the compound. As a matter of fact (though facts have come to have little to do with discussion of these matters), a child recognizes its dresses long before it identifies colors; and it learns to distinguish colors as *marks*, that is as *means* of more effective discrimination between different dresses—or toys or other objects. When the homogeneity of perceptual qualities and objects is acknowledged and firmly held to, one important phase of the so-called epistemological problem of perception assumes the proper form of a familiar logical situation—the relation of a sign, mark, to that which is signified.

Fourthly, the question of the spatial location of qualities perceived by means of the senses is one of physics and not of epistemology. The case of the whereabouts of illusory objects is usually cited as the final clincher to demonstrate the psychical character of the characteristic objects of sense-perception. Where is the ghost that isn't there? Where is the imaged tree which moves when the eye-ball is pushed? Where is the bent stick when the straight stick is plunged in water? It has even been suggested that mental or psychical may be defined as that which physical or public space refuses to accept and assign place to,[4] so conclusive is this type of question felt to be.

The source of this difficulty is failure to make a critical analysis of the conception of "where," of situs. Where, for example, is an explosion? Where is an echo? Where is the "magnetism" that causes a sensitized needle to assume a certain directional position? Wherever there is an event, there is interaction, and interaction entails the conception of a *field*. No "field" can be precisely delimited; it extends wherever the energies involved in the interaction operate and as far as any redistributions of energy are effected. The field can be limited *practically*, as can all matters of degree; it can not be existentially located with literal exactness. Thus the place of most *intense* disturbance in an earthquake may be located and, with sufficient variety of seismographic apparatus, the boundaries of its *appreciable* presence may be mapped out. But these boundaries are set practically by capacity to detect and record changes; they are not absolute in any existential sense. One might say that existentially the field of the earthquake is the entire universe since the redistribution of energies extends indefinitely. This would be correct, theoretically, though practically of no significance.

In similar fashion the bent rays of light in the case of the stick partly in air and partly in water are literally an interaction field determined by (presumably) electro-magnetic disturbances, physiological structures and a refracting agency. It is not "in" the organism, nor is it "at" a highly delimited spot in the environment. The place where light rays impinge on the refracting thing with its different angles of refraction in two media of different density may form one focus in the field; the point where the refracted rays impinge on the molecular structures forming the optical apparatus may be another focus. But these, like foci of an

4. Lovejoy, *Essays in Critical Realism*, p. 61.

ellipse, are determinations in a wider field. The sun—or other source of light—is a part of the "where" of the bent rays, just as much as some remote portions of the interior of the earth are a part of the "where" of an earthquake.

Specific location is always a relationship to a *further* event: it is additive in character. We "locate" an explosion *at* a given spot because the act of generating or preventing the explosion, the act of control of occurrence, is directed there. If we knew enough and had the power to occasion and to prevent earthquakes, we should undoubtedly say that an earthquake is *where* the act of control is applied. A disease involves the entire organism and (ultimately) some extra-organic interacting event, but its "seat" is where remedial measures most effectively take place. A man's body may be in Europe, since in certain respects he may be reached there most effectively, while his residence is in Florida and his domicile in New York. The demand to know "where" are the images of the tree that move when the eye-ball is pushed is an ambiguous question. Literally they are wherever a certain interaction of at least three factors is taking place. From the everyday practical standpoint, that of "common-sense," "where" signifies the point at which action should be directed to control the occurrence of the phenomenon.

The fact that "where" in ordinary usage contains a reference to an act, originating in an organic agent, is a commonplace. But unfortunately it is not usual to employ the commonplace in discussing questions of this sort. To "common-sense" a thing is located with respect to that locomotion or other movement of the organism which is required to attain or prevent certain results. That a thing is so many paces away in front, to the right and a little above, signifies that the human body must move so far ahead, swerve to one side and raise some part of itself in order to procure certain consequences. Every psychological book is full of instances of the fact that specific location is not inherent or intrinsic, but has reference to the actual or potential behavior of an organism in effecting a course of events. The location of the stick which is in the air is related to a certain habit of reaching and handling. This habit being adapted to a certain medium does not work correctly when the refraction of light occurs under unusual conditions. A wrong, an inefficient, unadapted act hence takes place. When the habit is re-made, specific location again takes place correctly. There does not appear to be any further mystery in the cases which are frequently employed to show that some objects of perception are mental in nature. Anyone who learns to use a microscope, or even a mirror, learns that specific location is a practical matter, not a literal existential one, and that unusual conditions of the coordination of acts of seeing and reaching occasion difficulty in locating until a new habit is set up. That certain images of light can not be located in space signifies, then, only that the practical act of reaching and grasping in their case, does not without pains and practice, fit into the established systems of habits which customarily determine the seat, residence, or situs of an affair, the latter being physically and literally a complex interaction, covering a vast field. Indeed, the field is so vast and illimitable that, strictly speaking, the interaction may be said to be "of" nature rather than "in" it, in the practical sense in which we quite properly use the terms "in" and "of." The theory criticized is thus also guilty of the third of the misconceptions we have mentioned. It passes surreptitiously from ordinary perceived spatial relations of perceived things to "physical" space in the sense of space as the object of physical science. If we stick strictly to physical terms, there is no peculiar problem, but only the ordinary scientific problem of determining a field. If we stick to empirical perceptual terms, there is only the problem of correct practical adjustments in reaching, grasping, handling, *etc.*

I do not suppose that the four misconceptions which have been considered exhaust the list of antecedent confusions and mistakes which bring about the conversion of a naturalistic view into an epistemological one. But they are important contributing factors. Until these preliminary ambiguities and shiftings have been got rid of, there seems to be little hope that continued discussion of the problem of perception which proceeds without any reference to them will bring us nearer to agreement and settlement. When they are disposed of, as far as there remain anything more than scientific questions of a familiar type, the residual problems concern metaphysical matters, such as import of the causal relationship and the nature and status of qualities.

Individuality and Experience

The interesting report of Dr. Munro in the October number of the *Journal of the Barnes Foundation* on the methods of picture-making employed in the classes of Professor Cizek in Vienna raises a question that has to be dealt with in every branch of instruction. The question develops in two directions, one suggested by his statement that it is impossible to exclude outside influences, and the other by his report that upon the whole the more original constructions are those of younger pupils, that older students seem gradually to lose interest, so that no prominent artist has been produced. The problem thus defined consists in the relation of individuality and its adequate development to the work and responsibilities of the teacher, representing accumulated experience of the past.

Unfortunately, the history of schools not only in art but in all lines shows a swing of the pendulum between extremes, though it must be admitted that the simile of the pendulum is not a good one, for the schools remain most of them, most of the time, near one extreme, instead of swinging periodically and evenly between the two. Anyway, the two extremes are external imposition and dictation and "free-expression." Revolt from the costly, nerve-taxing and inadequate results of mechanical control from without creates an enthusiasm for spontaneity and "development from within," as it is often phrased. It is found that children at first are then much happier in their work—anyone who has seen Cizek's class will testify to the wholesome air of cheerfulness, even of joy, which pervades the room—but gradually tend to become listless and finally bored, while there is an absence of cumulative, progressive development of power and of actual achievement in results. Then the pendulum swings back to

[First published in *Journal of the Barnes Foundation* 2 (January 1926): 1–6.]

regulation by the ideas, rules, and orders of some one else, who being maturer, better informed and more experienced is supposed to know what should be done and how to do it.

The metaphor of the pendulum is faulty in another respect. It seems to suggest that the solution lies in finding a mid-point between the two extremes which would be at rest. But what is really wanted is a change in the direction of movement. As a general proposition no one would deny that personal mental growth is furthered in any branch of human undertaking by contact with the accumulated and sifted experience of others in that line. No one would seriously propose that all future carpenters should be trained by actually starting with a clean sheet, wiping out everything that the past has discovered about mechanics, about tools and their uses and so on. It would not be thought likely that this knowledge would "cramp their style," limit their individuality, etc. But neither, on the other hand, have carpenters been formed by the methods often used in manual training shops where dinky tasks of a minute and technical nature are set, wholly independent of really making anything, having only specialized skill as their aim. As a rule carpenters are educated in their calling by working with others who have experience and skill, sharing in the simpler portions of the real undertakings, assisting in ways which enable them to observe methods and to see what results they are adapted to accomplish.

Such learning is controlled by two great principles: one is participation in something inherently worth while, or undertaken on its own account; the other, is perception of the relation of means to consequences. When these two conditions are met, a third consideration usually follows as a matter of course. Having had an experience of the meaning of certain technical processes and forms of skill there develops an interest in skill and "technique": the meaning of the result is "transferred" to the means of its attainment. Boys interested in base-ball as a game thus submit themselves voluntarily to continued practice in throwing, catching, batting, the separate elements of the game. Or boys who get interested in the game of marbles will practice to increase their skill in shooting and hitting. Just imagine, however, what would happen if they set these exercises as tasks in school, with no prior activity in the games and with no sense of what they were about or for, and without any such appeal to the social, or participating impulses, as takes place in games!

If we generalize from such a commonplace case as the education of artisans through their work, we may say that the customs, methods and *working* standards of the calling constitute a "tradition," and that initiation into the tradition is the means by which the powers of learners are released and directed. But we should also have to say that the urge or need of an individual to join in an undertaking is a necessary prerequisite of the tradition's being a factor in his personal growth in power and freedom; and also that he has to *see* on his own behalf and in his own way the relations between means and methods employed and results achieved. Nobody else can see for him, and he can't see just by being "told," although the right kind of telling may guide his seeing and thus help him see what he needs to see. And if he has no impelling desire of his own to become a carpenter, if his interest in being one is perfunctory, if it is not an interest in *being* a carpenter at all, but only in getting a pecuniary reward by doing jobs, the tradition will never of course really enter into and integrate with his own powers. It will remain, then, a mere set of mechanical and more or less meaningless rules that he is obliged to follow if he is to hold his job and draw his pay.

Supposing, again, that our imaginary pupil works for and with a master carpenter who believes in only one kind of house with a fixed design, and his aim is not only to teach his apprentice to make just that one kind of house, but to accept it with all his soul, heart and mind as the only kind of house that should ever be built, the very type and standard model of all houses. Then it is easy to see that limitation of personal powers will surely result, not merely, moreover, limitation of technical skill but, what is more important, of his powers of observation, imagination, judgment, and even his emotions, since his appreciations will be warped to conform to the one preferred style. The imaginary case illustrates what often happens when we pass from the education of artisans to that of artists. As a rule a carpenter has to keep more or less open; he is exposed to many demands and must be flexible enough to meet them. He is in no position to set up a final authority about ends and models and standards, no matter how expert he may be in methods and means. But an architect in distinction from a builder is likely to be an "authority"; he can dictate and lay down what is right and wrong, and thus prescribe certain ends and proscribe others. Here is a case where tradition is not enhancing and liberating, but is restrictive and enslaving. If he has pupils, he is a "master" and not an advanced fellow worker; his students are disciples rather than learners. Tradition is no longer tradition but a fixed and absolute convention.

In short, the practical difficulty does not reside in any antagonism of methods and rules and results worked out in past experience to individual desire, capacity and freedom. It lies rather in the hard and narrow and, we may truly say, uneducated habits and attitudes of teachers who set up as authorities, as rulers and judges in Israel. As a matter of course they know that as bare individuals they are not "authorities" and will not be accepted by others as such. So they clothe themselves with some tradition as a mantle, and henceforth it is not just "I" who speaks, but some Lord speaks through me. The teacher then offers himself as the organ of the voice of a whole school, of a *finished* classic tradition, and arrogates to himself the prestige that comes from what he is the spokesman for. Suppression of the emotional and intellectual integrity of pupils is the result; their freedom is repressed and the growth of their own personalities stunted. But it is not because of any opposition between the wisdom and skill of the past and the individual capacities of learners; the trouble lies in the habits, standards and ideas of the teacher. It is analogous to another case. There is no inherent opposition between theory and practice; the former enlarges, releases and gives significance to the latter; while practice supplies theory with its materials and with the test and check which keeps it sincere and vital. But there is a whole lot of opposition between human beings who set themselves up as practical and those who set themselves up as theorists, an irresolvable conflict because both have put themselves into a wrong position.

This suggests that the proponents of freedom are in a false position as well as the would-be masters and dictators. There is a present tendency in so-called advanced schools of educational thought (by no means confined to art classes like those of Cizek) to say, in effect, let us surround pupils with certain materials, tools, appliances, etc., and then let pupils respond to these things according to their own desires. Above all let us not suggest any end or plan to the students; let us not suggest to them what they shall do, for that is an unwarranted trespass upon their sacred intellectual individuality since the essence of such individuality is to set up ends and aims.

Now such a method is really stupid. For it attempts the impossible, which is always stupid; and it misconceives the conditions of independent thinking. There are a multitude of ways of reacting to surrounding conditions, and without some guidance from experience these reactions are almost sure to be casual, sporadic and ultimately fatiguing, accompanied by nervous strain. Since the teacher has presumably a greater background of experience, there is the same presumption of the right of a teacher to make suggestions as to what to do, as there is on the part of the head carpenter to suggest to apprentices something of what they are to do. Moreover, the theory literally carried out would be obliged to banish all artificial materials, tools and appliances. Being the product of the skill, thought and matured experience of others, they would also, by the theory, "interfere" with personal freedom.

Moreover, when the child proposes or suggests what to do, some consequence to be attained, whence is the suggestion supposed to spring from? There is no spontaneous germination in the mental life. If he does not get the suggestion from the teacher, he gets it from somebody or something in the home or the street or from what some more vigorous fellow pupil is doing. Hence the chances are great of its being a passing and superficial suggestion, without much depth and range—in other words, not specially conducive to the developing of freedom. If the teacher is really a teacher, and not just a master or "authority," he should know enough about his pupils, their needs, experiences, degrees of skill and knowledge etc., to be able (not to dictate aims and plans) to share in a discussion regarding what is to be done and be as free to make suggestions as any one else. (The implication that the teacher is the one and only person who has no "individuality" or "freedom" to "express" would be funny if it were not often so sad in its outworkings.) And his contribution, given the conditions stated, will presumably do more to getting something started which will really secure and increase the development of strictly individual capacities than will suggestions springing from uncontrolled haphazard sources.

The point is also worth dwelling upon, that the method of leaving the response entirely to pupils, the teacher supplying, in the language of the day, only the "stimuli," misconceives the nature of thinking. Any so-called "end" or "aim" or "project" which the average immature person can suggest in advance is likely to be highly vague and unformed, a mere outline sketch, not a suggestion of a definite result or consequence but rather a gesture which roughly indicates a field within which activities might be carried on. It hardly represents thought at all: it is a suggestion. The real intellectual shaping of the "end" or purpose comes during and because of the operations subsequently performed. This is as true of the suggestion which proceeds from the teacher as of those which "spontaneously" spring from the pupils, so that the former does not restrict thought. The advantage on the side of the teacher—if he or she has any business to be in that position—is the greater probability that it will be a suggestion which will permit and require thought in the subsequent activity which builds up a clear and organized conception of an end. There is no more fatal flaw in psychology than that which takes the original vague fore-feeling of some consequence to be realized as the equivalent of a *thought* of an end, a true purpose and directive plan. The thought of an end is strictly correlative to perception of means and methods. Only when, and as the latter becomes clear during the serial process of execution does the project and guiding aim and plan become evident and articulated. In the full sense of the word, a person becomes aware of what he wants to do and what he is about only when the work is actually complete.

The adjective "serial" is important in connection with the process of performance or execution. Each step forward, each "means" used, is a partial attainment of an "end." It makes clearer the character of that end, and hence suggests to an observing mind the next step to be taken, or the means and methods to be next employed. Originality and independence of thinking are therefore connected with the intervening process of execution rather than with the source of the initial suggestion. Indeed, genuinely fruitful and original suggestions are themselves usually the results of experience in the carrying out of undertakings. The "end" is not, in other words, an end or finality in the literal sense, but is in turn the starting point of new desires, aims and plans. By means of the process the mind gets power to make suggestions which are significant. There is now a past experience from which they can spring with an increased probability of their being worthwhile and articulate.

It goes without saying that a teacher may interfere and impose alien standards and methods during the operation. But as we have previously seen, this is not because of bringing to bear the results of previous experience, but because the habits of the teacher are so narrow and fixed, his imagination and sympathies so limited, his own intellectual horizon so bounded, that he brings them to bear in a wrong way. The fuller and richer the experience of the teacher, the more adequate his own knowledge of "traditions" the more likely is he, given the attitude of participator instead of that of master, to use them in a liberating way.

Freedom or individuality, in short, is not an original possession or gift. It is something to be achieved, to be wrought out. Suggestions as to things which may advantageously be taken, as to skill, as to methods of operation, are indispensable conditions of its achievement. These by the nature of the case must come from a sympathetic and discriminating knowledge of what has been done in the past and how it has been done.

Events and the Future

It is quite possible to use the word "event" as a fundamental term in science and yet carry over into the meaning of the
term implications which belong to an order of scientific conceptions which "event" is employed to replace, and which are
incompatible with satisfying the conditions which "event" is
selected to meet. An illustration of this fact, and of the philosophical consequences of it, is found in Broad's *Scientific
Thought*. Following Whitehead, Broad points out that "there are
many types of objects whose characteristic qualities need a certain minimum of duration to inhere in." For example, if nothing
is a mind which does not have memory, a long enough duration
to permit memory is clearly necessary to the existence of a mind.
Again, "Suppose that a certain sort of atom consisted of a nu-
cleus and an electron rotating about it at a certain characteristic
speed. Such an atom would need at least the duration of one
complete rotation to display its characteristic properties. . . . If
the duration of one complete rotation be sliced up into adjacent
successive parts, *the contents of the parts will differ in quality
from the contents of the whole*." [1]

I quote the passage because it gives an indispensable character
of anything which may be termed an event: namely, a qualitative
variation of parts with respect to the whole which requires duration in which to display itself. If we assume only qualitative homogeneity in a mind, we shall not have memory, and hence by
definition not a mind. For the later portion of the total duration,
even if *otherwise* exactly like the earlier, must, if there be memory, differ from it by recalling the previous state, and hence can
not be a mere unchanged persistence of the earlier.

1. Broad, *Scientific Thought*, p. 403, italics not in original.

[First published in *Journal of Philosophy* 23 (13 May 1926): 253–58.]

Unfortunately, however, Mr. Broad at once goes on to show that he does *not* regard qualitative variation to be involved in the definition of an event. He says "there may well be objects which are temporally homogeneous. This would mean that, however you divide up their *history*, the contents of the slices are the same as each other and as the whole in quality. . . . Now science regards the *ultimate* scientific objects as being spatio-temporally homogeneous. And it assumes that these ultimate scientific objects never begin or end. Thus the ultimate scientific objects are regarded as *eternal* in the sense of existing throughout all time. The only ultimate scientific changes are the groupings and re-groupings of such objects according to a single set of fundamental laws." [2]

Now I am not concerned here to try to show that there are no such *objects*. Mr. Broad says that he does not know whether the assumption that there are such objects is true or not, and I shall not profess to know that it is false. But one can assert on purely formal grounds that such objects are not events, nor parts of events. Eternal objects have no "history," much less a history which can be "divided." And if it is stated that such objects are the "temporally homogeneous" slabs out of which events or histories are composed, it is not evident how the union or co-adjacence of the timeless can give rise to time, nor how the qualitatively homogeneous can pass into the qualitatively heterogeneous; nor, to generalize, how "eternal objects" subject to a "single set of fundamental laws" can permit of *re*groupings, nor what conceivable meaning can attach to the phrase "ultimate scientific *changes*." The argument is not helped out by saying that the ultimate objects are eternal in the sense of "existing throughout all time." For unless there are changes and changes such that eternal objects can be put in correspondence with them, on the basis of which correspondence eternal objects may be said to have duration, there is no time for them to exist "throughout." There is also no sense in terming them *temporally* homogeneous. Their homogeneity with respect to temporality is utter irrelevancy to it. In short, the only logical significance which can be attached to the passage cited is one which makes "objects" logically prior to

2. *Ibid.*, p. 403, italics mine.

events, while it also sets serious barriers, to put it mildly, in the way of deriving events from objects as defined. While nominally much is made of events, the emphasis turns out Pickwickian.[3]

The bearing of the implication that (i) there are adjacent slabs of time which (ii) are qualitatively homogeneous with one another, appears in Broad's explicit discussion of time and the future, in an earlier part of the book, namely, Chapter Two. There he says that by event he is going to signify "anything which endures at all, no matter how long it lasts or whether it be *qualitatively alike or qualitatively different* in adjacent stages in its history."[4] Here we have an express statement that there may be stages of history which are qualitatively like each other. It is my purpose to show that this assumption determines the results at which he arrives with respect to time, especially as regards futurity. Assuming that the definition means just what it says, and that by qualitative likeness he intends identity, and not merely close similarity—which, of course, admits heterogeneity—there appears to be no basis whatever for the idea of "adjacent stages." Bare persistence is not history and it has no stages; the moment they are referred to as stages qualitative change is introduced. Stages mean differences. A persistent "duration" without change may be alleged to be part of a history when enclosed in a larger whole in which there is qualitative variation, but it can not be itself a history. And without a history what is meant by imputing endurance to the thing called "event"? But where there are adjacent stages, every such stage is an event or history, and hence it has stages, which are events. Or, every event comprises events and is itself comprised in an event.[5]

The only other way in which we can intelligibly speak of adjacent stages in what persists as qualitatively the same is in relation to some *other* event. If we have taken genuine stages of difference in M and have assigned a certain date of beginning and end to each of these, then we may compare M as to these stages with N,

3. Contrast with Whitehead's: "Objects are entities recognised as appertaining to events," *Principles of Natural Knowledge*, p. 81. There was, of course, no obligation upon Broad to follow Whitehead, but the thought of the latter so hangs together that it is not possible to borrow his conception of events, and then place "*recognita*" or objects behind and under events, without getting into precisely such difficulties as the above.
4. *Op. cit.*, p. 54; italics not in original text.
5. Whitehead, *The Principles of Natural Knowledge*, p. 61, 77.

and assign an identical duration (or some part of it) to N, and, by setting up a one-to-one correspondence between it and the stages of M, apportion it, in spite of its homogeneity. That we do thus divide into stages things which do not themselves exhibit *perceptible* differences is a well known fact. But to say that a, in spite of qualitative identity, is a temporal stage of N, is to assert that it can be put in one-to-one correspondence with α, which is a qualitative variation of M, standing in turn in specified relation to β, γ, δ, . . . other qualitative variations of M.

Given the conception of an event as something internally unchanged, it is clear that the beginning of an event, and the occurrence of a qualitative variation in an event (if there be any distinction between these two things), is something other than an event. So Mr. Broad quite logically says that qualitative changes "involve the coming into existence of an event," and that such a change, which he calls a *becoming*, is of such a peculiar character that it is misleading to term it a change. "When we say that a thing changes in quality, or that an event changes in pastness, we are talking of events that exist both before and after the moment at which the change takes place. But when an event becomes, it *comes into existence*; and it was not anything at all until it had become" (p. 68, italics in original text). From this it follows logically that past and present events exist, since they *have* become; future events do not exist at all, since they have not become. Thus it follows from his conception of the intrinsically homogeneous character of an event that the future occupies a status existentially which is radically different from that of past and present events. The "future is simply nothing at all" (p. 70). "A present event is defined as one which is succeeded by nothing"; "there is no such thing as ceasing to exist; what has become exists henceforth for ever" (p. 68 and p. 69). Thus the sum total of existence is always increasing; something becomes; when this event is past, a fresh slice of existence has been added to the total history of the world.

The distinction between "event" and "becoming" follows logically from his definition of event. Events become but they are not becomings. What is given us by Broad is thus a lot of unchanging things, termed, nevertheless, events, with abrupt insertions of changes; time in the usual sense would appear to proceed by jerks or interruptions. How this view is adjusted to any notion of causal continuity does not here concern us. The point is that it is indispensable to Broad's argument to speak of events as *that which* come into existence. But if an event *is* a becoming, it is not intelligible to speak of the eventing of an event; or the becoming of a becoming. And an event is a becoming if as an event it involves qualitative variation or heterogeneity throughout itself. A distinction between event and becoming can be drawn only if an event is conceived as a solid homogeneous slab throughout, that is, is conceived of as *not* an event or a history. Broad carries over into his nominal use of the term "event" considerations pertinent to modes of thought which attach to what we may call the "pre-event" era of scientific history.

The bearing upon "time" and the future should be fairly evident. If existences are histories or events in the sense of becomings, then past-present-future are on the same level, because all are phases of any event or becoming. Any becoming is from, to, through. Its fromness, or out-of-ness, is *its* pastness; its towardness or intrinsic direction, is *its* futurity; that through which the becoming passes is *its* presentness. No becoming can be perceived or thought of except as out of something into something, and this involves a series of transitions which, taken distributively, belong both to the "out-of" and the "into," or form a "through." The present has thus nothing privileged about it; it is as legitimate to speak of the present century or the present geological age as of the present "moment." The present is defined in relation to an "out-of" and by a future or "into," as truly as the past by the present.

Since without change into, there is no becoming or event, futurity is comprised directly in any and every event which can be said to be present, or, better, be said to *have* a phase of presentness.

On this basis it is mere fiction that we know pastness and futurity only by means of inference from presentness. Any experience of anything in being an experience of a becoming or event contains within itself qualities which are named pastness, presentness, and futurity. To recall a specific past event or to foresee or predict a future specific event requires inference, but in the same sense it demands inference to make a determinately specific judgment about anything said to be present. Psychologically, expectancy stands on the same level as memory; in the same sense in which the latter can be said to refer directly to the past, the former can be said to refer directly to the future. In fact, it is questionable whether psychologically the attitude of expectancy is not more usually co-present with observations of what is going on than that of recall. It is even possible that we so commonly ignore it just because it is so omnipresent that there is no need to make it an object of explicit attention.

Mr. Broad gives what seems to me a correct account of *judgments* about the future, but to make a false use of his analysis. It is true that we can not refer intellectually to *a* future event, if the future is dissevered from the present, for then it does not exist for us to refer to. But when he says that it is not true that a judgment involving the future can "mean anything that begins with the statement: 'There is an event'" (p. 76), he says something gratuitously unnecessary. The judgment involving the future is: "There is a going-on or a becoming such that it has a specified directional movement." To make the judgment about the future explicit is not to refer to a non-existent; it is to infer the further becoming of what is going-on. "It will probably rain tomorrow" asserts a quality of toward-whichness characteristic of what is happening to-day defined in terms of yesterdays. In its completeness it is a judgment regarding some out-of-which-through-which-into-which.

When Mr. Broad says that any judgment that professes to be about the future seems to "involve two peculiar and not further analysable kinds of assertion," one of which "asserts that further events *will* become" (italics mine), and the other that so-and-so "*will* characterize some of the events which *will* become" (italics mine), he simply restores under the name of "will" what he officially denies under the name of futurity.[6] "Will be" and the future tense are equivalents and both go back to an "it-is-going-to," where the going-to characterizes what *is*. "Will become" is equivalent to futurity, precisely because it does not refer to some *other* event wholly disconnected from the present, but to an event or becoming which is going-on. Hence the "was," the "is," when temporally limited to a phase of the going-on, and the "will be" all stand on the same level with respect to judgment. All of them as judgments are equally susceptible of error, but

6. *Op. cit.*, pp. 76–77.

that is because all involve inference. For to say that every event, or going-on, has a phase of pastness, presentness, and futurity is not to say that *what* has been, is, and will be, is immediately self-revealing, or that it can be determined without an intellectual or mediating factor.

To save space I have written somewhat dogmatically. But the argument is hypothetical. It contrasts what follows *if* an event is a becoming or involves qualitative changes throughout, with what follows if something nominally termed an event is defined so as to exclude internal heterogeneity. In my opinion, Mr. Broad first nominally introduces duration into his "events" and then takes pains to eliminate all temporality from them. Having done that, he is obliged to re-introduce time by a succession of arbitrarily assumed interruptions or jerks, called becomings.

The Meaning of Value

I hope it is not altogether too late to continue the discussion concerning the nature of value in which Mr. Prall and myself have previously engaged. I shall confine myself to two points, one of a primarily logical nature, and the second and, doubtless, the more important, a question of fact. The first, however, is involved, not only because of prior discussions, but because some statement about it seems to be necessary to clear the ground for a consideration of the issue as to fact. The first point concerns the ambiguity in the term "value," it being both a concrete and an abstract noun, in the former case designating (although metaphorically) a thing having value-quality and in the latter sense designating an essence, an entity of the sort that the scholastics called *ens rationis*. The second point concerns the *de facto* relationship of thought to cases of the *occurrence* of value.

I

In my article I raised *a* question regarding the use of the term "value," although not the one just mentioned. I queried whether in certain passages Dr. Prall did not sometimes use the term to designate a thing having value, and sometimes to denote the quality. There was nothing original in drawing attention to the possible ambiguity; it is almost a commonplace of discussion concerning value, however difficult it may be to avoid falling into the equivocation. I can not complain of any lack of definiteness in the reply made by Dr. Prall. It turns out that by "value" and "values" he does not mean either of these things, but rather the quality taken as itself an entity or essence. "Value has only its

[First published in *Journal of Philosophy* 22 (26 February 1925): 126–33. For Prall's article to which this is a rejoinder, see this volume, pp. 393–402.]

abstract meaning—the meaning of an abstract noun, that is; and when I use the plural *values* I mean also the plural of the same abstract noun. One says color and colors, red and reds, redness and rednesses, beauty and beauties; and such terms are, of course, used very frequently to indicate things 'having' the qualities. But the plurals are just as important and just as accurately used to indicate (*a*) a number of cases of the quality, or, if the term includes many qualities having this more general quality in common, to indicate (*b*) the quality in its various kinds (instead of number) of occurrences" (p. 119 [this volume, p. 395]). And again on the previous page. "So far as I know, I have always been careful to use *value* as the properly abstract noun that I take it to be." And on the same page it is expressly stated that value thus taken is a logical essence such as discourse might define. "Values in the strictest terms of discourse *are*; they have no existence, but they have being and reality, which is to say they are natures or characters or qualities—essences if we are to use the term of such metaphysical logicians as Plato and Leibniz and Spinoza and Mr. Santayana." And he endorses the position of Mr. Santayana that "nothing given exists"[1] so that, I take it, an *existence* having value represents an embodiment or actualization of what otherwise is eternal and a possibility.

I have no wish to raise difficulties captiously. But while I appreciate Mr. Prall's definite reply to my question, I am forced to believe that the reply complicates the question instead of simplifying it. I can understand, I hope, the theory of essences and universals as held by the school of metaphysicians to which Mr. Prall refers, and, irrespective of my own views as to the nature of essence, I respect consistent appeal to that doctrine. What I do not understand is Mr. Prall's appeal to it in view of his statements about the exclusive correlation of liking with value. For "liking," I take it, is used to indicate an existential event on the part of an existential creature. If this be so, it is logical to correlate liking with the coming into existence of value, the concrete embodying of eternal value-essence. But to say this is simply to take the position which I pointed out in my prior article [*Middle*

---

1. It does not seem to have occurred to Mr. Prall that his acceptance of this dictum is incompatible with his definition of value as constituted by liking. The obverse of this point is considered below.

Works 15 : 20 – 26] and which Mr. Prall expressly repudiates in the article now under consideration: *viz.*, definition in the sense of stating how a quality comes to exist as a possession or acquisition of a thing. I had always supposed that this was the sense and the only sense in which Mr. Santayana defined value as connected with liking, since he expressly distinguishes between the causal occurrence of things possessed of value and the nature of value as essence. Nor do I see how any one who holds the theory of essence in the Platonic-Leibnizian sense can attach any meaning to the proposition that value as an essence is constituted by liking. This sort of statement is precisely the sort of statement, I had always supposed, that gives members of that school the horrors. The position of Moore and Russell is surely the one that follows when one proclaims that he is dealing with value as essence. Mr. Santayana has sustained his particular position by making it clear that in connecting liking with value he is dealing with existence, not essence, that is to say, with causal or physical considerations.

Taking Mr. Prall literally, we have, I should say, a most curious reversal of positions. While he has accused me of over-rationalizing value, it is he who now makes value something wholly envisaged by reason. He has done so by treating abstract value as the only significant subject-matter of discussion, and by ruling out as irrelevant, or at least subordinate, the question of the causation of existences having value. And I am borne out in this conclusion by the fact that when Mr. Santayana deals with value as essence he insists that the theme and method are wholly dialectical—an explication or clarification of intent which brings one intent into systematic coherent relationship with other intents. Instead of defining value by liking as a feeling, he recognizes expressly that feeling is purely existential; he says "why any one values anything at all, or anything in particular, is a question of physics. . . . What ethics asks is not why a thing is called good, but whether it is good or not, whether it is right or not so to esteem it. Goodness, in this ideal sense, is not a matter of opinion, but of nature." And he accuses the utilitarian school because of its neglect of this distinction of having substituted a "dubious psychology for Socratic dialectic."[2]

2. *Life of Reason*, Vol. 5, *Reason in Science*, p. 172; pp. 214–15; p. 256.

II

I come now to the question of fact. I have held that the only thing which can be intelligibly discussed concerning value as such is the existential question—the question of how values come to be, *i.e.*, how things come to possess the quality of value. I have asserted that the theories which link value with liking, bias, interest, are in fact theories about how cases of value existentially occur. To this statement I have added another, namely, that only a liking, bias, interest, which includes thinking is an adequate causal condition of the presence of a thing having value. And to avoid misapprehension I explicitly state that this position does not imply that a dialectic of goods or values described by Mr. Santayana is either impossible or illegitimate. On the contrary, it is because the thing enstated as having value involves thought, that there is a character or general nature capable of development in thought, of comparison and synthesis. As Mr. Santayana points out, if liking were wholly a matter of feeling and not of intent or meaning embedded in feeling, there would be nothing to say.

The discussion of the previous section regarding value as essence confirms my position. It is significant that in restating his position Mr. Prall says that he means an affecto-motor attitude constitutes value in the sense of *being it*, not of generating, and adds: "For since I was asserting that the motor-affective relation constitutes the value, and since I had been careful to explain—Mr. Dewey quotes the clause—that 'in the *occurrence* of this relation the value . . . *occurs*,' I felt at liberty to say that the relation constituted the value. . . . The relation means the situation, the constituted relation with the two terms present. Further this relation can not *occur* without the attitude of the subject" (p. 120 [this volume, p. 396], italics not in original). And in defining the issue between us as regards the presence or absence of thought he says: "For value to *occur* or to *arise*, and to arise in the occurrence itself, there must be an attitude." And, again, he says the question is "What does the *occurrence* of the value-quality consist in? What is the nature of what *happens*, if value is to *occur* in the happening?" (Both quotations from p. 121 [this volume, pp. 397, 398]; italics all mine.) And he says that definition here is in the empirical form of pointing. As one points to a color, so in order to define value one points to this kind of situation where this kind of relation exists between a subject's attitude and an object. "Value is thus constituted in tropisms" (p. 122 [this volume, p. 398]).

I shall not here press the point that he has shifted the ground from his prior statement that he was defining an essence, something abstract, and is now asserting that the only way to "define" value is to point to existential situations in which the quality is concretely found—a position with which as an empiricist I wholly agree. Nor will I here urge the point that he has now taken his stand on the third of the ambiguous conceptions which I pointed out in the article to which he is replying—namely, not that liking constitutes or *is* value, but that liking is an ingredient or constituent in any situation having value quality; or that there is a constant correlation between the existence of likings and of value-situations. This position I admitted then and re-assert now. I quote his passages to define the issue of fact which, as far as I can see, is the important difference between us. For they make it clear that the question can be stated in this way: In the situations having value-quality, is liking the sole and exclusive ingredient from the side of the subject, or is thought also involved? However value be defined in the abstract, or whether it be indefinable or not, this question raises a definite issue of fact.

Since Mr. Prall says he gets from what I have said an irresistible "suggestion that value is not the creation of irrational preference, but is somehow at bottom rational" (p. 124 [this volume, p. 401]), I state as explicitly as possible that I regard liking as an indispensable ingredient or constituent in those situations which have value quality, but not as a *sufficient* ingredient or constituent. This position is, I hope, an intelligible one, even if it should turn out not to express the actual fact. It makes provision for the fundamentally irrational factor in situations having value, and makes no effort to explain that factor away or reduce it to something rational. (I might insert the remark that after having been the subject of so many animadversions on the alleged ground of my "irrationalism" and more specifically after having been treated with some contempt for giving such a large place to "interest" in education, I find it at least an amusing change to be charged with excessive rationalism.)

Differences as to matter of fact are not to be settled by argument; they are decided by competent observation, and I have no reason to suppose that my observation is more competent than that of Mr. Prall. But certain considerations may be presented which have a bearing on the kind of observations which need to be made. In the first place, when it is said that "thought" is involved in the attitude of the subject in the situation in which value occurs as a quality, the word "thought" requires definition—which I failed to give in my previous article. By thought I mean at least a *recognition of meaning*; and in meaning is implied reference beyond the present or immediate state, a reference to something ulterior or eventual: to something which, being outside the immediate state and yet implied in it, may be called, in the logical sense at least, "objective." [3]

The distinction between thoughtful liking and blind, *merely* impulsive, "liking" is certainly a familiar and obvious one; it is not invented *ad hoc* by me for purposes of identifying value situations. Mr. Prall has, I am sure, a respect for the word of Mr. Santayana which he has not for mine. I shall quote, accordingly, a passage. "No existence is of moment to a man, not even his own, unless it touches his will and fulfils or thwarts his *intent*. Unless he is *concerned* that existence *should* be of *specific kinds*, unless he is interested *in form*, he can hardly be interested in being" (*Op. cit.*, 5, 167; italics mine). Since we are not disputing about words, I should be willing to let the case rest on this one point: Does or does not Mr. Prall include in his conception of liking as a defining constituent in value-situations the element of *concern* for the *object* liked? If he does, I am willing to surrender the use of the word "thought," although I should be glad to have suggested some word to indicate recognition of meaning as such. In any event, it is this element of *concern for an object*, for a spe-

3. Mr. Prall, in the absence of any explicit statement on my part, was entitled to quote from me a definition of reflective thinking which includes problematic factors, doubt and search. While I hold that these elements are essential to the evaluating judgment which is, in some degree, a causal condition of the occurrence of the situation having value-quality, it is the *resultant* definitive meaning which characterizes the value situation itself, and which may be directly recognized or envisaged. In speaking of the attitude as one of "reflective apprehension" my use of the adjective "reflective" was unfortunate; in my own mind it was *apprehension* that was significant, and the adjective conveyed the idea stated in the next sentence: "embodying the *results* of much thoughtful interest."

cific kind of object, which I do not find included in bare animal appetition and assimilation.

In the second place, it is clear that Mr. Prall does not mean by liking a mere state of feeling, but an active attitude, a motor and selective act which not merely *is* a difference in consciousness, but which makes a difference to external things. It is of the nature of a tropism. Now a blind bias or appetite makes a difference as much as one having meaning and intent. But in a significant or thoughtful liking, meaning expresses awareness of objective difference as making, or of the *force* of the selective bias in altering the otherwise existent. It is connected with the concern that existence be of a certain sort rather than of another. It hence deserves the name of interest, as a blind liking does not save metaphorically.

It is for this reason that the good is capable of judgment, of development and comparison and connection and systematization in thought. For while in many cases there is no thought beyond that of a narrow and nearby difference, there is nothing in the nature of the case to limit the scope of the meaning inherent in the object of interest, the differences it imports. Accordingly, and this is the third consideration, the conception that mere liking is adequate to constitute a value situation makes no provision for the education and cultivation of taste and renders criticism, whether esthetic, moral, or logical, arbitrary and absurd. The conception of thoughtful liking, on the other hand, makes refinement and criticism intrinsic outgrowths of a factor already contained in the value situation.

When I find a writer who nominally holds the same conception as that advanced by Mr. Prall saying, "One topic of empirical importance is the education of discriminating appreciation, the attainment of progressive connoisseurship,"[4] I can not help feeling that the author virtually includes in his conception of bias, liking, or interest precisely the thought phase I am concerned to point out, and omits to make his inclusion explicit only because his chief interest is in upholding the general theory of

4. Bush, "Value and Causality," *Journal of Philosophy, Psychology and Scientific Methods*, Vol. 15, p. 91. [*The Middle Works of John Dewey, 1899–1924*, edited by Jo Ann Boydston (Carbondale: Southern Illinois University Press, 1982), 11:382.]

interest against theories of good which deny it. I am sorry that in his reply Mr. Prall did not go into this point and explain what he meant by just and unjust valuings and satisfactory and unsatisfactory values, and in general what he means by criticism, education, and cultivation in connection with such likings as exclude any element of thought and meaning. (See my original criticism, p. 621 [*Middle Works* 15 : 25].) His only allusion to my pointing out that he admitted "unsatisfactory values" (which flatly contradicts that mere immediate liking constitutes a value) is to say that there are negative values, values of disliking. Of course there are; but this was not the issue. The point concerned his admission that there were unsatisfactory values in cases of *liking*, "according as the subject's faculties are acute or not, and his training in specific fields thorough." I do not refer to this for the sake of charging a personal contradiction; any one may fall into a temporary lapse of thought as well as of speech. I refer to it because it seems to be so obviously true and so highly important. And I do not see how its truth and importance are consistent with any theory of value except the thought-liking theory. Mere likings may differ in intensity; they may differ in quality; but by definition they can not differ as to constitution of values. Upon this doctrine a more "acute" liking may determine a more intense value, and more thorough training may constitute a *different* value. But this can not, on the liking theory, mean a difference as to valuableness of value; it can not imply improvement or cultivation or refinement or education in any eulogistic sense of these terms; it can not imply anything as to the desirableness of the change; or that one value is more "satisfactory" than another. It means only that one liking has replaced another and hence one value been substituted for another—as if a man had abandoned tea for coffee or coffee for Postum, for no cause at all except a bare change in immediate liking.

It is just because I hold, as I take Mr. Prall to hold, that educated interest or taste is, ultimately, supreme, the *unum necessarium*, in morals (where it is called conscience), in matters intellectual (where it is called insight), as well as in esthetics where it is more usually called taste, that the case for taste should not be weakened, and made easy of attack by non-empirical and non-humanist theories. It is the omission and denial of meaning and intent in that "liking" which constitutes good which give rise to the remote and transcendental type of theories of value— whether of the idealistic variety of Bosanquet, Münsterberg *et al.*, or of the realistic type of Moore and Russell. The empirical theories which rule out and deny the intelligible and objective factor of meaning are the chief bulwarks of "transcendental" rationalism. It is because I so thoroughly agree with what I take to be the ulterior spirit and aims of Mr. Prall that I would fain see an adequate basis for them provided.

Value, Objective Reference and Criticism

In some writings of mine on judgments of value considered as evaluations, there was no attempt to reach or state any conclusion as to the nature of value itself.[1] The position taken was virtually this: *No matter what* value is or is taken to be, certain traits of evaluative judgments as judgments can be formulated. One can assuredly consider the nature of impersonal judgments, such as "it rains," without going into the physical and meteorological constitution of rain. So it seemed possible to consider the nature of value-judgments (as evaluations, not just statements about values already had) without consideration of value, just as, once more, one might discuss deliberation without analysis of things deliberated upon.

The outcome soon showed the mistake. There was a tactical error in connection with the present status of the discussion. There was much interest in value, and little in the theory of judgments, and my essay to disentangle the two only gave the impression that I was trying in a roundabout way to insinuate a peculiar theory concerning value itself, or else that because I did not discuss value I thought it of little importance as compared with instrumentalities. But the error was more than one of mode of presentation, as, indeed, might have occurred to me in considering the analogy between evaluation judgments and deliberation. For if deliberation constitutes a distinctive type of judgment, it is because there is a distinctive type of subject-matter; not that it is necessary to go into details about special matters deliberated upon, but that certain generic traits need to be registered. For as Aristotle remarked long ago, we do not deliberate concerning

---

1. *Essays in Experimental Logic*, essay on "Judgments of Practice," pp. 335–442 [*Middle Works* 8:14–82], and the *Philosophical Review*, "Valuation and Experimental Knowledge," vol. 31, pp. 325–51 [*Middle Works* 13:3–28].

[First published in *Philosophical Review* 34 (July 1925): 313–32.]

necessary things, or things that have happened, but only about things still contingent. Hence to make out that deliberation is representative of a distinctive logical type, it is necessary to show that genuinely contingent subject-matter exists. And my theory regarding evaluation judgment involved a similar implication regarding value as its subject-matter. The present article is, accordingly, an attempt to supply the deficiency by showing that the nature of value is such as not only to permit of but to require the general type of judgment sketched in the previous writings.

I

In undertaking this task, it is possible to evade the question of the definability or indefinability of value. Obviously, value is definable in the sense that things possessing it can be identified and marked off and the property which serves as the ground of their demarcation can be indicated. Definition by pointing or denotation is indeed the ultimate recourse in all empirical matters, and that is the only kind of definition required as a preliminary for our purpose. Thus Ogden and Richards in their chapter on the Theory of Definition say that "symbolisation" is the simplest, most fundamental type of definition, and illustrate its nature as follows: "If we are asked to what 'orange' refers, we may take some object which is orange and say 'Orange' is a symbol which stands for This. . . . But, it will be said, This merely tells us that 'orange' is applicable in *one* case; what we wish to know is how it is applicable in general. This generalisation may be performed . . . by the use of similarity relationships. We may say 'Orange' applies to this and to all things similar in respect to colour."[2]

As it would be mere affectation to undertake the task of such empirical pointing *de novo*, discussion may be abbreviated by setting out from the widely held belief that wherever value is found there something called bias, liking, interest is also found, while conversely, wherever these acts, attitudes or feelings are found, there also and only there is value found.[3] Such a one to

2. *The Meaning of Meaning*, pp. 217–18.
3. Perry, on "The Definition of Value," *Journal of Philosophy, Psychology and Scientific Methods*, Vol. 11, pp. 141–62. Prall, *University of California Pub-*

one correspondence leaves us with many questions unsettled, as will shortly appear, but it suffices for the purposes of a *prima facie* identification.

The questions left unsettled cluster about the import of the terms "liking," "bias," "interest," etc. That these terms are vague and ambiguous I should have supposed to be a notorious fact, were it not that so many writers of this school seem to assume that their meaning is determinate, uniform and agreed upon; so much so that, with the exception of Perry and Santayana, they do nothing more than to mention them. For purposes of controversy, against the theories of value which deny correlation of value with any human or subjective attitude, such a procedure doubtless suffices. But for an understanding of value, some correlation being conceded, it is fatally defective.

For the conceptions are used so broadly and diversely as to be *specifically* meaningless. Instead of pointing to any discriminable group of objects, the gesture is a sweeping one to a very extensive section of the horizon. Thus Picard gives as synonyms "like, demand, admire, approve, wish, want, etc.," and seems to feel that the requirement of specification is met by saying that these are all expressive of *feeling*. Yet it is a notorious fact that "feeling" is one of the vaguest terms in all psychological literature, being sometimes used to express any kind of emotion or affection, sometimes to cover "conative" tendencies, impulse and desire, and sometimes restricted to an experience of pleasure and pain. Obviously wish, want, demand are what are usually called conative, while admire and approve are affectional attitudes, with the implication of an ideational content. What is more important is the fact that want, desire, wish, demand, all imply the

lications in Philosophy, Vol. 3, No. 2 (with bibliography), "Study in the Theory of Value," pp. 179–290; *Ibid.*, Vol. 4, pp. 77–103, "The Present Status of the Theory of Value"; *Journal of Philosophy*, Vol. 20, pp. 128–37, "In Defense of a *Worthless* Theory of Value"; *Ibid.*, Vol. 21, pp. 117–25, "Value and Thought-Process." Santayana, *Winds of Doctrine*, pp. 138–54. Picard, *Values, Immediate and Contributory* (N.Y., 1920), and "The Psychological Basis of Value," *Journal of Philosophy, Psychology and Scientific Methods*, Vol. 17, pp. 11–20. Bush, "Value and Causality," *Journal of Philosophy, Psychology and Scientific Methods*, Vol. 15, pp. 85–96 [*Middle Works* 11:375–87]. Kallen, "Value and Existence," *Journal of Philosophy, Psychology and Scientific Methods*, Vol. 11, pp. 264–76, and essay of the same title in *Creative Intelligence*, pp. 409–67.

lack or absence of an object, a longing or craving for something not given, while admire and approve, though they may attach to either the present or the absent, do not involve a craving to bring some absent and lacking object into realized existence. And if we add another term usually included, namely, "enjoyment," it is clear that value defined in its terms entails the actual presence or givenness of the object enjoyed, and is in so far antipodal to want, wish and demand.

Certainly a large arc of the horizon is already subtended. But we cannot stop here. Want and desire are notoriously ambiguous. Sometimes they are used to denote attitudes which connote the presence of an idea, an idea of the object wanted; sometimes they are used to express a wholly blind affair, blind, that is, as respects even a dim and shadowy conception or representation of an object. The same point comes out more clearly in the use of the words bias and interest. I do not say that these terms are heteronyms; but bias readily suggests an attitude prior to thought and wholly independent of an idea, while interest, to most minds, connotes interest *in* something mentally recognized; a concern for, if not actual identification of the affectional attitude with some*thing*, instead of, like bias, a blind tendency toward something. At all events, we have little in the way of definition until we know whether the element of idea is or is not excluded.

The distinction just made points to another phase which must be specified. Bias, whether blind or not, and interest both point to an active factor, one of concern and caring, a tendency to look after, to further, promote, the well-being of something outside one's self. They are of course attitudes of the subject, but they are attitudes which involve (whether consciously or not) an object *qua* object, as enjoyment for example need not do, and as "feeling" in some of its many meanings does not. And it is notorious that the same ambiguity is attached to "love" and "affection." Sometimes they are used to designate a simple *state* of a subject, and sometimes an attitude that goes out to and cultivates, exacts, the well-being of its objects.

The same distinction may be stated in another way. Is the attitude of the subject described as liking, preference, interest, bias, understood in a behavioristic sense or in the sense of a state or process of consciousness as the latter are defined by introspective psychology? The distinction may be made clearer by a quotation from Santayana: "Desire and will, in the proper psychological sense of these words, are incidental phases of consciousness. . . . At the same time the words desire and will are often used, in a mythical or transcendental sense, for those material dispositions and instincts by which vital and moral units are constituted."[4] Now I have not found that most writers even raise the question as to the sense in which they use such a word as preference; whether to designate the bare "feeling," or state, of contentment in contrast with some feeling of discomfort, or to mean what common sense usually means—an active tendency to go out after, or to maintain and hold onto one object to the active elimination, exclusion or warding off of another. It makes however an enormous difference, even apart from the inclusion or exclusion of the ideational factor, which meaning is implied; an enormous difference, that is, for the identification of value. For the first rules out of the "definition" of value an element of "objective reference" while the other implicates it.

I should perhaps have included the name of Prall among those who have at least attempted to specify the idea of liking. He expressly states that it is "affecto-motor," and denies that it includes any element of thought or judgment; and in his last writing says, "Value is thus constituted in tropisms, if you like." Such phrases seem definitive in recognizing an act toward an object, in thinking of an object as integrated in the act. Yet in the immediate context (p. 122 [this volume, p. 398]) he says, "values to be such are felt and the feeling of an animal that has any feeling is *all* that is needed to give a situation where there is value." Hence what he means is probably only that a tropism is the *cause* of a feeling, while value connects with feeling as such. The same impression is derived from p. 124 [this volume, p. 401], where he speaks of Woodworth's intimating that feeling is the "body's instantaneous impulse to accept or to be rid of." Now if it is an act of acceptance and getting rid of which identifies liking and hence value, then the objective reference (contained in any behavioristic account) is indubitable. But he seems to mean rather that feeling can itself be genetically accounted for on the basis of such

---

4. *Winds of Doctrine*, pp. 145 f. I do not know how the use of the terms "proper" and "mythical" respectively are to be reconciled with the position of Mr. Santayana discussed in the sequel, but the distinction is clear, independent of these epithets.

responses, while the feeling, no matter how caused, is what constitutes value. At all events, there is a dilemma. If the terms "affecto-motor" and tropism are taken seriously, then liking is not a feeling but is an act, having objective consequences and relationships like any act. If "feeling" is the key-word, then the apparent specification procured by the words affecto-motor and tropisms is wholly illusory, and we are left with that psychological morass of vagueness and ambiguities, "feeling," as our determinant of value.

The more one reflects upon the vast scope of the terms which are used to name the attitude which is used to distinguish cases of value, and notes how these terms denote incompatible as well as diverse attitudes, and notes also that the method of escape from these inconsistencies is recourse to some word which is neutral only because it is vague and ambiguous, the more, I think, will one be ready to admit that the gesture of pointing has been so indefinite in the instances under discussion, that all it points to is some region of the horizon of experience in which a personal or at least animal attitude is implicated, and an attitude which is *not* primarily cognitive in nature. Yet denial that "liking" is cognitive need not preclude a perception of an object, nor moreover of an object so connected with liking as in some sense to justify as well as to evoke it. For example, Mr. Prall, who in his latest writing seems to feel obliged to eliminate entirely any intellectual element, had written earlier: "It is the perception not merely of the features themselves that counts, but of the features of objects as responsible for the likings these objects have called out. This is the basis of appreciation and of critical evaluations." [5]

Readings in this field have accordingly convinced me of the justness of the remarks of Ogden and Richards. [6] In distinguishing between words that are used symbolically to stand for and refer to an object, and words used emotively, and after saying that the emotive use is more common than is usually allowed for, they go on to say: "The word 'good' may be taken as an example. It seems probable that the word is essentially a collection of homonyms, such that the set of things, roughly, those in connec-

5. *Univ. of Calif. Publications*, Vol. 4, p. 100.
6. *The Meaning of Meaning*, pp. 227–28, in connection with a discussion of the theory of definition.

tion with which we have heard it pronounced in early years (a good bed, a good kick, a good baby, a good God) have no common characteristic. But another use of the word is often asserted to occur . . . where 'good' is alleged to stand for a unique unanalysable concept. . . . This peculiar ethical use of 'good' is, we suggest, a purely emotive use. When so used the word stands for nothing whatever, and has no symbolic function. Thus, when we so use it in the sentence '*This* is good,' we merely refer to *this*, and the addition of 'is good' makes no addition whatever to our reference. When, on the other hand, we say '*This* is red,' the addition of 'is red' to 'this' does symbolise an extension of our reference, namely, to some other red thing. But 'is good' has no comparable *symbolic* function; it serves only as an emotive sign expressing our attitude to *this*, and perhaps evoking similar attitudes in other persons, or inciting them to actions of one kind or another." (In a footnote, it is explained that this assertion of a purely emotive status refers only to the alleged indefinable "good"; not to uses of "This is good" where "good" refers to "this" in a way that also refers to other things similar to "this" in a designated respect.)

If I may put my own gloss on these words, I should say that such an emotive situation is exemplified when a child spontaneously claps his hands in the presence of some affair, perhaps saying, in addition, "Goody-goody." "Goody-goody," in the words of our authors, "merely refers to *this*"; it makes no addition to or difference in the emotive attitude itself. It is as ejaculatory as the clapping of the hands. It has *meaning*, (the "symbolic reference" of the authors) only for the bystander who is familiar with an intelligent, not-purely-emotive use of "good," a use which implies reference to something beyond the attitude itself. To seek in such a case for a meaning and then to use this meaning to "define" good, is like seeking for an intrinsic meaning in "Oh, Oh!" Some bystander may impute meaning to a sigh, through taking it, because of reference to objects other than the sigh, as the expression of a saddened state. But the sigh as mere immediate existence has no such meaning; it is emotive only.

These considerations point to two conclusions. There exist direct attitudes of an affective kind toward things. They are more than feelings; they are motive or motor in being emotive. They doubtless are accompanied by or result in "feelings"—that is, they have their own qualitative colorings. The most fundamental of these attitudes are undoubtedly—taking biological considerations as well as more direct observations into account—appropriation, assimilation, on one hand, and exclusion, elimination, on the other hand. Certain acts of going-out to meet, and of turning away from may properly be regarded as minor degrees of these acts, or as partial assimilations and rejections. For, biologically, it is clear that these latter acts are temporal operations, not instantaneously complete, so they have lesser and fuller phases. So conceived, "liking" might be generically defined as the act of welcoming, greeting; "disliking" as the act of spewing out, getting rid of. And in recognizing that an organism tends to take one or other of these two attitudes to *every* occurrence to which it reacts at all, we virtually include such acts as admitting, accepting, tolerating as fainter cases of greeting, and such acts as omitting, passing quickly by or over, etc., as fainter cases of expulsion.

The second point is that while these acts, attitudes and dispositions do not in their *immediate occurrence* define, or confer any meaning upon "good" (since immediately they are nothing but the acts which are, so that "liking" denotes not good or a good thing but just the act of liking), nevertheless they may be indispensable ingredients in the meaning "good." It is possible, namely, that nothing would be in existence to which the word "good" might intelligibly refer if there were not things which are directly assimilated and spewed forth. In this case, these acts would be necessary although not sufficient conditions of value. In other words, we are back to the need of further specification, of differential qualification, of the attitude involved in the experience of value.

Ogden and Richards "in passing" suggest as a definition of good "that which we approve of approving." If we identify the "approving" which is the object of approving with what the text calls "greeting," then the "approving of" it clearly cannot be just the *same* approving over again (for this would be equally emotive), but designates approving with a qualification—presumably reflective approval in some sense of reflective. Again, Mr. Prall finds an example of the attitude he holds to constitute value in a ruminating cow, chewing its cud. And of this act, he says: "She is having elementary esthetic enjoyment in each chew, or perhaps more strictly in each impulse to go on chewing, ruminating, *contemplating*, as an infant is having such enjoyment when it chews on a teething ring, or Aristotle's God when he contemplates the universe."[7] Far be it from me to dogmatize on the precise nature of the experience of animal, infant or God. But it is significant that Mr. Prall takes the distinctively human and metaphorical meaning of "ruminating"—namely, as meditative, contemplating—and attributes it to cow and infant. Possibly he is justified. I am not informed. But *if* the act be of such a kind, then it is the act of assimilating *qualified*, not in its bare occurrence. And since the qualification is by some*thing* contemplated, or by an objective reference, whether to cud, or to impulse and its consequences, or to the Aristotelian rational universe, to which the rudimentary or developed esthetic enjoyment is attached, the enjoyment is not bare feeling. The act is thus characterized by more than bare feeling; it and feeling alike are qualified by the objects to which they are directed and attached. Objective differences of a specifiable nature thus inhere in them.

This is more than can be said of the mere ejaculatory attitudes of greeting and riddance. As far as I can see there is nothing in the wide universe which may not at certain times, by certain agents, and under certain circumstances be accepted or rejected: another way of reaching the conclusion that these acts fail to define good and bad. Only when the acts are qualified by some as yet unmentioned differential condition do they have any force which is discriminative of a "this" (instead of being "this" over again *in toto*) and which is additive, lining up the "this" selected with other things "similar in some designated respect."

II

In Mr. Perry's article, a definite and significant qualification is introduced. He defines value as satisfaction, fulfillment, consummation of interest, and uses this differential complex to discriminate the otherwise simple term "liking."[8] He is also explicit as to the implication of objective reference. "There must be

7. *Journal of Philosophy*, Vol. 21, p. 122 [this volume, p. 399], italics mine.
8. *Op. cit.*, pp. 149, 150.

a term toward which interest or bias is directed. There can be no liking or disliking unless there be something liked or disliked." And we might add, as even more to the point, there can be no value except as there is some object in which the liking is fulfilled or frustrated.[9] Moreover, he explicitly recognizes the difference between the attitude of enjoying which involves possession and presence and that of desiring, attempt to get or get rid of, which involves absence and movement. He asks, "Does value consist at bottom in *having* what you like or dislike, or in *getting* what you like or dislike?" He replies that since neither quiescent enjoyment alone nor progressive effort alone appear satisfactory notions, the two dispositions may be unified. "This appears possible if we recognize the motor factor in feeling and the factor of prospective possession in desire. To like a present object is to seek to prolong it; and is thus not a purely static phenomenon after all. To consummate desire is to achieve the object by the expenditure of effort, and is thus not merely a matter of non-possession."[10]

The qualifications thus introduced seem to me wholly in the right direction. I do not propose to criticize them, but to point out what seem to me the implications of this objective reference thereby introduced, as to an ideal or ideational factor in value. In further discussion, I go beyond anything said or suggested by Mr. Perry, and of course he is not to be held to any endorsement of the use made of his conceptions.

In fulfillment of interest, as involving both active movement (even if only movement to retain and perpetuate) and possessive enjoyment (if only in present anticipation) there is found, obviously and truistically, change, movement, and a change or movement such that it is marked by tendency to pass from one relation between subject and object to another relation between them. This difference of relationships is, of course, contained in the idea of fulfilling, consummating; it implies a change from a relatively non-fulfilling status of the object with respect to the attitude of the subject into a relatively fulfilling status. It thus involves a mediate factor in the liking which defines value or good.

9. Incidentally, it may be pointed out that this conception allows for the fact, which the other theory does not, that disliking may be connected with a *positive* value or good—namely, when it is adequately fulfilled.

10. *Op. cit.*, p. 150.

It precludes any definition of value in terms of any purely momentary attitude.

It might be questioned whether the idea of fulfillment is not in general and of necessity an idea which implies a temporal process characterized by a particular *kind* of change, namely, tendency in a direction which introduces qualitative difference between beginning and terminus. Nothing, it can reasonably be argued, is fulfillment except as referred to an antecedent state and a process of development or growth out of it into something else. But in this case, it is not necessary to appeal to these general considerations. By description, the kind of fulfillment which is in question is one which unites movement and possession.

It is therefore pertinent, and it would seem logically obligatory, to specify the nature of this change which takes place. In the first place—this point is tautological, but advisable to make explicit—it is not just a change in or of the subject; it is a change in the *relation* of subject and object, such that any change which takes place in the subject, (such as from uneasiness to complacency or from quiescent comfort to active enjoyment) is conditioned upon the change in its relation to the object. The change in the state of the subject as such—like a bare change in its feelings—does not identify any case of value. Secondly and more definitely, the change in the relationship of subject and object may be described as a change from relative distance or absence to possession and presence; from insecurity to security, from unreadiness to readiness, from *de facto* appropriation or assimilation to an assimilation recognized to be the fruit or end-term of the activity—the choice and preference—of the subject.

This conception introduces into the very constitution of value objective reference, and thus factors which are ideational and open to inquiry. This is the same as saying that *a* value not being immediate is also not final in the sense of being so conclusive that it is closed to criticism and revision. A thing may be taken to be a good and yet not be a good, just as a thing may be taken to be red and yet not be red. Much of the talk about "immediate" value confuses, I believe, a number of different things. Immediacy of the quality in the abstract means nothing except that valueness is valueness; it is what it is. The assertion that a particular thing which has been taken to be a value *is* a value is, on the other hand, an additive and instructive statement, "synthetic" in the Kantian sense. It signifies that the thing has been found, upon suitable examination and test, to possess the quality attributed to it. As such, the quality is of course "immediate"; any quality is immediate when it exists. But this is far from signifying that the thing in question possesses it in an immediate, that is an unconditioned, self-evident and unquestionable way just because a given "feeling" is instantaneously present.

It is reasonable to suppose that the property of being a food on the part of any thing is relative to the organic function of nutrition. Because an animal is hungry it seeks food. Were there no such things as nutritive assimilation and hunger there would be no such things as food; the plants and animals that now serve as foods might exist just the same, but they would not be foods. Nevertheless being hungry does not constitute a thing into a food, although it leads to a thing being taken or treated as a food. The matter of *being* a food is *eventual*; it depends upon what happens after the food is taken as food, whether it nourishes or not. And this is an objective matter, capable of investigation and ascertainment on an objective basis. If value be defined as fulfillment of interest, the analogy between "liking" and hunger on one side, and food and value on the other is, I think, clear and instructive. Value may be ascribed or imputed, just as a particular substance may be taken into the system *for* food. And the ascription or imputation may in both cases consist in a manner of behavior, of treatment, rather than in any reasoned-out process. But since the existence of value depends upon the outcome—the fulfilling or institution of a determinate change of relationship—the thing may not after all *be* a value. The taking and finding, as an immediate affair, is at a venture; it is hypothetical; it postulates a subsequent process which as matter of fact may not take place. And it is, I suppose, a commonplace that even the most ardent desires and seekings often end in disappointment and disillusion; the thing sweet in the seeking turns out bitter in taste actually achieved. It is almost a proverb that things pleasant in anticipation are not so pleasant in realized possession. This fact is just what should be expected on the theory which connects value with a specifically and objectively conditioned mode of "liking"; it is difficult to see how it is to be reconciled with the theory that liking as bare immediate feeling is enough to determine a value.

I hesitate to involve Mr. Perry in any liability for my account, since there are in his article occasional indications that he does not mean by fulfilling, consummating interest in a temporal, objectively conditioned process. He may mean that the mere momentary presence of a thing as an object or recipient of "interest" is a fulfillment of the latter. The importance of the issue justifies a hypothetical discussion of this position. He says of the "alleged tertiary qualities of value" that they appear "to be either modes of attitude or impulse, and thus motor, or sensory qualia which are localizable in the body. . . . Similarly I conclude that interest is not an immediate cognition of value qualities in its object, but is a mode of the organism, enacted, sensed, or possibly felt, and qualifying the object through being a response to it." [11] The more obvious meaning of this passage is that interest can be treated as an immediate, in the sense of instantaneous, condition of the organism, and that its immediate play upon, or direction toward, an object constitutes that object a value. I arise in the morning tired and cross, and in as far as that attitude expresses itself toward things and persons they are thereby clothed with negative value. Such a view, however, is contrary to the apparent meaning of the passage regarding the implication of "progressive effort" along with present enjoyment. Apart from a question of consistency, we have the fact that the inclusion of "progressive effort" leads to conclusions that are to my mind in agreement with the findings of common-sense experience. When I give way to irritability, I *feel* as if things were of negative value, I *take* them that way, but the contrast of such cases with the instances in which there is progressive movement reveals that things and persons which I *felt* towards in this antagonistic way on this account may fulfill interest and hence really have value. This, of course, is the same as saying that bare feeling and instantaneous taking are not enough to determine value, or that feeling is not its adequate sign and proof. [12]

11. *Op. cit.*, p. 153.
12. As the clause "interest is not an immediate cognition of value qualities in its object" indicates, Mr. Perry is here discussing another question, namely, whether or no appreciation, liking, interest, etc., in constituting value is also a knowledge or judgment of it. Hence the passage cannot be taken as conclusive upon the point raised in the text. Upon the fact that the experience of value is not a judgment or knowledge of value, I agree, of course, with Mr. Perry.

If the idea of fulfillment of interest be taken in its natural sense, then every experience in which value figures is one in which there is an idea, or thought, of the relation which some object bears to the furthering or frustrating of interest. The state of being bored is all one with the fact that an object is now stale, flat and unprofitable—that is, with the fact that it is so taken. The state of being highly sanguine is all one with a future desired object being taken to be practically sure of attainment. The state of being covetous is all one with the fact that a certain object is taken to be one which must if possible be possessed. Experience shows that as a matter of fact objective reference precedes subjective reference. Reference to a subject instead of to an object is extrinsic and reflective. It is indeed only another mode of objective reference; that is, some tediousness of the object is accounted for in terms of an unusual state of the subject. Otherwise to say "I am bored" and "It is tedious" are merely two phrases to express exactly the same fact.

The doctrine that appreciation or prizing, cherishing, holding dear, liking as fulfillment of interest, includes an element of thought, an idea which is at least an implicit judgment, means then that there is an idea of an object and of the object's connection with the self (or that of the self with it), such as may be appealed to in order to justify, confirm, or render dubious or false the imputation of value to the object. This clearly is not at all to assert nor to imply that the judgment in question is one of value. It is of an object. But this idea of an object is an ingredient or constituent in a non-cognitive appreciation. Failure to distinguish between judgment of an object and judgment of value is the reason why, I take it, critics have charged me with holding that the experience of value is itself rational, judgmental, instead of primarily an affecto-motor one.

III

We come now to the explicit discussion of the ideational or ideal factor. A reference to so-called presuppositional or grounded values will serve to make the transition. There are values of the following sort: A man esteems a picture, thinking it to have been painted by Leonardo; if he finds reason to hold it is an imitation, his liking alters. Or a man admires a building, thinking it is made of stone; he finds it constructed of painted lath and his immediate affectional attitude changes. Now the hypothesis argued for in the previous section may be thus stated: *Every* case of value is a case of a presuppositional value, their generic presupposition being: Any thing is "liked" or esteemed as (on the ground that) it is taken to further or retard a moving preference for one object rather than another.

The significance of this position for the topic in hand is evident. A presupposition may be in agreement with or contrary to fact. Hence the "liking" may be well or ill grounded; in an intelligible sense the value will then be true or false; or more correctly, only apparent or else genuine and "real." The distinction between apparent and real good, whether in matters economic, ethical, esthetic or logical, thus has a basis and a valid import. Mr. Perry in speaking of presuppositional values says such values "may be tested by determining the truth or falsity of the assumptions which mediate them. . . . A valuation [appreciation] that is undisturbed or fortified by increased light is in a special sense a true valuation or a genuine value." [13] Now if all cases of the occurrence of values are cases of grounded values, then they are all either ill or well grounded, and are subject to examination, to reflective inquiry on account of factors contained within them.

The treatment of Santayana may be used as the basis of a discussion of the nature of judgment of values. Physics, the science of existence, is but half of science, and feeling, as existential, is subject-matter of physics. The other half, the more interesting and fundamental half of science, is dialectic. This, not being founded on existence, is founded on intent. "No existence is of moment to a man, not even his own, unless it touches his will, and fulfils or thwarts his intent. . . . The flying moment must be loaded with obloquy or excellence if its passage is not to remain a dead fact." [14] Ethics and mathematics are two applications of dialectic. "Purposes need dialectical articulation as much as essences do, and without an articulate and fixed purpose, without an ideal, action would collapse into mere motion or conscious change." [15] "So a man who is in pursuit of things for the good

13. *Op. cit.*, p. 160.
14. *Life of Reason*, Vol. 5, p. 167.
15. *Ibid.*, p. 200.

that is in them must recognise and (if reason avails) must pursue what is good in all of them. Strange customs and unheard-of thoughts may then find their appropriate warrant." [16] Questions regarding the good, he says, are more or less habitually involved in confusion, because physical and dialectical questions are not distinguished. "Why any one values anything at all, or anything in particular, is a question of physics; it asks for the causes of interest, judgment, and desire. To esteem a thing good is to express certain affinities between that thing and the speaker; and if this is done with self-knowledge and with knowledge of the thing, so that the felt affinity is a real one, the judgment is invulnerable and cannot be asked to rescind itself." [17] And he goes on to say that the science of ethics has naught to do with causes: "What ethics asks is not why a thing is called good, but whether it is good or not, whether it is right or not so to esteem it. Goodness, in this ideal sense, is not a matter of opinion, but of nature. For intent is at work and the question is whether the thing or situation responds to that intent. . . . To judge whether things are *really* good intent must be made to speak; and if this intent may itself be judged later, that happens by virtue of other intents comparing the first with their own direction."

The necessity for intent in any event that constitutes a value is equivalent to recognition of the objective mediation which has been insisted upon. The purpose of the quotations at this point, however, is not so much to confirm the account given by appeal to authority, as it is to indicate the nature of knowledge of the good. The passages indicate what the chapter on "Rational Morality" makes still more explicit, (i) that this knowledge is essentially clarification of intent, through (ii) explication of what it implies, so that a man becomes aware of what other things he intends in intending this particular object, so that (iii) such an explication inevitably leads to comparison of different intents and to unification, organization of various intents into a comprehensive harmonized, a consistent and far-seeing, plan of life, while (iv) in the course of this process new goods, and hence intents, present themselves while things good in first intent are discovered not to *be* good, because their realization implies thwarting of other and more inclusive intents.

16. *Ibid.*, p. 201.
17. *Ibid.*, p. 214.

To this exposition of Socratic morality I have nothing to add. It assumes intents and intents as *expressing*, conveying, not merely issuing from, vital bias. The account of why a particular intent occurs is existential, psychological, a discovery of a man's blood and training, the happenings of his brain cells and fibres. But he says that ethics begins where this causal inquiry leaves off.[18] The question I would raise is whether there is not a closer connection between the causal and dialectical inquiries than Mr. Santayana allows.

To raise this question is not to doubt that confusion and harm result when propositions pertinent to the two inquiries are confused. It signifies rather that (i) the dialectic itself can be accomplished only by the aid of causal, existential inquiries, and (ii) that its outcome can be made effective in life only by the aid of existential inquiries. In this case, physics—as defined by Mr. Santayana—is an indispensable ingredient of moral theory and practice, and not merely an unavoidable preliminary. And in saying this I do not think I go contrary to the spirit, the intent, of Mr. Santayana's writing, although there is an immediate or physical clash with some of his statements. For, to take the second and simpler point first, he certainly would be the first to uphold that in dealing with values, which are "the principle of perspective in science no less than of rightness in life,"[19] the outcome of dialectic is futile unless it be embodied in some change of direct intent. Since dialectic of value exists for the sake of intent and value, incarnation in existence is its own goal and consummation, and not an extraneous "application." Clearly the question of how effective embodiment is to take place, is an existential question, and it will be skilfully or unsuccessfully handled in the degree in which we have a technique based on knowledge of matters of fact, anthropological, historical, physiological.

This principle applies, it seems to me, equally to the first mentioned point. The greater the moral importance of dialectic, the greater is the importance of the performance of the required dialectic. And dialectic is not self-executing; its performance is a matter of occurrence, that is, of existence; it can be secured only in virtue of causal considerations. To initiate a development and clarification requires an *intent* over and above the intent to be

18. *Ibid.*, p. 215.
19. *Ibid.*, p. 217.

clarified. This additional intent depends, by description, upon a pertinent and congenial liking. Mr. Santayana's own chapters on morality are a persuasive invitation to add a new liking or a more urgent liking to the likings we already have, namely a liking for reason. And he knows well enough that the success of any such effort, the property that differentiates it from futile preaching, is command of an effective causal technique.[20] All this, I take it, is simply an amplification of the principle of Mr. Santayana that physics and dialectic meet at both top and bottom, beginning and end, together with a recognition that these beginnings and endings are constantly recurrent, not remote from each other —that is, any stage of the dialectical development expresses recourse to an occurrence instead of being self-perpetuating.

The conclusions to be drawn from such a position are general, applying to esthetic and logical criticisms as well as moral. In the first place, there is the development of intent constituting what is sometimes called "immanent" criticism. This involves at least a disclosure of meaning. In the case of literary criticism, for example, the clarification of an author's intent will include a clearer manifestation than the text affords—or at least, one which renders it easier of access and understanding. This is the prime requirement, and without it a book may be reviewed, praised or blamed but not criticized. Then there may be a survey of his various meanings, a synthesis with a view to determining consistency and range, the coherence of the values contained and implied from their own point of view. And this operation may revise meanings set forth, may reveal new and unexpected values, and in so far be itself "creative."

From the existential point of view, criticism will undertake an inquiry into the source of the "liking" which is expressed in the author's point of view, the quality and direction of his intents. This approach or attack (in the literal sense) will of course depend upon, and, in the degree of its sincerity, reveal the critic's own bias and interest. The saying "*De gustibus, non disputandum*," however, is either just a maxim of politeness or a stupid saying—a precept of courtesy if taken as a warning against that

20. See pp. 234–38, pages which it seems to me evince an excursion into Spinozistic naturalism, and an acknowledgment that Socratic dialectic must be supplemented by the causal art of constructing a just society in order that dialectic may either occur or be effective.

disputing which consists in a sheer pitting of likings against each other, the "You are" and "You aren't" of childish quarrels; stupid if it means that likings cannot be gone behind, or be made subject to inquiry as to their productive causes and consequences. Too often the saying erects our own ignorance and incapacity into an inherent trait of values. For it must be admitted that the psychological, biographical, social and historical knowledge which would make possible an effective causal discussion of likings is largely conspicuous for its absence. But it is silly to take this practical limitation as if it were something inhering in the very nature of tastes and their objects. Even as it is, an intelligent and honest judge can usually reveal to a person something instructive about the source and workings of the likings that are expressed in his intents and values which he did not know himself—provided, this disclosure is made the objective of criticism.

IV

We now return to our original topic and problem. Criticisms as judgments are like judgments of deliberation in that they imply that the subject-matter, values or goods, always contain a reference beyond what is directly given. Wherever there is appreciation, esteeming, prizing, cherishing, there is something over and above momentary enjoyment, and this surplusage is a sense of the objective relationships of what is enjoyed—its status as fulfilling prior tendencies and contributing to further movements.[21] A valuative judgment is therefore not a mere statement that a certain thing has been liked; it is an investigation of the *claims* of the thing in question to be esteemed, appreciated, prized, cherished. This involves the old and familiar distinction between an apparent and a real good, so that, subject to the

21. Thus viewed, the gap between the type of definition which has been considered and the seemingly more objective definition of Brown—adequacy of potentiality—and of Sheldon—help in completing or furthering some tendency already present—is not so great as at first sight seems; the disparity between them and any definition in terms of purely immediate liking is absolute. See Brown, "Value and Potentiality," *Journal of Philosophy, Psychology and Scientific Methods*, Vol. 11, pp. 29–37; Sheldon, "An Empirical Definition of Value," *ibid.*, pp. 113–24.

meaning given these terms upon the basis of our prior discussion, the object of all criticism is to determine whether an apparent good, something taken to be good, under more or less hidden and unavowed conditions, or "presuppositions," actually meets and satisfies these conditions. This article is too long to permit of any attempt to show that such critical judgments are of the nature of judgments of practise or what should be done, but if it has been successful in accomplishing what it set out to do, it clears the ground for the identification.

The Ethics of Animal Experimentation

Different moralists give different reasons as to why cruelty to animals is wrong. But about the fact of its immorality there is no question, and hence no need for argument. Whether the reason is some inherent right of the animal, or a reflex bad effect upon the character of the human being, or whatever it be, cruelty, the wanton and needless infliction of suffering upon any sentient creature, is unquestionably wrong. There is, however, no ethical justification for the assumption that experimentation upon animals, even when it involves some pain or entails, as is more common, death without pain,—since the animals are still under the influence of anaesthetics,—is a species of cruelty. Nor is there moral justification for the statement that the relations of scientific men to animals should be under any laws or restrictions save those general ones which regulate the behavior of all men so as to protect animals from cruelty. Neither of these propositions conveys, however, the full truth, for they are couched negatively, while the truth is positive. Stated positively, the moral principles relating to animal experimentation would read as follows:—

1. Scientific men are under definite obligation to experiment upon animals so far as that is the alternative to random and possibly harmful experimentation upon human beings, and so far as such experimentation is a means of saving human life and of increasing human vigor and efficiency.

2. The community at large is under definite obligations to see to it that physicians and scientific men are not needlessly hampered in carrying on the inquiries necessary for an adequate performance of their important social office of sustaining human life and vigor.

Let us consider these propositions separately.

[First published in *Atlantic Monthly* 138 (September 1926): 343–46.]

I

When we speak of the moral right of competent persons to experiment upon animals in order to get the knowledge and the resources necessary to eliminate useless and harmful experimentation upon human beings and to take better care of their health, we understate the case. Such experimentation is more than a right; it is a duty. When men have devoted themselves to the promotion of human health and vigor, they are under an obligation, no less binding because tacit, to avail themselves of all the resources which will secure a more effective performance of their high office. This office is other than the mere lessening of the physical pain endured by human beings when ill. Important as this is, there is something much worse than physical pain, just as there are better things than physical pleasures.

The person who is ill not merely suffers pain but is rendered unfit to meet his ordinary social responsibilities; he is incapacitated for service to those about him, some of whom may be directly dependent upon him. Moreover, his removal from the sphere of social relations does not merely leave a blank where he was; it involves a wrench upon the sympathies and affections of others. The moral suffering thus caused is something that has no counterpart anywhere in the life of animals, whose joys and sufferings remain upon a physical plane. To cure disease, to prevent needless death, is thus a totally different matter, occupying an infinitely higher plane, from the mere palliation of physical pain. To cure disease and prevent death is to promote the fundamental conditions of social welfare; is to secure the conditions requisite to an effective performance of all social activities; is to preserve human affections from the frightful waste and drain occasioned by the needless suffering and death of others with whom one is bound up.

These things are so obvious that it almost seems necessary to apologize for mentioning them. But anyone who reads the literature or who hears the speeches directed against animal experimentation will recognize that the ethical basis of the agitation against it is due to ignoring these considerations. It is constantly assumed that the object of animal experimentation is a selfish willingness to inflict physical pain upon others simply to save physical pain to ourselves.

On the moral side, the whole question is argued as if it were merely a balancing of physical pain to human beings and to animals over against each other. If it were such a question, the majority would probably decide that the claims of human suffering take precedence over that of animals; but a minority would doubtless voice the opposite view, and the issue would be, so far, inconclusive. But this is not the question. Instead of being the question of animal physical pain against human physical pain, it is the question of a certain amount of physical suffering to animals—reduced in extent to a minimum by the precautions of anaesthesia, asepsis, and skill—against the bonds and relations which hold people together in society, against the conditions of social vigor and vitality, against the deepest of shocks and interferences to human love and service.

No one who has faced this issue can be in doubt as to where the moral right and wrong lie. To prefer the claims of the physical sensations of animals to the prevention of death and the cure of disease—probably the greatest sources of poverty, distress, and inefficiency, and certainly the greatest sources of moral suffering—does not rise even to the level of sentimentalism.

It is accordingly the duty of scientific men to use animal experimentation as an instrument in the promotion of social well-being; and it is the duty of the general public to protect these men from attacks that hamper their work. It is the duty of the general public to sustain them in their endeavors. For physicians and scientific men, though having their individual failings and fallibilities like the rest of us, are in this matter acting as ministers and ambassadors of the public good.

II

This brings us to the second point: What is the duty of the community regarding legislation that imposes special restrictions upon the persons engaged in scientific experimentation with animals? That it is the duty of the State to pass general laws against cruelty to animals is a fact recognized by well-nigh all civilized States. But opponents of animal experimentation are not content with such general legislation; they demand what is in effect, if not legally, class legislation, putting scientific men under peculiar surveillance and limitation. Men in slaughterhouses, truck drivers, hostlers, cattle and horse owners, farmers and stable keepers, may be taken care of by general legislation; but educated men, devoted to scientific research, and physicians, devoted to the relief of suffering humanity, need some special supervision and regulation!

Unprejudiced people naturally inquire after the right and the wrong of this matter. Hearing accusations of wantonly cruel deeds—actuated by no higher motive than passing curiosity—brought against workers in laboratories and teachers in classrooms, at first they may be moved to believe that additional special legislation is required. Further thought leads, however, to a further question: If these charges of cruelty are justified, why are not those guilty of it brought up for trial in accordance with the laws already provided against cruelty to animals? Consideration of the fact that the remedies and punishments already provided are not resorted to by those so vehement in their charges against scientific workers leads the unprejudiced inquirer to a further conclusion.

Agitation for new laws is not so much intended to prevent specific instances of cruelty to animals as to subject scientific inquiry to hampering restrictions. The moral issue changes to this question: What ought to be the moral attitude of the public toward the proposal to put scientific inquiry under restrictive conditions? No one who really asks himself this question—without mixing it up with the other question of cruelty to animals that is taken care of by already existing laws—can, I imagine, be in doubt as to its answer. Nevertheless, one consideration should be emphasized. *Scientific inquiry has been the chief instrumentality in bringing man from barbarism to civilization, from darkness to light, while it has incurred, at every step, determined opposition from the powers of ignorance, misunderstanding, and jealousy.*

It is not so long ago, as years are reckoned, that a scientist in a physical or chemical laboratory was popularly regarded as a magician engaged in unlawful pursuits, or as in impious converse with evil spirits, about whom all sorts of detrimental stories were circulated and believed. Those days have gone; generally speaking, the value of free scientific inquiry as an instrumentality of social progress and enlightenment is acknowledged. At the same time, it is possible, by making irrelevant emotional appeals and obscuring the real issues, to galvanize into life something of the old spirit of misunderstanding, envy, and dread of science. The point at issue in the subjection of animal experimenters to special supervision and legislation is thus deeper than at first sight appears. In principle it involves the revival of that animosity to discovery and to the application to life of the fruits of discovery which, upon the whole, has been the chief foe of human progress. It behooves every thoughtful individual to be constantly on the alert against every revival of this spirit, in whatever guise it presents itself.

III

It would be agreeable to close with these positive statements of general principles; but it is hardly possible to avoid saying a few words regarding the ethics of the way in which the campaign against animal experimentation is often waged. Exaggerated statements, repetitions of allegations of cruelty which have never been proved or even examined, use of sporadic cases of cruelty to animals in Europe a generation or two ago as if they were typical of the practice in the United States today, refusal to accept the testimony of reputable scientific men regarding either their own procedure or the benefits that have accrued to humanity and to the brute kingdom itself from animal experimentation, uncharitable judgment varying from vague insinuation to downright aspersion—these things certainly have an ethical aspect which must be taken into account by unbiased men and women desirous that right and justice shall prevail.

It is also a fair requirement that some kind of perspective and proportion shall be maintained in moral judgments. Doubtless more suffering is inflicted upon animals in a single day in a single abattoir in some one city of our country than in a year, or years, in all the scientific and medical laboratories of all the United States. Do they come into court with clean hands who complacently, without protest and without effort to remedy or to alleviate existing evils, daily satisfy their own physical appetites at the cost of the death of animals after suffering, in order then to turn around and cry out against a relatively insignificant number of deaths occurring, after skilled precautions against suffering, in the cause of advancement of knowledge for the sake of the relief of humanity? Surely, until it is finally decided that the taking of animal life for human food is wrong, there is something morally unsound in any agitation which questions the right to take animal life in the interests of the life and health of men, women, and children, especially when infinitely more precautions are used to avoid animal suffering in the latter case than in the former.

Affective Thought

Traditional theories in philosophy and psychology have accustomed us to sharp separations between physiological and organic processes on the one hand and the higher manifestations of culture in science and art on the other. The separations are summed up in the common division made between mind and body. These theories have also accustomed us to draw rigid separations between the logical, strictly intellectual, operations which terminate in science, the emotional and imaginative processes which dominate poetry, music and to a lesser degree the plastic arts, and the practical doings which rule our daily life and which result in industry, business and political affairs. In other words, thought, sentiment or affectivity and volition have been marked off from one another. The result of these divisions has been the creation of a large number of problems which in their technical aspect are the special concern of philosophy, but which come home to every one in his actual life in the segregation of the activities he carries on, the departmentalizing of life, the pigeon-holing of interests. Between science's sake, art for art's sake, business as usual or business for money-making, the relegation of religion to Sundays and holy-days, the turning over of politics to professional politicians, the professionalizing of sports, and so on, little room is left for living, for the sake of living, a full, rich and free life.

Recent advances in some fundamental generalizations regarding biological functions in general and those of the nervous system in particular have made possible a definite conception of continuous development from the lower functions to the higher. Interestingly enough, this breaking-down of fixed barriers between physiological operations and the far reaches of culture in

[First published in *Journal of the Barnes Foundation* 2 (April 1926): 3–9.]

science and art has also removed the underpinning from beneath the separation of science, art and practical activity from one another. There has long been vague talk about the unity of experience and mental life, to the effect that knowledge, feeling and volition are all manifestations of the same energies, etc.; but there has now been put in our hands the means by which this talk may be made definite and significant.

Naturally, the variety of physiological details involved has not yet been adequately organized nor has there been time to digest them and get their net results. In any case, the writer is not an expert in this field, and even if he were this would hardly be the place to expound them. But some of their net results are easy of comprehension, and they have a definite bearing upon art and its connection with the normal processes of life.

We may begin with the field of reasoning, long supposed to be preempted by pure intellect, and to be completely severed, save by accident, from affectivity and desire and from the motor organs and habits by which we make our necessary practical adjustments to the world about us. But a recent writer, Rignano, working from a biological basis, has summed up his conclusions as follows: "The analysis of reasoning, the highest of our mental faculties, has led us to the view that it is constituted entirely by the reciprocal play of the two fundamental and primordial activities of our psyche, the intellectual and the affective. The first consist in simple mnemonic evocations of perceptions or images of the past; the second appear as tendencies or aspirations of our mind towards a certain end to be attained, towards which reasoning itself is directed."[1]

An isolated quotation fails, of course, to bring out the full force of the points made. But what is summed up here under the idea of "affectivity" is that an organism has certain basic needs which cannot be supplied without activity that modifies the surroundings; that when the organism is in any way disturbed in its "equilibration" with its environment, its needs show themselves as restless, craving, desiring activity which persists until the acts thus induced have brought about a new integration of the organism and its relation to the environment. Then it is shown that thinking falls within the scope of this principle; reasoning is a

1. Rignano, *The Psychology of Reasoning*, p. 388.

phase of the generic function of bringing about a new relationship between organisms and the conditions of life, and like other
phases of the function is controlled by need, desire and progressive satisfactions.

Rignano calls the other phase "intellectual." But the context
shows that the basic principle here is one of practical adjustments. Past experiences are retained so that they may be evoked
and arranged when there is need to use them in attaining the new
end set by the needs of our affective nature. But the retention is
not intellectual. It is a matter of organic modifications, of change
of disposition, attitude and habit. The "stuff" from which thinking draws its material in satisfying need by establishing a new
relation to the surroundings is found in what, with some extension of the usual sense of the word, may be termed habits:
namely, the changes wrought in our ways of acting and undergoing by prior experiences. Thus the material of thought all
comes from the past; but its purpose and direction is future, the
development of a new environment as the condition of sustaining a new and more fully integrated self.

It thus turns out, though the argument is too technical to be
developed on this occasion, that the great gap which is traditionally made between the lower physiological functions and the
higher cultural ones, is due first to isolating the organism from
the environment, failing to see the necessity of its integration
with environment, and secondly, to neglect of the function of
needs in creating ends, or consequences to be attained. So when
"ends" are recognized at all, it has been thought necessary to call
in some higher and independent power to account for them. But
the connection of ends with affectivities, with cravings and desires, is deep-seated in the organism, and is constantly extended
and refined through experience. Desire, interest, accomplishes
what in the traditional theory a pure intellect was evoked to accomplish. More and more expansive desires and more varied and
flexible habits build up more elaborate trains of thought; finally,
the harmonies, consistencies and comprehensive structures of
logical systems result.

Reasoning and science are thus obviously brought nearer to
art. The satisfaction of need requires that surroundings should
be changed. In reasoning, this fact appears as the necessity for
experimentation. In plastic art it is a common-place. Art also explicitly recognizes what it has taken so long to discover in sci-

ence; the control exercised by emotion in re-shaping natural conditions, and the place of the imagination, under the influence of desire, in re-creating the world into a more orderly place. When so-called nonrational factors are found to play a large part in the production of relations of consistency and order in logical systems, it is not surprising that they should operate in artistic structures. Indeed, it may be questioned whether any scientific systems extant, save perhaps those of mathematics, equal artistic structures in integrity, subtlety and scope, while the latter are evidently more readily and widely understood, and are the sources of a more widespread and direct satisfaction. These facts are explicable only when it is realized that scientific and artistic systems embody the same fundamental principles of the relationship of life to its surroundings, and that both satisfy the same fundamental needs. Probably a time will come when it will be universally recognized that the differences between coherent logical schemes and artistic structures in poetry, music and the plastics are technical and specialized, rather than deep-seated.

In the past we have had to depend mostly upon phrases to explain the production of artistic structures. They have been referred to genius or inspiration or the creative imagination. Contemporary appeal to the Unconscious and the Racial Unconscious are the same thing under a new name. Writing the word with a capital letter and putting "the" before it, as if it were a distinct force, gives us no more light than we had before. Yet unconscious activities are realities, and the newer biology is making it clear that such organic activities are just of the kind to re-shape natural objects in order to procure their adequate satisfaction, and that the re-shaped object will be marked by the features known to belong to works of art.

It is a common-place that recurrence in place and time, rhythm, symmetry, harmony, modulation, suspense and resolution, plot, climax and contrasting let down, emphasis and intervals, action and retardation, unity, being "all of a piece," and inexhaustible variety, are means, in varying ways, to meet the requirements of different media, of all artistic productions. These are just the traits which naturally characterize objects when the environment is made over in consonance with basic organic requirements. On the other hand, the fact that the spectator and auditor "click" so intimately and intensely in the face of works of art is accounted for. By their means there are released old, deep-seated habits or engrained organic "memories," yet these old habits are deployed in new ways, ways in which they are adapted to a more completely integrated world so that they themselves achieve a new integration. Hence the liberating, expansive power of art.

The same considerations explain the fact that works of art of a new style have to create their own audience. At first there is experienced largely the jar of dissonance with the superficial habits most readily called into play. But changes in the surroundings involve correlated changes in the organism, and so the eye and ear gradually become acclimatized. The organism is really made over, is reorganized in effecting an adequate perception of a work of art. Hence the proper effect of the latter is gradually realized, and then what was first condemned as *outré* falls into its serial place in the history of artistic achievement.

In *The Art in Painting*, Mr. Barnes has shown that plastic form is the *integration of all plastic means*. In the case of paintings, these are color, line, light and space. By means of their relations to one another, design is affected: design, namely in line patterns, in surface masses, in three-dimensional solids, and in spatial intervals—the "room" about objects whether up and down, side to side, front and back. And Mr. Barnes has shown that it is the kind and degree of integration of plastic means in achieving each of the elements of design taken by itself and also the integration of each with all the others, which constitutes the objective standard for value in painting. From the psychological standpoint, this integration in pictures means that a correlative integration is effected in the total set of organic responses; eye activities arouse allied muscular activities which in turn not merely harmonize with and support eye activities, but which in turn evoke further experiences of light and color, and so on. Moreover, as in every adequate union of sensory and motor actions, the background of visceral, circulatory, respiratory functions is also consonantly called into action. In other words, integration in the object permits and secures a corresponding integration in organic activities. Hence, the peculiar well-being and rest in excitation, vitality in peace, which is characteristic of aesthetic enjoyment.

Defective value can, of course, be judged by the same measure. Some one of the elements may be deficient; thereby adequate support is not given to the functioning of the other elements and a corresponding lack of vitality in response occurs or even a feeling of frustration and bafflement. Or, what is more likely to happen in pictures that may conventionally attain celebrity for a time, some factor is overaccentuated—so that while vision is captured and impressed for the moment, the final reaction is partial and one-sided, a fatiguing demand being made upon some organic activities which are not duly nourished and reinforced by the others.

Thus it is not too much to say that the statement of an objective criterion of value in paintings set forth for the first time by Mr. Barnes will make possible in time an adequate psychological, even physiological, analysis of aesthetic responses in spectators, so that the appreciation of paintings will no longer be a matter of private, absolute tastes and *ipse dixits*.

By the use of the same conception of integration of specified means, Mr. Barnes has also for the first time given us the clue to the historical development of modern painting in terms of paintings themselves. In the earlier period, integration is in considerable measure achieved by means extraneous to the painting itself, such as associated subject-matter in the religious or prior (academic) tradition, or by undue reliance upon familiar associations between light and shade and spatial positions. The history of art shows a tendency to secure variety and relationship in plastic form by means of the element most truly distinctive of painting, namely, color. Lines, for example, have ceased to be hard and fast clear-cut divisions (in which case they are more or less nonintegrative), and are determined by subtle meetings of color-masses which upon close examination are found to melt into one another. Similarly, light and shade were long employed on the basis of every-day practical associations to give the impression of solidity. But artists capable of greater differentiation and integration of their experiences in terms of color itself experimented in conveying tri-dimensional relationships by means of variations and juxtapositions in color. Then color was employed to build up structural solidity and its variations in single objects. Painters have also learned to render action and movement, not by depending upon associations with extraneous experiences—which always lead to an overaccentuation of some one feature, light or line, as in depicting exaggerated muscular poses—but by use of the relations of forms to one another, in connection with spatial intervals, this end being attained by use of color as means. The fact that this more subtle and complete integration usually involves deformation or distortion of familiar forms—that is, conflicts with associations formed outside the realm of painting—accounts for the fact that they are greeted at first with disdainful criticism. But in time a new line of organic associations is built up, formed on the basis of unalloyed aesthetic experiences, and deformations—what are such from the practical every-day standpoint—cease to give trouble and to be annoying. They become elements in a genuine and direct aesthetic grasp.

From the standpoint of the analysis of pictures, there is nothing new in these remarks to any one familiar with Mr. Barnes's book. I have recurred to them only because the objective analysis of Mr. Barnes is in the first place so thoroughly in accord with the present trend of fundamental biological conceptions, and, secondly, because it makes possible an application of these biological conceptions to the whole field of artistic structures and aesthetic criticism. It then becomes possible to break down the traditional separation between scientific and intellectual systems and those of art, and also to further the application of the principle of integration to the relationship of those elements of culture which are so segregated in our present life—to science, art, in its variety of forms, industry and business, religion, sport and morals. And it is daily being more evident that unless some integration can be attained, the always increasing isolations and oppositions consequent upon the growth of specialization in all fields, will in the end disrupt our civilization. That art and its intelligent appreciation as manifested especially in painting is itself an integrating experience is the constant implication of the work of the Barnes Foundation as that is reflected in *The Art in Painting*. For to make of paintings an educational means is to assert that the genuine intelligent realization of pictures is not only an integration of the specialized factors found in the paintings as such, but is such a deep and abiding experience of the nature of fully harmonized experience as sets a standard or forms a habit for all other experiences. In other words, paintings when taken out of their specialized niche are the basis of an educational experience which counteracts the disrupting tendencies of the hard-and-fast specializations, compartmental divisions and rigid segregations which so confuse and nullify our present life.

Art in Education—and
Education in Art

In a recent review of an inspiring book [this volume, p. 221], Whitehead's *Science and the Modern World*, limitations of space compelled me to omit reference to many of its significant considerations. One of these was a plea for the inclusion of aesthetic appreciation in the scheme of life and of education. The plea is the more significant because based on a fundamental philosophical principle, not just upon miscellaneous eulogies assembled ad hoc. To quote some of his own words:

There is something between the gross specialised values of the practical man, and the thin specialised values of the mere scholar. Both types have missed something; and if you add together the two sets of values, you do not obtain the missing elements. What is wanted is an appreciation of the infinite variety of vivid values achieved by an organism in its proper environment. When you understand all about the sun and all about the atmosphere and all about the rotation of the earth, you may still miss the radiance of the sunset. There is no substitute for the direct perception of the concrete achievement of a thing in its actuality. We want concrete fact with a high light thrown on what is relevant to its preciousness.

Art and aesthetic appreciation is what is missing, "art" denoting any selective activity by which concrete things are so arranged as to elicit attention to the distinctive values realizable by them.

Aesthetic appreciation and art so conceived are not additions to the real world, much less luxuries. They represent the only ways in which the individualized elements in the world of nature and man are grasped. Science assumes *that* there are such individual realizations in which something exists immediately for its

[First published in *New Republic* 46 (24 February 1926): 11–13.]

own sake, but it passes over *what* they are: it does so because its business is elsewhere, namely in the relations which they have to other things. Without aesthetic appreciation we miss the most characteristic as well as the most precious thing in the real world. The same is true of "practical" matters, that is, of activity limited to effecting technical changes, changes which do not affect our enjoyable realizations of things in their individualities. Modern preoccupation with science and with industry based on science has been disastrous; our education has followed the model which they have set. It has been concerned with intellectual analysis and formularized information, and with technical training for this or that field of professionalized activity, a statement as true, upon the whole, of the scholar in the classics or in literature or in the fine arts themselves as of specialists in other branches.

The result is disastrous because it strengthens the tendency to professionalism, or the setting of minds in grooves. "The fixed person for the fixed duties, who in older societies was such a godsend, in the future will be a public danger." The physical celibacy of the learned class of the Middle Ages is now repeated in a "celibacy of the intellect divorced from the concrete contemplation of the complete facts." Again, the outcome is disastrous because it leads men to take abstractions as if they were realities. The social effects are seen in traditional political economy with its abstractions from concrete individual human lives, the theory only reflecting, however, the actual abstractions which reign practically in industry. It is disastrous because it has fixed attention upon competition for control and possession of a fixed environment rather than upon what art can do to *create* an environment; and because it has led to the middle-class complacent regard for comfort and security in a moving world, while "in the immediate future there will be less security than in the immediate past, less stability." It is disastrous because civilization built upon these principles cannot supply the demand of the soul for joy, or freshness of experience; only attention through art to the vivid but transient values of things can effect such refreshment. Such refreshments, themselves transient, yet discipline the inmost being of man, a discipline "not distinct from enjoyment, but by reason of it," since they shape the soul to a permanent appreciation of values beyond its former self.

Such an indictment of existing culture upon both its scientific and industrial sides with the claim that aesthetic appreciation inspired by art is the missing element, raises the question of the intrinsic connection between education and the arts. In a recent review, Mr. Leo Stein made an adverse criticism of the book on *The Art in Painting* written by Mr. A. C. Barnes, on the ground that the book was unfavorably affected by Mr. Barnes's interest in education as exemplified in his creation of the Barnes Foundation as an educational institution.[1] The assertion raises in its implications the question of what painting as an art is in relation to education. Is art in painting so foreign to education and education so foreign to art that they must be kept apart, or is art intrinsically educative, intrinsically, by its very existence, and not by virtue of any didactic purpose to which it is subordinated? The answer to the question is clear enough from the standpoint of such a philosophy as that of Mr. Whitehead. The book and the Foundation which it represents propound the question in a definite form which properly affords the point of departure for a more specific consideration of the general theme.

The book is written from the conviction that art as displayed in painting is inherently educative. But paintings do not educate at present till we are educated to enjoy, to realize, their educative potentialities. The need of prior education flows from many sources. Part of the reasons are stated in what has been drawn from Mr. Whitehead: the submergence of aesthetic appreciation by the ruling tendencies of our present culture. We are unconsciously educated away from art in painting in advance. But they are also more specific. They spring from the disposition of artists, or at least "connoisseurs," to set art on a pedestal, to make of it something esoteric, something apart from values inherent in all experiences of things in their full integrity, and something apart from the constant needs of the everyday man. This attitude is fostered in turn by the customs of institutionalized museums and the habits of professional critics. The celibacy of the intellect has found its way into galleries and histories of art, into books about painters and paintings. The strong social current setting against aesthetic realization is reinforced by influences which not only give the would-be enjoyer of paintings no directive as-

1. The *New Republic*, Winter Literary Section, Dec. 2, 1925.

sistance, but which actually confuse and mislead. For they fix observation upon everything except what is vital—the eliciting of attention to the distinctive values realizable in all things, when these values are selected and heightened by the painter's eye and hand. The book in question attempts, as does the educational Foundation, a reversal of this process.

Since Mr. Stein omitted in his review to state the principles by which Mr. Barnes achieves the reversal, I may be excused for stating them. One of them is that the painter realizes the heightened appreciative enjoyment of the scenes of nature and human life by thorough-going integration of the elements proper to painting, namely, color, including light, line, spatial arrangement, the latter including surface pattern, solidity and depth. Plastic form or design is the result of the merging, the interpenetration of these elements, and is not to be identified with the effect of any one of them taken by itself—which, in fact, only leads to an overaccentuation of some one feature detracting from the aesthetic effect of the whole. This interpenetration or integration is then the vital thing, comparable to what, in Mr. Whitehead's terminology, is the interplay of individual values such that every part of the whole reflects the aspects of every other part, as the whole reflects aspects of nature extending far beyond the scene specifically displayed. To be educated for the educative function of paintings is thus to learn to see this integration in the whole and in its every part. The other element in education is recognition of a continuing tradition which works in the individual artist, but not by way of enslavement—which defines academic art. Every significant painter in respecting and using the tradition adds something to it from his own personal vision and emotion, and his addition is qualitative, transforming.

Such a statement as has just been made is, of course, merely preliminary; by itself it is nothing. It becomes something by being applied in detail to the definite analysis of a large number of paintings from the time of Giotto to the present day. We come back to the two questions already asked. In the first place, is art intrinsically an education and an imperatively needed education of the human being? In the second place, is education needed to help human beings to see paintings so that their educative function may be realized? I am loath to believe that Mr. Stein would answer either of these questions in the negative; I do not suppose he belongs to the esoterics who would treat art in paintings or elsewhere as a mystery for the few. In this case, difference in appraisal of particular artists or paintings means little or nothing in itself. For the essence of what Mr. Barnes offers is method and a criterion based on that method. If the method is right then errors in specific appraisals must be corrected by the use of the method.

Method means or is intelligence at work; denial of the existence of any attainable method signifies, therefore, continuation of the present chaos and impotency of aesthetic appreciation: that is, continued non-performance of that educative function from absence of which our civilization is suffering so disastrously. I shall not obtrude my own opinion as to the worth of the method. But the existence of the Foundation and the book which presents its leading ideas of method are a challenge. They assert that aesthetic appreciation inspired and directed by art is a rightful and imperatively urgent demand of the common man; they assert that method, intelligence, may be employed not just by a few critics for the delectation or information of a small circle, but so that everyone may be educated to obtain what art in paintings has to give. They make the latter assertion by proffering in general and in detail a method, showing it in operation. They raise therefore a problem of immense importance in education, a problem intimately and vitally connected with the greatest weakness in existing education, a weakness disastrously affecting every phase of contemporary life. It is this fact which gives the book a quality incommensurate with that of other "treatises" on painting and art and which calls for criticism which is correspondingly out of the usual sort.

What Is the Matter
with Teaching?

American educational theory is the most advanced to be found in the world. It is a recognized source of progressive educational movements in Japan, China, Australia, Russia, Turkey, South Africa as well as western Europe. Those schools in the United States in which this theory is put in operation are an inspiration to modern schools all over the world. And what is most significant is that these schools are a good deal more than models for improvement in this or that new detail. They have furnished new and revolutionary ideas of what schools are for; of what they are capable of effecting in transforming lives of boys and girls, and of how the transformation is brought about. It is in elementary education that this work has been accomplished; no such striking advance is found in high schools or colleges.

Nevertheless the vast mass of American elementary schools show no trace of the influence of advanced educational theory or practise. They are practically what they have been for the last fifty years; worse, one is tempted to say, but that perhaps is an exaggeration. In the big cities they are by and large big scholastic factories, efficiently managed for the American commercial specialty—mass production of standardized products at lowest cost. In the rural districts they are dead, dispirited, poorly equipped, with the air of carrying on a losing struggle.

What is the cause of this contrast? this contradiction? In a word, the answer is found in the old saying: As is the teacher, so is the school. Yet this answer tells us only where to look for the problem; it does not solve the problem. Teachers are an effect of social conditions before they are a cause of schools.

Why are the teachers of our elementary schools what they are? What selected them? What keeps them what they are? The responsibility is found in the community; we can not unload it on

[First published in *Delineator* 107 (October 1925): 5–6, 78.]

the teachers, for they are symptoms, products of our own beliefs, desires, ideals, and what we are satisfied with. To find out what is the matter with the schools, we have to make an examination of teachers; to find out what is the matter with the teachers, we have to examine ourselves.

As a people, we profess to believe in education above everything else. We have succeeded in making ourselves believe in this profession. Critics are taken in by it, and ridicule our alleged faith as a blind religion and our devotion to schools as a cult, a superstitious mummery. But what is the test of the depth and sincerity of a faith? Only acts show whether a professed belief is living or is a form of words. In the case of education the actions which serve as a test are: First, are we willing to pay, to give, to sacrifice, to get and keep in our elementary schools the kind of men and women teachers who alone can make our schools be what they should be? And, secondly, apart from money for salaries and equipment of schools for educational work, what are we willing to do in the way of esteem, respect, social prestige, hearty backing? For neither question is the answer very encouraging, least of all for elementary schools.

Immediately after the war the shortage of teachers was such as to compel some attention to the question of adjustment of wages in the face of the rise in the cost of living. The Red scare helped also, at least as far as high school and college teachers were concerned, since there was a fear that poorly paid "intellectuals" would be attracted toward Bolshevism. But symptoms only, not causes, were then dealt with, and that remains true to-day. Salaries were increased with reference to quantity and not quality. The aim was simply to pay what was demanded in order to get enough teachers to go around, such as they were; not to find out what would be required to attract and hold the best men and women within the schools.

In spite of the readjustment of wage scales, the shortage is still all but chronic in many regions, and in many rural districts there are fewer schools and fewer teachers to-day than there were ten years ago. A serious feature in the situation is that while elementary teaching is lessening in attractiveness, other callings are gaining in competitive power, especially for women. It is not necessary to point out how many avenues formerly closed to women are now open to them. The "invasion" of business, if not of the professions, by women is a commonplace. Moreover, the higher paid positions in business are becoming more and more accessible, so that ambitious women see something ahead to beckon them on. In contrast the pulling power of the elementary teaching vocation on the financial side is almost pitiable.

Ten years ago one of the greatest problems of the women's colleges in placing their graduates was to find anything but a poorly paid teaching profession for them to go into. The more enterprising institutions made a business of diversifying opportunities. So rapid has been the change that one of the colleges which took up this matter most seriously found a few years ago that its courses to prepare students for teaching were almost without students. In less than ten years teaching sank from an almost monopolistic role among gainful occupations for women down toward the lower half of the list.

The other side of this story is that as cultivated women coming from homes with a tradition of culture find teaching less and less attractive, keeping school presents itself to another class of girls as an opportunity to take a step upward beyond the place of their parents in the social scale. In the larger cities a constantly increasing ratio of elementary school teachers come from daughters of immigrants of, as a rule, not more than one generation's standing.

I have no sympathy with the highbrow and "Nordic" slurs passed upon our recent immigrants. I only point out that it is impossible to secure in large numbers from this particular class any high grade of cultivation, occupied as the families have been with getting a bare economic foothold, and that the pathetic eagerness for education displayed by many of this immigrant class does not compensate for the generations of intellectual starvation which has produced this hunger.

In one form and another, the depths of culture are contained in the resources of the mother tongue, and not much can be expected from teachers to whom the daily language is still largely an external instrument and not an organ of the soul.

Another proof of the seriousness of the financial aspect of the question is the extent of the "labor turn-over." I spare the reader any attempt at statistics upon this point as upon that of salaries. Any one can take judicial notice of the fact that even in the cities where preparation and advancement are best organized from a mechanical point of view, the number of teachers who abandon their calling is very large. This signifies in practise that young and unexperienced girls are flowing in a steady stream into the elementary schools, only, after they have obtained some experience and some professional sense and outlook, to be replaced by others, equally crude, who have also resorted to teaching as a temporary stop-gap pending marriage or the taking up of some more lucrative pursuit. And this is the situation at its best!

In the country districts as a whole there is hardly even a pretense of the maintenance of professional standards and spirit. Teaching is no more a profession than washing dishes and taking care of the baby at home. It is an improvised occupation easily taken up and easily laid aside, largely pursued to fill in because it does not involve as much social stigma as going out to service and exacts little if any more special training than is acquired by any one who has himself or herself been at school. If these words seem harsh or exaggerated, let it be remembered that there is little prospect of any great improvement in our schools throughout the country as a whole until we get rid of our feeling of complacency.

Finally, let us bear in mind that all conditions are at the worst in elementary schools. A large part of even the educated part of the community is still under the shadow of the old belief that anybody who is in possession of his five senses and who has himself or herself learned to read, write and figure, knows enough to teach *little* children, at least if he or she "be handy with the children." It is not too much to say that psychological science has in the last few years practically proved the prophetic insight of a few great educational reformers who asserted that the early years are the most important, because at this period all the underlying emotional habits and unconscious attitudes are being formed. The scientific demonstration is the more impressive because it has come mainly from physicians who in dealing with abnormalities have been forced to trace them to their origin in badly adjusted personal and social relationships in childhood.

It may be that this scientific demonstration will mark the beginning of a new era in education. But if so, the epoch is still in the future. Parents and teachers alike are still committed to the absurdity that the older a person is, and the more fixed, closed and specialized his habits, the more important are skill and learning in his guardians and teachers, while in the plastic years in which habits are being formed for the whole of life, habits which are fundamental and general, the human being may safely be left to chance, ignorance and inexpertness. I sometimes think that this absurdity is itself more than enough to account for all the failures of all our educational efforts, and that until it is remedied all our energies spent in other directions are wasted. See what happens. As a rule the most inexperienced teachers and those who receive the lowest rate of pay are given the youngest children. Because the latter are the easiest to teach, they shall receive the supposedly poorest teachers. Then because being the easiest to teach and learn, and having been started by acquiring habits in the most haphazard and misfit ways, we will pay subsequent teachers more and more to try and correct the results of prior poor teaching and learning! So it works out that we college teachers, who by the nature of the case can do the least in forming fundamental habits, although most, of course, in imparting specialized skill and knowledge, get the highest pay for the fewest hours of work.

It is not all a joke if I say that we can measure the dawn of a serious faith in education by the manifestation of willingness to pay the highest wages going to those who actively direct the education of the youngest. We shall then begin by setting new teachers to deal with older and relatively case-hardened specimens, and as they prove their fitness promote them to teach younger children whose education is so much more important just because they are much, so much easier, to teach wrong. As for high-school and college students, once started right they would largely educate one another, together with the contacts which they would naturally seek with those specially skilled and learned in the lines in which their curiosity had been aroused.

In devoting so much of my space to the pecuniary side, I do not imply that right education can be bought out of hand like a material commodity. I have in mind the will to pay adequately as a sign and test of the genuineness and depth of our professed faith and interest in the cause of popular education. My first question is really part of my second: What is the degree and quality of our esteem, our working respect for education as measured by our attitude toward those who pursue it? Judged by our desire to make the calling materially attractive, it is pretty low, and the intangibles and imponderables of the case bear out the conclusions indicated by the material factor. Who pays the piper calls the tune.

Consider first the conditions with which teaching is surrounded. It is a commonplace of those scientific principles to which allusion was made at the outset that no two children are alike, that no two learn in just the same way, or are, strictly speaking, capable of being compared, measured and graded on a basis of just quantity, more and less. Nevertheless the number of pupils to a teacher may average anywhere above thirty-six, this being regarded as about the lowest number under most favorable conditions. Consequently quantity becomes the controlling consideration. The teacher is compelled to instruct in batches and on a basis of uniformity. Everything tends automatically to lock-step treatment in teaching and discipline. To cover so much ground with every pupil, to have each one go through as nearly as possible the same motions as every other, is the same thing as to discourage originality and depress individuality.

What if the teacher believes in encouraging independent thought and creative impulse? The pressure of circumstances gives her no opportunity; she is forced to fall in line; she is a part of the machine. Uniformity gives speed, and speed alone enables her to get over the ground that she is required to cover.

Human beings were not constructed to operate like machines; they need more leeway and variety of action. Hence the teacher is under constant nervous strain from the abnormality of her life. The type of nervous fatigue and overstrain which marks the school is as easily recognizable as that found in the overdriven factory worker.

In the teacher it goes deeper and leaves behind it a great organic irritability. For the factory hand is only working against machines. The school hand is working against other human beings who also rebel against being treated as machines. The strain and irritation is more than doubled. Then the teacher looks for the first chance to escape from the treadmill. The vicious circle keeps on.

Generalization regarding the social esteem in which elementary teachers are held is probably foolish, since it is not likely that the same rule holds for the country as a whole. What is needed is a careful collection of data made by investigation of selected parts of the country. Upon the whole, however, elementary teachers seem to be approaching the status of upper-class servants; save that their conduct and movement are subject to a closer watch and stricter censorship. What is galling to those with brains and is surely driving them from the profession is that they are not expected to have any ideas of their own on any controverted social and moral subjects. Wo be to them if in an unguarded moment they permit a dull class in geography, or history or civil government to be enlivened by a discussion of some contemporary topic in which the appearance of heretical ideas is permitted. These things are in the keeping of the local branch of the American Legion, of the hardware merchant and bank cashier and the local board of education.

Colorless intellectual conformity, blank vacuousness, is the estate to which the teacher is called. Even in her amusements and what is commonly called "social life," the teacher must be not only blameless and circumspect, but neutral and subservient. Consciously and still more by unconscious selection and elimination, the teaching profession is insured against the presence of vigorous, many-sided and rich personalities, from whom alone something positive and constructive might be expected.

The ever-thickening wall which divides the classroom teacher and the adminstrative officer is another sign of the degraded esteem in which the elementary teacher is held. When the community thinks with some degree of respect and honor of an "educator," it is the principal and superintendent who is thought of. Within the system promotion and increase of pay are almost equivalents of getting out of teaching and into that professional mystery termed administration. The further away one is from children and from the only place where education takes place, the direct contact of mind and mind, the greater is the probability that one will be an educational authority and looked up to with respect and envy. In the name of scientific administration and close supervision, the initiative and freedom of the actual teacher are more and more curtailed. By means of achievement and mental tests carried on from the central office, of a steadily issuing stream of dictated typewritten communications, of minute and explicit syllabi of instruction, the teacher is reduced to a living phonograph. In the name of centralization of responsibility and of efficiency and even science, everything possible is done to make the teacher into a servile rubber stamp. After we have either thus scared away intellectual creativeness and originality, or else segregated it in offices remote from fertilizing contact with child life which is touched only through statistics and standardized tests, we wonder why all the energy and zeal expended upon education bears so little fruit!

If I have assumed the role of a Jeremiah, I have indeed left out of the account many true and encouraging things which might have been said. But I have not invented or exaggerated the dark spots. As are the teachers, so are the schools. That is the one fundamental and unalterable principle of sound pedagogy. But when we take stock of the work of the schools, when we criticize and undertake reforms, we are willing and anxious to tinker with everything else. We are not willing to ask just what keeps out of the occupation of teaching mature, rich, free, independent personalities.

I should look upon the present situation with more equanimity, if there were more disposition to drop our preoccupation with the mechanics and externals of efficiency, and concentrate upon one question. What can be done to liberate teachers, to free their personalities and minds from all the petty economic, social and administrative restrictions which so frequently hem them in and repress them?

The "Socratic Dialogues" of Plato [1]

Every student of Plato knows what advance has been made in interpreting many of the dialogues of Plato, notably *Euthydemus*, *Theaetetus*, etc., by detection of contemporary schools of philosophy, especially the Cynics, Cyrenaics and Megarics, figuring under the guise of Sophists of a by-gone generation. But interpreters who employ this idea as a matter of course for dialogues from the "middle period" on, still cling piously to the idea of a genuinely Socratic early period. They hold that the themes and general tenor of the *Lesser Hippias*, *Laches*, *Lysis*, *Charmides*, etc., are genuinely Socratic, even when they are not claimed to be literal reports. This is an extraordinary tribute to Plato's dramatic power. But in my judgment it leaves us without the key to understanding these early dialogues, and also without a clew to their relation to the later dialogues. It is worth while to adopt a contrary hypothesis and proceed in a reverse direction. We may assume that while the dialogues are indubitably early ones, they are aimed at rival thinkers who claimed to be true Socratics. They are intended to show that the views which these rival thinkers advance are full of confusion and contradictions. The joke, so transparently clear to Plato's own audience, is

1. The purpose of this paper is to present a point of view for interpreting the Platonic dialogues rather than to develop that point of view into an adequate piece of scholarly research. This fact accounts for the absence of references to important literature. One reference must be made, however, that to Karl Joël's articles on *Der λόγος Σωκρατιχός* in the *Archiv für Geschichte der Philosophie*, Vol. 8, p. 466, and Vol. 9, p. 50, 1895–6. These articles are the source of the method used in this paper, and have guided me in reading Plato since I became acquainted with them. I acknowledge also indebtedness to Benn for the conviction that the Sophists were divided into two schools, one naturalistic and the other humanistic and that this division accounts for the form which many problems assume in Plato.

[First published in *Studies in the History of Ideas*, ed. Department of Philosophy, Columbia University (New York: Columbia University Press, 1925), 2:1–23.]

heightened by putting the confutation in the mouth of Socrates himself. He ironically shows that the views derived from him are not capable of maintaining themselves against an elementary examination.

The purpose of the dialogues, however, is not just to ridicule Plato's rivals in philosophy. It is also to bring out the nature of certain problems and to define them in such a way as to prepare for a constructive treatment. It goes without saying that Plato was intensely sensitive to the ideas and problems of other thinkers. He advanced in his own development by mastering and absorbing the thoughts of others. It was almost inevitable that there should be an early period in which he was chewing upon the systems of rival schools, when he felt that he had a grasp on their problems, on the elements of truth in them, and on the points where they went wrong, and when he was more concerned to confute them as systems and elicit their problematic factors than to offer his independent solutions. My hypothesis is that this phase of his development constitutes the so-called Socratic period.

Before entering upon a detailed discussion we may consider some antecedent probabilities. In the first place, there is the bare fact of the rival groups in Athens, a number of them taking the name of Socrates, while others like the literary-rhetorical group attacked all philosophers. Also we know that dialogues centering about the figure of Socrates, were a common mode of literary composition, the rhetoricians attacking Socrates, the philosophers replying and putting him in a good light, and also attacking one another if not by name then by masked identifications easily penetrated. The probability that Plato reserved the expression of his antagonism to the Megarics, to Antisthenes, etc., to a comparatively late period, that his dramatic and competitive spirit did not fasten upon his contemporaries from the start, seems slight. Those who conceive that in early youth Plato's arrogant and self-assured spirit humbly devoted itself to his master and to thinkers of a by-gone age, and wrote dialogues intended (as even Gomperz holds) merely to show the dialectic superiority of Socrates to the men of Socrates' own time, do not seem to observe ordinary psychological canons. They make no effort to recover the contemporary scene.

Philosophical rivalry was also bound up with political factionalism. The aristocratic connections of Plato made him a ready mark for the gibes of the "democratic" Cynic school. Moreover he was "state-minded," while the Cynics were anti-political. And while the Cyrenaics preached accommodation to society and utilization of all its benefits, they also preached that the wise man would abstain from active political participation, while the Plato who later taught that philosophers should be rulers can hardly have been innocent of political bias in his early period. In view of Socrates' own abstention from political life, it is evident that the other "Socratics" had a *prima-facie* case against Plato with respect to their genuine discipleship, and that Plato would have to devise a plausible reason to account for Socrates' practical deviation from the theories he attributed to him. When Plato became interested in the physical speculations of the Pre-Socratics he suffered from a similar embarrassment, a liability to attack as not a true Socratic, which the Cynics at least would force home to him.

Every reader of Plato knows how much of obscurity and confusion is found in his choice of topics, in the sequence of problems and arguments, in the peculiar turns given to the arguments, and how frequently obvious sophisms are attributed to Socrates. He knows also to what little avail commentators have wrestled with these difficulties. It seems likely that if we had as full records of the other schools of his day as we have of Plato's own writings, we should be in possession of the key, and that until further manuscripts are discovered we shall be at a loss. Upon the whole it seems less hazardous to use Plato to piece out the reconstruction of other thinkers of his day than it is to interpret Plato while ignoring them. At least we can adopt the hypothesis that when somebody in a dialogue seriously presents a view which is criticized by Socrates we have an echo of some teaching of some contemporary school. The allusion may be quite direct, so that any cultivated person in Athens could immediately locate its bearing. It may be indirect, a generalized reference to some doctrine that had given Plato pause, and by wrestling with which he had advanced a stage in his own thought. Today in reading James, Royce and Santayana any careful reader can find a multitude of such indirect and perhaps often subconscious cross-references; a common intellectual background of Harvard is presupposed. And any scheme of philosophical interpretation is inept which forgets that every thinker thinks against as well as with the views of his contemporaries and associates. It is especially inept when applied to the Athenian temperament and social conditions. Today we write direct criticism, naming our antagonist. The urbane, competitive, dramatic, prestige-seeking Greek adopted a veiled method.

Coming more closely to the contents of the early dialogues, we are met by the well known fact that in each dialogue Socrates subjects to hostile criticism views which are Socratic in tenor, views, moreover, which he himself accepts in the dialogue, while deploring his inability to establish them satisfactorily, and which afterwards reappear, in modified and deepened form, in Plato's constructive dialogues. The interpreters who claim that these dialogues are Socratic are full of ingenious explanations of why Socrates attacks his own doctrines. Jowett is hardly to be cited for philosophical acumen, but his naïveté makes him worth quoting. Of the *Charmides* he says "we see with surprise that Plato, who in his other writings identifies good and knowledge, here opposes them"; of the *Lysis* that "Socrates has allowed himself to be carried away by a sort of eristic or illogical logic"; of the *Laches* that the knowledge which is identified with virtue is "here lost in an unmeaning and transcendental conception"; of the *Protagoras* that the truth advanced by Socrates "is paradoxical or transcendental." And yet Jowett rests sure in the faith that all these dialogues in spite of their transcendental and dialectic character belong genuinely to the homely, practical Socrates! It surely would be much simpler to hold that the "Socratic" views and methods which are criticized are those of men pretending to speak in Socrates' name, which Plato then ridicules in the name of Socrates himself, involving them in obscurity.

More specifically the main theme of these earlier dialogues is the relation of knowledge, virtue and the good. Secondary but derived topics are the unity and plurality of virtues, and the teachability of virtue; that is, knowledge and virtue in process of becoming. It is incredible that Plato would have represented Socrates questioning his own thesis, the connection of virtue and knowledge, and of both as means to an end of benefit or good, unless there had arisen conceptions of knowledge, virtue and good which Plato was interested in criticizing and repudiating. In the *Lesser Hippias*, Socrates *from certain premisses* drives the argument to the conclusion that only the good man can do injustice involuntarily. The premisses have a specious Socratic coloring in the analogy of moral knowledge and virtue with the knowledge and skill of artisans. But when Hippias says he cannot accept the conclusion, Socrates says "Neither can I." No wonder many have rejected the authenticity of the dialogue when it seems to end in a *reductio ad absurdum* of a genuine Socratic doctrine. But the case stands otherwise if what is criticized is the *Antisthenean* interpretation of Socratic knowledge and skill. Of Antisthenes at least this much is known. He began as a rhetorician and literary interpreter, especially of Homer. After becoming acquainted with Socrates late in life, he expounded, by means of allegorical symbolism, Homer as a teacher of Socratic morals. He preached return to nature along with the necessity of strict discipline of the passions and desires, in order that man may be free or self-possessed and self-sufficient. He opposed institutions, especially political ones, to nature on the ground that they were either conventional or arbitrary. Governments taught injustice, deceit, intrigue and introduced luxury and corruption. Aside from the poets—allegorically understood—the artisans are those who have knowledge. They know their business, their material, their objects. Their art is skill, virtue. They obtain it by discipline, by practice, based on natural aptitudes. Among the arts some are false since they are concerned with luxuries, others natural, because dealing with and meeting the necessities of nature, food, shelter and clothing. The truly independent soul will unite as many of these arts as possible in himself so as to be free. This self-sufficiency is good or happiness.

In this account appears a genuine Socratic element, but interpreted in a way which differs radically from that of Plato. We note especially the exaltation of practice over logical and theoretical science as means of attaining virtue, and the attack not merely on existing institutions but on the political state as such. In the former point, Antisthenes was influenced by the Megaric dialectic, except that instead of using it to deny plurality and establish the unity of good, being and truth, dialectic was regarded as merely of negative use, to refute others who connect true knowledge with the use of a logical method. We know from other dialogues that Plato's standing term for the Cynics was uncultivated, uneducated, which by the time of Aristotle had become a technical name for all who denied the value of logical method. Upon the political side, we know the pains which Plato took to show that knowledge, in the form of correct opinion of death and other things which arouse fear, can be generated and maintained only in an organized state which is ruled by the truly wise.

The trend of the dialogue is now obvious. Hippias appears as a rhetorician. His theme is Homer. He is the master of all arts, and self-sufficient. Then it is shown that the man who is the master of an art is just the one who is able to deceive others, and the artist or craftsman who can deceive others voluntarily is better than the one who deceives accidentally. The analogy is then extended to objects, artificial ones, like rudders, bows, natural ones like the eye. Then it is shown of the soul also as a tool or organ having a function. Hence the wise in anything, who in Socratic fashion, is defined as virtuous and hence able to produce good or benefit, is also the one who can produce at will either good or evil; the capable soul is the one who can do injustice voluntarily and the only one who can.

The conclusion is irresistible, given the premises. But we recall that Plato's great contribution to discussion, the one he borrows from geometry and prides himself upon contributing to philosophy, is that all such premisses are hypotheses, defining problems, and that the value of the conclusion consists in its explication of the meaning of the premisses. The premiss here is the Cynic identification of knowledge and virtue with the wisdom and skill of the artisan. Absurdity results because this view is carried over to moral virtues. The reason for the absurdity is clearly indicated. What is true of relative ends, ends that ultimately are only means, has been assumed to be true of real or absolute ends, the goods of the soul. As is so often pointed out in other dialogues, the physician knows what health is and how to attain it. The good of health, or whether it would be better to die, he does not and cannot, as physician, know. A supreme science, a science of Good and ends in themselves is thus clearly indicated, and the absence of it is shown to be the weakness of Hippias as a representative of a rival school.[2] The one who knows this ultimate good cannot possibly act unjustly either voluntarily or involuntarily.

2. Cf. the Republic, 505, that if we knew everything else perfectly but did not know the essential form of the good it would not profit us.

In the *Laches*, reference to distinctive schools is highly indirect, but reference to the problem which divided the schools is obvious. Laches is a conservative, opposed to all philosophizing, but a Spartanizer, and as such attached to exercise and practise as the means of attaining virtue, and also a strong believer in original natural aptitudes. He is, so to speak, a Cynic without knowing it. Nicias, on the contrary, is a lover of culture and philosophic discussion; he is a humanist. He introduces his conception of the virtue of courage as connected with wisdom as something he had heard from Socrates—a sufficient warning to the wise. He expressly denies that the knowledge of specialists or artisans is the kind of wisdom searched for. He also denies that *natural* courage, lacking forethought, is in any sense a virtue. He points to the need of a theoretical knowledge of grounds of things to be feared, a knowledge different in kind from that of the artisan. Like Plato he is a critic of Cynic morals. Yet Plato criticizes him.

The thing which stands out is that if the difficulty is to be overcome, there must be different kinds or degrees of knowledge and hence of virtues. Nicias is impaled on a dilemma. Without knowledge, there is no courage; there must be knowledge of danger, of threatening evil. But with perfect knowledge, there would be complete knowledge of evil and of good, hence no fear, but only prudence, and hence no possibility of courage. Nothing could point more clearly to the need of some genuine knowledge which although genuine is less than wisdom. In the *Meno* as well as in the *Theaetetus*, right opinion is introduced, and right opinion exactly answers the difficulty for both courage and temperance. The exact definitions are given in the *Republic*, where courage is defined as opinion, not perfect knowledge, an opinion about the things which should and should not be feared based upon the laws of the state as formulated by the truly wise. The opinion is embodied in custom by the latter. The problems of the unity and plurality of virtues and of the teachability of virtue are thus both solved.[3]

3. It will be recalled that the *Protagoras* ends with a reversal of the original positions, Socrates finally holding that virtue is teachable under certain conditions. Protagoras had treated citizens as they happen to exist in present states as its teachers. The discussion apparently switches to the problem of the unity and plurality of virtues—to the perplexity of many commentators. But the solu-

It is strange that Plato's negative dialectic should have persuaded so many of his interpreters against Plato's own express teachings, that he held to an exclusive unity of virtue, and to a denial of the need of practise or habit in attaining and maintaining virtue. The fault is perhaps Aristotle's, because of his charge that Plato ignored the necessity of practise to safeguard man from the seductions of the passions. But the view is contrary to fact. Temperance and courage involve knowledge; but since they exist in the realm of change and therefore in that of practical art, they demand skill acquired through exercise and formed into habit. The too common refusal in spite of the *Republic* to recognize Plato's own position is largely connected with the interpretation of the early ethical dialogues as Socratic. Regard them as dialectic refutations of thinkers claiming to be Socratic, and their positions are not only consistent with the teachings of the *Republic* but state the problems whose solutions are there given. If Nicias had perceived that, given knowledge of ends and goods which do not change, a virtue and knowledge become possible which are attained by *practise under the direction of the truly wise*, he would have escaped the dilemma. But Nicias stands where the Cyrenaics stood. He is Socratic enough to proclaim the importance of knowledge for virtue. He does not, as Plato does, see that knowledge, even in the form of right opinion as to things which change such as pleasures and pains, depends upon insight into Being—that which does not change.

The discussion of *sophrosyne* in the *Charmides* is complementary, though considerably more complicated. It is to be noted that the figures of the dialogue are Plato's friends and relatives and that the atmosphere is a friendly non-controversial one; while at the same time the arguments, as far as Critias is concerned, are quite formal and turn on highly technical points, such as the existence and meaning of self-relation, the difference between knowledge *that* we know and *what* we know; between specific particular knowledge and abstract universal knowledge. The dialogue also distinguishes carefully the meaning of terms,

tion of one question is the solution of the other. In a state ruled by the wise, the unity of knowledge and of virtue maintained by the wise renders possible right opinion, a plurality of virtues and the teachability of virtues—all in the realm of generation—for the many.

and the distinction is serious although there is some humor about Prodicus as their real author. It seems to me that only a paucity of historic imagination can attribute such themes to the historic Socrates, especially as they are just the technical distinctions with which Plato positively occupies himself.

The point upon which Critias is finally tripped gives the key to the problem of the dialogue and to its reserved solution, if not quite clearly to the philosophical school masked by Critias. The latter has set up a science of sciences as the wisdom which gives the virtue of sophrosyne. The science of the good is expressly *subordinated* by him to this science. In prior discussion in the dialogue it has been shown that it is the special sciences which give special goods, like health, etc., and that a science of science is of no avail in obtaining them, and that the only science which is of final use is the science of the good itself. Thus the argument of Critias has been going in a circle. Not the life according to knowledge makes men act rightly and be happy, even if all sciences be included, but the life according to only *one* science, *that of good and evil.* Here is an obvious hint, expanded to the full doctrine of the *Republic*, that the science of the Good is the ultimate science, not a subordinate one, and that knowledge of knowledge (that is, logic) is subordinated to it, not *vice-versa.*[4]

The dialogue does not lack for other hints. Socrates after rejecting the idea that the wisdom which gives virtue is identical with a knowledge of the nature of knowledge, quite gratuitously remarks that such a knowledge would be useful to the *learner*, making learning easier, clearer and also enabling him whenever

4. The correspondence with the *Republic*, 505, is almost point for point. The multitude call pleasure the good, but even those whose "*definition* identifies pleasure and the good are forced to admit the existence of evil (harmful) pleasures." The more enlightened call the good *phronesis.* "And you are aware, my friend, that the advocates of the latter opinion are unable to explain what they mean by insight, and are compelled at last to explain it as insight into the good, and are in a ridiculous difficulty." The reference to some well-known philosophic doctrine and to a well-known criticism of it is unmistakable. Of course, critics have recognized the similarity to the argument and conclusion of *Laches*, but holding that the latter is genuinely Socratic have been much puzzled to explain it. But in fact we have here the explicit assertion of a supreme science of objective good which is negatively indicated in *Laches* as the key to any true knowledge of knowledge, and as a superior knowledge and virtue. Compare also *Republic*, 509, where it is expressly said that knowledge *resembles* the Good but *is* not (the) good absolutely or without qualification.

he has any knowledge to test the knowledge of others; and that the trouble has been that we have been seeking from knowledge of knowledge (or logic), something more than it can yield. Still earlier after criticizing the doctrine of self-relation (which is obviously akin to an undoubted later Platonic notion) he contents himself by saying that in some cases it is inadmissible, namely in number, as that is relativistically defined, while with respect to other things a "great man" is needed to determine whether an absolute, or self-related exists, and how wisdom is connected with it.

The reference here to number and computation is surely ironical and the irony is part of the confutation of Critias. Plato had no false modesty in thinking himself the great man who could solve the problem of the self-related! and in other dialogues he expressly denies the relative character of number. Since a half is also a double (with respect to something else) mathematics cannot be a science of relatives of this sort. (See *Phaedo*, 101, and *Republic*, 438, 439 and 479.) Critias after defining number as required for a proper utilitarian computation of the good as relative and then arguing from it to a self-related—knowledge of knowledge—is guilty of self-contradiction. The popular notion that the Cyrenaics identified virtue with pleasure as well as pleasure with the good is absurd. They identified virtue with knowledge of the greater pleasure; this can be attained only by computation or calculation. A sensation of pleasure may have been regarded as the most certain knowledge of good, but this kind of knowledge, taken by itself, could hardly be the kind of knowledge which gives skill, art, virtue. Discrimination of lesser from greater pleasures, or knowledge of knowledge, is required. From independent sources we know that the Aristippeans esteemed dialectic as a tool and that, although they were humanists rather than naturalists, they prized knowledge of nature so far as that conduced to human welfare—a motive which finally drew them to the atomists for their cosmology, and which finds its final expression in Lucretius. As compared with the Cynics, Plato regarded them as "refined." [5]

Even if *Protagoras* be not classed as a "Socratic" dialogue, (it certainly belongs in the same group as those just considered) it is

5. See *Theaetetus*, 156; *Philebus*, 53.

worth turning aside a moment from the *Charmides* to note the similarity of atmosphere. The Protagoras of the dialogue called by that name is less obviously a caricature, or mask, than he appears in the *Theaetetus*. But he is equally Cyrenaic in temper. In accord with his usual method of reasoning from premises hypothetically adopted, Socrates starts with the identification of good and pleasure. The argument then shows that pleasures differ in quantity, and hence measurement is required—compare the computation of Charmides. Hence knowledge of measurement stands higher than pleasure. The science of number and measure is explicitly reserved for later discussion. Note also that even in the *Protagoras*, the concept of number as relative is not questioned; that is, Plato admits a discussion in terms of greater and less. Of course it may be contended that Plato at this period had not himself advanced beyond this notion, and that it was only later that, by realizing the absolute nature of number, he succeeded in straightening himself out on the topic of pleasure and its connections with knowledge and with good. But if we adopt the hypothesis, not violent in the case of a mathematician, that Plato already had his insight as regards number, we find everything dovetailing with remarkable precision. Pleasures are relative, in the realm of becoming. As such they are greater and less. A hedonist, one who does not rise above the plane of generation, must then, if he is Socratic at all in retaining an identification of knowledge and virtue, define virtue as knowledge of greater and less. Thereby he lets in calculation and measurement as superior pleasure. Submit number and measure to examination, and they are found to take us into the region of the self-related or absolute—out of generation into being. The dialectic is perfect.

A point in the earlier part of the *Protagoras* is worth notice with respect to the *Laches* and *Charmides*. When courage comes under discussion, Protagoras takes a depreciative view of it; it is not like other virtues; it is a mere gift of nature. But Socrates controverts him by showing that an element of knowledge is required if courage is a virtue, and thus affiliates it to the other virtues. To the Cyrenaic, military courage must have been a barbarous virtue, fit for animals, wildmen, soldiers, and Cynics and others living according to nature. Civilized, cultivated human beings living by art and friendship have no call for it save as they lapse into a state of nature. Notice the humanistic element in the assertion that "The worst of men in a civilized state are better than savages who have no education nor courts and laws," and contrast this view with the view of the Cynics that laws and states are devices of the powerful to advance their own interests. Recall also that the end of philosophy to the Cyrenaics was to enable its adepts to live without laws as other men lived because of laws. The temper of Protagoras is everywhere that of the Cyrenaics: an appreciation of the value of human arts, specially social arts, as the source of all cultivation and truly human delights, together with a condescending tolerance toward the masses who have to live by custom because they have not risen to the plane of insight, *phronesis*, and of whole-mindedness in estimating pleasures. We should at least glance also at the discussion of fearlessness of soul which the wise man displays in the face of thought of death and other evils.

Protagoras, like the Cyrenaics, is a humanist, not a naturalist. He solves the question of the teaching of virtues by a glorification of the social in humane arts. The art of government is the bond of society. Zeus tells Hermes not to distribute the social arts as technical crafts are distributed—to the experts or few, but to all, since otherwise states cannot exist. All have some share in reverence, justice and wisdom. The social order is the great teacher of the virtues. The doctrine is precisely that of the *Republic*—with a difference. The *existing* state teaches vice rather than virtue; it is the great sophist, the corrupter of men's affections and opinions. Introduce into the state a class of men who really know and give them control of the laws—the ultimate educators of men—and the humanistic ideal becomes a reality. But it is impossible to secure the needed class of wise men without training in dialectic, mathematics and understanding of nature. Thus Plato develops his synthesis of the motifs which were scattered and disjoined among contemporary schools. The "Socratic" dialogues are the critical preparatory try-outs.

We have, however, too long turned aside from the *Charmides*. Note the conclusive reason for rejecting the knowledge of knowledge as the true wisdom. Nicias has appealed to the arts, especially the non-mechanical arts—the latter being the stronghold of the Cynics. But it is clear that the physician judges and is judged by his knowledge of health, not by his knowledge of knowledge.[6] To know health we should have to have the special knowledge which the physician has. Now we know from a multitude of other passages in Plato that while we can trust the physician, the carpenter, the competent artist and artisan in any sphere, to know his own subject-matter and how to attain it, he does not know the end of his own end, the good of his good. That is, the physician does not know when or why health is really a good to his patient. He does not know of the limits of his own knowledge.[7] Hence the need of another kind of wisdom, that of the man who knows goods that are always goods and who can judge special goods in the light of his knowledge of real and final good—the philosopher as Plato conceived him. Place knowledge of the good above knowledge of knowledge—which then becomes dialectic based on mathematics—and the whole argument becomes as clear in its positive implications as it is in its negative criticisms. Knowledge of the real good will enable us to utilize the physician's knowledge, without having to descend to becoming physicians ourselves, and to fix and test its limits. That Socrates could carry a discussion as near as this to Plato's own most characteristic ethical idea without knowing what he was doing and where he was going may be asserted, but it puts a strain on credulity.

The previous argument has assumed a kinship of Critias to the Cyrenaic school. But we hardly know with sufficient certainty when the affiliation of Cyrenaic humanism with atomistic naturalism began, though we know that the alliance finally became firmly established. If we can assume that the alliance was already under way when Plato wrote, the context of the dialogue becomes clearer. It was pleasures of mind which the Cyrenaics ar-

6. The reader's attention is again invited to the "unmeaning and transcendental" nature of this concept of knowledge of knowledge on the basis of the ordinary interpretation. Where does it come from? Why is it introduced? What does it mean? Identify primary knowledge with the experience of pleasure, and knowledge of knowledge with the estimate of present pleasures in respect to future pleasures, and knowledge of knowledge gets a definite significance and historic context. Its quick conversion into knowledge of self also becomes something more than a vicious dialectic pun.

7. That is the objection to democracy, to the rule of mechanics etc. Within their own affairs they trust the expert, the "one"—him who knows. But in public affairs which are concerned with more ultimate good, each claims knowledge for himself, and establishes judgment and rule by the many incompetent.

rived at as a consequence of their comparison of pleasures, that and pleasures of friendship. Moreover natural science was at least a pleasure of mind even if intrinsically of slight importance as compared with knowledge of the humane arts. Also it was a bulwark against the fears and pains bound up with superstitions about death and the gods. If we turn to Democritus we know that he was ethically a hedonist, and that he held that only a man who was wise—defined as insight into natural causes—could discriminate among pleasures, and judge pleasures and pains truly. Admit the Democritean contention of the connection of virtue with knowledge and its hedonistic aim, and the supreme virtue becomes discretion, discernment, sophrosyne. It yields self-control as its immediate fruit.

Critias shows no obvious signs of the atomists' interest in knowledge of nature. He stands nearer the Cyrenaics than to the atomists. But there must have been an approximation from both sides with respect to their common ethical ground, pleasure and the good. A person starting from the school of Socrates with the identification of virtue with knowledge of present pleasure in terms of causes and remote pleasures, and identifying the good with pleasure, would have met halfway a Democritean who started with atoms and ended with ability to discriminate among pleasures and pains on the basis of knowledge of their natural causes. The two would differ only in emphasis.

It is noteworthy that when Plato permits Socrates to drop his playful badgering, Socrates twice admits that such a knowledge of knowledge as Critias has in mind would insure order and happiness. Each man would act according to his own science, and no man professing an art, whether military affairs, medicine, or government, would be able to impose upon others. Prediction of the future would come under the control of the man who understands the causes which produce things in past, present, and future alike. So far would discrimination of what we know and do not know reach. The household and state would be well-ordered and happiness would reign.

Analogy with the *Republic* lies on the face. The discussion passes over from the innocent Charmides to Critias when virtue is defined as doing one's business, and doing is expressly contrasted with making—the business of artisans. It is connected with doing worthy deeds. The general likeness to the *Republic* is obvious. Most important is the passage in the *Republic*, 443, where justice is identified with an inward doing, and temperance—the virtue under discussion in the *Charmides*—with the resulting inward harmony which also secures self-mastery. Critias was, so to speak, all right up to a certain point. His trouble was that he identified the highest virtue or knowledge with knowledge of knowledge instead of with knowledge of the real and permanent end or good. He then had no criterion left, except the criterion of the crafts which he repudiates, to judge the proper work, doing, business, of the different parts of the soul. The passage with its reference to putting a house in order should be compared with *Charmides*, 171. Note also in the context, *Republic*, 444, the likening of justice to health in that both imply that the powers of body and soul are arranged so that they "master and are mastered by one another in accord with nature."

The importance attached to ability to distinguish between real knowledge and false and conventional belief is as Democritean as it is Platonic. Plato here criticizes the notion that this ability can be had by means of knowledge of knowledge. It can be had only by knowledge of ends or goods in themselves. Self-knowledge is indeed fundamentally important. It constitutes sophrosyne; it is manifested in ability to discriminate and measure among pleasures and pains; it is a condition of self-control. So far there is agreement. But Democritus held that this self-knowledge in the form of knowledge of knowledge can be attained by knowledge of natural causes. Plato holds that knowledge of physical causes, being in the realm of generation, is useful, but only when there is first a knowledge of ends which are final. Here is touched upon, at least by indirection, the difference between the two great systems of antiquity.

Our last paragraphs, however, emphasize more than the facts warrant a Democritean element in the views allotted to Critias. It is enough that the position is Cyrenaic with probable atomistic affiliations, which could hardly be stressed with a man of the world like Critias as the leading figure. The dialogue begins with Charmides who defines temperance or sophrosyne as gentleness or quietness or moderation. Is it fanciful to see here an allusion to the well-known Cyrenaic identification of true pleasures with gentle motions? Note also the reference to a charm which brings health, which is connected with treating the part in the light of the whole. The charm came from Thrace; Democritus was a Thracian. Sophrosyne means health of soul. The knowledge of health possessed by the physician is the pivot upon which the argument turns at each critical stage. When at the close the argument is about to come to the conviction that knowledge which ensures virtue and so happiness is knowledge of the good, not knowledge of knowledge, Socrates asks if it is knowledge of health they are in search of, and Critias replies that that is near the truth. Note the contemptuous attitude taken throughout toward practical knowledge of the kind possessed by craftsmen. Note again how the soothsayer's knowledge is introduced. Socrates refers to the knowledge of the future possessed by the prophet as making one happy. Critias interrupts and says, "Yes, but there are others as well as prophets who have such knowledge." Socrates replies, "Yes, those who know the past and present, as well as the future."[8] The passage suggests not only the importance attached by all hedonists to knowing future pleasures and pains in order to control present enjoyments, but also the knowledge of real things, irrespective of time claimed by atomists.

The argument clearly points to a school of aristocratic and cultivated leanings, which identified the highest virtue, art or knowledge with the health of the soul, which held that health of soul is connected with a science of self just as health of body is connected with the physician's science, and that the science of self, or knowledge of knowledge, enables a man and a city to discriminate between true and pretended knowledge in himself and in others, and hence secures self-control and order. If we substitute for temperance fearlessness of soul—which we know was a prized virtue of the atomists—there are many parallels between the temperance of Critias and the courage of Nicias though Critias occupies a much more advanced plane in dialectics.

The chief difficulty in more specific interpretation lies in the failure of Plato to make reference to atomism specific. This holds

8. The soothsayer appears in *Laches*, too. Here he cannot really know future sufferings and ills, because he does not know grounds or causes but only their signs. Hence he does not know whether future pains are really to be feared or not, whether they are evil, even when he "knows" that they are going to happen. Hence he has to be "under" the general, who has a knowledge of the things to be really feared and hoped for.

of his entire philosophy. His only serious intellectual rival, Democritus, his only rival in breadth and depth, Plato consistently ignores. Although Plato borrowed from him the concept of fixed forms, ideas or schemas, as the sole objects of true knowledge, and although the cleavage between the two systems is the deepest found in philosophy, Plato, so free in his references to other philosophers, never gives a hint of the existence of Democritus. Perhaps the "although" should be changed to "because." At all events, we come here upon the most serious difficulty in the way of a more specific interpretation of Platonic controversial references.

We are struggling today with the ethical problems of Plato's time. We assert rival views more vehemently. But perhaps we consider them less urbanely and with less of lucid intellectual method. The claims of discipline, of culture, of natural science and of an alleged more ultimate knowledge of ends, are still opposed to one another. Past discussion seems to have choked us with its debris rather than enlightened us. We project our mental muddiness and one-sidedness upon the Sophists, and laying our sins upon them fail to recognize that, comparatively speaking, the Sophists were direct and honest and that it is we who are sophisticated. If we cannot get instruction by recurring to the Platonic scene, we may at least discover the charm of free and direct mental play directed to the fundamental themes of life.

Substance, Power and Quality in Locke

According to the ordinary interpretation, Locke explicitly set forth a distinction between ideas as mental and natural objects as physical, while he held that all knowledge of the latter is by means of the former. He thus forced the question of knowledge to take this form: How can ideas which are mental truly represent or know objects which are radically different in kind from themselves? The difficulty of the question was accentuated because Locke divided ideas into two kinds, one of which resembled the objects while the other possessed no likeness to them. I am far from denying that the tenor of Locke's teaching points towards the positions just stated, or that it was practically inevitable that subsequent students of Locke should have been led to them as conclusions. But in this paper I wish to set forth, from a study of Locke himself, the conviction that Locke did not start out with any such conception; that it has an historical source which it is quite possible to point out, and that if Locke had avoided becoming entangled with traditional conceptions which are inconsistent with his own positive teachings, he might have developed an empirical theory of knowledge which would neither contain nor suggest the epistemological problem referred to above.

What is significant and original in Locke is his insistence that knowledge consists in the perception of a *relation*. It is true that he defines this as a relation between ideas. But it is also true that Locke was in no sense the originator of the doctrine that the object of knowledge is an idea; such was the teaching of the schools, using idea not to denote anything mental or psychical, but to signify "form," "species." And officially and intentionally Locke did not depart from this conception: by idea he means, as

[First published in *Philosophical Review* 35 (January 1926): 22–38.]

he says, simply "the immediate object of the mind in thinking"—thinking being used in the Cartesian sense to denote the act of being aware of. It is an *object* of mind; it is the real object as it becomes the object of awareness; it is not a state or content of mind, any more than it was with the scholastics. Where Locke departs from scholastic and classic theory is in holding that knowledge is not the apprehension of form or idea as such, but is the apprehension of a relation between forms or ideas.

But Locke was also obviously influenced by the new physical science, by Boyle, Newton and other representatives of the new physics. Now this new physics had no use for species and forms in the classic sense. It substituted minute corpuscles mathematically or quantitatively defined. Let one deny the metaphysical reality of species and forms (ideas) in the old sense and still retain that part of the old theory which holds that the form or idea is the immediate object of the mind in knowing, and one enters upon a course which is full of snares and inconsistencies—as Locke found to his cost and to the perverting of pretty much all English theories of knowledge, psychological and epistemological, since his day.

But this is not the whole of the story. If knowledge is perception of relations, and if knowledge is to have to do with real natural existence, then Locke should have concluded that existence, as the subject-matter of knowledge, is inherently relational. But Locke did not have the courage of his convictions; or rather he did not have the perspicacity of his convictions; he did not see what they implied. He retained the old notion of separate, independent substances, each of which has its own inner constitution or essence. Knowledge which grasps only relations—such as were the staple of the new physics—cannot grasp an inner essence, which remains accordingly hidden and mysterious. In final analysis, the opposition between the inner constitution and essence (which Locke retained from prior metaphysics) and the relations which are knowable (his own contribution) is the source of the opposition which we are familiar with as the Lockian contrast between idea and object.

Nor is this quite the whole of the story. In the older metaphysics causation meant an operating and compelling force, emanating from substances and by some mysterious influence producing change in other substances. Clearly a relational theory of knowledge calls for quite a different notion of causation, if it is to have any place at all in the structure of knowledge. Any thorough-going acknowledgment of the implications of the relational theory of knowledge would soon have arrived at the conclusion that causality signifies simply the relation of orderly seriality among events. In this case the discovery that certain qualities (like colors) are "caused" by material corpuscles in conjunction with organic physiological structures would have been simply to discover one interesting and important succession in a single and homogeneous order of natural events. It would not have implied a mysterious power in physical objects to produce "ideas" in something totally different, namely, mind. But Locke retained the old conception of causation as well as of independent substances. In consequence he is constantly forced to move in the direction of the doctrine that the order of ideas is of one sort of existence and that of things (substances) is of another kind, while they are yet so related that the order of independent substances is the causally productive source of the order of ideas, while the latter is cognitively representative of the former, and the sole evidence of its existence. Here are all the materials of the epistemological problem, and if Locke did not make the implications explicit, his successors soon did so.[1]

I

The usual statement of Locke's position concerning primary and secondary qualities fails to convey it in Locke's own terms. The Lockian terms are concerned with distinction of qualities in respect to *substances*, not in respect to being physical and mental, or objective and subjective. He makes a threefold distinction of qualities, not a dual one. The first kind corresponds in form to the traditional "essential" attributes, though

1. The following from James gives a clear statement of the terms of this "problem": "Conceived objects must show sensible effects or else be disbelieved. And the effects, *even though reduced to relative unreality* when their causes come to view (as heat which molecular vibrations *make unreal*) are yet the things upon which our knowledge of the causes rests. Strange mutual dependence this, in which the appearance needs the reality in order to exist, but the reality needs the appearance in order to be known!" *Psychology*, Vol. 2, p. 301; italics mine.

differing radically in content. And this fact locates his primary contradiction. For his statement of the concrete nature of what he terms primary qualities is such as absolutely to destroy the classic distinction between essence, properties, accidents and relations. Primary qualities are according to him such as "are utterly inseparable from the body in what state soever it be; such as . . . it constantly keeps." Like essence in classic thought they make it what it is; they constitute its formal cause. But instead of being such affairs as stoniness, humanity, etc., together with, in the case of physical substances, certain "sensible forms," they are "solidity, extension, figure, and mobility." Physical substances according to him are particles or corpuscles whose nature or essence is to have such properties. Since such properties, however, are not absolute but relational, he was in reality doing away with the old notion of substances, and along with it destroying the old notion of formal constitutive essence.

His secondary qualities are almost frankly relational in the modern sense of relational. They are powers in substances to produce by means of their primary qualities certain effects in us, such effects as colors, sounds, smells, tastes, etc. It is, be it noted, the power to produce which is called secondary, not the effects themselves. Then there is a "third sort," namely, the power of the primary properties to produce changes in other things—such as the power of fire by its primary qualities of bulk, texture and motion of particles to produce a new consistency in wax. More explicitly, it is the "power that is in any body by reason of the particular constitution of its primary qualities, to make such a change in the bulk, figure, texture and motion of *another body*, as to make it operate on our senses differently from what it did before."[2]

Taken strictly and literally, then, there is first a distinction between properties which are inherently, always and absolutely, in the substance, without which it cannot exist at all, and others which characterize a connection with other things and which do not exist except where acting and being acted upon are found. Of the latter there are two sorts. There are those which designate power to produce effects like softness, weight, or acceleration in other things, and those which designate power to produce

2. *Essay*, Book II, Chap. VIII, 9, 10, 23; *cf.* Book II, Chap. XXIII, 7, 9.

qualities like pain, griping, color, noise, taste by acting upon the senses of an organic body. In both cases, the distinction depends upon maintaining a fixed separation between intrinsic essential properties and relational extrinsic ones. And, as before noted, the properties selected by Locke as intrinsically constitutive apart from acting and being acted upon, namely, bulk, figure, motion and situation are precisely the properties which in physical science are now treated as relational, not absolute.[3]

II

The extent to which Locke retained the formal conceptions of substance and essence while assigning to them a concrete content which negated the traditional meanings, is clear enough in his treatment of substance. Nominally he reduces it to an unknown substrate, which is a step toward eliminating it in its classic sense. But he retains the conception that things have essential natures. Thus, while he holds empirical (or "nominal") essences to be abstract ideas employed for the purpose of sorting (classifying) and discriminating, he never questions the existence of *real* essences. They are the "constitution of the insensible parts of a body upon which" the sensible qualities depend. Essence is the "*foundation* of all those qualities which are the ingredients of our complex idea." Or, more formally, "by this real essence I mean the real constitution of anything, which is the foundation of all those properties which are combined in and are found constantly to co-exist with the nominal essence; that particular constitution which everything has within itself, *without any relation to anything without it.*"[4] Scores of passages could be quoted to the effect that this ultimate and intrinsic constitution is that upon which *all* the properties of things depend and from which they flow. "What is that texture of parts, that real essence,

3. Of course I am ignoring the notion that there is a difference in kind between changes produced in the senses and those produced in other things. But this neglect is justified for two reasons. First, Locke thought *both* of them to be arbitrary, or due to the fact that God had affixed certain powers to things, and secondly any difference of kind that exists is relevant not to the discussion of qualities as such, but to quite a different matter, namely, the theory of ideas.
4. *Essay*, Book III, Chap. VI, 2, 3, 6; Book III, Chap. III, 15; italics are of course mine.

that makes lead and antimony fusible, wood and stones not?" "It is true every substance that exists has its peculiar constitution, whereon depend those sensible qualities and powers we observe in it."[5] "By what right is it that fusibility comes to be a part of the essence signified by the word gold, and solubility but a property of it? or why is its colour part of its essence, and its malleableness but a property? That which I mean is this, that these all being but properties, *depending on its real constitution*, and nothing but powers, either active or passive in relation to other bodies, no one has authority to determine the signification of the word gold (as referred to such a body existing in nature) more to one collection of ideas as found in that body than to another."[6] In his chapters on knowledge he is constantly referring to the "real constitution of the minute parts on which their qualities do depend"; "the real constitution of substances whereon our simple ideas depend and which really is the cause of the strict union of some of them with one another, and the exclusion of others."[7]

III

The customary account of Locke misrepresents him by treating secondary qualities as something found in the mind, while to Locke, as we have seen, they signify the power of certain properties of substance to produce certain effects "in us"—to employ his favorite and ambiguous phrase. This renders it necessary to consider more definitely his theory of power and causation, and of relations. Because of a wavering use of the word "relation," it is well to begin with the latter. Locke follows the classic tradition which opposes "relations" to essence as the extrinsic to the intrinsic. The stock example of relation is "quan-

5. Book III, Chap. VI, 9, 13.
6. Book III, Chap. IX, 17.
7. Book IV, Chap. III, 14; Book IV, Chap. IV, 12. Compare, in this controversy with Stillingfleet, such expressions as "the real essence is that internal constitution of things, from which their powers and properties flow": the essence "is in every thing that internal constitution, or frame, or modification of the substance which God in his wisdom and good pleasure thinks fit to give to every particular creature, when he gives it a being." English edition of 1823, Vol. IV, p. 82. "There is an internal constitution of things on which their properties depend. This your lordship and I are agreed of, and this we call the real essence," p. 87.

tity" which varies without alteration of essence; a thing may be more or less, greater or smaller, without ceasing to be what it is; hence, quantity is an "accident." Like every accident or non-essential change, it depends upon matters outside the thing itself; it is a relation, not a property, since not flowing from essence. While following this tradition, Locke also associates relation with comparison. "When the mind so considers one thing that it does as it were bring it to and set it by another, and carries its view from one to the other—this is, as the words import, relation and respect; and the denominations given to positive things intimating that respect, and serving as marks to lead the thought beyond the subject itself denominated, to something distinct from it are what we call relatives; and the things so brought together, related." Examples are whiter in contrast with white; husband in contrast with man; father and son; servant, captain, enemy, patron; bigger and less; cause and effect, etc. And he remarks "Change of Relation may be without any Change in the subject." Caius remains Caius, although he ceases to be father, when his son dies. Also we have clear ideas of the relation when the ideas of the things related are "obscure and imperfect."[8] This fact is of great significance in connection with mathematics and morals as demonstrative sciences.

Relations are thus opposed by Locke to the intrinsic constitution of a thing and also to the properties which directly depend upon this essence. And what is more important for our present purposes it is also marked off from what he terms connexion, both "necessary connexion" and "real coexistence" or as he frequently terms it "going together."[9]

Unfortunately, however, on one occasion at least Locke indulges in change in his ordinary linguistic usage. And by what is almost a fatality, this lapse occurs in connection with his discussion of power. This he treats as a simple idea, and one got from both sensation and reflection. But he says: "I confess power includes in it some kind of relation (a relation to action or change),

8. Book II, Chap. XXV, 1, 2, 5; compare Book IV, Chap. II, 15.
9. Much of T. H. Green's polemic against Locke with respect to relations being the "workmanship of the understanding" turns upon nothing more serious than failure to notice that while *usually* Locke employs "relation" in the restricted sense noted above, he never doubts that substances themselves have real and necessary *connexions* with one another.

as, indeed, which of our ideas, of whatever kind soever, when attentively considered does not? For our ideas of extension, duration and number, do they not all contain in them a secret relation of the parts? Figure and motion have something relative in them much more visibly; and sensible qualities, as colours and smells, &c., what are they but the powers of different bodies in relation to our perception, &c.? And, if considered in the things themselves, do they not depend upon the bulk, figure, texture and motion of the parts? All of which include some kind of relation in them. Our idea, therefore, of power, I think may well have a place amongst other simple ideas, and be considered one of them, being one of those that makes a principal ingredient in our complex ideas of substance, as we shall hereafter have occasion to observe." [10]

Obviously relation is here used in the sense of connexion, not in the sense in which it designates things taken by the mind in comparison with other things. For in the same sense in which power contains relation, simple ideas do so also. Locke never doubted that "power" designates a real efficacy in things to generate or receive changes in or from other things, any more than he doubted the existence of disconnected substances each having its own essence or internal constitution.

Before following up this idea, it will be well however to devote a little space to his conception of connexion as a real union in things as distinct from relation dependent upon the mind's act of comparison. In the first place, this notion underlies his treatment of the association of ideas. If "connexion" were mental, association would play the same role in his thinking that it comes to play in James Mill and successors. But Locke uses the notion only to account for abnormalities and eccentricities, unreasonable antipathies, superstitions, etc. Beside the case of belief in goblins, he cites the sad plight of the young man who having learned to dance in a room where there was a trunk in a certain position could only dance in that room or in another room where there was a similar piece of "household stuff" in a like position. "Associations" are due to chance or custom; whence "jargon becomes sense, demonstration is given to absurdity and consistency to nonsense." "It is the foundation of the greatest er-

10. Book II, Chap. XXI, 3; compare Chap. XXIII, 37, yellow, fusibility, etc., being "nothing but so many relations to other substances"; also XXXI, 2, 8.

rors in the world." It unites things in themselves "disjoined." In contrast to these casual connections stand those in which "our ideas have a *natural* correspondence and connexion one with another; it is the office and excellency of *reason* to trace these, and hold them together in that union and correspondence which is founded in their peculiar being." [11]

Again it will be recalled that Locke correlates knowledge with certainty, assent with probability. And in a striking, though neglected passage, he says: "As knowledge is no more arbitrary than perception; so, I think, assent is no more in our power than knowledge. When the agreement of any two ideas appears to our minds, whether immediately or by the assistance of reason, I can no more refuse to perceive, no more avoid knowing it, than I can avoid seeing what I turn my eyes to and look upon in daylight; and what upon full examination I find the most probable I cannot deny my assent to." He adds that it is "by stopping our inquiry" that we hinder both knowledge and assent. [12] Locke here declares that even assent (opinion, belief) is objectively controlled and that with a proper use of faculties, degrees of assent exactly follow degrees of probable connection in subject-matter. Probability is calculated, in other words, rather than guessed at, and belief follows objective connections as much as does knowledge or certainty. The most conclusive evidence, however, is found in his whole treatment of the nature of knowledge as that is given in the fourth book of the *Essay*. To take this matter up at this point would involve needless repetition, so here we simply point out that all physical knowledge is to him knowledge of coexistence or conjunction, and that our physical knowledge does not go beyond probability just because *necessary connexion* is the sole ground for assertion of *universal* coexistence. And necessary connexion we cannot arrive at because of our inability to penetrate the inner constitution or essence of substances. In other words, only because Locke assumes that essence is the basis of necessary connexion in things, does he hold that *we* cannot attain to certainty in physical science. Eliminate this assumption of necessary connexion as equivalent to or derived from es-

11. Book II, Chap. XXXIII, 5, 7, 16, 18; *cf.* Book III, Chap. VI, 28, "the mind puts none together which are not supposed to have a union in nature," also Book III, Chap. IX, 13; Book IV, Chap. IV, 12.
12. Book IV, Chap. XX, 16.

sence in substances themselves, and his argument takes on quite a different temper and import.

We return, now, to his consideration of "power"—that is, of efficiency. As we have already seen, the distinction between qualities is made by Locke in terms of the distinction between essence which is intrinsically constitutive and power which involves the action of essence of things upon other things. The *idea* of power is derived by observation of the change of sensible ideas, "in things without" and also, through reflection, by observation of the change in ideas "by the determination of its own choice." He adds that since it is two-fold, "viz., as able to make, or able to receive, any change," it may be worth considering whether matter has anything but passive power and whether we should not "direct our minds to the consideration of God and spirits, for the clearest ideas of active powers."[13] So self-evident, indeed, does the real existence of power appear to Locke, that he passes on at once to the discussion of liberty of the will and moral issues.[14]

In the next chapter but one, namely Chap. XXIII, entitled "Of Our Complex Ideas of Substance," it is repeatedly asserted that "powers justly make a great part of our complex ideas of substance" (10). And he returns in this connection to the topic of primary and secondary qualities. One clause is worth adding to the previous citations: "The sensible secondary qualities are nothing but the powers those substances have to produce several ideas in us by our senses; which ideas are not in the things themselves *otherwise than as anything is in its cause.*" In his discussion of material substance he simplifies somewhat his previous statements regarding both essential or primary qualities and power. The former are reduced to "cohesion of solid and separable parts," "figure" being a consequence; the latter to power "of communicating motion by impulse."[15] Here we have perhaps his nearest approximation to the physical concepts of mass and mo-

---

13. It is hardly too much to say that Berkeley is implicit in this suggestion while it is reasonably certain that Hume's so-called sceptical denial of substance and of causation is based upon Locke's doctrine of our inability to perceive necessary connection among empirical objects.
14. Book II, Chap. XXIII, 1, 2, and following.
15. Book II, Chap. XXIII, 9, 17.

tion, with the implication that mass is closest to the inner essence, while causal power consists in imparting and receiving motion.

His unquestioned belief in causation as real power or efficacy is not brought into doubt by the fact that he discusses "cause and effect" as a relation. For the chapter[16] makes it evident that it is the correlativity of *cause and effect* which he has in mind. Power is the real thing behind both terms of this relation. "We cannot but observe that several particular, both qualities and substances begin to exist; and that they receive their existence from the due application and operation of some other being." "A cause is that which makes any other thing begin to be; and an effect is that which had its beginning from some other thing."[17] In other words while the mind gets the ideas by comparison, what it compares is the action and reception of power. "The idea of beginning to be is necessarily connected with the idea of some operation."[18]

IV

We come now to the bearing of these considerations upon the theory of knowledge. The traditional and current theory is that the difficulty with which Locke labors is the epistemological dilemma: things which we immediately know are mental and we know physical or "objective" things only by the intervention of these mental things, while these mental things are themselves the effect of physical things. Given these premises there is certainly an epistemological problem distinct from any metaphysical or cosmological problem. But Locke's own theory is that we know essences of substances only through their powers, and powers only through their effects (which, as we have directly to do with them, he terms ideas of sensation or sensible qualities); and as we are not able to trace any *necessary* connexion between the effects and their operative efficacious causes, we have no certain knowledge of the connexion of the effects with one another. That is, we can know *in general* that the essence of

16. Book II, Chap. XXVI.
17. *Ibid.*, 1, 2.
18. *Works*, IV, 61–62.

things is the bulk, contexture, figure and number of particles which have the power of communicating motion, but we cannot know the particular properties which produce in any particular case the particular effect or quality which is immediately present or with which we are in contact.[19] The difficulty is not that primary qualities are physical while secondary are mental, but that we cannot ascertain the *necessary connexion* which physically exists between causative powers and their effects.

"Yellowness is not actually in gold; but it is a *power* in gold to produce that idea in us by our eyes, when placed in a due light; and the heat, which we cannot leave out of our ideas of the sun, is no more really in the sun, than the white colour it introduces into wax. These are both equally *powers* in the sun, *operating*, by the motion and figure of its sensible parts, so on a *man*, as to *make* him have the idea of heat; and so on wax, as to *make* it capable to *produce in a man* the idea of white. Had we senses acute enough to discern the minute particles of bodies and the real constitution on which their sensible properties depend, I doubt not that they would produce quite different ideas in us: and that which is now the yellow colour of gold would then disappear, and instead of it we should see an admirable texture of parts, of a certain size and figure."[20]

As the quotation intimates, the difficulty is that our organs of perception are not fitted to yield effects which are comparable in subtlety and minuteness to the real structure or constitution of things, and hence we can never establish the detailed and specific necessary connexions that exist between causes and effects. For that reason, *and for that reason alone*, we cannot make universal and necessary statements, or attain knowledge (certainty) regarding the relations of the effects (ideas) to one another. If, to cite his favorite example, we knew the inner constitution upon which depend fusibility of gold and its solubility in *aqua regia*, we should be able to know whether the connection between solubility and fusibility is necessary and universal, or whether it is contingent and severable. The same thing holds for the connection of yellowness with these other properties. If we had such knowledge of the inner constitution of gold as would enable us

19. *Essay*, Book II, Chap. XXXI, 6.
20. Book II, Chap. XXIII, 10, 11; italics mine.

to see how its minute particles produce yellowness and also how they produce fusibility, we should have an exact criterion of the degree of closeness or looseness of connexion between yellowness and fusibility.

A statement which he makes in his controversy with Stillingfleet is worth quoting at length. The Bishop of Worcester had reproved Locke for complaining of the lack of certainty in our knowledge of things. In reply Locke says: "To say that if we knew the real essences or internal constitutions of those beings, some of whose properties we know, we should have much more certain knowledge concerning those things and their properties, I am sure is true, and I think no faulty complaining." After saying that we are, as it is, certain that some beings exist and that some properties are the properties of those beings, he goes on: "But there are other very desirable certainties, or other parts of knowledge concerning those same things, which we may want. . . . Knowing the colour, figure and smell of hyssop, I can, when I see hyssop, know so much as that there is a certain being in the world, endued with such distinct powers and properties; and yet I may justly complain that I want something in order to certainty that hyssop will cure a bruise or a cough, or that it will kill moths; or, used in a certain way, harden iron, or a hundred other useful properties that may be in it, which I shall never know; and yet might be certain of if I knew the real essences or internal constitutions of things upon which their properties depend." [21]

If Locke had held that the limits and uncertainty of our propositions about physical things were due to the fact that we know by means of ideas which are different in kind from the things, it would have been the easiest thing in the world for him to say so.

21. *Works*, Vol. IV, pp. 81–82. Compare *Essay*, Book III, Chap. VI, 3, 9, also, Chap. XI, 22: "If the formal constitution of this shining, heavy, ductile thing (from whence all these its properties flow) lay open to our senses, as the formal constitution or essence of a triangle does, the signification of the word gold might as easily be ascertained as that of triangle." And Book IV, Chap. VI, 10: "Could any one discover the necessary connexion between malleableness and the colour or weight of gold, or any other part of the complex idea signified by that name, he might make a certain universal proposition concerning gold in this respect; and the real truth of this proposition 'that all gold is malleable' would be as certain as of this, 'the three angles of all right-lined triangles are all equal to two right ones.'"

But that to which he actually assigns the limitations of our physical knowledge is that "the *Connexion between most simple Ideas* is unknown." In his own words, knowledge of such connexion is "very narrow and scarce any at all," for the "simple ideas whereof our complex ideas of substances are made up are, for the most part, such as carry with them in their own nature, no visible necessary connexion or inconsistency with any other simple ideas." And the reason is "not knowing the root they spring from, not knowing what size, figure and texture of parts they are on which depend and from which result those qualities which make our complex idea of gold, it is impossible that we should know what other qualities result from or are incompatible with the same constitution of the insensible parts of gold, and so must always co-exist with the complex idea we have of it, or else are inconsistent with it." [22] To paraphrase Hume's saying about causation (the underlying idea of which he must have derived from Locke), for all we can know any quality may go with or coexist with any other quality in the make up of an empirical thing. But Locke still holds that *if* we knew its inner constitution, we should be able to *deduce* just what qualities go together and the degree of their uniform and universal connection. In one sense, Locke's contention is of an idea which has become a commonplace since his day: namely, that of existences there are no universal propositions, the latter being possible only where deduction applies.

Thus Locke says: "I doubt not but if we could discover the figure, size, texture and motion of the minute constituent parts of any two bodies, we should know *without trial* several of their operations one upon another; as we do now know the properties of a square or a triangle. . . . We should be able to tell *beforehand* that rhubarb will purge, hemlock kill, and opium make a man sleep. . . . But whilst we are destitute of senses acute enough to discover the minute particles of bodies, and to give us ideas of their mechanical affections, we must be content to be ignorant of their properties and ways of operation; nor can we be assured about them any further than some few trials we make are able to reach." [23]

22. Book IV, Chap. III, 11.
23. Book IV, Chap. III, 25.

The same general idea is repeated several times in this chapter upon the "Extent of Human Knowledge"; and also in Chapter VI on "Universal Propositions." Paragraph 11 of the latter chapter is noteworthy for the explicit distinction it makes between the internal essence and the properties that flow directly from it and the properties that are due to "extrinsical causes." "Put a piece of gold anywhere by itself, separate from the reach and influence of all other bodies, it will immediately lose all its colour and weight, and perhaps malleableness too; which for all I know would be changed into a perfect friability." Certainly Locke does not intend to imply that weight is a "subjective" or "mental" state but that it depends upon connexion with other things—namely, gravitation. Hence the passage is particularly instructive as to what is signified by "secondary" qualities in general. As he summarizes the matter: "Things however absolute and entire they seem in themselves, are but retainers to other parts of nature for that which they are most taken notice of by us." In this passage Locke seems almost on the verge of denying the very existence of ultimate disconnected things, a denial which would have radically altered his whole conception of knowledge,[24] but he immediately returns to the idea of the absolute, intrinsic essence of things as that which, so to say, *ought* to be known, but which cannot be known, because qualities due to connexions with other things so overlay them. (The main thesis as to knowledge of coexistence is repeated also in Chap. XII, on "Improvement of Our Knowledge.")

To continue quotations is perhaps to gild gold and paint the lily, but the fact that Locke applies exactly the same logic to the matter of the perception of degree of likeness among *secondary qualities* seems to be crucially conclusive. Different degrees (shades) of color depend upon the size, position, number and motion of minute insensible corpuscles. Therefore they may be *really* different although they are *sensibly* alike to us. We cannot *know* (have certainty) as to the degrees of similarity existing between two whitenesses. "Not knowing, therefore, what number of particles, nor what motion of them, is fit to produce any precise degree of whiteness, we cannot *demonstrate* the certain equality of any two degrees of whiteness; because we have no

24. See Whitehead, *Principles of Natural Knowledge*, Chap. I.

certain standard to measure them by, nor means to distinguish every the least real difference." [25] This passage in itself completely refutes the current notion that Locke's secondary qualities are states of consciousness or of mind. If they were, their appearance would be their being; if they were alike in "consciousness" they would *be* alike. It is safe to issue a challenge to anyone who holds the traditional interpretation to explain this passage.

It is no part of the present enterprise to set forth just what Locke's positive theory of knowledge becomes when his theory of existence is made to square with his theory of knowledge. It is plain, however, that unless existences are in some aspect or phase connected instead of disconnected, and that unless the connectedness of things (or things in their connectedness) is the proper object of knowledge, there is an unbridgeable gap between things and any knowledge which operates, as Locke's does, in terms of the perception of connexions. It is enough for our present purpose that Locke repeatedly sets forth the gist of what his theory becomes when revised. "Ideas" are so connected together in experience that they serve with varying degrees of probability to point to and distinguish the complex interconnected wholes of which an "idea" is a part. A certain yellowness enables us to distinguish gold from silver, a taste wine from water, and so on. And this function, as he repeatedly states, answers all our purposes: in fact, as he says in one passage, it would probably prove embarrassing if we could detect the inner essence, while other things remain as they now are. [26] In short, it is enough if the connectedness of things is such as to render possible the relationship of *implication* and the act of *inference*. Berkeley put his finger on the point when he said: "The connexion of ideas does not imply the relation of cause and effect, but only of a mark or sign with the things signified." [27]

With this substitution, a distinction between those qualities which Locke calls secondary and those which he calls primary remains of value, though the Lockian interpretation is altered.

25. Book IV, Chap. II, 11–13.
26. Book II, Chap. XXIII, 12. The main thesis is also stated in Book II, Chap. XXXII, 14, 15; Book III, Chap. VI, 30; Book III, Chap. IX, 15; Book IV, Chap. I, 6; Chap. XI, 7; Chap. XII, 11; Chap. XVI, 6; and *Works*, Vol. IV, p. 76–77.
27. *Principles of Human Knowledge*, Part One, 65.

Primary qualities cease to be the counterparts of traditional essential attributes and the efficacious causes of secondary; they are those qualities of things which serve as the most accurate, dependable and comprehensive signs; the qualities most important and most available for reasoning in the *implication* relation. Sweetness has turned out to be a much less valuable *sign* than is the "bulk, number and texture" of extended parts.

William James in
Nineteen Twenty-Six[1]

It would be hard to say just how it happened, but the immediate effect of re-reading this volume of extraordinarily well selected and arranged extracts from the writings of William James was to set me wondering about the impact of the World War upon the intellectual life of the United States. The volume, together with its penetrating introductory interpretation of the thought of William James, brings home to one afresh how precisely and adequately Mr. James expressed a certain phase of American life-experience. The volume also deepens one's sense of the gap, the seemingly impassable chasm, that exists between the America of today and that of the nineties and nineteen hundreds whence dates the intellectual achievement of William James. What and why is this paradox?

Why should the most genuinely characteristic of American voices sound today as if coming to us from a by-gone and finished age? The weight of the paradox is increased when one remembers the contrast between the attitude of professional colleagues toward him while his work was doing and his established position today. Well do I remember the tone of thirty years ago. A great psychologist, certainly, but as to his ill-advised forays into philosophy, there was an amused and pitying condescension. Yet his ideas of an open universe with its plural and unfinished directions, its irregularities and hazards, its novelties and its unadjusted cross-currents which seemed so wantonly heretical, have already become, I will not say everywhere accepted, yet commonplaces of discussion, though only twenty-five years have passed. One thing is sure: he was a prophet of the future; all

1. *The Philosophy of William James*, Drawn from his own Works, with an Introduction by Horace M. Kallen, of the New School for Social Research. New York: The Modern Library, 1925.

[First published in *New Republic* 47 (30 June 1926): 163–65.]

the vital currents of science and philosophy have set in the direction in which he pointed. Yet the more certain is his place in general philosophy, his place as a thinker among the thinkers of the
world, the more uncertain does it appear whether he is a permanent spokesman for the spirit of the United States, or whether he
summed up an age, the pioneer age, of the country when it was
passing from the actual scene. Is the spirit to which he gave articulation gone, gone not to return, and shall men henceforth read
him simply for what is universally human in his insights, as the
first forerunner in the world of philosophy of the new orienta-
tion to proceed from the science of nature? Or is that for which
he spoke an abiding, an indestructible, possession of American
life? Will Americans go back to him simply for reminiscence and
compensation, or for invigoration and girding of loins? Merely
to ask the questions occasions a certain depression.

If you wish to know what it was in American life that William
James stood for, no better answer can be found than that given
by Mr. Kallen in his Introduction. Mr. James gave intellectual
expression to the life of the pioneer who made the country.
There is similarity between the personal, the private, experiences
of James whereby his own thought was nurtured and "the free
responses of the American people to the American scene." The
latter have to do "with the unprecedented, the hazardous, the
unpredictable in the adventure of the white man on the American continent. . . . They are most at play in the effort of the pioneer; the will to believe at one's own risk in the outcome of an
enterprise the success of which is not guaranteed in advance is
what they sum up to. Freedom, risk, effort, novelty and an inde-
terminate future all are involved in them." Thus "the private experience of William James and the public experience of Europeans making a home in the American wilderness coincide. . . .
Each is an assertion of the autonomy and naturalness of the individual; of his freedom to win to such success or excellence as is
within his scope, on his own belief, in his own way, by his own
effort, at his own risk during his unending struggle to live in this
changing world which was not made for him, this altogether *un*-
guaranteed world."

But the pioneer has gone. He remains, as Mr. Kallen reminds
us, only in the romanticism of the "western" motion-pictures.
Organization and regimentation appropriate to the technology

of mass production have taken his place. It was not many years ago that Mr. Wells thought to sum up his impressions of this country by reading everything in terms of an unrestrained "individualism." But save as "individualism" was used in a technical sense to denote a temper of indifference to political or governmental action, Mr. Wells was even then interpreting this country not for what it was, but for what it had been and had ceased to be. The temper of science has moved since the day of James to the intimation of an open and irregular universe; but our own human scene has become relatively trimmed and closed. The older instinctive and unconscious individuality has given way to a self-conscious individualism which expresses its liberality chiefly in rebellion against what are called Puritanic restrictions in personal conduct, while "personal liberty" and liberalism find their apotheosis in the declaration of the inalienable right to patronize a bootlegger. We talk much more about individualism and liberty than our ancestors. But as so often happens, when anything becomes conscious, the consciousness is compensatory for absence in practice.

It happened that I was reading these selections from James at the same time with Graham Wallas's *The Art of Thought*. It would be difficult to frame an interpretation of the pioneer spirit more divergent from the one just stated than that set forth by Mr. Wallas. The divergence is immensely significant in the present context. Mr. Wallas finds the surviving influence of the pioneer mind the chief obstacle to a development of independent intellectual life in this country. To him "pioneer" is almost synonymous with Philistine contempt for thought as a high-brow futility; synonymous with the conforming Fundamentalist in religion; with strenuous effort directed toward future material gain and achievement at the expense of present enjoyment and leisure. In piquant contrast with the writing of Mr. Kallen, he happens to instance William James as the antithesis of the pioneer mind. Any controversy as to which interpretation of the pioneer spirit is correct would be idle. All sensible persons would admit that "the pioneer spirit" as an entity, as a concept, is something artificially selected and constructed; it allows opportunity of choice from among the traits of the actual pioneer men and women, who, being human, were mixed like the rest of us. But the significant thing is that the free, hazarding, individualistic

quality has so receded that when a commentator on contemporary conditions looks for present relics of a pioneer mind, he
finds them precisely in those characters of the American scene
which lie, a smothering blanket, upon intellectual and moral
individuality.

Unbidden the query arises whether the popular view of "pragmatism" and of Mr. James as its author does not itself testify to a
subtle perversion of the reality of James's thought, a perversion
which is itself indicative of the change which has come about
along with the substitution of a machine-made world for the
out-door world of the pioneer. If I mistake not some of the
laudatory renown of William James at present springs from attributing to him a view of "consequences" which he had by anticipation bitterly denounced. It was he who said that the weakest point in American character was the tendency to worship
"the bitch-goddess, Success." Yet perhaps some of the vogue of
pragmatism among us—as well as of the adverse criticism of foreigners—is the notion that it is somehow a philosophy of, for
and by success. There is little room to doubt that in the little less
than twenty years since the volume called *Pragmatism* was published, there has taken place a certain transformation of values;
some things which were foremost with James have fallen into the
background, and things slighted by him have come to the front.

However it may be with the popular interpretation of the
pragmatic thought of James, the pragmatism of American life is
the predominance of business. A recent American writer[2] has
quoted from the head of one of the departments of the United
States Chamber of Commerce to the following effect: "Capitalism is today triumphant and the American business man, as its
conspicuous exponent, occupies a position of leadership which
the business man has never held before." The citation is backed
up by another from no less an authority than Henry Ford. "Our
whole competitive system, our whole creative expression, all the
play of our faculties seem to be centered around material production and its by-products of success and wealth." Mr. Otto
goes on to say the most ominous feature of the situation is not
the general absorption in business, deplorable as that is. "Far

2. *Natural Laws and Human Hopes*, by M. C. Otto, Henry Holt and Company,
1926.

worse, is the threatened assumption by business men of leader-ship in man's aspirational life." "Backed by unnumbered speeches before 'service' clubs and articles in business magazines, and aided by the ramifying arm of governmental agencies, the propa-ganda for 'practical idealism' is going forward."

The cardinal doctrines of the gospel according to business as set forth by Mr. Otto—and I know of no more ominously sig-nificant remarks—are, first, that the hopes upon which men set their hearts are to be dictated by business men; secondly, the technological means for the realization of these hopes are to be furnished by men of science; and, thirdly, the apprenticeship nec-essary to prepare the rising generation to take its place quickly and efficiently in the industrial system is to be supervised by edu-cators, while the chief responsibility of religious teachers is to fos-ter devotion to those moral and religious codes which are needed to hold the mass of men to habits of sobriety and industry.

We are not, I think, here far away from our theme of the para-doxical relation of William James and American life. The pas-sage suggests the enormous contrast that may exist within the compass of a common conception. That thought, speculation, theory should have a definite meaning in particular consequences in human life was certainly the teaching of William James. The doctrine was an articulate expression of something native in our scene. Yet the distance between it and the current pragmatism which Mr. Otto perceives and condemns is more significant than any difference between any American and any non-American philosophy. It indicates a civil war, an internal split. In which di-rection are we to move: in that marked out by James or in that which seems to be controlling today? Did William James catch a passing and perhaps expiring note and idealize it by imbuing it with his own personality? Or did he penetrate to a reality which is abiding and which will surely manifest itself through the su-perficial froth and foam which temporarily conceal it?

Bishop Brown:
A Fundamental Modernist

That the fundamentalists stole a march on their opponents in the selection of epithets by which to characterize the religious issues at stake I have had occasion to point out previously in the *New Republic*. It is evident that the modernists are themselves more or less at fault in this matter, not just because they have accepted the word, but because of an intellectual vagueness which attends their convictions. At least to one outside of the controversy, to one not attached to either wing, religious "liberalism" as stated by its adherents seems to be essentially transitional, mediating, in character. Its psychological value to many persons in easing strain cannot be doubted; no one can deny that there is a social value in movements which modulate from one position to another in a way which avoids the crises and breakdowns incident to abrupt changes. But it is in the interest of intellectual coherence and integrity that the direction of a movement of transition should be recognized, that there should be some clear perception of the outcome to which the moving logic of the situation points.

Bishop William Montgomery Brown has in his lifetime traversed the whole course; he has done it knowingly, aware of where he started and where he has come out. He has moved from one fundamentalism to another creed equally fundamental. He is therefore more than a modernist; he has surrendered a supernaturalism connected with the authority of tradition and the institution of the church for a naturalism connected with the authority of investigation and the institution of science. Yet no reader with a spark of sympathy can gainsay his repeated assertions that at the end he is as religious, in his own conviction indeed more religious than when he was an orthodox bishop in the

[First published in *New Republic* 48 (17 November 1926): 371–72.]

Protestant Episcopal Church, where he was more than usually successful in rehabilitating dying churches and founding new ones. His recent book (*My Heresy*, published by the John Day Company, New York) breathes the confidence, assurance, of a faith which knows that it is founded on an indestructible Rock of Ages.

That is the fact which gives interest to the record of the spiritual development of Bishop Brown—the reality of religion so impregnates his life as well as his book that it is difficult to fancy even his ecclesiastic enemies failing to think of him, in spite of his deposition, as Bishop. In his intellectual conceptions, his ideas of the nature of belief, of authority, of the objects of faith and aspiration, he has swung full circle. But the circle is inscribed within an atmosphere which is everywhere religious; nowhere does it cross the boundary. For this reason the movement which the book records has a typical significance which is absent from most heresies. The history of the disowned ardent cleric presents what is lacking in the activities of most modernists: the attainment of a location and a possession which is as fundamental as that of any ecclesiastic who arrogates to himself the title of fundamentalist. Because of this fact, his career makes clear an issue obscured in most recent controversy: What is the foundation of a vital religious experience in this present time?

The intellectual naïveté, the innocence and virginity, of Bishop Brown's temperament is an agency in clarifying the situation. His book as a book is too argumentative, too concerned with making a conclusion definite and strong in the mind of the reader, to be the subtly illuminating "spiritual autobiography" which a literary egoist would have made of the material at hand. But in spite of the reiterated striking of the same note which at times imparts heaviness to the book, the fact is made to stand out that the successive steps of Bishop Brown in "heresy" (surely it cannot be long before the word will be permanently embalmed in quotation marks) represent a succession of widenings and deepenings of faith. His clerical career did not end in a defrocking because he discovered from time to time that he believed less, but because from time to time he discovered that absence of faith in man and knowledge were bound up with the beliefs which he had previously held. Others who had shared these beliefs remained in their unbelief; his faith moved on.

Thus he found himself without desire, without expectation on his part, moved, rather than moving, from one level to another. Each crisis found him with the naïve belief that his brethren in the faith would respond as soon as he communicated to them the new revelation, that is, the new perception of scientific and social realities, which had been forced upon him; that, even if they did not actively approve and go with him, they would at least acknowledge his right and duty to follow the light which he had seen. Each time the refusal he encountered, refusals to enter even in imagination into the new and larger ways of truth in which he must walk in order to remain true to the faith which was in him, compelled him to further thought to search for the reasons for the refusal. Only at the very end, at the close of his trial by the bishops and by reason of the character of the trial, was he forced to the conclusion that "My Heresy" consisted essentially in the fact that he had placed faith in truth and reality above and below all other articles of faith. Only then, upon his appeal, did he turn to the business of making the issue clear, of getting written plain upon the record the official attitude of the Church. Till then he had only striven to share the faith which possessed him, even as he had striven to bring others to the faith when he was still orthodox of the orthodox, ecclesiastic of the ecclesiastics. Doubtless history knows many instances of faith which from childhood to old age remained childlike. But the instances in which childlike faith persisted while passing from extremes of literalism and dogmatism to doubt and denial of a personal God, personal immortality and the historic existence of Jesus, are certainly rare.

The way out and onward which Bishop Brown found for himself and which he offered others who would be religious while living in full communion with the present intellectual and social world is the way of symbolic interpretation: Yield glad and complete allegiance to whatever truths are anywhere discovered and treat the formulae in which bygone ages stated their faith as symbols of what humanity now feels, knows and aspires to do. There are many, also heretics from the standpoint of the churches, whom the method leaves cold. They have no more interest in retaining as symbolism the Old and New Testament, the Apostles and Nicene Creed, than they have in giving a symbolic interpretation to Plato or Virgil. But even they realize that the church is an historic institution and one with which the religious life of most men has been bound up; they realize that piety to the traditions which are closely associated with deep emotional experiences is a thing to be respected; they know that the church as an institution, and personal piety to the sources from which the ideal life of man has been so largely nourished, are confronted with the problem of adaptation to the intellectual and social realities of present life. The way of symbolism is with respect to these things a fundamental release, emancipation and inspiration. The issue which the trials of Bishop Brown for heresy have written clear and large upon the record is whether the Christian churches are to continue surrendering to symbolism one after another of the special items of the old beliefs and formulae, when the coercion of accomplished facts leaves no other course open, while clinging obstinately to literalism and dogmatism as to others; or whether it will voluntarily and graciously concede to all men the fullest liberty of symbolic interpretation of any and all articles and items, reserving its faith for the realities of life itself. Upon the decision of this issue the future of Protestantism depends. Bishop Brown is no intellectual giant; he makes no claim to great scholarship. But his sincere and genuine faith in spiritual fundamentals has accomplished more in making the issue clear than has been effected by men of greater intellectual stature and profounder scholarship. In comparison with this achievement the crudities and eccentricities which may accompany some of the symbolic interpretations which commend themselves to Bishop Brown are of no importance. He is a fundamentalist in religion, though a heretic in traditional supernaturalism.

America's Responsibility

The "Practical Idealism" of the United States has perhaps assumed a pharisaical tinge due to over-advertising. Like another fine thing and fine word, "service," it has been cheapened by the use to which it has been put by self-seekers and by those who grab at any idealistic phrase which is current in order to advance any cause in which they are interested. Nevertheless there is an immense fund of goodwill and desire to be of help to those in need diffused among the American people. This is no especial credit to us; it would be a shame were it otherwise. It was born of pioneer conditions, fostered by the mobility of life and the need of improvising cooperative adjustments to meet new conditions, and is demanded by the amplitude of our resources on account of which so many are raised above the pressure of personal need. Much of the energy which in other countries drives along political channels goes in this country in voluntary unions devoted to the public welfare.

Causes of American Aloofness

This fund of goodwill, in spite of all appearances to the contrary, still exists with respect to international affairs. There are definite causes for our attitude of aloofness from European struggles and problems. Large portions of our population migrated here in order to escape ills of one sort or another from which they suffered across the sea. They wanted to get away mentally and morally as well as physically; they still want to forget. In a pinch they are for their old country as against some other country, but in general they are anti-European. The diver-

[First published in *Christian Century* 43 (23 December 1926): 1583–84.]

sity of our immigrant population is another factor. There is hardly a national group which has not a tradition of fear, suspicion, hostility toward some other European nation which is its historic enemy. One of the conditions required in order that these different groups may live in amity on this side of the water is that there should have been a tacit agreement to put European questions in the background, to leave them alone as far as possible. Otherwise our politics and our social life would have continued and repeated all the historic strifes of Europe.

Physical distance inevitably carries with it a certain amount of psychological isolation. The mass of people occupied with the things which have to be done in their daily life have little leisure and little call to give much thought to affairs going on in remote places. All the forces of self-preservation work automatically against mixing in matters, especially political ones, which are so far away as to be beyond adequate knowledge, not to say beyond control. Minding one's own business is a form of conduct that commends itself even more nationally than domestically. Consider how close the British Isles are to the continent of Europe, and yet how her whole traditional policy up to very recent years has made in the direction of isolation. Isolation is not a high ideal but it denotes a better state of things than one of meddling which involves the meddler in unpleasant complications and does no one else any good in the end. There is something humorous in the rebukes and advice freely handed out to Americans regarding the selfishness and futility of American isolation, in view of the century old similar policies of Great Britain in spite of her much closer and more numerous contacts.

The War as an Educational Factor

Even such a cursory summary as these remarks would be woefully incomplete were there not mentioned the disillusionments following the war. The outcome of the war served as an enormous political education; I do not say a complete or adequate one. But the prevalent feeling of having been fooled—prevailing even among those who think we would have to do the same thing over under like circumstances, only in a different spirit—together with the withdrawal which accompanies this feeling, is not a mere emotional gesture due to temporary fatigue and disgust. It is attended with a much greater knowledge than the American people had before of the realities of European racial and economic rivalries, political intrigues and diplomatic methods. Few have taken the trouble to go into the details of the discussion of war guilt. But great masses of people are convinced that the war merely reflected the European state of mind and of politics. They see, in spite of Locarno and one or two other favorable occurrences, no marked sign that the state of the European mind and politics has undergone any change, save such as is due to exhaustion. Fundamentally the attitude of aloofness is due to a determined aversion to mixing in the complications of European strife, intrigue and mutual treacheries. There is a natural aversion to experiencing the troubles incident to getting mixed up with such a situation. But there is more than that. There is a firm belief that the whole American situation and tradition in international matters is radically diverse from the European system.

Two Systems

This need not imply that we think we are morally better. Admission that present Europeans are not to blame for what they have inherited, nor we deserving because of what we have inherited, does not affect the fact. That fact is the important thing, and the fact is that the two systems are different. The notion that we can really be of help to Europe by joining in their affairs on terms that are set by their unhappy international and diplomatic heritage seems to me silly. We shall simply be drawn in, and our system assimilated to theirs.

What has been said may be taken superficially as a justification of a policy of isolation on our part. The intention is wholly different. A few of the causes of the tendency toward isolation have been stated. Even should one regard them all as evil—which they certainly are not—they exist as facts and help determine the situation. Any realistic thinker, one who wishes not just to be idealistic in his private inner consciousness but to see ideals carried out, must take them into account. They stand as a solid block against certain methods which are most urged upon us as methods of cooperating with European recovery and of assisting the cause of world peace. The efforts in question come from many high-minded and devoted men and women. But they are pathetic. The whole set and movement of American affairs dooms them to disappointment. The fact that the conscious fund of American idealism with respect to international friendship has gone so largely into such impossible channels is a large part of the explanation of why the genuine practical idealism of the American people has remained latent and ineffective.

Thus we come to the real purpose of the statement regarding the causes of American aloofness. Upon what terms and along what lines can American sentiment, belief and action be mobilized in behalf of the supreme cause of international understanding and goodwill? The attempt to force them into channels which are opposed to their very nature results only in increasing aloofness, in promoting indifference, or even antagonism. The campaign for the league court, and its fate, should demonstrate this fact to any persons with open eyes. It is a pity, a tragedy, to see so much potential energy for good go to waste because of misdirection, while so much more potential energy, which might be roused into activity for international peace, remains passive and inert.

Europe and America

I am accordingly addressing an appeal to those who have been actively and energetically concerned with bringing Europe and the United States together in behalf of world peace and amity. Why not search for a method and agency of operation which calls into play all the actual and latent practical idealism of the country? Why not seek means which are in accord with American tradition and outlook, measures whose consequences do not involve getting implicated in the heritage of European war politics, and which will afford Europe an opportunity to free herself from that incubus? Is there anything the United States can do for Europe half as important as to share in emancipating her from the legalized war system? It is not just the results of the last war which weigh down Europe, which reduce her, which threaten her civilization. It is even more the prospects of the next war, and the next. It is the war system. Relieved from that dead weight and overhanging menace, no one believes that Europe has not enough resources—material, intellectual, moral—to recover herself, and become a leader in the friendly rivalry of civilizations. Anything which we do or can do that serves in whatever way, direct or indirect, closely or remotely, to perpetuate the war system, is a disservice to Europe. Let the practical idealism of the United States do for Europe the one thing that Europe most needs and the one thing which is most in harmony with American tradition and aspirations, and in time all other needed things will be added.

The search for such a method and agency would quickly reach its mark. It is already at hand. It is embodied in the resolution of Senator Borah and the suggested treaty of Mr. Levinson. I have yet to hear an objection which did not boil down to a conviction that the proposal does not meet European conditions, that it ignores the past conflicts of the European states and the crying demand of these states for guarantees and security. Well, that is just the glory of the scheme. It *is* remote from *existing* political conditions in Europe, which are at once the fruit of the war system and the seeds of future war. Any other scheme than the outlawry of war in basing its guarantees upon force is a guarantee of war. Any security that rests upon the threat of war assures war. As far as the argument implies that Europe is so wedded by its past to the war system that it will neither help itself nor be helped by others out of it, it proves too much. If Europe is determined upon suicide nothing can be done. But the adoption of such a pessimistic attitude is unjustified. It will remain unjustified until the United States has put itself squarely behind the outlawry of the war system, has made clear the terms upon which Europe and the United States can cooperate for peace and in peace, and has then been refused by Europe.

The first responsibility rests with this country. It must first commit itself by the adoption of the Borah resolution and of the measures that are sequels to it. In spite of all the enthusiasm the idea has aroused, it is not yet committed. If the committal is delayed, the responsibility will not lie wholly upon those who are indifferent to the rest of the world and to the ties which bind us to it, nor wholly upon those who are skeptical about the possibility of lasting peace and goodwill among nations, nor upon those who accept war as the final arbiter of national disputes. It will rest in some measure with those impractical idealists who waste and divert the energies of the country upon projects which will never appeal to the citizenship of the country. There is such a thing as knowing so much about the details of the European situation that the mind is held enslaved by them and thinks in terms of the European tradition and system, proposing a mitigation here and a palliation there. There are times and places where a basic point of view and a broad outlook are demanded, and where attention to the trees forbids a sight of the jungle. The sole fundamental issue is the outlawry or the perpetuation of the war system.

America and the Far East

During the great famine in China I happened to be present when a number of Americans in Peking were discussing the relations of the United States and China. One of them, a business man, was complaining of the great difficulty in getting Americans to invest their money in China for industrial and commercial purposes. He started from the fact that an engineering scheme which would have been of undoubted benefit to China, since it involved a reclamation project that would prevent floods, had failed because of the refusal of Americans to put in their money, although a fair return would have been assured. He contrasted this holding back with the amount of money which had just been voluntarily contributed by benevolence for the relief of famine sufferers. The amount given was several millions more than the amount which had been refused as a loan. He asserted, and not wholly in a whimsical spirit, that the only way to finance China's needs in the United States was to appeal to the churches and philanthropically inclined persons on the basis of benevolence, not profit.

I have often thought that his remarks furnished, in a way, a symbol of the underlying relations of the two countries. Of course there are American business relations with China, and some of them have a good deal at stake. And yet they are hardly typical of the situation. In a true sense, our concern with China is parental rather than economic. All parental sentiments are somewhat mixed: they usually contain an economic factor; there is the hope that the children may be of assistance later on. Yet expectation of financial gain is not the essence of parental feeling.

The largest American investments both of human beings and of capital in China are in missions, education and philanthropy.

[First published in *Survey* 56 (1 May 1926): 188.]

Europeans, accustomed to continental methods, usually take it as a matter of course that these developments were made designedly with commercial or political ends in view. In fact, Americans are not infrequently complimented by Europeans upon the far-sighted shrewdness with which our country has laid its plans in the Far East. To those who know the real history of events this implication is absurd. But nonetheless a definite situation has been created; our relations with China are primarily cultural. We have gone there with ideas and ideals, with sentiments and aspirations; we have presented a certain type of culture to China as a model to be imitated. As far as we have gone at all, we have gone *in loco parentis*, with advice, with instruction, with example and precept. Like a good parent we would have brought up China in the way in which she should go. There is a genial and generous aspect to all this. But nonetheless it has created a situation, and that situation is fraught with danger.

Our diplomatic and political role has been largely paternal. From the time of Burlingame down we have been, as far as we have been anything, protective. The doctrine of the Open Door, of maintaining the territorial integrity of China, ran with our own interests. The remission of the Boxer indemnity for educational purposes is known to all, but John Hay undoubtedly rendered a greater service to China in limiting the claims and exactions of European nations; as far as any one person outside of China saved China from division it was John Hay. We have not done as much positively as we pride ourselves upon; but from the negative side, by absence of aggression, by smoothing things down when we could without great trouble to ourselves, we have played a paternal role.

Such a part arouses expectations which are not always to be met. Expectations may be unreasonable and yet their not being met may arouse disappointment and resentment. There is something of this sort in the temper of China towards us today: a feeling that we have aroused false hopes only to neglect the fulfilment of obligations involved in the arousal. On the other side, parents are rarely able to free themselves from the notion that gratitude is due them; failure to receive it passes readily into anger and dislike. Unless this country has more than the average amount of parental understanding, it may soon be charging China with ingratitude.

The more serious danger, however, springs from the fact that China is rapidly growing up. In sentiment, if not in effective action, it is attaining its majority. It will henceforth resent more and more any assumption of parental tutelage even of a professedly benevolent kind. Signs of the resentment are already apparent. Missions and even schools are no longer welcome if they assume an air of superiority either as to what they have to offer or in their administration. The Chinese feel that a new day for them has arrived and that foreigners, even those with the best of intentions, must accommodate themselves to it. They are free in their imputation of bad motives whenever foreign interests do not respond. Politically also, the Chinese no longer wish for any foreign guardianship. If this country should not take the lead in relieving them of judicial and tariff tutelage, what we may have done in the past will be quickly forgotten.

There is a crisis in most families when those who have been under care and protection grow to the point of asserting their independence. It is the same in the family of nations. Obviously primary responsibility rests with the mature and experienced. In the next ten years we shall probably need much patience, tolerance, understanding and good-will to alter our traditional parental attitude, colored as it has been by a temper of patronage, conscious or unconscious, into one of respect and esteem for a cultural equal. If we cannot successfully make the change, the relationship of this country with the entire Far East will take a decided turn for the worse.

Highly Colored White Lies

A month or two ago reports emanating from Germany told of alleged secret clauses in the Russo-Japanese treaty, according to which the two countries had made a combination against Europe and the United States in respect to Asia in general and China in particular. It even went into detail as to the number of Chinese soldiers that were to be trained for the army of the combination. It is not difficult to imagine behind this report the desire of some German to arouse apprehension in our minds lest Germany, rebuffed by continued ill-treatment from the western world, should finally throw in her lot with an Asiatic combination. The late Kaiser's evocation of the Yellow Peril was met, even before the War, in the minds of some Americans at least, by the spectre of a German-Russian-Japanese combination, often with China thrown in, to add bulk to the ghost.

Within the last few days cable tolls have been paid to make known to us at considerable length the speech of a French public man who prophesied the next great war, more terrible than any which had yet happened. This war is to be between Asia and the rest of the world, the United States meeting the brunt of the attack. As the speech was made and reported at just the time when, according to other reports, the French government was frowning upon another Washington disarmament conference, it is hardly cynical to suppose that this particular spectacle of horror was painted to wean the American mind from interest in premature disarmament, and to suggest that in the venture we might need assistance from French arms.

A few weeks ago, in the debate in the English Parliament on the Singapore fortification matter, a representative of the Cabinet, in response to a query from MacDonald, is reported to have

[First published in *New Republic* 42 (22 April 1925): 229–30.]

said in effect that citizens of the United States would probably look with favor upon making Singapore a strong naval base, because of the influence of its proximity to the Philippines in case of war between the United States and Japan. Considering the offense such a remark was bound to give to Japan, the late ally of Great Britain, it is hardly likely that this indiscretion was intended merely to placate sentiment in this country with respect to the Singapore measure. The secretary who made the statement could hardly have failed to know that the remark would be taken throughout Asia, including India as well as Japan and China, to mean that there is an understanding or entente of some kind between Great Britain and America with reference to Asiatic affairs. It is reasonable to infer that was the impression he meant to create by his remark.

Let it not be thought that these three European countries are more at fault in this matter than we ourselves. Representatives of interests of our navy have systematically been doing what they can to create in our minds a fear of Japan. They have fostered every suspicion and every alarm that could possibly lodge and take root among us. They, too, have talked about the prospective union of Japan and Russia; they have not hesitated to try to disturb our historic friendly feeling toward China by silly stories about the Bolshevizing of China and its prospective union with Soviet interests against the rest of the world. In private, if not in public, they cause it to be understood that Japanese agents are busy in India, encouraging and subsidizing the independent nationalistic movement there with a view to getting the assistance of the man power of India in the future struggle with the United States.

A few weeks ago cartoons in an American paper depicted two alternative scenes. Either this country must line up actively with the European powers, taking a responsible interest in their affairs, really uniting with them in forming their international policy, or we shall finally be united with them in slavery under the heel of yellow and brown races. It is easy to see the motives back of the other highly colored propagandas. This particular case looks like a gratuitous attack of foolishness, since even the most fanatic devotee of our entrance into the League of Nations could hardly have thought of this argument. Nevertheless it is but one of many signs of the attempt to create the belief that at some time or other and probably reasonably soon there is going to be an armed conflict either between all the colored races and the white, or else between the United States and some of the colored races. A version of the future conflict which is a slight variant of the color scheme is the prophecy of union of all the Moslem peoples in a war for extermination on one side or the other against the Christian peoples. One reads outgivings of this sort occasionally from official followers of Christ.

It is easy to say that intelligent people pay no attention to such reports. That is precisely what makes them dangerous. Anyone who will keep track of the statements and rumors of which these given are but casual samples, will be surprised and perhaps appalled to discover how numerous and varied they are, and what a constant stream of them runs into men's minds. The very stupidity which causes sensible persons to neglect them or turn aside in disgust gives them an entrance into the minds of many whose knowledge of foreign affairs is next to nothing. It is of no use to point out to these persons that the interests of Japan and Russia in Asia are as antagonistic as ever they were, and that even now the activities of the Soviet government, which has retained the old imperialism of the Tsar plus a new efficiency, is creating friction with both Japan and China in Outer and Inner Mongolia respectively. It is useless to point out that China is historically and constitutionally afraid of both Russia and Japan, and plays one off against the other as the situation dictates. It is of no use to point out that India is going to be more than occupied for generations with her own internal problems equally whether she remains a British dependency or becomes independent. And it is equally useless to point out that the so-called Moslem world is a medley of particularistic and centrifugal tribes, petty states and interests which nothing short of a miracle will bring into a semblance of unity. It is equally useless to point out the industrial impotency of the people who are combined to make up the scarecrow. Ignorance is invincible.

It is consequently more than useless to point out that these reports calculated to arouse dread of an Asiatic menace in general and a Japanese one in particular, come from opposite sources and are moved by inconsistent springs. For the few who discount them on that account there are thousands who are moved by the consensus of their result. For they all tend toward a single outcome in practice, no matter how logically contradictory they are to one another. The springs of public opinion are being poisoned at their source. The Nordic and race myth is meantime cooperating to the same result. While comparatively insignificant in its direct influence, because it is confined to a small group, the professional intellectuals, it nevertheless may have serious weight in the end just because it reinforces the prejudiced sentiments of an ignorant mass.

Possibly it might arouse suspicions of another and more useful sort to note that in all this flood of rumors, coming from so many different sources, it is the United States which is elected to stand in the van of the inevitable conflict. The inevitable race conflict is a romantic myth without the attractiveness of most romance. But its consequences are definite and concrete and the United States is the chief sufferer. Few Americans probably even know of the Supreme Court decision making it impossible for East Indians to become naturalized in this country. Fewer still know of the activities of our government, seemingly under the special instigation of the patriotic Mr. Beck, to make the decision retroactive by cancelling the citizenship of the small number previously naturalized, leaving them literally without a country. Millions, however, know the fact in India, and our educational and other influence has received a tremendous blow in that country in consequence.

Our Senate with its rude slap at Japanese pride has prevented two or three hundred Japanese a year from migrating to this country. In consequence, American business interests have suffered greatly in loss of contracts in Japan, while, an affair of infinitely greater importance, the growth of democratic ideas in Japan, the one thing calculated to increase American prestige there, has undergone its chief setback, and the anti-American influence of the imperialistic and bureaucratic class has received a reinforcement which is most welcome to it.

It is too much to say that Chinese sentiment has as yet turned definitely against us, but it is known to all in contact with the Chinese educated classes, whether at home or among the student body in this country, that many Chinese are beginning seriously to ask whether the United States is going back on its traditional policy of friendly detachment, and is approaching a union or understanding with European policies of economic and political aggression.

Simply from the standpoint of self-interest, we need to ask

whether it is not time to call a halt on the circulation and influence of these silly reports and prophecies. And from the larger standpoint of the influence of the United States in the world in making for peace and good will among nations, it is imperative to give heed to the question. It will be a tragic pity if the thoughts and activities of those among us who conceive themselves peculiarly internationally minded become so fixed on the European situation, and upon the importance of counteracting isolationist policies in that quarter, that they become blind and indifferent to the change that is steadily going on in American sentiment with reference to our relations to the continent of Asia. There among the reawakening peoples is a natural and legitimate field for the exercise of whatever is sound in historic American ideas and ideals: and there it is where our power for good is being most systematically undermined.

Is China a Nation
or a Market?

If it were not a fact and a fact of a kind more or less familiar, the Conference now in solemn conclave in Peking would be incredible. The orthodox axiom of all "sound political science" is national sovereignty; in practice no phase of political independence is more jealously guarded than the right to control taxation and to levy tariffs, whether for revenue or for the rearing of infant industries. In session in Peking are representatives of the three great democracies of the world, Great Britain, the United States and France, each professing unqualified faith in the right of independent nations to self-government. In addition there is a wide-spread hostility to everything which smacks of "internationalism"; for are not the "Reds" internationalists, and are not the Reds a menace? From these premises, one would hardly conclude that the Conference in Peking sits an international assembly held to take part in governing China; that it arrogates to itself one of the most "sacred" functions of sovereignty, that of fixing the tariff on foreign goods, and that it has no notion of yielding any more to the expressed desire and purpose of China concerning its own affairs than it shall find necessary in order to avoid serious trouble.

It is doubtless highly theoretical to call attention to such flagrant discrepancies between political theory and practice. Nevertheless it may be one way to induce the American public to visualize the Chinese scene, and to realize that the State department of the United States has soon to decide whether it will continue to engage in the regulation of the internal affairs of China, contrary to the practically united will of the Chinese people, or whether it will have the courage and initiative to act in not merely a democratic but a decent way in permitting financial self-government to the Chinese government. There is no reason

[First published in *New Republic* 44 (11 November 1925): 298–99.]

to doubt the kind sentiments of the State department; in all probability it means well by China, and its expressions of good-will are not hypocritical camouflage. But the department is influenced by precedent, by routine, by the etiquette of diplomacy which might more easily fear a breach of manners toward other nations than a breach of justice towards China. And it is also exposed to direct and more or less powerful influence from business interests that want in behalf of their own pockets to keep the tariff of China on foreign goods at the lowest possible point. Is it too much to hope that the general public shall have an active concern in the decisions which are to be made, and shall bring greater pressure to bear upon the State department to act in a fair, humane and democratic way, than self-interest and hidden groups bring to bear in the opposite direction? It is futile to lecture the general public on its responsibilities in this matter; it is fed up with foreign responsibilities and wants to be left alone. But it may do no harm to assert with all possible emphasis that in China at present the American people is on trial, and that the attitude taken toward tariff autonomy by the United States will determine for long years the attitude taken by the Chinese towards us. Are our professions of goodwill to China sincere? Are our assertions of greater disinterestedness than animates other nations genuine? Or are they a combination of Pharisaism, sentimentality and highfaluting talk? That is the issue in the minds of most Chinese, and the way the American people meets the tariff question may determine for a generation the moral and political alignment of the Chinese people to western civilization in general and to American ideas and institutions in particular.

Needless to say the illogical position of interference of democratic nations, themselves highly nationalistic, and mostly addicted to protective tariffs, with the internal affairs of China grew up gradually for historic reasons, and so was tolerated until it became familiar and a vested interest. At the outset, the Chinese people were indifferent, and it is almost correct to say that the Chinese government invited the interference. In the past, it has not worked altogether badly; considerable good came of it. If international conferences to help regulate the affairs of individual nations were the rule and not an exception confined to countries so weak that they can be safely meddled with, there might even be something to say for continuing the practice in China. But the past is not the present, and present China is bent upon a radical break with the past in all that concerns its own management of its own affairs. The danger is that diplomats will not face the reality and extent of this change, and will palter, compromise, truckle over details, do as little as they possibly can, and trust to future events to be able to get away with their evasion of the issue. It is not too much to say that unless the International Conference takes action which looks in a definite and stated way towards the resumption of Chinese tariff autonomy, not at some vague future time when all shall be well with the government of China but at a specified date under specified conditions, public opinion in China will force any Chinese government that may exist to resume tariff autonomy in defiance of the powers, and that at no distant date. To put the matter at its lowest level, it might be as well to make a virtue of necessity, and by anticipating events get the credit for a just and sensible act.

It is understood that the powers are willing to permit China to level duties up to ten or fifteen percent. Japan is reported to have sprung a surprise by volunteering at the first meeting to agree to a raise up to twelve and a half percent. One feels helpless to comment adequately upon the situation. If the imagination will only work and think of a similar conference called to pass upon the affairs of France or Italy, or the United States, or even of a third-rate European power, there will be no need for any comment; a sense of the indignation and resentment of an awakened China and of the danger of giving cause for its continued growth, will take care of the affair. But it is more than the amount of tariff which China is to be permitted to levy that is under consideration. It is also proposed to decide for China what China shall do with the moneys when they are raised. There is a story that the assent of Japan to the American proposal of a Conference was secured by a tacit agreement that the United States would join in urging that the added funds be employed to pay off the Nishihara loans by Japan. The story may well be false—but it may also have a grain of fact in it. Doubtless China should meet her foreign obligations. But in view of the fact that these loans were made at a time when the Anfu pro-Japanese party was in power at Peking and are universally regarded as part of the betrayal of China to foreign interests, it is obvious that the popularity and prestige of the Conference will not be increased by any such proposals. And this situation illustrates the danger which now attends upon every pretension of foreign powers to decide China's domestic affairs for her. Some decisions as to the use to be made by China of additional funds would be less unpopular than some others, but any attempt to decide and to enforce decision, anything more than advice which in the present entangled condition of Chinese finance is legitimate, will surely make trouble instead of alleviating an already troubled situation.

It is trite to say that in the present condition of the world nations can no longer do the sort of thing which once they did as a matter of course and with impunity. But that trite fact is the essence of the Chinese situation. The only question is whether it is to be recognized only by small bits, grudgingly, and by yielding to trouble after it has broken out, or whether it will be recognized at once in its full force and whole-heartedly. If the United States shows a disposition to compromise, to postpone, to take half steps and quarter steps, to evade, to depend upon time-honored formulae that have nothing to do with the present situation, the case, difficult enough at best as between the powers, is lost in advance. If it leads with a definite and thoroughgoing policy of which financial autonomy for China is a central feature, something definite will be accomplished.

The American public should bear in mind that there is no question of even what is called national honor and prestige at stake. There is only a vested interest. Reduced to its lowest terms, the question for American citizens to form a judgment upon is whether they wish the power of the United States government to be used to promote, at the expense of China and of the good relations of China and the United States, the pecuniary interests of a small group of manufacturers, merchants, commission agents and exporters. They are doubtless all enthusiastic high-tariff men at home, but they want to retain a cheap and easy hold on Chinese markets by keeping down the rate of duty. At bottom, this is what the solemn and dignified International Conference at Peking is about, in spite of the fact that it is possible to overlay this ground-work with many important but irrelevant matters. The issue is simple enough so that even a people sick of foreign questions and policies should be able to pass upon it, and do so with promptness and efficacy. Do we wish China to be treated as a free and self-respecting people should be treated or as a market upon which to dump goods for the pecuniary profit of a small number?

We Should Deal with China as Nation to Nation

In the recent number of the *Survey* dealing with Oriental problems in their connection with the United States, Mr. Lewis Gannett reports a conversation with General Chiang Kai-shek in Canton. According to Mr. Gannett, the Chinese leader said: "Thinking men in China hate America more than they hate Japan . . . Japan talks to us in ultimatums; she says frankly she wants special privileges—extraterritoriality, tariff control—in China. We understand that and know how to meet it. The Americans come to us with smiling faces and friendly talk; but in the end your government acts just like the Japanese. And we, disarmed by your fair words, do not know how to meet such insincerity."

I have no way of knowing how far such statements are representative of Chinese opinion. To some extent they are perhaps colored by local feeling at Canton, which resents the support given by the American government to the Peking government. But nevertheless it is significant that they are held by such a representative person as Chiang Kai-shek. Probably most Americans, including those sympathetic with China, will feel that the statements are unfair, and will incline to be irritated. I do not think they are fair either, but I quote them not to controvert them, but to indicate the great difficulty nations have in understanding each other. For I do not think that American opinion about China, and about the relations of the United States to China, are very fair either as a rule. Yet I do not think that on either side there is a *desire* to be anything but fair—leaving out the case of those who have something to gain by misrepresentations.

The conclusion I would draw is that official and governmental relations ought to be such that the misunderstandings and unfair

[First published in *Chinese Students' Monthly* 21 (May 1926): 52–54.]

statements which develop will do as little harm as is possible. I recognize the great truth in what is constantly said about the importance of nations' understanding one another, appreciating one another's Culture, etc. This is all true. But such understanding and appreciation is of very slow growth, and it will be a long, long time before it will develop to a point where it can be counted upon to regulate international relations. Persons of the same country, of the same culture and tradition, even persons of the same family, find great difficulty in properly understanding one another. We are not as yet sufficiently civilized or sufficiently scientific in our methods to understand one another. I do not believe that for a very long time the mass of Americans are going to see the Orientals as they see and feel themselves, nor do I know any reason why we should expect the mass of Orientals to judge us from the standpoint we take in estimating our own conduct.

It may seem harsh to say that we have to count, for a long time in the future, upon a large measure of misunderstanding between peoples. But I think a frank recognition of this fact would afford a measure of security and protection. It would lessen the amount of exasperation and irritation that grows up when a misunderstanding is revealed and patent. Above all, it would, as has been already suggested, indicate that the great thing is so to direct public policies that the inevitable misunderstandings will, when they arise, be shorn of power to result in practical harm.

It is because I believe that present American governmental policies in China tend to invest misunderstandings with power to work actual evil that I would see those policies changed. It is quite "natural" that state departments and diplomats should follow traditional policies. One of these traditional policies is that western nations should unite and pursue a common policy in China instead of each nation conducting its diplomacy independently. It is easy to see how from a historical point of view the method grew up. The inertia of diplomacy, the desire to follow precedents, the feeling that it is risky to do anything new, all operate to induce the American state department to continue to act in concert with the foreign offices of other nations in dealing with China. But because I believe it increases international misunderstanding between China and the United States, because it clothes these misunderstandings with power to work practical evil, and because it prevents our state department from actively manifesting and executing what is at least the passive desire of most Americans, I am opposed to it. I think that we should at once deal with China as nation to nation, and leave other nations to pursue a similar independent course. A policy of complete non-intervention may not seem benevolent, but I do not believe that any nation at present is wise enough or good enough to act upon an assumption of altruism and benevolence toward other nations. Till conditions have changed, the great thing is to leave one another alone, and give each nation a chance to manage its own affairs, no matter how inadequate and incompetent the management may seem to us to be.

I think our present policy has also a tendency to prevent Chinese from facing frankly their own situation. As long as the unequal treaties exist, and as long as foreign nations encroach politically—or economically with political support—upon Chinese territory, the Chinese people will use this fact as an alibi. It will minimize its own responsibility for the bad condition of its own affairs and will throw all the blame upon foreigners. Only China can straighten out Chinese affairs. It seems to me that one reason they are not tackling the job with greater energy and persistence is because they can allege foreign policies, including that of the United States, as long as we engage in the diplomatic concert as an excuse. At present, in my opinion—and I recognize how readily opinion may be mistaken—thought and energy that should be directed by Chinese upon their own internal affairs are diverted largely to criticising and blaming foreigners. This is natural; we all love alibis and excuses. But the United States should, as far as it is concerned, abrogate all special privileges and one-sided relations so that the attention of the Chinese may centre upon improving their own conditions.

Another reason which has great weight with me in making me believe that our government should change its policy is that when a certain result is seen to be sure to come about sooner or later in any case, it is the part of good-sense to anticipate that result, and see to it that it comes about earlier, and with the least possible disturbance and ill-will. In any case, the present one-sided relations with China cannot continue indefinitely. I do not agree with those who think that they can be abrogated without some disturbance, and without some harm resulting to China itself. But with the growing development of national sentiment in

China, these evils and disturbances are in my opinion slight in comparison with those which will take place if things are allowed to drift until China of her own initiative and without negotiation with other nations denounces the existing treaties and arrangements.

The Problem of Turkey

During the early part of one's stay in Turkey, one is haunted by the feeling that there is a thin but impenetrable veil between his vision and the realities of the country. There is an almost physical impulsion to hunt for some slight rents that may serve as a peephole, as there is a physical irritation at not being able to find it. What lies open to the eye is confused, obscure, ambiguous, inconsistent. One cannot escape the idea that close-by there exists a vantage point from which the facts would assume order and significance. And the resulting exasperation is increased rather than diminished by the realization that perhaps there is no veil, no concealed meaning; that the uncertainty lies in the elements of the situation.

One day a Turkish friend remarked that life in Turkey since the great war had been very hard; that it was almost impossible for a person with enough education to be aware of what was going on not to be a pessimist; that he was doubtful, although himself a teacher, whether the extension of education under existing conditions was desirable since the only happy persons were the fishermen and peasants who did not know enough to take cognizance of anything but their immediate surroundings and acts. "We are living in a fog. In no respect do we know what is going to happen, any more than we know how to bring to pass the things we wish to have happen. It is hard living when everything around one is so obscure that one cannot see his road six paces in advance!"

I do not know that this conversation gives the complete explanation of the perplexity of a visitor. But it so fell in with the trend of additional knowledge and observations that it seemed to be much nearer the heart of the situation than are the cocksure as-

[First published in *New Republic* 41 (7 January 1925): 162–63.]

criptions of inexplicable and self-contradictory events to some definite policy on the part of those in control of Turkey's destiny. During the years of the war of independence the course of action was clear, once a few determined teachers like Mustapha Kemal had described and proclaimed it. To expel the invader, to abandon all ambitions which interfered with the unity and independence of Turkey, to assert, against every other nation, a l'outrance, the will of Turkey to be its own independent master in its own abode; such a course of action was as clear as it was urgent. But the achievement of this primary task brought to the fore all the elements of inner weakness and confusion, the heritage from the old absolutism of irresponsible religious and political power.

To the outsider accustomed to think of the war as now six years in the past, it comes as a shock to assist, as we have been doing the last few weeks, in celebrations of anniversaries of the events of the year 1922 which brought the three-and-a-half years' war-after-the-war to a close. And the reminder of the nearness of the war struggle, a struggle literally for existence carried on against seemingly hopeless odds, renders one aware that the war-psychology, which has been growing dim with us and which we are glad to forget, still hangs on in Turkey. Indeed, during the first of these two post-war years, until the second conference of Lausanne, it was not certain whether the war might not be renewed. Hence it seemed necessary for Turkey to keep alive enough of the war spirit to meet the threatening emergency. When we think how much longer than one year the suspicions, animosities and fears of the war-mind persisted among us, in spite of our infinitely greater remoteness from the scene of combat and destruction; when we think of the stupid and shameful things we did under the dominion of this hangover, we can perhaps begin to appreciate the state of mind which leads the Turks at present to do things which show both dislike of the foreigner and a short-sighted sense of their own interests.

Dread and dislike are always intensified by uncertainty and its accompanying impotency. The foreigner has much to answer for in Turkey, and this fact induces undiscriminating hostility to the foreigner as if he were a single collective entity, an antagonism shown in ways which are often more damaging to Turks than to those at whom they are directed. These acts are not so much the manifestations of a definite and consistent policy as they are expressions of an emotional condition that has nothing to do with that policy: as when the charge is brought against an American school that its buildings are painted blue and white—the Greek colors—or against a teacher in an American school that he spoke more highly of ancient Byzantine architecture in Constantinople than of later Turkish architecture—an appreciation which proves that he is dangerously pro-Greek! It is useless and harmful, I think, to seek for deeper motives behind such acts than such as actuated inflamed American patriots in the years immediately after the war.

Given a period of internal tranquility and such acts will cease as the emotions from which they spring subside. But the intrinsic uncertainty and obscurity to which they afford a momentary relief will not pass so readily. In certain respects, Turkey at present is more stable, both internally and externally, than any one of its Balkan neighbors. But the transformation of a military and theocratic despotism, whose interests required that its subjects be more barbarous than civilized, into a secular democratic state, a transformation undertaken in the midst of a terrible exhaustion following upon almost fifteen years of uninterrupted foreign wars, is no easy task.

Ever since the president of the new republic took up his seemingly hopeless task, he has been distinguished for a certain realistic facing of facts. In such speeches of his as I have been able to read in translations no note recurs so often as the warning against entertaining illusions. In a speech which he made recently at the anniversary of the expulsion of the Greeks from Brusa he said that much as the Turks had suffered from foreign foes, their greatest sufferings had been inflicted upon them from within and by their own rulers; and that the woes from which Turkey was now suffering were due to the fact that their ancient rulers had not been able or willing to lead their people into the society of civilized nations. In another recent speech, made at the laying of the corner-stone of a memorial to The Unknown Soldier on the ground of the final decisive battle of August, 1922, he said that difficult as was the struggle against the invading foe, that fight was much easier than the economic and social battle which must be won if Turkey was to become an integral part of the civilized world.

The two sayings define the problem of Turkey in its larger outlines. The Turkish state has been a military state in which the fighting spirit was stimulated and sustained by an unquestioned identification of the ambition of the ruler with the requirements of a blind religious faith. The power, the superiority, of the Ottoman Empire was one of arms, and its administration always relied upon the force of arms, fused with religious faith, to make good all its other defects. Now that the nation of Turkey has consigned the Ottoman Empire in both its political and theocratic phases to a grave from which there is no resurrection, it finds itself held back by the very traditions, military and theocratic, out of which it is struggling to escape. Is it any wonder that action is inconsistent, that tendencies are ambiguous, and that a fog hangs over the situation? No person of any intelligence expects such a problem to be resolved in the twinkling of an eye. But also no informed person has any doubt about the sincerity of those engaged in the struggle to effect the alteration. Their sincerity, one may say, is an accentuation of the problem; if they were not so sincere, their task would not be so hard. Of success or failure no mortal can speak with complacency, but I am sorry for those who have no inkling of the heroism of the effort that is being made.

The economic aspect of the problem is marked by the same inner perplexity. Turkey was long by turns the spoiled darling and the hapless victim of the European great powers. Money was loaned to her recklessly in hope of returns to come from concessions granted with equal recklessness. Turkey never had to face the questions of natural economy which every self-respecting independent nation has to deal with. Well might she exclaim that the way of the transgressor is made easy, while that of the repentant prodigal nation is lonely and hard. Owing to the constant quest of foreign nations for concessions, Turkey, in the person of its authorities, has a somewhat exaggerated idea of the value of its natural resources and has still a tendency to seek some magic source for wealth, an arbitrary protective tariff and the elimination of the foreigner from industry and commerce being much in favor just now. It professes, and sincerely I personally believe, a great desire for foreign aid both in technical skill and in capital. But its inexperience in economic matters and its too great experience of foreign wiles, combine to render it unwilling to meet the conditions under which alone it is possible to secure capital and skill. If this meant a mere postponement of industrial development, it would not be serious. But Turkey is in a severe economic crisis which almost threatens the disappearance of the middle class. Its two greatest immediate needs, schools and a competent and honest civil administration, will require a marked economic revival.

Silly as is the comparison of the problem of Turkey with that of China, it is impossible for one who has known something of both countries to abstain from making it. The quantitative disparity, the slight population of Turkey compared with that of China, is in some degree offset by the strategic position occupied by Turkey, as the bridge between Europe and Asia, and between northern Russian Europe and the south. Both have the same problem of transformation, a change which can be effected only from within however much it may be required by external relations. But Turkey has a military and religious tradition which China lacks, while China possesses skill in industry and trade which is lacking in Turkey. The military prowess of Turkey has made it possible for her to protect her independence in the final crisis as it was not possible for pacific China. But the struggle for economic development and for culture in art, science and philosophy may well prove more taxing for Turkey than for China. The ultimate ground for confidence is in the fact that the Turks have that intangible something which we call character. They have virility, sobriety of outlook and sincerity of purpose.

The handicap imposed upon them by the old régime is enormous. It is double: part of it is real in the heritage of ignorance and of lack of economic ability; part of it consists in the reputation which Turkey acquired and which, by foreign ignorance and by the design of interested foreign powers, leads other nations to deny to present-day Turkey a genuine change of spirit and aim. If refusal to admit the reality of the change persists the refusal may do much to prevent Turkey from receiving the assistance it needs to make the change effective and permanent. In that case the belief of liberal Turks that the most powerful enemies of the modernization of Turkey have been the professedly modern and democratic states of Europe, will receive another confirmation.

Church and State in Mexico

The events constituting the conflict of church and government in Mexico have been so fully reported in the press that there is little which a newcomer on the ground, like myself, can add. Politics and religion are the two subjects, in any case, which one cannot help approaching with a certain amount of parti pris. In this particular case one can receive about as many diverse accounts of the motives which explain the conduct of either side, and as many different prognostications as to the future, as the number of persons with whom one converses. However, there has gradually formed in my mind a certain deposit of impressions regarding the present situation and its probable movement, which I shall expose, with the understanding that it is simply a matter of certain net results which have emerged from the confusion and conflict of opinions, and not a claim to reveal any inner truths or hidden facts.

In the first place, the technical cause of the strike of the church is of greater importance than has been attached to it in most of the accounts which I have run across in the papers of the United States. On July 3, 1926, President Calles issued a series of regulations, giving effect, via the penal code, to the provisions of the constitution of 1917. Most of these rules were not only restatements, verbally exact, of the terms of the constitution, but they also related to accomplished facts, adding only definite penalties for cases of violation. Such accomplished facts included the dissolution of monastic orders; the denial of the right of incorporation or legal "personality" to religious bodies; the exclusion of all foreigners from the right to exercise religious functions and to teach religion in schools; the title in the state, of all properties of religious bodies (churches and objects of art, jewels, etc., in

[First published in *New Republic* 48 (25 August 1926): 9–10.]

them, as well as real estate); the limitation of all religious services to the interior of churches; the denial of the right to wear a
distinctive religious garb or emblems outside of churches; the denial to the clergy of the right to engage in politics, to comment
on political affairs, (also denied to religious periodicals), and the
complete laicizing of *primary* education, whether in public or
private schools.

This legislation, embodied as already stated in the organic law
of Carranza's time which put in legal form the achievements of
the revolution, and itself consummated the revolution of Juárez
in 1857, is obviously drastic and thorough. Equally obvious to
the eye of one acquainted with history, the constitution marked
a stadium in the struggle of church and state which has been
going on for several centuries in all modern nations, and which
has ended in all European states in the definite subordination of
the church to civil authority. What is distinctive in the Mexican
laws is the extreme thoroughness with which anti-clerical legislation has been carried out. Upon this legislation itself I do not
propose to comment; one's attitude toward it will depend upon
one's social and political philosophy, and one's view of the nature of religion, and its connection with organized political life.
The usual defense of its unusually drastic character, as compared
with that of even most other anti-clerical legislation, is of course
the monopolistic character of the past history of the church, its
almost universal association with anti-republican tendencies,
and the hold of the priests upon the ignorant rural Indian population, by which was directed its intellectual, political and economic as well as its religious activity, without any corresponding
contribution to education or well-being. To this has to be added,
the distinct anti-foreign phase of the nationalistic side of the revolution; the claim is made that the exploitation of the natives by
the clergy, economic and political, has been greatly increased and
exasperated by the presence of foreign bishops and priests, especially Spanish and Italian. This fact, or alleged fact, has a bearing, as will be indicated shortly, upon the rules and penalties
which are the immediate cause of the present clerical strike.

The constitution also contained a provision, which had not
however been put into effect, that all priests and preachers
should register, stating the particular church building with
which their ministrations were connected, and that the registra-

tion should be vouched for by ten citizens of the locality. The regulations of July 3 set August 1 as the date by which this registration should be accomplished, assigning heavy penalties for clergy who should officiate after that date without having registered. Technically the abandonment by the clergy of all religious rites and offices, including preaching and the sacraments, turns upon this one regulation. The clergy were forbidden from above to register; and, as the method by which they would then be protected from civil penalties for failure to register, were authorized to suspend all offices.

When one inquires into the reasons and motives for this attitude on the part of the archbishops, one plunges into the arena of rumor, not to say gossip. The reason officially assigned is that this move, coming after all the other restrictions put upon the church, was of so definitely an anti-religious nature as to render it impossible for the church to exercise its God-given functions; that the regulations in their totality were contrary to divine and "natural" law, and hence null. Rumors of an extreme character are to the effect that it was hoped to create the impression that the state had itself closed the churches, thereby arousing a popular reaction which would weaken if not overthrow the government; the more moderate theory is that it was intended to create a popular reaction which would demand and secure from the federal congress and the state legislative bodies an amendment of the constitution. If the first expectation was entertained events have definitely negated it; upon this score, the government has won a complete victory; barring a few sporadic incidents complete order has been obtained, and the position of the government of President Calles was never stronger, perhaps never so strong. The more moderate expectation takes us into the region of prophecy; I can only register my impression that it is extremely unlikely to be fulfilled.

The position of the government is simple. The provision for registration is in the constitution; hence the resistance of the clergy is but another manifestation that the church still regards itself as superior to civil law. The registration is held to be a necessary consequence of the nationalization of ecclesiastical properties. Granted this premise, the state must know who is responsible for the care and preservation of the buildings and their treasures. Furthermore such registration is the only means by which clergy of foreign birth can be prevented from returning and resuming their activities. My own guess is this anti-foreign bias, so marked in all revolutionary "backward" countries, is the factor which counts most. On the surface there is now a complete deadlock; there are rumors of an adjustment already on foot, but they spread one day to be denied the next. To one accustomed to the legalistic procedures of the Anglo-Saxon world, it seems as if the issue could be settled and church offices resumed only by a complete surrender on one side or the other. But here in Mexico some acquainted with the native psychology say that it will be settled rather by a gradual filtration of parish priests. There are already a few cases of individual submission to the law.

There has been a schismatic movement to form a Mexican Catholic church in contradistinction to the Roman Catholic church. So far it is largely abortive. But state control of church properties gives the government some leverage. The church cannot educate the people to do without its services; there are some good reasons for thinking that the pressure of the mass of the faithful will be directed toward ensuring the resumption of the services of the church rather than toward any change of the constitution. There is no organized public opinion in Mexico; and personal opinion as to the attitude of the mass of inert and ignorant peasants varies with the attitude of the one who gives the judgment. But the church can hardly escape paying the penalty for the continued ignorance and lack of initiative which it has tolerated if not cultivated. In short, such popular organization as exists is with the government and not with the church; and this fact, as far as it goes, is the sole basis for predicting the future.

The regulations in question were issued by the President. This fact is eloquent as to political conditions. Congress even when in session does not make the important laws. It authorizes the President to issue what are in effect decrees putting the constitution into effect in this and that respect. Mexico is a republic, but effective democratic government is largely in the future. There is something humorous in the attitude of those, among whom are many foreigners including American fellow-countrymen, who sigh for the "strong-man" government of Díaz. There is a strong-man government in existence, but it operates mostly against foreign interests instead of in their behalf, as was the case with

Díaz. The only well organized force in the country, outside of the army, is the labor unions, and they are officially behind the government; the demonstration and parade of August 1 proved that fact. The power of the army in politics has been much curbed, and even if there were generals willing to advance their own prospects by rebelling against the government, which is the usual method of starting revolutions, they are, by common consent, practically powerless as long as the embargo of the United States against arms remains in force.

But in my opinion "liberals" in other countries can hardly appeal to existing democratic liberalism in Mexico in support of the policy of the government. The fact of the case is that the revolution in Mexico is not completed. There is not a single manifesto which does not refer to the Principles of the Revolution; it is from the standpoint of completing the revolution that events in Mexico must be judged, not from that of legalities and methods of countries where political and social institutions are stabilized. This fact accounts for the great diversity of judgment on the present crisis which one finds among intelligent people. If upon the whole they think the revolution is a good thing for Mexico, they support the government's side though regretting the harshness with which some of its measures have been executed. If they dislike the revolution, they are quite sure that the present struggle originated from anti-religious rather than political motives. Under these circumstances, one with only a short and superficial acquaintance with Mexican conditions is perhaps entitled to fall back on general historical knowledge, and see in the conflict a belated chapter in the secular struggle of church and state for superior political authority, complicated, as it has so often been in the past, with anti-foreign sentiment. From this standpoint, one may also prophesy on general historic grounds, not on the basis of knowledge of local conditions, what the outcome will be, the victory of the national state. Again, following history, the conclusion would be that Catholics as a whole will in the end, though the end may be remote in Mexico, be better off than when they had too easy and too monopolistic a possession of the field.

Mexico's Educational Renaissance

Mexicans interested in education are given to calling attention to the fact that President Calles began his career as a rural school teacher. In one of his earlier political announcements he summed up his program in two policies: economic liberation, and the development of public education. Most foreign residents are perforce familiar with the operations of the first factor in the program—which they usually call Bolshevism; not many have taken the trouble to acquaint themselves with the second.

At the outset, we may dispose of the formal features of the situation. The schools are of three categories: federal, state and municipal. The latter are decreasing, being taken over by the states, while federal activity is growing more rapidly than state; moreover, the figures regarding the latter are well kept and accessible, while statistics for state schools are often not organized, nor easily attainable. Elementary education covers six years, of which the first four are, legally, compulsory. Actually about four children out of ten of the school population are in public schools. There are no statistics for private schools, but, before the closing of the Catholic institutions it is a fair guess that about one-half of the children were in some school.

In the federal district, the government is spending four times as much as was spent in the heyday of the Díaz régime; in some of the larger towns, there are not as yet, owing to the destructions of the revolutionary period, as many state and municipal schools as in 1910. Five open-air schools have been started in Mexico City and suburbs during the present year, where 800 to 1,000 children are cared for at an expense for the plant of from ten to twenty thousand dollars. This type of school, the creation

[First published in *New Republic* 48 (22 September 1926): 116–18.]

of the present school administration, under Doctor Puig, is artistic, hygienic and well adapted to the climate, and the low expense will make possible the provision of accommodation for all children of required school age in the federal district in a short time.

Until recently there was no secondary education in Mexico excepting the schools which prepared for the university; four high schools have been opened recently and are crowded. There is also a federal normal school, housed and equipped in a way equal to any in the world, with five thousand pupils of both sexes, including children in the practice school. A regional normal school for each state is planned. The flourishing National University has ten thousand students, a large number being women; its Rector, Doctor Pruneda, is much interested in exchange of students and teachers, and during a visit to the United States in the coming autumn will arrange for such exchanges with our own country, a consummation which is to be hoped for. As it is, the University maintains, under the direction of Doctor Montaño, a truly unique summer school for North Americans (one learns in a Spanish-American country to temper the arrogance of our ordinary "American"), attended during the past summer by more than three hundred persons, mainly teachers, from the United States.

The most interesting as well as the most important educational development is, however, the rural schools: which means, of course, those for native Indians. This is the cherished preoccupation of the present régime; it signifies a revolution rather than renaissance. It is not only a revolution for Mexico, but in some respects one of the most important social experiments undertaken anywhere in the world. For it marks a deliberate and systematic attempt to incorporate in the social body the Indians who form 80 percent of the total population. Previous to the revolution, this numerically preponderant element was not only neglected, but despised. Those who attack the revolution complacently ignore the fact that it was the inevitable outcome of this policy of contemptuous disregard for the mass of the people, a disregard which affected every phase of life: educational, for example, since the Díaz administration did not establish a single rural school for Indians. In spite of the difficulty in securing teachers, there are now 2,600 such schools, 1,000 of which were opened during the last year, which it is hoped to raise to 2,000 during the coming year. It is estimated that if ten years of tranquility are secured, there will be schools for the entire school population, and illiteracy, as far as the new generation is concerned, will be wiped out.

This educational revolution not only represents an effort to incorporate the indigenous population into the social life and intellectual culture of Mexico as a whole, but it is also an indispensable means of political integration for the country. Nothing in Mexico can be understood without bearing in mind that until a few years ago the Indians were economically enslaved, intellectually disinherited and politically eliminated. Even the present church-state crisis roots, at many points, in this fact. Because of the absence of rural schools, the only common force which touched the life of all the people was the church; and it is putting it moderately to say that the influence of the clergy did not make for social and political integration. The fact that the country priests have used their enormous influence over the souls of their parishes to oppose the establishment of rural schools has been at least one factor in causing the drastic decree for the laicizing of all primary schools.

The difficulties in creating a moral and political entity out of Mexico are so enormous that they often seem insuperable; one most readily pictures the general state of the country by thinking of early colonial days in the United States, with a comparatively small number of settlements of a high civilization surrounded by Indian peoples with whom they have but superficial contact. The fact that the Mexican Indians have a settled agricultural life, a much higher culture and greater resistance than our own Indians but increases the difficulty of the situation. Add to this fact that the Indians are anything but homogeneous among themselves, divided into some thirty different tribes, intensely self-centred, jealous of their autonomy, prizing an isolation which is accentuated by geographical conditions, and we begin to have a faint idea of the problem which the revolutionary government is facing as systematically as all previous régimes dodged it. It is evidence of the still superficial character of our democratic ideas that the average foreign resident in Mexico, including those from the United States, assumes that the problem is incapable of solution, and that the only way out is "strong" oligarchical rule. One might think that the gallant attempt of the revolutionary government would win recognition if but for its gallantry, even from those who think the cause is doomed, but the sporting instinct of the average Anglo-Saxon (happily there are exceptions) appears to be as specialized as is his democratic creed.

Much more interesting than statistics are the spirit and aims which animate these rural schools. Mr. Saenz, the first subsecretary of education (who once taught in the Lincoln School in New York), stated in a lecture recently at the University of Chicago that "nowhere have I seen better examples of a socialized school than in some of these rural schools in Mexico." I am willing to go further and say that there is no educational movement in the world which exhibits more of the spirit of intimate union of school activities with those of the community than is found in this Mexican development. I have long had a pet idea that "backward" countries have a great chance educationally; that when they once start in the school-road they are less hampered by tradition and institutionalism than are countries where schools are held by customs which have hardened through the years. But I have to confess that I have never found much evidence in support of this belief that new countries, educationally new, can start afresh, with the most enlightened theories and practices of the most educationally advanced countries. The spirit and aims of Indian rural schools as well as of the Normal School of Mexico revived my faith.

Much of the actual work is, it goes without saying, crude, as crude as are the conditions under which it is done. But it is the crudeness of vitality, of growth, not of smug conventions. Whether or not it is the uprooting effect of long continued revolutions I do not know; but along with the bad effects of so many and so rapid social dislocations, there is evident everywhere a marked spirit of experimentation, a willingness "to try anything once," and most things more than once. Given the good start which now exists, the great need is continuity of policy, and it is seriously to be hoped that changes of political administration will not lead to abrupt shifts of educational plan.

Neither as to buildings, course of study nor preparation of teachers has the mistake of over-elaborateness been made. Of the thousand federal rural schools opened during the last year almost every one was furnished without cost to the nation by the people of the locality, mainly by the parents who wanted their children to have the opportunities at present denied them. To judge from those which I saw in the state of Tlaxcala, they are mainly old buildings, sometimes churches, sometimes houses, which had been ruined and were restored for school use. In an Indian village not far from Mexico City, the six grades were housed in six different adobe dwelling-houses offered by the parents in lieu of any available building. Every school has a garden attached, and it is characteristic of the aesthetic temperament of the Indian that although the vegetable section may be neglected, the flower garden is sure to be gay and well cared for.

The simplicity of the buildings and the genial climate make for a simple curriculum: reading, writing and, when necessary, the speaking of Spanish as a matter of course; some "figuring," local geography, national history with emphasis upon the heroes of Independence and the Revolution, and then for the remainder, industrial education, chiefly agricultural, and such home industries, weaving, pottery, etc., as are characteristic of the neighborhood. (It is part of the general "socialistic" policy of the present government to foster the development of "small industries," carried on in the home, and cooperatively managed, as an offset to the invasion of large, capitalistic and therefore for the most part foreign industries.) In many places there is much attention to music and to design in the plastic arts, for both of which things the Indians display a marked genius. As a rule, if what we saw may be depended upon as evidence, the designs in the small rural schools were much better, even though the work was crude, than in the industrial schools of the city, where department store art has made a lamentable invasion. If the rural schools can succeed in preserving the native arts, aesthetic traditions and patterns, protecting them from the influence of machine-made industry, they will in that respect alone render a great service to civilization. Fortunately the influence of Vasconcelos, the former minister of education, and of Doctor Gamio, the distinguished anthropologist, was strongly employed for the maintenance of the indigenous arts and crafts. At the present time the National University has a woman, herself a cultivated musician, constantly occupied in traveling throughout the country collecting the folk-songs, words and music, in which Mexico is rich almost without parallel in contemporary countries.

As for instruction, the leading idea is that any teacher is better than none, provided there is a native man or woman who can read and write and is devoted. For the most part, they receive their professional instruction after they begin teaching. One of the most interesting features of teacher training is the "cultural missions." The "missionaries" (this is their title) go to some country town, gather the rural teachers of the immediate district, and for three weeks the staff gives intensive instruction. The work is not theoretical pedagogy. There is always an instructor in physical training (almost every school in Mexico, no matter how remote, now has a playground and a basketball field). A social worker is present, usually a woman, who gives instruction in hygiene, first aid, vaccination, and the rudiments of the care of children, etc. There are also a teacher of chorus singing, a specialist in hand industries, instructed to employ as far as possible local materials, and finally, a specialist in school organization and methods of teaching. The task of the latter is, however, chiefly to coordinate the academic teaching of the schools with agricultural and manual industries.

During the last school year, the missionaries worked in six states and next year's budget carries an increase of half a million pesos for extension of the work. At the same time, the federal bureau is sending small libraries as fast as possible to all schools, and the aim is to make each one the centre of a new life for its neighborhood, intellectual, recreational and economic. Night schools are held in each building, to which come young men and women who are to work during the day; their eagerness to learn is symbolized in the fact that they walk miles to reach the place of instruction, each one bringing a candle by whose glimmering light the studying is done. And the Indian teachers work practically all day and then again in the evening for a wage of four pesos a day.

The ruling educational catch-word is escuela de acción. It is a common complaint that the graduates of the former schools have marvelous memories, but no initiative and little independent responsibility. This fact has been cited to me scores of times as a convincing indication of the limits of the mentality of the Mexican. I am sceptical in advance of all such psychological generalizations; as long as pupils were dealing with traditional studies in the traditional way, the material was so isolated from their experience that memory was their sole reliance. Now that "activity"—not always to be sure with adequate organization or intellectual content—is the guiding principle, and the "project method" is all but officially adopted as the basis of the school program, there is sure to be a change. Practice falls short of ideals, and the program is much better executed in some places than in others. But I believe that the brightest spot in the Mexico of today is its educational activity. There is vitality, energy, sacrificial devotion, the desire to put into operation what is best approved in contemporary theory, and above all, the will to use whatever is at hand.

We in the United States who have pursued such a different policy with our Indian population are under an obligation to understand and to sympathize. The policy of incorporating the Indians into modern life is of such extraordinary difficulty, its execution demands so much time, peace and tranquility, that any action on our part which puts added obstacles in its way is simply criminal. One can sympathize with foreigners in Mexico who find that their legal rights are not assured; yet from the standpoint of business in the long run as well as from that of human development, vested legalities are secondary to the creation of an integrated people. Foreign interference in any and every form means immediate increased instability and this unsettlement means in turn the prolongation of those internal divisions which have been the curse of Mexico; it means a deliberate cultivation of all seeds of turbulence, confusion and chaos.

From a Mexican Notebook

It is possible that little things, things apparently insignificant, will count for more in the future of Mexico than sensational affairs which newspapers have headlined. During the early days of August, 1926, when excitement was at its height, the walls of Mexico blossomed out with posters, large and small, instructing the population to wash their hands before eating. They were issued by the bureau of propaganda of the Department of Public Health. They are one symptom among many of an intensive and systematic campaign to improve the physical and hygienic habits of the people. The rector of the University, himself a physician, lectures regularly to the inspectors of primary schools in the federal district upon social hygiene. Home-visitors are already at work in connection with the schools, and the federal normal school has a two years' course to train these go-betweens, whose duties are largely centred upon improving conditions of health. School medical inspection has been instituted. City schools are being provided with open-air swimming pools. Old residents say that one of the most striking changes is in the interest in outdoor sports. Before the revolution the common people were hardly permitted to enter Chapultepec Park, which is certainly one of the most beautiful of the world; now it has many children's playgrounds which are in constant use. During this autumn, Olympic games for Central America will be held in Mexico City.

An interesting manifestation of transitional movements is the growth of "new thought." There is in Mexico City a centre of the Impersonal Life. For the benefit of those as ignorant as I was, it may be said that the movement originated in a book with that title published in Akron, O. Whether it reached Mexico along with automobile tires I do not know. But purely by means of a

[First published in *New Republic* 48 (20 October 1926): 239–41.]

translation—of which over twenty thousand copies have now been sold—it made its way, and there is now a centre of the faith with four thousand adherents, holding two meetings a week. The members have come mostly from the educated classes, who have deserted the church, and have now filled the religious void with "new thought." My statement in answer to a question that I had never happened to hear of the book or the movement in the United States was received with obvious scepticism. The inquirer, himself a physician, was prepared to hear that I was the author of the book. The bookstores are filled with translations of different types of occult literature. Probably more copies of Orison Swett Marden than of any other American author are sold in Mexico—except Nick Carter. One of the two leading dailies of Mexico City recently published an article on North American culture in which after a reference to Emerson it was pointed out that Marden's is today *the* philosophy of the United States.

Mexico is the land of contradictions. This fact, so baffling that it keeps the visitor in an unrelieved state of foggy confusion, is at the same time the most natural of all its phenomena. The newest and the oldest exist side by side without mixing and also inextricably combined. The result is the Mexico of today; if I seek a single adjective by which to describe it, "incredible" is the word that comes to mind. Fifteen years ago farm labor was in a state of complete serfdom, in fact a slavery as effective as that of Negroes in the United States before the Civil War. Industrial labor was unorganized and oppressed. Today Mexico has, on the statute books, the most advanced labor legislation of any contemporary state; and the "syndicates" are the greatest single power in the land. The streets blaze forth the signs of the offices of the different unions more prominently than in any place I have ever visited. Five years ago the marchers in a May Day procession in Mexico City could be counted in the hundreds; now they amount to fifty or sixty thousand.

Human life is cheap; men with full cartridge belts and revolvers are seen everywhere on the street and in trains. A few weeks ago several politicians were shot at crowded mid-day in the street which is Mexico's union of Broadway and Fifth Avenue. But any accident in a mine must be reported at once to the government bureau in Mexico City, and if it is serious enough to result in any miners being taken to the hospital, word of it must be telegraphed. The coexistence of customs that antedate the coming of the Spaniards, that express early colonial institutions, and that mark the most radical of contemporary movements, intellectual and economic, accounts for the totally contradictory statements about every phase of Mexican life with which the visitor is flooded; it makes impossible any generalization except that regarding the combination of the most stiff-necked conservatism and the most unrestrained and radical experimentalism.

One of the picturesque elements of contemporary Mexican life is the religious life of the natives, where Catholic rites have been superimposed upon pre-conquest creeds and cults. A resident in the state of Oaxaca told me of seeing an altar on the top of a mountain to the god of rain where, just before the coming of the rainy season, pilgrims poured the blood of turkeys upon the ground and offered the breasts on the altar. These same peasants pour an offering of soup upon the newly plowed grounds just before planting, and make a similar offering after the harvest is gathered. And Oaxaca is not the most primitive state of Mexico. A professor in the University in Mexico City tells of being invited to the opening of a rural school in the mountains not far from Mexico City. In response to inquiries, the mayor, an Indian, informed him that he was a socialist and was also taking part in the ceremony of the adoration of the Virgin which was going on. Asked for an explanation of the seeming anomaly, the village chief replied that he was a socialist because the government had made the village a Pueblo—that is, granted it self-government—while he was adoring the Virgin because the charter arrived on the saint's day. A not dissimilar story concerns the revival of worship of the old god of rain after a drought, where the rites were terminated with the advice of the old idol to purchase a new robe for the Virgin in the parish church. Priests are nowhere as numerous as are churches, and in many remote districts the churches are in the charge of locally elected major-domos, who conduct services except during the annual or semi-annual visit of a priest.

Some of the most beautiful pottery of the country is made in an Indian village of a few thousand inhabitants about ten miles out of Guadalajara. The entire family works together in the industry, squatting on the ground for the shaping and painting; the methods are those of centuries ago; not even a potter's wheel is used. The patterns, while not identical with the primitive, are genuinely indigenous, observing a traditional type with spontaneous individual inventions. The school authorities had the sense to remove formal instruction in drawing from the schools when they found the taught designs were being copied. But halfway between this town and Guadalajara there is another pottery centre where the stores are filled—together with some specimens of Tonalá work—with all the monstrosities of commercialized European and North American "art." Unfortunately, but naturally, in the minds of the well-to-do, the native pottery with its extraordinarily beautiful rhythms of pattern and color is associated with the life of the peons; conspicuous consumption favors the use of artistic monstrosities. With the rise of the standard of living among the common people, it will be increasingly difficult to maintain the native arts. Fortunately enlightened educators, including the section of the federal department of education for indigenous culture, are working against the tide; whether with success remains to be determined.

Among the contradictions of Mexico is the union of anti-foreign, and anti-American, feeling with the disposition to imitate foreign things and methods, especially those of the United States. In some sense, the "Americanization" of the country appears to be an inevitable process, both for good and for evil. The Ford car and the movie are already working a revolution. English is practically the only foreign language taught in the schools, including even the national military school. The large emigration from Mexico into the United States is having a reflex effect. Increasing numbers of Mexican youth are sent to the United States for their schooling. In regard to large classes of goods, those from the United States control the markets, even in remote districts, and pervasively affect the habits of the people.

The close contact of the most industrially advanced country of the world with an industrially backward country but one possessed of enormous natural resources, the contact of a people having an industrialized, Anglo-Saxon psychology with a people of Latin psychology (in so far as it is not pre-colonial) is charged with high explosives. But the most definite impression of the many confused and uncertain impressions I carry away is that slow permeation is so inevitable, under existing conditions of industry, commerce, travel and other means of distributing goods and ideas, that its great enemies are those who, impatient for immediate profit and judging affairs only from the standpoint of their own economic and legal psychology, would hasten the process. Their attitude and operations in the past are the chief cause of the deliberate efforts of the revolutionary government to handicap the economic invasion of the United States. Every activity on their part which looks even remotely and indirectly toward our intervention or even interference, only delays the natural process. It also increases, under the title of "stabilizing Mexican conditions," the inherent instability of the country. An ironical element of the situation is that those business interests which at home clamor for the free play of "natural" economic law and forces and which deplore governmental action, in Mexico distrust this factor and clamor for political and diplomatic action.

Finally, while one hears denunciation of the Mexican government from American business men, especially those engaged in mining and oil, what they say about Mexican "bolshevism" is mild in comparison with their language about the activity—or inactivity—of our own State Department. Judging from their attitude, those in our country who are interested in maintaining good relations between the two countries have more cause for gratitude to our own government than they are aware of.

Reviews

Practical Democracy

The Phantom Public, by Walter Lippmann.
New York: Harcourt, Brace and Co., 1925.
205 pages. $2.

Walter Lippmann has followed his analysis of Public Opinion with a shorter and, if possible, even more pregnant, essay on The Public itself—the being or creature which forms and voices the opinion which is said to govern the state. His estimate of this being is condensed in his title: *The Phantom Public*. Yet, in the end, it appears that it is the public of democratic theorists which is the phantom, and that Mr. Lippmann believes there is a public, or rather many publics, which, although volatile, elusive, ignorant and shy may, by appropriate means be caught, precipitated, formed and informed, and be induced occasionally to appear—in public, one might say. And he believes that when properly treated and re-educated, these publics may with some considerable degree of efficacy and profit intervene in settling political questions, that is, in the conduct of government. Hence, while one might cite passages which, if divorced from their context, would give the impression that Mr. Lippmann was permanently "off" democracy, Mr. Lippmann's essay is in reality a statement of faith in a pruned and temperate democratic theory, and a presentation of methods by which a reasonable conception of democracy can be made to work, not absolutely, but at least better than democracy works under an exaggerated and undisciplined notion of the public and its powers.

Thus, to my own mind at least, his contribution is constructive. The measure of the extent to which the romantic notion of democracy is tempered in his account is that, even under much improved conditions, the public is not to govern but is to intervene, and intervene not continuously, but at critical junctures. Nevertheless, I can imagine a book similar to that of Mr. Lippmann being written at a time when the general atmosphere

[First published in *New Republic* 45 (2 December 1925): 52–54.]

was not one of disenchantment, of fear of humbuggery, of protest against pretentiousness, of being over-fed with indigestible issues, which would be taken as pre-eminently a positive contribution to the workings of democratic forms of government. In short, the book expresses a revolt not against democracy but against a theory of democracy which, to paraphrase a quotation from Bentham at the close of the book, has distracted the understanding and inflamed the passions, and thereby enormously increased the difficulties of democratic government. For to be workable democracy demands allayed passions and clarified understanding.

The book is clear, extraordinarily so considering the fundamental and controverted issues it raises. Even if a summary of its argument were called for, Mr. Lippmann has already provided one covering its main points, which is better than any this reviewer could furnish. After stating certain tests by which public opinion might be guided in performing the function he assigns to it, he goes on to say that while he does not set great store by these especial tests, he does attach great importance to the *nature* of these tests, since that depends upon underlying principles. The negative aspects of these tests come first; and in them are resumed his criticisms of the enthusiastic, unchastened democratic theory. Executive action is not for the public. The intrinsic merits of a question are not for it. The intellectual anticipation of a problem, its analysis and solution, are not for the public. The specific technical, intimate criteria required in the handling of a question are not for the public. The development of the reasons for these conclusions and a statement of what is left for the public to do in such a situation take up the first two-thirds of the book.

The argument turns essentially upon a distinction between the few insiders and the many outsiders, the insiders being the active forces, the outsiders being spectators, bystanders. "The actual governing is made up of a multitude of arrangements on specific questions by particular individuals." Governing not only is so made but it must be. Things are not done in general, they are done by somebody in particular. The things to be done in government are largely technical and professional. They are sufficiently complex so that they have to be the main business of some persons. The modern state is so large that the decisions made and the executions initiated are necessarily remote from the mass of citizens; modern society is not only not visible, but it is not intelligible continuously and as a whole. And, even occasionally, most of its special problems are not to be grasped by the outsider, who after all has his own life to lead, his own personal and domestic problems to deal with. Even in the city-state of Aristotle's time it was a problem how the gap between the limited capacities of the citizen and the complexity of his environment was to be bridged. The answer of Aristotle "that the community must be kept simple and small" is no longer possible of realization—nor, Mr. Lippmann might well have added, is the other part of Aristotle's solution, namely, that effective citizenship be restricted to men of leisure. The older democratic dogma has broken down just because it assumed an omnicompetent citizen and the limitless capacity of public opinion. The extent of the failure of that doctrine is seen in the fact that in the last thirty years the ratio of the popular to the eligible vote has declined from eight out of ten to five out of ten.

The contrast often drawn between the efficiency of private action in business and the laxity and inertia of governmental action is not in truth a contrast between public and private enterprises, but between "men doing specific things and men attempting to command general results." The latter is in reality impossible; there is not enough unity in society; there is not enough common knowledge; and even if there were, action in general is nonsense. The pretense of a common mind and general action in behalf of things at large has only bred fictions, and these fictions have increased confusion, have put a premium on deceptions and propaganda. "The making of a general will out of a multitude of general wishes is not a Hegelian mystery, but an art well known to leaders, politicians and steering committees. It consists essentially in the use of symbols which assemble emotions after they have been detached from their ideas." The outcome of course is that action is as much determined in private by a few insiders as ever it was. But falsification has come in; acting for ends of their own, they claim to be the agents of a public will and to have public support and sanction, and to get the latter as a working force, they bamboozle the public.

The growth of communities in size and complexity has compelled organization on a vast scale. The effect has been "to concentrate decision in central governments, in distant executive offices, in caucuses and in steering committees." Thus upon one side are those who actually make decisions but can cover up the fact that they make them, what they are, and how they are made, and pretend to be giving effect only to some popular mandate: at the other extreme, there is the politically confused, uncertain, more or less futile and discouraged electorate. "The lengthening of the interval between conduct and experience, between cause and effect, has nurtured a cult of self-expression in which each thinker thinks about his own thoughts and has subtle feelings about his feelings. That he does not in consequence deeply affect the course of affairs is not surprising."

The positive function of the public is, then, to intervene occasionally upon the work of the insiders, by taking the part of some of the insiders against others, to judge coarse and overt acts, and to learn to throw its weight to this or the other inside group by using some phases of external action as samples. To accomplish its task the public needs criteria; these are framed with the intent that the public may discriminate between the group whose policies genuinely further the public interest and those who are making use of the public to promote private ends. The essential point in arriving at this distinction is to find out which of the inside parties is least willing to submit its claims to open inquiry and least willing to abide by the result of adequate publicity. For the path of reason is the path of willingness to follow some regular rule; lacking insight into the substance of rationality in different proposals, the public may at least judge of its form, its method and spirit. Unwillingness to submit a case to inquiry is a sure sign of aversion to the regularity of reason and law.

This is only a summary and is dry, while Mr. Lippmann's full discussion, although abbreviated, is juicy. But I hope it may serve to indicate the spirit of the restrictions which Mr. Lippmann would have the public observe; observe, because they lie in the nature of the case: namely, the specific and complex nature of the problems; the remoteness of the public, and the preoccupation of its units with their own work and amusements. To the summary should be added, to avoid misconception, that Mr. Lippmann means by "insiders" something more than *political* insiders; more than governmental administrators and more than managers of machines. For they in many respects are outsiders. In industrial and economic questions it is, I take it, the active industrial leaders, whether capitalists or labor leaders, who are the insiders, and so on. Thus in effect Mr. Lippmann's argument is a powerful plea, from a new angle of approach, for decentralization in governmental affairs; a plea for recognition that actual government, whether or no we like it, must be carried on by nonpolitical agencies, by organs which we do not conventionally regard as having to do with government.

In spite of references to the decline of the activity of the electorate, the real import of Mr. Lippmann's criticism is, I suppose, that the electorate still attempts altogether too much; in the language of the older laissez-faire school, it is given to meddling.

One is struck, it may be noted in passing, by the fact that Mr. Lippmann makes no reference to the theories which would organize different social activities functionally, by occupational activities and interests. Probably the reference involved too much of an excursion into remote and speculative matters to tempt him. But it is difficult to see how even occasional intervening action of the general public is to be made effective in the ways which he postulates until the group activities upon which it is to operate are better organized and more open to recognition, more exposed to that "identification of the partisan" and his purposes which is the aim of democratic technique. It is at least arguable that Mr. Lippmann's conception cannot be made workable without something that approximates a "guild" or "soviet"—please note I do not say Bolshevist—organization.

It may be doubted whether Mr. Lippmann's criticisms are not aimed in some degree at a man of straw. I would not say that no one has ever held the theory of democracy which he assumes to be the orthodox theory. But it is safe to say that such notions come for the most part after the fact; they are, in current cant, "rationalizations" of an accomplished fact. To borrow the language of James Harvey Robinson, democracy did not emerge as the realization of an ideal, good or bad. What is called popular government is rather the consequence of a large and varied number of particular happenings. It was Carlyle, no friend of democracy, who said that given the printing-press, democracy was inevitable.

It is open to doubt whether the spokesmen of democracy ever

conceived its functions very differently from Mr. Lippmann's thought of them. To be the judge and the umpire in last resort, to be able to compel submission of important issues to popular judgment, to force political governors to appear now and then on trial before their constituents so as to give a reckoning of their stewardship; such, I think, were the not immoderate pretensions in the main of the men who actually forwarded the democratic movement in government.

That the difficulties in the way of intelligent performance of even such restricted tasks have immensely increased in later days, there can be no doubt. And this change makes necessary just such reconsiderations as Mr. Lippmann gives us. But it also renders his revision, when stripped of the logical irrelevance of Mr. Lippmann's obvious dislike of some of the recent misguided activities of the public—exemplified in prohibition and in the legislation of Tennessee—a contribution to the technique of democratic government rather than a far-reaching criticism of it. It would be enlightening, as well as interesting, to get from Mr. Lippmann's pen a detailed analysis of the relation of prohibitory legislation to public opinion and popular voting. A discussion of the suitability of the affair for popular decision would clarify the whole subject. Is the objection one to the national public concerning itself with the issue at all, or is it to the kind of action taken? Presumably the former, since if it were the latter, the obvious recourse is continued appeal to democratic practice to modify its prior action. But if the former, then it would be interesting to know what protection there is, on any theory, against extreme and sweeping action on the part of those in power when they feel strongly on any question. Certainly, sumptuary legislation is not an invention of democratic government; and it is nonpolitical features of modern society, such things as rapid and complex intercommunication by railways and newspapers which makes possible the present extensive mode of sumptuary legislation. Certainly Mr. Lippmann would be the last to trust to precepts and exhortation to governors to behave themselves to give protection from unwise legislation. But what is the way out? I do not see that the problem is more relevant to democratic government than to any other form. If it is now more acute, it is The Great Society which makes it so.

Granting the unwisdom of, say, prohibition or legislation

about the teaching of science, it is hardly credible that faith in the omnipotence of the voter, in the existence of infallible public opinion and in the divine right of the majority has much to do with the matter. Not a particular theory of democracy, but dislike of the liquor traffic animated the prohibitionists, a dislike entertained from one point of view by moralists who regard cards, drinking and dancing as inventions of the devil; from another point of view by those whose deity is thrift or wealth, by large employers of labor, and by those who dreaded the political power of the saloon—and from many other points of view as well. And it is ardent theological conviction, of a kind, that animates those who pass anti-evolutionary legislation.

If it be said that democratic institutions give the publics in question their opportunity to pass the laws, the reply is that the statement is true, but its implications take an accident for the essence. The Catholic Church is hardly a democratic body, but Darwin is on the Index; and if the Church were in complete control of schools, its action would not be less extreme than that of Tennessee fundamentalists. For those who think that the divine right which once belonged to ecclesiastics, and was then inherited by kings, has descended upon the populace, it is an undoubted gain to be taught that democracy is not automatic protection against abuse of power. But in any case the trouble seems to spring from stupidity, intolerance, bullheadedness and bad education, whether these traits decorate a monarch, ornament an oligarchy or supply the moral insignia of the populace.

I do not for a moment suppose that these remarks militate against the great value of Mr. Lippmann's discussion. But perhaps they suggest the need of further analysis, which should take account primarily of the inherent problems and dangers the Great Society has brought with it, with respect to which the weakness of democracy seems symptomatic rather than causal. They suggest that helpful as may be the improvement of the present technique by such criteria as Mr. Lippmann indicates, the further organization of society itself is the only sure road out. They suggest also the need of further discussion of publicity in relation to the public. The ethical improvement of the press would still come far short of meeting the question. The ultimate question is scientific and artistic: the question of making the press a continuous, systematic and effective revelation of social movements, including the desires and intents of the various groups of insiders. This is an artistic as well as an intellectual problem, for it supposes not only a scientific organization for discovering, recording and interpreting all conduct having a public bearing, but also methods which make presentation of the results of inquiry arresting and weighty. I do not suppose that most persons buy sugar because of belief in its nutritive value; they buy from habit and to please the palate. And so it must be with buying the facts which would prepare various publics in particular and the wider public in general to see private activities in their public bearings and to deal with them on the basis of the public interest.

I have omitted any reference to the feature of Mr. Lippmann's book which most appealed to the reviewer in his capacity of professional philosopher. Mr. Lippmann makes effective and penetrating use of the pluralistic tendencies of contemporary thought, including the theory that intelligence operates not of its own momentum but to adjust conflicts and resolve specific difficulties. This philosophical background gives his book a reach and force which distinguish it from almost all other contemporary writing in the field of affairs, and of which this review fails to take adequate account. But this notice is already too long, and with the editor's permission I hope to return to this phase of the matter later.

The Changing Intellectual Climate

Science and the Modern World, by A. N. Whitehead. New York: Macmillan Co., 1925. 296 pages. $3.

There is news in the realm of mind. The intellectual climate, the mentality, which has prevailed for three centuries is changing. The presages of this change have already shown themselves in the natural sciences; since the trend of these sciences has determined the problems, materials and tools of thought for some three hundred years, this veering of the natural sciences imports nothing less than a new mental attitude. Such in effect is the news reported in these Lowell lectures of Professor Whitehead. According to him, the change is not short of revolutionary. A change in mentality is the most significant, the most practically effective, of all changes. "It builds cathedrals before the workmen have moved a stone, and it destroys them before the elements have worn down their arches. It is the architect of the buildings of the spirit, and it is also their solvent—and the spiritual precedes the material." The book is more than an announcement of the arrival of the new mentality; it is also a record of the "great adventure" of reason since the advent of natural science in the late sixteenth century, and an account of the new ideas, associated with the doctrines of relativity and the quantum theory, which have disclosed the limitations of that adventure and which have initiated a new venture of thought.

The paradox of the scientific movement has been its extraordinary success within a defined region, and the perplexity, the enfeeblement, almost paralysis it has wrought outside that region. Its success has been associated with its strict adherence to mechanical ideas, to a materialistic view of the world. Technically, yet fundamentally, that view, those ideas, were the result of certain general abstractions regarding the nature of space and time, for generalized abstractions are the means by which mind ap-

[First published in *New Republic* 45 (17 February 1926): 360–61.]

proaches and masters the concrete. Indeed, the characteristic which has marked the recent age has been precisely "a vehement and passionate interest in the relation of general principles to irreducible and stubborn facts. All the world over and at all times there have been practical men, absorbed in 'irreducible and stubborn facts'; all the world over and at all times there have been men of philosophic temperament who have been absorbed in the weaving of general principles. It is the *union* of passionate interest in the detailed facts, with equal devotion to abstract generalisation, which forms the novelty in our present society. Previously it has appeared sporadically and as if by chance." The crisis, the change in intellectual climate, is due to the collapse of the ultimate ideas about space and time upon which science has been building. "The stable foundations of physics have broken up: also for the first time physiology is asserting itself as an effective body of knowledge, as distinct from a scrap-heap. The old foundations of scientific thought are becoming unintelligible. Time, space, matter, material, ether, electricity, mechanism, organism, configuration, structure, pattern, function, all require reinterpretation. What is the sense of talking about a mechanical explanation when you do not know what you mean by mechanics?"

The reader would derive a totally false impression, however, if he inferred that Mr. Whitehead's book is but another version of the oft-played game, in which some breakdown of older scientific ideas is interpreted as a triumph of traditional religious ideas. On the contrary, the difficulty with religious ideas in recent times has been their obstinate resistance to intellectual change. For science, on the contrary, "a clash of doctrines is not a disaster, it is an opportunity. In formal logic, a contradiction is the signal of defeat: but in the evolution of real knowledge it marks the first step in progress towards a victory." Religion has been on the defensive; it has proclaimed certain notions to be vital, only to be compelled to surrender them; its history is a history of undignified retreats. But when "Darwin or Einstein proclaims theories which modify our ideas, it is a triumph for science. We do not go about saying there is another defeat for science, because its old ideas have been abandoned. We know that another step of scientific insight has been gained."

The collapse of the older scientific abstractions in the face of new concrete facts is then an opportunity, and scientific men are rising to the occasion. Since the older science rested upon certain abstract conceptions of space and time, the newer science instead of patching up details and muddling along, is going to the root of the matter; it is radically revising its ulterior abstractions regarding space and time, a revision for which mathematicians had already prepared the way. This fact is, of course, what makes the scientific change so difficult for the layman to grasp; it is not easy to modify notions regarding space and time which have been bred in our intellectual bone since man was: for the scientific revolution of the seventeenth century, the "century of genius" as Whitehead fittingly terms it in his historical retrospect, after all but clarified and simplified man's traditional ideas about the space-time characters of the world in which he lives. Even the scientific man and the philosopher who builds upon science still have to approach the new ideas through a complex mathematical medium; the new ideas are not yet intuitive and spontaneous. Only psychological adaptation through familiar use can work the needed change. Yet Mr. Whitehead, although he does not succeed in making the new ideas intuitive, that is, appreciated in terms of naïve, everyday experience, does succeed in a wonderful way in giving readers a sense for the nature of the change and what it imports.

Technically stated, it is the substitution for the idea of mechanism of the idea of organism. Every concrete reality is of the nature of an organism; that is, it is a whole which endures or has a history, which develops, and which as a whole both reflects into itself the life-history of other organisms and in some degree dominates the energies of its constituent parts. Traditional physical science totally ignored the inner and qualitative characteristics of these organisms, of vital and intrinsically energizing individuals. "The atomic material entities which are considered in physical sciences are merely these individual enduring entities, conceived in abstraction from everything except what concerns their mutual interplay in determining each other's historical routes of life-history." Science took, as it were, certain external relations among the realities as if they were the realities themselves. This is the fallacy of "misplaced concreteness," growing out of the fallacy of the doctrine of "simple location." This latter doctrine, which as already indicated, is essentially a generalized abstraction regarding space, attempted to build up wholes out of simple, independent units having only relations of position and extension (shape and size), and of locomotion; that is, changes of position, size and shape. The entire scheme of mechanical materialism is the logical outcome. The result was denial or doubt as to the reality of genuine individuality, purpose, value and history as development, as anything more than a reshuffling of spatial units. As a consequence, philosophy was divorced from science; it like religion adopted a defensive and apologetic attitude, a defender of mind and the things of the mind, but with a defense which reduced mind to a subjective anomaly set over against the world, and making good only as it infected the reality of the natural world with its own subjectivity. The ideas of the new science put an end to the divorce between philosophy and science, not by some trick of "reconciliation," but by effecting a new synthesis of subject-matter in terms of enduring, energetic organisms as the realities of science itself.

The mind is so full of muddled compromises and half-truths that what has just been said may be taken by some to indicate that Mr. Whitehead claims that science has repudiated mechanism in behalf of something called "vitalism." Nothing could be further from the truth. "Vitalism," as he points out, is itself a defensive and dualistic doctrine; it admits old-fashioned mechanism for a certain province, and then arbitrarily makes a cleft in nature for the sake of "saving" something from the sway of mechanism. The doctrine of "organic mechanism" to which science is leading retains with slight modifications of detail the triumphs of mechanical science, including their application to human organisms, personal minds, but points out that the mechanical doctrines deal not with the realities themselves, but with their influence upon one another's life-routes. It does not superimpose superior beings transcending the laws of nature upon the natural objects with which physics is concerned.

Limits of space have compelled me to confine myself to the barest bones of Mr. Whitehead's argument. I hope it may induce some to go to the book itself, the most significant restatement for the general reader of the present relations of science, philosophy and the issues of life which has yet appeared. If the intelligent reader omits the chapters on Relativity, the Quantum Theory, Abstraction and God, he may have difficulties with some detailed passages, but none, I think, in getting the spirit and movement of thought. The book is alive with suggestions regarding the bearing of the scientific change upon the deeper issues of society. I wish in closing to point to simply one of these. He remarks that "biology has aped the manners of physics"; he might have added that with only the tools of the old science at command it was obliged to do so. At the present time, psychology is also aping the manners of physics, and with the consequence, as far as the influence of an influential school is concerned, of mechanizing education and social relations—in the precise sense in which Whitehead shows that mechanism has collapsed in physics itself. It is one of the tragedies of that professionalized specialism of science which Mr. Whitehead reveals and criticizes, that the humane sciences are always adopting and using in the sphere of psychology, education and human relations, materials and methods which the more advanced physical sciences are abandoning. If the psychological school which claims to be the only genuine "Behaviorism" could read and digest the physical ideas which this book sets forth an immense amount of misleading and confusing intellectual activity would be saved the next generation. Psychology emancipated to deal with the behavior of organisms as genuine organisms would be a very different thing in itself and in its educational and social bearings from a Behaviorism which adopts uncritically the basic abstractions which have collapsed in their own region. It would cease taking the behavior of fragments of an organism as if they were the whole of behavior. Without such an abandonment, it will carry into human activity and education, with the pretended prestige of science, ideas which are depressing and enfeebling to what is most valuable in human beings, and which most require some type of scientific control.

A Key to the New World

Education and the Good Life, by Bertrand Russell. New York: Boni and Liveright, 1926. 319 pages. $2.50.

There are many who ridicule American faith in education, calling it a religion, which it often is, but treating it as a peculiarly jejune form of superstition. Yet it need not be superstitious, unless all faith in the possibility of a world better than that in which we live be condemned as unreasonable. Such condemnation seems to be itself peculiarly dogmatic. For until we have tried seriously and systematically (and I think only a few zealots would hold that mankind has yet tried intelligently and patiently) we do not and cannot know how far the world can be made a better and sweeter place in which to live. We may, indeed, mistake the object of our faith, and take something to be education which is not a proper object of devotion. But until all aspiration for something better and all faith in future possibilities have been eliminated from human beings, I know of no kind of faith in the undemonstrated as reasonable and as gracious as that which centres our hopes and ambitions in the possibilities to be achieved by education. Till mankind is wholly cynical from defeat this faith will always burn afresh.

I call Mr. Bertrand Russell's book a fine contribution to the literature of education as religion. Toward its conclusion he says: "I have now tried to bring before the reader the wonderful possibilities which are now open to us. Think what it would mean: health, freedom, happiness, kindness, intelligence, all nearly universal. In one generation, if we chose, we could bring the millennium." The conviction, even if stopped somewhat short of anticipating the millennium, is the more striking because of its contrast with the spirit which animated some of Mr. Russell's writings during and immediately after the War. One could appreciate, indeed, in the very bitterness of what sounded like cyn-

[First published in *New Republic* 46 (19 May 1926): 410–11.]

ical pessimism the note of a thwarted idealism: if he had not cared so much, if he had possessed the ordinary degree of polite indifference, his disappointment with man would not have found so harsh an outlet. In this book, the flame of hope burns again with a steady and clear light.

Since Mr. Russell himself mentions repeatedly the fact that he has two young children, it is not, I hope, an impertinence to connect his renewal of faith with that most astounding of all human experiences, the renewing of life in the young. Volumes, I suppose, have been written about the renewal of vegetable life in the round of the seasons. Such renewal is casual, intermittent and trivial compared with that taking place every time a human birth occurs. This birth is the eternal reminder of the possibility of a new and different world; and though as time goes by the hope is frustrated and the tragedy of dissipation, so much greater than the obvious tragedy of direct defeat, recurs, yet the promise constantly returns. A new life, a life as yet one of potentiality, will signify to man the possibility of a different world until all hope dies from the human breast. Were it not for the fact that Bernard Shaw had himself no children, I should always have marveled at the limitations he has displayed in the treatment of the relation of elders and youth. There is enough of cruelty and misunderstanding to be sure between them, but I do not recall a single intimation on his part that the relation between them can be other than one of veiled indifference or polite indifference. Yet it is one of the happiest and most intellectually stimulating to be found anywhere in life. There is beauty and joy in watching the growth of a plant, the putting forth of a flower, the development of a work of art or a scientific research. Yet none of these exceeds the healthy joy, the play of varied curiosity, the drama of suspense and change, that accompanies the gradual awakening of a human life.

I should, however, probably do Mr. Russell a disservice if I continued in this strain. For the chief characteristic of his book is its enlightened empirical common sense. There are no far-reaching generalizations in it, no attempt at an underlying scientific or philosophic groundwork. It is rather a series of comments and homilies upon a large diversity of topics, with almost a minimum of generalized theorizing—apart from its unflagging faith in the union of knowledge and affection. The book is in the best

English tradition. Though more than two hundred years have intervened between John Locke on education and the present book, one who knows his Locke can hardly fail to be reminded on almost every page of the latter. There is the same trust in reasonableness and freedom, in mutual confidence, in the sure response of children to intelligent, affectionate treatment; the same aversion to pampering and coddling; the same insistence upon the value of curiosity and the necessity for not checking it; the pervading belief that if a child is constantly confronted with facts which he cannot dodge he will form his opinions objectively, and that his relapse into wishful thinking and fantasy is always to be put at the door of some adult who has encouraged him in forming this habit. Aside from differences made by the advance of science since Locke's day and the growth of democracy, the only outstanding difference is that Mr. Russell's book shows an aesthetic sensitiveness which Locke, if he had it, successfully covered up.

Fidelity to the English tradition is seen in the fact that eleven of the nineteen chapters are given to the education of character. Under this head are chapters on The First Year, Fear, Play and Fancy, Constructiveness, Selfishness and Property, Truthfulness, Punishment, Importance of Other Children, Affection and Sympathy, Sex Education, the Nursery-School. The enlightened common sense of the book may be indicated by a quotation from the first of these chapters: "Do not let the child feel fear if you can possibly help it. If it is ill, and you are anxious, hide your anxiety very carefully, lest it should pass to the child by suggestion. Avoid everything that might produce excitement. And do not minister to the child's self-importance by letting it see that you mind if it does not sleep or eat or evacuate as it should. . . . Never let the child think that a necessary normal action, such as eating which ought to be a pleasure, is something that you desire, and that you want it to do so to please you. If you do, the child soon perceives that it has acquired a new source of power, and expects to be coaxed into actions which it ought to perform spontaneously"—the last being a truly Lockeian touch. The chapter on Fear emphasizes a point which pervades the whole book: the loss and maiming that comes to life in all its forms at present from the presence of habits of fear so ingrained as for the most part to have become unconscious. The chapter on Play and Fancy indicates the pervasive sense of inferiority in children, and the reliance upon play and fancy by children as a means of developing compensatory sense of power. Taken in connection with the chapter on Affection and Sympathy a reader open to conviction may derive a knowledge of what is useful and what is not for the parent in current Freudianism. There is a kind of unbaked radicalism prevalent which compels half-educated persons to think that anything and everything which has a radical flavor must perforce be true. Mr. Russell's reputation for "radicalism" may give weight to his words when he says that the attempt to find sex symbolism in children's play is "utter moonshine," and when he denies, except for rare morbid cases, the existence of the much touted Oedipus complex in the relation of parents and children. He wisely remarks that because Freudians have failed to recognize the instinctive differences in the affection of husband and wife, parents for children and children for parents, they have been rendered, in a sense, ascetics as regards the relations of parents and children. Certainly as far as most American families are concerned, it is the desire for power on one hand and the desire on the other hand for being recognized as individuals who count for something in their own behalf, which is the ultimate root of most difficulties between children and parents.

If I pass over the introductory chapters which deal with general principles and the concluding chapters which discuss Intellectual Education, it is not because they do not contain much of value, stated in a forcefully clear manner. But upon fundamentals there is perhaps nothing new to be said about education, and Mr. Russell does not strain after originality. He is content with good sense illuminatingly uttered. The book is addressed to parents, rather than to teachers and professed "educationists," and parents dealing with younger children in the home will profit most from the book. That a man of Mr. Russell's standing should have perceived that it is worth while to devote himself to studying the life of little children and the way in which that life may be rendered fruitful is something at which to rejoice. That fact, even more than any special words of wisdom which he has expressed, makes the book notable. "It is education that gives us bad qualities, and education that must give us the opposite virtues. Education is the key to the new world." In closing I cannot think of a better summary of the spirit of the book than words which I borrow from a student: "In the past our energies have mainly gone to checking the operations of will instead of to a positive development of those intellectual attitudes which would give human beings command of the activities of the will."

The Art of Thought

The Art of Thought, by Graham Wallas.
New York: Harcourt, Brace and Co., 1926.
314 pages. $2.75.

There are at least three ways of reading Mr. Wallas's last book. Each way would determine its own standard of judgment, and the application of the different standards would yield divergent judgments as to its value. It may be read as a series of essays, half-literary and half-psychological, having to do with thinking, its direction and improvement; its psychic relatives such as emotion, habit; and its successes and failures. Upon the whole, one would then judge it a reasonably happy blend of literature and science, neither great letters nor profound science, but always readable, often sagacious, still more often suggestive, with a sufficient store of nuggets to be retained as treasures, though without penetrating insights that cleave to the heart of the subject. That is to say, as an essayist, he is not an Emerson, nor as a psychologist, a William James. As a literary document, the book suggests the card index too much (there must be three hundred names cited in the index), and the same quality makes it rather scrappy as a work of science.

One who knows Mr. Wallas's interest in politics and who is aware of our author's sense of the intimate connection of social control and organization with the primary facts of human nature might read the book in quite another way. By The Art of Thought such a one would understand the method by which intelligence may be brought to bear analytically and systematically upon the conduct of social life. Such an expectation is fostered not only by the reputation of Mr. Wallas, but by the opening passages of the book itself. They appear in the synoptic table of contents in this form: "Men have recently increased their power over Nature, without increasing the control of that power by thought. We can make war more efficiently, but cannot prevent

[First published in *New Republic* 47 (16 June 1926): 118–19.]

war; we can explore the world, but cannot contrive an interracial world-policy; and the same want of intellectual control exists, within each nation, in politics, philosophy and art."

If there are any who read this book, they will, if they persist in so interpreting it, surely be disappointed. The first sentences of the book arouse the expectation, but the same sentences taken in their context explain the lack of its fulfillment. "It is a commonplace that, during the last two centuries, men have enormously increased their power over nature without increasing the control of that power by thought. In the sphere of international and interracial relations, our chemists and engineers are now contriving, by technical methods whose subtlety would have been inconceivable to our grandfathers, plans for the destruction of London and Paris; but when French and British statesmen meet to prevent those plans from being put into operation, they find it no easier than would the leaders of two Stone Age tribes to form a common purpose." Placed where it is, the passage seems to set forth the problem of the book. But the cue is misleading. For it is obvious that there is an art of thought in matters of physical science or technology, and that the antithesis between control of nature and power of thought is, in that respect, wholly false. What is lacking, from the standpoint of this problem, is simply an art of thought with respect to human affairs comparable with that already attained in physical matters. This contrast raises an interesting problem, probably the most important problem which the world now faces. Is there a legitimate possibility of an art of social thought which is one with increase of control, or is the idea a dream? If it is a legitimate possibility, how is it to be realized?

Such a question, however, is in no sense a psychological problem. The development of natural science is not due to the fact that individual thinkers have learned a better intimately personal art of managing their own thoughts. It is due to the formation of an objective technique of instruments and external procedures together with the accumulation of prior results which direct from without the growth of pertinent problems and fruitful hypotheses. But it is the personal and psychological problem alone with which Mr. Wallas deals. There is no approach to a consideration of the political and economic conditions which stand in social affairs in the way of the development of methods of objective intellectual behavior employing means which almost automatically direct the thoughts of individuals as such. Mr. Wallas is concerned not with this objective control, but with the control which individual thinkers can achieve inside their own minds.

It would not be fair to Mr. Wallas to say that his psychological standpoint is wholly introspective and internal. But it is, I think, both fair and pertinent to say that his interest is pedagogical. And the reader and critic who take the book from this point of view will, it seems to me, judge it in its proper perspective. Mr. Wallas, as everybody knows, is an old and highly successful teacher. It would seem as if an interest in the working of the minds of students and in the ways by which these mental workings can be rectified ought to be capable of being taken for granted as existing in all teachers. Unfortunately such an interest is rare. Mr. Wallas has it in a marked degree, and I mistake not this book is the outcome of that interest and those who approach it from this angle will not be disappointed. For Mr. Wallas does not conceive that "study" is simply coming into possession of the ideas and facts stated by others, much less their words. He takes it to mean independent, which is original and creative, thought. He has generalized his pedagogical interest, and attempted to outline the processes which productive thinkers actually employ. In Chapter Four he gives the gist of his conclusions. There are two stages of thinking, the first and last, which are capable of the more formal and conscious regulation, and two which are less so. Preparation, the first stage, is the period of accumulating knowledge, defining or deliberately laying out the field, employing rules of search in amassing and classifying material, and in breaking it up into definite problems. Then comes a period of incubation, which is a period of voluntary abstention from conscious mental work on the material and problems which have eventuated in the first stage. The third stage is called "illumination," the appearance of flashes of insight, which is followed by that of "verification," where again conscious or deliberate effort comes into play. Among the most suggestive remarks of Wallas are those which concern "intimation" as a sub-process of the "illumination" stage; that is, the phase of the rising or dawning of some fringe association. Wallas points out a considerable part of the success of original thinkers is due to ability to grasp and hold these transitory and shadowy intimations.

The reading public is so dominated by labels that there is perhaps some danger that *The Art of Thought* will not find the audience where it can be most useful. It ought to be in the hands of teachers, especially in the hands of teachers of teachers and of those in training to be teachers in normal schools and colleges. It is hardly systematic enough for a text, but it would be valuable collateral reading. For American students, the emphasis upon the need of leisurely incubation, of allowing the mind free play without too conscious painful control, of adventuring in that border-ground just this side of mere fancy where most original ideas are born, is of especial value.

The Public and Its Problems

Prefatory Note

This volume is the result of lectures delivered during the month of January, nineteen hundred and twenty-six, upon the Larwill Foundation of Kenyon College, Ohio. In acknowledging the many courtesies received, I wish to express also my appreciation of the toleration shown by the authorities of the College to delay in publication. The intervening period has permitted a full revision and expansion of the lectures as originally delivered. This fact will account for an occasional reference to books published in the interval.

J.D.

1. Search for the Public

If one wishes to realize the distance which may lie between "facts" and the meaning of facts, let one go to the field of social discussion. Many persons seem to suppose that facts carry their meaning along with themselves on their face. Accumulate enough of them, and their interpretation stares out at you. The development of physical science is thought to confirm the idea. But the power of physical facts to coerce belief does not reside in the bare phenomena. It proceeds from method, from the technique of research and calculation. No one is ever forced by just the collection of facts to accept a particular theory of their meaning, so long as one retains intact some other doctrine by which he can marshal them. Only when the facts are allowed free play for the suggestion of new points of view is any significant conversion of conviction as to meaning possible. Take away from physical science its laboratory apparatus and its mathematical technique, and the human imagination might run wild in its theories of interpretation even if we suppose the brute facts to remain the same.

In any event, social philosophy exhibits an immense gap between facts and doctrines. Compare, for example, the facts of politics with the theories which are extant regarding the nature of the state. If inquirers confine themselves to observed phenomena, the behavior of kings, presidents, legislators, judges, sheriffs, assessors and all other public officials, surely a reasonable consensus is not difficult to attain. Contrast with this agreement the differences which exist as to the basis, nature, functions and justification of the state, and note the seemingly hopeless disagreement. If one asks not for an enumeration of facts, but for a definition of the state, one is plunged into controversy, into a medley of contradictory clamors. According to one tradition, which claims to derive from Aristotle, the state is associated and harmonized life lifted to its highest potency; the state is at once the keystone of the social arch and is the arch in its wholeness. According to another view, it is just one of many social institutions, having a narrow but important function, that of arbiter in the conflict of other social units. Every group springs out of and realizes a positive human interest; the church, religious values; guilds, unions and corporations, material economic interests, and so on. The state, however, has no concern of its own; its purpose is formal, like that of the leader of the orchestra who plays no instrument and makes no music, but who serves to keep other players who do produce music in unison with one another. Still a third view has it that the state is organized oppression, at once a social excrescence, a parasite and a tyrant. A fourth is that it is an instrument more or less clumsy for keeping individuals from quarreling too much with one another.

Confusion grows when we enter subdivisions of these different views and the grounds offered for them. In one philosophy, the state is the apex and completion of human association, and manifests the highest realization of all distinctively human capacities. The view had a certain pertinency when it was first formulated. It developed in an antique city-state, where to be fully a free man and to be a citizen participating in the drama, the sports, the religion and the government of the community were equivalent affairs. But the view persists and is applied to the state of to-day. Another view coordinates the state with the church (or as a variant view slightly subordinates it to the latter) as the secular arm of Deity maintaining outward order and decorum among men. A modern theory idealizes the state and its activities by borrowing the conceptions of reason and will, magnifying them till the state appears as the objectified manifestation of a will and reason which far transcend the desires and purposes which can be found among individuals or assemblages of individuals.

We are not concerned, however, with writing either a cyclopedia or history of political doctrines. So we pause with these arbitrary illustrations of the proposition that little common ground has been discovered between the factual phenomena of political behavior and the interpretation of the meaning of these phenomena. One way out of the impasse is to consign the whole matter of meaning and interpretation to political philosophy as distinguished from political science. Then it can be pointed out that futile speculation is a companion of all philosophy. The moral is to drop all doctrines of this kind overboard, and stick to facts verifiably ascertained.

The remedy urged is simple and attractive. But it is not possible to employ it. Political facts are not outside human desire and judgment. Change men's estimate of the *value* of existing political agencies and forms, and the latter change more or less. The different theories which mark political philosophy do not grow up externally to the facts which they aim to interpret; they are amplifications of selected factors among those facts. Modifiable and altering human habits sustain and generate political phenomena. These habits are not wholly informed by reasoned purpose and deliberate choice—far from it—but they are more or less amenable to them. Bodies of men are constantly engaged in attacking and trying to change some political habits, while other bodies of men are actively supporting and justifying them. It is mere pretense, then, to suppose that we can stick by the *de facto*, and not raise at some points the question of *de jure*: the question of by what right, the question of legitimacy. And such a question has a way of growing until it has become a question as to the nature of the state itself. The alternatives before us are not factually limited science on one hand and uncontrolled speculation on the other. The choice is between blind, unreasoned attack and defense on the one hand, and discriminating criticism employing intelligent method and a conscious criterion on the other.

The prestige of the mathematical and physical sciences is great, and properly so. But the difference between facts which are what they are independent of human desire and endeavor and facts which are to some extent what they are because of human interest and purpose, and which alter with alteration in the latter, cannot be got rid of by any methodology. The more sincerely we appeal to facts, the greater is the importance of the distinction between facts which condition human activity and facts which are conditioned by human activity. In the degree which we ignore this difference, social science becomes pseudo-science. Jeffersonian and Hamiltonian political ideas are not merely theories dwelling in the human mind remote from facts of American political behavior. They are expressions of chosen phases and factors among those facts, but they are also something more: namely, forces which have shaped those facts and which are still contending to shape them in the future this way and that. There is more than a speculative difference between a theory of the state which regards it as an instrument in protecting individuals in the rights they already have, and one which conceives its function to be the effecting of a more equitable distribution of rights among individuals. For the theories are held and applied by legislators in congress and by judges on the bench and make a difference in the subsequent facts themselves.

I make no doubt that the practical influence of the political philosophies of Aristotle, the Stoics, St. Thomas, Locke, Rousseau, Kant and Hegel has often been exaggerated in comparison with the influence of circumstances. But a due measure of efficacy cannot be denied them on the ground which is sometimes proffered; it cannot be denied on the ground that ideas are without potency. For ideas belong to human beings who have bodies, and there is no separation between the structures and processes of the part of the body that entertains the ideas and the part that performs acts. Brain and muscles work together, and the brains of men are much more important data for social science than are their muscular system and their sense organs.

It is not our intention to engage in a discussion of political philosophies. The concept of the state, like most concepts which are introduced by "The," is both too rigid and too tied up with controversies to be of ready use. It is a concept which can be approached by a flank movement more easily than by a frontal attack. The moment we utter the words "The State" a score of intellectual ghosts rise to obscure our vision. Without our intention and without our notice, the notion of "The State" draws us imperceptibly into a consideration of the logical relationship of various ideas to one another, and away from facts of human activity. It is better, if possible, to start from the latter and see if we are not led thereby into an idea of something which will turn out to implicate the marks and signs which characterize political behavior.

There is nothing novel in this method of approach. But very much depends upon what we select from which to start and very much depends upon whether we select our point of departure in order to tell at the terminus what the state *ought* to be or what it *is*. If we are too concerned with the former, there is a likelihood that we shall unwittingly have doctored the facts selected in order to come out at a predetermined point. The phase of human action we should *not* start with is that to which direct causative power is attributed. We should not look for state-forming forces. If we do, we are likely to get involved in mythology. To explain the origin of the state by saying that man is a political animal is to travel in a verbal circle. It is like attributing religion to a religious instinct, the family to marital and parental affection, and language to a natural endowment which impels men to speech. Such theories merely reduplicate in a so-called causal force the effects to be accounted for. They are of a piece with the notorious potency of opium to put men to sleep because of its dormitive power.

The warning is not directed against a man of straw. The attempt to derive the state, or any other social institution, from strictly "psychological" data is in point. Appeal to a gregarious instinct to account for social arrangements is the outstanding example of the lazy fallacy. Men do not run together and join in a larger mass as do drops of quicksilver, and if they did the result would not be a state nor any mode of human association. The instincts, whether named gregariousness, or sympathy, or the sense of mutual dependence, or domination on one side and abasement and subjection on the other, at best account for everything in general and nothing in particular. And at worst, the alleged instinct and natural endowment appealed to as a causal force themselves represent physiological tendencies which have previously been shaped into habits of action and expectation by means of the very social conditions they are supposed to explain. Men who have lived in herds develop attachment to the horde to which they have become used; children who have perforce lived in dependence grow into habits of dependence and subjection. The inferiority complex is socially acquired, and the "instinct" of display and mastery is but its other face. There are structural organs which physiologically manifest themselves in vocalizations as the organs of a bird induce song. But the barking of dogs and the song of birds are enough to prove that these native tendencies do not generate language. In order to be converted into language, native vocalization requires transformation by extrinsic conditions, both organic and extra-organic or environmental: formation, be it noted, not just stimulation. The cry of a baby can doubtless be described in purely organic terms, but the wail becomes a noun or verb only by its consequences in the responsive behavior of others. This responsive behavior takes the form of nurture and care, themselves dependent upon tradition, custom and social patterns. Why not postulate an "instinct" of infanticide as well as one of guidance and instruction? Or an "instinct" of exposing girls and taking care of boys?

We may, however, take the argument in a less mythological form than is found in the current appeal to social instincts of one sort or another. The activities of animals, like those of minerals and plants, are correlated with their structure. Quadrupeds run, worms crawl, fish swim, birds fly. They are made that way; it is "the nature of the beast." We do not gain anything by inserting instincts to run, creep, swim and fly between the structure and the act. But the strictly organic conditions which lead men to join, assemble, foregather, combine, are just those which lead other animals to unite in swarms and packs and herds. In describing what is common in human and other animal junctions and consolidations we fail to touch what is distinctively human in human associations. These structural conditions and acts may be *sine qua nons* of human societies; but so are the attractions and repulsions which are exhibited in inanimate things. Physics and chemistry as well as zoology may inform us of some of the conditions without which human beings would not associate. But they do not furnish us with the *sufficient* conditions of community life and of the forms which it takes.

We must in any case start from acts which are performed, not from hypothetical causes for those acts, and consider their consequences. We must also introduce intelligence, or the observation of consequences *as* consequences, that is, in connection with the acts from which they proceed. Since we must introduce it, it is better to do so knowingly than it is to smuggle it in in a way which deceives not only the customs officer—the reader—but ourselves as well. We take then our point of departure from the objective fact that human acts have consequences upon others, that some of these consequences are perceived, and that their perception leads to subsequent effort to control action so as to secure some consequences and avoid others. Following this clew, we are led to remark that the consequences are of two kinds, those which affect the persons directly engaged in a transaction, and those which affect others beyond those immediately concerned. In this distinction we find the germ of the distinction between the private and the public. When indirect consequences are recognized and there is effort to regulate them, something having the traits of a state comes into existence. When the consequences of an action are confined, or are thought to be confined, mainly to the persons directly engaged in it, the transaction is a private one. When A and B carry on a conversation together the action is a trans-action: both are concerned in it; its results pass, as it were, across from one to the other. One or other or both may be helped or harmed thereby. But, presumably, the consequences of advantage and injury do not extend beyond A and B; the activity lies between them; it is private. Yet if it is found that the consequences of conversation extend beyond the two directly concerned, that they affect the welfare of many others, the act acquires a public capacity, whether the conversation be carried on by a king and his prime minister or by Catiline and a fellow conspirator or by merchants planning to monopolize a market.

The distinction between private and public is thus in no sense equivalent to the distinction between individual and social, even if we suppose that the latter distinction has a definite meaning. Many private acts are social; their consequences contribute to the welfare of the community or affect its status and prospects. In the broad sense any transaction deliberately carried on between two or more persons is social in quality. It is a form of associated behavior and its consequences may influence further associations. A man may serve others, even in the community at large, in carrying on a private business. To some extent it is true, as Adam Smith asserted, that our breakfast table is better supplied by the convergent outcome of activities of farmers, grocers and butchers carrying on private affairs with a view to private profit than it would be if we were served on a basis of philanthropy or public spirit. Communities have been supplied with works of art, with scientific discoveries, because of the personal delight found by private persons in engaging in these activities. There are private philanthropists who act so that needy persons or the community as a whole profit by the endowment of libraries, hospitals and educational institutions. In short, private acts may be socially valuable both by indirect consequences and by direct intention.

There is therefore no necessary connection between the private character of an act and its non-social or anti-social character. The public, moreover, cannot be identified with the socially useful. One of the most regular activities of the politically organized community has been waging war. Even the most bellicose of militarists will hardly contend that all wars have been socially helpful, or deny that some have been so destructive of social values that it would have been infinitely better if they had not been waged. The argument for the non-equivalence of the public and the social, in any praiseworthy sense of social, does not rest upon the case of war alone. There is no one, I suppose, so enamored of political action as to hold that it has never been shortsighted, foolish and harmful. There are even those who hold that the presumption is always that social loss will result from agents of the public doing anything which could be done by persons in their private capacity. There are many more who protest that some special public activity, whether prohibition, a protective tariff or the expanded meaning given the Monroe Doctrine, is baleful to society. Indeed every serious political dispute turns upon the question whether a given political act is socially beneficial or harmful.

Just as behavior is not anti-social or non-social because privately undertaken, it is not necessarily socially valuable because carried on in the name of the public by public agents. The argument has not carried us far, but at least it has warned us against identifying the community and its interests with the state or the politically organized community. And the differentiation may dispose us to look with more favor upon the proposition already advanced: namely, that the line between private and public is to be drawn on the basis of the extent and scope of the consequences of acts which are so important as to need control, whether by inhibition or by promotion. We distinguish private and public buildings, private and public schools, private paths and public highways, private assets and public funds, private persons and public officials. It is our thesis that in this distinction we find the key to the nature and office of the state. It is not without significance that etymologically "private" is defined in opposition to "official," a private person being one deprived of public position. The public consists of all those who are affected by the indirect consequences of transactions to such an extent that it is deemed necessary to have those consequences systematically cared for. Officials are those who look out for and take care of the interests thus affected. Since those who are indirectly affected are not direct participants in the transactions in question, it is necessary that certain persons be set apart to represent them, and see to it that their interests are conserved and protected. The buildings, property, funds, and other physical resources involved in the performance of this office are *res publica*, the common-wealth. The public as far as organized by means of officials and material agencies to care for the extensive and enduring indirect consequences of transactions between persons is the *Populus*.

It is a commonplace that legal agencies for protecting the persons and properties of members of a community, and for redressing wrongs which they suffer, did not always exist. Legal institutions derive from an earlier period when the right of self-help obtained. If a person was harmed, it was strictly up to him what he should do to get even. Injuring another and exacting a penalty for an injury received were private transactions. They were the affairs of those directly concerned and nobody else's direct business. But the injured party obtained readily the help of friends and relatives, and the aggressor did likewise. Hence consequences of the quarrel did not remain confined to those immediately concerned. Feuds ensued, and the blood-quarrel might implicate large numbers and endure for generations. The recognition of this extensive and lasting embroilment and the harm wrought by it to whole families brought a public into existence. The transaction ceased to concern only the immediate parties to it. Those indirectly affected formed a public which took steps to conserve its interests by instituting composition and other means of pacification to localize the trouble.

The facts are simple and familiar. But they seem to present in embryonic form the traits that define a state, its agencies and officers. The instance illustrates what was meant when it said that it is fallacy to try to determine the nature of the state in terms of direct causal factors. Its essential point has to do with the enduring and extensive consequences of behavior, which like all behavior proceeds in ultimate analysis through individual human beings. Recognition of evil consequences brought about a common interest which required for its maintenance certain measures and rules, together with the selection of certain persons as their guardians, interpreters, and, if need be, their executors.

If the account given is at all in the right direction, it explains the gap already mentioned between the facts of political action and theories of the state. Men have looked in the wrong place. They have sought for the key to the nature of the state in the field of agencies, in that of doers of deeds, or in some will or purpose back of the deeds. They have sought to explain the state in terms of authorship. Ultimately all deliberate choices proceed from somebody in particular; acts are performed by somebody, and all arrangements and plans are made by somebody in the most concrete sense of "somebody." Some John Doe and Richard Roe figure in every transaction. We shall not, then, find the public if we look for it on the side of originators of voluntary actions. Some John Smith and his congeners decide whether or not to grow wheat and how much, where and how to invest money, what roads to build and travel, whether to wage war and if so how, what laws to pass and which to obey and disobey. The actual alternative to deliberate acts of individuals is not action by the public; it is routine, impulsive and other unreflected acts also performed by individuals.

Individual human beings may lose their identity in a mob or in a political convention or in a joint-stock corporation or at the polls. But this does not mean that some mysterious collective agency is making decisions, but that some few persons who know what they are about are taking advantage of massed force to conduct the mob their way, boss a political machine, and manage the affairs of corporate business. When the public or state is involved in making social arrangements like passing laws, enforcing a contract, conferring a franchise, it still acts through concrete persons. The persons are now officers, representatives of a public and shared interest. The difference is an important one. But it is not a difference between single human beings and a collective impersonal will. It is between persons in their private and in their official or representative character. The quality presented is not authorship but authority, the authority of recognized consequences to control the behavior which generates and averts extensive and enduring results of weal and woe. Officials are indeed public agents, but agents in the sense of factors doing the business of others in securing and obviating consequences that concern them.

When we look in the wrong place we naturally do not find what we are looking for. The worst of it is, however, that looking in the wrong place, to causal forces instead of consequences, the outcome of the looking becomes arbitrary. There is no check on it. "Interpretation" runs wild. Hence the variety of conflicting theories and the lack of consensus of opinion. One might argue *a priori* that the continual conflict of theories about the state is itself proof that the problem has been wrongly posed. For, as we have previously remarked, the main facts of political action, while the phenomena vary immensely with diversity of time and place, are not hidden even when they are complex. They are facts of human behavior accessible to human observation. Existence of a multitude of contradictory theories of the state, which is so baffling from the standpoint of the theories themselves, is readily explicable the moment we see that all the theories, in spite of their divergence from one another, spring from a root of shared error: the taking of causal agency instead of consequences as the heart of the problem.

Given this attitude and postulate, some men at some time will find the causal agency in a metaphysical nisus attributed to nature; and the state will then be explained in terms of an "essence" of man realizing itself in an end of perfected Society. Others, influenced by other preconceptions and other desires, will find the required author in the will of God reproducing through the medium of fallen humanity such an image of divine order and justice as the corrupt material allows. Others seek for it in the meeting of the wills of individuals who come together and by contract or mutual pledging of loyalties bring a state into existence. Still others find it in an autonomous and transcendent will embodied in all men as a universal within their particular beings, a will which by its own inner nature commands the establishment of external conditions in which it is possible for will to express outwardly its freedom. Others find it in the fact that mind or reason is either an attribute of reality or is reality itself, while they condole that difference and plurality of minds, individuality, is an illusion attributable to sense, or is merely an appearance in contrast with the monistic reality of reason. When various opinions all spring from a common and shared error, one is as good as another, and the accidents of education, temperament, class interest and the dominant circumstances of the age decide which is adopted. Reason comes into play only to find justification for the opinion which has been adopted, instead of to analyze human behavior with respect to its consequences and to frame polities accordingly. It is an old story that natural philosophy steadily progressed only after an intellectual revolution. This consisted in abandoning the search for causes and forces and turning to the analysis of what is going on and how it goes on. Political philosophy has still in large measure to take to heart this lesson.

The failure to note that the problem is that of perceiving in a discriminating and thorough way the consequences of human action (including negligence and inaction) and of instituting measures and means of caring for these consequences is not confined to production of conflicting and irreconcilable theories of the state. The failure has also had the effect of perverting the views of those who, up to a certain point, perceived the truth. We have asserted that all deliberate choices and plans are finally the work of single human beings. Thoroughly false conclusions have been drawn from this observation. By thinking still in terms of causal forces, the conclusion has been drawn from this fact that the state, the public, is a fiction, a mask for private desires for power and position. Not only the state but society itself has been pulverized into an aggregate of unrelated wants and wills. As a logical consequence, the state is conceived either as sheer oppression born of arbitrary power and sustained in fraud, or as a pooling of the forces of single men into a massive force which single persons are unable to resist, the pooling being a measure of desperation since its sole alternative is the conflict of all with all which generates a life that is helpless and brutish. Thus the state appears either a monster to be destroyed or as a Leviathan to be cherished. In short, under the influence of the prime fallacy that the problem of the state concerns causal forces, individualism, as an ism, as a philosophy, has been generated.

While the doctrine is false, it sets out from a fact. Wants, choices and purposes have their locus in single beings; behavior which manifests desire, intent and resolution proceeds from them in their singularity. But only intellectual laziness leads us to conclude that since the form of thought and decision is individual, their content, their subject-matter, is also something purely personal. Even if "consciousness" were the wholly private matter that the individualistic tradition in philosophy and psychology supposes it to be, it would still be true that consciousness is *of* objects, not of itself. Association in the sense of connection and combination is a "law" of everything known to exist. Singular things act, but they act together. Nothing has been discovered which acts in entire isolation. The action of everything is along with the action of other things. The "along with" is of such a kind that the behavior of each is modified by its connection with others. There are trees which can grow only in a forest. Seeds of many plants can successfully germinate and develop only under conditions furnished by the presence of other plants. Reproduction of kind is dependent upon the activities of insects which bring about fertilization. The life-history of an animal cell is conditioned upon connection with what other cells are doing. Electrons, atoms and molecules exemplify the omnipresence of conjoint behavior.

There is no mystery about the fact of association, of an interconnected action which affects the activity of singular elements. There is no sense in asking how individuals come to be associated. They exist and operate in association. If there is any mystery about the matter, it is the mystery that the universe is the kind of universe it is. Such a mystery could not be explained without going outside the universe. And if one should go to an outside source to account for it, some logician, without an excessive draft upon his ingenuity, would rise to remark that the outsider would have to be connected with the universe in order to account for anything in it. We should still be just where we started, with the fact of connection as a fact to be accepted.

There is, however, an intelligible question about human association:—Not the question how individuals or singular beings come to be connected, but how they come to be connected in just those ways which give human communities traits so different from those which mark assemblies of electrons, unions of trees in forests, swarms of insects, herds of sheep, and constellations of stars. When we consider the difference we at once come upon the fact that the consequences of conjoint action take on a new value when they are observed. For notice of the effects of connected action forces men to reflect upon the connection itself; it makes it an object of attention and interest. Each acts, in so far as the connection is known, in view of the connection. Individuals still do the thinking, desiring and purposing, but *what* they think of is the consequences of their behavior upon that of others and that of others upon themselves.

Each human being is born an infant. He is immature, helpless, dependent upon the activities of others. That many of these dependent beings survive is proof that others in some measure look out for them, take care of them. Mature and better equipped beings are aware of the consequences of their acts upon those of the young. They not only act conjointly with them, but they act in that especial kind of association which manifests interest in the consequences of their conduct upon the life and growth of the young.

Continued physiological existence of the young is only one phase of interest in the consequences of association. Adults are equally concerned to act so that the immature learn to think, feel, desire and habitually conduct themselves in certain ways. Not the least of the consequences which are striven for is that the young shall themselves learn to judge, purpose and choose from the standpoint of associated behavior and its consequences. In fact, only too often this interest takes the form of endeavoring to make the young believe and plan just as adults do. This instance alone is enough to show that while singular beings in their singularity think, want and decide, *what* they think and strive for, the content of their beliefs and intentions is a subject-matter provided by association. Thus man is not merely *de facto* associated, but he *becomes* a social animal in the make-up of his ideas, sentiments and deliberate behavior. *What* he believes, hopes for and aims at is the outcome of association and intercourse. The only thing which imports obscurity and mystery into the influence of association upon what individual persons want and act for is the effort to discover alleged, special, original, society-making causal forces, whether instincts, fiats of will, personal, or an immanent, universal, practical reason, or an indwelling, metaphysical, social essence and nature. These things do not explain, for they are more mysterious than are the facts they are evoked to account for. The planets in a constellation would form a community if they were aware of the connections of the activities of each with those of the others and could use this knowledge to direct behavior.

We have made a digression from consideration of the state to the wider topic of society. However, the excursion enables us to distinguish the state from other forms of social life. There is an old tradition which regards the state and completely organized society as the same thing. The state is said to be the complete and inclusive realization of all social institutions. Whatever values result from any and every social arrangement are gathered together and asserted to be the work of the state. The counterpart of this method is that philosophical anarchism which assembles all the evils that result from all forms of human grouping and attributes them *en masse* to the state, whose elimination would then bring in a millennium of voluntary fraternal organization. That the state should be to some a deity and to others a devil is another evidence of the defects of the premises from which discussion sets out. One theory is as indiscriminate as the other.

There is, however, a definite criterion by which to demarcate the organized public from other modes of community life. Friendships, for example, are non-political forms of association. They are characterized by an intimate and subtle sense of the fruits of intercourse. They contribute to experience some of its most precious values. Only the exigencies of a preconceived theory would confuse with the state that texture of friendships and attachments which is the chief bond in any community, or would insist that the former depends upon the latter for existence. Men group themselves also for scientific inquiry, for religious worship, for artistic production and enjoyment, for sport, for giving and receiving instruction, for industrial and commercial undertakings. In each case some combined or conjoint action, which has grown up out of "natural," that is, biological, conditions and from local contiguity, results in producing distinctive consequences—that is, consequences which differ in kind from those of isolated behavior.

When these consequences are intellectually and emotionally appreciated, a shared interest is generated and the nature of the interconnected behavior is thereby transformed. Each form of association has its own peculiar quality and value, and no person in his senses confuses one with another. The characteristic of the public as a state springs from the fact that all modes of associated behavior may have extensive and enduring consequences which involve others beyond those directly engaged in them. When these consequences are in turn realized in thought and sentiment, recognition of them reacts to remake the conditions out of which they arose. Consequences have to be taken care of, looked out for. This supervision and regulation cannot be effected by the primary groupings themselves. For the essence of the consequences which call a public into being is the fact that they expand beyond those directly engaged in producing them. Consequently special agencies and measures must be formed if they are to be attended to; or else some existing group must take on new functions. The obvious external mark of the organization of a public or of a state is thus the existence of officials. Government is not the state, for that includes the public as well as the rulers charged with special duties and powers. The public, however, is organized in and through those officers who act in behalf of its interests.

Thus the state represents an important although distinctive and restricted social interest. From this point of view there is nothing extraordinary in the preeminence of the claims of the organized public over other interests when once they are called into play, nor in its total indifference and irrelevancy to friendships, associations for science, art and religion under most circumstances. If the consequences of a friendship threaten the public, then it is treated as a conspiracy; usually it is not the state's business or concern. Men join each other in partnership as a matter of course to do a piece of work more profitably or for mutual defense. Let its operations exceed a certain limit, and others not participating in it find their security or prosperity menaced by it, and suddenly the gears of the state are in mesh. Thus it happens that the state, instead of being all absorbing and inclusive, is under some circumstances the most idle and empty of social arrangements. Nevertheless, the temptation to generalize from these instances and conclude that the state generically is of no significance is at once challenged by the fact that when a family connection, a church, a trade union, a business corporation, or an educational institution conducts itself so as to affect large numbers outside of itself, those who are affected form a public which endeavors to act through suitable structures, and thus to organize itself for oversight and regulation.

I know of no better way in which to apprehend the absurdity of the claims which are sometimes made in behalf of society politically organized than to call to mind the influence upon community life of Socrates, Buddha, Jesus, Aristotle, Confucius, Homer, Vergil, Dante, St. Thomas, Shakespeare, Copernicus, Galileo, Newton, Boyle, Locke, Rousseau and countless others, and then to ask ourselves if we conceive these men to be officers of the state. Any method which so broadens the scope of the state as to lead to such conclusion merely makes the state a name for the totality of all kinds of associations. The moment we have taken the word as loosely as that, it is at once necessary to distinguish, within it, the state in its usual political and legal sense. On the other hand, if one is tempted to eliminate or disregard the state, one may think of Pericles, Alexander, Julius and Augustus Caesar, Elizabeth, Cromwell, Richelieu, Napoleon, Bismarck and hundreds of names of that kind. One dimly feels that they must have had a private life, but how insignificant it bulks in comparison with their action as representatives of a state!

This conception of statehood does not imply any belief as to the propriety or reasonableness of any particular political act, measure or system. Observations of consequences are at least as subject to error and illusion as is perception of natural objects. Judgments about what to undertake so as to regulate them, and how to do it, are as fallible as other plans. Mistakes pile up and consolidate themselves into laws and methods of administration which are more harmful than the consequences which they were originally intended to control. And as all political history shows, the power and prestige which attend command of official position render rule something to be grasped and exploited for its own sake. Power to govern is distributed by the accident of birth or by the possession of qualities which enable a person to obtain office, but which are quite irrelevant to the performance of its representative functions. But the need which calls forth the organization of the public by means of rulers and agencies of government persists and to some extent is incarnated in political fact. Such progress as political history records depends upon some luminous emergence of the idea from the mass of irrelevancies which obscure and clutter it. Then some reconstruction occurs which provides the function with organs more apt for its fulfillment. Progress is not steady and continuous. Retrogression is as periodic as advance. Industry and inventions in technology, for example, create means which alter the modes of associated behavior and which radically change the quantity, character and place of impact of their indirect consequences.

These changes are extrinsic to political forms which, once established, persist of their own momentum. The new public which is generated remains long inchoate, unorganized, because it cannot use inherited political agencies. The latter, if elaborate and well institutionalized, obstruct the organization of the new public. They prevent that development of new forms of the state which might grow up rapidly were social life more fluid, less precipitated into set political and legal molds. To form itself, the public has to break existing political forms. This is hard to do because these forms are themselves the regular means of instituting change. The public which generated political forms is passing away, but the power and lust of possession remains in the hands of the officers and agencies which the dying public instituted. This is why the change of the form of states is so often effected only by revolution. The creation of adequately flexible and responsive political and legal machinery has so far been beyond the wit of man. An epoch in which the needs of a newly forming public are counteracted by established forms of the state is one in which there is increasing disparagement and disregard of the state. General apathy, neglect and contempt find expression in resort to various short-cuts of direct action. And direct action is taken by many other interests than those which employ "direct action" as a slogan, often most energetically by intrenched class-interests which profess the greatest reverence for the established "law and order" of the existing state. By its very nature, a state is ever something to be scrutinized, investigated, searched for. Almost as soon as its form is stabilized, it needs to be re-made.

Thus the problem of discovering the state is not a problem for theoretical inquirers engaged solely in surveying institutions which already exist. It is a practical problem of human beings living in association with one another, of mankind generically. It is a complex problem. It demands power to perceive and recognize the consequences of the behavior of individuals joined in groups and to trace them to their source and origin. It involves selection of persons to serve as representatives of the interests created by these perceived consequences and to define the functions which they shall possess and employ. It requires institution of a government such that those having the renown and power which goes with the exercise of these functions shall employ them for the public and not turn them to their own private benefit. It is no cause for wonder, then, that states have been many, not only in number but in type and kind. For there have been countless forms of joint activity with correspondingly diverse consequences. Power to detect consequences has varied especially with the instrumentalities of knowledge at hand. Rulers have been selected on all kinds of different grounds. Their functions have varied and so have their will and zeal to represent common interests. Only the exigencies of a rigid philosophy can lead us to suppose that there is some one form or idea of The State which these protean historic states have realized in various degrees of perfection. The only statement which can be made is a purely formal one: the state is the organization of the public effected through officials for the protection of the interests shared by its members. But what the public may be, what the officials are, how adequately they perform their function, are things we have to go to history to discover.

Nevertheless, our conception gives a criterion for determining how good a particular state is: namely, the degree of organization of the public which is attained, and the degree in which its officers are so constituted as to perform their function of caring for public interests. But there is no *a priori* rule which can be laid down and by which when it is followed a good state will be brought into existence. In no two ages or places is there the same public. Conditions make the consequences of associated action and the knowledge of them different. In addition the means by which a public can determine the government to serve its interests vary. Only formally can we say what the best state would be. In concrete fact, in actual and concrete organization and structure, there is no form of state which can be said to be the best: not at least till history is ended, and one can survey all its varied forms. The formation of states must be an experimental process. The trial process may go on with diverse degrees of blindness and accident, and at the cost of unregulated procedures of cut and try, of fumbling and groping, without insight into what men are after or clear knowledge of a good state even when it is achieved. Or it may proceed more intelligently, because guided by knowledge of the conditions which must be fulfilled. But it is still experimental. And since conditions of action and of inquiry and knowledge are always changing, the experiment must always be retried; the State must always be rediscovered. Except, once more, in formal statement of conditions to be met, we have no idea what history may still bring forth. It is not the business of political philosophy and science to determine what the state in general should or must be. What they may do is to aid in creation of methods such that experimentation may go on less blindly, less at the mercy of accident, more intelligently, so that men may learn from their errors and profit by their successes. The belief in political fixity, of the sanctity of some form of state consecrated by the efforts of our fathers and hallowed by tradition, is one of the stumbling-blocks in the way of orderly and directed change; it is an invitation to revolt and revolution.

As the argument has moved to and fro, it will conduce to clearness to summarize its steps. Conjoint, combined, associated action is a universal trait of the behavior of things. Such action has results. Some of the results of human collective action are perceived, that is, they are noted in such ways that they are taken account of. Then there arise purposes, plans, measures and means, to secure consequences which are liked and eliminate those which are found obnoxious. Thus perception generates a common interest; that is, those affected by the consequences are perforce concerned in conduct of all those who along with themselves share in bringing about the results. Sometimes the consequences are confined to those who directly share in the transaction which produces them. In other cases they extend far beyond those immediately engaged in producing them. Thus two kinds of interests and of measures of regulation of acts in view of consequences are generated. In the first, interest and control are limited to those directly engaged; in the second, they extend to those who do not directly share in the performance of acts. If, then, the interest constituted by their being affected by the actions in question is to have any practical influence, control over the actions which produce them must occur by some indirect means.

So far the statements, it is submitted, set forth matters of actual and ascertainable fact. Now follows the hypothesis. Those indirectly and seriously affected for good or for evil form a group distinctive enough to require recognition and a name. The name selected is The Public. This public is organized and made effective by means of representatives who as guardians of custom, as legislators, as executives, judges, etc., care for its especial interests by methods intended to regulate the conjoint actions of individuals and groups. Then and in so far, association adds to itself political organization, and something which may be government comes into being: the public is a political state.

The direct confirmation of the hypothesis is found in the statement of the series of observable and verifiable matters of fact. These constitute conditions which are sufficient to account, so it is held, for the characteristic phenomena of political life, or state activity. If they do, it is superfluous to seek for other explanation. In conclusion, two qualifications should be added. The account just given is meant to be generic; it is consequently schematic, and omits many differential conditions, some of which receive attention in subsequent chapters. The other point is that in the negative part of the argument, the attack upon theories which would explain the state by means of special causal forces and agencies, there is no denial of causal relations or connections among phenomena themselves. That is obviously assumed at every point. There can be no consequences and measures to regulate the mode and quality of their occurrence without the causal nexus. What is denied is an appeal to *special* forces outside the series of observable connected phenomena. Such causal powers are no different in kind to the occult forces from which physical science had to emancipate itself. At best, they are but phases of the related phenomena themselves which are then employed to account for the facts. What is needed to direct and make fruitful social inquiry is a method which proceeds on the basis of the interrelations of observable acts and their results. Such is the gist of the method we propose to follow.

2. Discovery of the State

If we look in the wrong place for the public we shall never locate the state. If we do not ask what are the conditions which promote and obstruct the organization of the public into a social group with definite functions, we shall never grasp the problem involved in the development and transformation of states. If we do not perceive that this organization is equivalent to the equipment of the public with official representatives to care for the interests of the public, we shall miss the clew to the nature of government. These are conclusions reached or suggested by the discussion of the last hour. The wrong place to look, as we saw, is in the realm of alleged causal agency, of authorship, of forces which are supposed to produce a state by an intrinsic *vis genetrix*. The state is not created as a direct result of organic contacts as offspring are conceived in the womb, nor by direct conscious intent as a machine is invented, nor by some brooding indwelling spirit, whether a personal deity or a metaphysical absolute will. When we seek for the origin of states in such sources as these, a realistic regard for facts compels us to conclude in the end that we find nothing but singular persons, you, they, me. We shall then be driven, unless we have recourse to mysticism, to decide that the public is born in a myth and is sustained by superstition.

There are many answers to the question: What is the public? Unfortunately many of them are only restatements of the question. Thus we are told that the public is the community as a whole, and a-community-as-a-whole is supposed to be a self-evident and self-explanatory phenomenon. But a community as a *whole* involves not merely a variety of associative ties which hold persons together in diverse ways, but an organization of all elements by an integrated principle. And this is precisely what we are in search of. Why should there be anything of the nature of an all-inclusive and regulative unity? If we postulate such a thing, surely the institution which alone would answer to it is humanity, not the affairs which history exhibits as states. The notion of an inherent universality in the associative force at once breaks against the obvious fact of a plurality of states, each localized, with its boundaries, limitations, its indifference and even hostility to other states. The best that metaphysical monistic philosophies of politics can do with this fact is to ignore it. Or, as in the case of Hegel and his followers, a mythical philosophy of history is constructed to eke out the deficiencies of a mythical doctrine of statehood. The universal spirit seizes upon one temporal and local nation after another as the vehicle for its objectification of reason and will.

Such considerations as these reinforce our proposition that the perception of consequences which are projected in important ways beyond the persons and associations directly concerned in them is the source of a public; and that its organization into a state is effected by establishing special agencies to care for and regulate these consequences. But they also suggest that actual states exhibit traits which perform the function that has been stated and which serve as marks of anything to be called a state. Discussion of these traits will define the nature of the public and the problem of its political organization, and will also operate to test our theory.

We can hardly select a better trait to serve as a mark and sign of the nature of a state than a point just mentioned, temporal and geographical localization. There are associations which are too narrow and restricted in scope to give rise to a public, just as there are associations too isolated from one another to fall within the same public. Part of the problem of discovery of a public capable of organization into a state is that of drawing lines between the too close and intimate and the too remote and disconnected. Immediate contiguity, face to face relationships, have consequences which generate a community of interests, a sharing of values, too direct and vital to occasion a need for political organization. Connections within a family are familiar; they are matters of immediate acquaintance and concern. The so-called blood-tie which has played such a part in demarcation of social units is largely imputed on the basis of sharing immediately in the results of conjoint behavior. What one does in the household affects others directly and the consequences are appreciated at once and in an intimate way. As we say, they "come home." Special organization to care for them is a superfluity. Only when the tie has extended to a union of families in a clan and of clans in a tribe do consequences become so indirect that special measures are called for. The neighborhood is constituted largely on the same pattern of association that is exemplified in the family. Custom and measures improvised to meet special emergencies as they arise suffice for its regulation.

Consider the village in Wiltshire so beautifully described by Hudson: "Each house has its centre of human life with life of bird and beast, and the centres were in touch with one another, connected like a row of children linked together by their hands; all together forming one organism, instinct with one life, moved by one mind, like a many-coloured serpent lying at rest, extended at full length upon the ground. I imagined the case of a cottager at one end of the village occupied in chopping up a tough piece of wood or stump and accidentally letting fall his heavy sharp axe on to his foot, inflicting a grievous wound. The tidings of the accident would fly from mouth to mouth to the other extremity of the village, a mile distant; not only would each villager quickly know of it, but have at the same time a vivid mental image of his fellow villager at the moment of his misadventure, the sharp glittering axe falling on to his foot, the red blood flowing from the wound; and he would at the same time feel the wound in his own foot and the shock to his system. In like manner all thoughts and feelings would pass freely from one to another, though not necessarily communicated by speech; and all would be participants in virtue of that sympathy and solidarity uniting the members of a small isolated community. No one would be capable of a thought or emotion which would seem strange to the others. The temper, the mood, the outlook of the individual and the village, would be the same."[1] With such a condition of intimacy, the state is an impertinence.

For long periods of human history, especially in the Orient, the state is hardly more than a shadow thrown upon the family and neighborhood by remote personages, swollen to gigantic form by religious beliefs. It rules but it does not regulate; for its

1. W. H. Hudson, *A Traveller in Little Things*, pp. 110–12.

rule is confined to receipt of tribute and ceremonial deference. Duties are within the family; property is possessed by the family. Personal loyalties to elders take the place of political obedience. The relationships of husband and wife, parent and children, older and younger children, friend and friend, are the bonds from which authority proceeds. Politics is not a branch of morals; it is submerged in morals. All virtues are summed up in filial piety. Wrongdoing is culpable because it reflects upon one's ancestry and kin. Officials are known but only to be shunned. To submit a dispute to them is a disgrace. The measure of value of the remote and theocratic state lies in what it does *not* do. Its perfection is found in its identification with the processes of nature, in virtue of which the seasons travel their constant round, so that fields under the beneficent rule of sun and rain produce their harvest, and the neighborhood prospers in peace. The intimate and familiar propinquity group is not a social unity within an inclusive whole. It is, for almost all purposes, society itself.

At the other limit there are social groups so separated by rivers, seas and mountains, by strange languages and gods, that what one of them does—save in war—has no appreciable consequences for another. There is therefore no common interest, no public, and no need nor possibility of an inclusive state. The plurality of states is such a universal and notorious phenomenon that it is taken for granted. It does not seem to require explanation. But it sets up, as we have noted, a test difficult for some theories to meet. Except upon the basis of a freakish limitation in the common will and reason which is alleged to be the foundation of the state, the difficulty is insuperable. It is peculiar, to say the least, that universal reason should be unable to cross a mountain range and objective will be balked by a river current. The difficulty is not so great for many other theories. But only the theory which makes recognition of consequences the critical factor can find in the fact of many states a corroborating trait. Whatever is a barrier to the spread of the consequences of associated behavior by that very fact operates to set up political boundaries. The explanation is as commonplace as is the thing to be explained.

Somewhere between associations that are narrow, close and intimate and those which are so remote as to have only infrequent and casual contact lies, then, the province of a state. We do not find and should not expect to find sharp and fast demarcations. Villages and neighborhoods shade imperceptibly into a political public. Different states may pass through federations and alliances into a larger whole which has some of the marks of statehood. This condition, which we should anticipate in virtue of the theory, is confirmed by historical facts. The wavering and shifting line of distinction between a state and other forms of social union is, again, an obstacle in the way of theories of the state which imply as their concrete counterpart something as sharply marked off as is the concept. On the basis of empirical consequences, it is just the sort of thing which should occur. There are empires due to conquest where political rule exists only in forced levies of taxes and soldiers, and in which, though the word state may be used, the characteristic signs of a public are notable for their absence. There are political communities like the city-states of ancient Greece in which the fiction of common descent is a vital factor, in which household gods and worship are replaced by community divinities, shrines, and cults: states in which much of the intimacy of the vivid and prompt personal touch of the family endures, while there has been added the transforming inspiration of a varied, freer, fuller life, whose issues are so momentous that in comparison the life of the neighborhood is parochial and that of the household dull.

Multiplicity and constant transformation in the forms which the state assumes are as comprehensible upon the hypothesis proposed as is the numerical diversity of independent states. The consequences of conjoint behavior differ in kind and in range with changes in "material culture," especially those involved in exchange of raw materials, finished products and above all in technology, in tools, weapons and utensils. These in turn are immediately affected by inventions in means of transit, transportation and intercommunication. A people that lives by tending flocks of sheep and cattle adapts itself to very different conditions than those of a people which ranges freely, mounted on horses. One form of nomadism is usually peaceful; the other warlike. Roughly speaking, tools and implements determine occupations, and occupations determine the consequences of associated activity. In determining consequences, they institute publics with different interests, which exact different types of political behavior to care for them.

In spite of the fact that diversity of political forms rather than uniformity is the rule, belief in *the* state as an archetypal entity persists in political philosophy and science. Much dialectical ingenuity has been expended in construction of an essence or intrinsic nature in virtue of which any particular association is entitled to have applied to it the concept of statehood. Equal ingenuity has been expended in explaining away all divergencies from this morphological type, and (the favored device) in ranking states in a hierarchical order of value as they approach the defining essence. The idea that there is a model pattern which makes a state a *good* or true state has affected practice as well as theory. It, more than anything else, is responsible for the effort to form constitutions offhand and impose them ready-made on peoples. Unfortunately, when the falsity of this view was perceived, it was replaced by the idea that states "grow" or develop instead of being made. This "growth" did not mean simply that states alter. Growth signified an evolution through regular stages to a predetermined end because of some intrinsic nisus or principle. This theory discouraged recourse to the only method by which alterations of political forms might be directed: namely, the use of intelligence to judge consequences. Equally with the theory which it displaced, it presumed the existence of a single standard form which defines *the* state as the essential and true article. After a false analogy with physical science, it was asserted that only the assumption of such a uniformity of process renders a "scientific" treatment of society possible. Incidentally, the theory flattered the conceit of those nations which, being politically "advanced," assumed that they were so near the apex of evolution as to wear the crown of statehood.

The hypothesis presented makes possible a consistently empirical or *historical* treatment of the changes in political forms and arrangements, free from any overriding conceptual domination such as is inevitable when a "true" state is postulated, whether that be thought of as deliberately made or as evolving by its own inner law. Intrusions from non-political internal occurrences, industrial and technological, and from external events, borrowings, travel, migrations, explorations, wars, modify the consequences of preexisting associations to such an extent that new agencies and functions are necessitated. Political forms are also subject to alterations of a more indirect sort. Developments of better methods of thinking bring about observation of consequences which were concealed from a vision which used coarser intellectual tools. Quickened intellectual insight also makes possible invention of new political devices. Science has not indeed played a large role. But intuitions of statesmen and of political theorists have occasionally penetrated into the operations of social forces in such a way that a new turn has been given to legislation and to administration. There is a margin of toleration in the body politic as well as in an organic body. Measures not in any sense inevitable are accommodated to after they have once been taken; and a further diversity is thereby introduced in political manners.

In short, the hypothesis which holds that publics are constituted by recognition of extensive and enduring indirect consequences of acts accounts for the relativity of states, while the theories which define them in terms of specific causal authorship imply an absoluteness which is contradicted by facts. The attempt to find by the "comparative method" structures which are common to antique and modern, to occidental and oriental states, has involved a great waste of industry. The only constant is the function of caring for and regulating the interests which accrue as the result of the complex indirect expansion and radiation of conjoint behavior.

We conclude, then, that temporal and local diversification is a prime mark of political organization, and one which, when it is analyzed, supplies a confirming test of our theory. A second mark and evidence is found in an otherwise inexplicable fact that the quantitative scope of results of conjoint behavior generates a public with need for organization. As we already noted, what are now crimes subject to public cognizance and adjudication were once private ebullitions, having the status now possessed by an insult proffered by one to another. An interesting phase of the transition from the relatively private to the public, at least from a limited public to a larger one, is seen in the development in England of the King's Peace. Justice until the twelfth century was administered mainly by feudal and shire courts, courts of hundreds, etc. Any lord who had a sufficient number of subjects and tenants decided controversies and imposed penalties. The court and justice of the king was but one among many, and primarily concerned with royalty's tenants, servants, properties and dignities. The monarchs wished, however, to increase their revenues and expand their power and prestige. Various devices were invented and fictions set up by means of which the jurisdiction of kingly courts was extended. The method was to allege that various offenses, formerly attended to by local courts, were infractions of the king's peace. The centralizing movement went on till the king's justice had a monopoly. The instance is significant. A measure instigated by desire to increase the power and profit of the royal dynasty became an impersonal public function by bare extension. The same sort of thing has repeatedly occurred when personal prerogatives have passed into normal political processes. Something of the same sort is manifested in contemporary life when modes of private business become "affected with a public interest" because of quantitative expansion.

A converse instance is presented in transfer from public to private domain of religious rites and beliefs. As long as the prevailing mentality thought that the consequences of piety and irreligion affected the entire community, religion was of necessity a public affair. Scrupulous adherence to the customary cult was of the highest political import. Gods were tribal ancestors or founders of the community. They granted communal prosperity when they were duly acknowledged and were the authors of famine, pestilence and defeat in war if their interests were not zealously attended to. Naturally when religious acts had such extended consequences, temples were public buildings, like the agora and forum; rites were civic functions and priests public officials. Long after theocracy vanished, theurgy was a political institution. Even when disbelief was rife, few there were who would run the risk of neglecting the ceremonials.

The revolution by which piety and worship were relegated to the private sphere is often attributed to the rise of personal conscience and assertion of its rights. But this rise is just the thing to be accounted for. The supposition that it was there all the time in a submerged condition and finally dared to show itself reverses the order of events. Social changes, both intellectual and in the internal composition and external relations of peoples, took place so that men no longer connected attitudes of reverence or disrespect to the gods with the weal and woe of the community. Faith and unbelief still had serious consequences, but these were now thought to be confined to the temporal and eternal happiness of the persons directly concerned. Given the other belief, and persecution and intolerance are as justifiable as is organized hostility to any crime; impiety is the most dangerous of all threats to public peace and well-being. But social changes gradually effected as one of the new functions of the life of the community the rights of private conscience and creed.

In general, behavior in intellectual matters has moved from the public to the private realm. This radical change was, of course, urged and justified on the ground of intrinsic and sacred private right. But, as in the special case of religious beliefs, it is strange, if this reason be accepted, that mankind lived so long in total unawareness of the existence of the right. In fact, the idea of a purely private area of consciousness, where whatever goes on has no external consequences, was in the first instance a product of institutional change, political and ecclesiastic, although, like other beliefs, once it was established it had political results. The observation that the interests of the community are better cared for when there is permitted a large measure of personal judgment and choice in the formation of intellectual conclusions, is an observation which could hardly have been made until social mobility and heterogeneity had brought about initiation and invention in technological matters and industry, and until secular pursuits had become formidable rivals to church and state. Even yet, however, toleration in matters of judgment and belief is largely a negative matter. We agree to leave one another alone (within limits) more from recognition of evil consequences which have resulted from the opposite course rather than from any profound belief in its positive social beneficence. As long as the latter consequence is not widely perceived, the so-called natural right to private judgment will remain a somewhat precarious rationalization of the moderate amount of toleration which has come into being. Such phenomena as the Ku Klux and legislative activity to regulate science show that the belief in liberty of thought is still superficial.

If I make an appointment with a dentist or doctor, the transaction is primarily between us. It is my health which is affected and his pocket-book, skill and reputation. But exercise of the professions has consequences so wide-spread that the examination and licensing of persons who practice them becomes a public matter. John Smith buys or sells real estate. The transaction is effected by himself and some other person. Land, however, is of prime importance to society, and the private transaction is hedged about with legal regulations; evidence of transfer and ownership has to be recorded with a public official in forms publicly prescribed. The choice of a mate and the act of sexual union are intimately personal. But the act is the condition of bearing of offspring who are the means of the perpetuation of the community. The public interest is manifested in formalities which are necessary to make a union legal and for its legal termination. Consequences, in a word, affect large numbers beyond those immediately concerned in the transaction. It is often thought that in a socialistic state the formation and dissolution of marriages would cease to have a public phase. It is possible. But it is also possible that such a state would be even more alive than is the community at present to the consequences of the union of man and woman not only upon children but upon its own well-being and stability. In that case certain regulations would be relaxed, but there might be imposed stringent rules as to health, economic capacity and psychologic compatibility as preconditions of wedlock.

No one can take into account all the consequences of the acts he performs. It is a matter of necessity for him, as a rule, to limit his attention and foresight to matters which, as we say, are distinctively his own business. Any one who looked too far abroad with regard to the outcome of what he is proposing to do would, if there were no general rules in existence, soon be lost in a hopelessly complicated muddle of considerations. The man of most generous outlook has to draw the line somewhere, and he is forced to draw it in whatever concerns those closely associated with himself. In the absence of some objective regulation, effects upon them are all he can be sure of in any reasonable degree. Much of what is called selfishness is but the outcome of limitation of observation and imagination. Hence when consequences concern a large number, a number so mediately involved that a person cannot readily prefigure how they are to be affected, that number is constituted a public which intervenes. It is not merely that the combined observations of a number cover more ground than those of a single person. It is rather that the public itself, being unable to forecast and estimate all consequences, establishes certain dikes and channels so that actions are confined within prescribed limits, and insofar have moderately predictable consequences.

The regulations and laws of the state are therefore misconceived when they are viewed as commands. The "command" theory of common and statute law is in reality a dialectical consequence of the theories, previously criticized, which define the state in terms of an antecedent causation, specifically of that theory which takes "will" to be the causal force which generates the state. If a will is the origin of the state, then state-action expresses itself in injunctions and prohibitions imposed by its will upon the wills of subjects. Sooner or later, however, the question arises as to the justification of the will which issues commands. Why should the will of the rulers have more authority than that of others? Why should the latter submit? The logical conclusion is that the ground of obedience lies ultimately in superior force. But this conclusion is an obvious invitation to trial of forces to see where superior force lies. In fact the idea of authority is abolished, and that of force substituted. The next dialectical conclusion is that the will in question is something over and above any private will or any collection of such wills: is some overruling "general will." This conclusion was drawn by Rousseau, and under the influence of German metaphysics was erected into a dogma of a mystic and transcendent absolute will, which in turn was not another name for force only because it was identified with absolute reason. The alternative to one or other of these conclusions is surrender of the causal authorship theory and the adoption of that of widely distributed consequences, which, when they are perceived, create a common interest and the need of special agencies to care for it.

Rules of law are in fact the institution of conditions under which persons make their arrangements with one another. They are structures which canalize action; they are active forces only as are banks which confine the flow of a stream, and are commands only in the sense in which the banks command the current. If individuals had no stated conditions under which they come to agreement with one another, any agreement would either terminate in a twilight zone of vagueness or would have to cover such an enormous amount of detail as to be unwieldy and unworkable. Each agreement, moreover, might vary so from every other that nothing could be inferred from one arrangement as to the probable consequences of any other. Legal rules state certain conditions which when met make an agreement a contract. The terms of the agreement are thereby canalized within manageable limits, and it is possible to generalize and predict from one to another. Only the exigencies of a theory lead one to hold that there is a command that an agreement be made in such and such a form.[2] What happens is that certain conditions are set such that *if* a person conform to them, he can count on certain consequences, while if he fails to do so he cannot forecast consequences. He takes a chance and runs the risk of having the whole transaction invalidated to his loss. There is no reason to interpret even the "prohibitions" of criminal law in any other way. Conditions are stated in reference to consequences which may be incurred if they are infringed or transgressed. We can similarly state the undesirable results which will happen if a stream breaks through its banks; if the stream were capable of foreseeing these consequences and directing its behavior by the foresight, we might metaphorically construe the banks as issuing a prohibition.

This account explains both the large arbitrary and contingent element in laws and their plausible identification with reason, dissimilar as are the two considerations. There are many transactions in which the thing of chief importance is that consequences be determinate in *some* fashion rather than that they be determined by some inherent principle to be just such and such. In other words, within limits it is indifferent what results are fixed by the conditions settled upon; what is important is that the consequences be certain enough to be predictable. The rule of the road is typical of a large number of rules. So is the fixing of sunset or of a specified hour as the exact time when the felonious entering of the premises of another takes on a more serious quality. On the other hand, rules of law are reasonable so that "reason" is appealed to by some as their fount and origin on the ground pointed out by Hume.[3] Men are naturally shortsighted, and the shortsightedness is increased and perverted by the influence of appetite and passion. "The law" formulates remote and long-run consequences. It then operates as a condensed available check on the naturally overweening influence of immediate desire and interest over decision. It is a means of doing for a person what otherwise only his own foresight, if thoroughly reasonable, could do. For a rule of law, although it may be laid down because

2. Judges make rules of law. On the "will" theory this is an encroachment on the legislative function. Not so, if the judges further define conditions of action.
3. *A Treatise of Human Nature*, Part II, sec. vii.

of a special act as its occasion, is formulated in view of an indefinite variety of other possible acts. It is necessarily a generalization; for it is generic as to the predictable consequences of a *class* of facts. If the incidents of a particular occasion exercise undue influence upon the content of a rule of law, it will soon be overruled, either explicitly or by neglect. Upon this theory, the law as "embodied reason" means a formulated generalization of means and procedures in behavior which are adapted to secure what is wanted. Reason expresses a function, not a causal origin. Law is reasonable as a man is sensible who selects and arranges conditions adapted to produce the ends he regards as desirable. A recent writer, who regards "reason" as that which generates laws, says, "A debt does not in reason cease to be a debt because time has passed, but the law sets up a limitation. A trespass does not cease in reason to be a trespass because it is indefinitely repeated, yet the law shows a tendency to admit an unresisted trespass in time to the status of right. Time, distance and chance are indifferent to pure reason; but they play their part in the legal order." [4] But if reasonableness is a matter of adaptation of means to consequences, time and distance are things to be given great weight; for they effect both consequences and the ability to foresee them and to act upon them. Indeed, we might select statutes of limitation as excellent examples of the kind of rationality the law contains. Only if reason is looked upon as "pure," that is as a matter of formal logic, do the instances cited manifest limitation of reason.

A third mark of the public organized as a state, a mark which also provides a test of our hypothesis, is that it is concerned with modes of behavior which are old and hence well established, engrained. Invention is a peculiarly personal act, even when a number of persons combine to make something new. A novel idea is the kind of thing that has to occur to somebody in the singular sense. A new project is something to be undertaken and set agoing by private initiative. The newer an idea or plan, the more it deviates from what is already recognized and established in practice. By the nature of the case an innovation is a departure from the customary. Hence the resistance it is likely to encounter. We, to be sure, live in an era of discoveries and inventions.

4. Hocking, *Man and the State*, p. 51.

Speaking generically, innovation itself has become a custom. Imagination is wonted to it; it is expected. When novelties take the form of mechanical appliances, we incline to welcome them. But this is far from always having been the case. The rule has been to look with suspicion and greet with hostility the appearance of anything new, even a tool or utensil. For an innovation *is* a departure, and one which brings in its train some incalculable disturbance of the behavior to which we have grown used and which seems "natural." As a recent writer has clearly shown, inventions have made their way insidiously; and because of some immediate convenience. If their effects, their long-run consequences, in altering habits of behavior had been foreseen, it is safe to say that most of them would have been destroyed as wicked, just as many of them were retarded in adoption because they were felt to be sacrilegious.[5] In any case, we cannot think of their invention being the work of the state.[6]

The organized community is still hesitant with reference to new ideas of a non-technical and non-technological nature. They are felt to be disturbing to social behavior; and rightly so, as far as old and established behavior is concerned. Most persons object to having their habits unsettled, their habits of belief no less than habits of overt action. A new idea *is* an unsettling of received beliefs; otherwise, it would not be a new idea. This is only to say that the production of new ideas is peculiarly a private performance. About the most we can ask of the state, judging from states which have so far existed, is that it put up with their production by private individuals without undue meddling. A state which will organize to manufacture and disseminate new ideas and new ways of thinking may come into existence some time, but such a state is a matter of faith, not sight. When it comes it will arrive because the beneficial consequences of new ideas have become an article of common faith and repute. It may, indeed, be said that even now the state provides those conditions of security which are necessary if private persons are to engage effectually in discovery and invention. But this service is a by-product; it is foreign to the grounds on which the conditions

5. Ayres, *Science: The False Messiah*, Chapter 4, "The Lure of Machinery."
6. The one obvious exception concerns the tools of waging war. With respect to them, the state has often shown itself as greedy as it has been reluctant and behindhand with reference to other inventions.

in question are maintained by the public. And it must be offset by noting the extent to which the state of affairs upon which the public heart is most set is unfavorable to thinking in other than technical lines. In any case, it is absurd to expect the public, because it is called in no matter how eulogistic a sense the state, to rise above the intellectual level of its average constituents.

When, however, a mode of behavior has become old and familiar, and when an instrumentality has come into use as a matter of course, provided it is a prerequisite of other customary pursuits, it tends to come within the scope of the state. An individual may make his own track in a forest; but highways are usually public concerns. Without roads which one is free to use at will, men might almost as well be castaways on a desert island. Means of transit and communication affect not only those who utilize them but all who are dependent in any way upon what is transported, whether as producers or consumers. The increase of easy and rapid intercommunication means that production takes place more and more for distant markets and it puts a premium upon mass-production. Thus it becomes a disputed question whether railroads as well as highways should not be administered by public officials, and in any case some measure of official regulation is instituted, as they become settled bases of social life.

The tendency to put what is old and established in uniform lines under the regulation of the state has psychological support. Habits economize intellectual as well as muscular energy. They relieve the mind from thought of means, thus freeing thought to deal with new conditions and purposes. Moreover, interference with a well-established habit is followed by uneasiness and antipathy. The efficiency of liberation from attention to whatever is regularly recurrent is reenforced by an emotional tendency to get rid of bother. Hence there is a general disposition to turn over activities which have become highly standardized and uniform to representatives of the public. It is possible that the time will come when not only railways will have become routine in their operation and management, but also existing modes of machine production, so that business men instead of opposing public ownership will clamor for it in order that they may devote their energies to affairs which involve more novelty, variation and opportunities for risk and gain. They might conceivably, even un-

274 THE PUBLIC AND ITS PROBLEMS

der a régime of continued private property in general, no more wish to be bothered with routinized operations than they would want to take over the care of public streets. Even now the question of the public's taking charge of the machinery of the manufacture of goods is less a matter of wholesale "individualism" versus "socialism" than it is of the ratio of the experimental and novel in their management to the habitual and matter-of-course; of that which is taken for granted as a condition of other things to that which is significant in its own operation.

A fourth mark of the public is indicated by the idea that children and other dependents (such as the insane, the permanently helpless) are peculiarly its wards. When the parties involved in any transaction are unequal in status, the relationship is likely to be one-sided, and the interests of one party to suffer. If the consequences appear serious, especially if they seem to be irretrievable, the public brings to bear a weight that will equalize conditions. Legislatures are more ready to regulate the hours of labor of children than of adults, of women than of men. In general, labor legislation is justified against the charge that it violates liberty of contract on the ground that the economic resources of the parties to the arrangement are so disparate that the conditions of a genuine contract are absent; action by the state is introduced to form a level on which bargaining takes place. Labor unions often object, however, to such "paternalistic" legislation on the ground that voluntary combinations to ensure collective bargaining is better for those concerned than action taken without the active participation of laborers. The general objection that paternalism tends to keep those affected by it permanently in the status of children, without an impetus to help themselves, rests on the same basis. The difference here is nevertheless not as to the principle that inequality of status may call for public intervention, but as to the best means of securing and maintaining equality.

There has been a steady tendency for the education of children to be regarded as properly a state charge in spite of the fact that children are primarily the care of a family. But the period in which education is possible to an effective degree is that of childhood; if this time is not taken advantage of the consequences are irreparable. The neglect can rarely be made up later. In the degree, then, that a certain measure of instruction and training is deemed to have significant consequences for the social body, rules are laid down affecting the action of parents in relation to their children, and those who are not parents are taxed—Herbert Spencer to the contrary notwithstanding—to maintain schools. Again, the consequences of neglect of safeguards in industries involving machines which are dangerous and those presenting unhygienic conditions, are so serious and irretrievable that the modern public has intervened to maintain conditions conducive to safety and health. Movements which aim at insurance against illness and old-age under governmental auspices illustrate the same principle. While public regulation of a minimum wage is still a disputed matter, the argument in behalf of it appeals to the criterion stated. The argument in effect is that a living wage is a matter of such serious indirect consequences to society that it cannot be safely left to the parties directly concerned, owing to the fact that immediate need may incapacitate one party to the transaction from effective bargaining.

In what has been said there is no attempt to lay down criteria to be applied in a predetermined way to ensure just such and such results. We are not concerned to predict the special forms which state action will take in the future. We have simply been engaged in pointing out the marks by which public action as distinct from private is characterized. Transactions between singular persons and groups bring a public into being when their indirect consequences—their effects beyond those immediately engaged in them—are of importance. Vagueness is not eliminated from the idea of importance. But at least we have pointed out some of the factors which go to make up importance: namely, the far-reaching character of consequences, whether in space or time; their settled, uniform and recurrent nature, and their irreparableness. Each one of these matters involves questions of degree. There is no sharp and clear line which draws itself, pointing out beyond peradventure, like the line left by a receding high tide, just where a public comes into existence which has interests so significant that they must be looked after and administered by special agencies, or governmental officers. Hence there is often room for dispute. The line of demarcation between actions left to private initiative and management and those regulated by the state has to be discovered experimentally.

As we shall see later, there are assignable reasons why it will be drawn very differently at different times and places. The very fact that the public depends upon consequences of acts and the perception of consequences, while its organization into a state depends upon the ability to invent and employ special instrumentalities, shows how and why publics and political institutions differ widely from epoch to epoch and from place to place. To suppose that an *a priori* conception of the intrinsic nature and limits of the individual on one side and the state on the other will yield good results once for all is absurd. If, however, the state has a definite nature, as it should have if it were formed by fixed causal agencies, or if individuals have a nature fixed once for all apart from conditions of association, a final and wholesale partitioning of the realms of personal and state activity is the logical conclusion. The failure of such a theory to reach practical solutions is, therefore, a further confirmation of the theory which emphasizes the consequences of activity as the essential affair.

In conclusion, we shall make explicit what has been implied regarding the relation to one another of public, government and state.[7] There have been two extreme views about this point. On one hand, the state has been identified with government. On the other hand, the state, having a necessary existence of its own, *per se*, is said then to proceed to form and employ certain agencies forming government, much as a man hires servants and assigns them duties. The latter view is appropriate when the causal agency theory is relied upon. Some force, whether a general will

7. This is a convenient place for making explicit a qualification which has to be understood throughout but which is slighted in the text. The words "government" and "officers" are taken functionally, not in terms of some particular structure which is so familiar to us that it leaps to the eyes when these words are used. Both words in their functional meaning are much wider in application than what is meant when we speak, say, of the government and officers of Great Britain or the United States. In households, for example, there have usually been rule and "heads"; the parents, for most purposes the father, have been officers of the family interest. The "patriarchal family" presents an emphatic intensification, on account of comparative isolation of the household from other social forms, of what exists in lesser degree in almost all families. The same sort of remark applies to the use of the term "states," in connection with publics. The text is concerned with modern conditions, but the hypothesis propounded is meant to hold good generally. So to the patent objection that the state is a very modern institution, it is replied that while modernity is a property of those *structures* which go by the name of states, yet all history, or almost all, records the exercise of analogous *functions*. The argument concerns these functions and the mode of their operation, no matter what word be used, though for the sake of brevity the word "state," like the words "government" and "officer," has been freely employed.

or the singular wills of assembled individuals, calls the state into being. Then the latter as a secondary operation chooses certain persons through whom to act. Such a theory helps those who entertain it to retain the idea of the inherent sanctity of the state. Concrete political evils such as history exhibits in abundance can be laid at the door of fallible and corrupt governments, while the state keeps its honor unbesmirched. The identification of the state with government has the advantage of keeping the mind's eye upon concrete and observable facts; but it involves an unaccountable separation between rulers and people. If a government exists by itself and on its own account, why should there be government? Why should there persist the habits of loyalty and obedience which permit it to rule?

The hypothesis which has been advanced frees us from the perplexities which cluster about both of these two notions. The lasting, extensive and serious consequences of associated activity bring into existence a public. In itself it is unorganized and formless. By means of officials and their special powers it becomes a state. A public articulated and operating through representative officers is the state; there is no state without a government, but also there is none without the public. The officers are still singular beings, but they exercise new and special powers. These may be turned to their private account. Then government is corrupt and arbitrary. Quite apart from deliberate graft, from using unusual powers for private glorification and profit, density of mind and pomposity of behavior, adherence to class-interest and its prejudices, are strengthened by position. "Power is poison" was the remark of one of the best, shrewdest and most experienced observers of Washington politicians. On the other hand, occupancy of office may enlarge a man's views and stimulate his social interest so that he exhibits as a statesman traits foreign to his private life.

But since the public forms a state only by and through officials and their acts, and since holding official position does not work a miracle of transubstantiation, there is nothing perplexing nor even discouraging in the spectacle of the stupidities and errors of political behavior. The facts which give rise to the spectacle should, however, protect us from the illusion of expecting extraordinary change to follow from a mere change in political agencies and methods. Such a change sometimes occurs, but when it does, it is because the social conditions, in generating a new public, have prepared the way for it; the state sets a formal seal upon forces already in operation by giving them a defined channel through which to act. Conceptions of "The State" as something *per se*, something intrinsically manifesting a general will and reason, lend themselves to illusions. They make such a sharp distinction between *the* state and *a* government that, from the standpoint of the theories, a government may be corrupt and injurious and yet The State by the same idea retain its inherent dignity and nobility. Officials may be mean, obstinate, proud and stupid and yet the nature of the state which they serve remain essentially unimpaired. Since, however, a public is organized into a state through its government, the state is as its officials are. Only through constant watchfulness and criticism of public officials by citizens can a state be maintained in integrity and usefulness.

The discussion also returns with some added illumination to the problem of the relation of state and society. The problem of the relation of individuals to associations—sometimes posed as the relation of *the* individual to society—is a meaningless one. We might as well make a problem out of the relation of the letters of an alphabet to the alphabet. An alphabet *is* letters, and "society" is individuals in their connections with one another. The mode of combination of letters with one another is obviously a matter of importance; letters form words and sentences when combined, and have no point nor sense except in some combination. I would not say that the latter statement applies literally to individuals, but it cannot be gainsaid that singular human beings exist and behave in constant and varied association with one another. These modes of conjoint action and their consequences profoundly affect not only the outer habits of singular persons, but their dispositions in emotion, desire, planning and valuing.

"Society," however, is either an abstract or a collective noun. In the concrete, there are societies, associations, groups of an immense number of kinds, having different ties and instituting different interests. They may be gangs, criminal bands; clubs for sport, sociability and eating; scientific and professional organizations; political parties and unions within them; families; religious denominations, business partnerships and corporations;

and so on in an endless list. The associations may be local, nation-wide and trans-national. Since there is no one *thing* which may be called society, except their indefinite overlapping, there is no unqualified eulogistic connotation adhering to the term "society." Some societies are in the main to be approved; some to be condemned, on account of their consequences upon the character and conduct of those engaged in them and because of their remoter consequences upon others. All of them, like all things human, are mixed in quality; "society" is something to be approached and judged critically and discriminatingly. "Socialization" of some sort—that is, the reflex modification of wants, beliefs and work because of share in a united action—is inevitable. But it is as marked in the formation of frivolous, dissipated, fanatical, narrow-minded and criminal persons as in that of competent inquirers, learned scholars, creative artists and good neighbors.

Confining our notice to the results which are desirable, it appears that there is no reason for assigning all the values which are generated and maintained by means of human associations to the work of states. Yet the same unbridled generalizing and fixating tendency of the mind which leads to a monistic fixation of society has extended beyond the hypostatizing of "society" and produced a magnified idealization of The State. All values which result from any kind of association are habitually imputed by one school of social philosophers to the state. Naturally the result is to place the state beyond criticism. Revolt against the state is then thought to be the one unforgivable social sin. Sometimes the deification proceeds from a special need of the time, as in the cases of Spinoza and Hegel. Sometimes it springs from a prior belief in universal will and reason and a consequent need of finding some empirical phenomena which may be identified with the externalization of this absolute spirit. Then this is employed, by circular logic, as evidence for the existence of such a spirit. The net import of our discussion is that a state is a distinctive and secondary form of association, having a specifiable work to do and specified organs of operation.

It is quite true that most states, after they have been brought into being, react upon the primary groupings. When a state is a good state, when the officers of the public genuinely serve the public interests, this reflex effect is of great importance. It renders the desirable associations solider and more coherent; indirectly it clarifies their aims and purges their activities. It places a discount upon injurious groupings and renders their tenure of life precarious. In performing these services, it gives the individual members of valued associations greater liberty and security: it relieves them of hampering conditions which if they had to cope with personally would absorb their energies in mere negative struggle against evils. It enables individual members to count with reasonable certainty upon what others will do, and thus facilitates mutually helpful cooperations. It creates respect for others and for one's self. A measure of the goodness of a state is the degree in which it relieves individuals from the waste of negative struggle and needless conflict and confers upon him positive assurance and reenforcement in what he undertakes. This is a great service, and there is no call to be niggardly in acknowledging the transformations of group and personal action which states have historically effected.

But this recognition cannot be legitimately converted into the monopolistic absorption of all associations into The State, nor of all social values into political value. The all-inclusive nature of the state signifies only that officers of the public (including, of course, law-makers) may act so as to fix conditions under which *any* form of association operates; its comprehensive character refers only to the impact of its behavior. A war like an earthquake may "include" in its consequences all elements in a given territory, but the inclusion is by way of effects, not by inherent nature or right. A beneficent law, like a condition of general economic prosperity, may favorably affect all interests in a particular region, but it cannot be called a whole of which the elements influenced are parts. Nor can the liberating and confirming results of public action be construed to yield a wholesale idealization of states in contrast with other associations. For state activity is often injurious to the latter. One of the chief occupations of states has been the waging of war and the suppression of dissentient minorities. Moreover, their action, even when benign, presupposes values due to non-political forms of living together which are but extended and reenforced by the public through its agents.

The hypothesis which we have supported has obvious points of contact with what is known as the pluralistic conception of the state. It presents also a marked point of difference. Our doctrine of plural forms is a statement of a fact: that there exist a plurality of social groupings, good, bad and indifferent. It is not a doctrine which prescribes inherent limits to state action. It does not intimate that the function of the state is limited to settling conflicts among other groups, as if each one of them had a fixed scope of action of its own. Were that true, the state would be only an umpire to avert and remedy trespasses of one group upon another. Our hypothesis is neutral as to any general, sweeping implications as to how far state activity may extend. It does not indicate any particular polity of public action. At times, the consequences of the conjoint behavior of some persons may be such that a large public interest is generated which can be fulfilled only by laying down conditions which involve a large measure of reconstruction within that group. There is no more an inherent sanctity in a church, trade-union, business corporation, or family institution than there is in the state. Their value is also to be measured by their consequences. The consequences vary with concrete conditions; hence at one time and place a large measure of state activity may be indicated and at another time a policy of quiescence and *laissez-faire*. Just as publics and states vary with conditions of time and place, so do the concrete functions which should be carried on by states. There is no antecedent universal proposition which can be laid down because of which the functions of a state should be limited or should be expanded. Their scope is something to be critically and experimentally determined.

3. The Democratic State

Singular persons are the foci of action, mental and moral, as well as overt. They are subject to all kinds of social influences which determine *what* they can think of, plan and choose. The conflicting streams of social influence come to a single and conclusive issue only in personal consciousness and deed. When a public is generated, the same law holds. It arrives at decisions, makes terms and executes resolves only through the medium of individuals. They are officers; they represent a Public, but the Public acts only through them. We say in a country like our own that legislators and executives are elected by the public. The phrase might appear to indicate that the Public acts. But, after all, individual men and women exercise the franchise; the public is here a collective name for a multitude of persons each voting as an anonymous unit. As a citizen-voter each one of these persons is, however, an officer of the public. He expresses his will as a representative of the public interest as much so as does a senator or sheriff. His vote may express his hope to profit in private purse by the election of some man or the ratification of some proposed law. He may fail, in other words, in effort to represent the interest entrusted to him. But in this respect he does not differ from those explicitly designated public officials who have also been known to betray the interest committed to them instead of faithfully representing it.

In other words, every officer of the public, whether he represents it as a voter or as a stated official, has a dual capacity. From this fact the most serious problem of government arises. We commonly speak of some governments as representative in contrast with others which are not. By our hypothesis all governments are representative in that they purport to stand for the interests which a public has in the behavior of individuals and groups. There is, however, no contradiction here. Those concerned in government are still human beings. They retain their share of the ordinary traits of human nature. They still have private interests to serve and interests of special groups, those of the family, clique or class to which they belong. Rarely can a person sink himself in his political function; the best which most men attain to is the domination by the public weal of their other desires. What is meant by "representative" government is that the public is definitely organized with the intent to secure this dominance. The dual capacity of every officer of the public leads to conflict in individuals between their genuinely political aims and acts and those which they possess in their non-political roles. When the public adopts special measures to see to it that the conflict is minimized and that the representative function overrides the private one, political institutions are termed representative.

It may be said that not until recently have publics been conscious that they were publics, so that it is absurd to speak of their organizing themselves to protect and secure their interests. Hence states are a recent development. The facts are, indeed, fatally against attribution of any long history to states provided we use a hard and fast conceptual definition of states. But our definition is founded on the exercise of a function, not on any inherent essence or structural nature. Hence it is more or less a verbal matter just what countries and peoples are called states. What is of importance is that the facts which significantly differentiate various forms from one another be recognized. The objection just urged points to a fact of great significance, whether the word "state" be used or not. It indicates that for long stretches of time the public role of rulers has been incidental to other ends for which they have used their powers. There has been a machinery of government, but it has been employed for purposes which in the strict sense are non-political, the deliberate advancement of dynastic interests. Thus we come upon the primary problem of the public: to achieve such recognition of itself as will give it weight in the selection of official representatives and in the definition of their responsibilities and rights. Consideration of this problem leads us, as we shall see, into the discussion of the democratic state.

Taking history as a whole, the selection of rulers and equipment of them with powers has been a matter of political accident. Persons have been selected as judges, executives and administrators for reasons independent of capacity to serve public interests. Some of the Greek states of antiquity and the examination system of China stand out for the very reason that they are exceptions to this statement. History shows that, in the main, persons have ruled because of some prerogative and conspicuous place which was independent of their definitively public role. If we introduce the idea of the public at all, we are bound to say that it was assumed without question that certain persons were fit to be rulers because of traits independent of political considerations. Thus in many societies the male elders exercised such rule as obtained in virtue of the mere fact that they were old men. Gerontocracy is a familiar and widespread fact. Doubtless there was a presumption that age was a sign of knowledge of group traditions and of matured experience, but it can hardly be said that this presumption was consciously the influential factor in giving old men a monopoly of rule. Rather they had it *ipso facto*, because they had it. A principle of inertia, of least resistance and least action, operated. Those who were already conspicuous in some respect, were it only for long gray beards, had political powers conferred upon them.

Success in military achievement is an irrelevant factor which has controlled the selection of men to rule. Whether or no "camps are the true mothers of cities," whether or no Herbert Spencer was right in declaring that government originated in chieftainship for war purposes, there is no doubt that, in most communities, the ability of a man to win battles has seemed to mark him out as a predestined manager of the civil affairs of a community. There is no need to argue that the two positions demand different gifts, and that achievement in one is no proof of fitness for the other. The fact remains. Nor do we have to look at ancient states for evidence of its effective operation. States nominally democratic show the same tendency to assume that a winning general has some quasi-divine appointment to political office. Reason would teach that oftentimes even the politicians who are most successful in instigating the willingness of the civilian population to support a war are by that very fact incapacitated for the offices of making a just and enduring peace. But the treaty of Versailles is there to show how difficult it is to make a shift of personnel even when conditions radically alter so that there is need for men of a changed outlook and interests. To those who have, it shall be given. It is human nature to think along the easiest lines, and this induces men when they want conspicuous leaders in the civil function to fasten upon those who are already conspicuous, no matter what the reason.

Aside from old men and warriors, medicine men and priests have had a ready-made, predestined vocation to rule. Where the community welfare is precarious and dependent upon the favor of supernatural beings, those skilled in the arts by which the wrath and jealousy of the gods are averted and their favor procured, have the marks of superior capacity to administer states. Success in living to an old age, in battle and in occult arts, have, however, been most signalized in the *initiation* of political régimes. What has counted most in the long run is the dynastic factor. *Beati possidentes*. The family from which a ruler has been taken occupies in virtue of that fact a conspicuous position and superior power. Preeminence in status is readily taken for excellence. Divine favor *ex officio* attends a family in which rule has been exercised for enough generations so that the memory of original exploits has grown dim or become legendary. The emoluments, pomp and power which go with rule are not thought to need justification. They not only embellish and dignify it, but are regarded as symbols of intrinsic worthiness to possess it. Custom consolidates what accident may have originated; established power has a way of legitimizing itself. Alliances with other potent families within and without the country, possession of large landed estates, a retinue of courtiers and access to revenues of the state, with a multitude of other things irrelevant to the public interest, establish a dynastic position at the same time that they divert the genuine political function to private ends.

An additional complication is introduced because the glory, wealth and power of rulers constitutes in itself an invitation to seize and exploit office. The causes which operate to induce men to strive for any shining object operate with increased appeal in the case of governmental power. The centralization and scope of functions which are needed in order to serve the interests of the public become, in other words, seductions to draw state officials into subserving private ends. All history shows how difficult it is for human beings to bear effectually in mind the objects for the nominal sake of which they are clothed with power and pomp; it shows the ease with which they employ their panoply to advance private and class interests. Were actual dishonesty the only, or even chief, foe, the problem would be much simpler. The ease of routine, the difficulty of ascertaining public needs, the intensity of the glare which attends the seat of the mighty, desire for immediate and visible results, play the larger part. One often hears it said by socialists justly impatient with the present economic régime that "industry should be taken out of private hands." One recognizes what they intend: that it should cease to be regulated by desire for private profit and should function for the benefit of producers and consumers, instead of being sidetracked to the advantage of financiers and stockholders. But one wonders whether those who so readily utter this saying have asked themselves into whose hands industry is to pass? Into those of the public? But, alas, the public has no hands except those of individual human beings. The essential problem is that of transforming the action of such hands so that it will be animated by regard for social ends. There is no magic by which this result can be accomplished. The same causes which have led men to utilize concentrated political power to serve private purposes will continue to act to induce men to employ concentrated economic power in behalf of non-public aims. This fact does not imply the problem is insoluble. But it indicates where the problem resides, whatever guise it assumes. Since officers of the public have a dual make-up and capacity, what conditions and what technique are necessary in order that insight, loyalty and energy may be enlisted on the side of the public and political role?

These commonplace considerations have been adduced as a background for discussion of the problems and prospects of democratic government. Democracy is a word of many meanings. Some of them are of such a broad social and moral import as to be irrelevant to our immediate theme. But one of the meanings is distinctly political, for it denotes a mode of government, a specified practice in selecting officials and regulating their conduct as officials. This is not the most inspiring of the different meanings of democracy; it is comparatively special in character. But it contains about all that is relevant to *political* democracy. Now the theories and practices regarding the selection and behavior of public officials which constitute political democracy have been worked out against the historical background just al-

luded to. They represent an effort in the first place to counteract
the forces that have so largely determined the possession of rule
by accidental and irrelevant factors, and in the second place an
effort to counteract the tendency to employ political power to
serve private instead of public ends. To discuss democratic government at large apart from its historic background is to miss its
point and to throw away all means for an intelligent criticism of
it. In taking the distinctively historical point of view we do not
derogate from the important and even superior claims of democracy as an ethical and social ideal. We limit the topic for discussion in such a way as to avoid "the great bad," the mixing of
things which need to be kept distinct.

Viewed as a historical tendency exhibited in a chain of movements which have affected the forms of government over almost
the entire globe during the last century and a half, democracy is
a complex affair. There is a current legend to the effect that the
movement originated in a single clear-cut idea, and has proceeded by a single unbroken impetus to unfold itself to a predestined end, whether triumphantly glorious or fatally catastrophic. The myth is perhaps rarely held in so simple and
unmixed a form. But something approaching it is found whenever men either praise or damn democratic government absolutely, that is, without comparing it with alternative polities.
Even the least accidental, the most deliberately planned, political
forms do not embody some absolute and unquestioned good.
They represent a choice, amid a complex of contending forces, of
that particular possibility which appears to promise the most
good with the least attendant evil.

Such a statement, moreover, immensely oversimplifies. Political forms do not originate in a once for all way. The greatest
change, once it is accomplished, is simply the outcome of a vast
series of adaptations and responsive accommodations, each to
its own particular situation. Looking back, it is possible to make
out a trend of more or less steady change in a single direction.
But it is, we repeat, mere mythology to attribute such unity of
result as exists (which is always easy to exaggerate) to single
force or principle. Political democracy has emerged as a kind of
net consequence of a vast multitude of responsive adjustments to
a vast number of situations, no two of which were alike, but
which tended to converge to a common outcome. The demo-

cratic convergence, moreover, was not the result of distinctively political forces and agencies. Much less is democracy the product *of* democracy, of some inherent nisus, or immanent idea. The temperate generalization to the effect that the unity of the democratic movement is found in effort to remedy evils experienced in consequence of prior political institutions realizes that it proceeded step by step, and that each step was taken without foreknowledge of any ultimate result, and, for the most part, under the immediate influence of a number of differing impulses and slogans.

It is even more important to realize that the conditions out of which the efforts at remedy grew and which made it possible for them to succeed were primarily non-political in nature. For the evils were of long standing, and any account of the movement must raise two questions: Why were efforts at improvement not made earlier, and, when they were made, why did they take just the form which they did take? The answers to both questions will be found in distinctive religious, scientific and economic changes which finally took effect in the political field, being themselves primarily non-political and innocent of democratic intent. Large questions and far-ranging ideas and ideals arose during the course of the movement. But theories of the nature of the individual and his rights, of freedom and authority, progress and order, liberty and law, of the common good and a general will, of democracy itself, did not produce the movement. They reflected it in thought; after they emerged, they entered into subsequent strivings and had practical effect.

We have insisted that the development of political democracy represents the convergence of a great number of social movements, no one of which owed either its origin or its impetus to inspiration of democratic ideals or to planning for the eventual outcome. This fact makes irrelevant both paeans and condemnations based upon conceptual interpretations of democracy, which, whether true or false, good or bad, are reflections of facts in thought, not their causal authors. In any case, the complexity of the historic events which have operated is such as to preclude any thought of rehearsing them in these pages, even if I had a knowledge and competency which are lacking. Two general and obvious considerations need, however, to be mentioned. Born in revolt against established forms of government and the state, the events which finally culminated in democratic political forms were deeply tinged by fear of government, and were actuated by a desire to reduce it to a minimum so as to limit the evil it could do.

Since established political forms were tied up with other institutions, especially ecclesiastical, and with a solid body of tradition and inherited belief, the revolt also extended to the latter. Thus it happened that the intellectual terms in which the movement expressed itself had a negative import even when they seemed to be positive. Freedom presented itself as an end in itself, though it signified in fact liberation from oppression and tradition. Since it was necessary, upon the intellectual side, to find justification for the movements of revolt, and since established authority was upon the side of institutional life, the natural recourse was appeal to some inalienable sacred authority resident in the protesting individuals. Thus "individualism" was born, a theory which endowed singular persons in isolation from any associations, except those which they deliberately formed for their own ends, with native or natural rights. The revolt against old and limiting associations was converted, intellectually, into the doctrine of independence of any and all associations.

Thus the practical movement for the limitation of the powers of government became associated, as in the influential philosophy of John Locke, with the doctrine that the ground and justification of the restriction was prior non-political rights inherent in the very structure of the individual. From these tenets, it was a short step to the conclusion that the sole end of government was the protection of individuals in the rights which were theirs by nature. The American revolution was a rebellion against an established government, and it naturally borrowed and expanded these ideas as the ideological interpretation of the effort to obtain independence of the colonies. It is now easy for the imagination to conceive circumstances under which revolts against prior governmental forms would have found its theoretical formulation in an assertion of the rights of groups, of other associations than those of a political nature. There was no logic which rendered necessary the appeal to the individual as an independent and isolated being. In abstract logic, it would have sufficed to assert that some primary groupings had claims which the state could not legitimately encroach upon. In that case, the celebrated modern antithesis of the Individual and Social, and the problem of their reconciliation, would not have arisen. The problem would have taken the form of defining the relationship which non-political groups bear to political union. But, as we have already remarked, the obnoxious state was closely bound up in fact and in tradition with other associations, ecclesiastic (and through its influence with the family), and economic, such as gilds and corporations, and, by means of the church-state, even with unions for scientific inquiry and with educational institutions. The easiest way out was to go back to the naked individual, to sweep away all associations as foreign to his nature and rights save as they proceeded from his own voluntary choice, and guaranteed his own private ends.

Nothing better exhibits the scope of the movement than the fact that philosophic theories of knowledge made the same appeal to the self, or ego, in the form of personal consciousness identified with mind itself, that political theory made to the natural individual, as the court of ultimate resort. The schools of Locke and Descartes, however much they were opposed in other respects, agreed in this, differing only as to whether the sentient or rational nature of the individual was the fundamental thing. From philosophy the idea crept into psychology, which became an introspective and introverted account of isolated and ultimate private consciousness. Henceforth moral and political individualism could appeal to "scientific" warrant for its tenets and employ a vocabulary made current by psychology:—although in fact the psychology appealed to as its scientific foundation was its own offspring.

The "individualistic" movement finds a classic expression in the great documents of the French Revolution, which at one stroke did away with all forms of association, leaving, in theory, the bare individual face to face with the state. It would hardly have reached this point, however, if it had not been for a second factor, which must be noted. A new scientific movement had been made possible by the invention and use of new mechanical appliances—the lens is typical—which focused attention upon tools like the lever and pendulum, which, although they had long been in use, had not formed points of departure for scientific theory. This new development in inquiry brought, as Bacon foretold, great economic changes in its wake. It more than paid its debt to tools by leading to the invention of machines. The use of machinery in production and commerce was followed by the creation of new powerful social conditions, personal opportunities and wants. Their adequate manifestation was limited by established political and legal practices. The legal regulations so affected every phase of life which was interested in taking advantage of the new economic agencies as to hamper and oppress the free play of manufacture and exchange. The established custom of states, expressed intellectually in the theory of mercantilism against which Adam Smith wrote his account of *The* (True) *Wealth of Nations*, prevented the expansion of trade between nations, a restriction which reacted to limit domestic industry. Internally, there was a network of restrictions inherited from feudalism. The prices of labor and staples were not framed in the market by higgling but were set by justices of the peace. The development of industry was hampered by laws regulating choice of a calling, apprenticeship, migration of workers from place to place,—and so on.

Thus fear of government and desire to limit its operations, because they were hostile to the development of the new agencies of production and distribution of services and commodities, received powerful reenforcement. The economic movement was perhaps the more influential because it operated, not in the name of the individual and his inherent rights, but in the name of Nature. Economic "laws," that of labor springing from natural wants and leading to the creation of wealth, of present abstinence in behalf of future enjoyment leading to creation of capital effective in piling up still more wealth, the free play of competitive exchange, designated the law of supply and demand, were "natural" laws. They were set in opposition to political laws as artificial, man-made affairs. The inherited tradition which remained least questioned was a conception of Nature which made Nature something to conjure with. The older metaphysical conception of Natural Law was, however, changed into an economic conception; laws of nature, implanted in human nature, regulated the production and exchange of goods and services, and in such a way that when they were kept free from artificial, that is political, meddling, they resulted in the maximum possible social prosperity and progress. Popular opinion is little troubled by questions of logical consistency. The economic theory of *laissez-faire,* based upon belief in beneficent natural laws which brought about harmony of personal profit and social benefit, was readily fused with the doctrine of natural rights. They both had the same practical import, and what is logic between friends? Thus the protest of the utilitarian school, which sponsored the economic theory of natural law in economics, against natural right theories had no effect in preventing the popular amalgam of the two sides.

The utilitarian economic theory was such an important factor in developing the theory, as distinct from the practice, of democratic government that it is worth while to expound it in outline. Each person naturally seeks the betterment of his own lot. This can be attained only by industry. Each person is naturally the best judge of his own interests, and, if left free from the influence of artificially imposed restrictions, will express his judgment in his choice of work and exchange of services and goods. Thus, barring accident, he will contribute to his own happiness in the measure of his energy in work, his shrewdness in exchange and his self-denying thrift. Wealth and security are the natural rewards of economic virtues. At the same time, the industry, commercial zeal, and ability of individuals contribute to the social good. Under the invisible hand of a beneficent providence which has framed natural laws, work, capital and trade operate harmoniously to the advantage and advance of men collectively and individually. The foe to be dreaded is interference of government. Political regulation is needed only because individuals accidentally and purposely—since the possession of property by the industrious and able is a temptation to the idle and shiftless—encroach upon one another's activities and properties. This encroachment is the essence of injustice, and the function of government is to secure justice—which signifies chiefly the protection of property and of the contracts which attend commercial exchange. Without the existence of the state men might appropriate one another's property. This appropriation is not only unfair to the laborious individual, but by making property insecure discourages the forthputting of energy at all and thus weakens or destroys the spring of social progress. On the other hand, this doctrine of the function of the state operates automatically as a limit imposed to governmental activities. The state is itself just only when it acts to secure justice—in the sense just defined.

The political problem thus conceived is essentially a problem of discovering and instating a technique which will confine the operations of government as far as may be to its legitimate business of protecting economic interests, of which the interest a man has in the integrity of his own life and body is a part. Rulers share the ordinary cupidity to possess property with a minimum of personal effort. Left to themselves they take advantage of the power with which their official position endows them to levy arbitrarily on the wealth of others. If they protect the industry and property of private citizens against the invasions of other private citizens, it is only that they may have more resources upon which to draw for their own ends. The essential problem of government thus reduces itself to this: What arrangements will prevent rulers from advancing their own interests at the expense of the ruled? Or, in positive terms, by what political means shall the interests of the governors be identified with those of the governed?

The answer was given, notably by James Mill, in a classic formulation of the nature of political democracy. Its significant features were popular election of officials, short terms of office and frequent elections. If public officials were dependent upon citizens for official position and its rewards, their personal interests would coincide with those of people at large—at least of industrious and property-owning persons. Officials chosen by popular vote would find their election to office dependent upon presenting evidence of their zeal and skill in protecting the interests of the populace. Short terms and frequent elections would ensure their being held to regular account; the polling-booth would constitute their day of judgment. The fear of it would operate as a constant check.

Of course in this account I have oversimplified what was already an oversimplification. The dissertation of James Mill was written before the passage of the Reform Bill of 1832. Taken pragmatically, it was an argument for the extension of the suffrage, then largely in the hands of hereditary landowners, to manufacturers and merchants. James Mill had nothing but dread of pure democracies. He opposed the extension of the franchise to women.[1] He was interested in the new "middle-class" forming

1. This last position promptly called forth a protest from the head of the utilitarian school, Jeremy Bentham.

under the influence of the application of steam to manufacture and trade. His attitude is well expressed in his conviction that even if the suffrage were extended downwards, the middle-class "which gives to science, art and legislation itself its most distinguished ornaments, and which is the chief source of all that is refined and exalted in human nature, is that portion of the community of which the influence would ultimately decide." In spite, however, of oversimplification, and of its special historic motivation, the doctrine claimed to rest upon universal psychological truth; it affords a fair picture of the principles which were supposed to justify the movement toward democratic government. It is unnecessary to indulge in extensive criticism. The differences between the conditions postulated by the theory and those which have actually obtained with the development of democratic governments speak for themselves. The discrepancy is a sufficient criticism. This disparity itself shows, however, that what has happened sprang from no theory but was inherent in what was going on not only without respect to theories but without regard to politics: because, generally speaking, of the use of steam applied to mechanical inventions.

It would be a great mistake, however, to regard the idea of the isolated individual possessed of inherent rights "by nature" apart from association, and the idea of economic laws as natural, in comparison with which political laws being artificial are injurious (save when carefully subordinated), as idle and impotent. The ideas were something more than flies on the turning wheels. They did not originate the movement toward popular government, but they did profoundly influence the forms which it assumed. Or perhaps it would be truer to say that persistent older conditions, to which the theories were more faithful than to the state of affairs they professed to report, were so reenforced by the professed philosophy of the democratic state, as to exercise a great influence. The result was a skew, a deflection and distortion, in democratic forms. Putting the "individualistic" matter in a gross statement, which has to be corrected by later qualifications, we may say that "the individual," about which the new philosophy centered itself, was in process of complete submergence in fact at the very time in which he was being elevated on high in theory. As to the alleged subordination of political affairs to natural forces and laws, we may say that actual economic conditions were thoroughly artificial, in the sense in which the theory condemned the artificial. They supplied the man-made instrumentalities by which the new governmental agencies were grasped and used to suit the desires of the new class of business men.

Both of these statements are formal as well as sweeping. To acquire intelligible meaning they must be developed in some detail. Graham Wallas prefixed to the first chapter of his book entitled *The Great Society* the following words of Woodrow Wilson, taken from *The New Freedom*: "Yesterday and ever since history began, men were related to one another as individuals. . . . To-day, the every-day relationships of men are largely with great impersonal concerns, with organisations, not with other individuals. Now this is nothing short of a new social age, a new age of human relationships, a new stage-setting for the drama of life." If we accept these words as containing even a moderate degree of truth, they indicate the enormous ineptitude of the individualistic philosophy to meet the needs and direct the factors of the new age. They suggest what is meant by saying the theory of an individual possessed of desires and claims and endued with foresight and prudence and love of bettering himself was framed at just the time when the individual was counting for less in the direction of social affairs, at a time when mechanical forces and vast impersonal organizations were determining the frame of things.

The statement that "yesterday and ever since history began, men were related to one another as individuals" is not true. Men have always been associated together in living, and association in conjoint behavior has affected their relations to one another as individuals. It is enough to recall how largely human relations have been permeated by patterns derived directly and indirectly from the family; even the state was a dynastic affair. But none the less the contrast which Mr. Wilson had in mind is a fact. The earlier associations were mostly of the type well termed by Cooley[2] "face-to-face." Those which were important, which really counted in forming emotional and intellectual dispositions, were local and contiguous and consequently visible. Human beings, if they shared in them at all, shared directly and in a

2. C. H. Cooley, *Social Organization*, Ch. 3, on "Primary Groups."

way of which they were aware in both their affections and their beliefs. The state, even when it despotically interfered, was remote, an agency alien to daily life. Otherwise it entered men's lives through custom and common law. No matter how widespread their operation might be, it was not their breadth and inclusiveness which counted but their immediate local presence. The church was indeed both a universal and an intimate affair. But it entered into the life of most human beings not through its universality, as far as their thoughts and habits were concerned, but through an immediate ministration of rites and sacraments. The new technology applied in production and commerce resulted in a social revolution. The local communities without intent or forecast found their affairs conditioned by remote and invisible organizations. The scope of the latter's activities was so vast and their impact upon face-to-face associations so pervasive and unremitting that it is no exaggeration to speak of "a new age of human relations." The Great Society created by steam and electricity may be a society, but it is no community. The invasion of the community by the new and relatively impersonal and mechanical modes of combined human behavior is the outstanding fact of modern life. In these ways of aggregate activity the community, in its strict sense, is not a conscious partner, and over them it has no direct control. They were, however, the chief factors in bringing into being national and territorial states. The need of some control over them was the chief agency in making the government of these states democratic or popular in the current sense of these words.

Why, then, was a movement, which involved so much submerging of personal action in the overflowing consequences of remote and inaccessible collective actions, reflected in a philosophy of individualism? A complete answer is out of the question. Two considerations are, however, obvious and significant. The new conditions involved a release of human potentialities previously dormant. While their impact was unsettling to the community, it was liberating with respect to single persons, while its oppressive phase was hidden in the impenetrable mists of the future. Speaking with greater correctness, the oppressive phase affected primarily the elements of the community which were also depressed in the older and semi-feudal conditions. Since they did not count for much anyway, being traditionally the drawers of water and hewers of wood, having emerged only in a legal sense from serfdom, the effect of new economic conditions upon the laboring masses went largely unnoted. Day laborers were still in effect, as openly in the classic philosophy, underlying conditions of community life rather than members of it. Only gradually did the effect upon them become apparent; by that time they had attained enough power—were sufficiently important factors in the new economic régime—to obtain political emancipation, and thus figure in the forms of the democratic state. Meanwhile the liberating effect was markedly conspicuous with respect to the members of the "middle-class," the manufacturing and mercantile class. It would be short-sighted to limit the release of powers to opportunities to procure wealth and enjoy its fruits, although the creation of material wants and ability to satisfy them are not to be lightly passed over. Initiative, inventiveness, foresight and planning were also stimulated and confirmed. This manifestation of new powers was on a sufficiently large scale to strike and absorb attention. The result was formulated as the discovery of the individual. The customary is taken for granted; it operates subconsciously. Breach of wont and use is focal; it forms "consciousness." The necessary and persistent modes of association went unnoticed. The new ones, which were voluntarily undertaken, occupied thought exclusively. They monopolized the observed horizon. "Individualism" was a doctrine which stated what was focal in thought and purpose.

The other consideration is akin. In the release of new powers singular persons were emancipated from a mass of old habits, regulations and institutions. We have already noted how the methods of production and exchange made possible by the new technology were hampered by the rules and customs of the prior régime. The latter were then felt to be intolerably restrictive and oppressive. Since they hampered the free play of initiative and commercial activity, they were artificial and enslaving. The struggle for emancipation from their influence was identified with the liberty of the individual as such; in the intensity of the struggle, associations and institutions were condemned wholesale as foes of freedom save as they were products of personal agreement and voluntary choice. That many forms of association remained practically untouched was easily overlooked, just because they were matters of course. Indeed, any attempt to touch them, notably the established form of family association and the legal institution of property, were looked upon as subversive, as license, not liberty, in the sanctified phrase. The identification of democratic forms of government with this individualism was easy. The right of suffrage represented for the mass a release of hitherto dormant capacity and also, in appearance at least, a power to shape social relations on the basis of individual volition.

Popular franchise and majority rule afforded the imagination a picture of individuals in their untrammeled individual sovereignty making the state. To adherents and opponents alike it presented the spectacle of a pulverizing of established associations into the desires and intentions of atomic individuals. The forces, springing from combination and institutional organization which controlled below the surface the acts which formally issued from individuals, went unnoted. It is the essence of ordinary thought to grasp the external scene and hold it as reality. The familiar eulogies of the spectacle of "free men" going to the polls to determine by their personal volitions the political forms under which they should live is a specimen of this tendency to take whatever is readily seen as the full reality of a situation. In physical matters natural science has successfully challenged this attitude. In human matters it remains in almost full force.

The opponents of popular government were no more prescient than its supporters, although they showed more logical sense in following the assumed individualistic premise to its conclusion: the disintegration of society. Carlyle's savage attacks upon the notion of a society held together only by a "cash-nexus" are well known. Its inevitable terminus to him was "anarchy plus a constable." He did not see that the new industrial régime was forging social bonds as rigid as those which were disappearing and much more extensive—whether desirable ties or not is another matter. Macaulay, the intellectualist of the Whigs, asserted that the extension of suffrage to the masses would surely result in arousing the predatory impulses of the propertyless masses who would use their new political power to despoil the middle as well as upper class. He added that while there was no longer danger that the civilized portions of humanity would be overthrown by the savage and barbarous portions, it was possible that in the bosom of civilization would be engendered the malady which would destroy it.

Incidentally we have trenched upon the other doctrine, the idea that there is something inherently "natural" and amenable to "natural law" in the working of economic forces, in contrast with the man-made artificiality of political institutions. The idea of a natural individual in his isolation possessed of full-fledged wants, of energies to be expended according to his own volition, and of a ready-made faculty of foresight and prudent calculation is as much a fiction in psychology as the doctrine of the individual in possession of antecedent political rights is one in politics. The liberalist school made much of desires, but to them desire was a conscious matter deliberately directed upon a known goal of pleasures. Desire and pleasure were both open and above-board affairs. The mind was seen as if always in the bright sunlight, having no hidden recesses, no unexplorable nooks, nothing underground. Its operations were like the moves in a fair game of chess. They are in the open; the players have nothing up their sleeves; the changes of position take place by express intent and in plain sight; they take place according to rules all of which are known in advance. Calculation and skill, or dullness and inaptitude, determine the result. Mind was "consciousness," and the latter was a clear, transparent, self-revealing medium in which wants, efforts and purposes were exposed without distortion.

To-day it is generally admitted that conduct proceeds from conditions which are largely out of focal attention, and which can be discovered and brought to light only by inquiries more exacting than those which teach us the concealed relationships involved in gross physical phenomena. What is not so generally acknowledged is that the underlying and generative conditions of concrete behavior are social as well as organic: much more social than organic as far as the manifestation of *differential* wants, purposes and methods of operation is concerned. To those who appreciate this fact, it is evident that the desires, aims and standards of satisfaction which the dogma of "natural" economic processes and laws assumes are themselves socially conditioned phenomena. They are reflections into the singular human being of customs and institutions; they are not natural, that is, "native," organic propensities. They mirror a state of civilization. Even more true, if possible, is it that the form in which work is done, industry carried on, is the outcome of accumulated culture, not an original possession of persons in their own structure. There is little that can be called industry and still less that constitutes a store of wealth until tools exist, and tools are the results of slow processes of transmission. The development of tools into machines, the characteristic of the industrial age, was made possible only by taking advantage of science socially accumulated and transmitted. The technique of employing tools and machines was equally something which had to be learned; it was no natural endowment but something acquired by observing others, by instruction and communication.

These sentences are a poor and pallid way of conveying the outstanding fact. There are organic or native needs, of course, as for food, protection and mates. There are innate structures which facilitate them in securing the external objects through which they are met. But the only kind of industry they are capable of giving rise to is a precarious livelihood obtained by gathering such edible plants and animals as chance might throw in the way: the lowest type of savagery just emerging from a brute condition. Nor, strictly speaking, could they effect even this meagre result. For because of the phenomenon of helpless infancy even such a primitive régime depends upon the assistance of associated action, including that most valuable form of assistance: learning from others. What would even savage industry be without the use of fire, of weapons, of woven articles, all of which involve communication and tradition? The industrial régime which the authors of "natural" economy contemplated presupposed wants, tools, materials, purposes, techniques and abilities in a thousand ways dependent upon associated behavior. Thus in the sense in which the authors of the doctrine employed the word "artificial," these things were intensely and cumulatively artificial. What they were really after was a changed direction of custom and institutions. The outcome of the acts of those who were engaged in forwarding the new industry and commerce was a new set of customs and institutions. The latter were as much extensive and enduring conjoint modes of life as were those which they displaced; more so in their sweep and force.

The bearing of this fact upon political theory and practice is evident. Not only were the wants and intentions which actually operated functions of associated life, but they re-determined the forms and temper of this life. Athenians did not buy Sunday newspapers, make investments in stocks and bonds, nor want motor cars. Nor do we to-day want for the most part beautiful bodies and beauty of architectural surroundings. We are mostly satisfied with the result of cosmetics and with ugly slums, and oftentimes with equally ugly palaces. We do not "naturally" or organically need them, but we *want* them. If we do not demand them directly we demand them none the less effectively. For they are necessary consequences of the things upon which we have set our hearts. In other words, a community wants (in the only intelligible sense of wanting, effective demand) either education or ignorance, lovely or squalid surroundings, railway trains or ox-carts, stocks and bonds, pecuniary profit or constructive arts, according as associated activity presents these things to them habitually, esteems them, and supplies the means of attaining them. But that is only half the tale.

Associated behavior directed toward objects which fulfill wants not only produces those objects, but brings customs and institutions into being. The indirect and unthought-of consequences are usually more important than the direct. The fallacy of supposing that the new industrial régime would produce just and for the most part only the consequences consciously forecast and aimed at was the counterpart of the fallacy that the wants and efforts characteristic of it were functions of "natural" human beings. They arose out of institutionalized action and they resulted in institutionalized action. The disparity between the results of the industrial revolution and the conscious intentions of those engaged in it is a remarkable case of the extent to which indirect consequences of conjoint activity outweigh, beyond the possibility of reckoning, the results directly contemplated. Its outcome was the development of those extensive and invisible bonds, those "great impersonal concerns, organizations," which now pervasively affect the thinking, willing and doing of everybody, and which have ushered in the "new era of human relationships."

Equally undreamed of was the effect of the massive organizations and complicated interactions upon the state. Instead of the independent, self-moved individuals contemplated by the theory, we have standardized interchangeable units. Persons are joined together, not because they have voluntarily chosen to be united in these forms, but because vast currents are running which bring men together. Green and red lines, marking out political boundaries, are on the maps and affect legislation and jurisdiction of courts, but railways, mails and telegraph-wires disregard them. The consequences of the latter influence more profoundly those living within the legal local units than do boundary lines. The forms of associated action characteristic of the present economic order are so massive and extensive that they determine the most significant constituents of the public and the residence of power. Inevitably they reach out to grasp the agencies of government; they are controlling factors in legislation and administration. Not chiefly because of deliberate and planned self-interest, large as may be its role, but because they are the most potent and best organized of social forces. In a word, the new forms of combined action due to the modern economic régime control present politics, much as dynastic interests controlled those of two centuries ago. They affect thinking and desire more than did the interests which formerly moved the state.

We have spoken as if the displacement of old legal and political institutions was all but complete. That is a gross exaggeration. Some of the most fundamental of traditions and habits have hardly been affected at all. It is enough to mention the institution of property. The naïveté with which the philosophy of "natural" economics ignored the effect upon industry and commerce of the legal status of property, the way in which it identified wealth and property in the legal form in which the latter had existed, is almost incredible to-day. But the simple fact is that technological industry has not operated with any great degree of freedom. It has been confined and deflected at every point; it has never taken its own course. The engineer has worked in subordination to the business manager whose primary concern is not with wealth but with the interests of property as worked out in the feudal and semi-feudal period. Thus the one point in which the philosophers of "Individualism" predicted truly was that in which they did not predict at all, but in which they merely clarified and simplified established wont and use: when, that is, they asserted that the main business of government is to make property interests secure.

A large part of the indictments which are now drawn against technological industry are chargeable to the unchanged persistence of a legal institution inherited from the pre-industrial age. It is confusing, however, to identify in a wholesale way this issue with the question of private property. It is conceivable that private property may function socially. It does so even now to a considerable degree. Otherwise it could not be supported for a day. The extent of its social utility is what blinds us to the numerous and great social disutilities that attend its present working, or at least reconcile us to its continuation. The real issue or at least the issue to be first settled concerns the conditions under which the institution of private property legally and politically functions.

We thus reach our conclusion. The same forces which have brought about the forms of democratic government, general suffrage, executives and legislators chosen by majority vote, have also brought about conditions which halt the social and humane ideals that demand the utilization of government as the genuine instrumentality of an inclusive and fraternally associated public. "The new age of human relationships" has no political agencies worthy of it. The democratic public is still largely inchoate and unorganized.

4. The Eclipse of the Public

Optimism about democracy is to-day under a cloud. We are familiar with denunciation and criticism which, however, often reveal their emotional source in their peevish and un-discriminating tone. Many of them suffer from the same error into which earlier laudations fell. They assume that democracy is the product of an idea, of a single and consistent intent. Carlyle was no admirer of democracy, but in a lucid moment he said: "Invent the printing press and democracy is inevitable." Add to this: Invent the railway, the telegraph, mass manufacture and concentration of population in urban centres, and some form of democratic government is, humanly speaking, inevitable. Political democracy as it exists to-day calls for adverse criticism in abundance. But the criticism is only an exhibition of querulous-ness and spleen or of a superiority complex, unless it takes cognizance of the conditions out of which popular government has issued. All intelligent political criticism is comparative. It deals not with all-or-none situations, but with practical alternatives; an absolutistic indiscriminate attitude, whether in praise or blame, testifies to the heat of feeling rather than the light of thought.

American democratic polity was developed out of genuine community life, that is, association in local and small centres where industry was mainly agricultural and where production was carried on mainly with hand tools. It took form when English political habits and legal institutions worked under pioneer conditions. The forms of association were stable, even though their units were mobile and migratory. Pioneer conditions put a high premium upon personal work, skill, ingenuity, initiative and adaptability, and upon neighborly sociability. The township or some not much larger area was the political unit, the town meet-ing the political medium, and roads, schools, the peace of the community, were the political objectives. The state was a sum of such units, and the national state a federation—unless perchance a confederation—of states. The imagination of the founders did not travel far beyond what could be accomplished and understood in a congeries of self-governing communities. The machinery provided for the selection of the chief executive of the federal union is illustrative evidence. The electoral college assumed that citizens would choose men locally known for their high standing; and that these men when chosen would gather together for consultation to name some one known to them for his probity and public spirit and knowledge. The rapidity with which the scheme fell into disuse is evidence of the transitoriness of the state of affairs that was predicated. But at the outset there was no dream of the time when the very names of the presidential electors would be unknown to the mass of the voters, when they would plump for a "ticket" arranged in a more or less private caucus, and when the electoral college would be an impersonal registering machine, such that it would be treachery to employ the personal judgment which was originally contemplated as the essence of the affair.

The local conditions under which our institutions took shape is well indicated by our system, apparently so systemless, of public education. Any one who has tried to explain it to a European will understand what is meant. One is asked, say, what method of administration is followed, what is the course of study and what the authorized methods of teaching. The American member to the dialogue replies that in this state, or more likely county, or town, or even some section of a town called a district, matters stand thus and thus; somewhere else, so and so. The participant from this side is perhaps thought by the foreigner to be engaged in concealing his ignorance; and it would certainly take a veritable cyclopedic knowledge to state the matter in its entirety. The impossibility of making any moderately generalized reply renders it almost indispensable to resort to a historical account in order to be intelligible. A little colony, the members of which are probably mostly known to one another in advance, settle in what is almost, or quite, a wilderness. From belief in its benefits and by tradition, chiefly religious, they wish their children to know at least how to read, write and figure. Families can only rarely provide a tutor; the neighbors over a certain area, in

New England an area smaller even than the township, combine in a "school district." They get a schoolhouse built, perhaps by their own labor, and hire a teacher by means of a committee, and the teacher is paid from the taxes. Custom determines the limited course of study, and tradition the methods of the teacher, modified by whatever personal insight and skill he may bring to bear. The wilderness is gradually subdued; a network of highways, then of railways, unite the previously scattered communities. Large cities grow up; studies grow more numerous and methods more carefully scrutinized. The larger unit, the state, but not the federal state, provides schools for training teachers and their qualifications are more carefully looked into and tested. But subject to certain quite general conditions imposed by the state-legislature, but not the national state, local maintenance and control remain the rule. The community pattern is more complicated, but is not destroyed. The instance seems richly instructive as to the state of affairs under which our borrowed, English, political institutions were reshaped and forwarded.

We have inherited, in short, local town-meeting practices and ideas. But we live and act and have our being in a continental national state. We are held together by non-political bonds, and the political forms are stretched and legal institutions patched in an *ad hoc* and improvised manner to do the work they have to do. Political structures fix the channels in which non-political, industrialized currents flow. Railways, travel and transportation, commerce, the mails, telegraph and telephone, newspapers, create enough similarity of ideas and sentiments to keep the thing going as a whole, for they create interaction and interdependence. The unprecedented thing is that states, as distinguished from military empires, can exist over such a wide area. The notion of maintaining a unified state, even nominally self-governing, over a country as extended as the United States and consisting of a large and racially diversified population would once have seemed the wildest of fancies. It was assumed that such a state could be found only in territories hardly larger than a city-state and with a homogeneous population. It seemed almost self-evident to Plato—as to Rousseau later—that a genuine state could hardly be larger than the number of persons capable of personal acquaintance with one another. Our modern state-unity is due to the consequences of technology employed so as to facilitate the rapid and easy circulation of opinions and information, and so as to generate constant and intricate interaction far beyond the limits of face-to-face communities. Political and legal forms have only piecemeal and haltingly, with great lag, accommodated themselves to the industrial transformation. The elimination of distance, at the base of which are physical agencies, has called into being the new form of political association.

The wonder of the performance is the greater because of the odds against which it has been achieved. The stream of immigrants which has poured in is so large and heterogeneous that under conditions which formerly obtained it would have disrupted any semblance of unity as surely as the migratory invasion of alien hordes once upset the social equilibrium of the European continent. No deliberately adopted measures could have accomplished what has actually happened. Mechanical forces have operated, and it is no cause for surprise if the effect is more mechanical than vital. The reception of new elements of population in large number from heterogeneous peoples, often hostile to one another at home, and the welding them into even an outward show of unity is an extraordinary feat. In many respects, the consolidation has occurred so rapidly and ruthlessly that much of value has been lost which different peoples might have contributed. The creation of political unity has also promoted social and intellectual uniformity, a standardization favorable to mediocrity. Opinion has been regimented as well as outward behavior. The temper and flavor of the pioneer have evaporated with extraordinary rapidity; their precipitate, as is often noted, is apparent only in the wild-west romance and the movie. What Bagehot called the cake of custom formed with increasing acceleration, and the cake is too often flat and soggy. Mass production is not confined to the factory.

The resulting political integration has confounded the expectations of earlier critics of popular government as much as it must surprise its early backers if they are gazing from on high upon the present scene. The critics predicted disintegration, instability. They foresaw the new society falling apart, dissolving into mutually repellent animated grains of sand. They, too, took seriously the theory of "Individualism" as the basis of democratic government. A stratification of society into immemorial classes within which each person performed his stated duties according to his fixed position seemed to them the only warrant of stability. They had no faith that human beings released from the pressure of this system could hold together in any unity. Hence they prophesied a flux of governmental régimes, as individuals formed factions, seized power, and then lost it as some newly improvised faction proved stronger. Had the facts conformed to the theory of Individualism, they would doubtless have been right. But, like the authors of the theory, they ignored the technological forces making for consolidation.

In spite of attained integration, or rather perhaps because of its nature, the Public seems to be lost; it is certainly bewildered.[1] The government, officials and their activities, are plainly with us. Legislatures make laws with luxurious abandon; subordinate officials engage in a losing struggle to enforce some of them; judges on the bench deal as best they can with the steadily mounting pile of disputes that come before them. But where is the public which these officials are supposed to represent? How much more is it than geographical names and official titles? The United States, the state of Ohio or New York, the county of this and the city of that? Is the public much more than what a cynical diplomat once called Italy: a geographical expression? Just as philosophers once imputed a substance to qualities and traits in order that the latter might have something in which to inhere and thereby gain a conceptual solidity and consistency which they lacked on their face, so perhaps our political "common-sense" philosophy imputes a public only to support and substantiate the behavior of officials. How can the latter be public officers, we despairingly ask, unless there is a public? If a public exists, it is surely as uncertain about its own whereabouts as philosophers since Hume have been about the residence and make-up of the self. The number of voters who take advantage of their majestic right is steadily decreasing in proportion to those who might use it. The ratio of actual to eligible voters is now about one-half. In spite of somewhat frantic appeal and organized effort, the endeavor to bring voters to a sense of their privileges and duties has so far been noted for failure. A few preach the impotence of

1. See Walter Lippmann's *The Phantom Public*. To this as well as to his *Public Opinion*, I wish to acknowledge my indebtedness, not only as to this particular point, but for ideas involved in my entire discussion even when it reaches conclusions diverging from his.

all politics; the many nonchalantly practice abstinence and indulge in indirect action. Skepticism regarding the efficacy of voting is openly expressed, not only in the theories of intellectuals, but in the words of lowbrow masses: "What difference does it make whether I vote or not? Things go on just the same anyway. My vote never changed anything." Those somewhat more reflective add: "It is nothing but a fight between the ins and the outs. The only difference made by an election is as to who get the jobs, draw the salaries and shake down the plum tree."

Those still more inclined to generalization assert that the whole apparatus of political activities is a kind of protective coloration to conceal the fact that big business rules the governmental roost in any case. Business is the order of the day, and the attempt to stop or deflect its course is as futile as Mrs. Partington essaying to sweep back the tides with a broom. Most of those who hold these opinions would profess to be shocked if the doctrine of economic determinism were argumentatively expounded to them, but they act upon a virtual belief in it. Nor is acceptance of the doctrine limited to radical socialists. It is implicit in the attitude of men of big business and financial interests, who revile the former as destructive "Bolshevists." For it is their firm belief that "prosperity"—a word which has taken on religious color— is the great need of the country, that they are its authors and guardians, and hence by right the determiners of polity. Their denunciations of the "materialism" of socialists is based simply upon the fact that the latter want a different distribution of material force and well-being than that which satisfies those now in control.

The unfitness of whatever public exists, with respect to the government which is nominally its organ, is made manifest in the extra-legal agencies which have grown up. Intermediary groups are closest to the political conduct of affairs. It is interesting to compare the English literature of the eighteenth century regarding factions with the status actually occupied by parties. Factionalism was decried by all thinkers as the chief enemy to political stability. Their voice of condemnation is reechoed in the writing of early nineteenth-century American writers on politics. Extensive and consolidated factions under the name of parties are now not only a matter of course, but popular imagination can conceive of no other way by which officials may be selected and governmental affairs carried on. The centralizing movement has reached a point where even a third party can lead only a spasmodic and precarious existence. Instead of individuals who in the privacy of their consciousness make choices which are carried into effect by personal volition, there are citizens who have the blessed opportunity to vote for a ticket of men mostly unknown to them, and which is made up for them by an undercover machine in a caucus whose operations constitute a kind of political predestination. There are those who speak as if ability to choose between two tickets were a high exercise of individual freedom. But it is hardly the kind of liberty contemplated by the authors of the individualistic doctrine. "Nature abhors a vacuum." When the public is as uncertain and obscure as it is today, and hence as remote from government, bosses with their political machines fill the void between government and the public. Who pulls the strings which move the bosses and generates power to run the machines is a matter of surmise rather than of record, save for an occasional overt scandal.

Quite aside, however, from the allegation that "Big Business" plays the tune and pulls the strings to which bosses dance, it is true that parties are not creators of policies to any large extent at the present time. For parties yield in piece-meal accommodation to social currents, irrespective of professed principles. As these lines are written a weekly periodical remarks: "Since the end of the Civil War practically all the more important measures which have been embodied in federal legislation have been reached without a national election which turned upon the issue and which divided the two major parties." Reform of civil service, regulation of railways, popular election of senators, national income tax, suffrage for women, and prohibition are supported to substantiate the statement. Hence its other remark appears justified: "American party politics seem at times to be a device for preventing issues which may excite popular feeling and involve bitter controversies from being put up to the American people."

A negatively corroborating fact is seen in the fate of the Child Labor amendment. The need of giving to Congress power to regulate child labor, denied it by decisions of the Supreme Court, had been asserted in the platforms of all political parties; the idea was endorsed by the last three of the presidents belonging to the party in power. Yet so far, the proposed amendment to the

Constitution has not begun to secure the needed support. Political parties may rule, but they do not govern. The public is so confused and eclipsed that it cannot even use the organs through which it is supposed to mediate political action and polity.

The same lesson is taught by the breakdown of the theory of the responsibility of elected representatives to the electorate, to say nothing of their alleged liability to be called before the bar of the private judgment of individuals. It is at least suggestive that the terms of the theory are best met in legislation of the "pork-barrel" type. There a representative may be called to account for failure to meet local desire, or be rewarded for pertinacity and success in fulfilling its wishes. But only rarely is the theory borne out in important matters, although occasionally it works. But the instances are so infrequent that any skilled political observer could enumerate them by name. The reason for the lack of personal liability to the electorate is evident. The latter is composed of rather amorphous groups. Their political ideas and beliefs are mostly in abeyance between elections. Even in times of political excitement, artificially accelerated, their opinions are moved collectively by the current of the group rather than by independent personal judgment. As a rule, what decides the fate of a person who comes up for election is neither his political excellence nor his political defects. The current runs for or against the party in power and the individual candidate sinks or swims as runs the current. At times there is a general consensus of sentiment, a definite trend in favor of "progressive legislation" or a desire for a "return to normalcy." But even then only exceptional candidates get by on any basis of personal responsibility to the electorate. The "tidal wave" swamps some; the "landslide" carries others into office. At other times, habit, party funds, the skill of managers of the machine, the portrait of a candidate with his firm jaw, his lovely wife and children, and a multitude of other irrelevancies, determine the issue.

These scattered comments are not made in the belief that they convey any novel truth. Such things are familiar; they are the common-places of the political scene. They could be extended indefinitely by any careful observer of the scene. The significant thing is that familiarity has bred indifference if not contempt. Indifference is the evidence of current apathy, and apathy is testimony to the fact that the public is so bewildered that it cannot find itself. The remarks are not made with a view to drawing a conclusion. They are offered with a view to outlining a problem: What is the public? If there is a public, what are the obstacles in the way of its recognizing and articulating itself? Is the public a myth? Or does it come into being only in periods of marked social transition when crucial alternative issues stand out, such as that between throwing one's lot in with the conservation of established institutions or with forwarding new tendencies? In a reaction against dynastic rule which has come to be felt as despotically oppressive? In a transfer of social power from agrarian classes to industrial?

Is not the problem at the present time that of securing experts to manage administrative matters, other than the framing of policies? It may be urged that the present confusion and apathy are due to the fact that the real energy of society is now directed in all non-political matters by trained specialists who manage things, while politics are carried on with a machinery and ideas formed in the past to deal with quite another sort of situation. There is no particular public concerned in finding expert school instructors, competent doctors, or business managers. Nothing called a public intervenes to instruct physicians in the practice of the healing art or merchants in the art of salesmanship. The conduct of these callings and others characteristic of our time are decided by science and pseudo-science. The important governmental affairs at present, it may be argued, are also technically complicated matters to be conducted properly by experts. And if at present people are not educated to the recognition of the importance of finding experts and of entrusting administration to them, it may plausibly be asserted that the prime obstruction lies in the superstitious belief that there is a public concerned to determine the formation and execution of general social policies. Perhaps the apathy of the electorate is due to the irrelevant artificiality of the issues with which it is attempted to work up factitious excitement. Perhaps this artificiality is in turn mainly due to the survival of political beliefs and machinery from a period when science and technology were so immature as not to permit of a definite technique for handling definite social situations and meeting specific social needs. The attempt to decide by law that the legends of a primitive Hebrew people regarding the genesis of man are more authoritative than the results of scientific inquiry might be cited as a typical example of the sort of thing which is bound to happen when the accepted doctrine is that a public organized for political purposes, rather than experts guided by specialized inquiry, is the final umpire and arbiter of issues.

The questions of most concern at present may be said to be matters like sanitation, public health, healthful and adequate housing, transportation, planning of cities, regulation and distribution of immigrants, selection and management of personnel, right methods of instruction and preparation of competent teachers, scientific adjustment of taxation, efficient management of funds, and so on. These are technical matters, as much so as the construction of an efficient engine for purposes of traction or locomotion. Like it they are to be settled by inquiry into facts; and as the inquiry can be carried on only by those especially equipped, so the results of inquiry can be utilized only by trained technicians. What has counting heads, decision by majority and the whole apparatus of traditional government to do with such things? Given such considerations, and the public and its organization for political ends is not only a ghost, but a ghost which walks and talks, and obscures, confuses and misleads governmental action in a disastrous way.

Personally I am far from thinking that such considerations, pertinent as they are to administrative activities, cover the entire political field. They ignore forces which have to be composed and resolved before technical and specialized action can come into play. But they aid in giving definiteness and point to a fundamental question: What, after all, is the public under present conditions? What are the reasons for its eclipse? What hinders it from finding and identifying itself? By what means shall its inchoate and amorphous estate be organized into effective political action relevant to present social needs and opportunities? What has happened to the Public in the century and a half since the theory of political democracy was urged with such assurance and hope?

Previous discussion has brought to light some conditions out of which the public is generated. It has also set forth some of the causes through which a "new age of human relationships" has been brought into being. These two arguments form the premises which, when they are related to each other, will provide our answer to the questions just raised. Indirect, extensive, enduring and serious consequences of conjoint and interacting behavior call a public into existence having a common interest in controlling these consequences. But the machine age has so enormously expanded, multiplied, intensified and complicated the scope of the indirect consequences, has formed such immense and consolidated unions in action, on an impersonal rather than a community basis, that the resultant public cannot identify and distinguish itself. And this discovery is obviously an antecedent condition of any effective organization on its part. Such is our thesis regarding the eclipse which the public idea and interest have undergone. There are too many publics and too much of public concern for our existing resources to cope with. The problem of a democratically organized public is primarily and essentially an intellectual problem, in a degree to which the political affairs of prior ages offer no parallel.

Our concern at this time is to state how it is that the machine age in developing the Great Society has invaded and partially disintegrated the small communities of former times without generating a Great Community. The facts are familiar enough; our especial affair is to point out their connections with the difficulties under which the organization of a democratic public is laboring. For the very familiarity with the phenomena conceals their significance and blinds us to their relation to immediate political problems.

The scope of the Great War furnishes an urgent as well as convenient starting point for the discussion. The extent of that war is unparalleled, because the conditions involved in it are so new. The dynastic conflicts of the seventeenth century are called by the same name: we have only one word, "war." The sameness of the word too easily conceals from us the difference in significance. We think of all wars as much the same thing, only the last one was horrible beyond others. Colonies were drawn in: self-governing ones entered voluntarily; possessions were levied upon for troops; alliances were formed with remote countries in spite of diversities of race and culture, as in the cases of Great Britain and Japan, Germany and Turkey. Literally every continent upon the globe was involved. Indirect effects were as broad as direct. Not merely soldiers, but finance, industry and opinion were mobilized and consolidated. Neutrality was a precarious affair.

There was a critical epoch in the history of the world when the Roman Empire assembled in itself the lands and peoples of the Mediterranean basin. The World War stands out as an indubitable proof that what then happened for a region has now happened for the world, only there is now no comprehensive political organization to include the various divided yet interdependent countries. Any one who even partially visualizes the scene has a convincing reminder of the meaning of the Great Society: that it exists, and that it is not integrated.

Extensive, enduring, intricate and serious indirect consequences of the conjoint activity of a comparatively few persons traverse the globe. The similes of the stone cast into the pool, ninepins in a row, the spark which kindles a vast conflagration, are pale in comparison with the reality. The spread of the war seemed like the movement of an uncontrolled natural catastrophe. The consolidation of peoples in enclosed, nominally independent, national states has its counterpart in the fact that their acts affect groups and individuals in other states all over the world. The connections and ties which transferred energies set in motion in one spot to all parts of the earth were not tangible and visible; they do not stand out as do politically bounded states. But the war is there to show that they are as real, and to prove that they are not organized and regulated. It suggests that existing political and legal forms and arrangements are incompetent to deal with the situation. For the latter is the joint product of the existing constitution of the political state and the working of non-political forces not adjusted to political forms. We cannot expect the causes of a disease to combine effectually to cure the disease they create. The need is that the non-political forces organize themselves to transform existing political structures: that the divided and troubled publics integrate.

In general, the non-political forces are the expressions of a technological age injected into an inherited political scheme which operates to deflect and distort their normal operation. The industrial and commercial relations that created the situation of which the war is a manifestation are as evident in small things as great. They were exhibited, not only in the struggle for raw materials, for distant markets, and in staggering national debts, but in local and unimportant phenomena. Travelers finding themselves away from home could not get their letters of credit cashed even in countries not then at war. Stockmarkets closed on one hand, and profiteers piled up their millions on the other. One instance may be cited from domestic affairs. The plight of the farmer since the war has created a domestic political issue. A great demand was generated for food and other agricultural products; prices rose. In addition to this economic stimulus, farmers were objects of constant political exhortation to increase their crops. Inflation and temporary prosperity followed. The end of active warfare came. Impoverished countries could not buy and pay for foodstuffs up to even a pre-war level. Taxes were enormously increased. Currencies were depreciated; the world's gold supply centered here. The stimulus of war and of national extravagance piled up the inventories of factories and merchants. Wages and the prices of agricultural implements increased. When deflation came it found a restricted market, increased costs of production, and farmers burdened with mortgages lightly assumed during the period of frenzied expansion.

This instance is not cited because it is peculiarly important in comparison with other consequences which have happened, especially in Europe. It is relatively insignificant by contrast with them, and in contrast with the arousal of nationalistic sentiments which has everywhere taken place since the war in so-called backward countries. But it shows the ramifying consequences of our intricate and interdependent economic relations, and it shows how little prevision and regulation exist. The farming population could hardly have acted with knowledge of the consequences of the fundamental relations in which they were implicated. They could make a momentary and improvised response to them, but they could not manage their affairs in controlled adaptation to the course of events. They present themselves as hapless subjects of overwhelming operations with which they were hardly acquainted and over which they had no more control than over the vicissitudes of climate.

The illustration cannot be objected to on the ground that it rests upon the abnormal situation of war. The war itself was a normal manifestation of the underlying unintegrated state of society. The local face-to-face community has been invaded by forces so vast, so remote in initiation, so far-reaching in scope and so complexly indirect in operation, that they are, from the standpoint of the members of local social units, unknown. Man, as has been often remarked, has difficulty in getting on either with or without his fellows, even in neighborhoods. He is not more successful in getting on with them when they act at a great distance in ways invisible to him. An inchoate public is capable of organization only when indirect consequences are perceived, and when it is possible to project agencies which order their occurrence. At present, many consequences are felt rather than perceived; they are suffered, but they cannot be said to be known, for they are not, by those who experience them, referred to their origins. It goes, then, without saying that agencies are not established which canalize the streams of social action and thereby regulate them. Hence the publics are amorphous and unarticulated.

There was a time when a man might entertain a few general political principles and apply them with some confidence. A citizen believed in states' rights or in a centralized federal government; in free trade or protection. It did not involve much mental strain to imagine that by throwing in his lot with one party or another he could so express his views that his belief would count in government. For the average voter to-day the tariff question is a complicated medley of infinite detail, schedules of rates specific and *ad valorem* on countless things, many of which he does not recognize by name, and with respect to which he can form no judgment. Probably not one voter in a thousand even reads the scores of pages in which the rates of toll are enumerated and he would not be much wiser if he did. The average man gives it up as a bad job. At election time, appeal to some time-worn slogan may galvanize him into a temporary notion that he has convictions on an important subject, but except for manufacturers and dealers who have some interest at stake in this or that schedule, belief lacks the qualities which attach to beliefs about matters of personal concern. Industry is too complex and intricate.

Again the voter may by personal predilection or inherited belief incline towards magnifying the scope of local governments and inveigh against the evils of centralization. But he is vehemently sure of social evils attending the liquor traffic. He finds that the prohibitory law of his locality, township, county or state, is largely nullified by the importation of liquor from outside, made easy by modern means of transportation. So he becomes an advocate of a national amendment giving the central

government power to regulate the manufacture and sale of intox-
icating drinks. This brings in its train a necessary extension of
federal officials and powers. Thus to-day, the south, the traditional home of the states' rights doctrine, is the chief supporter
of national prohibition and Volstead Act. It would not be possible to say how many voters have thought of the relation between
their professed general principle and their special position on the
liquor question: probably not many. On the other hand, life-long
Hamiltonians, proclaimers of the dangers of particularistic local
autonomy, are opposed to prohibition. Hence they play a tune
ad hoc on the Jeffersonian flute. Gibes at inconsistency are, however, as irrelevant as they are easy. The social situation has been
so changed by the factors of an industrial age that traditional
general principles have little practical meaning. They persist as
emotional cries rather than as reasoned ideas.

The same criss-crossing occurs with reference to regulation of
railways. The opponent of a strong federal government finds,
being a farmer or shipper, that rates are too high; he also finds
that railways pay little attention to state boundaries, that lines
once local are parts of vast systems and that state legislation and
administration are ineffectual for his purpose. He calls for national regulation. Some partisan of the powers of the central
government, on the other hand, being an investor in stocks and
bonds, finds that his income is likely to be unfavorably affected
by federal action and he promptly protests against the vexatious
tendency to appeal to national aid, which has now become in his
eyes a foolish paternalism. The developments of industry and
commerce have so complicated affairs that a clear-cut, generally
applicable, standard of judgment becomes practically impossible. The forest cannot be seen for the trees nor the trees for
the forest.

A striking example of the shift of the actual tenor of doctrines—that is, of their consequences in application—is presented in the history of the doctrine of Individualism, interpreted
to signify a minimum of governmental "interference" with industry and trade. At the outset, it was held by "progressives," by
those who were protesting against the inherited régime of rules
of law and administration. Vested interests, on the contrary,
were mainly in favor of the old status. To-day the industrial-
property régime being established, the doctrine is the intellectual

bulwark of the standpatter and reactionary. He it is that now wants to be let alone, and who utters the war-cry of liberty for private industry, thrift, contract and their pecuniary fruit. In the United States the name "liberal," as a party designation, is still employed to designate a progressive in political matters. In most other countries, the "liberal" party is that which represents established and vested commercial and financial interests in protest against governmental regulation. The irony of history is nowhere more evident than in the reversal of the practical meaning of the term "liberalism" in spite of a literal continuity of theory.

Political apathy, which is a natural product of the discrepancies between actual practices and traditional machinery, ensues from inability to identify one's self with definite issues. These are hard to find and locate in the vast complexities of current life. When traditional war-cries have lost their import in practical policies which are consonant with them, they are readily dismissed as bunk. Only habit and tradition, rather than reasoned conviction, together with a vague faith in doing one's civic duty, send to the polls a considerable percentage of the fifty per cent. who still vote. And of them it is a common remark that a large number vote against something or somebody rather than for anything or anybody, except when powerful agencies create a scare. The old principles do not fit contemporary life as it is lived, however well they may have expressed the vital interests of the times in which they arose. Thousands feel their hollowness even if they cannot make their feeling articulate. The confusion which has resulted from the size and ramifications of social activities has rendered men skeptical of the efficiency of political action. Who is sufficient unto these things? Men feel that they are caught in the sweep of forces too vast to understand or master. Thought is brought to a standstill and action paralyzed. Even the specialist finds it difficult to trace the chain of "cause and effect"; and even he operates only after the event, looking backward, while meantime social activities have moved on to effect a new state of affairs.

Similar considerations account for depreciation of the machinery of democratic political action in contrast with a rising appreciation of the need of expert administrators. For example, one of the by-products of the war was the investment of the government at Muscle Shoals for the manufacture of nitrogen, a chemical product of great importance to the farmer, as well as to armies in the field. The disposition and utilization of the plant have become matters of political dispute. The questions involved, questions of science, agriculture, industry and finance, are highly technical. How many voters are competent to measure all the factors involved in arriving at a decision? And if they were competent after studying it, how many have the time to devote to it? It is true that this matter does not come before the electorate directly, but the technical difficulty of the problem is reflected in the confused paralysis of the legislators whose business it is to deal with it. The confused situation is further complicated by the invention of other and cheaper methods of producing nitrates. Again, the rapid development of hydro-electric and super-power is a matter of public concern. In the long run, few questions exceed it in importance. Aside from business corporations which have a direct interest in it and some engineers, how many citizens have the data or the ability to secure and estimate the facts involved in its settlement? One further illustration: Two things which intimately concern a local public are street-railway transportation and the marketing of food products. But the history of municipal politics shows in most cases a flare-up of intense interest followed by a period of indifference. Results come home to the masses of the people. But the very size, heterogeneity and mobility of urban populations, the vast capital required, the technical character of the engineering problems involved, soon tire the attention of the average voter. I think the three instances are fairly typical. The ramification of the issues before the public is so wide and intricate, the technical matters involved are so specialized, the details are so many and so shifting, that the public cannot for any length of time identify and hold itself. It is not that there is no public, no large body of persons having a common interest in the consequences of social transactions. There is too much public, a public too diffused and scattered and too intricate in composition. And there are too many publics, for conjoint actions which have indirect, serious and enduring consequences are multitudinous beyond comparison, and each one of them crosses the others and generates its own group of persons especially affected with little to hold these different publics together in an integrated whole.

The picture is not complete without taking into account the

many competitors with effective political interest. Political concerns have, of course, always had strong rivals. Persons have always been, for the most part, taken up with their more immediate work and play. The power of "bread and the circus" to divert attention from public matters is an old story. But now the industrial conditions which have enlarged, complicated and multiplied public interests have also multiplied and intensified formidable rivals to them. In countries where political life has been most successfully conducted in the past, there was a class specially set aside, as it were, who made political affairs their special business. Aristotle could not conceive a body of citizens competent to carry on politics consisting of others than those who had leisure, that is, of those who were relieved from all other preoccupations, especially that of making a livelihood. Political life, till recent times, bore out his belief. Those who took an active part in politics were "gentlemen," persons who had had property and money long enough, and enough of it, so that its further pursuit was vulgar and beneath their station. To-day, so great and powerful is the sweep of the industrial current, the person of leisure is usually an idle person. Persons have their own business to attend to, and "business" has its own precise and specialized meaning. Politics thus tends to become just another "business": the especial concern of bosses and the managers of the machine.

The increase in the number, variety and cheapness of amusements represents a powerful diversion from political concern. The members of an inchoate public have too many ways of enjoyment, as well as of work, to give much thought to organization into an effective public. Man is a consuming and sportive animal as well as a political one. What is significant is that access to means of amusement has been rendered easy and cheap beyond anything known in the past. The present era of "prosperity" may not be enduring. But the movie, radio, cheap reading matter and motor car with all they stand for have come to stay. That they did not originate in deliberate desire to divert attention from political interests does not lessen their effectiveness in that direction. The political elements in the constitution of the human being, those having to do with citizenship, are crowded to one side. In most circles it is hard work to sustain conversation on a political theme; and once initiated, it is quickly dismissed with a yawn. Let there be introduced the topic of the mechanism and accomplishment of various makes of motor cars or the respective merits of actresses, and the dialogue goes on at a lively pace. The thing to be remembered is that this cheapened and multiplied access to amusement is the product of the machine age, intensified by the business tradition which causes provision of means for an enjoyable passing of time to be one of the most profitable of occupations.

One phase of the workings of a technological age, with its unprecedented command of natural energies, while it is implied in what has been said, needs explicit attention. The older publics, in being local communities, largely homogeneous with one another, were also, as the phrase goes, static. They changed, of course, but barring war, catastrophe and great migrations, the modifications were gradual. They proceeded slowly and were largely unperceived by those undergoing them. The newer forces have created mobile and fluctuating associational forms. The common complaints of the disintegration of family life may be placed in evidence. The movement from rural to urban assemblies is also the result and proof of this mobility. Nothing stays long put, not even the associations by which business and industry are carried on. The mania for motion and speed is a symptom of the restless instability of social life, and it operates to intensify the causes from which it springs. Steel replaces wood and masonry for buildings; ferro-concrete modifies steel, and some invention may work a further revolution. Muscle Shoals was acquired to produce nitrogen, and new methods have already made antiquated the supposed need of great accumulation of water power. Any selected illustration suffers because of the heterogeneous mass of cases to select from. How can a public be organized, we may ask, when literally it does not stay in place? Only deep issues or those which can be made to appear such can find a common denominator among all the shifting and unstable relationships. Attachment is a very different function of life from affection. Affections will continue as long as the heart beats. But attachment requires something more than organic causes. The very things which stimulate and intensify affections may undermine attachments. For these are bred in tranquil stability; they are nourished in constant relationships. Acceleration of mobility disturbs them at their root. And without abiding attachments associations are too shifting and shaken to permit a public readily to locate and identify itself.

The new era of human relationships in which we live is one marked by mass production for remote markets, by cable and telephone, by cheap printing, by railway and steam navigation. Only geographically did Columbus discover a new world. The actual new world has been generated in the last hundred years. Steam and electricity have done more to alter the conditions under which men associate together than all the agencies which affected human relationships before our time. There are those who lay the blame for all the evils of our lives on steam, electricity and machinery. It is always convenient to have a devil as well as a savior to bear the responsibilities of humanity. In reality, the trouble springs rather from the ideas and absence of ideas in connection with which technological factors operate. Mental and moral beliefs and ideals change more slowly than outward conditions. If the ideals associated with the higher life of our cultural past have been impaired, the fault is primarily with them. Ideals and standards formed without regard to the means by which they are to be achieved and incarnated in flesh are bound to be thin and wavering. Since the aims, desires and purposes created by a machine age do not connect with tradition, there are two sets of rival ideals, and those which have actual instrumentalities at their disposal have the advantage. Because the two are rivals and because the older ones retain their glamor and sentimental prestige in literature and religion, the newer ones are perforce harsh and narrow. For the older symbols of ideal life still engage thought and command loyalty. Conditions have changed, but every aspect of life, from religion and education to property and trade, shows that nothing approaching a transformation has taken place in ideas and ideals. Symbols control sentiment and thought, and the new age has no symbols consonant with its activities. Intellectual instrumentalities for the formation of an organized public are more inadequate than its overt means. The ties which hold men together in action are numerous, tough and subtle. But they are invisible and intangible. We have the physical tools of communication as never before. The thoughts and aspirations congruous with them are not communicated, and hence are not common. Without such communication the public will remain shadowy and formless, seeking spasmodically for itself, but seizing and holding its shadow rather than its substance. Till the Great Society is converted into a Great Community, the Public will remain in eclipse. Communication can alone create a great community. Our Babel is not one of tongues but of the signs and symbols without which shared experience is impossible.

5.   Search for the Great Community

We have had occasion to refer in passing to the distinction between democracy as a social idea and political democracy as a system of government. The two are, of course, connected. The idea remains barren and empty save as it is incarnated in human relationships. Yet in discussion they must be distinguished. The idea of democracy is a wider and fuller idea than can be exemplified in the state even at its best. To be realized it must affect all modes of human association, the family, the school, industry, religion. And even as far as political arrangements are concerned, governmental institutions are but a mechanism for securing to an idea channels of effective operation. It will hardly do to say that criticisms of the political machinery leave the believer in the idea untouched. For, as far as they are justified—and no candid believer can deny that many of them are only too well grounded—they arouse him to bestir himself in order that the idea may find a more adequate machinery through which to work. What the faithful insist upon, however, is that the idea and its external organs and structures are not to be identified. We object to the common supposition of the foes of existing democratic government that the accusations against it touch the social and moral aspirations and ideas which underlie the political forms. The old saying that the cure for the ills of democracy is more democracy is not apt if it means that the evils may be remedied by introducing more machinery of the same kind as that which already exists, or by refining and perfecting that machinery. But the phrase may also indicate the need of returning to the idea itself, of clarifying and deepening our apprehension of it, and of employing our sense of its meaning to criticize and remake its political manifestations.

Confining ourselves, for the moment, to political democracy, we must, in any case, renew our protest against the assumption that the idea has itself produced the governmental practices which obtain in democratic states: General suffrage, elected representatives, majority rule, and so on. The idea has influenced the concrete political movement, but it has not caused it. The transition from family and dynastic government supported by the loyalties of tradition to popular government was the outcome primarily of technological discoveries and inventions working a change in the customs by which men had been bound together. It was not due to the doctrines of doctrinaires. The forms to which we are accustomed in democratic governments represent the cumulative effect of a multitude of events, unpremeditated as far as political effects were concerned and having unpredictable consequences. There is no sanctity in universal suffrage, frequent elections, majority rule, congressional and cabinet government. These things are devices evolved in the direction in which the current was moving, each wave of which involved at the time of its impulsion a minimum of departure from antecedent custom and law. The devices served a purpose; but the purpose was rather that of meeting existing needs which had become too intense to be ignored, than that of forwarding the democratic idea. In spite of all defects, they served their own purpose well.

Looking back, with the aid which *ex post facto* experience can give, it would be hard for the wisest to devise schemes which, under the circumstances, would have met the needs better. In this retrospective glance, it is possible, however, to see how the doctrinal formulations which accompanied them were inadequate, one-sided and positively erroneous. In fact they were hardly more than political war-cries adopted to help in carrying on some immediate agitation or in justifying some particular practical polity struggling for recognition, even though they were asserted to be absolute truths of human nature or of morals. The doctrines served a particular local pragmatic need. But often their very adaptation to immediate circumstances unfitted them, pragmatically, to meet more enduring and more extensive needs. They lived to cumber the political ground, obstructing progress, all the more so because they were uttered and held not as hypotheses with which to direct social experimentation but as final truths, dogmas. No wonder they call urgently for revision and displacement.

Nevertheless the current has set steadily in one direction: toward democratic forms. That government exists to serve its community, and that this purpose cannot be achieved unless the community itself shares in selecting its governors and determining their policies, are a deposit of fact left, as far as we can see, permanently in the wake of doctrines and forms, however transitory the latter. They are not the whole of the democratic idea, but they express it in its political phase. Belief in this political aspect is not a mystic faith as if in some overruling providence that cares for children, drunkards and others unable to help themselves. It marks a well-attested conclusion from historic facts. We have every reason to think that whatever changes may take place in existing democratic machinery, they will be of a sort to make the interest of the public a more supreme guide and criterion of governmental activity, and to enable the public to form and manifest its purposes still more authoritatively. In this sense the cure for the ailments of democracy is more democracy. The prime difficulty, as we have seen, is that of discovering the means by which a scattered, mobile and manifold public may so recognize itself as to define and express its interests. This discovery is necessarily precedent to any fundamental change in the machinery. We are not concerned therefore to set forth counsels as to advisable improvements in the political forms of democracy. Many have been suggested. It is no derogation of their relative worth to say that consideration of these changes is not at present an affair of primary importance. The problem lies deeper; it is in the first instance an intellectual problem: the search for conditions under which the Great Society may become the Great Community. When these conditions are brought into being they will make their own forms. Until they have come about, it is somewhat futile to consider what political machinery will suit them.

In a search for the conditions under which the inchoate public now extant may function democratically, we may proceed from a statement of the nature of the democratic idea in its generic social sense.[1] From the standpoint of the individual, it consists in having a responsible share according to capacity in forming and directing the activities of the groups to which one belongs and in

1. The most adequate discussion of this ideal with which I am acquainted is T. V. Smith's *The Democratic Way of Life*.

participating according to need in the values which the groups sustain. From the standpoint of the groups, it demands liberation of the potentialities of members of a group in harmony with the interests and goods which are common. Since every individual is a member of many groups, this specification cannot be fulfilled except when different groups interact flexibly and fully in connection with other groups. A member of a robber band may express his powers in a way consonant with belonging to that group and be directed by the interest common to its members. But he does so only at the cost of repression of those of his potentialities which can be realized only through membership in other groups. The robber band cannot interact flexibly with other groups; it can act only through isolating itself. It must prevent the operation of all interests save those which circumscribe it in its separateness. But a good citizen finds his conduct as a member of a political group enriching and enriched by his participation in family life, industry, scientific and artistic associations. There is a free give-and-take: fullness of integrated personality is therefore possible of achievement, since the pulls and responses of different groups reenforce one another and their values accord.

Regarded as an idea, democracy is not an alternative to other principles of associated life. It is the idea of community life itself. It is an ideal in the only intelligible sense of an ideal: namely, the tendency and movement of some thing which exists carried to its final limit, viewed as completed, perfected. Since things do not attain such fulfillment but are in actuality distracted and interfered with, democracy in this sense is not a fact and never will be. But neither in this sense is there or has there ever been anything which is a community in its full measure, a community unalloyed by alien elements. The idea or ideal of a community presents, however, actual phases of associated life as they are freed from restrictive and disturbing elements, and are contemplated as having attained their limit of development. Wherever there is conjoint activity whose consequences are appreciated as good by all singular persons who take part in it, and where the realization of the good is such as to effect an energetic desire and effort to sustain it in being just because it is a good shared by all, there is in so far a community. The clear consciousness of a communal life, in all its implications, constitutes the idea of democracy.

Only when we start from a community as a fact, grasp the fact in thought so as to clarify and enhance its constituent elements, can we reach an idea of democracy which is not utopian. The conceptions and shibboleths which are traditionally associated with the idea of democracy take on a veridical and directive meaning only when they are construed as marks and traits of an association which realizes the defining characteristics of a community. Fraternity, liberty and equality isolated from communal life are hopeless abstractions. Their separate assertion leads to mushy sentimentalism or else to extravagant and fanatical violence which in the end defeats its own aims. Equality then becomes a creed of mechanical identity which is false to facts and impossible of realization. Effort to attain it is divisive of the vital bonds which hold men together; as far as it puts forth issue, the outcome is a mediocrity in which good is common only in the sense of being average and vulgar. Liberty is then thought of as independence of social ties, and ends in dissolution and anarchy. It is more difficult to sever the idea of brotherhood from that of a community, and hence it is either practically ignored in the movements which identify democracy with Individualism, or else it is a sentimentally appended tag. In its just connection with communal experience, fraternity is another name for the consciously appreciated goods which accrue from an association in which all share, and which give direction to the conduct of each. Liberty is that secure release and fulfillment of personal potentialities which take place only in rich and manifold association with others: the power to be an individualized self making a distinctive contribution and enjoying in its own way the fruits of association. Equality denotes the unhampered share which each individual member of the community has in the consequences of associated action. It is equitable because it is measured only by need and capacity to utilize, not by extraneous factors which deprive one in order that another may take and have. A baby in the family is equal with others, not because of some antecedent and structural quality which is the same as that of others, but in so far as his needs for care and development are attended to without being sacrificed to the superior strength, possessions and matured abilities of others. Equality does not signify that kind of mathematical or physical equivalence in virtue of which any one element may be substituted for another. It denotes effective regard for whatever is distinctive and unique in each, irrespective of physical and psychological inequalities. It is not a natural possession but is a fruit of the community when its action is directed by its character as a community.

Associated or joint activity is a condition of the creation of a community. But association itself is physical and organic, while communal life is moral, that is emotionally, intellectually, consciously sustained. Human beings combine in behavior as directly and unconsciously as do atoms, stellar masses and cells; as directly and unknowingly as they divide and repel. They do so in virtue of their own structure, as man and woman unite, as the baby seeks the breast and the breast is there to supply its need. They do so from external circumstances, pressure from without, as atoms combine or separate in presence of an electric charge, or as sheep huddle together from the cold. Associated activity needs no explanation; things are made that way. But no amount of aggregated collective action of itself constitutes a community. For beings who observe and think, and whose ideas are absorbed by impulses and become sentiments and interests, "we" is as inevitable as "I." But "we" and "our" exist only when the consequences of combined action are perceived and become an object of desire and effort, just as "I" and "mine" appear on the scene only when a distinctive share in mutual action is consciously asserted or claimed. Human associations may be ever so organic in origin and firm in operation, but they develop into societies in a human sense only as their consequences, being known, are esteemed and sought for. Even if "society" were as much an organism as some writers have held, it would not on that account be society. Interactions, transactions, occur *de facto* and the results of interdependence follow. But participation in activities and sharing in results are additive concerns. They demand *communication* as a prerequisite.

Combined activity happens among human beings; but when nothing else happens it passes as inevitably into some other mode of interconnected activity as does the interplay of iron and the oxygen of water. What takes place is wholly describable in terms of energy, or, as we say in the case of human interactions, of force. Only when there exist *signs* or *symbols* of activities and of their outcome can the flux be viewed as from without, be arrested for consideration and esteem, and be regulated. Lightning strikes and rives a tree or rock, and the resulting fragments take up and continue the process of interaction, and so on and on. But when phases of the process are represented by signs, a new medium is interposed. As symbols are related to one another, the important relations of a course of events are recorded and are preserved as meanings. Recollection and foresight are possible; the new medium facilitates calculation, planning, and a new kind of action which intervenes in what happens to direct its course in the interest of what is foreseen and desired.

Symbols in turn depend upon and promote communication. The results of conjoint experience are considered and transmitted. Events cannot be passed from one to another, but meanings may be shared by means of signs. Wants and impulses are then attached to common meanings. They are thereby transformed into desires and purposes, which, since they implicate a common or mutually understood meaning, present new ties, converting a conjoint activity into a community of interest and endeavor. Thus there is generated what, metaphorically, may be termed a general will and social consciousness: desire and choice on the part of individuals in behalf of activities that, by means of symbols, are communicable and shared by all concerned. A community thus presents an order of energies transmuted into one of meanings which are appreciated and mutually referred by each to every other on the part of those engaged in combined action. "Force" is not eliminated but is transformed in use and direction by ideas and sentiments made possible by means of symbols.

The work of conversion of the physical and organic phase of associated behavior into a community of action saturated and regulated by mutual interest in shared meanings, consequences which are translated into ideas and desired objects by means of symbols, does not occur all at once nor completely. At any given time, it sets a problem rather than marks a settled achievement. We are born organic beings associated with others, but we are not born members of a community. The young have to be brought within the traditions, outlook and interests which characterize a community by means of education: by unremitting instruction and by learning in connection with the phenomena of overt association. Everything which is distinctively human is learned, not native, even though it could not be learned without native structures which mark man off from other animals. To learn in a human way and to human effect is not just to acquire added skill through refinement of original capacities.

To learn to be human is to develop through the give-and-take of communication an effective sense of being an individually distinctive member of a community; one who understands and appreciates its beliefs, desires and methods, and who contributes to a further conversion of organic powers into human resources and values. But this translation is never finished. The old Adam, the unregenerate element in human nature, persists. It shows itself wherever the method obtains of attaining results by use of force instead of by the method of communication and enlightenment. It manifests itself more subtly, pervasively and effectually when knowledge and the instrumentalities of skill which are the product of communal life are employed in the service of wants and impulses which have not themselves been modified by reference to a shared interest. To the doctrine of "natural" economy which held that commercial exchange would bring about such an interdependence that harmony would automatically result, Rousseau gave an adequate answer in advance. He pointed out that interdependence provides just the situation which makes it possible and worth while for the stronger and abler to exploit others for their own ends, to keep others in a state of subjection where they can be utilized as animated tools. The remedy he suggested, a return to a condition of independence based on isolation, was hardly seriously meant. But its desperateness is evidence of the urgency of the problem. Its negative character was equivalent to surrender of any hope of solution. By contrast it indicates the nature of the only possible solution: the perfecting of the means and ways of communication of meanings so that genuinely shared interest in the consequences of interdependent activities may inform desire and effort and thereby direct action.

This is the meaning of the statement that the problem is a moral one dependent upon intelligence and education. We have in our prior account sufficiently emphasized the role of technological and industrial factors in creating the Great Society. What was said may even have seemed to imply acceptance of the deterministic version of an economic interpretation of history and institutions. It is silly and futile to ignore and deny economic facts. They do not cease to operate because we refuse to note them, or because we smear them over with sentimental idealizations. As we have also noted, they generate as their result overt and external conditions of action and these are known with various degrees of adequacy. What actually happens in consequence of industrial forces is dependent upon the presence or absence of perception and communication of consequences, upon foresight and its effect upon desire and endeavor. Economic agencies produce one result when they are left to work themselves out on the merely physical level, or on that level modified only as the knowledge, skill and technique which the community has accumulated are transmitted to its members unequally and by chance. They have a different outcome in the degree in which knowledge of consequences is equitably distributed, and action is animated by an informed and lively sense of a shared interest. The doctrine of economic interpretation as usually stated ignores the transformation which meanings may effect; it passes over the new medium which communication may interpose between industry and its eventual consequences. It is obsessed by the illusion which vitiated the "natural economy": an illusion due to failure to note the difference made in action by perception and publication of its consequences, actual and possible. It thinks in terms of antecedents, not of the eventual; of origins, not fruits.

We have returned, through this apparent excursion, to the question in which our earlier discussion culminated: What are the conditions under which it is possible for the Great Society to approach more closely and vitally the status of a Great Community, and thus take form in genuinely democratic societies and state? What are the conditions under which we may reasonably picture the Public emerging from its eclipse?

The study will be an intellectual or hypothetical one. There will be no attempt to state how the required conditions might come into existence, nor to prophesy that they will occur. The object of the analysis will be to show that *unless* ascertained specifications are realized, the Community cannot be organized as a democratically effective Public. It is not claimed that the conditions which will be noted will suffice, but only that at least they are indispensable. In other words, we shall endeavor to frame a hypothesis regarding the democratic state to stand in contrast with the earlier doctrine which has been nullified by the course of events.

Two essential constituents in that older theory, as will be

recalled, were the notions that each individual is of himself equipped with the intelligence needed, under the operation of self-interest, to engage in political affairs; and that general suffrage, frequent elections of officials and majority rule are sufficient to ensure the responsibility of elected rulers to the desires and interests of the public. As we shall see, the second conception is logically bound up with the first and stands or falls with it. At the basis of the scheme lies what Lippmann has well called the idea of the "omnicompetent" individual: competent to frame policies, to judge their results; competent to know in all situations demanding political action what is for his own good, and competent to enforce his idea of good and the will to effect it against contrary forces. Subsequent history has proved that the assumption involved illusion. Had it not been for the misleading influence of a false psychology, the illusion might have been detected in advance. But current philosophy held that ideas and knowledge were functions of a mind or consciousness which originated in individuals by means of isolated contact with objects. But in fact, knowledge is a function of association and communication; it depends upon tradition, upon tools and methods socially transmitted, developed and sanctioned. Faculties of effectual observation, reflection and desire are habits acquired under the influence of the culture and institutions of society, not ready-made inherent powers. The fact that man acts from crudely intelligized emotion and from habit rather than from rational consideration, is now so familiar that it is not easy to appreciate that the other idea was taken seriously as the basis of economic and political philosophy. The measure of truth which it contains was derived from observation of a relatively small group of shrewd business men who regulated their enterprises by calculation and accounting, and of citizens of small and stable local communities who were so intimately acquainted with the persons and affairs of their locality that they could pass competent judgment upon the bearing of proposed measures upon their own concerns.

Habit is the mainspring of human action, and habits are formed for the most part under the influence of the customs of a group. The organic structure of man entails the formation of habit, for, whether we wish it or not, whether we are aware of it or not, every act effects a modification of attitude and set which directs future behavior. The dependence of habit-forming upon those habits of a group which constitute customs and institutions is a natural consequence of the helplessness of infancy. The social consequences of habit have been stated once for all by James: "Habit is the enormous fly-wheel of society, its most precious conservative influence. It alone is what keeps us within the bounds of ordinance, and saves the children of fortune from the uprisings of the poor. It alone prevents the hardest and most repulsive walks of life from being deserted by those brought up to tread therein. It keeps the fisherman and the deck-hand at sea through the winter; it holds the miner in his darkness, and nails the countryman to his log-cabin and his lonely farm through all the months of snow; it protects us from invasion by the natives of the desert and the frozen zone. It dooms us all to fight out the battle of life upon the lines of our nurture or our early choice, and to make the best of a pursuit that disagrees, because there is no other for which we are fitted and it is too late to begin again. It keeps different social strata from mixing."

The influence of habit is decisive because all distinctively human action has to be learned, and the very heart, blood and sinews of learning is creation of habitudes. Habits bind us to orderly and established ways of action because they generate ease, skill and interest in things to which we have grown used and because they instigate fear to walk in different ways, and because they leave us incapacitated for the trial of them. Habit does not preclude the use of thought, but it determines the channels within which it operates. Thinking is secreted in the interstices of habits. The sailor, miner, fisherman and farmer think, but their thoughts fall within the framework of accustomed occupations and relationships. We dream beyond the limits of use and wont, but only rarely does revery become a source of acts which break bounds; so rarely that we name those in whom it happens demonic geniuses and marvel at the spectacle. Thinking itself becomes habitual along certain lines; a specialized occupation. Scientific men, philosophers, literary persons, are not men and women who have so broken the bonds of habits that pure reason and emotion undefiled by use and wont speak through them. They are persons of a specialized infrequent habit. Hence the idea that men are moved by an intelligent and calculated regard for their own good is pure mythology. Even if the principle of self-love actuated behavior, it would still be true that the *objects* in which men find their love manifested, the objects which they take as constituting their peculiar interests, are set by habits reflecting social customs.

These facts explain why the social doctrinaires of the new industrial movement had so little prescience of what was to follow in consequence of it. These facts explain why the more things changed, the more they were the same; they account, that is, for the fact that instead of the sweeping revolution which was expected to result from democratic political machinery, there was in the main but a transfer of vested power from one class to another. A few men, whether or not they were good judges of their own true interest and good, were competent judges of the conduct of business for pecuniary profit, and of how the new governmental machinery could be made to serve their ends. It would have taken a new race of human beings to escape, in the use made of political forms, from the influence of deeply engrained habits, of old institutions and customary social status, with their inwrought limitations of expectation, desire and demand. And such a race, unless of disembodied angelic constitution, would simply have taken up the task where human beings assumed it upon emergence from the condition of anthropoid apes. In spite of sudden and catastrophic revolutions, the essential continuity of history is doubly guaranteed. Not only are personal desire and belief functions of habit and custom, but the objective conditions which provide the resources and tools of action, together with its limitations, obstructions and traps, are precipitates of the past, perpetuating, willy-nilly, its hold and power. The creation of a *tabula rasa* in order to permit the creation of a new order is so impossible as to set at naught both the hope of buoyant revolutionaries and the timidity of scared conservatives.

Nevertheless, changes take place and are cumulative in character. Observation of them in the light of their recognized consequences arouses reflection, discovery, invention, experimentation. When a certain state of accumulated knowledge, of techniques and instrumentalities is attained, the process of change is so accelerated, that, as to-day, it appears externally to be the dominant trait. But there is a marked lag in any corresponding change of ideas and desires. Habits of opinion are the toughest of all habits; when they have become second nature, and are supposedly thrown out of the door, they creep in again as stealthily and surely as does first nature. And as they are modified, the alteration first shows itself negatively, in the disintegration of old beliefs, to be replaced by floating, volatile and accidentally snatched up opinions. Of course there has been an enormous increase in the amount of knowledge possessed by mankind, but it does not equal, probably, the increase in the amount of errors and half-truths which have got into circulation. In social and human matters, especially, the development of a critical sense and methods of discriminating judgment has not kept pace with the growth of careless reports and of motives for positive misrepresentation.

What is more important, however, is that so much of knowledge is not knowledge in the ordinary sense of the word, but is "science." The quotation marks are not used disrespectfully, but to suggest the technical character of scientific material. The layman takes certain conclusions which get into circulation to be science. But the scientific inquirer knows that they constitute science only in connection with the methods by which they are reached. Even when true, they are not science in virtue of their correctness, but by reason of the apparatus which is employed in reaching them. This apparatus is so highly specialized that it requires more labor to acquire ability to use and understand it than to get skill in any other instrumentalities possessed by man. Science, in other words, is a highly specialized language, more difficult to learn than any natural language. It is an artificial language, not in the sense of being factitious, but in that of being a work of intricate art, devoted to a particular purpose and not capable of being acquired nor understood in the way in which the mother tongue is learned. It is, indeed, conceivable that sometime methods of instruction will be devised which will enable laymen to read and hear scientific material with comprehension, even when they do not themselves use the apparatus which is science. The latter may then become for large numbers what students of language call a passive, if not an active, vocabulary. But that time is in the future.

For most men, save the scientific workers, science is a mystery in the hands of initiates, who have become adepts in virtue of following ritualistic ceremonies from which the profane herd is excluded. They are fortunate who get as far as a sympathetic appreciation of the methods which give pattern to the complicated apparatus: methods of analytic, experimental observation, mathematical formulation and deduction, constant and elaborate check and test. For most persons, the reality of the apparatus is found only in its embodiments in practical affairs, in mechanical devices and in techniques which touch life as it is lived. For them, electricity is *known* by means of the telephones, bells and lights they use, by the generators and magnetos in the automobiles they drive, by the trolley cars in which they ride. The physiology and biology they are acquainted with is that they have learned in taking precautions against germs and from the physicians they depend upon for health. The science of what might be supposed to be closest to them, of human nature, was for them an esoteric mystery until it was applied in advertising, salesmanship and personnel selection and management, and until, through psychiatry, it spilled over into life and popular consciousness, through its bearings upon "nerves," the morbidities and common forms of crankiness which make it difficult for persons to get along with one another and with themselves. Even now, popular psychology is a mass of cant, of slush and of superstition worthy of the most flourishing days of the medicine man.

Meanwhile the technological application of the complex apparatus which is science has revolutionized the conditions under which associated life goes on. This may be known as a fact which is stated in a proposition and assented to. But it is not known in the sense that men understand it. They do not know it as they know some machine which they operate, or as they know electric light and steam locomotives. They do not understand *how* the change has gone on nor *how* it affects their conduct. Not understanding its "how," they cannot use and control its manifestations. They undergo the consequences, they are affected by them. They cannot manage them, though some are fortunate enough—what is commonly called good fortune—to be able to exploit some phase of the process for their own personal profit. But even the most shrewd and successful man does not in any analytic and systematic way—in a way worthy to compare with the knowledge which he has won in lesser affairs by means of the stress of experience—know the system within which he operates. Skill and ability work within a framework which we have not created and do not comprehend. Some occupy strategic positions which give them advance information of forces that affect the market; and by training and an innate turn that way they have acquired a special technique which enables them to use the vast impersonal tide to turn their own wheels. They can dam the current here and release it there. The current itself is as much beyond them as was ever the river by the side of which some ingenious mechanic, employing a knowledge which was transmitted to him, erected his saw-mill to make boards of trees which he had not grown. That within limits those successful in affairs have knowledge and skill is not to be doubted. But such knowledge goes relatively but little further than that of the competent skilled operator who manages a machine. It suffices to employ the conditions which are before him. Skill enables him to turn the flux of events this way or that in his own neighborhood. It gives him no control of the flux.

Why should the public and its officers, even if the latter are termed statesmen, be wiser and more effective? The prime condition of a democratically organized public is a kind of knowledge and insight which does not yet exist. In its absence, it would be the height of absurdity to try to tell what it would be like if it existed. But some of the conditions which must be fulfilled if it is to exist can be indicated. We can borrow that much from the spirit and method of science even if we are ignorant of it as a specialized apparatus. An obvious requirement is freedom of social inquiry and of distribution of its conclusions. The notion that men may be free in their thought even when they are not in its expression and dissemination has been sedulously propagated. It had its origin in the idea of a mind complete in itself, apart from action and from objects. Such a consciousness presents in fact the spectacle of mind deprived of its normal functioning, because it is baffled by the actualities in connection with which alone it is truly mind, and is driven back into secluded and impotent revery.

There can be no public without full publicity in respect to all consequences which concern it. Whatever obstructs and restricts publicity, limits and distorts public opinion and checks and distorts thinking on social affairs. Without freedom of expression, not even methods of social inquiry can be developed. For tools can be evolved and perfected only in operation; in application to observing, reporting and organizing actual subject-matter; and this application cannot occur save through free and systematic communication. The early history of physical knowledge, of Greek conceptions of natural phenomena, proves how inept become the conceptions of the best endowed minds when those ideas are elaborated apart from the closest contact with the events which they purport to state and explain. The ruling ideas and methods of the human sciences are in much the same condition to-day. They are also evolved on the basis of past gross observations, remote from constant use in regulation of the material of new observations.

The belief that thought and its communication are now free simply because legal restrictions which once obtained have been done away with is absurd. Its currency perpetuates the infantile state of social knowledge. For it blurs recognition of our central need to possess conceptions which are used as tools of directed inquiry and which are tested, rectified and caused to grow in actual use. No man and no mind was ever emancipated merely by being left alone. Removal of formal limitations is but a negative condition; positive freedom is not a state but an act which involves methods and instrumentalities for control of conditions. Experience shows that sometimes the sense of external oppression, as by censorship, acts as a challenge and arouses intellectual energy and excites courage. But a belief in intellectual freedom where it does not exist contributes only to complacency in virtual enslavement, to sloppiness, superficiality and recourse to sensations as a substitute for ideas: marked traits of our present estate with respect to social knowledge. On one hand, thinking deprived of its normal course takes refuge in academic specialism, comparable in its way to what is called scholasticism. On the other hand, the physical agencies of publicity which exist in such abundance are utilized in ways which constitute a large part of the present meaning of publicity: advertising, propaganda, invasion of private life, the "featuring" of passing incidents in a way which violates all the moving logic of continuity, and which leaves us with those isolated intrusions and shocks which are the essence of "sensations."

It would be a mistake to identify the conditions which limit free communication and circulation of facts and ideas, and which thereby arrest and pervert social thought or inquiry, merely with overt forces which are obstructive. It is true that those who have ability to manipulate social relations for their own advantage have to be reckoned with. They have an uncanny instinct for detecting whatever intellectual tendencies even remotely threaten to encroach upon their control. They have developed an extraordinary facility in enlisting upon their side the inertia, prejudices and emotional partisanship of the masses by use of a technique which impedes free inquiry and expression. We seem to be approaching a state of government by hired promoters of opinion called publicity agents. But the more serious enemy is deeply concealed in hidden entrenchments.

Emotional habituations and intellectual habitudes on the part of the mass of men create the conditions of which the exploiters of sentiment and opinion only take advantage. Men have got used to an experimental method in physical and technical matters. They are still afraid of it in human concerns. The fear is the more efficacious because like all deep-lying fears it is covered up and disguised by all kinds of rationalizations. One of its commonest forms is a truly religious idealization of, and reverence for, established institutions; for example in our own politics, the Constitution, the Supreme Court, private property, free contract and so on. The words "sacred" and "sanctity" come readily to our lips when such things come under discussion. They testify to the religious aureole which protects the institutions. If "holy" means that which is not to be approached nor touched, save with ceremonial precautions and by specially anointed officials, then such things are holy in contemporary political life. As supernatural matters have progressively been left high and dry upon a secluded beach, the actuality of religious taboos has more and more gathered about secular institutions, especially those connected with the nationalistic state.[2] Psychiatrists have discovered that one of the commonest causes of mental disturbance is an underlying fear of which the subject is not aware, but which leads to withdrawal from reality and to unwillingness to think things through. There is a social pathology which works powerfully against effective inquiry into social institutions and conditions. It manifests itself in a thousand ways; in querulousness, in impotent drifting, in uneasy snatching at distractions, in ideal-

2. The religious character of nationalism has been forcibly brought out by Carlton Hayes, in his *Essays on Nationalism*, especially Chap. 4.

ization of the long established, in a facile optimism assumed as a cloak, in riotous glorification of things "as they are," in intimidation of all dissenters—ways which depress and dissipate thought all the more effectually because they operate with subtle and unconscious pervasiveness.

The backwardness of social knowledge is marked in its division into independent and insulated branches of learning. Anthropology, history, sociology, morals, economics, political science, go their own ways without constant and systematized fruitful interaction. Only in appearance is there a similar division in physical knowledge. There is continuous cross-fertilization between astronomy, physics, chemistry and the biological sciences. Discoveries and improved methods are so recorded and organized that constant exchange and intercommunication take place. The isolation of the humane subjects from one another is connected with their aloofness from physical knowledge. The mind still draws a sharp separation between the world in which man lives and the life of man in and by that world, a cleft reflected in the separation of man himself into a body and a mind, which, it is currently supposed, can be known and dealt with apart. That for the past three centuries energy should have gone chiefly into physical inquiry, beginning with the things most remote from man such as heavenly bodies, was to have been expected. The history of the physical sciences reveals a certain order in which they developed. Mathematical tools had to be employed before a new astronomy could be constructed. Physics advanced when ideas worked out in connection with the solar system were used to describe happenings on the earth. Chemistry waited on the advance of physics; the sciences of living things required the material and methods of physics and chemistry in order to make headway. Human psychology ceased to be chiefly speculative opinion only when biological and physiological conclusions were available. All this is natural and seemingly inevitable. Things which had the most outlying and indirect connection with human interests had to be mastered in some degree before inquiries could competently converge upon man himself.

Nevertheless the course of development has left us of this age in a plight. When we say that a subject of science is technically specialized, or that it is highly "abstract," what we practically mean is that it is not conceived in terms of its bearing upon human life. All *merely* physical knowledge is technical, couched in a technical vocabulary communicable only to the few. Even physical knowledge which does affect human conduct, which does modify what we do and undergo, is also technical and remote in the degree in which its bearings are not understood and used. The sunlight, rain, air and soil have always entered in visible ways into human experience; atoms and molecules and cells and most other things with which the sciences are occupied affect us, but not visibly. Because they enter life and modify experience in imperceptible ways, and their consequences are not realized, speech about them is technical; communication is by means of peculiar symbols. One would think, then, that a fundamental and ever-operating aim would be to translate knowledge of the subject-matter of physical conditions into terms which are generally understood, into signs denoting human consequences of services and disservices rendered. For ultimately all consequences which enter human life depend upon physical conditions; they can be understood and mastered only as the latter are taken into account. One would think, then, that any state of affairs which tends to render the things of the environment unknown and incommunicable by human beings in terms of their own activities and sufferings would be deplored as a disaster; that it would be felt to be intolerable, and to be put up with only as far as it is, at any given time, inevitable.

But the facts are to the contrary. Matter and the material are words which in the minds of many convey a note of disparagement. They are taken to be foes of whatever is of ideal value in life, instead of as conditions of its manifestation and sustained being. In consequence of this division, they do become in fact enemies, for whatever is consistently kept apart from human values depresses thought and renders values sparse and precarious in fact. There are even some who regard the materialism and dominance of commercialism of modern life as fruits of undue devotion to physical science, not seeing that the split between man and nature, artificially made by a tradition which originated before there was understanding of the physical conditions that are the medium of human activities, is the benumbing factor. The most influential form of the divorce is separation between pure and applied science. Since "application" signifies recognized bearing upon human experience and well-being, honor of what is "pure" and contempt for what is "applied" has for its outcome a science which is remote and technical, communicable only to specialists, and a conduct of human affairs which is haphazard, biased, unfair in distribution of values. What is applied and employed as the alternative to knowledge in regulation of society is ignorance, prejudice, class-interest and accident. Science is converted into knowledge in its honorable and emphatic sense *only* in application. Otherwise it is truncated, blind, distorted. When it is then applied, it is in ways which explain the unfavorable sense so often attached to "application" and the "utilitarian": namely, use for pecuniary ends to the profit of a few.

At present, the application of physical science is rather *to* human concerns than *in* them. That is, it is external, made in the interests of its consequences for a possessing and acquisitive class. Application *in* life would signify that science was absorbed and distributed; that it was the instrumentality of that common understanding and thorough communication which is the precondition of the existence of a genuine and effective public. The use of science to regulate industry and trade has gone on steadily. The scientific revolution of the seventeenth century was the precursor of the industrial revolution of the eighteenth and nineteenth. In consequence, man has suffered the impact of an enormously enlarged control of physical energies without any corresponding ability to control himself and his own affairs. Knowledge divided against itself, a science to whose incompleteness is added an artificial split, has played its part in generating enslavement of men, women and children in factories in which they are animated machines to tend inanimate machines. It has maintained sordid slums, flurried and discontented careers, grinding poverty and luxurious wealth, brutal exploitation of nature and man in times of peace and high explosives and noxious gases in times of war. Man, a child in understanding of himself, has placed in his hands physical tools of incalculable power. He plays with them like a child, and whether they work harm or good is largely a matter of accident. The instrumentality becomes a master and works fatally as if possessed of a will of its own—not because it has a will but because man has not.

The glorification of "pure" science under such conditions is a rationalization of an escape; it marks a construction of an asylum of refuge, a shirking of responsibility. The true purity of knowledge exists not when it is uncontaminated by contact with use and service. It is wholly a moral matter, an affair of honesty, impartiality and generous breadth of intent in search and communication. The adulteration of knowledge is due not to its use, but to vested bias and prejudice, to one-sidedness of outlook, to vanity, to conceit of possession and authority, to contempt or disregard of human concern in its use. Humanity is not, as was once thought, the end for which all things were formed; it is but a slight and feeble thing, perhaps an episodic one, in the vast stretch of the universe. But for man, man is the centre of interest and the measure of importance. The magnifying of the physical realm at the cost of man is but an abdication and a flight. To make physical science a rival of human interests is bad enough, for it forms a diversion of energy which can ill be afforded. But the evil does not stop there. The ultimate harm is that the understanding by man of his own affairs and his ability to direct them are sapped at their root when knowledge of nature is disconnected from its human function.

It has been implied throughout that knowledge is communication as well as understanding. I well remember the saying of a man, uneducated from the standpoint of the schools, in speaking of certain matters: "Sometime they will be found out and not only found out, but they will be known." The schools may suppose that a thing is known when it is found out. My old friend was aware that a thing is fully known only when it is published, shared, socially accessible. Record and communication are indispensable to knowledge. Knowledge cooped up in a private consciousness is a myth, and knowledge of social phenomena is peculiarly dependent upon dissemination, for only by distribution can such knowledge be either obtained or tested. A fact of community life which is not spread abroad so as to be a common possession is a contradiction in terms. Dissemination is something other than scattering at large. Seeds are sown, not by virtue of being thrown out at random, but by being so distributed as to take root and have a chance of growth. Communication of the results of social inquiry is the same thing as the formation of public opinion. This marks one of the first ideas framed in the growth of political democracy as it will be one of the last to be fulfilled. For public opinion is judgment which is formed and entertained by those who constitute the public and is about public affairs. Each of the two phases imposes for its realization conditions hard to meet.

Opinions and beliefs concerning the public presuppose effective and organized inquiry. Unless there are methods for detecting the energies which are at work and tracing them through an intricate network of interactions to their consequences, what passes as public opinion will be "opinion" in its derogatory sense rather than truly public, no matter how widespread the opinion is. The number who share error as to fact and who partake of a false belief measures power for harm. Opinion casually formed and formed under the direction of those who have something at stake in having a lie believed can be *public* opinion only in name. Calling it by this name, acceptance of the name as a kind of warrant, magnifies its capacity to lead action estray. The more who share it, the more injurious its influence. Public opinion, even if it happens to be correct, is intermittent when it is not the product of methods of investigation and reporting constantly at work. It appears only in crises. Hence its "rightness" concerns only an immediate emergency. Its lack of continuity makes it wrong from the standpoint of the course of events. It is as if a physician were able to deal for the moment with an emergency in disease but could not adapt his treatment of it to the underlying conditions which brought it about. He may then "cure" the disease—that is, cause its present alarming symptoms to subside—but he does not modify its causes; his treatment may even affect them for the worse. Only continuous inquiry, continuous in the sense of being connected as well as persistent, can provide the material of enduring opinion about public matters.

There is a sense in which "opinion" rather than knowledge, even under the most favorable circumstances, is the proper term to use—namely, in the sense of judgment, estimate. For in its strict sense, knowledge can refer only to what *has* happened and been done. What is still *to be* done involves a forecast of a future still contingent, and cannot escape the liability to error in judgment involved in all anticipation of probabilities. There may well be honest divergence as to policies to be pursued, even when plans spring from knowledge of the same facts. But genuinely public policy cannot be generated unless it be informed by knowledge, and this knowledge does not exist except when there is systematic, thorough, and well-equipped search and record.

Moreover, inquiry must be as nearly contemporaneous as possible; otherwise it is only of antiquarian interest. Knowledge of history is evidently necessary for connectedness of knowledge. But history which is not brought down close to the actual scene of events leaves a gap and exercises influence upon the formation of judgments about the public interest only by guess-work about intervening events. Here, only too conspicuously, is a limitation of the existing social sciences. Their material comes too late, too far after the event, to enter effectively into the formation of public opinion about the immediate public concern and what is to be done about it.

A glance at the situation shows that the physical and external means of collecting information in regard to what is happening in the world have far outrun the intellectual phase of inquiry and organization of its results. Telegraph, telephone, and now the radio, cheap and quick mails, the printing press, capable of swift reduplication of material at low cost, have attained a remarkable development. But when we ask what sort of material is recorded and how it is organized, when we ask about the intellectual form in which the material is presented, the tale to be told is very different. "News" signifies something which has just happened, and which is new just because it deviates from the old and regular. But its *meaning* depends upon relation to what it imports, to what its social consequences are. This import cannot be determined unless the new is placed in relation to the old, to what has happened and been integrated into the course of events. Without coordination and consecutiveness, events are not events, but mere occurrences, intrusions; an event implies that out of which a happening proceeds. Hence even if we discount the influence of private interests in procuring suppression, secrecy and misrepresentation, we have here an explanation of the triviality and "sensational" quality of so much of what passes as news. The catastrophic, namely, crime, accident, family rows, personal clashes and conflicts, are the most obvious forms of breaches of continuity; they supply the element of shock which is the strictest meaning of sensation; they are the *new* par excellence, even though only the date of the newspaper could inform us whether they happened last year or this, so completely are they isolated from their connections.

So accustomed are we to this method of collecting, recording and presenting social changes, that it may well sound ridiculous to say that a genuine social science would manifest its reality in the daily press, while learned books and articles supply and polish tools of inquiry. But the inquiry which alone can furnish knowledge as a precondition of public judgments must be contemporary and quotidian. Even if social sciences as a specialized apparatus of inquiry were more advanced than they are, they would be comparatively impotent in the office of directing opinion on matters of concern to the public as long as they are remote from application in the daily and unremitting assembly and interpretation of "news." On the other hand, the tools of social inquiry will be clumsy as long as they are forged in places and under conditions remote from contemporary events.

What has been said about the formation of ideas and judgments concerning the public apply as well to the distribution of the knowledge which makes it an effective possession of the members of the public. Any separation between the two sides of the problem is artificial. The discussion of propaganda and propagandism would alone, however, demand a volume, and could be written only by one much more experienced than the present writer. Propaganda can accordingly only be mentioned, with the remark that the present situation is one unprecedented in history. The political forms of democracy and quasi-democratic habits of thought on social matters have compelled a certain amount of public discussion and at least the simulation of general consultation in arriving at political decisions. Representative government must at least seem to be founded on public interests as they are revealed to public belief. The days are past when government can be carried on without any pretense of ascertaining the wishes of the governed. In theory, their assent must be secured. Under the older forms, there was no need to muddy the sources of opinion on political matters. No current of energy flowed from them. Today the judgments popularly formed on political matters are so important, in spite of all factors to the contrary, that there is an enormous premium upon all methods which affect their formation.

The smoothest road to control of political conduct is by control of opinion. As long as interests of pecuniary profit are powerful, and a public has not located and identified itself, those who have this interest will have an unresisted motive for tampering with the springs of political action in all that affects them.

Just as in the conduct of industry and exchange generally the technological factor is obscured, deflected and defeated by "business," so specifically in the management of publicity. The gathering and sale of subject-matter having a public import is part of the existing pecuniary system. Just as industry conducted by engineers on a factual technological basis would be a very different thing from what it actually is, so the assembling and reporting of news would be a very different thing if the genuine interests of reporters were permitted to work freely.

One aspect of the matter concerns particularly the side of dissemination. It is often said, and with a great appearance of truth, that the freeing and perfecting of inquiry would not have any especial effect. For, it is argued, the mass of the reading public is not interested in learning and assimilating the results of accurate investigation. Unless these are read, they cannot seriously affect the thought and action of members of the public; they remain in secluded library alcoves, and are studied and understood only by a few intellectuals. The objection is well taken save as the potency of art is taken into account. A technical high-brow presentation would appeal only to those technically high-brow; it would not be news to the masses. Presentation is fundamentally important, and presentation is a question of art. A newspaper which was only a daily edition of a quarterly journal of sociology or political science would undoubtedly possess a limited circulation and a narrow influence. Even at that, however, the mere existence and accessibility of such material would have some regulative effect. But we can look much further than that. The material would have such an enormous and widespread human bearing that its bare existence would be an irresistible invitation to a presentation of it which would have a direct popular appeal. The freeing of the artist in literary presentation, in other words, is as much a precondition of the desirable creation of adequate opinion on public matters as is the freeing of social inquiry. Men's conscious life of opinion and judgment often proceeds on a superficial and trivial plane. But their lives reach a deeper level. The function of art has always been to break through the crust of conventionalized and routine consciousness. Common things, a flower, a gleam of moonlight, the song of a bird, not things rare and remote, are means with which the deeper levels of life are touched so that they spring up as desire and thought. This process is art. Poetry, the drama, the novel, are proofs that the problem of presentation is not insoluble. Artists have always been the real purveyors of news, for it is not the outward happening in itself which is new, but the kindling by it of emotion, perception and appreciation.

We have but touched lightly and in passing upon the conditions which must be fulfilled if the Great Society is to become a Great Community; a society in which the ever-expanding and intricately ramifying consequences of associated activities shall be known in the full sense of that word, so that an organized, articulate Public comes into being. The highest and most difficult kind of inquiry and a subtle, delicate, vivid and responsive art of communication must take possession of the physical machinery of transmission and circulation and breathe life into it. When the machine age has thus perfected its machinery it will be a means of life and not its despotic master. Democracy will come into its own, for democracy is a name for a life of free and enriching communion. It had its seer in Walt Whitman. It will have its consummation when free social inquiry is indissolubly wedded to the art of full and moving communication.

6.   The Problem of Method

Perhaps to most, probably to many, the conclusions which have been stated as to the conditions upon which depends the emergence of the Public from its eclipse will seem close to denial of the possibility of realizing the idea of a democratic public. One might indeed point for what it is worth to the enormous obstacles with which the rise of a science of physical things was confronted a few short centuries ago, as evidence that hope need not be wholly desperate nor faith wholly blind. But we are not concerned with prophecy but with analysis. It is enough for present purposes if the problem has been clarified:—if we have seen that the outstanding problem of the Public is discovery and identification of itself, and if we have succeeded, in however groping a manner, in apprehending the conditions upon which the resolution of the problem depends. We shall conclude with suggesting some implications and corollaries as to method, not, indeed, as to the method of resolution, but, once more, the intellectual antecedents of such a method.

The preliminary to fruitful discussion of social matters is that certain obstacles shall be overcome, obstacles residing in our present conceptions of the method of social inquiry. One of the obstructions in the path is the seemingly engrained notion that the first and the last problem which must be solved is the relation of the individual and the social:—or that the outstanding question is to determine the relative merits of individualism and collective or of some compromise between them. In fact, both words, individual and social, are hopelessly ambiguous, and the ambiguity will never cease as long as we think in terms of an antithesis.

In its approximate sense, anything is individual which moves and acts as a unitary thing. For common sense, a certain spatial separateness is the mark of this individuality. A thing is one when it stands, lies or moves as a unit independently of other things, whether it be a stone, tree, molecule or drop of water, or a human being. But even vulgar common sense at once introduces certain qualifications. The tree stands only when rooted in the soil; it lives or dies in the mode of its connections with sunlight, air and water. Then too the tree is a collection of interacting parts; is the tree more a single whole than its cells? A stone moves, apparently alone. But it is moved by something else and the course of its flight is dependent not only upon initial propulsion but upon wind and gravity. A hammer falls, and what was one stone becomes a heap of dusty particles. A chemist operates with one of the grains of dust, and forthwith it disappears in molecules, atoms and electrons—and then? Have we now reached a lonely, but not lonesome, individual? Or does, perhaps, an electron depend for its single and unitary mode of action upon its connections, as much as the stone with which we started? Is its action also a function of some more inclusive and interacting scene?

From another point of view, we have to qualify our approximate notion of an individual as being that which acts and moves as a unitary thing. We have to consider not only its connections and ties, but the consequences with respect to which it acts and moves. We are compelled to say that for some purposes, for some results, the tree is the individual, for others the cell, and for a third, the forest or the landscape. Is a book or a leaf or a folio or a paragraph, or a printer's em *the* individual? Is the binding or the contained thought that which gives individual unity to a book? Or are all of these things definers of an individual according to the consequences which are relevant in a particular situation? Unless we betake ourselves to the stock resort of common sense, dismissing *all* questions as useless quibbles, it seems as if we could not determine an individual without reference to differences made as well as to antecedent and contemporary connections. If so, an individual, whatever else it is or is not, is not just the spatially isolated thing our imagination inclines to take it to be.

Such a discussion does not proceed upon a particularly high nor an especially deep level. But it may at least render us wary of any definition of an individual which operates in terms of separateness. A *distinctive* way of behaving in conjunction and *con-*

nection with other distinctive ways of acting, not a self-enclosed way of acting, independent of everything else, is that toward which we are pointed. Any human being is in one respect an association, consisting of a multitude of cells each living its own life. And as the activity of each cell is conditioned and directed by those with which it interacts, so the human being whom we fasten upon as individual *par excellence* is moved and regulated by his associations with others; what he does and what the consequences of his behavior are, what his experience consists of, cannot even be described, much less accounted for, in isolation.

But while associated behavior is, as we have already noted, a universal law, the fact of association does not of itself make a society. This demands, as we have also seen, perception of the consequences of a joint activity and of the distinctive share of each element in producing it. Such perception creates a common interest; that is concern on the part of each in the joint action and in the contribution of each of its members to it. Then there exists something truly social and not merely associative. But it is absurd to suppose that a society does away with the traits of its own constituents so that it can be set over against them. It can only be set over against the traits which they and their like present in some *other* combination. A molecule of oxygen in water may act in certain respects differently than it would in some other chemical union. But *as* a constituent of water it acts as water does as long as water is water. The only intelligible distinction which can be drawn is between the behaviors of oxygen in *its* different relations, and between those of water in *its* relations to various conditions, not between that of water and the oxygen which is conjoined with hydrogen in water.

A single man when he is joined in marriage is different in that connection to what he was as single or to what he is in some other union, as a member, say, of a club. He has new powers and immunities, new responsibilities. He can be contrasted with *himself* as he behaves in other connections. He may be compared and contrasted with his wife in their distinctive roles within the union. But *as* a member of the union he cannot be treated as antithetical to the union in which he belongs. *As* a member of the union, his traits and acts are evidently those which he possesses in virtue of it, while those of the integrated association are what they are in virtue of his status in the union. The only reason we fail to see this, or are confused by the statement of it, is because we pass so easily from the man in one connection to the man in some other connection, to the man not as husband but as business man, scientific investigator, church-member or citizen, in which connections his acts and their consequences are obviously different to those due to union in wedlock.

A good example of the fact and of the current confusion as to its interpretation is found in the case of associations known as limited liability joint-stock companies. A corporation as such is an integrated collective mode of action having powers, rights, duties and immunities different from those of its singular members *in their other connections*. Its different constituents have also diverse statuses—for example, the owners of stock from the officers and directors in certain matters. If we do not bear the facts steadily in mind, it is easy—as frequently happens—to create an artificial problem. Since the corporation can do things which its individual members, *in their many relationships outside of their connections in the corporation*, cannot do, the problem is raised as to the relation of the corporate collective union to that of individuals *as such*. It is forgotten that as members of the corporation the individuals themselves are different, have different characteristics, rights and duties, than they would possess if they were not its members and different from those which they possess in other forms of conjoint behavior. But what the individuals may do legitimately *as* members of the corporation in their respective corporate roles, the corporation does, and vice versa. A collective unity may be taken *either* distributively *or* collectively, but when taken collectively it is the union of its distributive constituents, and when taken distributively, it is a distribution of and within the collectivity. It makes nonsense to set up an antithesis between the distributive phase and the collective. An individual cannot be opposed to the association of which he is an integral part nor can the association be set against its integrated members.

But groups may be opposed to one another, and individuals may be opposed to one another; and an individual as a member of different groups may be divided within himself, and in a true sense have conflicting selves, or be a relatively disintegrated individual. A man may be one thing as a church member and another thing as a member of the business community. The difference may be carried as if in water-tight compartments, or it may become such a division as to entail internal conflict. In these facts we have the ground of the common antithesis set up between society and the individual. Then "society" becomes an unreal abstraction and "*the* individual" an equally unreal one. Because *an* individual can be disassociated from this, that and the other grouping, since he need not be married, or be a church-member or a voter, or belong to a club or scientific organization, there grows up in the mind an image of a residual individual who is not a member of any association at all. From this premise, and from this only, there develops the unreal question of how individuals come to be united in societies and groups: *the* individual and *the* social are now opposed to each other, and there is the problem of "reconciling" them. Meanwhile, the genuine problem is that of adjusting groups and individuals to one another.

The unreal problem becomes particularly acute, as we have already noted in another connection, in times of rapid social change, as when a newly forming industrial grouping with its special needs and energies finds itself in conflict with old established political institutions and their demands. Then it is likely to be forgotten that the actual problem is one of reconstruction of the ways and forms in which men unite in associated activity. The scene presents itself as the struggle of the individual as such to liberate himself from society as such and to claim his inherent or "natural" self-possessed and self-sufficing rights. When the new mode of economic association has grown strong and exercises an overweening and oppressive power over other groupings, the old fallacy persists. The problem is now conceived as that of bringing individuals as such under the control of society as a collectivity. It should still be put as a problem of readjusting social relationships; or, from the distributive side, as that of securing a more equable liberation of the powers of all individual members of all groupings.

Thus our excursion has brought us back to the theme of method, in the interest of which the excursion was taken. One reason for the comparative sterility of discussion of social matters is because so much intellectual energy has gone into the supposititious problem of the relations of individualism and collectivism at large, wholesale, and because the image of the antithesis infects so many specific questions. Thereby thought is diverted from the only fruitful questions, those of investigation into factual subject-matter, and becomes a discussion of concepts. The "problem" of the relation of the concept of authority to that of freedom, of personal rights to social obligations, with only a subsumptive illustrative reference to empirical facts, has been substituted for inquiry into the *consequences* of some particular distribution, under given conditions, of specific freedoms and authorities, and for inquiry into what altered distribution would yield more desirable consequences.

As we saw in our early consideration of the theme of the public, the question of what transactions should be left as far as possible to voluntary initiative and agreement and what should come under the regulation of the public is a question of time, place and concrete conditions that can be known only by careful observation and reflective investigation. For it concerns consequences; and the nature of consequences and the ability to perceive and act upon them varies with the industrial and intellectual agencies which operate. A solution, or distributive adjustment, needed at one time is totally unfitted to another situation. That social "evolution" has been either from collectivism to individualism or the reverse is sheer superstition. It has consisted in a continuous re-distribution of social integrations on the one hand and of capacities and energies of individuals on the other. Individuals find themselves cramped and depressed by absorption of their potentialities in some mode of association which has been institutionalized and become dominant. They may think they are clamoring for a purely personal liberty, but what they are doing is to bring into being a greater liberty to share in other associations, so that more of their individual potentialities will be released and their personal experience enriched. Life has been impoverished, not by a predominance of "society" in general over individuality, but by a domination of one form of association, the family, clan, church, economic institutions, over other actual and possible forms. On the other hand, the problem of exercising "social control" over individuals is in its reality that of regulating the doings and results of some individuals in order that a larger number of individuals may have a fuller and deeper experience. Since both ends can be intelligently attained only by knowledge of actual conditions in their modes of operation and their consequences, it may be confidently asserted that the chief enemy of a social thinking which would count in public affairs is the sterile and impotent, because totally irrelevant, channels in which so much intellectual energy has been expended.

The second point with respect to method is closely related. Political theories have shared in the absolutistic character of philosophy generally. By this is meant something much more than philosophies of the Absolute. Even professedly empirical philosophies have assumed a certain finality and foreverness in their theories which may be expressed by saying that they have been non-historical in character. They have isolated their subject-matter from its connections, and any isolated subject-matter becomes unqualified in the degree of its disconnection. In social theory dealing with human nature, a certain fixed and standardized "individual" has been postulated, from whose assumed traits social phenomena could be deduced. Thus Mill says in his discussion of the logic of the moral and social sciences: "The laws of the phenomena of society are, and can be, nothing but the laws of the actions and passions of human beings united together in the social state. Men, however, in a state of society are still men; their actions and passions are obedient to the laws of *individual* human nature."[1] Obviously what is ignored in such a statement is that "the actions and passions" of individual men are in the concrete what they are, their beliefs and purposes included, because of the social medium in which they live; that they are influenced throughout by contemporary and transmitted culture, whether in conformity or protest. What is generic and the same everywhere is at best the organic structure of man, his biological make-up. While it is evidently important to take this into account, it is also evident that none of the *distinctive* features of *human* association can be deduced from it. Thus, in spite of Mill's horror of the metaphysical absolute, his leading social conceptions were, logically, absolutistic. Certain social laws, normative and regulative, at all periods and under all circumstances of proper social life were assumed to exist.

The doctrine of evolution modified this idea of method only superficially. For "evolution" was itself often understood non-historically. That is, it was assumed that there is a predestined

1. J. S. Mill, *Logic*, Book VI, ch. 7, sec. 1. Italics mine.

course of fixed stages through which social development must proceed. Under the influence of concepts borrowed from the physical science of the time, it was taken for granted that the very possibility of a social science stood or fell with the determination of fixed uniformities. Now every such logic is fatal to free experimental social inquiry. Investigation into empirical facts was undertaken, of course, but its results had to fit into certain ready-made and second-hand rubrics. When even *physical* facts and laws are perceived and used, social change takes place. The phenomena and laws are not altered, but invention based upon them modifies the human situation. For there is at once an effort to regulate their impact in life. The discovery of malaria does not alter its existential causation, intellectually viewed, but it does finally alter the facts from which the production of malaria arises, through draining and oiling swamps, etc., and by taking other measures of precaution. If the laws of economic cycles of expansion and depression were understood, means would at once be searched for to mitigate if not to do away with the swing. When men have an idea of how social agencies work and their consequences are wrought, they at once strive to secure consequences as far as desirable and to avert them if undesirable. These are facts of the most ordinary observation. But it is not often noted how fatal they are to the identification of social with physical uniformities. "Laws" of social life, when it is genuinely human, are like laws of engineering. If you want certain results, certain means must be found and employed. The key to the situation is a clear conception of consequences wanted, and of the technique for reaching them, together with, of course, the state of desires and aversions which causes some consequences to be wanted rather than others. All of these things are functions of the prevalent culture of the period.

While the backwardness of social knowledge and art is of course connected with retarded knowledge of human nature, or psychology, it is also absurd to suppose that an adequate psychological science would flower in a control of human activities similar to the control which physical science has procured of physical energies. For increased knowledge of human nature would directly and in unpredictable ways modify the workings of human nature, and lead to the need of new methods of regulation, and so on without end. It is a matter of analysis rather than of prophecy to say that the primary and chief effect of a better psychology would be found in education. The growth and diseases of grains and hogs are now recognized as proper subjects of governmental subsidy and attention. Instrumental agencies for a similar investigation of the conditions which make for the physical and moral hygiene of the young are in a state of infancy. We spend large sums of money for school buildings and their physical equipment. But systematic expenditure of public funds for scientific inquiry into the conditions which affect the mental and moral development of children is just beginning, and demands for a large increase in this direction are looked upon askance.

Again, it is reported that there are more beds in hospitals and asylums for cases of mental disturbance and retardation than for all diseases combined. The public pays generously to take care of the results of bad conditions. But there is no comparable attention and willingness to expend funds to investigate the causes of these troubles. The reason for these anomalies is evident enough. There is no conviction that the sciences of human nature are far enough advanced to make public support of such activities worth while. A marked development of psychology and kindred subjects would change this situation. And we have been speaking only of antecedent conditions of education. To complete the picture we have to realize the difference which would be made in the methods of parents and teachers were there an adequate and generally shared knowledge of human nature.

But such an educational development, though intrinsically precious to the last degree, would not entail a control of human energies comparable to that which already obtains of physical energies. To imagine that it would is simply to reduce human beings to the plane of inanimate things mechanically manipulated from without; it makes human education something like the training of fleas, dogs and horses. What stands in the way is not anything called "free-will," but the fact that such a change in educational methods would release new potentialities, capable of all kinds of permutations and combinations, which would then modify social phenomena, while this modification would in its turn affect human nature and its educative transformation in a continuous and endless procession.

The assimilation of human science to physical science represents, in other words, only another form of absolutistic logic, a kind of physical absolutism. We are doubtless but at the beginning of the possibilities of control of the physical conditions of mental and moral life. Physiological chemistry, increased knowledge of the nervous system, of the processes and functions of glandular secretions, may in time enable us to deal with phenomena of emotional and intellectual disturbance before which mankind has been helpless. But control of these conditions will not determine the uses to which human beings will put their normalized potentialities. If any one supposes that it will, let him consider the applications of such remedial or preventive measures to a man in a state of savage culture and one in a modern community. Each, as long as the conditions of the social medium remained substantially unaltered, will still have his experience and the direction of his restored energies affected by the objects and instrumentalities of the human environment, and by what men at the time currently prize and hold dear. The warrior and merchant would be better warriors and merchants, more efficient, but warriors and merchants still.

These considerations suggest a brief discussion of the effect of the present absolutistic logic upon the method and aims of education, not just in the sense of schooling but with respect to all the ways in which communities attempt to shape the disposition and beliefs of their members. Even when the processes of education do not aim at the unchanged perpetuation of existing institutions, it is assumed that there must be a mental picture of some desired end, personal and social, which is to be attained, and that this conception of a fixed determinate end ought to control educative processes. Reformers share this conviction with conservatives. The disciples of Lenin and Mussolini vie with the captains of capitalistic society in endeavoring to bring about a formation of dispositions and ideas which will conduce to a preconceived goal. If there is a difference, it is that the former proceed more consciously. An experimental social method would probably manifest itself first of all in surrender of this notion. Every care would be taken to surround the young with the physical and social conditions which best conduce, as far as freed knowledge extends, to release of personal potentialities. The habits thus formed would have entrusted to them the meeting of future social requirements and the development of the future state of society. Then and then only would all social agencies that are available operate as resources in behalf of a bettered community life.

What we have termed the absolutistic logic ends, as far as method in social matters is concerned, in a substitution of discussion of concepts and their logical relations to one another for inquiry. Whatever form it assumes, it results in strengthening the reign of dogma. Their contents may vary, but dogma persists. At the outset we noted in discussion of the state the influence of methods which look for causal forces. Long ago, physical science abandoned this method and took up that of detection of correlation of events. Our language and our thinking is still saturated with the idea of laws which phenomena "obey." But in his actual procedures, the scientific inquirer into physical events treats a law simply as a stable correlation of changes in what happens, a statement of the way in which one phenomenon, or some aspect or phase of it, varies when some other specified phenomenon varies. "Causation" is an affair of historical sequence, of the order in which a series of changes takes place. To know cause and effect is to know, in the abstract, the formula of correlation in change, and, in the concrete, a certain historical career of sequential events. The appeal to causal forces at large not only misleads inquiry into social facts, but it affects equally seriously the formation of purposes and policies. The person who holds the doctrine of "individualism" or "collectivism" has his program determined for him in advance. It is not with him a matter of finding out the particular thing which needs to be done and the best way, under the circumstances, of doing it. It is an affair of applying a hard and fast doctrine which follows logically from his preconception of the nature of ultimate causes. He is exempt from the responsibility of discovering the concrete correlation of changes, from the need of tracing particular sequences or histories of events through their complicated careers. He knows in advance the sort of thing which must be done, just as in ancient physical philosophy the thinker knew in advance what must happen, so that all he had to do was to supply a logical framework of definitions and classifications.

When we say that thinking and beliefs should be experimental, not absolutistic, we have then in mind a certain logic of method, not, primarily, the carrying on of experimentation like that of laboratories. Such a logic involves the following factors:

First, that those concepts, general principles, theories and dialectical developments which are indispensable to any systematic knowledge be shaped and tested as tools of inquiry. Secondly, that policies and proposals for social action be treated as working hypotheses, not as programs to be rigidly adhered to and executed. They will be experimental in the sense that they will be entertained subject to constant and well-equipped observation of the consequences they entail when acted upon, and subject to ready and flexible revision in the light of observed consequences. The social sciences, if these two stipulations are fulfilled, will then be an apparatus for conducting investigation, and for recording and interpreting (organizing) its results. The apparatus will no longer be taken to be itself knowledge, but will be seen to be intellectual means of making discoveries of phenomena having social import and understanding their meaning. Differences of opinion in the sense of differences of judgment as to the course which it is best to follow, the policy which it is best to try out, will still exist. But opinion in the sense of beliefs formed and held in the absence of evidence will be reduced in quantity and importance. No longer will views generated in view of special situations be frozen into absolute standards and masquerade as eternal truths.

This phase of the discussion may be concluded by consideration of the relation of experts to a democratic public. A negative phase of the earlier argument for political democracy has largely lost its force. For it was based upon hostility to dynastic and oligarchic aristocracies, and these have largely been reft of power. The oligarchy which now dominates is that of an economic class. It claims to rule, not in virtue of birth and hereditary status, but in virtue of ability in management and of the burden of social responsibilities which it carries, in virtue of the position which superior abilities have conferred upon it. At all events, it is a shifting, unstable oligarchy, rapidly changing its constituents, who are more or less at the mercy of accidents they cannot control and of technological inventions. Consequently, the shoe is now on the other foot. It is argued that the check upon the oppressive power of this particular oligarchy lies in an intellectual aristocracy, not in appeal to an ignorant, fickle mass whose interests are superficial and trivial, and whose judgments are saved from incredible levity only when weighted down by heavy prejudice.

It may be argued that the democratic movement was essentially transitional. It marked the passage from feudal institutions to industrialism, and was coincident with the transfer of power from landed proprietors, allied to churchly authorities, to captains of industry, under conditions which involved an emancipation of the masses from legal limitations which had previously hemmed them in. But, so it is contended in effect, it is absurd to convert this legal liberation into a dogma which alleges that release from old oppressions confers upon those emancipated the intellectual and moral qualities which fit them for sharing in regulation of affairs of state. The essential fallacy of the democratic creed, it is urged, is the notion that a historic movement which effected an important and desirable release from restrictions is either a source or a proof of capacity in those thus emancipated to rule, when in fact there is no factor common in the two things. The obvious alternative is rule by those intellectually qualified, by expert intellectuals.

This revival of the Platonic notion that philosophers should be kings is the more taking because the idea of experts is substituted for that of philosophers, since philosophy has become something of a joke, while the image of the specialist, the expert in operation, is rendered familiar and congenial by the rise of the physical sciences and by the conduct of industry. A cynic might indeed say that the notion is a pipe-dream, a revery entertained by the intellectual class in compensation for an impotence consequent upon the divorce of theory and practice, upon the remoteness of specialized science from the affairs of life: the gulf being bridged not by the intellectuals but by inventors and engineers hired by captains of industry. One approaches the truth more nearly when one says that the argument proves too much for its own cause. If the masses are as intellectually irredeemable as its premise implies, they at all events have both too many desires and too much power to permit rule by experts to obtain. The very ignorance, bias, frivolity, jealousy, instability, which are alleged to incapacitate them from share in political affairs, unfit them still more for passive submission to rule by intellectuals. Rule by an economic class may be disguised from the masses; rule by experts could not be covered up. It could be made to work only if the intellectuals became the willing tools of big economic interests. Otherwise they would have to ally themselves with the masses, and that implies, once more, a share in government by the latter.

A more serious objection is that expertness is most readily attained in specialized technical matters, matters of administration and execution which postulate that general policies are already satisfactorily framed. It is assumed that the policies of the experts are in the main both wise and benevolent, that is, framed to conserve the genuine interests of society. The final obstacle in the way of any aristocratic rule is that in the absence of an articulate voice on the part of the masses, the best do not and cannot remain the best, the wise cease to be wise. It is impossible for highbrows to secure a monopoly of such knowledge as must be used for the regulation of common affairs. In the degree in which they become a specialized class, they are shut off from knowledge of the needs which they are supposed to serve.

The strongest point to be made in behalf of even such rudimentary political forms as democracy has already attained, popular voting, majority rule and so on, is that to some extent they involve a consultation and discussion which uncover social needs and troubles. This fact is the great asset on the side of the political ledger. De Tocqueville wrote it down almost a century ago in his survey of the prospects of democracy in the United States. Accusing a democracy of a tendency to prefer mediocrity in its elected rulers, and admitting its exposure to gusts of passion and its openness to folly, he pointed out in effect that popular government is educative as other modes of political regulation are not. It forces a recognition that there are common interests, even though the recognition of *what* they are is confused; and the need it enforces of discussion and publicity brings about some clarification of what they are. The man who wears the shoe knows best that it pinches and where it pinches, even if the expert shoemaker is the best judge of how the trouble is to be remedied. Popular government has at least created public spirit even if its success in informing that spirit has not been great.

A class of experts is inevitably so removed from common interests as to become a class with private interests and private knowledge, which in social matters is not knowledge at all. The ballot is, as often said, a substitute for bullets. But what is more significant is that counting of heads compels prior recourse to methods of discussion, consultation and persuasion, while the essence of appeal to force is to cut short resort to such methods. Majority rule, just as majority rule, is as foolish as its critics charge it with being. But it never is *merely* majority rule. As a practical politician, Samuel J. Tilden, said a long time ago: "The means by which a majority comes to be a majority is the more important thing": antecedent debates, modification of views to meet the opinions of minorities, the relative satisfaction given the latter by the fact that it has had a chance and that next time it may be successful in becoming a majority. Think of the meaning of the "problem of minorities" in certain European states, and compare it with the status of minorities in countries having popular government. It is true that all valuable as well as new ideas begin with minorities, perhaps a minority of one. The important consideration is that opportunity be given that idea to spread and to become the possession of the multitude. No government by experts in which the masses do not have the chance to inform the experts as to their needs can be anything but an oligarchy managed in the interests of the few. And the enlightenment must proceed in ways which force the administrative specialists to take account of the needs. The world has suffered more from leaders and authorities than from the masses.

The essential need, in other words, is the improvement of the methods and conditions of debate, discussion and persuasion. That is *the* problem of the public. We have asserted that this improvement depends essentially upon freeing and perfecting the processes of inquiry and of dissemination of their conclusions. Inquiry, indeed, is a work which devolves upon experts. But their expertness is not shown in framing and executing policies, but in discovering and making known the facts upon which the former depend. They are technical experts in the sense that scientific investigators and artists manifest *expertise*. It is not necessary that the many should have the knowledge and skill to carry on the needed investigations; what is required is that they have the ability to judge of the bearing of the knowledge supplied by others upon common concerns.

It is easy to exaggerate the amount of intelligence and ability demanded to render such judgments fitted for their purpose. In the first place, we are likely to form our estimate on the basis of present conditions. But indubitably one great trouble at present is that the data for good judgment are lacking; and no innate faculty of mind can make up for the absence of facts. Until secrecy, prejudice, bias, misrepresentation, and propaganda as well as sheer ignorance are replaced by inquiry and publicity, we have no way of telling how apt for judgment of social policies the existing intelligence of the masses may be. It would certainly go much further than at present. In the second place, *effective* intelligence is not an original, innate endowment. No matter what are the differences in native intelligence (allowing for the moment that intelligence can be native), the actuality of mind is dependent upon the education which social conditions effect. Just as the specialized mind and knowledge of the past is embodied in implements, utensils, devices and technologies which those of a grade of intelligence which could not produce them can now intelligently use, so it will be when currents of public knowledge blow through social affairs.

The level of action fixed by *embodied* intelligence is always the important thing. In savage culture a superior man will be superior to his fellows, but his knowledge and judgment will lag in many matters far behind that of an inferiorly endowed person in an advanced civilization. Capacities are limited by the objects and tools at hand. They are still more dependent upon the prevailing habits of attention and interest which are set by tradition and institutional customs. Meanings run in the channels formed by instrumentalities of which, in the end, language, the vehicle of thought as well as of communication, is the most important. A mechanic can discourse of ohms and amperes as Sir Isaac Newton could not in his day. Many a man who has tinkered with radios can judge of things which Faraday did not dream of. It is aside from the point to say that if Newton and Faraday were now here, the amateur and mechanic would be infants beside them. The retort only brings out the point: the difference made by different objects to think of and by different meanings in circulation. A more intelligent state of social affairs, one more informed with knowledge, more directed by intelligence, would not improve original endowments one whit, but it would raise the level upon which the intelligence of all operates. The height of this level is much more important for judgment of public concerns than are differences in intelligence quotients. As Santayana has said: "Could a better system prevail in our lives a better order would establish itself in our thinking. It has not been for want of keen senses, or personal genius, or a constant order in the outer world, that mankind has fallen back repeatedly into barbarism and superstition. It has been for want of good character, good example, and good government." The notion that intelligence is a personal endowment or personal attainment is the great conceit of the intellectual class, as that of the commercial class is that wealth is something which they personally have wrought and possess.

A point which concerns us in conclusion passes beyond the field of intellectual method, and trenches upon the question of practical re-formation of social conditions. In its deepest and richest sense a community must always remain a matter of face-to-face intercourse. This is why the family and neighborhood, with all their deficiencies, have always been the chief agencies of nurture, the means by which dispositions are stably formed and ideas acquired which laid hold on the roots of character. The Great Community, in the sense of free and full intercommunication, is conceivable. But it can never possess all the qualities which mark a local community. It will do its final work in ordering the relations and enriching the experience of local associations. The invasion and partial destruction of the life of the latter by outside uncontrolled agencies is the immediate source of the instability, disintegration and restlessness which characterize the present epoch. Evils which are uncritically and indiscriminately laid at the door of industrialism and democracy might, with greater intelligence, be referred to the dislocation and unsettlement of local communities. Vital and thorough attachments are bred only in the intimacy of an intercourse which is of necessity restricted in range.

Is it possible for local communities to be stable without being static, progressive without being merely mobile? Can the vast, innumerable and intricate currents of trans-local associations be so banked and conducted that they will pour the generous and abundant meanings of which they are potential bearers into the smaller intimate unions of human beings living in immediate contact with one another? Is it possible to restore the reality of the lesser communal organizations and to penetrate and saturate their members with a sense of local community life? There is at present, at least in theory, a movement away from the principle of territorial organization to that of "functional," that is to say, occupational, organization. It is true enough that older forms of territorial association do not satisfy present needs. It is true that ties formed by sharing in common work, whether in what is called industry or what are called professions, have now a force which formerly they did not possess. But these ties can be counted upon for an enduring and stable organization, which at the same time is flexible and moving, only as they grow out of immediate intercourse and attachment. The theory, as far as it relies upon associations which are remote and indirect, would if carried into effect soon be confronted by all the troubles and evils of the present situation in a transposed form. There is no substitute for the vitality and depth of close and direct intercourse and attachment.

It is said, and said truly, that for the world's peace it is necessary that we understand the peoples of foreign lands. How well do we understand, I wonder, our next door neighbors? It has also been said that if a man love not his fellow man whom he has seen, he cannot love the God whom he has not seen. The chances of regard for distant peoples being effective as long as there is no close neighborhood experience to bring with it insight and understanding of neighbors do not seem better. A man who has not been seen in the daily relations of life may inspire admiration, emulation, servile subjection, fanatical partisanship, hero worship; but not love and understanding, save as they radiate from the attachments of a near-by union. Democracy must begin at home, and its home is the neighborly community.

It is outside the scope of our discussion to look into the prospects of the reconstruction of face-to-face communities. But there is something deep within human nature itself which pulls toward settled relationships. Inertia and the tendency toward stability belong to emotions and desires as well as to masses and molecules. That happiness which is full of content and peace is found only in enduring ties with others, which reach to such depths that they go below the surface of conscious experience to form its undisturbed foundation. No one knows how much of the frothy excitement of life, of mania for motion, of fretful discontent, of need for artificial stimulation, is the expression of frantic search for something to fill the void caused by the loosening of the bonds which hold persons together in immediate community of experience. If there is anything in human psychology to be counted upon, it may be urged that when man is satiated with restless seeking for the remote which yields no enduring satisfaction, the human spirit will return to seek calm and order within itself. This, we repeat, can be found only in the vital, steady, and deep relationships which are present only in an immediate community.

The psychological tendency can, however, manifest itself only when it is in harmonious conjunction with the objective course of events. Analysis finds itself in troubled waters if it attempts to discover whether the tide of events is turning away from dispersion of energies and acceleration of motion. Physically and externally, conditions have made, of course, for concentration; the development of urban, at the expense of rural, populations; the corporate organization of aggregated wealth, the growth of all sorts of organizations, are evidence enough. But enormous organization is compatible with demolition of the ties that form local communities and with substitution of impersonal bonds for personal unions, with a flux which is hostile to stability. The character of our cities, of organized business and the nature of the comprehensive associations in which individuality is lost, testify also to this fact. Yet there are contrary signs. "Community" and community activities are becoming words to conjure with. The local is the ultimate universal, and as near an absolute as exists. It is easy to point to many signs which indicate that unconscious agencies as well as deliberate planning are making for such an enrichment of the experience of local communities as will conduce to render them genuine centres of the attention, interest and devotion for their constituent members.

The unanswered question is how far these tendencies will re-establish the void left by the disintegration of the family, church and neighborhood. We cannot predict the outcome. But we can assert with confidence that there is nothing intrinsic in the forces which have effected uniform standardization, mobility and remote invisible relationships that is fatally obstructive to the return movement of their consequences into the local homes of mankind. Uniformity and standardization may provide an underlying basis for differentiation and liberation of individual potentialities. They may sink to the plane of unconscious habituations, taken for granted in the mechanical phases of life, and deposit a soil from which personal susceptibilities and endowments may richly and stably flower. Mobility may in the end supply the means by which the spoils of remote and indirect interaction and interdependence flow back into local life, keeping it flexible, preventing the stagnancy which has attended stability in the past, and furnishing it with the elements of a variegated and many-hued experience. Organization may cease to be taken as an end in itself. Then it will no longer be mechanical and external, hampering the free play of artistic gifts, fettering men and women with chains of conformity, conducing to abdication of all which does not fit into the automatic movement of organization as a self-sufficing thing. Organization as a means to an end would reenforce individuality and enable it to be securely itself by enduing it with resources beyond its unaided reach.

Whatever the future may have in store, one thing is certain. Unless local communal life can be restored, the public cannot adequately resolve its most urgent problem: to find and identify itself. But if it be reestablished, it will manifest a fullness, variety and freedom of possession and enjoyment of meanings and goods unknown in the contiguous associations of the past. For it will be alive and flexible as well as stable, responsive to the complex and world-wide scene in which it is enmeshed. While local, it will not be isolated. Its larger relationships will provide an inexhaustible and flowing fund of meanings upon which to draw, with assurance that its drafts will be honored. Territorial states and political boundaries will persist; but they will not be barriers which impoverish experience by cutting man off from his fellows; they will not be hard and fast divisions whereby external separation is converted into inner jealousy, fear, suspicion and hostility. Competition will continue, but it will be less rivalry for acquisition of material goods, and more an emulation of local groups to enrich direct experience with appreciatively enjoyed intellectual and artistic wealth. If the technological age can provide mankind with a firm and general basis of material security, it will be absorbed in a humane age. It will take its place as an instrumentality of shared and communicated experience. But without passage through a machine age, mankind's hold upon what is needful as the precondition of a free, flexible and many-colored life is so precarious and inequitable that competitive scramble for acquisition and frenzied use of the results of acquisition for purposes of excitation and display will be perpetuated.

We have said that consideration of this particular condition of the generation of democratic communities and an articulate democratic public carries us beyond the question of intellectual method into that of practical procedure. But the two questions are not disconnected. The problem of securing diffused and seminal intelligence can be solved only in the degree in which local communal life becomes a reality. Signs and symbols, language, are the means of communication by which a fraternally shared experience is ushered in and sustained. But the wingèd words of conversation in immediate intercourse have a vital import lacking in the fixed and frozen words of written speech. Systematic and continuous inquiry into all the conditions which affect association and their dissemination in print is a precondition of the creation of a true public. But it and its results are but tools after all. Their final actuality is accomplished in face-to-face relationships by means of direct give and take. Logic in its fulfillment recurs to the primitive sense of the word: dialogue. Ideas which are not communicated, shared, and reborn in expression are but soliloquy, and soliloquy is but broken and imperfect thought. It, like the acquisition of material wealth, marks a diversion of the wealth created by associated endeavor and exchange to private ends. It is more genteel, and it is called more noble. But there is no difference in kind.

In a word, that expansion and reenforcement of personal understanding and judgment by the cumulative and transmitted intellectual wealth of the community which may render nugatory the indictment of democracy drawn on the basis of the ignorance, bias and levity of the masses, can be fulfilled only in the relations of personal intercourse in the local community. The connections of the ear with vital and out-going thought and emotion are immensely closer and more varied than those of the eye. Vision is a spectator; hearing is a participator. Publication is partial and the public which results is partially informed and formed until the meanings it purveys pass from mouth to mouth. There is no limit to the liberal expansion and confirmation of limited personal intellectual endowment which may proceed from the flow of social intelligence when that circulates by word of mouth from one to another in the communications of the local community. That and that only gives reality to public opinion. We lie, as Emerson said, in the lap of an immense intelligence. But that intelligence is dormant and its communications are broken, inarticulate and faint until it possesses the local community as its medium.

Miscellany

1946 Introduction to
The Public and Its Problems

This book was written some twenty years ago. It is my belief that intervening events confirm the position about the public and its connection with the state as the political organization of human relationships that was then presented. The most obvious consideration is the effect of the Second World War in weakening the conditions to which we give the name "Isolationism." The First World War had enough of that effect to call the League of Nations into being. But the United States refused to participate. And, while out-and-out nationalism was a prime factor in the refusal, it was reinforced by the strong belief that, after all, the main purpose of the League was to preserve the fruits of victory for the European nations that were on the winning side. There is no need to revive old controversies by discussing how far that belief was justifiable. The important fact for the issue here discussed is that the *belief* that such was the case was a strongly actuating consideration in the refusal of the United States to join the League. After the Second World War, this attitude was so changed that the country joined the United Nations.

What is the bearing of this fact upon the position taken in the book regarding the public and the connection of the public with the political aspects of social life? In brief, it is as follows: The decline, (though probably not for a rather long future time the obliteration) of Isolationism is evidence that there is developing the sense that relations between nations are taking on the properties that constitute a public, and hence call for some measure of political organization. Just what the measure is to be, how far political authority is to extend, is a question still in dispute. There are those who would hold it to the strictest possible construction of the code for the United Nations adopted at San

[First published in *The Public and Its Problems: An Essay in Political Inquiry* (Chicago: Gateway Books, 1946): iii–xi.]

Francisco. There are others who urge the necessity of altering the code so as to provide for a World Federation having wide political authority.

It is aside from the point here under consideration to discuss which party is right. The very fact that there are two parties, that there is an active dispute, is evidence that the question of the relations between nations which in the past have claimed and exercised singular sovereignty has now definitely entered the arena of political problems. It is pointed out in the text of this book that the scope, the range, of the public, the question of where the public shall end and the sphere of the private begin, has long been a vital political problem in domestic affairs. At last the same issue is actively raised about the relations between national units, no one of which in the past has acknowledged *political* responsibility in the conduct of its policies toward other national units. There has been acknowledgment of *moral* responsibility. But the same thing holds good in relations that are private and non-political; the chief difference is the greater ease with which moral responsibility broke down in the case of relationships between nations. The very doctrine of "Sovereignty" is a complete denial of political responsibility.

The fact that this issue is now within the active scope of political discussion also bears out another point made in the text. The matter at issue is in no way one between the "social" and the "non-social," or between that which is moral and that which is immoral. No doubt the feeling on the part of some that the moral responsibility which concerns the relations between nations should be taken more seriously played a part in bringing about a greater emphasis on the fact that the consequences of these relations demand some kind of political organization. But only the ultra-cynical have ever denied in the past the existence of some moral responsibility. Sufficient proof of this is found in the fact that, in order to interest the citizens of any genuinely modern people in an actual war, it has been necessary to carry on a campaign to show that *superior* moral claims were on the side of a war policy. The change of attitude is not fundamentally an affair of moral conversion, a change from obdurate immorality to a perception of the claims of righteousness. It results from greatly intensified recognition of the factual consequences of war. And this increased perception is in turn mainly due to the fact that modern wars are indefinitely more destructive and that the destruction occurs over a much wider geographical area than was the case in the past. It is no longer possible to argue that war brings positive good. The most that can be said is that it is a choice of the lesser moral evil.

The fact that the problem of the scope of the political relations between nations has now entered the arena of political discussion, goes to confirm another point emphasized in the book. The same problem of where the line is to be drawn between affairs left to private consideration and those subject to political adjudication is *formally* a universal problem. But with respect to the actual content taken by the problem, the question is always a *concrete* one. That is, it is a question of specifying factual consequences, which are never inherently fixed nor subject to determination in terms of abstract theory. Like all facts subject to observation and specification, they are spatial-temporal, not eternal. *The State* is pure myth. And, as is pointed out in the text, the very notion of the state as a universal ideal and norm arose at a particular space-time juncture to serve quite concrete aims.

Suppose for example that the idea of federation, as distinct from both isolation and imperial rule, is accepted as a working principle. Some things are settled, but not the question of just what affairs come within the jurisdiction of the Federated Government and which are excluded and remain for decision by national units as such. The problem of what should be included and what excluded from federated authority would become acute. And in the degree in which the decision on this point is made intelligently, it will be made on the ground of foreseen, concrete consequences likely to result from adopting alternative policies. And just as in the case of domestic political affairs, there will be the problem of discovering something of common interest amid the conflict of separate interests of the distinctive units. Friendship is not the cause of arrangements that serve the common interests of several units, but the outcome of the arrangements. General theory might indeed be helpful; but it would serve intelligent decision only if it were used as an aid to foreseeing factual consequences, not directly *per se*.

Thus far, I have kept discussion within what I find to be the field of facts sufficiently evident so that any one who so desires can take note of them. I come now to a point that trenches actively upon the field of important, unsettled hypotheses. In the second chapter of the text, changes in "material culture" are mentioned as an important factor in shaping the concrete conditions which determine the consequences that are of the kind called "public" and that lead to some sort of political intervention. If there were ever any reasonable doubt of the import of technological factors with respect to socially significant human consequences, that time is well past. Nor is the importance of technological development confined to domestic issues, great as it is in this field. The enormously increased destructiveness of war, previously mentioned, is the immediate outcome of modern technological developments. And the frictions and conflicts which are the immediate occasion of wars are due to the infinitely multiplied and more intricate points of contact between peoples which in turn are the direct result of technological developments.

So far we are still within the bounds of the observable facts of the transactions that occur between national units in the same way they occur between the members of a given domestic unit. The unsettled question that now looms as the irrepressible conflict of the future pertains to the actual range of the economic factor in determination of specific consequences. As will be seen by consulting the index, s.v. "Economic Forces and Politics," the immense influence exercised by economic aspects of modern life receives attention. But as far as concerned political relations between national units, the question then had to do mainly with special issues such as tariffs, most favored treatment, retaliation, etc. The view that economics is the *sole* condition affecting the entire range of political organization and that present day industry imperatively demands a certain single type of social organization has been a *theoretical* issue because of the influence of the writings of Marx. But, in spite of the revolution in Soviet Russia, it was hardly an immediate *practical* issue of international politics. Now it is definitely becoming such an issue, and present signs point to its being a *predominant* issue in determining the future of international political relationships.

The position that economics is the sole conditioning factor of political organization, together with the position that all phases and aspects of social life, science, art, education and all the agencies of public communication included, are determined by the type of economy that prevails is identical with that type of life to which the name "totalitarian" justly applies. Given the view that there is but one form of economic organization that properly fulfills social conditions, and that one country of all the peoples of the earth has attained that state in an adequate degree, there is in existence an outstanding and overshadowing practical problem.

For Soviet Russia has now arrived at a state of power and influence in which an intrinsically totalitarian philosophy has passed from the realm of theory into that of the practical political relations of the national states of the globe. The problem of adjusting the relations of states sufficiently democratic to put a considerable measure of trust in free inquiry and open discussion, as a fundamental method in peaceable negotiation of social conflicts, with the point of view that there is but one Truth, fixed and absolute and hence not open to inquiry and public discussion, is now a vital one. Although my own belief as to where the line of social progress is to be drawn between the two positions is firmly in accord with that of the great majority of members of democratic states, I am not here concerned with considerations of right and wrong, of truth or falsity. I cannot refrain, however, from pointing out how the world situation bears out the hypothesis that the matter of the scope or range and of the seriousness of the factual consequences of associated human transactions is the determining factor in affecting social behavior with *political* properties too evident to be ignored. The problem of discovering and implementing politically areas of common interest is henceforth imperative.

There is one other point that demands attention. The text points out in a number of places, firstly, that *noting* of consequences is an indispensable condition over and above their mere occurrence and, secondly, that this noting (on anything like an adequate scale) depends upon the state of knowledge at the time, especially upon the degree to which the kind of method called scientific is applied to social affairs. Some of us have been insisting for some time that science bears exactly the same relation to the progress of culture as do the affairs acknowledged to be technological (like the state of invention in the case, say, of tools and machinery, or the progress reached in the arts, say, the medical). We have also held that a considerable part of the remediable evils of present life are due to the state of imbalance of scientific method with respect to its application to physical facts on one side and to specifically human facts on the other side; and that the most direct and effective way out of these evils is steady and systematic effort to develop that effective intelligence named scientific method in the case of human transactions.

Our theorizing on this point cannot be said to have had much effect. The relative importance of the consequences of events which are of the nature of theorizing, and of events which are so overt as to force themselves upon general attention is well exhibited in what has followed upon the fission of the atom. Its consequences are so impressive that there is not only a clamor, approaching a Babel, about the utility and disutility of physical sciences, but some aspects of the control of science in the interest of social well-being have entered the arena of politics,—of governmental discussion and action. In evidence, it is enough to point to the controversy going on in the Congress of the United States as these pages are written as to civilian and military participation in control, and in the United Nations as to the best method in general of managing the needed control.

Aspects of the *moral* problem of the status of physical science have been with us for a long time. But the consequences of the physical sciences, though immeasurably important to industry, and through industry in society generally, failed to obtain the kind of observation that would bring the conduct and state of science into the specifically *political* field. The use of these sciences to increase the destructiveness of war was brought to such a sensationally obvious focus with the splitting of the atom that the political issue is now with us, whether or no.

There are those who not only insist upon taking an exclusively moralistic view of science but who also insist upon doing so in an extremely one-sided way. They put the blame for the present evils on physical science as if it were a causal entity *per se*, and not a human product which does what prevailing human institutions exact of it. They then use the evils that are apparent as a ground for the subjection of science to what they take to be moral ideals and standards, in disregard of the fact, hortatory preaching aside, there is no method of accomplishing this subordination save setting up some institution equipped with absolute authority—the sure way to restore the kind of conflict that once marked the attempt of the Church to control scientific inquiry. The net outcome of their position, were it adopted, would not be the subordination of science to ideal moral aims, in disregard of political or public interests, but the production of political despotism with all the moral evils which attend that mode of social organization.

Science, being a human construction, is as much subject to human use as any other technological development. But, unfortunately, "use" includes misuse and abuse. Holding science to be an entity by itself, as is done in most of the current distinctions between science as "pure" and "applied," and then blaming it for social evils, like those of economic maladjustment and destruction in war, with a view to subordinating it to moral ideals, is of no positive benefit. On the contrary, it distracts us from using our knowledge and our most competent methods of observation in the performance of the work they are able to do. This work is the promotion of effective foresight of the consequences of social policies and institutional arrangements.

Dedication Address of the Barnes Foundation

In two of the telegrams just read, one referred to this educational work, which is being dedicated today, as "monumental," and another referred to it as "epoch-making." These telegrams both came from the other side of the water, and while I certainly should not say they exemplified the old saying about a prophet and his honor in his own country, I think they do indicate that sometimes people at a distance see things in a truer perspective than we who are nearer. So I wish to express my deep felt appreciation of the honor of being associated in any way today with the initiation of this genuinely monumental and epoch-making enterprise. I wish to express my conviction, my most profound conviction, that we are really celebrating here today one of the most significant steps taken in this country for freedom of pictorial or plastic art, for art in education, and also for what is genuine and forward-moving throughout the whole field of education. This institution today, like any institution on a momentous occasion, looks both forward and backward. The Associate Director of Education has already told you something of the immediate past and prospects for the immediate future. I suppose most who come here today, who see these pictures and hear of the use which it is expected will be made of them, have their gaze for the most part turned toward the future. It is very natural that they should think of this as an opening and beginning, an initiation. But after all, we can hardly understand of what it is the opening and initiation, if we do not recall years of past history. These years show us that it is not so much just an opening, a fresh start, we are celebrating today, as it is an opening out, a continuation, an extension of ideas, activities, that have long been in operation in the past.

[First published in *Journal of the Barnes Foundation* 1 (May 1925): 3–6, from an address delivered at Merion, Pa., 19 March 1925.]

On the one hand there is the connection of this building and these pictures with the business which the active staff of the Foundation has built up. It is not simply that the money earned through the activity of these people in business made possible this adventure, but that the activity was also the source of the ideas, the experience, ideals, expectations and plans, which are incarnate here and which are, to a very large extent, a memorial of the past work of the people who have been engaged in the enterprise. From the first, if I may refer to the words of a previous speaker, there has been in this development the union, that trinity of power, action, achievement, in the practical sense of the word, with the cultivation of intelligence, of method which is intelligence, and of that intrinsic interest and joy in work which makes any activity aesthetic.

These beautiful grounds and trees (a genuine part of the educational work of this Foundation) are also a memorial of the love and affection which Captain Wilson has through so many years devoted to this particular aesthetic phase of Nature. The further development of the Arboretum will, fortunately, continue to have the advantage of the experience of Captain Wilson, as he is one of the Trustees. In addition, the artistic and scientific purposes of the grounds will be under the especial charge of Mrs. Barnes, the Vice-President of the Foundation. Under her direction the beauty of the surroundings will be a worthy setting for the beauty within, while through arrangements still to be made, the outdoor facilities will also become part of the educational resources of the Foundation.

The one reason to my mind why this enterprise, this Foundation, is entitled to be called epoch-making, monumental—is that it is not simply a building for the collection of pictures and the dissemination of knowledge about pictures. It is, rather, the expression of a profound belief that all the daily activities of life, the necessary business and commercial activities of life, may be made intrinsically significant, may be made sources of joy to those who engage in them so that they can put their whole beings, not merely their hands and a small section of their brain, but their feelings and emotions, into what they are doing. And while there can be no doubt that the stimulus came from the founder himself, the results would not have been possible except for the zeal and intelligence of his co-workers, all of the men and women who for many years have shared with him the satisfactions as well as the labors of attempting that which, if it is not quite unique, is almost unique in social activities: namely, the carrying on of a business which is successful as a business but which uses intelligence instead of mere force and mere mechanical efficiency, which rewarded all those engaged in it not only by pecuniary remuneration but also by the reward of the cultivation and development of their own souls.

It is, I think, significant that you will find in this gallery one of the finest collections in the world of African art, which records the aesthetic activities of individuals whose names are not known, probably have not been known for centuries. For it suggests that members of the Negro race, of people of African culture, have also taken a large part in the building up of the activity which has culminated in this beautiful and significant enterprise. I know of no more significant, symbolic contribution than that which the work of the members of this institution have made to the solution of what sometimes seems to be not merely a perplexing but a hopeless problem—that of race relations. The demonstration that two races may work together successfully and cooperatively, that the work has the capacity to draw out from our Negro friends something of that artistic interest and taste in making the contribution which their own native temperament so well fits them to make, is something to be dwelt upon in a celebration like this. We may well rejoice at every demonstration of the artistic capacity of any race which has been in any way repressed or looked upon as inferior. It is the demonstration of this capacity for doing beautiful and significant work which gives the best proof of the fundamental quality, and equality, of all people. It serves, as the telegram said, the cause of bringing all people from all over the world together in greater harmony.

Others will touch more fittingly upon the most especial activities which are to be carried on here. But I have spoken very poorly, indeed, if at least I have not made it clear that this is not an artistic or aesthetic educational enterprise in that narrow and exclusive sense of the word which considers Fine Art and Painting in the way which Sunday is often related to week-days and work-days. Art is not something apart, not something for the few, but something which should give the final touch of meaning, of consummation, to all the activities of life. So I am sure this work is not only going to spread in universities and schools as we have heard today it is spreading, but that it also will affect the public schools. It is agreed that one of the weakest points in our public school educational system is that while it gives some training in mechanical, technical things, while it conveys a certain amount of useful information and ideas, yet it is still largely public in name only. It does not yet touch what is most common, most fundamental, most demanding public recognition—an appreciation of the place occupied in all human activity by that intelligent method which is the essence of art and by the liberated and enjoyable methods which are the result of the presence of art.

While it is always dangerous to attempt the role of prophet, I feel confident we can open our eyes and look into the years ahead, to see radiating from this institution, from the work of this Foundation, influences which are going to effect education in the largest sense of that word: development of the thoughts and emotions of boys and girls, youths, men and women all over this country, and to an extent and range and depth which makes this, to my mind, one of the most important educational acts, one of the most profound educational deeds, of the age in which we are living.

Literature or Mathematics?

Is the *Boys' Own Arithmetic*, by Raymond Weeks (Dutton), literature, mathematics or a play of humor? All three doubtless, but it is also, for him who reads intelligently, a compendium of sound pedagogical sense. Its real theme is wider than numerical problems. It is a protest, none the less effective for being humorously couched, against all the methods which separate "subjects" from human life and activity. If it also involves some irony at the expense of those who attempt to connect their special subjects with human life in a forced and artificial way, it is none the worse for it.

[First published in *School and Society* 21 (27 June 1925): 786.]

Foreword to
The Story of Philosophy

Having had the privilege of reading an advance copy of Dr. Durant's *Story of Philosophy*, I am glad of the opportunity to commend such an admirable piece of intellectual work, as to its substance and its literary form. Philosophical thinkers are wont to make high claims for the human value of philosophy, as a comprehensive survey of life and as an analysis of fundamentals. But philosophic writing is often so specialized and technical that even educated readers, unless professionally trained, are repelled rather than attracted. Dr. Durant has distilled the essential thought of a series of important writers and has presented it in a way which is human and readable. While the work is one of popularization, it is also much more than that as popularization is usually conceived. The work is thoroughly scholarly. Dr. Durant has gone to the original writings and not to second-hand sources. He has selected the thinkers who are expounded with good judgment; his expositions are accurate as well as clear; his personal comments are always intelligent and useful. He has shown remarkable skill in selecting quotations that are typical, that give the flavor of the author, and that are readable. In fine he has humanized rather than merely popularized the story of philosophy. It is a pleasure to do anything which may assist in making known such a thoroughly useful book. Teachers and students in universities as well as the general reader have much to gain from it.

[First published in William James Durant's *The Story of Philosophy* (New York: Simon and Schuster, 1926): v.]

Scholasticism

What opinion do you, as a non-Scholastic philosopher, have of Scholasticism?

In reply to your very interesting letter I will make the following statements:

It is difficult to make any sweeping generalization regarding the attitude of non-Scholastic philosophers toward Scholasticism at the present time. The neglect of Scholasticism is in part due to psychological and pedagogical reasons rather than to logical ones. There are, of course, certain fashions, to use a harsh term, in thought as well as in other matters, and the neglect of the Scholastic system is in some measure due to the fact that the thinkers and writers outside of the Catholic Church do not have at present a lively interest in the problems and issues with which Scholasticism is primarily concerned. It is my impression, however, that there is now a growing interest, connected partly with the revival of realistic theories of knowledge, and partly with increased study of Aristotle and consequent interest in the relation of mediaeval thinkers to the Aristotelian system.

The chief causes for indifference rather than positive unfriendliness are these: (1) The fact that non-Scholastic thinkers have mostly been brought up in the Protestant tradition and have,—more or less unconsciously,—identified Scholasticism with the theological dogmas which they do not accept. The teachers themselves were educated under these influences. The courses in the history of philosophy given in institutions under Protestant auspices emphasize the Greek thought and modern

[First published as one of thirty-three responses in *Present-Day Thinkers and the New Scholasticism: An International Symposium* (St. Louis: B. Herder Book Co., 1926): 29–31.]

movement since Bacon, rather than Scholastic philosophy, and consequently the habit of neglect tends to perpetuate itself. (2) A more objective cause of this attitude of mind is, I think, the decay of acute interest, if not actual belief, in the content of Christian revelation. (3) The Scholastic method seems too rationalistic and not sufficiently empirical to appeal to one school of contemporary thought, while those who are rationalistically inclined seem to prefer at present to follow the model set by recent mathematics. (4) The development of natural science since the formulation of the main tenets of Scholasticism, and the fact that it does not seem possible to find harmony between the points of view developed in this science and the positions of Scholastic philosophy, is another reason. The new problems, moreover, which the development of modern science (in its methods and results) introduced, are more widely and intensely appreciated than the problems with which Scholasticism is concerned. (5) The rise of many new social and political problems upon which Scholasticism does not appear to throw any light, because it had been developed in a period before these presented themselves.

As to bringing about a better understanding, the only suggestion that occurs to me in connection with this point is the desirability of a presentation of the main points of Scholasticism apart from a definite reference to the theological doctrines of the Church, and a more sympathetic interest in at least problems of modern empirical and rationalistic philosophers than has been displayed by some of those writing from the Scholastic point of view. What I mean is, a tendency which I have occasionally observed in some of these writers to assume that the truth is so finally and clearly stated in Scholasticism that most modern European philosophy is a kind of wilful and perverse aberration. Now while there is a growing dissatisfaction with many of the results of eighteenth and nineteenth century philosophy, there are probably no non-Scholastic thinkers who do not believe that they represent a sincere attempt to deal with genuine problems.

Appendix

Value and Thought-Process
By David Wight Prall

In the nature of the case the questions that Mr. Dewey has put so specifically in his comment[1] on an article of mine on the subject of value,[2] seem to me in part gratuitous. The answering of them, however, will doubtless conduce, as he says, to clearing up the issue. But Mr. Dewey's first sentence, "Strictly speaking there *are* no such things as values," is so very much to the point that I may be excused at the beginning for adding a comment which seems to me significant, a comment which Mr. Dewey apparently thinks it not necessary to make. Things are never values: they are said to have value, which is thus an adjective of things. But this seems to mean for Mr. Dewey that values in the strict sense of the term *are* not at all; for he italicizes *are*, and when he says broadly that there are no such things as values, *things* would seem to be used in its widest sense, as meaning entities, realities, individuals. There are, of course, no such existent things as values; but there are such entities, such realities, such individual forms as values. If there were not it would be foolish, as Mr. Dewey perhaps thinks it is—I am not sure of his opinion here—to discuss anything but the one question to which he chiefly confines himself, *viz.*, What brings about or is responsible for the fact that things come to be valuable? But values in the strictest terms of discourse *are*; they have no existence, but they have being and reality, which is to say that they are natures or characters or qualities—essences, if we are to use the term of such metaphysical logicians as Plato and Leibniz and Spinoza and of Mr. Santayana.

1. This Journal, Vol. 20, No. 23, pp. 617–22 (1923). [*Middle Works* 15: 20–26.]
2. This Journal, Vol. 20, No. 5, pp. 128–37 (1923). [*Middle Works* 15: 338–48.]
[First published in *Journal of Philosophy* 21 (28 February 1924): 117–25, as a rejoinder to Dewey's article "Values, Liking, and Thought" (*Middle Works* 15: 20–26). For Dewey's rejoinder to Prall, see this volume, pp. 69–77.]

Plato, indeed, made essence into a sort of transcendent existence; Leibniz, while he tried to keep it a pure possibility, still gave it a place in God's existence and a right to demand attention as worthy of existence, an actual tendency to exist on its own account, "each possible thing having the right to claim existence in proportion to the perfection which it involves."[3] Spinoza kept the distinction clearer. Attribute, for example, was that which the intellect perceives as the essence of Substance, but Substance as such, in its existence, or even in all its essence, intellect must fail to perceive. It is true that the essence of Substance involves its existence; but the case of Substance is unique, and the true definition in the case of each existent *thing* involves nothing but its nature,—involves, that is to say, only its essence, leaving its existence entirely unaccounted for.[4] Mr. Santayana is still more insistent on the distinction; it is maintained from the very beginning of *The Life of Reason*: "What exists at any instant, if you arrest and name it, turns out to have been an embodiment of some logical essence such as discourse might define."[5] It is only such a defining of value that I have ever attempted; but such defining seems to me important.

So far as I know, I have always been careful to use *value* as the properly abstract noun that I take it to be. Mr. Dewey considers it legitimate to use the word in a looser sense, not, as I should think, warranted in any accurate discussion, to mean *things valued*. It is by taking my use of the word to carry this sense, a usage which he now and then permits himself, that he very generously puts into my sentences a meaning that he considers sound. He wishes not to believe that I mean to assume the "wholly undemonstrated and in point of fact inconceivable position" that my theorizing distinctly indicates, until I assert that I do. By thus generously giving me the benefit of the ambiguity, however, he is very easily able to show that what he takes to be the main issue between us, which he states several times with precision, resolves itself in the proposition that judgment is as definitely constitutive of value as is "an appreciation that embodies a minimum of thought," "a liking that excludes thought," "the liking of a pig for his swill," if you choose.

3. *Monadology*, 51, 54.
4. Spinoza, *Ethics*, Part I, Proposition VIII, note 2.
5. *Op. cit.*, Vol. I, p. 24.

This issue Mr. Dewey has certainly made clear, and I may as well make it equally clear that this seems to me not "the only intelligible subject of discussion," and furthermore that while I do—and, as Mr. Dewey's quotations show, *did* in the article discussed by him—not only admit, but very specially assert, that judgment may help in the acquisition of the values[6] that things may acquire, I do not admit that in the total complex situation in which alone value occurs, judgment plays the kind of part that is played by an attitude that excludes judgment. This is beside the point for much of Mr. Dewey's argument, but it seems to me an intelligible and significant assertion. If it is trite and obvious, it is for all that not generally admitted. That is the only excuse for the present essay in repetition.

Before I answer Mr. Dewey's specific questions, let me, however, make perfectly unambiguous the proposition above in which I said that Mr. Dewey resolved the issue, *viz.*, that judgment is as definitely constitutive of value as bare liking. *To be constitutive* means here *to go to make up* as an essential element or part in a total situation. *Value* has only its abstract meaning—the meaning of an abstract noun, that is; and when I use the plural *values* I mean also the plural of the same abstract noun. One says color and colors, red and reds, redness and rednesses, beauty and beauties; and such terms are, of course, used very frequently to indicate things "having" the qualities. But the plurals are just as important and just as accurately used to indicate (*a*) a number of cases of the quality, or, if the term includes many qualities having this more general quality in common, to indicate (*b*) the quality in its various kinds (instead of number) of occurrences. There are under *a* the different values of my pen and my typewriter; and there are ordinarily supposed to be not only numerically different cases of value, but also various kinds of value. Thus there are under *b* moral, ethical, and esthetic values, again in the plural and again not meaning things at all. So that this plural need involve no ambiguity. I am sorry if I have seemed to be speaking ambiguously in the use of the term in this way, even though such usage has given the opportunity for generosity in interpretation. The values are not the pen or the typewriter itself, nor moral acts, but the values that these are said to have, as a

6. *Valuity* seems to me not a happy coinage, and at least here unnecessary.

book may be said to have its own style, and authors their various styles; if the style is the man, surely it is his character or essence; not his existence, but his way of existence, his quality.

Now, having indicated an answer in general, let me be more specific. First there are the three questions which Mr. Dewey puts at the bottom of page 621 [*Middle Works* 15:25], and which he specifically asks to have answered. The sentence which he finds so full of ambiguity and which demands these answers to clear it, is to the following effect: "The values of my theory in so far as they have any common elements to justify grouping them under the term *value* at all can be shown to be constituted in the motor-affective relation which constitutes immediate value." The answers to the numbered questions are enough, I think, to show what the questions were. (1) The plural, *values*, at the beginning has the same signification as the singular, *value*, in italics. (2) The term *immediate value* refers to value in precisely the same sense of the word. (3) *Constitutes* is used in the sense of *being*, Mr. Dewey's first alternative possibility. For since I was asserting that the motor-affective relation constitutes the value, and since I had been careful to explain—Mr. Dewey quotes the clause—that "in the occurrence of this relation the value . . . occurs," I felt at liberty to say that the relation constituted the value, thinking that my analysis of the situation made my meaning clear. The relation means the situation, the constituted relation with the two terms present. Further, this relation can not occur without the attitude of the subject, while any object whatever will do for the other term; for any object whatever may conceivably be liked, while only a particular kind of subject with a particular kind of attitude can do the liking. Hence it seemed to me not very ambiguous to say that the liking-relation constitutes the value. At least I hope that there can be no ambiguity in my present statement.

"But how can a relation *be* a quality?" Mr. Dewey asks. "To identify qualities with relations seems meaningless; value is not one of the related terms of the . . . situation . . . it is a quality of a situation consisting of related things." My answer is that the two things in the relation are an animal organism and something to which the organism reacts. And it is when this reaction takes place that the relation is established and that that which the organism takes as its object is said in ordinary parlance to have value. As Mr. Dewey enunciates the alternatives open to me on page 620 [*Middle Works* 15 : 23 – 24], the same point is involved. No. 1 here is not only the meaning required for my argument, as he sees and notes, but the meaning intended, a meaning which Mr. Dewey says he does not understand. The issue then comes to be, since we are agreed on the situation as involving the same three factors, *viz.*, a subject, an object, and an attitude which relates them, just what this attitude is and whether judgment is included in it or not. My contention is that it is not; that for value to occur or to arise, and to arise in the occurrence itself, there must be an attitude; but I wish to say at the same time that this attitude is like the pig's towards his swill,—not a thoughtful attitude, like Mr. Dewey's towards a problem he is engaged upon.

But Mr. Dewey here takes my description of the attitude as "contemplative liking," so that he finds it easy to indicate my real difficulty, one which he finds insuperable because meaningless. "How," he asks—and the question is obviously rhetorical— "how can contemplation fail to be thoughtful; how can it exclude judgment?" This I shall even have the temerity to try and make clear, for above all others this seems to me the issue at stake. Mr. Dewey's greater interest is in what causes things to become valuable, and in his solution of this problem I follow him; except that I feel that in laying such stress on judgment and thought he is over-emphasizing their importance, the importance of a logical and practical activity. So far as I know, what causes anything to take on value is very largely just such thinking as he indicates in the last sentence of his article; but what I should wish to emphasize is a non-practical, non-intellectual activity. Since he admits the importance of both kinds, there is no serious theoretical issue between us here. Certainly Mr. Dewey's practical judgments, as he calls them, are a large part of the process that "enstates" values, as he has previously put it. Since, however, desires, likings, bare motor-affective attitudes also help, I can not see why he finds *valuing* as distinct from *valuation* an unfortunate word. It would be so in his context, perhaps; it seems to me not so in mine. But he would be right at this point in saying that the issue which he wishes resolved is still open, *viz.*, the issue as to "whether appreciation . . . does or does not include an element of reflective apprehension." If *reflective* means thoughtful or logical or judgmental, I think that such an element is not included. This is, if I have followed at all, what I must now make clear.

The question then is, what does the occurrence of the value-quality consist in? What is the nature of what happens, if value is to occur in the happening? What are the elements of the situation we have agreed to talk about?

To answer this question is, of course, to define the indefinable, if definition must always be of the Leibnizian form—red is a color. But there is another sort of definition which empiricists have always used, the kind that is of the form—this is red, accompanied by a gesture that points to something that *is* red. It is in this sense only that red exists, and it is in this sense that value exists. Neither of them exists, I suppose, in the sense that the substance of nature itself exists, a moving chaos in which we knock against other chaotic elements. As Mr. Santayana puts it, nothing given exists; and I had made up my mind to that long ago. But I have not made up my mind to the impossibility of empirical definitions, nor to the impossibility of so framing causal laws and descriptions of functions that discourse becomes intelligible, communicable, and useful. So I can say that value is there where the relation above described comes to be. The value is there as the quality of this spatio-temporal happening. And it only comes to be there when the substance of an animal so reacts upon the substances about it that the animal feels pleased or displeased. Value is thus constituted in tropisms, if you like. For value, esse *is* percipi; values to be such are felt, and the feeling of the animal that has any feeling is all that is needed to give a situation where there is value, for feelings are had only by reaction to stimulus, and stimulus comes from an independent substantial source—perhaps within the animal's own body—whose *esse* is not *percipi* at all, but whose qualities are empirically *what* they are because the stimulus is what it is and the animal's attitude what *it* is.

Mr. Dewey's pig and his swill is as good an illustration as any, although I should prefer, since I must give a meaning to the term *contemplation*, a cat in the sun or a ruminating cow. Here by good luck we have the very synonym for contemplative. In human beings the attitude is the attitude of a habitually more practical and thoughtful animal, but an animal attitude it remains; and the ruminating cow, the cud she chews, and the feeling of acceptance instead of riddance that keeps her chewing, comprise a very good case of a situation in which value occurs. As she keeps on chewing the value *re*curs—an esthetic value, I hope; for I suppose that the cow is not grinding predigested corn into milk, nor even preparing supplies to keep up her necessary strength. She is having elementary esthetic enjoyment in each chew, or perhaps more strictly in each impulse to go on chewing, ruminating, contemplating; as an infant is having such enjoyment when it chews on a teething ring, or Aristotle's God when he contemplates the universe. For while this species of contemplation was certainly akin to psychological process, Aristotle's God was surely not doing what Mr. Dewey calls thinking.[7] As Mr. Taylor translates, God, instead of really thinking, was only "thinking of thought," in an "activity of immobility."[8] How, indeed, could he have been thinking, with the whole moving universe which he knew by heart immediately present to his mind, seen by him in pure intuition, in the one case in which there could be immanent knowledge, the case, that is, where there could be no knowledge at all? All the relativity of the actual motion was lost, I suppose, and the whole paradox of an Unmoved Mover seems on this basis a very plausible, nay intelligible, idea. What would be *un*-intelligible, what always has been unintelligible, is a *moving* mover. What indeed could call forth thought in such a situation? Plato has described this same thrilling, but thoughtless, contemplation in the *Phaedrus*. Montaigne's neat eulogy of the permanent pleasure of sex intercourse, Dr. Johnson's equally pat notion of the perfect life as driving with a pretty woman, and Browning's sentimental, but barbarous, "Last Ride" all give us the same notion of heaven. It is a thoughtless place; there is no judging in heaven; the Last Judgment has been made. Even the Christian God has stopped thinking, and there is only the timeless music of the twanging harps, which is eternal without needing to endure.

Value occurs instantaneously. It is an occurrence that defies literal analysis, but symbolically language can indicate, *i.e.*, point out, the kind of an occurrence that it is.

7. See *How We Think*, p. 9 [*Middle Works* 6:188], where Mr. Dewey says that there are involved in every reflective act "a state of perplexity, hesitation, doubt" and "an act of search," *etc.*
8. A. E. Taylor, *Aristotle*, p. 50.

If this is a "wholly undemonstrated" position, it is because it could not conceivably be demonstrated except by just this kind of careful indication. And if it is "in point of fact inconceivable," that is true of all occurrences as such, whether they are occurrences of quality or of philosophical opinions upon the nature of a particular quality called value. Can Mr. Dewey *demonstrate* occurrence except by pointing to it? Or can he—can logic itself?—make transition conceivable? The occurrence of value is a case of the occurrence of quality, of a transition, and is *therefore* not literally conceivable.

But put it more simply—in psychological terms. What Mr. Dewey says that I need to prove is that contemplative liking excludes thought. This, I understand him, would effectively refute the one part of his double contention at the bottom of page 617 [*Middle Works* 15 : 20–21], which asserts that judgment is a necessary "constituent part of the total complex situation having valuity." The other part of his contention I do not deny, as I have made clear above. But why need there be judgment in contemplative liking? When we listen to music, and in the few moments when our attention recurs in strong enough pulsations so that we really hear it, we do not think. There are no problems; there is no need to think; there is no "thought-provoking situation" to force us on. Rather we rest in the barest feeling. We rest as the pig would rest with his swill if there were no other pigs to get ahead of him, and if he did not have to perform so many difficult practical operations to devour it. But we rest also as Aristotle's God does,—unmoved, not thinking; or as any mortal does in the face of beauty which is really his. One does not thoughtfully contemplate works of art unless one is trying to re-express them in another medium or thinking up things to say about them, or trying to remember what some one else has already said. One is simply struck with them, with form itself; art moves us instantaneously or not at all. It may take years before we see anything very complex as beautiful; but when we do, it is at a glance, between breaths. So esthetic trances have been mistaken for eternity,[9] which occurs, I suppose, instead of enduring. It has been clearly seen by poets, and now at last by philosophers in Italy, that poetry is essentially lyrical, of a moment. This is

9. A minor and modern instance is Rupert Brooke's "Dining-Room Tea."

why Goethe says that art for most of us is fragments, and only for great minds the one immediately present whole which it is to the poet himself. And it is this type of experience, entirely undemonstrated, as any experience must needs be to be experience at all, that I mean by contemplative liking.

If, as Mr. Woodworth seems to think,[10] feeling is the body's instantaneous impulse to accept or to be rid of, then this is the hint of a psychological account of esthetic contemplation at its root. But I am not explaining how it can happen, but trying to say what the essential nature of the happening itself is—to define it by pointing it out.

Mr. Dewey has treated my article with careful consideration. Perhaps it seems ungracious to refuse the charity he offers by way of my "ambiguities"; but the central point on which we differ seems to me of the greatest significance, and we differ by a world. For I can not help finding in Mr. Dewey's insertion of thought and judgment into value, even into the process that makes things valuable one over against another, the process that he calls evaluation,—I can not help seeing here a suggestion that value is not the creation of irrational preference, but is somehow at bottom rational. I have indeed spoken of just preferences and values; those which, when one is all that a human being can come to be by training in perception and feeling, one will naturally have or appreciate. There is no difficulty in having the word *justice* mean something here, which it really does mean. On the contrary, it is only by the admission of preference as the beginning of reason and justice that one can be a naturalist at all, or a scientific student of morals. For if evolution means anything, if biological science has validity or value, then mind occurs in nature, and reason is born of the irrational; it is an irrational existence before it is anything else and in order to be anything else. As beginnings are never conceivable, Hume to the contrary notwithstanding, so the beginnings of rationality can only be what was not rational and became so, an obviously "inconceivable" occurrence. The first step to make the thought process what it is was not a thoughtful step. It was an animal attitude, accepting or rejecting appearances, as it felt them good or bad. Value came first.

10. R. S. Woodworth, *Psychology*, pp. 177–78.

But this is not the place to dilate upon the theme of reason and its ordered universe, floating in an inconceivably vaster irrational and unknown chaos of possibilities. I can only hope that Mr. Dewey will think that I mean to hold the inconceivable position that I do with at least as much ground in my well-working sub-consciousness—I take it to be my natural soul, which does all my thinking and theorizing too—as in my expressed argument. One of his questions I have failed to answer. How can there be values which are not valuable? There can not be. But there can be dis-likes as well as likes, and so negative values as well as positive. Mr. Dewey may find that the present discourse has only the for-mer sort of value. It seems to me, however, that I have at least shown that I mean quite unambiguously something; that most of what I mean does not interfere with accepting Mr. Dewey's doc-trine of valuation judgments, except in so far as this doctrine suggests that such judgments are integral to the occurrence of value itself; and that the rest of what I mean bears on the nature of value, however indefinable value may be because it is an ulti-mate category, a mere event, the occurrence of one specific sort of quality, or more rigorously, the specific sort of quality that is present to mind as the essence of the thoughtless situation indicated.

Notes

These notes, keyed to the page and line numbers of the present edition, explain references to matters not found in standard sources.

179.18   Mr. Beck] James Montgomery Beck, a Philadelphia lawyer who served as U.S. assistant attorney general from 1900–1903 and later as a congressional representative from Pennsylvania (1927–34), was a leading Republican critic of Woodrow Wilson's policies. The Immigration Act of 1917, passed by Congress over the second veto of President Wilson, created a "barred zone" based on degrees of longitude and latitude, and thus eliminated all of India as a source of immigration. Beck welcomed Warren G. Harding's election as a triumph for conservatism; in 1922, while Beck was serving as solicitor general for the Harding administration, the U.S. Supreme Court confirmed the exclusion law for Asiatics. Humiliated and puzzled Indians called American democracy a hypocrisy. Not until 1946 did Congress mitigate the situation with the passage of the India Immigration and Naturalization Bill.

183.32–33   Nishihara loans] Japanese Prime Minister Terauchi Masatake, intent on advancing Japanese interests in China through profits from his country's World War I boom, supported Chinese military growth by supplying arms and financing for such purchases. China contracted with Japan for more than $80 million in loans from 1916 to 1918; secret negotiations were conducted by Terauchi's old acquaintance and director of the Bank of Korea, Nishihara Kamezō. Nishihara thus bypassed Japanese governmental channels such as the Foreign Office and the Yokohama Specie Bank, causing negative publicity in Japan when the loans were revealed. Even the Japanese minister in Peking charged that he and his officials were bypassed in financing which vitally affected Japanese policy toward China.

Woodrow Wilson responded by deciding that the influence of the Nishihara loans had grown so rapidly that the U.S. would reverse an earlier decision and allow American participation in a new consortium to loan China money as an offset to Japanese financial activities.

The Nishihara loans, given to old Chinese warlords fighting each other, were viewed as a contribution to backwardness and imperialism by a Young China struggling toward reform and nationalism.

In Japan, the Nishihara loans came to be regarded as a financial disaster; they were given without security, wasted by recipients, and left Japan with bad debts after China defaulted in the 1920s. Moreover, the loans soured China's attitude toward Japan for its attempt to collect interest on the principal.

218.38–39   The Great Society] Dewey's usage of this term derives from a book with the same title written by Graham Wallas in 1914 and dedicated to Walter Lippmann. As a participant in this intellectual triumvirate of the 1920s, Dewey reviewed Lippmann's *Public Opinion* previous to this article and, six months later, he analyzed Graham Wallas's *The Art of Thought* in the *New Republic* (see this volume, pp. 231–34).

Textual Apparatus

Textual Principles and Procedures
Textual Notes
Textual Commentary
Emendations List
Alterations in Typescripts
Line-end Hyphenation
Substantive Variants in Quotations
Checklist of Dewey's References

Index

Textual Principles and Procedures
By Fredson Bowers

Except for his correspondence, these volumes of *The Later Works of John Dewey, 1925–1953*, offer a definitive critical text of all Dewey's published writings arranged in a generally chronological order.

A text may be called "definitive," or "established," (a) when an editor has exhaustively determined the authority, in whole and in part, of all preserved documents containing the work under examination; (b) when the text is then based on the most authoritative documents produced in the work's publishing history; and (c) when the complete textual data of all appropriate documents are recorded, together with a full account of all emendatory divergences from the edition chosen as copy-text (the basis for the edited text), so that the student may recover the meaningful (substantive) readings of any document used in the preparation of the edited text.

A text may be called "critical" when an editor does not simply reprint any single document without modification but instead intervenes to correct the faults or aberrations of the copy-text on editorial authority or to alter it by reference to the corrections and revisions of some authoritative edition later than the edition or manuscript chosen as copy-text.[1]

The first step in the establishment of a critical text is the determination of the exact forms of the texts in the early editions and of the facts about their relationship one to another. An important distinction must be made immediately between an "edition" and a "printing" or "impression." Technically, an edition comprises a particular typesetting, without regard for the number of printings made at different times from this typesetting and its plates.[2]

---

1. Various terms used here to describe textual principles and operations are discussed at length in Fredson Bowers, "Established Texts and Definitive Editions," *Philological Quarterly* 41 (1962): 1–17; and in "Textual Criticism," *The Aims and Methods of Scholarship in Modern Languages and Literatures*, 2d ed., ed. James Thorpe (New York: Modern Language Association of America, 1970), pp. 29–54.
2. In the present edition the use of the bibliographical terms "edition," "impression" (or "printing"), "issue," and "state" follows that recommended in Fredson Bowers, *Principles of Bibliographical Description* (Princeton: Princeton

Textual variation is most commonly found when for one reason or another a publisher decides to order a new typesetting, since changes are inevitable in the mechanical process of transmitting the words from the copy to the new form. Some of these changes may have authority if Dewey himself took the opportunity presented by the new edition to correct or to revise his work; the remaining changes can have no authority since they emanate from the publisher's readers or the compositors and may run the gamut from normal house-styling to positive though inadvertent error.

Textual variation may also occur, however, between printings within the same edition, since alterations of various kinds can be made in the plates in preparation for running off more copies to form a new impression, or printing. Often these changes originate with the publisher, whose readers have seen misprints or other actual or fancied errors in the earlier printing and now take the opportunity to correct the plates. Although these corrections may prove to be so necessary or desirable that an editor will wish to accept them, they can have no basic authority, of course, when they were not ordered by Dewey himself. Moreover, it may happen that in the course of resetting a line to conform to the publisher's requested correction the printer may make other changes in order to justify the new line or he may inadvertently make a different error not caught by the casual proofreading often adopted for plate-changes. In addition, similar errors may be found when for purely mechanical reasons, such as damage to plates in storage between printings, or an attempt to refurbish excessive wear attacking a plate, the printer without the knowledge of the publisher or author may reset a page in whole or in part to make a new plate or extensively to modify an old one.

To establish texts for the present edition, all true editions of any work up to Dewey's death in 1952 have been collated, all their variants recorded, and a decision made whether in any part the new editions seem to contain authorial revision, or whether on the whole they represent no more variation than is normally to be anticipated in a series of unattended reprints. When new editions do give evidence that they were revised by the author, an attempt is thereupon made to distinguish his corrections and revisions from the normal variation of publisher and printer that can have no authority.

Ordinarily, Dewey did not revise his work merely for stylistic felicity but instead to clarify, amplify, and sometimes even to alter his meaning. For this reason, the nature of the changes usually provides sufficient evidence to determine whether or not Dewey had himself revised a new

---

University Press, 1949; offset by Russell and Russell, New York, 1962), pp. 379–426.

edition. Meaningful revisions such as Dewey ordered made in *Individu-alism, Old and New* are always recognizable owing to their particular nature or extent. However, corrections, as distinguished from revisions, made by a publisher's reader are almost impossible to separate from the corrections of an author unless they seem to bring variants into confor-mity with house-style, in which case their non-authoritative origin is manifest.

As remarked, not only every new edition but even every printing dur-ing an author's lifetime carries within itself the possibility for authorial correction or revision that an editor must take into account. Hence the first step in the establishment of the present text has been the collection of all known editions and impressions of each work, followed by the determination of their order and relationship from the examination of internal as well as external evidence. That is, publishers' markings may indicate the order of separate impressions, as found in D. C. Heath and Company's reprints of *How We Think*; but sometimes no external evi-dence is available, or else (like a failure to change the date on a title page) it is untrustworthy, and then internal evidence based on the wear and deterioration of the plates, combined with their repair, must be uti-lized to separate one otherwise indistinguishable impression from an-other and to determine its order in the printing history of the plates.

Such evidence has been gathered by the scrupulous examination of available copies of every known edition—for articles, primarily by sight collation and for books, primarily on the Hinman Collator. The ma-chine collations have enabled discovery of the alterations made from time to time in the book plates during their printing history, all of which have been recorded so that the evidence may be made available of the total body of facts from which the editors worked. This full stemma, then, of the total number of editions and impressions of any Dewey work, and their order, establishes the necessary physical base for pro-ceeding to the critical investigation of the complete body of evidence about textual variation and its order of development, a matter that has a crucial bearing upon the determination of the authority of the variants in any given edition or impression.

Modern critics have come to a general agreement about the following propositions for the determination of authority in the process of editing a definitive edition that attempts to establish an author's text, in every respect. For overall authority, nothing can take the place of the manu-script that was used by the printer, because it stands in the closest rela-tion to the author's intentions. In only one respect can the printed edi-tion manufactured from this manuscript exceed the manuscript in authority, and that is in the specific alterations made in proof by the author, which give us his final revised intentions. When proof-sheets are not preserved, it is the editor's task to isolate these important readings from other variants such as errors made by the compositor that were overlooked in the proofreading. The distinction between authorial revision in proof and compositorial sophistication of a text is not always easy to make, but informed critical and bibliographical investigation of the corpus of substantive variants between manuscript and printed text will ordinarily yield satisfactory results.

That is, when meaning is involved distinctions can be made. But when meaning is not involved, as in the hundreds and sometimes thousands of variations between manuscript and print in respect to spelling, punctuation, capitalization, and word-division, the inevitable assumption holds—especially if a holograph manuscript were the printer's copy, or close to it—that the author has not engaged himself to vast sums of overcharges for proof-alterations in these matters, and that the ordinarily expected house-styling has taken place, sometimes initiated by a publisher's reader, but always concluded by the compositors.

A distinction develops, hence, between the words of a text—the "substantives"—and the forms that these words take in respect to their spelling, punctuation, capitalization, or division, what are known as the "accidentals" of a text.[3] Editorial criticism may attempt to assess the authority of the substantives, but one must take it that, especially as against a printer's-copy manuscript, no printed edition can have full authority in respect to the accidentals.

On the other hand, some authors—and Dewey was often among these—are extremely careless in the inscribing or typing of the accidentals in their manuscripts, since they may be relatively indifferent to anomalies and expect the printer to set all right for publication. Thus in some respects it is not uncommon to find that the printed edition's accidentals may be superior to those of the manuscript in matters of consistency and even correctness. Yet every author whether consciously or unconsciously, and often whether consistently or inconsistently, does use at least some of the forms of the accidentals of his text as a method for conveying meaning. For example, Dewey frequently capitalized words he expected to be taken as concepts, thus distinguishing them in meaning from non-capitalized forms of the same words. That he was not con-

---

3. The use of these terms, and the application to editorial principles of the divided authority between both parts of an author's text, was chiefly initiated by W. W. Greg, "The Rationale of Copy-Text," *Studies in Bibliography* 3 (1950–51): 19–36. For extensions of the principle, see Fredson Bowers, "Current Theories of Copy-Text," *Modern Philology* 68 (1950): 12–20; "Multiple Authority: New Concepts of Copy-Text," *The Library*, 5th ser., 27 (1972): 81–115; "Remarks on Eclectic Texts," *Proof* 4 (1974): 31–76, all reprinted in *Essays in Bibliography, Text, and Editing* (Charlottesville: University Press of Virginia, 1975). See also his "Greg's 'Rationale of Copy-Text' Revisited," *Studies in Bibliography* 31 (1978): 90–161.

sistent does not alter the fact that he used such a device, which an editor must respect.

It follows that the words of the printed first edition usually have in general a superior, although not a unique, authority over those of the manuscript form of the text in view of the ever-present possibility that substantive variants in the print can represent authorial revision in lost stages of proof. On the other hand, the author's accidentals, insofar as they are viable in correctness or consistency, have an authority in manuscript superior to that in the printed form that has undergone the ministrations of copyreaders and compositors.

In these circumstances, a critical text—which is to say an eclectic text—will endeavor to join both authorities by printing each of the two major elements in the text from the form that is uniquely superior in its closeness to the author's own habits or intentions, although either element may be altered as necessary by editorial intervention to restore true authority, or purity.

This editorial principle can be extended logically to the situation when an author's manuscript has not been preserved. In this circumstance the first edition, which is the only edition set directly from the author's manuscript, must necessarily take the place of the manuscript as the prime authority. If the author has not intervened to alter matters in any subsequent impression or edition, this first edition remains the single authority for both parts of the text and must therefore become the copy-text or basis for the definitive edition, although subject to editorial correction. Later impressions or editions may unauthoritatively alter, and even correct, the text, but unless the author has himself ordered such alterations the changes have no authority and may only suggest necessary or advisable corrections to an editor. Indeed, the usual history of a text in these circumstances is one of chronological degeneration into ever more corrupt readings.

On the other hand, when in a later impression or edition the author makes his own revisions and corrections, these represent his altered intentions which must be respected by the editor. Special circumstances may call for special treatment, however, and thus two specific exceptions to the rule will be discussed later. At present it is necessary to remark only that the general principles of editing a text in critical form call for the editorial acceptance of an author's altered wishes. The earlier readings should be recorded, because they must be made available to the reader concerned to study their historical position in the development of the author's thought; but in the text itself they obviously must be superseded by the author's final intentions in cases when the editor proposes to print only a single combined text. The substantive readings of a revised impression or edition, then, have a general authority superior to those in a preceding form.

Early editors were inclined to take as copy-text the last edition of a work published in the author's lifetime, on the supposition that if he had corrected or revised it this edition would contain the maximum authority. This procedure is no longer current, for in relieving the editor of the necessity to demonstrate that any authorial revision had indeed taken place it usually resulted (in cases when no authoritative intervention had occurred) in an editorial reprint of the most corrupt edition of all. And even when somewhere in the publishing history authoritative revision had appeared, the naive editorial acceptance of *all* substantive variants in the last edition as necessarily authorial produced an unscholarly mixture of true revisions side by side with the inevitable corruptions of a reprint.

No uncritical acceptance of *all* substantive readings in any edition, whether or not revised, therefore, meets modern standards of scholarly textual criticism. It is the duty of an editor to assess all the variants that have accumulated in a text during its history and to choose on critical and bibliographical evidence those that appear to be authorial while rejecting those that appear to be printers' corruptions.[4]

As suggested above, however, in cases when the manuscript is not available the accidentals of a first edition must necessarily be more authoritative, as a whole, than those of any later reprint. House-styled as in part these first-edition accidentals may be, the fact that they were set directly from the author's manuscript will often have influenced the compositors to adopt the manuscript forms; and in any event, they must necessarily represent a closer approximation of the manuscript accidentals than can any reprint, which is only one printed edition further house-styled and set from another printed edition. What changes in the accidentals may take place in a revised edition at the order of an author are often impossible to isolate, but they must necessarily be fewer than the substantive alterations that were the chief reason for his intervention, especially with an author like Dewey.

On the modern textual principle of divided authority, therefore, the copy-text for this edition of Dewey remains stable as the earliest authority closest to the author, usually the first edition;[5] and hence the ac-

4. As a case history the first edition of Nathaniel Hawthorne's *The House of the Seven Gables* may be cited. In this, scrupulous editorial investigation established that two-thirds of the substantive variants between the manuscript and first edition were unauthoritative in the print and were to be rejected. See the Centenary Edition of Hawthorne, vol. 2 (Columbus: Ohio State University Press, 1965), pp. xlvii–lviii.

5. Few early Dewey holograph manuscripts were preserved; a number of his own typescripts for articles published after Dewey moved to Columbia University in 1905, however, do exist. These suggest that the copy given to the printer might vary widely in legibility and in styling. According to his associates, Dewey usually composed on the typewriter with a margin-stop set at the left

cidentals for Dewey's texts are established as those of the first editions printed from his manuscripts whenever the manuscripts themselves are not extant. If it is ascertained that no authorial revision or correction took place in any subsequent impression or edition, the first edition remains the final authority for the substantives as well. On the other hand, when substantive revisions are made in later impressions or editions, and when these are of a nature that permit their incorporation into a single critical text, those variants believed to be authorial are adopted in preference to readings of the first edition, and thus an eclectic text is established that combines the highest authority in respect to the substantives drawn from the revised forms of the text with the highest authority of the accidentals drawn from the edition closest to the manuscript source. In short, in this form of critical text the copy-text remains the first edition, but into the texture of its accidentals are inserted the revised readings that have been selectively ascertained to represent Dewey's altered intentions.

When special circumstances exist, exceptions may be made to this now classic formulation of the principles of copy-text and the treatment of revised editions. First, like some other authors Dewey occasionally revised a work so extensively that it is necessary to print both the original and its rewritten revision for the benefit of readers concerned to read each version in its proper historical setting. Matter and idea may be so complexly and thoroughly altered in a revision (as in the first chapter of *Experience and Nature*, or *Ethics*, or *How We Think*) as to make impracticable the reader's reconstruction of the earlier form from the conventional list of variants. The two-text principle is sometimes the only answer to otherwise insoluble textual problems.

---

but seldom at the right, with the result that some words might be typed on the platen instead of on the paper. Customarily the machine was set for double- or triple-spacing; revisions and additions were then typed in so that the final page might look as if it had been single-spaced. Handwritten comments might also be added, as well as handwritten revisions of the typed material. From the 'thirties on, Dewey made extensive use of professional typing services, but even during those years, friends, colleagues, and trusted former students are known to have helped put materials in shape for the printer.

Dewey was characteristically indifferent about his spelling and hyphenation, although more consistent in handwritten than in his typewritten material; however, Dewey's punctuation in both typescripts and manuscripts, since it was more closely related to exact meaning, was treated with greater care. One of Dewey's long-time editors in Henry Holt and Co. has stated, "I tried a number of times to 'improve' his style, but whenever I made a substantial change I found that I also had changed the sense and therefore had to reinstate the original. I did go over many passages with him and he improved them. He permitted us to use our house style, but I kept as close to the original as I could." Letter from Charles A. Madison, 25 June 1964, Center for Dewey Studies, Southern Illinois University at Carbondale.

Second, revision may be less extensive than that requiring the printing of both texts and in all such cases the practical possibility is present, therefore, of contriving the usual eclectic or critical text that would incorporate the revisions in the texture of the original. Yet in special circumstances it may happen that such a lesser revision—usually at a considerably later time—may so blot out or recast the essential ideas and point of view of the original and its corpus of ideas as to create what are, in effect, two ideologically independent documents. True, the apparatus list of the rejected earlier readings would still enable a reader to reconstruct the original and its differing content. Nevertheless, the presentation among the *Early Works* and *Middle Works* of such an eclectic text based on the later revised substantives would occasionally clash sharply with and distort the historical perspective of the development of Dewey's thought gained by the chronological presentation of his works in the present edition. It would be a distinct anomaly, for example, suddenly to come in the *Middle Works* upon a developed body of ideas, as in a revised critical text, that Dewey, in fact, was not fully to formulate until the *Later Works*. Yet to restrict the appearance of the text to the *Later Works* in its revised form would leave too important a gap in the continuity of the *Early* or *Middle Works* volumes. Thus whenever this marked ideological difference exists in a revision, the original early version has been printed in the *Works* volumes in its proper historical position. However, since this second category differs from the first in that a collational apparatus can enable a reader to sift the differences between the two versions, a historical collation of the variant substantive readings in the revised publication that was to appear during the years covered by the *Later Works* volumes has been incorporated in the apparatus for the original form of the text in the earlier volume. A reader of such an early text, therefore, can if he wishes simultaneously investigate the nature of the later revisions. Nevertheless, since a reader of the *Later Works* volumes may also be interested in the contemporary revised form for a study of Dewey's intellectual progress, a special note in the *Later Works* volumes will refer him to these necessary collations elsewhere.

In the process of editing, the principle has been adopted that each separate work is to be treated as an independent unit in respect to its accidentals. That is, each unit has its own problems of copy-text, with inevitable variation in the nature of the printer's copy and the house-styling given it, ranging from that found in all sorts of journals to that required by different book-publishers. Thus, certain features may vary both within and between independent works in the present edition. For example, the heaviness or lightness of punctuation may differ markedly between articles published in different journals. Although one or other style may in some features approximate more closely what is known of Dewey's general punctuational characteristics, no editor can attempt to reconstruct the probable manuscript readings in these respects. Hence, except for the correction of presumptive error and an occasional clarification, the variable punctuation systems of the copy-texts must stand, for no certainty can obtain about the recovery of an author's exact punctuation in any given instance. On the other hand, Dewey's own spellings are ordinarily known, and it is no problem to recover these few characteristics of the manuscripts from the variety of American house-stylings given the spellings of his different works. Thus the editor has felt free to emend the spelling accidentals throughout to coincide with Dewey's practice, but always with a record so that the copy-text readings can be recovered from the apparatus provided. Only when Dewey himself was inconsistent in his spelling of certain words and when it is impossible to determine his preferred forms from manuscripts are inconsistent spellings not only between different copy-texts but also within a copy-text itself permitted to stand without a choice made between them.

Except for the small amount of silent alteration listed below, every editorial change in the chosen copy-text has been recorded, with its immediate source, and the original copy-text reading has been provided, whether in the substantives or the accidentals. The complete account will be found in the lists of emendations.

In most texts that have a reprinting history a certain number of variants will be positive errors or else unnecessary changes that are unauthoritative and have not been adopted by the present editors. All substantives of this kind have been recorded whether occurring in new impressions or in new editions.[6] However, when as in a new edition the text is reset throughout, the number of accidentals changes would be too large to list. In addition, since all such accidentals variants that seem to be either authoritative or advisable changes will have been incorporated as emendations of the copy-text, no useful purpose would be served by listing the hundreds and hundreds of discarded publishers' or printers' unauthoritative normalizings of the texts on which they had worked.

Since the number of rejected variants of the kind noted above that qualify for recording[7] is comparatively limited, no separate list has ordinarily been made and this group of historical variants has usually been incorporated with the appropriate emendations lists.

In the emendations lists an asterisk prefixed to the page-line number

6. Changes made in the plates that correct errors that would otherwise have been corrected in the copy-text by editorial intervention (see below) are recorded for the sake of completeness.
7. Such rejected readings from editions later than the copy-text are to be distinguished from copy-text readings rejected in favor of subsequent revision or correction, which of course are recorded as emendations.

indicates that the emendation, or the refusal to emend, recorded in this item is discussed in the Textual Notes that precede that list. These Textual Notes may also discuss readings for which no entry appears in the emendations lists.

In special cases separate lists within the textual material may substitute for part of the basic emendations list. For example, material the first edition of which falls within the period of the *Later Works* may have been substantially revised at a still later time but not so extensively as to call for parallel or separately reprinted texts of the two versions. Thus, as explained on p. 413 in reference to the treatment of certain revised works first printed in the *Early* or *Middle Works* volumes, a new form of list may appear in the *Later Works* when an extensive revision of an original copy-text herein printed can be reconstructed from a table of the substantive variants instead of being separately printed as an independent text.

When Dewey's manuscript, whether in the form of a holograph or typescript, serves as copy-text, a separate list entitled "Alterations in Manuscript(s) [or Typescript(s)]" records Dewey's changes in those documents, using the notational system illustrated in the present volume (*Later Works* Volume 2).[8]

A number of silent alterations have been made in the copy-text. These concern chiefly the mechanical or typographical presentation of the text and have nothing whatever to do with meaning, else they would have been recorded.

The most general class of these silent alterations has to do with Dewey's system of references whether within the text, in footnotes, or in lists of authorities that he might append. These references have been checked for accuracy, and the details of capitalization, punctuation, and of bibliographical reference have been normalized for the reader's convenience. When a reference is within the text, its form may be condensed following Dewey's own pattern when the expanded information required by the reader to check the reference will be found in an appended list of authorities. Except for the silent emendations mentioned and corrections which appear in the emendations lists, Dewey's footnotes are kept in their original form and position, since their references are completed in the appended Checklist of Dewey's References.

In all volumes, a list of substantive variants between Dewey's quotations and his source has also been provided as a supplement to the Checklist of Dewey's References. In most of Dewey's edited texts, quotations have been retained just as he wrote them even though not

---

8. This method of transcribing variants and alterations is described by Fredson Bowers in "Transcription of Manuscripts: The Record of Variants," *Studies in Bibliography* 29 (1976): 212–64.

always strictly accurate, since that was the form on which he was founding his expressed ideas. The section entitled Substantive Variants in Quotations gives the correct quotation and will be helpful to the reader in determining whether Dewey had the source open before him or was relying on his memory. However, every substantive variant is studied for evidence of errors not attributable to Dewey; these are corrected in the text and recorded in the Emendations List.

All references in footnotes or within the text (and also in the rejected readings of the copy-text) that relate to points taken up within the work in question (whether by backward or by forward reference) have had the appropriate pages of the present edition substituted for their original page numbers applying to the copy-text itself.

A second large class of silent alterations concerns itself with the works that Dewey published in England, wherein the English printer had styled in his own manner the American spellings, punctuation system, and other forms of the accidentals or general presentation such as the formal or typographical features of the punctuation. For the convenience of American readers, and in some part as a means of automatically returning to certain undoubted features of the manuscripts that served as printer's copy, the elements in such copy-texts that were styled in the English manner have been silently Americanized when these run contrary to what can be established as Dewey's own usage. Thus words like "emphasise" have been altered silently to "emphasize," "colour" to "color"; and the position of punctuation in relation to quotation marks has been altered to American usage. On the other hand, when a Dewey copy-text typeset in America exhibits some of these same British conventions, consistency with normal emendation principles demands that the editor's alterations to standard American usage or to Dewey's own ascertained style be treated as formal emendations. Hence the reader of these texts may expect that the English publications will have been silently normalized—in these respects only—to American (and to Dewey's) usage, but that in all texts originating in the United States similar emendations for normalizing purposes will be recorded.

For the rest, the silent changes are mechanical and concern themselves with making regular some anomalous typographical conventions or use of fonts, expanding most abbreviations, and so on. Typical examples are removing periods and dashes after headings and dates and signatures at the close of articles, and changing the font of syntactical punctuation after roman or italic words (or in italic passages) to follow a logical system. Roman numbers in chapter headings are silently altered to arabic, as are all references to them.

These remarks concern the general treatment of most texts in the present series. When unusual features call for unusual treatment, special notice in the respective textual commentaries will be given of modifications or of additions. The intent of the editorial treatment both in large and in small matters, and in the recording of the textual information, has been to provide a clean reading text for the general user, with all the specialized material isolated for the convenience of the specialist who wishes to consult it.

The result has been to establish in the wording Dewey's final intentions in their most authoritative form divorced from verbal corruption whether in the copy-text or in subsequent printings or editions. To this crucial aim has been added the further attempt to present Dewey's final verbal intentions within a logically contrived system of accidentals that in their texture are as close as controlled editorial theory can establish to their most authoritative form according to the documentary evidence that has been preserved for each work.

January 1982

Textual Notes

This list discusses readings adopted in the critical text, whether emendation or retention of copy-text readings where emendation might have been expected.

40.14   Althusius] Within Dewey's sentence structure, "the former" referred to Laski. However, by "the former" Dewey clearly meant the earlier jurist, Johannes Althusius, a German who established the theory of the state as a hierarchy of constituent groups. Laski's views expanded on and diverged from those of the founder.

47.23   causal] Rejection of the *Philosophy and Civilization* emendation is imperative here, given the context. Dewey argues that sense qualities have no invidiously psychical character but that "sense" indicates something about conditions giving rise to the quality rather than anything about the nature of the content. So, when speaking of sensory, sensible or sense qualities, Dewey makes no casual or chance reference; rather, he refers to causal conditions.

51.23   organ.] Based on the typescript's space after "organ" and subsequent capitalization of "Red" not followed by a comma, an editorial emendation has been made, restoring Dewey's original intent.

51.37   of a sign, mark, to] *Philosophy and Civilization*'s comma after "mark" has been accepted in connection with substantive changes within the same phrase.

51.38   is signified] During the process of revision in the earlier part of this sentence, "is" may have been inadvertently omitted. Therefore the copy-text reading has been restored due to possible oversight in composition.

54.17   "of."] Given the context of the sentence, where the corresponding prepositions are stated earlier, it is clear that Dewey meant to repeat "in" and "of."

54.33   settlement.] Dewey's alterations in his typescript indicate that he originally ended the essay at this point. He entered then x'd-out his signature and "Columbia University." The last sentence, by virtue of its uneven alignment and lighter type, was clearly Dewey's afterthought.

54.37   causal] Rejection of the substantive change from this essay's last publication is based on Dewey's discussion of metaphysical matters. Because of the content, substitution of "casual" for "causal" cannot be justified.

63.6   in quality] The word "in," found in Dewey's typescript and also in the original source, *Scientific Thought* by Charlie Dunbar Broad, had been omitted in the *Journal of Philosophy* publication.

66.35–36   presentness] Given the pattern of usage at 66.31 and 68.2, along with the context in which Dewey discusses elements of time, "presence" has been emended here.

370.25–26   inexhaustible] The absence of the prefix on "exhaustible," uncorrected in the 1946 republication of Dewey's book, would appear, given the intended meaning of the sentence, to be an inadvertent oversight in composition.

Textual Commentary

Volume 2 of *The Later Works of John Dewey, 1925–1953* comprises thirty-four items for the years 1925 to 1927; Dewey's writings for 1925, with the exception of *Experience and Nature*, and all of his works from 1926 are included, as well as his 1927 book, *The Public and Its Problems*. Twenty-four of these items are essays, twenty-two of which were published in journals. The other two essays appeared in *Studies in the History of Ideas*, a collective endeavor by members of the Department of Philosophy, Columbia University, to increase American contributions to the history of culture. The remaining items are four book reviews and five miscellaneous pieces, including Dewey's dedication address at the Albert Barnes Foundation and his 1946 introduction to the republished *The Public and Its Problems*.

Nine essays appeared in more than one publication but do not present copy-text problems; as with the remaining twenty-five items published once, the only authoritative appearance before this edition has necessarily served as copy-text. Even though the existence of only a single previous text eliminates textual problems, some commentary on the origin and reception of several of these items can reveal Dewey's writing habits and activities during 1925–1927 as well as connect these writings to the rest of the Dewey corpus; those items are, accordingly, discussed first and comments on textual choices follow the general discussion.

While visiting Japan and China in 1919–1921, Dewey had contracted with the *New Republic* for a series of articles on oriental culture. The last two of these essays, "Highly Colored White Lies" and "Is China a Nation or a Market?" appeared in *New Republic* on 22 April and 11 November 1925. Social and political analyst Walter Lippmann had complimented Dewey's observations in a letter: "The material you have written . . . for the New Republic . . . seem to me models of what political reporting ought to be. The American attitude toward the Far East is becoming increasingly impatient and bewildered while propagandist writing holds the field."[1]

1. Lippmann to Dewey, 14 June 1921, Walter Lippmann Papers, Special Collections, Yale University Library, New Haven, Conn.

"America and the Far East," published in *Survey* on 1 May 1926, and "We Should Deal with China as Nation to Nation," written for the May 1926 issue of *Chinese Students' Monthly*, completed Dewey's analysis of the Orient. Copy-text for these four Japan-China articles is their first known appearance in these three journals; *Characters and Events*, a collection of Dewey's writings edited by Joseph Ratner (New York: Henry Holt and Co., 1929), republished all of the oriental as well as the Turkish essays, but without Dewey's intervention and hence has no editorial authority.

During his 1920–21 stay in Peking, Dewey almost certainly met newly appointed United States Ambassador to China, Charles R. Crane.[2] Crane, a member of the 1919 Inter-Allied Commission on Mandates in Turkey and president of the Board of Trustees of the American College for Girls in Constantinople, later initiated and financed Dewey's two-month 1924 trip to Turkey. There, at the invitation of Sefa Bey, Turkish Minister of Public Instruction,[3] Dewey evaluated the country's educational system.[4]

After his return from Turkey, Dewey responded to the rapid changes in that country's life with another series of articles in the *New Republic*. The last of the Turkish essays, "The Problem of Turkey," appeared on 7 January 1925 and that appearance serves as copy-text for this edition.[5]

Four of this volume's items were republished in Dewey's collection of essays *Philosophy and Civilization* (New York: Minton, Balch and Co., 1931). Copy-text for "The Development of American Pragmatism," in which Dewey summed up his theory of learning by doing, is its first publication, in *Studies in the History of Ideas*, edited by Dewey's col-

2. A banker and Chicago manufacturer of valves and fittings, Crane became a world traveler and philanthropist. Because of Crane's interest in Asia, Woodrow Wilson had appointed him an adviser on Eastern Affairs at the Paris Peace Conference. See Arthur Benington, "The Growing Menace to the British Empire," *New York World*, 8 April 1923.

3. Robert M. Scotten to Secretary of State Charles Evans Hughes, 23 September 1924, Diplomatic Branch, National Archives, Washington, D.C. [*The Middle Works of John Dewey, 1899–1924*, ed. Jo Ann Boydston, 15:418–20. Carbondale: Southern Illinois University Press, 1983.]

4. Dewey's previously unpublished "Preliminary Report," prepared while he was still in Turkey, appears in *Middle Works* 15:301–7. His later and definitive thirty-page report, sent to the Turkish Ministry of Public Instruction and called *Report and Recommendation upon Turkish Education* [*Middle Works* 15:273–97], was first published in Turkish in 1939, and again in 1952. The English version was published in 1960 with the title *The John Dewey Report* (Ankara: Research and Management Bureau of the Ministry of Education, 1960), pp. 1–27.

5. Four previous essays on Turkish life, all published in *New Republic*, appear in *Middle Works* 15: "Secularizing a Theocracy," pp. 128–33; "Angora, the New," pp. 134–38; "The Turkish Tragedy," pp. 139–43; "Foreign Schools in Turkey," pp. 144–49.

leagues in the Department of Philosophy, Columbia University (New York: Columbia University Press, 1925).

"Corporate Personality," another essay that was republished in *Philosophy and Civilization*, initially appeared with the title "The Historical Background of the Corporate Legal Personality" in the April 1926 *Yale Law Journal*, which serves as copy-text here.

The third essay from this volume republished in *Philosophy and Civilization* (PC) was "A Naturalistic Theory of Sense-Perception." PC's publication was based on the essay's first appearance in *Journal of Philosophy* on 22 October 1925. Copy-text for the present edition has been Dewey's original typescript in the Journal of Philosophy Collection, Rare Books and Manuscripts, Columbia University Libraries, New York City.

"Affective Thought," the fourth essay republished in *Philosophy and Civilization*, had appeared twice earlier, initially with the title "Affective Thought in Logic and Painting" in the April 1926 *Journal of the Barnes Foundation*, and later in the Barnes Foundation's collection of essays, *Art and Education* (Merion, Pa.: Barnes Foundation Press, 1929). The essay's first publication has served as copy-text here.

Dewey's extended friendship with the founder of the Barnes Foundation dated from the academic year 1917–18, when Albert C. Barnes participated at the age of forty-five in one of Dewey's seminars at Columbia University. Barnes's excellent collection of French art, built with profits generated by his invention and manufacture of a silver nitrate solution called Argyrol, was housed at the Barnes Foundation in Merion, Pennsylvania; Dewey was in time appointed educational adviser and consultant to the staff of the foundation.[6] Dewey's "Dedication Address" for the ceremony at the Barnes Foundation, on 19 March 1925, appears in the Miscellany section of this volume. Copy-text is its only publication as the lead article in the first issue of the *Journal of the Barnes Foundation*, in May 1925.

That same summer Dewey accompanied Barnes on a brief tour of European art museums. In his correspondence with another collector of French paintings, Leo Stein, Dewey described Barnes's influence on him, saying that "Barnes has enormously advanced the recognition and statement of factors which enter objectively into the valuation of pictures— this belief is due to hearing him talk about pictures in the Louvre [and Prado] last summer as well as reading his book."[7]

The book to which Dewey referred was *The Art of Painting*, written by Barnes and published by the foundation in 1925. Barnes dedicated

6. George Dykhuizen, *The Life and Mind of John Dewey* (Carbondale: Southern Illinois University Press, 1973), pp. 221–22.
7. Dewey to Stein, 9 January 1926, James Rowland Angell Papers, Special Collections, Yale University Library, New Haven, Conn.

his book to Dewey, "whose conceptions of experience, of method, of education, inspired the work of which this foundation is a part."[8]

On 4 December 1925, after forwarding the proofs of "Affective Thought in Logic and Painting" to the *Journal of the Barnes Foundation* for publication, Dewey responded to Barnes's praise:

> You much exaggerate the article I sent you in relation to your own book [*The Art of Painting*]. I got the points as relates to painting entirely from you and have only linked them up with some other ideas which I came to in quite a different connection. I am writing an introduction to logical theory; that is I'm giving a course in which Im trying to sum up and round out my scattered ideas on that topic, and incidentally trying to use the lectures as the basis for getting the main points down in writing. All of the first part of the piece I sent you were lifted from that context, almost bodily. It was while I was working out what I call the biological foundations of thinking that I prepared this material and while in the course of it I felt there was a real connection with your treatment of painting. In other words the two experiences sort of blended in my mind. I didn't feel that I had taken time to work out the connection very well, so Im glad if the two parts of the article struck you as reasonably welded. I thought maybe it would seem rather externally stuck on, tho I feel there is a real connection.[9]

In his ongoing discussion of the esthetics of art with Leo Stein, Dewey further clarified his intentions with regard to "Affective Thought": "the psychological analysis of experience which ought to be the basis [of esthetics] doesnt exist as yet; I have tried to suggest another mode of approach in a little article which will come out in the next number of the journal of the Barnes Foundation, starting from Rignano's Psychology of Reasoning."[10]

Dewey continued to explore the relationship between life and art with his essay "Individuality and Experience." It is the fifth of nine items in this volume for which more than one possibly authoritative text exists. The article's first appearance, in the January 1926 *Journal of the*

---

8. Barnes, *The Art of Painting* (Merion, Pa.: Barnes Foundation Press, 1925), p. v.

9. Dewey to Barnes, 4 December 1925, Joseph Ratner/John Dewey Papers, Special Collections, Morris Library, Southern Illinois University at Carbondale. Both Dewey and Barnes authorized Joseph Ratner's photocopying of the Barnes-Dewey correspondence, the originals of which have not been available for research at the Barnes Foundation. All references here are to the copies in the Ratner/Dewey Papers.

10. Dewey to Stein, 22 February 1926, Angell Papers.

Barnes Foundation, has been selected as copy-text. Its republication in *Art and Education*, where Dewey's essays appeared with those of Barnes, art authority Laurence Buermeyer, and Barnes Foundation director of education, Violetta de Mazia, provides minor corrections which have been accepted as emendations.

Another subject that occupied Dewey's attention for a number of years was the theory of value. His essays relating to the problem and objects of value, published in the *Journal of Philosophy, Psychology and Scientific Methods* in 1913 and 1918,[11] caught the imagination of David Wight Prall, a noted philosopher and teacher at the University of California at Berkeley. In 1921 Prall wrote a monograph criticizing Dewey's conception of values as related to judgments.[12] Dewey's first response to Prall, in "Valuation and Experimental Knowledge,"[13] sparked a written debate between the two in the *Journal of Philosophy* from 1923 through 1925.[14] Dewey's final response to Prall, entitled "The Meaning of Value" and published in the *Journal of Philosophy* on 26 February 1925, appears in this volume. Although this article ended the Dewey-Prall exchange in the public print, Dewey himself sought throughout his lifetime to evolve a more complete philosophy of value.

For the essay entitled "Events and the Future," first published in *Journal of Philosophy* on 13 May 1926, the present edition uses a divided copy-text. Dewey's typescript in the Journal of Philosophy Collection, Rare Books and Manuscripts, Columbia University Libraries, serves as basic copy-text but, as only the first half is extant, the *Journal of Philosophy* published version serves as copy-text for the remaining portion of the essay, beginning at 67.4. Dewey's changes in the incomplete typescript, both by hand and at the typewriter, are recorded in the Alterations in Typescripts—"Events and the Future."

The three remaining items with multiple texts can be discussed as a group because of their similar publishing history. From 5 July to 21 August 1926 Dewey lectured to more than 500 American students at the Sixth Session of the Mexican National University Summer School in

11. "The Problem of Values," *Journal of Philosophy, Psychology and Scientific Methods* 10 (8 May 1913): 268–69; "The Objects of Valuation," ibid. 15 (9 May 1918): 253–58 [*Middle Works* 7:44–46; *Middle Works* 11:3–9].

12. "A Study in the Theory of Value," *University of California Publications in Philosophy* 3 (1921): 179–290.

13. *Philosophical Review* 31 (July 1922): 325–51 [*Middle Works* 13:3–28].

14. Rejoinder by Prall, "In Defense of a *Worthless* Theory of Value," *Journal of Philosophy* 20 (1 March 1923): 128–37 [*Middle Works* 15:338–48]; reply by Dewey, "Values, Liking, and Thought," *Journal of Philosophy* 20 (8 November 1923): 617–22 [*Middle Works* 15:20–26]; rejoinder by Prall, "Value and Thought-Process," *Journal of Philosophy* 21 (28 February 1924): 117–25 [*The Later Works of John Dewey, 1925–1953*, ed. Jo Ann Boydston, 2:393–402. Carbondale: Southern Illinois University Press, 1984].

Mexico City.[15] American Consul General Alexander W. Weddell reported to Secretary of State Frank B. Kellogg that Dewey lectured "on 'Advanced Educational Problems' and on 'Contemporary Philosophical Thought.'"[16]

Dewey's contact with American and Mexican students and professors, as well as with local educators and politicians, led to a series of *New Republic* articles: "Church and State in Mexico," 25 August 1926, pp. 9–10; "Mexico's Educational Renaissance," 22 September 1926, pp. 116–18; "From a Mexican Notebook," 20 October 1926, pp. 239–41. Copy-text for all three essays is this first appearance. That the editors of the *New Republic* were pleased with Dewey's observations is clear; they republished the three articles in their Dollar Book series volume entitled *Impressions of Soviet Russia and the Revolutionary World: Mexico—China—Turkey* (New York: New Republic, Inc., 1929). Dewey lightly edited the essays for book publication; his revisions and corrections have been accepted as emendations of the journal copy-text.

The treasurer of the *New Republic*, Daniel Mebane, singled out the article "Mexico's Educational Renaissance" to forward to President Calvin Coolidge. Attached to the essay was a letter which read:

> Dr. Dewey's high place in our national life is so universally acknowledged that I need make no apology for thus attempting to insure his report on educational progress in Mexico reaching your desk. I am confident that you, and Mrs. Coolidge as well, have the greatest concern for people struggling to advance themselves in public education, and the case of Mexico is one requiring sympathy as well as understanding.[17]

Indeed, Dewey's three essays described the changing national life of Mexico under the leadership of President Plutarco Elías Calles, who had been elected two years before Dewey's arrival.

> Despite the opposition of conservative forces, Calles was breaking up the large landed estates, advancing the rights of labor, expanding and reforming education, restricting the rights of foreign commercial and industrial interests, and severely limiting the powers and activities of the Catholic clergy in Mexico.[18]

15. Edward Davis, Military Attaché, U.S. Embassy in Mexico City, 18 May 1926, Record Group 165, Records of the War Department General and Special Staffs, Military and Intelligence Division, National Archives, Washington, D.C.
16. Weddell to Kellogg, 10 June 1926, Report #671, Index Bureau, State Department, National Archives.
17. Mebane to Coolidge, 22 September 1926, Division of Mexican Affairs, State Department, National Archives.
18. Dykhuizen, *Life and Mind of John Dewey*, p. 232.

Just as he had earlier reflected in the *New Republic* on his travels to China and Turkey, Dewey now pieced together the complex elements of Mexican national growth in his new series of essays for that journal. He clearly sympathized with the revolutionary movement in that country and his experiences there, according to his daughter Jane, "confirmed his belief in the power and necessity of education to secure revolutionary changes to the benefit of the individual, so that they cannot become mere alterations in the external form of a nation's culture."[19]

Alice Dewey had accompanied her husband to Mexico during the summer of 1926. Illness forced her return to New York City midway in the visit. After Dewey's return from Mexico and while writing the *New Republic* articles, he tended Alice in her declining health. During the spring of 1927, Dewey took a leave of absence from Columbia University in order to remain with his wife.

Since 1921 Dewey had written articles on behalf of the American Committee for the Outlawry of War. His essays, a response to the failure of the Covenant of the League of Nations to mandate an international ban on war, were encouraged by longtime friend and Chicago attorney, Salmon O. Levinson.[20] On 18 March 1925 Levinson wrote to Dewey, "I do hope you are revolving in your mind the greatly desired article on 'What is Law'. . . . While we felt somewhat under pressure during the supposed crusade of the Christian Century, I believe that an article now will be more timely than then."[21]

Subsequently Dewey's essay "American Responsibility" appeared in *Christian Century* on 23 December 1926, urging the forthright exercise of America's practical idealism by the adoption of Senator William E. Borah's resolution to outlaw the war system.[22] Copy-text for this essay

19. Jane M. Dewey, "Biography of John Dewey," in *The Philosophy of John Dewey*, The Library of Living Philosophers, ed. Paul A. Schilpp (Evanston: Northwestern University Press, 1939), 1:42.

20. Dewey's writing also included a foreword to the 1921 pamphlet *Outlawry of War* [*Middle Works* 13:411]. This pamphlet was the publication of the newly organized American Committee for the Outlawry of War, founded by Levinson. Voluminous correspondence passed between Levinson, leader of the movement headquartered in Chicago, and Dewey, who initiated the New York City branch.

   Dewey had written articles on the outlawry of war movement as early as 1918. Levinson's essay "The Legal Status of War," *New Republic* 14 (1918): 171–73 [*Middle Works* 11:388–92], prompted Dewey's reply, "Morals and the Conduct of States," *New Republic* 14 (1918): 232–34 [*Middle Works* 11:122–26].

21. Levinson to Dewey, 18 March 1925, Salmon O. Levinson Papers, Special Collections, The Joseph Regenstein Library, University of Chicago.

22. On 14 February 1923 Borah, after many contacts with Levinson, had introduced a resolution that placed the Senate on record as supporting the outlawry of war principle.

is this only previous appearance. Internal headings, probably supplied by an editor, have been retained to ensure Dewey's focus.

Articles by social and political analyst Walter Lippmann, first a supporter of the outlawry of war movement and later its formidable adversary, prompted Dewey to write two essays.[23] Prior to their disagreements on the outlawry of war issue, Dewey had reviewed Lippmann's *Public Opinion* in the *New Republic* on 3 May 1922,[24] stating that "There is no book I've read in a very long time from which I learned so much or rec'd so many suggestions."[25] Dewey's review of Lippmann's subsequent book *The Phantom Public*, entitled "Practical Democracy" and published in *New Republic* on 2 December 1925, appears in this volume. The two Lippmann books Dewey reviewed, still part of his personal library,[26] contain underlining and marginalia throughout whole sections. They clearly stimulated Dewey's interest, already whetted by legal questions growing out of the outlawry of war movement, in the changing nature of American government. Indeed, Dewey concluded in his review of *The Phantom Public* that Mr. Lippmann's remarks on the weakness of our democracy "suggest the need of further analysis. . . . I hope to return to this phase of the matter later."[27]

This natural evolution of ideas resulted in *The Public and Its Problems*. On 24 February 1927, Dewey wrote to Columbia University colleague Herbert Schneider, "I have just sent to Holt the mss of a 50 thousand word book called The Public and Its Problems, based on some lectures I gave a year ago at Kenyon College [at Gambier, Ohio, where Dewey delivered several lectures upon the Larwill Foundation in January 1926], in which I have t[r]ied to state in a somewhat popular manner my ideas about politics and its methods."[28]

Dewey's application of philosophy to politics was warmly received by critics,[29] who found *The Public and Its Problems* stimulating and

23. Lippmann's essay "The Outlawry of War" appeared in *Atlantic Monthly* 132 (1923): 245–53 [*Middle Works* 15:404–17]. Dewey responded in the *New Republic* with "What Outlawry of War Is Not" on 3 October 1923 and "War and a Code of Law" on 24 October 1923 [*Middle Works* 15:115–21 and 122–27]. These two articles became the sixteen-page pamphlet published by the American Committee for the Outlawry of War with the title *Outlawry of War: What It Is and Is Not, A Reply to Walter Lippmann* (Chicago, 1923).

24. *New Republic* 30 (1922): 286–88 [*Middle Works* 13:337–44].

25. Dewey to Lippmann, 4 May 1922, Lippmann Papers.

26. John Dewey Papers, Special Collections, Morris Library, Southern Illinois University at Carbondale.

27. See this volume, pp. 219–20.

28. Dewey to Schneider, Dewey Papers.

29. The following reviews appeared: R. E. Park, *American Journal of Sociology* 34 (1928): 1192–94; *Boston Transcript*, 12 November 1927, p. 8; Alfred Stiernotte, *Humanist* 7 (September 1947): 96–97; Stephen C. Pepper, *Inter-*

cogent, with "a lively historical sense" which illustrated "an interesting conception of social development based on human nature and its habits, and avoiding the extremes of economic determinism and the theory of the omnicompetent individual." [30]

Favorable reviews noted, for example, that "Professor Dewey has done much suggestive and forceful writing; but none better than this," [31] and were typified by William Ernest Hocking's comments in *Journal of Philosophy*:

> Dewey always accomplishes more than his title implies. . . . The cure for the ills of democracy is, for Dewey, . . . more democracy— not in the sense of more machinery, but in the sense of more adequate grasp of the idea. The Great Community must be ushered in by more day-to-day knowledge of socially significant truth, by a current social enquiry freely pursued and freely disseminated, and by the enlisting of art in the presenting of that scientific self-knowledge whose fascination, in our present jaded state of interest, our public does not understand. These are presently pertinent means to a goal which Dewey . . . regards as persistent, simply because it is "the idea of community life itself" and can not be abandoned. [32]

The *New Republic*, as might be expected, explored Walter Lippmann's influence on Dewey's interest in the problems of contemporary democracy. Robert M. Lovett concluded his review by stating that Dewey sets forth his indispensable conditions for organization of a democratic public "with such persuasive earnestness that they become to others the basis of a renewed faith and a lively hope, a guide to action as well as belief." [33]

While Harold Laski in the *Saturday Review of Literature* noted the "immense influence" of Lippmann, he called *The Public and Its Problems* "extraordinarily suggestive; also, like everything of his I am for-

national Journal of Ethics 38 (1927–28): 478–80; William Ernest Hocking, Journal of Philosophy 26 (6 June 1929): 329–35; O. de Selincourt, Mind, n.s. 37 (July 1928): 368–70; Monist 40 (October 1930): 640; Robert M. Lovett, New Republic 52 (24 August 1927): 22–23; Virgil Michel, New Scholasticism 2 (April 1928): 210–12; Sterling Lamprecht, New York Herald Tribune Books, 27 November 1927, p. 4; Robert Luther Duffus, New York Times Book Review, 23 October 1927, p. 15; Thomas Vernor Smith, Philosophical Review 38 (March 1929): 177–80; Harold J. Laski, Saturday Review of Literature 4 (15 October 1927): 198–99; Henry Neumann, Survey 59 (1 November 1927): 162–63; William B. Munro, Yale Review 17 (April 1928): 610–12.

30. De Selincourt, Mind, n.s. 37 (July 1928): 370.
31. Munro, Yale Review 17 (April 1928): 611.
32. Hocking, Journal of Philosophy 26 (6 June 1929): 329, 333.
33. Lovett, New Republic 52 (24 August 1927): 22–23.

tunate enough to know, it is quite extraordinarily difficult." [34] *Survey* reviewer Henry Neumann observed that "Professor Dewey brings a cooling intelligence to play upon exaggerated conceptions of the importance of the state and also upon the newer pessimism with respect to democracy." [35] In the *New York Times Book Review*, Robert Duffus stated that any reader who is willing to tackle "so hard-packed a discussion" by "one of the clearest thinkers, though not always the most lucid writer . . . will be well repaid." [36]

Twelve years later, Dewey himself wrote former student Hu Shih:

> Probably the best balanced of my writings is The Public and its Problems, and also the most "instrumental", at least by implication, for it brings out more the principle of relativity. . . . but unfortunately [I] did not make that fact explicitly conscious to myself and so not to readers. . . . I had meant . . . to emphasize—what was implicit but not explicit in my earlier statements—the absolute importance of democratic action in determining the policies of the government—for only by means of "government by the people" can government *for* the people be made secure. [37]

Hu Shih sent a copy of Dewey's letter to Joseph Ratner, another former student of Dewey's, who responded, "Indeed, the last chapters of the Public could have been written by any body else. . . . In fact, Dewey was far too much influenced by Lippmann's Public Opinion in those chapters." [38] However, delighted by Dewey's evolution of a genuinely "instrumental" theory of the state, whereby human activity becomes an "instrument" developed to solve social problems, Ratner concluded that "Dewey in The Public (Ch.II) wrote better than he knew." [39]

Henry Holt and Company published *The Public and Its Problems* in 1927 and kept it in print for fourteen years, using a single set of plates. All copies of the book examined have only the copyright date; no further indications of multiple printings appear. Comparison of the texts of these volumes on the Hinman Collator reveals no variants. On 21 October 1941, Charles A. Madison of Holt's College Editorial Department wrote to Dewey, "We are sincerely sorry not to be able to keep *The Public and Its Problems* in print any longer, but you will understand that unless a book commands a sufficient sale we cannot very well continue to keep it in print." [40]

34. Laski, *Saturday Review of Literature* 4 (15 October 1927): 198.
35. Neumann, *Survey* 59 (1 November 1927): 162.
36. Duffus, *New York Times Book Review*, 23 October 1927, p. 15.
37. Dewey to Hu Shih, 27 October 1939, Ratner/Dewey Papers.
38. Ratner to Hu Shih, 12 November 1939, Ratner/Dewey Papers.
39. Ibid.
40. Madison to Dewey, 21 October 1941, Holt Publishing Company Archives, Princeton University Library, Princeton, N.J.

By 6 May 1942 *The Public and Its Problems* was out of print and Dewey signaled his intentions in a reply to Madison. "Since . . . you do not intend to reprint, will you kindly let me know how I may obtain the plates and the right to use them."[41] Henry Holt and Company informed Dewey that the plates were available at scrap metal value of $15.00 and agreed to convey to Dewey all publishing rights to *The Public and Its Problems*.[42] Earle H. Balch of G. P. Putnam's Sons interceded at this point, negotiating the transfer of copyright from Holt to Dewey. Balch also wrote that Dewey "has asked me to take care of the matter of plates because he has no place to store them and we are glad to do so for him."[43]

In 1946, Gateway Press used the plates to reprint *The Public and Its Problems* with a new introduction by Dewey which appears in this volume. Copy-text for the present edition is the copyright deposit copy A 996499; it has been sight collated against the last (Chicago: Gateway, 1946) impression of *The Public and Its Problems* and their texts found to be identical.

As mentioned earlier, Dewey gathered essays that had been previously published for his collection *Philosophy and Civilization* (New York: Minton, Balch and Co., 1931). The substantive changes throughout, whether revisions or corrections, reflect the author's intentions and perspective some years after his initial writing.

"The Development of American Pragmatism," first published in *Studies in the History of Ideas*, appeared six years later in *Philosophy and Civilization* (PC), which is cited as the first appearance of seventy-five changes adopted for the present edition.

To prepare the article for republication, Dewey made many revisions, such as completely rewriting the sentence at 10.25–27, italicizing for emphasis at 4.32, 9.29, 9.31, 15.36, 18.17, and shifting to the present tense at 8.4, 8.5, 8.18, and at 10.8. Two errors in *Studies in the History of Ideas* were corrected in PC: "as" to "is" at 18.11, "on" to "to" at 21.11. Dewey changed sentence divisions for reemphasis at 12.32 and 21.21. Other substantive alterations seem to have been made in the interest of clarification: for example, Dewey changed "explanation" to "interpretation" at 7n.13, "greatly" to "indefinitely" at 8.40, "terms" to "concepts" at 9.31–32, "because" to "when" at 12.10, and "constitute" to "establish" at 14.13.

"Corporate Personality" first appeared in *Yale Law Journal* (YL); fifty-one corrections and revisions made for its republication in *Philoso-*

41. Dewey to Madison, 6 May 1942, Holt Archives.
42. H. G. Bristol to Dewey, 13 May 1942, Holt Archives. Dewey may have contracted with Holt for the publication of future writings when he signed the agreement from Peking in 1919 to publish his Imperial University lectures as *Reconstruction in Philosophy*.
43. Balch to H. G. Bristol, 25 May 1942, Holt Archives.

phy and Civilization (PC) have been accepted here as emendations. These include the shift in noun-verb agreement, from "wars confer" to "war confers" at 33n.5, and the correction of one typographic and two spelling errors found in YL: "the" to "that" at 30n.8, "ecclesiatic" to "ecclesiastic" at 33.25, and "Hobbessian" to "Hobbesian" at 40n.19. Examples of Dewey's revision to alter meaning are the change from "it" to "him" at 24.19, "less" to "more without" at 28.16, "conceded" to "promoted" at 36.18. One substantive change has been rejected in favor of the copy-text reading: at 36.20, the PC insertion of "it" incorrectly restructured the sentence and altered Dewey's meaning. Because of their accuracy and consistency, the law citations, with capitalized and abbreviated journal titles as well as page numbers signaling both essay beginnings and quotation locations, have been preserved, even though they differ stylistically from usual Dewey references and were almost certainly supplied by an earlier editor.

"A Naturalistic Theory of Sense-Perception" first appeared in *Journal of Philosophy* (JP) on 22 October 1925 and was republished in *Philosophy and Civilization* (PC); these publications are cited as the first appearance of fifty-six emendations to the typescript (TS), which has served as copy-text. The PC version of the essay agrees with JP in a number of substantive variants, indicating that Dewey selected the first publication as his basic text for PC.

Variants between PC and JP are mainly revisions for clarity and felicity, with few changes affecting content. Slight alterations of meaning occur at 46.26, where "accepting" is substituted for "taking," and at 47.19–20, where "because of" is substituted for "through." PC inserts a period at 44.22 that shifts emphasis, a change accepted as authoritative. However, PC's alteration of TS and JP "causal" to "casual" at 47.23 and 54.37 has been considered a printer's error and rejected. Another omission in both JP and PC at 47.17–18—"leads to difficulties in statement and which"—was probably Dewey's own revision in proof, along with the change of TS "obscure" to "obscures" for agreement, and both have been accepted here as emendations. At 51.37–38, Dewey revised in PC to eliminate the JP "implication, of" and to add "a" before "sign" and a comma after "mark" but failed to note the omission of TS "is"; the PC final revision has been accepted and "is" has been restored from TS.

The Emendations List for "A Naturalistic Theory of Sense-Perception" functions also as a historical collation, as it includes variants among the three available versions. Dewey's extensive typed alterations, made in the process of composition, as well as JP's inked editorial alterations in the TS prior to publication, mainly punctuating, italicizing, and supplying of omitted letters, appear in Alterations in Typescripts—"A Naturalistic Theory of Sense-Perception."

"Affective Thought," which appeared initially with the title "Affective

Thought in Logic and Painting" in the April 1926 *Journal of the Barnes Foundation*, is the fourth essay to be republished in *Philosophy and Civilization* (PC). The eight PC emendations include the substitutions of "that" for "which" at 105.32 and a semicolon for "and," at 106.34. Two corrections occur: "recurrence" replaces "repetition" at 107.31, and "means" replaces "marks" at 107.35. In addition to the shift in noun-verb agreement at 107.39, the repositioning of the phrase "re-shaping natural conditions" at 107.1–2 clarifies Dewey's meaning. Republication in *Art and Education* provided no substantive changes.

"Individuality and Experience" also appeared initially in the *Journal of the Barnes Foundation* 2 (January 1926): 1–6. Its republication in *Art and Education*, a collection of essays published by the Barnes Foundation Press in 1929, is noted as the first appearance of two emendations, both transpositions of punctuation marks.

Dewey's articles on Mexico first appeared in the *New Republic*: "Church and State in Mexico," 25 August 1926, pp. 9–10; "Mexico's Educational Renaissance," 22 September 1926, pp. 116–18; and "From a Mexican Notebook," 20 October 1926, pp. 239–41. Their republication in *Impressions of Soviet Russia and the Revolutionary World: Mexico–China–Turkey* (ISR) is cited as the first appearance of a total of eight emendations: five emendations in "Church and State," one in "Educational Renaissance," and two in "Mexican Notebook," all corrections of the original publication. They include the insertion of a date for clarification at 195.20 and 206.5, the spelling correction of "Carrazana's" to "Carranza's" at 195.9, and the addition of the accent on "Juárez" at 195.10. In addition, ISR shifts the apostrophe from "childrens'" to "children's" at 206.22.

B.A.W.

Emendations List

All emendations in both substantives and accidentals introduced into the copy-text are recorded in the list that follows, with the exception of the changes in formal matters described below. The copy-text for each item is identified at the beginning of the list of emendations in that item; for the items that had a single previous printing, no abbreviation for the copy-text appears in the list itself. Page-line number at left is from the present edition; all lines of print except running heads are counted. The reading to the left of the square bracket is from the present edition; following the bracket is an abbreviation for the source of the emendation.

W means Works—the present edition—and is used for emendations made here for the first time. The symbol WS (Works Source) is used to indicate emendations made within Dewey's quoted material that restore the spelling, capitalization, and some required substantives of his source (see Substantive Variants in Quotations).

For emendations restricted to punctuation, the curved dash ~ means the same word(s) as before the bracket; the inferior caret ∧ indicates the absence of a punctuation mark. The abbreviation [*om.*] means the reading before the bracket was omitted in the editions and impressions identified; [*not present*] is used where appropriate to signal material not appearing in identified sources. The abbreviation [*rom.*] means roman type and is used to signal the omission of italics; [*ital.*] means italic type and is used to signal the omission of roman type. *Stet* used with an edition or impression abbreviation indicates a substantive reading retained from an edition or impression subsequently revised; the rejected variant follows the semicolon. The asterisk before an emendation page-line number indicates that the reading is discussed in the Textual Notes.

A number of formal, or mechanical, changes have been made throughout:

1. Periods have been deleted after titles of essays appearing in this volume.

2. Superior numbers have been assigned consecutively to Dewey's footnotes throughout an item.

3. Book and periodical titles are in italic type; articles and sections of books are in quotation marks. Book and journal titles have been supplied and expanded where necessary. The form of Dewey's documentation, wherever unclear, has been made consistent. Periods after roman numerals have been deleted, and abbreviations regularized where necessary.

4. Periods and commas have been brought within quotation marks. Single quotation marks have been changed to double when not inside quoted material; however, opening or closing quotation marks have been supplied where necessary and recorded.

5. Chapter headings have been deleted and arabic numbers placed before the chapter titles in *The Public and Its Problems*.

The following spellings have been editorially regularized to the known Dewey usage appearing before the brackets:

centre(s)]   center   304.11, 304.23, 345.11, 369.30
common sense (noun)]   common-sense   30.22, 31.3
cooperate (all forms)]   coöperate   179.2–3, 203.21, 280.11, 384.21
coordinate (all forms)]   coördinate   204.18, 239.25, 347.27
coordinate (all forms)]   co-ordinate   15.4, 17.8
meagre]   meager   300.17
naïveté]   naiveté   127.16
preeminence]   preëminence   253.13, 285.17
preempted]   preëmpted   105.16
preexisting]   preëxisting   264.38
reechoed]   reëchoed   309.36
reestablish]   reëstablish   369.32–33
reenforce (all forms)]   reënforce   280.14, 280.37, 291.22, 294.31,
        328.20, 370.15, 371.27
role(s)]   rôle   5.18, 10.16, 18.13, 51.7, 51.8, 118.13, 123.6, 148.28,
        265.5, 283.12, 283.29, 284.7, 286.27, 302.10, 332.34, 353.35,
        354.26, 385.13
zoology]   zoölogy   243.22

The Development of American Pragmatism

Copy-text for this article is its publication in *Studies in the History of Ideas*, ed. Department of Philosophy (New York: Columbia University Press, 1925), 2:353–77. The republication in *Philosophy and Civilization* (New York: Minton, Balch and Co., 1931), pp. 13–35 (PC), is cited as the first appearance of seventy-five emendations.

3.8   avoiding] PC; avoids
3.9   their aims] PC; of their aims
4.1   especially interested,] PC; especially
4.2   concerned,] PC; ~∧
4.19   or else] PC; or
4.30   Make Our] W; *Make Our* PC; *make our*
4.31   doctrine. Peirce's effort was to] PC; doctrine in the efforts
         which he made to
4.32   *experience*] PC; [*rom.*]
5.23   concepts. Pragmatism] PC; concepts. [¶] Pragmatism
5.25–26 life. [¶] It] PC; life. It
5.30–31 the greatest generality of meaning] PC; the most general
         meaning
5.36   narrow] PC; too narrow
6.4   "practically."] PC; ∧ ~. ∧
6.18   neo-Kantian] W; neo-kantian
7.23   term "truth,"] PC; term,
7n.2   211] W; 210
7n.4   Anglo-Saxon] WS; ~∧~
7n.6   acts] WS; facts
7n.13   interpretation] PC; explanation
8.4   is] PC; was
8.5   are] PC; were
8.7–8   educator and humanist] PC; educator
8.14   of] PC; in
8.18   is] PC; was
8.40   indefinitely] PC; greatly
9.29   *meaning*] PC; [*rom.*]
9.31   *value*] PC; [*rom.*]
9.31–32 concepts] PC; terms
10.8   cherishes] PC; cherished
10.16   than do] PC; than
10.17   should] PC; would
10.25   all such proof. Above] PC; all evidence of this nature, and
         above
10.27–28 choose . . . his] PC; choose, his
11.23   reasoning] PC; resasoning
11.32   any] PC; the
11.33   led] PC; brought
12.10   when] PC; because
12.23   failure] PC; fail
12.29   empiricism, but] PC; empiricism
12.32   action. And] PC; action, and

13.33   as yet mere] PC; mere
13n.3   lead to] PC; become
13n.6   recently] PC; just recently
14.13   establish] PC; constitute
14.16   it] PC; that it
14.29,31,35   neo-Kantian(s)] W; neo-kantian(s)
14.36   Kantianism] W; kantianism
14.40   are, more or less,] PC; are
15.25   is among some] PC; is in one
15.25   pages] PC; aspects
15.29   discrete] W; discreet
15.36   *a-priorism*] PC; [*rom.*]
16.21   Effects] W; Rôle
16.31   on] PC; by
16.31   by] PC; under some
17.6   and there] PC; there
17.12   the] PC; its
17.13   of its] PC; in its
17.14   the] PC; its
17.23   predicate] PC; attribute
17.23   possible] PC; corresponding
17.24   habit] PC; the habit
17.24   manner] PC; the manner
17.24   should] PC; must
17.28   original] PC; same
18.1   neo-Hegelian] W; neo-hegelian
18.3   object] PC; own object
18.3–4   necessary] PC; possible
18.11   is] PC; as
18.17   *re*constituting] PC; reconstituting
18.18   it] PC; them
18.22   true in its place] PC; true
18.23–24 judgment.] PC; judgment in its place.
18.25   things] PC; facts
18.30   This] PC; The
18.30   more and more] PC; more
18.38   should be] PC; is
18.39   continues] PC; merely continues
20.21   on our practices] PC; in our thought
20.36   and] PC; and of
20.39   ∧by "a] W; "∼ ∧∼
21.8   indispensable] PC; sole and indispensable
21.10–11 he only reacts] PC; he need only react

21.11   to] PC; on
21.21   pursue. It] PC; pursue, but it
21.29   all men] PC; all

Corporate Personality

Copy-text for this article is its publication in *Yale Law Journal* 35
(1926): 655–72 (YL). The republication in *Philosophy and Civilization*
(New York: Minton, Balch and Co., 1931), pp. 141–65 (PC), is cited as
the first appearance of fifty-one emendations.

22.1   Corporate Personality] PC; THE HISTORIC
          BACKGROUND OF CORPORATE LEGAL PERSONALITY
23n.6   lawyerlike] WS; lawyer-like
23n.7–8   *Has . . . Corporations?*] W; *Theory of Corporations in
          Common Law*
23n.12   Maitland, 3 *Collected*] W; 3 Maitland, *Collected*
24.19   him] PC; it
24.30   sphere∧ so that] PC; sphere, until
24.38   whatnot] W; what not
25.17–18 unconsciously led] PC; been a controlling principle
          although usually made unconsciously, leading
26.5–6   adopted . . . "organism,"] PC; adopted all the extreme
          analogies with an "organism" into his corporate unit,
26.10   for the writing] PC; the writing
26.14   may] PC; will
26.36   right-duties. And] PC; right-duties, and
26n.1   Maitland, . . . Gierke] W; Gierke, *Political Theories of the
          Middle Age*
26n.2   1900] W; 1902
26n.2   xxvi.] W; xxvi (translated and prefaced by Maitland).
26n.3   *personnalité morale*] W; *Personnalité Morale*
26n.4   5] W; 1
28.16   more without] PC; less
28n.1   *Love,*] W; ~∧
29.24–25 their having] PC; having
29.29   and produce] PC; or have
29.33   to decide what] PC; what
29.34–35 while it is] PC; but it becomes
30.4   reference] PC; recurrence
30.11   "beings." Certain] PC; "beings." It is true that he adds "will"
          as a secondary defining element. Certain

30n.9   that] PC; the
30n.19   *volitions* from] PC; *volitions from*
30n.21   *personnalité juridique*] W; *Personalité Juridique*
31n.7   Kant's] PC; the latter's
32.9   are] PC; is
32.22   Middle Ages] PC; middle ages
32.25   of] PC; between
32.25   with] PC; and
32n.10   A] PC; One
33.3   particularly upon] PC; particularly
33.25   ecclesiastic] PC; ecclesiatic
33n.5   war.] PC; wars.
33n.5   war confers] PC; these wars confer
33n.6   affects] PC; affect
33n.17   1198] WS; 1196
33n.17–18   *A History of Political*] W; *Political*
34.23   that goes] PC; going
34.25   Middle Age] PC; middle age
34n.1   *deutsche*] W; *deutches*
34n.1–2   *Genossenschaftsrecht*] W; *Genossenschaftrecht*
34n.13   hypostases] W; hyspostases
35.12   this claim] PC; its claims
36.10   that of] PC; as far as
36.10–11   the power] PC; power
36.11   bodies.] PC; bodies is concerned
36.15   *legal power*] PC; [*rom.*]
36.18   promoted] PC; conceded
36.20   might] *stet* YL; it might PC
37.1   respect of] PC; respecting
37.10   on] PC; as
37.21   it was] PC; the corporation was
38.12   from] PC; which arise from
38.17   unity] PC; line
38.18   throughout] PC; through
38.35   all] PC; both
39.3   power∧] PC; power, as
*40.14   Althusius] W; the former
40.19   so as to] PC; to
40.20–21   held that] PC; in
40n.19   Hobbesian] PC; Hobbessian
41n.12   *Overtoun*] W; *Overtown*
41n.14   Vinogradoff] W; Vinagradoff
41n.20   alternative possibility omitted] PC; omitted alternative possibility

41n.24   State] WS; state
42.21   stated] PC; said
42n.5   205–6] W; 205
42n.8   (1924–1925)] W; (1924)
43.9   had] PC; has
43.10   to deny] PC; in order to deny

A Naturalistic Theory of Sense-Perception

Copy-text for this article is the typescript (TS), personally typed by Dewey, in the Journal of Philosophy Collection, Rare Books and Manuscripts, Columbia University Libraries, New York, N.Y. The article's publication in *Journal of Philosophy* 22 (22 October 1925): 596–605 (JP), and its republication in *Philosophy and Civilization* (New York: Minton, Balch and Co., 1931), pp. 188–201 (PC), are cited as the first appearance of fifty-six emendations. This list also serves as a historical collation of the three documents.

44.1–2   A Naturalistic Theory of Sense-Perception] W; A Naturalistic
         Theory of Sense∧Perception PC; THE NATURALISTIC
         THEORY OF PERCEPTION BY THE SENSES. JP, TS
44.9   specify] PC, JP; specify TS
44.9   acts] PC, JP; other acts TS
44.10   However∧] TS; ~, PC, JP
44.11   the traits] PC; special traits JP, TS
44.13   employed instrumentalities] PC, JP; instrumentalities
         employed TS
44.15   question] PC; questions JP, TS
44.21–22 blindness] PC, JP; blindnesss TS
44.22   muscular] PC; of muscular JP, TS
44.22   refraction] PC; of refraction JP, TS
44.22–23 lens. . . . how] PC; lens, and in general the participation
         of JP, TS
44.23   interact with] PC; with JP, TS
45.11–12 employed] PC; of its occurrence JP, TS
45.12   produced, yet its] PC, JP; produced. Its TS
45.14   "sense"] PC, JP; these TS
45.17   sense-*organs*,] TS; ~-~∧ PC, JP
45.18   connections∧] TS; ~, PC, JP
45.19   there] PC; this JP, TS
45.27   quality] PC, JP; qualities TS
45.29   all perception] PC; perception JP, TS

46.2   occurs] PC, JP; ocurs TS
46.24   thing?] PC, JP; thing?¹ TS
46.26   accepting] PC; taking JP, TS
46n.7   *ueberhaupt.*] PC, JP; ~.. TS
47.3   velocity] PC, JP; veleocity TS
47.4   tracks∧] TS; ~, PC, JP
47.14   is∧ however∧] TS; ~, ~, PC, JP
47.17–18 underbrush which obscures vision.] PC, JP; underbrush
          which leads to difficulties in statement and which obscure
          vision. TS
47.19–20 because of] PC; through JP, TS
*47.23   causal] JP, TS; casual PC
47.26   "intelligible"] PC, JP; "intelligble" TS
47.27   kinds] PC; kind JP, TS
47.32; 48.8 sense∧organs] TS; ~-~ PC, JP
47n.1–2 *Journal of Philosophy*] W; Journal PC; JOURNAL JP;
          JOURNAL TS
48.7   that] PC; which JP, TS
48.8   the generation of which] PC; whose generation JP; whose
          generration TS
48.8   play] PC; have JP, TS
48.9   pervasively] PC, JP; prevasively TS
48.9–10 ambiguity. This] PC; ambiguity which JP, TS
48.16   through] PC, JP; though TS
48.24   *etc.* Now] PC, JP; *etc..* Now TS
48n.4   not to denote an] PC, JP; to denote not any TS
48n.7   sense-organs] TS; ~∧~ PC, JP
49.5   water∧] TS; ~, PC, JP
49.14   ways.] TS; ~ : PC, JP
49.15   arrangements] PC, JP; arrangments TS
49.37   when] PC; which when JP, TS
49.38   while when] PC; when JP, TS
49.38–39 it presents] PC; presents JP, TS
49.40   like] PC; which is JP, TS
50.5   connection.] PC, JP; ~∧ TS
50.6   "appearance∧"] TS; "~," PC, JP
50.20   fact] PC; facts JP, TS
50.20   is] PC; are JP, TS
50.24   conditions∧] TS; ~, PC, JP
50.32   physical] PC, JP; phsycical TS
50.33   interpretation∧] PC, JP; ~, TS
50.36–37 to signify] PC, JP; as signifying TS
51.5   perception∧"] TS; ~," PC, JP

51.5   like] PC; as JP, TS
51.16   perceived;] PC, JP; ~;; TS
*51.23   organ.] W; ~, PC, JP; ~ₐ TS
51.23   Redₐ] TS; ~, PC, JP
51.23   a quality] PC, JP; quality TS
51.28–29   the compound] PC, JP; as complex TS
*51.37   of a sign, mark, to] PC; of implication, of sign, markₐ to JP;
          of implication, or of sign, markₐ and TS
*51.38   is signified] *stet* TS; signified PC, JP
52.32   structuresₐ] TS; ~, PC, JP
53.5   event:] TS; ~; PC, JP
53.19   interaction] PC, TS; interacton JP
53.26   "common-senseₐ"] TS; "~-~," PC, JP
53.27   to that] PC; to the JP, TS
54.9–10   grasping] PC; grasping does not JP, TS
54.10   case, does not] PC; case, JP; case,, TS
54.14   that,] PC, JP; ~,—, TS
*54.17   "of."] W; "at." PC, JP, TS
54.35   familiar] PC, JP; familar TS
*54.37   causal] JP, TS; casual PC
54.37   qualities.] PC; qualities./COLUMBIA UNIVERSITY. JOHN
          DEWEY. JP; Columbia University John Dewey TS

Individuality and Experience

Copy-text for this article is its publication in *Journal of the Barnes Foundation* 2 (January 1926): 1–6. The republication in *Art and Education* (Merion, Pa.: Barnes Foundation Press, 1929), pp. 175–83 (AE), is cited as the first appearance of two emendations.

56.31–32   "technique":] AE; "~:"
56.35   boysₐ] W; ~,
57.38–39   "authority";] AE; "~;"

Events and the Future

Copy-text for part of this article (pp. 62.1–67.3) is the incomplete type-script (TS), personally typed by Dewey, in the Journal of Philosophy Collection, Rare Books and Manuscripts, Columbia University Librar-ies, New York, N.Y. The article's publication, in *Journal of Philosophy* 23 (13 May 1926): 253–58 (JP), has served as copy-text for the re-mainder of the article (pp. 67.4–68.14).

62.2   word] JP; word an
62.14   "Suppose] *stet* TS; "suppose
*63.6   in quality] *stet* TS; quality
63.32   correspondence] JP; correpsondence
64.3   Pickwickian.³] JP; Pickwickian.³³
64.7   Chapter] JP; Chpater
64.21   mean] JP; means
64n.1   recognised] WS; recognized
64n.2   p. 81] *stet* TS; 81
64n.4   together] JP; toegther
65.1   to *N*,] JP; to ,
65.2   one-to-one] JP; ~ₐ~ₐ~
65.27   from] JP; to
65.29   nothing";] W; ~;"
65.31   for ever] WS; forever
66.17–18 towardness] JP; towardsness
66.18   direction, is] *stet* TS; direction, it
66.26   out-of] JP; ~ₐ~
66.32   On . . . is] JP; It is on this basis
*66.35–36 presentness] W; presence
66.36   recall] JP; recal
67.1   can] JP; [*not present*]
67.14   event'"] W; ~'ₐ
67.26   analysable] WS; analyzable

The Meaning of Value

Copy-text for this article is its publication in *Journal of Philosophy* 22 (26 February 1925): 126–33.

73.3   in] WS; by
74.6   subject] W; subjeect
74.23   mine).] W; ~.)

Value, Objective Reference and Criticism

Copy-text for this article is its publication in *Philosophical Review* 34 (July 1925): 313–32.

78n.2   442] W; 389
79.19   symbolisation] WS; symbolization
79.25   generalisation] WS; generalization

79.28   colour] WS; color
80n.1   3] W; II
80n.2   Value," pp. 179–290;] W; Value;"
80n.2   pp. 77–103] W; p. 77
80n.3   Value";] W; ~;"
80n.3   37] W; 36
80n.3–4 Defense] W; Defence
80n.4   Value";] W; ~;"
80n.4   pp. 117–25,] W; [*not present*]
80n.5   Thought-Process] W; ~ˌ~
80n.6   *Contributory*ˌ] W; ~,
84.4–5   unanalysable] WS; unalyzable
84.11   symbolise] WS; symbolize
84.18   "good";] W; "~;"
84.20   respect.)] W; ~).
84.25   *this*";] W; ~;"
89.3   "immediate";] W; "~;"
89.38   "liking";] W; "~;"
92n.2   Vol.] W; Pt.
93.1   recognise] WS; recognize
93.6   any one] WS; anyone
94.9   Santayana] W; Sanatayana
95.16   there is] W; there are

Affective Thought

Copy-text for this article is its publication in *Journal of the Barnes Foundation* 2 (April 1926): 3–9 (BF). The republication in *Philosophy and Civilization* (New York: Minton, Balch and Co., 1931), pp. 117–25 (PC), is cited as the first appearance of eight emendations.

104.1   Affective Thought] PC; Affective Thought in Logic and
         Painting
104.11   arts] *stet* BF; art PC
105.11   this would] PC; this JOURNAL would
105.32   that] PC; which
106.34   thought;] PC; thought and,
107.1–2 control . . . conditions,] PC; control of re-shaping natural
         conditions exercised by emotion,
107.9   structures] W; structure
107.31   recurrence] PC; repetition
107.35   means] PC; marks

107.39   "click"] PC; "clicks"
108.27   eye‸activities] W; ~-~

Art in Education—and Education in Art

Copy-text for this article is its publication in *New Republic* 46 (24 February 1926): 11–13.

111.11,12   specialised] WS; specialized

What Is the Matter with Teaching?

Copy-text for this article is its publication in *Delineator* 107 (October 1925): 5–6, 78.

116.1   Is] W; is
116.1   Matter] W; matter
116.22   lowest] W; lost

The "Socratic Dialogues" of Plato

Copy-text for this article is its publication in *Studies in the History of Ideas*, ed. Department of Philosophy (New York: Columbia University Press, 1925), 2 : 1–23.

124.6,n.9   Sophists] W; sophists
124n.5   Σωχράτιχος] W; Σωκράτικος
125.28   identifications] W; indentifications
127.19   them";] W; ~;"
127.20   logic";] W; ~;"
127.22   conception";] W; ~;"
129n.1   the] W; [*ital.*]
132n.1   *Republic*,] W; ~‸
133.19   utilitarian] W; utiliatarian
138.12–13   *Republic*,] W; ~‸
138.38   Cyrenaic] W; Cyreanic

Substance, Power and Quality in Locke

Copy-text for this article is its publication in *Philosophical Review* 35 (January 1926): 22–38.

144.26   explicitly] W; explicity
145.25, 154.14   co-exist] WS; coexist
146.6; 152.12,20; 153.17,n.7; 155.9   colour] WS; color
146n.1   Book III, Chap. VI] W; Same chapter
146n.6   every thing] WS; everything
146n.10–11   essence,] W; ~∧
147.9   other—] WS; ~;
147.17   Relation] WS; relation
147.17   Change] WS; change
148.5   colours] WS; colors
148.6,7   &c.] WS; etc.
148.11   amongst] WS; among
150.12   change,"] W; ~, ∧
153n.6   connexion] WS; connection
153n.10   malleable'] W; ~∧
153n.10   of this] WS; fo this
154.2   *Connexion*] WS; *connexion*
154.3   *Ideas*] WS; *ideas*

William James in Nineteen Twenty-Six

Copy-text for this article is its publication in *New Republic* 47 (30 June 1926): 163–65.

161.16   bitch-goddess, Success] WS; bitch∧goddess, success
161.34   centered] WS; centred

Bishop Brown: A Fundamental Modernist

Copy-text for this article is its publication in *New Republic* 48 (17 November 1926): 371–72.

163.6   the *New Republic*] W; these columns

America's Responsibility

Copy-text for this article is its publication in *Christian Century* 43 (23 December 1926): 1583–84.

167.17   welfare] W; welware
168.19   Isles] W; isles

171.31   war∧system] W; ∼-∼

America and the Far East

Copy-text for this article is its publication in *Survey* 56 (1 May 1926): 188.

174.18   Burlingame] W; Burlinghame

Highly Colored White Lies

Copy-text for this article is its publication in *New Republic* 42 (22 April 1925): 229–30.

176.1   Highly∧Colored] W; ∼-∼
178.22   Outer] W; outer
178.22   Inner] W; inner

Is China a Nation or a Market?

Copy-text for this article is its publication in *New Republic* 44 (11 November 1925): 298–99.

183.32–33   Nishihara] W; Nishahara

We Should Deal with China as Nation to Nation

Copy-text for this article is its publication in *Chinese Students' Monthly* 21 (May 1926): 52–54.

185.5–6,20   Chiang Kai-shek] W; Chang Kai∧Shek
186.4   another's] W; anothers'
187.24   mistaken—] W; ∼∧

The Problem of Turkey

Copy-text for this article is its publication in *New Republic* 41 (7 January 1925): 162–63.

193.11   strategic] W; stragetic

Church and State in Mexico

Copy-text for this article is its publication in *New Republic* 48 (25 August 1926): 9–10. The republication in *Impressions of Soviet Russia and the Revolutionary World: Mexico—China—Turkey* (New York: New Republic, Inc., 1929), pp. 113–19 (ISR), is cited as the first appearance of five emendations.

195.14   results] ISR; impressions
195.20   July 3, 1926,] ISR; July 3,
195.9   Carranza's] ISR; Carrazana's
195.10   Juárez] ISR; Juarez
195.38   however] ISR; previously
197.38, 198.1   Díaz] W; Diaz

Mexico's Educational Renaissance

Copy-text for this article is its publication in *New Republic* 48 (22 September 1926): 116–18. Its republication in *Impressions of Soviet Russia and the Revolutionary World: Mexico—China—Turkey* (New York: New Republic, Inc., 1929), pp. 119–29 (ISR), is cited as the first appearance of one emendation.

199.24, 200.38   Díaz] W; Diaz
203.23   industries.) In] ISR; industries. (In

From a Mexican Notebook

Copy-text for this article is its publication in *New Republic* 48 (20 October 1926): 239–41. The republication in *Impressions of Soviet Russia and the Revolutionary World: Mexico—China—Turkey* (New York: New Republic, Inc., 1929), pp. 168–80 (ISR), is cited as the first appearance of two emendations.

206.5   August, 1926,] ISR; August,
206.22   children's] ISR; childrens'

Practical Democracy

Copy-text for this article is its publication in *New Republic* 45 (2 December 1925): 52–54.

217.4   Mr. Lippmann's] W; Mr$_\wedge$ Lippman's

The Changing Intellectual Climate

Copy-text for this article is its publication in *New Republic* 45 (17 February 1926): 360–61.

222.9–10   generalisation] WS; generalization
222.16   scrap-heap] WS; ~$_\wedge$~
225.30   require] W; requires

A Key to the New World

Copy-text for this article is its publication in *New Republic* 46 (19 May 1926): 410–11.

228.23   Nursery-School] WS; ~$_\wedge$~
229.38   makes] W; make

Review of *The Art of Thought*

Copy-text for this article is its publication in *New Republic* 47 (16 June 1926): 118–19.

232.1   interracial] WS; inter-racial
234.3   hands] W; hand

The Public and Its Problems

Copy-text for this work is the copyright deposit copy A 996499 (New York: Henry Holt and Co., 1927).

239.7   corporations,] W; ~$_\wedge$
244.16   Catiline] W; Cataline
261.11   centre] WS; center
261.12   centres] WS; centers
261.15   many-coloured] WS; many-colored
270n.3   of] W; *on*
272n.1   Ayres] W; Ayers
288.12   made it] W; it made

295.12   every-day] WS; everyday
295.13   organisations] WS; organizations
295.26   ever] WS; even
311.1   Constitution] W; constitution
314.6   has] W; have
320.24   mobility] W; nobility
326.23   *post*] W; *posto*
335.12   countryman] WS; country-man
335.12   log-cabin] WS; ∼∧∼
341n.1−2 Carlton] W; Carleton
359.35   permutations] W; premutations
*370.25−26 inexhaustible] W; exhaustible

Dedication Address of the Barnes Foundation

Copy-text for this article is its publication in *Journal of the Barnes Foundation* 1 (1925): 3−6.

384.13,22   Negro] W; negro

Alterations in Typescripts

In the two lists that follow appear Dewey's changes both at the typewriter and by hand in the typescripts for "A Naturalistic Theory of Sense-Perception" and "Events and the Future." All alterations made during the course of Dewey's writing and revision appear here except for strengthened letters to clarify a word, irrelevant typed letters attached to a word, false starts for the same word, transposition of letters in a legible word, and a few mendings over illegible letters. The word(s) before the bracket refers to the original typescript. If the typescript has been emended or the spelling regularized, a grid # before the entry means the reading of the present edition is in the Emendations List.

Both essays were first published in *Journal of Philosophy* (JP); the typescripts contain inked changes made by an in-house editor which appear here as JP. These subsequent alterations are clearly distinguished from Dewey's hand by the intensity of ink, broader pen point, and rounded letter formation. JP revisions consist of additional commas, some underlining, and inconsistent transposition of periods and end quotation marks. Since JP regularly changed single quotation marks to double, these formal alterations do not appear in this list.

In addition, Dewey's typescript for "Events and the Future" lacks a final page, apparently lost some time after JP publication. The incomplete typescript corresponds with pp. 62.1–67.3 in this volume.

For alterations by Dewey and JP, which appear to the right of the bracket, the abbreviation *del.* is used to show material marked out in ink except when pencil is specifically mentioned; any alteration noted as *added* is also in ink unless pencil is specified. For material deleted at the typewriter, *x'd-out* is used. The abbreviation *alt.* is used to identify material altered in some way from an earlier form; if altered by hand, the medium is given; if the medium is not mentioned, it is to be assumed the alteration was typewritten. *Ov.* means inscribed over original letters, not interlined; *ab.* means interlined above without a caret unless a caret is specified; *bel.* means interlined below without a caret unless mentioned. When an addition is a simple interlineation, the formula is *intrl.* or *intrl. w. caret*. When a deletion positions the interlineation, *intrl.* is dropped and the formula reads *ab. del.* 'xyz'; *w. caret ab. del.* 'xyz'; or *ab. x'd-out* 'xyz.' All carets were made by hand; when a caret accompanies a typewritten interlineation, it is in ink unless pencil is noted. When carets are used with handwritten alterations, they are in the same medium as the alteration.

In brief, with respect to medium, only the abbreviation *del.* and the words *added* and *caret* always apply to handwritten changes made in ink unless pencil is specified; in all other instances—*ab., ov., intrl., insrtd., alt., bel., bef., aft.*—the change was made at the typewriter unless the medium is specified. Inasmuch as most additions are interlined, the medium will ordinarily appear, as in *intrl. in ink* or *intrl. in pencil*. Use of *intrl.* alone always means a typewritten interlineation. The abbreviations *bef.* (before) and *aft.* (after) signal a change made on the same line, whether original line or interline.

When an alteration, usually of a word or two, has been typed or written directly below the original line, the formula is *bel.* 'xyz.' The abbreviated word *insrtd.* refers to marginal additions that cannot be called interlines but are of the same nature. In alterations involving more than one line, the solidus / signals the end of a line. When an alteration itself has been revised, that revision is transcribed between square brackets immediately following the single word alteration to which it refers.

Alterations in "A Naturalistic Theory of Sense-Perception"

#44.1–2   THE NATURALISTIC THEORY OF PERCEPTION BY
  THE SENSES.] *underl. in ink three times; period del.* JP
44.3   In] 'I' *circled;* 'n' *underl. in ink three times* JP
44.4   objects] *aft. pencil del.* 'certain'
44.4–5   bodily] *aft. pencil del.* 'specified'
44.5   etc.] *underl. in ink*
44.7   the] *intrl. w. caret*
44.7   nature of] *in ink ab.* 'perceiving'
44.7   perceiving] *bef. x'd-out* 'as an act'
44.7–8   conveys information] *intrl. w. caret aft. intrl. del.* 'it'
44.8   of perceiving] *intrl. in ink w. caret*
44.9   phrases] *bef. del.* 'take writing, ['w' *in ink*] painting,
  engraving as acts and'
44.9   tools] *aft. x'd-out* 'the'
#44.9   other acts] *bel. in ink w. guideline aft. del.* 'they'
44.10   place.] *bef. x'd-out* 'The connection between'
44.10   However] *intrl. in ink*
44.10   in each case] *moved from bef.* 'modified' *w. caret and
  guideline*

44.10   the] 't' *ov.* 'T'

44.11   by] *bef. pencil del.* 'the'

#44.11   special traits] *in ink w. caret ab. del.* 'character'

44.11   organs and] *intrl. w. caret*

44.12   which] *aft. x'd-out* 'employed'

44.13   results?] *aft. x'd-out* 'outcome'

44.14   led] *alt. in ink fr.* 'lead'; *bef. pencil del.* 'directly'

44.16   their] *alt. fr.* 'there'

44.17   but] *bef. pencil del.* 'the'

44.17   mechanical] *aft. pencil del.* 'the'

44.18   Similarly,] *comma added*

44.19   ears,] *comma added* JP

44.19   etc.,] *underl. in ink; period and comma added* JP

44.19   in] *bef. x'd-out* 'per'

44.20   functions] *aft. x'd-out* 'consequence'

44.23   external] *intrl. w. caret*

44.25   all] *aft. pencil del.* 'note that'

44.28   the nature of] *intrl. w. caret*

44.29   or] *alt. in ink fr.* 'nor'

44.29   peculiar] *bef. pencil del.* 'in their kind'

44.30   about] *w. caret in pencil ov.* 'in'

44.30   them.] *bef. pencil del.* 'They are problems of the interaction ['with one another' *intrl.*] of natural conditions in generating certain results.'

44.31   prefixed] *aft. x'd-out* 'also'

45.1   Colors] 'C' *in ink ov.* 'c'; *aft. del.* 'Hence'

45.2   etc.,] *underl. in ink; comma added* JP

45.2   named] 'nam' *ov.* 'cal'

45.2   "sense-qualities."] *period and quot. transposed* JP

45.2   Here] 'H' *in ink ov.* 'h'; *aft. del.* 'But'

45.6   usage] *alt. fr.* 'use'

45.6   house] *bef. x'd-out* 'is'

45.7   that] *aft. pencil del.* 'of course'

45.7   the operation] 'the' *in pencil ov.* 'an' *aft. x'd-out* 'a process'

45.8   is misled] *ab. x'd-out* 'would be'

45.8   word] *aft. x'd-out* 'phrase'

45.9   or] *aft. x'd-out comma*

45.11   means] *bef. pencil del.* 'or condition'

#45.12   Its] *ab. x'd-out* 'The'

45.12   uses,] *comma added*

45.13   when] *in ink ab. pencil del. illeg. word*

45.13   produced are] *in pencil w. caret ab. pencil del. illeg. word and* 'quite'

45.16   short,] *comma added*

45.17   sense-*organs*,] *comma added*

45.20   this] *alt. fr.* 'the'

45.21   in any natural sequence] *ab. x'd-out* 'with any natural event'

45.21   a] *in ink ov.* 'the'

45.22   interacting] *aft. pencil del.* 'the'

45.24   lies] *aft. x'd-out* 'may be'

45.24   epistemological] *aft. x'd-out* 'theory'

45.24–25   sense-perceptions;] *semicolon added*

45.30   one] *aft. pencil del.* 'always'

45.31   the] *aft. del.* 'and'

45.31   between] *insrtd. in pencil w. caret and guideline*

45.34   say] *bef. pencil del.* 'that'

45.35   water.] *w. guideline bef. del.* 'a cat or dog, land or water, perceived. It is'

45.35   The] *intrl. in pencil*

45.35   is] *intrl. in pencil w. caret*

45.35   one] *ab. del.* 'the *concrete* object or'

45.35   factual] *aft. x'd-out* 'subjec'

45.36   subject-matter] *aft. x'd-out* 'object'

45.37   that] *in ink ov.* 'a'

45.38   perception] *aft. x'd-out* 'sense-'

45.38   is] *in ink ab. del.* 'being'

45.39   because of] *in ink w. caret ab. del.* 'by'

45.40   and hence the] *intrl. in ink w. caret*

46.1   in kind] *in ink ab. del.* 'in generic nature and not just in specifiable relationships'

46.1   a] *in ink ov.* 'an'

46.1   problem] *aft. del.* 'inevitable'

46.1   is] *aft del.* 'of adjustment or reconciliation' *and x'd-out* 'presents'

#46.2   ocurs] *intrl. in ink w. caret*

46.2   in] *aft. del.* 'applies with equal inevitableness and greater force ['force' *x'd-out*] problematic force'

46.2   contrast] *aft. del.* 'the'

46.2   things] *aft. x'd-out* 'obje'

46.2   as] *aft. x'd-out* 'in'

46.3   (or reflectively determined)] *parens. added*

46.3–4   in . . . objects,] *intrl. in ink w. caret*

46.4   In] 'I' *in ink ov.* 'i'; *aft. del.* 'While'

46.4   theory] *in ink w. guideline bel. del.* 'case'

46.4   and,] *comma added* JP

46.5   say,] *comma added* JP

46.7   perception;] *semicolon in ink ov. comma* JP

46.8   on] *in ink ov. illeg. word* JP

46.8   theory,] *in ink ab. del.* 'case'
46.9   reality,"] *comma and quot. transposed* JP
46.9   else] *intrl. w. caret*
46.10   the one] 'the' *in ink aft.* 'of'
46.10   that of] *intrl. w. caret*
46.12   is,] *comma added* JP
46.12   therefore,] *comma added* JP
46.13   question.] *period in ink*
46.13   Until] 'U' *ov.* 'u' *in ink; aft. del.* 'and'
46.14   problem] *aft. x'd-out* 'question'
46.16   Is] 'I' *ov.* 'i'; *aft. x'd-out* 'Does'
46.18   traits] *aft. pencil del.* 'specific'
46.18   of the] 'of' *aft. pencil del.* 'of'
46.20   to . . . pictures?[1]] *ab. del.* 'to red perception and green perception'; 'etching' *alt. fr.* 'etched' *aft. x'd-out* 'an'; *comma added;* '1' *in ink w. guideline*
46.22   "sensory"] *intrl.*
46.22   affecting] *alt. fr.* 'affected'
46.22   qualifying] *alt. fr.* 'qualified'
46.22   throughout] *bef. x'd-out* 'by'
46.23   the being] *aft. x'd-out* 'being'
46.23   thereby] *intrl. in pencil w. caret aft. del.* 'thus'
#46.24 thing?[1]] '1' *in ink w. guideline*
46.25   question is] 'question' *aft. x'd-out* 'problem'
46.26   factual] *intrl. w. caret*
46.26   assigned] *aft. x'd-out* 'usually'
46.29   need] *in ink w. caret ab. del.* 'will here'
46.30   affairs] *in ink w. caret ab. del.* 'facts'
46.31   place] *insrtd. in ink bef.* 'in'
46.31   an] *intrl. w. caret aft. x'd-out* 'these'
46.31   image] *final* 's' *x'd-out*
46n.1   [1]The] '1' *w. guideline*
46n.1   not] *intrl. w. caret*
46n.3   nature] *aft. x'd-out* 'exact'
46n.6   added] *underl. in ink*
46n.7   effect] *intrl. in ink w. caret aft. del.* 'consequences'
47.1   a] *in ink ov.* 'the'
#47.3   veloecity] *ab. x'd-out* 'rapidity'
47.4   removal;] *semicolon in ink ov. comma*
47.4   etc.,] *underl. in ink; period and comma added*
47.4–5 to . . . illusions.] *intrl. w. caret*
47.8   difficulties".[2]] '2' *in ink w. guideline*
47.11   unique] *aft. x'd-out* 'kind of'; *del.* 'a'

47.12   meaning, as here used,] *intrl. in ink w. caret aft. del.* 'here not being qualities of objects as such but'

47.14   Discussion] 'D' *in ink ov.* 'd'; *aft. del.* 'The'

47.15   diverse] *intrl. w. caret*

47.15   theories] *bef. x'd-out* 'of'

47.16   inherited] *aft. del.* 'that we have'

47.16   This paper] *in ink* ['T' *ov.* 't'; *aft. del.* 'Hence'] *ab. del.* 'So I shall reserve* ['discussion of' *intrl. in ink w. caret, then del.*] the factual consideration until'

47.16   is given to] *intrl. in ink w. caret and guideline*

47.17   effort] *bef. del.* 'has been made'

#47.17   underbrush . . . and] 'which' *in ink ov.* 'that'; 'in' *in ink ab. del.* 'of'; 'and' *bef. del.* 'to'

47.17   which] *in ink w. caret ab. del.* 'that'

#47.17−18   obscure] *alt. in ink fr.* 'obscures'

47.20   persisted] *aft. del.* 'is'

47.20   that] *in ink ov.* 'which'

47.20   had] *alt. in ink fr.* 'have'

47.22   sensible] *underl. in ink*

47.23   of] *bef. x'd-out* 'rer—'

47.24   metaphysical] *aft. x'd-out* 'cre' *ov.* 'the'

47.24   once] *intrl. in ink w. caret*

47.24−25   obtained,] *comma added*

47.25−26   distinction] 'ion' *intrl. in ink w. caret*

47.28   set] *in ink ov.* 'was'

47.28   the] *aft. x'd-out* 'and intrinsic' ['c' *ov. final* 'i']

47.29   of nature] 'of' *intrl. in ink w. caret*

47.30   qua] *underl. in ink*

47.31   natural] *intrl. in ink w. caret*

47.31   animals, including man,] *w. caret ab. x'd-out* 'man'

47.33   sense] *aft. del.* 'the'

47.34   into] *in ink ov.* 'as'

47.34   sensory] *intrl. in ink w. caret*

47.35   forms,] *comma added*

47.35   hand,] *comma added*

47.37   premises] *alt. in ink fr.* 'premisses'

47n.1   ²Durant] '2' *in ink w. guidelines*

47n.1   Durant] *aft. del.* 'Dr.'

#47n.1   JOURNAL] *underl. in ink twice*

48.3   causality")‚] *quot., paren. and comma added*

#48.8   whose] *in ink ov.* 'the'

#48.8   generration] *first* 'r' *in ink w. line-end hyphen*

48.8   sense] *aft. del.* 'of which'

48.8   to be] *intrl. in ink w. caret*
48.9   things,] *aft. x'd-out* 'thing'; *comma added*
48.11   candle-flames,] *comma added*
48.11   etc.] *underl. in ink* JP
48.12   qualities] *aft. del.* 'the'
48.14   (or] *paren. added*
48.17   brain,] *comma added*
48.17   in turn] *solidus in ink betw. words*
48.19   words,] *comma added*
48.19–20   organism,] *comma added*
48.22   The] 'T' *in ink ov.* 't'
48.22   true,] *comma added*
48.22   course,] *comma added*
48.24   of] *aft. x'd-out* 'of / of'
48.24   images,] *comma added*
#48.24   etc., etc..] *underl. in ink*
48.24   moment's] *apostrophe added* JP
48.25   tree] *aft. x'd-out* 'tress'
48.25   finger,] *comma added*
48.25   such] *intrl.*
48.25   objects] *bef. x'd-out* 'which'
48.25   as] *intrl.*
48.26   can not] *solidus in ink betw. words*
48.27   things,] *comma added*
48.27   the] *in ink. ab. del.* 'their own'
48.28   of the epistemologists,] *intrl. w. caret*; *comma added*
48.28   groups] *aft. x'd-out* 'on'
48.29   of] *intrl. w. caret*
48.29   equivalent] *alt. fr.* 'equivalents'
48.29   "images."] *period and quot. transposed* JP; *aft. x'd-out* 'ing'
48.30   Locke's] *apostrophe added*
48.30   language,] *comma added*
48.32   from] *in ink ov.* 'to'
48.32   order,] *comma added*
48n.1–9   ³Locke, . . . 19.] *separated fr. text w. guidelines*; *comma added*; 'footnote' *insrtd. in ink twice*
48n.1   for example,] *intrl. w. caret*; *comma added*
48n.1–2   qualities,] *comma added* JP
48n.2   retains the older terminology,] *ab. x'd-out* 'sensible'
48n.2   qualities,"] *comma and quot. transposed* JP
48n.4   uses] *alt. in ink fr.* 'use' *aft. del.* 'does not'
#48n.4   to] *aft.* 'not' *intrl. in ink w. caret and del.*
#48n.4   not] *intrl. in ink w. caret*

#48n.4   any] *alt. in ink fr.* 'an'

  48n.4   existence,] *comma added*

  48n.9   "reflection."] *period and quot. transposed* JP

  48n.9   *Essay*] *underl. in ink* JP

  49.1–3   And . . . qualities.] *intrl. in ink*

  49.4   The] *aft.* '(1)' *in ink then del.*

  49.4   a] *in ink ov.* 'the'

  49.4   quality] *aft. del.* 'sensible'

  49.4   as] *aft. x'd-out* 'is, in other words,'

  49.5   tree,] *aft. intrl. w. caret then del.* ', in other words,'

  49.5   *etc.,*] *underl. in ink; period and comma added*

  49.5–6   disturbances.] *period alt. in ink fr. comma*

  49.6   The latter] *intrl. in ink w. caret aft. del.* 'which'

  49.6   contrasted] *bef. x'd-out* 'not only'

  49.6   with] *intrl. w. caret*

  49.6   thing,] *comma added*

  49.6–7   the finger,] *intrl. in ink w. caret*

  49.7   color] *in ink ab. del.* 'sense'

  49.7   quality.] *period added bef. x'd-out* 'a fact of which the phenomenal idealist always is ready to take advantage against every form of 'representative realism'.'

  49.10   distortion,] *comma added*

  49.11   from a distance as] *ab. x'd-out* 'possibly'

  49.13   or other] *intrl. in ink w. caret*

  49.14   the] *added*

  49.14   (1)] *added*

  49.14   molecular] *aft. x'd-out* 'physical'

  49.15   in] *intrl. in ink w. caret*

  49.17   form] *ab. x'd-out* 'object'

  49.18   "real"] *quots. added*

  49.18   (physical)] *parens. added*

  49.19   they and it] *in pencil w. caret ab. del.* 'all'

  49.19–20   "appearances"] *quots. added*

  49.20   due] *aft. x'd-out* 'of'

  49.20   physical,] *comma added*

  49.21   "Appearance"] 'A' *ov.* 'a'; *aft. del.* 'And it is hard to say ['see' *intrl. in ink, then del. ab. del.* 'say'] that'

  49.21   here] *aft. del.* 'has'

  49.21   has no] *in ink. w. caret ab. del.* 'any'

  49.22   effects used,] 'effects' *alt. in ink fr.* 'effect'; 'used' *aft. del.* 'which are'; *comma added*

  49.22   as] *aft. x'd-out* 'howver'

  49.22   inquiry,] *comma added*

49.23   their cause.] *aft. x'd-out* 'the causes'

49.23–24   problems] *aft. del.* 'only'

49.24   involved] *intrl. in ink w. caret*

49.29   full] *intrl. w. caret*

49.30   placed] *alt. fr.* 'places'

49.37   placed] *aft. del.* 'it is'

49.38   form,] *comma added; bef. x'd-out* 'in'

49.38   when] *insrtd. in ink*

49.38–39   presents] *aft. del.* 'it'

49.40   form] *bef. x'd-out* 'with'

49.40   narrow] *aft. x'd-out* 'stra'

50.2   round] *aft. x'd-out* 'flat and'; *solidus bef.* 'round'

50.2–3   the entire] *in ink w. caret ab. del.* 'a a particular'

50.3   as] *bef. x'd-out* 'there'

50.3   some] *intrl.*

50.4   random,] *comma added*

50.4   or] *intrl. in ink w. caret*

50.4   jumble,] *comma added*

50.4   are] *aft. x'd-out* 'may b'

50.5   principle] *aft. del.* 'a common'

#50.5   connection] *in ink w. guideline ab. del.* 'reference'; *aft. intrl. and del.* 'serial'

50.6   "appearance"] *bef. del. dash*

50.8   and] *alt. in ink w. caret fr.* 'an'

50.9   formula] *bef. del.* 'or principle' *and x'd-out* 'or'

50.10   "It,"] *comma and quot. transposed; underl. in ink, then del.* JP

50.12   can not] *solidus betw. words*

50.12   a] *added* JP

50.15   mode,] *comma added*

50.17   others] *alt. in ink fr.* 'other' JP

50.19   others] *alt. in ink fr.* 'other' JP

50.24   etc.,] *underl. in ink* JP

50.24   their] *in ink w. caret ab. x'd-out* 'antecedents'

50.24   conditions] *bef. x'd-out comma*

50.25   physical] *intrl. in ink w. caret*

50.25   other,] *comma added*

50.29   , say,] *intrl. w. caret; commas added*

50.30   vice-versa,] *underl. in ink* JP

50.31   by] *intrl. w. caret*

50.31   considering] *aft. del. and x'd-out* 'from'; *solidus betw. words*

50.32   from] *in ink ov.* 'to' JP

#50.32   phsycical] 'h' *intrl. w. caret*
50.33   from] *in ink ov.* 'from' JP
#50.33   interpretation,] *comma added*
50.33   arises] *intrl. in ink w. caret and guideline*
50.33   if] *intrl. bel. w. guideline*
50.36   Let] *aft.* '¶'
#50.37   signifying] *intrl. w. caret aft. x'd-out* 'meaning'
50.37   effects,] *comma added*
51.1   "appear."] *period and quot. transposed* JP
51.2   signifies] *w. caret ab. x'd-out* 'means'
51.2   of,"] *comma and quot. transposed* JP
51.2   physical] *intrl. w. caret*
51.3   or] *aft. x'd-out* 'oor' [*second* 'o' *ov.* 'f']
51.3   is the "appearance"] *intrl. in ink w. caret*
51.4   signifies] *aft. x'd-out* 'means'
51.4   immediately] *intrl. w. caret*
51.5   in contrast] *solidus betw. words*
51.7   coin,] *comma alt. fr. period bef. x'd-out* 'Then the shifting from'
51.7   a] *in ink ov.* 'the'
51.7   particular] *intrl. in ink w. caret*
#51.7   rôle] *circumflex added* JP
#51.7–8   the . . . actor.] *in ink w. caret ab. del.* 'the human being who is the actor'; *circumflex added to* 'rôles' JP
51.9   idea] *aft. x'd-out* 'pro'
51.10   "real,"] *comma and quot. transposed* JP
51.13   ¶In] *aft. del.* 'these distinct types of relations; the confusion generates the / epistemological problem of perception.'
51.13   place,] *comma added*
51.14   psychological] *aft. x'd-out* 'the'
51.15   simple] *aft. x'd-out* 'those'
51.15   sensed] *in ink w. caret and guideline bef. intrl. then del.* 'perceived' *ab. x'd-out* 'seen before'
51.15   before] *insrtd.*
51.16   or] *bef. x'd-out* 'velee'
#51.16   is perceived;;] *intrl. in ink w. caret bef. undel. semicolon*
51.17   orange] *aft. x'd-out* 'etc.'
51.17   color] *intrl. w. caret*
51.17   etc.] *underl. in ink* JP
51.18   surrendered,] *comma added*
51.21   *discriminated*] *intrl. w. caret; underl. in ink*
51.22   perceptual] *intrl. in ink w. caret*
51.22   discrimination] *bef. del.* 'in perception'

51.26   which] *intrl. in ink w. caret*
51.27   chemical] *intrl. w. caret*
51.28   simple] *aft. x'd-out* 'distinct from water'
51.28   different] *aft. x'd-out* 'distin'
#51.28–29   from water as complex.] *intrl. in ink w. caret*
51.29   a] *intrl. bel.* JP
51.31   it] *in ink ov.* 'he'
51.31   colors;] *semicolon alt. in ink fr. comma*
51.31   learns] *in ink w. caret ab. del.* 'usually comes'
51.32   *marks*,] *bef. x'd-out* 'or means'
51.32   is] *alt. fr.* 'as'
51.32   *means* of] *solidus betw. words*
51.34   homogeneity] *aft. x'd-out* 'homh'
51.34   of] *bef. del.* 'the'
51.34   perceptual] *intrl. in ink w. caret*
51.34   objects] *aft. del.* 'the'
51.34   is] *aft. del.* 'which are perceived by use of the senses'
51.36   assumes] *in ink ab. del.* 'takes'
51.36   proper] *intrl. in ink w. caret*
#51.37   implication,] *in ink ab. del.* 'simple and complex'
#51.37–38   , or . . . signified.] *added*
51.39–40   perceived by means of] *ab. x'd-out* 'perceived through'
51.40–52.1   epistemology.] *aft. del.* 'psychology / or'
52.1   whereabouts] 's' *intrl. w. caret*
52.2   clincher] *bef. x'd-out* 'in case'
52.3   character of] *bef. x'd-out* 'sense some'
52.4   imaged] *aft. x'd-out* 'tree'
52.5   when] *aft. x'd-out* 'in'
52.6   It] 'I' *ov.* 'i'; *aft. x'd-out* 'And'
52.6   suggested] *bef. x'd-out* 'to defin'
52.7   defined as] *solidus betw. words*
52.8   and] *aft. x'd-out* 'with'
52.8   to,⁴] *comma added*; '4' *in ink ov.* '#'
52.10   to] *aft. x'd-out* 'to'
52.11   "where,"] *comma and quot. transposed* JP
52.11   for example,] *intrl.*
52.14   event,] *comma added*
52.14   interaction,] *aft. pencil del.* 'an'; *comma added in pencil*
52.14–15   interaction entails] *intrl. in pencil w. caret*
52.15   of] *bef. x'd-out* 'field'
52.15   *field*] *bef. pencil del. illeg. word*
52.15   No] *bef. pencil del. illeg. word*
52.16   the energies] 'the' *intrl. in ink*

52.17   interaction] *bef. x'd-out* 'are'

52.17   any] *intrl. in ink w. caret aft. x'd-out* 'the'

52.18   limited] *bef. x'd-out comma*

52.19   degree;] *semicolon alt. in ink fr. comma*

52.19   it can] *in ink ab. del.* 'but'

52.19   be] *intrl. in ink w. caret*

52.19   located] *intrl. in ink w. caret*

52.19   with] *bef. pencil del.* 'any' *and x'd-out* 'pre'

52.20   most] *aft. x'd-out* 'greatest intensity'

52.20   *intense] underl. in ink*

52.20   disturbance in] *ab. x'd-out* 'disurbance of'

52.23   are] *bef. x'd-out* 'evidently'

52.25   existentially] *ab. x'd-out* 'actually'

52.27   correct,] *comma added* JP

52.27–28   theoretically,] *comma added* JP

52.30   literally] *bef. x'd-out* 'a file a'

52.32   structures] *aft. x'd-out* 'menchanisms'

52.32   and] *bef. intrl. then del.* 'that of the'

52.32   a refracting] 'a' *added; aft. x'd-out* 'the structure', *del.* 'of the', *x'd-out* 'molecular reflecting'

52.33   organism,] *comma added*

52.33   "at"] *aft. x'd-out* 'a'

52.33   spot] *aft. x'd-out* 'spatian'

52.34   place] *aft. x'd-out* 'situs'

52.34   rays] *aft. x'd-out* 'rights'

52.34   the] *bef. x'd-out* 'th'

52.36   may] *in ink w. caret ab. del.* 'my'

52.37   structures] *first* 't' *added* JP

52.37   forming the] 'the' *insrtd. in ink*

52n.1   ⁴ *Essays . . . p. 61.] separated fr. text w. guidelines;* '4' *in ink ov.* '#'; 'Essays in Critical Realism,' *underl. in ink, comma added* JP; 'p. 61.' *added*

53.5   location] *bef. del.* 'in the case of any event which is constittuted as an interaction'

53.5   a relationship to a] *intrl. w. caret and guideline aft. intrl. then x'd-out* 'due to a'

53.5   *further] aft. x'd-out* 'a'

53.8   occurrence,] *comma added*

53.8   is directed] *in ink w. caret ab. del.* 'centres'

53.11   is] *alt. in ink fr.* 'was'

53.13   measures] *bef. x'd-out* 'would'

53.15   while] *intrl. in ink w. caret*

53.15   is] *in ink ov.* 'be'

53.15   in Florida] *solidus in ink betw. words*

53.16   The] 'T' *in ink ov.* 't'; *aft. del.* 'Thus'

53.19   taking] *aft. x'd-out* 'foun'

53.19   From] 'F' *in ink ov.* 'f'

53.20   "common-sense,"] *comma and quot. transposed* JP

53.21   the] *ab. x'd-out* 'at what'

53.21   at which] *ab. x'd-out* 'should'

53.21   should] *intrl. w. caret*

53.23   in ordinary usage] *intrl. w. caret and guideline*

53.23   contains] *ab. x'd-out* 'denotes in ordinary usage'

53.24   commonplace.] *period alt. in ink fr. comma*

53.24   But] 'B' *in ink ov.* 'b'

53.28   attain or prevent certain results] *in ink w. caret ab. del.* 'deal with it'

53.29   That] *intrl. w. caret*

53.29   a thing] 'a' *ov.* 'A'

53.29   away in front,] *ab. x'd-out* 'way,'

53.31   raise] *in ink w. caret ab. del.* 'lift'

53.32   procure] *intrl. in ink w. caret aft. del.* 'control'

53.33   instances] *bef. del.* 'which deal with'

53.33   of the] 'of' *intrl. in ink w. caret*

53.34   intrinsic,] *comma added*

53.35   effecting] *alt. in ink fr.* 'effects'

53.36   which is] *intrl. w. caret bef. intrl. then del.* 'all'

53.38   the refraction of light occurs] *ab. x'd-out* 'the stick reflects light'

53.38–39   under] *in ink ov.* 'in'

53.39   unusual conditions.] *solidus in ink betw. words*; *in ink ab. del.* 'two different media'

54.6   conditions] *bef. del.* 'of the coordination of the optical and manual factors in an [*intrl.*] act, the'

54.6   of the] *insrtd. in ink*

54.6   acts of] *intrl. in ink w. caret*

54.7   reaching] *bef. del.* 'as acts'

54.7   in locating] *intrl. in ink w. caret and guideline*

54.8   can not] *solidus in ink betw. words*

54.8   located] *in ink ab. del.* 'placed'

54.8   space] *alt. fr.* 'spaces'

54.9   that] *intrl. in ink w. caret*

54.9–10   grasping] *bef. del.* 'does not without pains and practice, fit into the general system of habits which customarily determine the seat, residence or situs of a [*alt. fr.* 'an'] complex interaction.'

#54.10   case,,] *first comma added* JP; *bef. del.* 'fit', *undel. comma*
 54.10   practice,] *aft. x'd-out* 'tro'
 54.10   fit] *intrl. in ink w. caret*
 54.12   an affair,] *in ink w. caret ab. del.* 'that which'
 54.12   the latter being] *intrl. in ink w. caret*
 54.13   literally] *aft. x'd-out* 'ei'; *bef. del. illeg. word*
 54.13   covering] *aft. x'd-out* 'occupying'
#54.14   that,—,] *first comma and dash added* JP; *bef. x'd-out* 'spring', *undel. comma*
 54.15   "of"] *underlining del.* JP
 54.16   quite] *intrl. w. caret*
#54.17   "at."] *period and quot. transposed* JP
 54.17   theory] *bef. x'd-out* 'con-/tained in'
 54.17   thus] *ab. x'd-out* 'also'
 54.17   also] *intrl. in ink w. caret*
 54.21   terms,] *comma added*
 54.22–23 but . . . field.] *intrl. in ink w. caret*
 54.23   If] 'I' *in ink ov.* 'i'; *aft. del.* 'and'
 54.23   terms,] *comma added*
 54.24   correct] *intrl. w. caret*
 54.25   handling, *etc.*] *comma added, underl. in ink* JP
 54.28   mistakes] *bef. x'd-out* 'that / affect the'
 54.33–34 settlement.] *ab. x'd-out* 'Columbia University', 'John Dewey'
#54.34–37 When . . . Dewey.] *added*
 54.34   remain] *in ink ab. del.* 'is'
 54.35   the] *alt. in ink fr.* 'there'
 54.35–36 residual problems concern] *in ink w. two carets ab. del.* 'are the'
 54.36   matters,] *in ink w. caret ab. del.* 'problems of the'
 54.36   such as] *intrl. in ink w. caret*
 54.37   and the] 'and' *bef. del.* 'of'
#54.37+   Columbia University.] *period added, underl. twice w. guideline* JP
#54.37+   John Dewey.] *period added, underl. twice* JP

Alterations in "Events and the Future"

 62.2   word] *in ink w. caret ab. del.* 'term'
 62.3   term] *intrl. in ink w. caret aft. del.* 'one'
 62.4–5   an order of scientific conceptions] *in ink w. caret and guideline ab. del.* 'the' *and illeg. word*

62.5   employed] *bef. del.* 'in / order'
62.5   replace,] *comma added*
62.6   with] *bef. x'd-out* 'the'
62.7   fact,] *bef. x'd-out* 'is found'
62.8–9   *Scientific Thought*] *underl. in ink* JP
62.11   in."] *period and quot. transposed* JP
62.14   Again,] *intrl. in ink w. caret*
62.14   "Suppose] 'S' *in ink ov.* 's'; *quot. added*
62.20   *whole.*"[1]] '1' *in ink ov.* '#' *w. pencil guideline and brkt.* JP
62.21   indispensable] *bef. x'd-out* 'trait'
62.22   namely,] *bef. x'd-out* 'the'
62.23–24   requires duration] *aft. del.* 'which'; *solidus in ink betw.* words
62.24   in] *aft. x'd-out* 'to'
62.24   If] *aft. x'd-out* 'Even is'
62.25   have] *aft. del.* 'also' *and pencil del.* 'not'
62.26   duration,] *comma added*
62.27   like] *alt. in ink fr.* 'alike'
62.27   earlier,] *comma added*
62.27   be] *in ink ov.* 'is'
62.27–28   memory,] *comma added*
62.28   state] *ab. x'd-out* 'state'
62.28–29   can not] *solidus in ink betw. words*
62n.1   [1]Broad] '1' *in ink ov.* '#' JP
62n.1   *Scientific Thought*] *underl. in ink* JP
63.1   Unfortunately, however,] *intrl. in ink w. caret aft. del.* 'But'
63.2   not] *underl. in ink*
63.2   regard] *bef. del.* 'such'
63.2   to be] *in ink w. caret ab. del.* 'as'
63.4   homogeneous] *alt. in ink w. caret fr.* 'homogenous'
63.6   Now] 'w' *intrl. w. caret* JP
63.8   homogeneous] *alt. in ink w. caret fr.* 'homogenous'
63.12–13   fundamental] *aft. x'd-out* 'scientific'
63.13   laws."[2]] '2' *in ink ov.* '#'; *period and quot. transposed*
63.14   try to] *intrl. w. caret*
63.15   the] *alt. fr.* 'there'
63.19   "history,"] *comma added*; *comma and quot. transposed* JP
63.20   "divided."] *aft. x'd-out* 'divided'; *period and quot. transposed* JP
63.24   homogeneous] *alt. w. caret fr.* 'homogenous'
63.28   *changes.*"] *underl. in ink*; *period and quot. transposed* JP
63.29   throughout] *aft. x'd-out* 'throught'
63.30   time."] *period and quot. transposed* JP
63.30   such that] *intrl. w. caret*

63.30   eternal] *aft. x'd-out* 'with which the'

63.31   in] *bef. x'd-out and del.* 'some'

63.31   with them,] *intrl. w. caret and guideline*

63.31   on] *intrl. w. caret aft. del.* 'on'

#63.32   correpsondence] *intrl. w. caret and guideline*

63.32   eternal objects] *bef. del.* 'they'

63.33   "throughout."] *period and quot. transposed* JP; *solidus betw. words*

63.33   There] *aft. x'd-out* 'In this case,'; 'T' *ov.* 't'

63.34   them] *bef. x'd-out* 'qualitatively'

63.34   homogeneous] *solidus betw. second* 'o' *and* 'g'

63.36   short,] *comma added*

63.37   logically] *alt. w. caret fr.* 'logical'

63n.1   ² *Ibid.*] '2' *in ink ov.* '#' *w. guideline and brkt.; underl.*

63n.1   403,] *comma ov. period*

63n.1   italics mine.] *added*

64.2   While] *aft. del.* 'In short,'; 'W' *in ink ov.* 'w'

64.3   emphasis] *aft. x'd-out* 'import'

64.3   Pickwickian] *aft. del.* 'to be'

#64.3   Pickwickian.³] '3' *added in ink aft. undel. footnote* '3' JP

#64.7   Chpater Two] *initial letters capitalized in ink*

64.8   by] *aft. solidus in ink*

64.8   he] *aft. solidus in ink*

64.9   all,] *marked to close up in ink*

64.9   no] *aft. solidus in ink*

64.10–11   history."] *period and quot. transposed* JP

64.12   stages] *aft. x'd-out* 'different'

64.16   that by] *solidus in ink betw. words*

64.17   which,] *comma added*

64.17   course,] *comma added*

64.17   heterogeneity—] *comma del., dash added*

64.18   stages."] *period and quot. transposed* JP

64.19   the] *aft. x'd-out* 'because'

64.22   alleged to be] *intrl. w. caret*

64.23   whole] *bef. x'd-out* 'withou'

64.23   can not] *solidus in'ink betw. words*

64.24–25   And without . . . "event"?] *added*

64.25   "event"?] *bef. del.* 'A means of difference and without them there is no history.'; 'No¶' *intrl. in ink, circled*

64.25   But where] *in ink w. caret and guideline ab. del.* 'If'

64.26   stages] *bef. x'd-out* 'in an event'

64.26   every] *aft del.* 'then'

64.26   or history] *intrl. w. caret*

64.27   event] *bef. x'd-out* 'is composed'

64.27   comprises] *ab. x'd-out* 'of'
64.28   itself] *intrl.*
64.28   event.⁵] '5' *in ink ov.* '6' *in ink ov.* '#'
64.29   The] *aft.* '¶' *in ink*
64.29   speak of] *solidus in ink betw. words*
64.29–30   adjacent] *bef. x'd-out* 'changes'
64.30   stages] *alt. fr.* 'states'
64.30   is] *bef. x'd-out* 'by compar'
64.31   *other*] *underl. in ink*
64.31   taken] *ab. x'd-out* 'found'
64.31   stages] *alt. fr.* 'states'
64.32   M] *underl. in ink*
64.33   M as to] *underl. in ink* JP; *in ink w. caret ab. x'd-out* 'it'
64.33   stages] *alt. fr.* 'states'
64.33   N,] *underl. in ink* JP
64n.1   ³Contrast] '3' *in ink w. guideline bel. del.* '3'
64n.2   events,"] *comma and quot. transposed* JP
64n.2   *Principles of Natural Knowledge*] *underl. in ink* JP
64n.2   was,] *comma added*
64n.2   course,] *comma added*
64n.4   hangs] *alt. in ink fr.* 'hand'
64n.5   then] *intrl. in ink w. caret bef. del.* 'at the same time'
64n.5   events,] *comma added*
64n.6   the] *alt. in ink fr.* 'these.'
64n.6   above.] *added*
64n.7   ⁴Op. cit.] '4' *ov.* '#'; *brkt. w. guidelines*; *underl. in ink*
64n.8   ⁵Whitehead] '5' *aft. brkt. w. guideline*; '6' *in ink del.*
64n.8   *The Principles of Natural Knowledge*, p. 61, 77.] *added;*
         underl. in ink JP
65.1   an identical] *ab. x'd-out* 'corresponding'
65.1   (or some part of it)] *intrl. in ink w. caret aft. del.* 'M'
#65.1   to] *bef. del.* 'it'
65.1   and,] *comma added*
65.2   by] *ab. x'd-out* 'may break'
65.2   setting] *alt. w. caret fr.* 'set'
65.2   between] *aft. x'd-out* 'between its port'
65.3   M,] *underl. in ink* JP; *comma added*
65.3   it,] 't' *in ink ov. illeg. letter*
65.3   in spite] *solidus in ink betw. words*
65.3   its] *aft. x'd-out* 'the'
65.4   themselves] *intrl. in ink w. caret*
65.5   fact.] *bef. del.* 'But this fact does not justify us / in ignoring
         its complex relational character.'
65.5   But] *intrl. in ink w. caret*

65.5   to] 't' *in ink ov.* 'T'

65.5   a] *underl. in ink*

65.6   a] *intrl. in ink w. caret*

65.6   N,] *underl. in ink* JP; *bef. x'd-out* 'in'

65.6   to] *aft. x'd-out* 'simply'

65.7   α,] *added and underl.* JP; *comma added*

65.7   which] *bef. x'd-out* 'in turn'

65.8   M,] *underl. in ink* JP; 'M' *in ink ov.* 'N'

65.8   in turn] *intrl. w. caret and guideline*

65.9   β, γ, δ,] *added*

65.9   M.] *underl. in ink* JP; 'M' *in ink ov.* 'N'

65.10   something] *intrl. in ink w. caret*

65.11   it] *aft. del.* 'and'

65.11   and] *in ink ov.* 'or'

65.12   if] *aft. solidus and opening paren. in ink*

65.12   be] *in ink ov.* 'is'

65.15   event,"] *quot. added*

65.22   become"] *bef. del. period*

65.22   p.] *slash to indicate lower case*

65.23   past] *aft. x'd-out* 'the'

65.23   events] *bef. del.* 'both'

65.23   exist,] *comma added*

65.23   have] *underl. in ink*

65.26   character] *aft. x'd-out* 'event'

65.26   status] *aft. x'd-out* 'radically'

65.28   all"] *bef. del. period*

65.28   p.] *slash to indicate lower case*

65.29   defined] *aft. x'd-out* 'succeeded by nothing at all'

#65.29   nothing;"] *semicolon and quot. transposed*

65.29   "there] *aft. x'd-out* 'there'

#65.31   forever"] *bef. del. period*

65.31   p. 68] *slash to indicate lower case*

65.36   his] *in ink ov.* 'the'

65.37   lot] *aft. x'd-out* 'so'

65.38   termed,] *comma added*

65.38   nevertheless,] *comma added*

66.2   argument] *aft. del.* 'to Broad's'

66.3   come] *aft. del.* 'become or'

66.3   existence.] *period alt. fr. semicolon;* 'they become, but are not becomings.' *intrl. in ink w. caret, then pencil del.*

66.3   if] *bef. x'd-out* 'the event is'

66.3   becoming,] *comma added*

66.4   it] *aft. x'd-out* 'there are not related as'

66.4   event;] *semicolon alt. in ink fr. comma*
66.4   or] *in ink w. caret aft. del. illeg. word* [*intrl.*] *ab. del. illeg.*
          word
66.5   if] *alt. fr.* 'is'
66.6−7   throughout] *close-up signal betw. syllables*
66.7   itself.] *intrl. in ink w. caret*
66.7   event] *aft. x'd-out* 'an'
66.8   an] *aft. x'd-out* 'th'
66.9   is conceived of as] 'is' *ov.* 'as'; *intrl. in ink w. caret*
66.9   not] *underl. in ink*
66.9   event] *comma del.*
66.10   Broad] *aft. del.* 'That'
66.10   carries] *alt. in ink fr.* 'carry'; *aft. del.* 'is shown to'
66.10   "event"] *quots. added*
66.13   and the future] *intrl. in ink w. caret*
66.13−14 evident.] *bef. del.* 'If becoming. / is *of* events, Broad's
          conclusions as to past, present and future may [*in*
          ink] / logically follow. But'
66.14   If] 'I' *in ink ov.* 'i'
66.14   existences] *aft. x'd-out* 'things are events or'
66.14   are] *aft. x'd-out* 'or hisot'
66.15   on] *aft. x'd-out* 'alive and all'
66.17   pastness] *alt. w. caret fr.* 'past'
#66.17−18 towardsness] 'to' *in ink ov. illeg. letters bef. x'd-out* 'or'
66.18   or] *intrl.*
66.18   its] *underl. in ink*
66.19   its] *underl. in ink*
66.20   something,] *comma added*
66.21   involves] *bef. del.* 'a'
66.21   a series of] *intrl. in ink w. caret*
66.21   transitions] *alt. in ink fr.* 'transition'
66.21   which,] *comma added*
66.21−22 taken distributively,] *intrl. in ink w. caret*
66.22   belong] *alt. in ink fr.* 'belongs'
66.22   "into,"] *comma and quot. transposed* JP
66.22   form] *intrl. in ink w. caret*
66.23   "through."] *period and quot. transposed* JP
66.25   "moment."] *period and quot. transposed* JP
66.25   defined] *bef. x'd-out* 'by'
66.26   an] *in ink w. caret ab. del.* 'a past, or'
66.26   future] *bef. x'd-out* ' 'or'
66.26   "into,"] *comma and quot. transposed* JP
66.26   truly] *aft. x'd-out* 'well'

66.28   Since . . . no] *ab. x'd-out* 'And without the future, or the 'into' there'

66.28–29   futurity] *alt. fr.* 'future'; *aft. x'd-out* 'a'

66.30   be said to *have*] 'be said' *intrl. in ink w. caret*

66.30   phase] *aft. del.* 'present'

66.30–31   of presentness.] *added aft. del. period*

#66.32   on this basis] *intrl. in ink w. caret*

66.33   by] *aft. x'd-out* 'from'

66.35   named] *alt. in ink fr.* 'names'; *bef. del.* 'as'

#66.35–36   presence,] *comma added*

66.36   specific] *ab. x'd-out* 'particular'

66.37   requires] *aft. x'd-out* 'involve'

66.39   Psychologically,] *comma added*

67.1   latter] *final* 's' *x'd-out; bef. solidus in ink*

67.1   can be said to] *intrl. in ink w. caret and guideline*

67.1   refer] *alt. in ink fr.* 'refers'

67.1   directly] *intrl. in ink w. caret*

67.2   can be said to] *intrl. in ink w. caret and guideline*

67.2   refer] *alt. in ink fr.* 'refers'

67.2   directly] *intrl. in ink w. caret*

67.2   In fact] *solidus in ink betw. words*

Line-end Hyphenation

I. Copy-text list.

The following are the editorially established forms of possible compounds that were hyphenated at the ends of lines in the copy-text:

19.5	neo-realism	224.18	half-truths
19.7	re-adaptation	252.13	non-political
20.40	today	264.35	non-political
78.26	subject-matter	273.31	reenforced
102.18	today	274.14	one-sided
107.18	deep-seated	275.4	safeguards
109.37	overaccentuation	279.14	narrow-minded
122.1	upper-class	286.11	sidetracked
122.11	hardware	286.12	stockholders
125.34	self-assured	286.24	make-up
126.38−39	subconscious	288.20	non-political
158.26	cross-currents	297.12	short-sighted
162.29	today	299.5	full-fledged
168.14	self-preservation	306.2	schoolhouse
184.18	thoroughgoing	306.24	non-political
187.28−29	one-sided	307.4	piecemeal
189.8−9	close-by	311.9−10	"pork-barrel"
189.30	cocksure	312.16	non-political
190.30	hangover	315.29	non-political
202.17	school-road	316.1	Stockmarkets
206.22−23	playgrounds	326.28	one-sided
207.10	bookstores	335.1	habit-forming
208.34	semi-annual	343.40	well-being
213.16	re-educated	349.4	subject-matter
218.32	intercommunication	355.30	readjusting
219.24	bullheadedness	370.20	reestablished

II. Critical-text list.

In transcriptions from the present edition, no line-end hyphens in ambiguously broken possible compounds are to be retained except the following:

20.7	re-commencing	209.19	anti-foreign
22.7	non-legal	215.14	omni-competent
51.35	so-called	217.7	non-political
61.22	co-adjacence	218.30	non-political
68.3	self-revealing	227.35	far-reaching
71.20	over-rationalizing	245.11	short-sighted
76.38	non-humanist	259.27	self-evident
100.21	well-being	299.12	above-board
104.18	pigeon-holing	301.9	ox-carts
121.13	lock-step	306.31	self-governing
126.3	anti-political	310.7	under-cover
138.20	Self-knowledge	310.13	to-day
138.24	self-knowledge	311.9	"pork-barrel"
147.3	non-essential	314.33	self-governing
183.22	third-rate	325.29	re-make
184.15	time-honored	348.31	To-day
187.28	one-sided	357.11	subject-matter
187.36	one-sided	357.37	non-historically
189.8	close-by	364.14	high-brows
202.7	sub-secretary	370.40	many-colored
209.5	half-way	383.12	epoch-making

Substantive Variants in Quotations

Dewey's substantive variants in quotations have been considered important enough to warrant this special list. Dewey represented source material in varying ways, from memorial paraphrase to verbatim copy, in some places citing his source fully, in others mentioning only authors' names, and, in still others, omitting documentation altogether. All material inside quotation marks, except that obviously being emphasized or restated, has been searched out; Dewey's citations have been verified and, when necessary, emended. All quotations have been retained as they appear in the copy-text, with the exceptions noted below, all of which are recorded in the Emendations List.

Although Dewey, like other scholars of the period, was unconcerned about precision in matters of form, many of the changes in quotations appearing in his published material may well have occurred in the printing process. For example, comparing Dewey's quotations with the originals reveals that some editors and compositors house-styled the quoted materials as well as Dewey's own. Therefore, in the present edition, the spelling and capitalization of the source have been restored. In cases of possible compositorial or typographical errors, corrections either of substantives or accidentals, including spelling and capitalization, that restore original readings are noted as WS emendations (Works—the present edition—emendations derived from Dewey's Source). Moreover, Dewey frequently changed or omitted punctuation in quoted material. Only when such changes or omissions have substantive implications, the punctuation of the source has been restored; these changes are also recorded in the Emendations List with the symbol WS.

The present list is therefore restricted to substantive variants in quotations; for a complete reconstruction of the sources from which Dewey quoted, it is necessary to consult the Emendations List in conjunction with this list.

Dewey often did not indicate that he had omitted material from his source. Omitted short phrases appear in this list; omissions of more than one line are noted by a bracketed ellipsis [. . .]. Italics in source material have been treated as substantives. Both Dewey's omitted and added italics are noted here.

Differences between Dewey's quotations and the source attributable to the context in which the quotation appears, such as changes in number or tense, are not recorded.

In cases where Dewey translated the source, the reference appears in the Checklist of Dewey's References, but no correction of the quotation is included here.

Notations in this section follow the formula: page-line numbers from the present edition, followed by the lemma, then a bracket. After the bracket, the original form appears, followed by the author's surname, shortened source-title from the Checklist of Dewey's References, and the page-line reference to the source, all in parentheses.

The Development of American Pragmatism

4.8   experimental] experimentalist (Peirce, "Pragmatism," 163.9)

4.37   pragmatist] pragmaticist (Peirce, "Pragmatism," 174.2)

5.5   pragmatist] pragmaticist (Peirce, "Pragmatism," 178.25)

5.8   generals] those generals (Peirce, "Pragmatism," 178.28)

6.27   beliefs are] belief? . . . involves (Peirce, "Ideas," 291.15–19)

6.27   really rules for action,] the establishment in our nature of a rule of action, (Peirce, "Ideas," 291.19)

6.27–29   and . . . action,] or, say for short, a *habit*. (Peirce, "Ideas," 291.19–20)

6.36   prefer to] prefer for our purposes this evening to (James, *Collected Essays*, 412.7–8)

7.4   the particular] particular (James, *Meaning*, 209.22)

7.5–6   inert—'Pragmata'] inert. [. . .] 'Pragmata' (James, *Meaning*, 209.23–210.2)

7.6   plurality—particular] plurality; [. . .] But particular (James, *Meaning*, 210.3–13)

7n.5   It is] Man, [. . .] is (James, *Meaning*, 210n.4–10)

7n.6   philosophy without words] [*ital.*] (James, *Meaning*, 210n.10)

7n.6   gestures and of acts] [*ital.*] (James, *Meaning*, 210n.11)

7n.7   particular] [*ital.*] (James, *Meaning*, 210n.12)

9.13–14   find . . . at] find out what definite difference it will make to you and me, at (James, *Collected Essays*, 413.31–414.1)

9.14–15   a determinate moment of our lives] definite instants of our life (James, *Collected Essays*, 414.1–2)

9.15–16   if . . . true] if this world-formula or that world-formula be the one which is true (James, *Collected Essays*, 414.2–3)

11.14–17   looking . . . facts]   [*ital.*] (James, *Pragmatism*,
     54.24–55.3)
16.2–5   The pursuance . . . mentality]   [*ital.*] (James, *Psychology*,
     1:8.11–13)
16.16–18   the only . . . of]   [*ital.*] (James, *Psychology*, 2:335.3–5)
16.18   mind]   *the mind* (James, *Psychology*, 2:335.4–5)
20.39   intelligence]   light (Höffding, *Modern Philosophy*, 457.12)
20.39   progress]   in progress (Höffding, *Modern Philosophy*,
     457.12)
20.40   humanity]   in humanity (Höffding, *Modern Philosophy*,
     457.12–13)

Corporate Personality

23n.6   rules]   the rules (Pollock, "Theory of Corporations,"
     220.19)
23n.6   art,]   art'—the lawyer's art, no other being in question—
     (Pollock, "Theory of Corporations," 220.19–20)
26.1   is a]   is no fiction, no symbol, no piece of the State's
     machinery, no collective name for individuals, but a
     (Maitland, Introduction, xxvi.3–4)
33n.8–9   in the]   The (Lindsay, "State in Recent Political Theory,"
     130.16)
33n.15–16   ecclesiastic theory]   ecclesiastical theory (Dunning,
     Political Theories, 163.1)
33n.16   ecclesiastic power]   ecclesiastical power (Dunning, *Political
     Theories*, 163.2)
37n.5   imagine]   imagine that (Machen, "Corporate Personality,"
     348.19)
40.1   supports]   support (Barnes, *Sociology*, 30.18)
43.5   by the very]   from the very (Dicey, "Combination Laws,"
     513.25)
43.6   composed]   constituted (Dicey, "Combination Laws,"
     513.26)

Events and the Future

62.10   objects]   object (Broad, *Thought*, 403.2)
62.14   sort]   kind (Broad, *Thought*, 403.9)
62.16   speed]   rate (Broad, *Thought*, 403.11)
63.5   you]   you choose to (Broad, *Thought*, 403.21)
63.5   of]   of all (Broad, *Thought*, 403.22)

64.8   which]   that (Broad, *Thought*, 54.24)
64.10   in adjacent]   at adjacent (Broad, *Thought*, 54.26)
65.15   an event]   events (Broad, *Thought*, 67.32)
65.19   events]   entities (Broad, *Thought*, 68.7)
65.28   is simply]   be literally (Broad, *Thought*, 70.5)
65.29   which]   that (Broad, *Thought*, 68.13)
65.30   ceasing]   [*ital.*] (Broad, *Thought*, 69.24)
67.14   is]   [*ital.*] (Broad, *Thought*, 76.25)
67.25–26 involve . . . assertion]   makes certain assertions of a quite
          peculiar and not further analysable kind (Broad, *Thought*,
          77.15–16)

The Meaning of Value

69.27   Value]   [*ital.*] (Prall, "Value," 119.30)
70.17   they]   that they (Prall, "Value," 118.16)
70.19   Mr.]   of Mr. (Prall, "Value," 118.18)
74.21   existence]   existences (Santayana, *Life*, 5:167.15)
74n.10   embodying]   embodies (Dewey, "Values, Liking, and
          Thought," 622.16) [*Middle Works* 15:26.7]
74n.10   *results*]   [*rom.*] (Dewey, "Values, Liking, and Thought,"
          622.16) [*Middle Works* 15:26.8]

Value, Objective Reference, and Criticism

79.21   to what]   what (Ogden and Richards, *Meaning*, 217.34)
79.21   refers]   refers to (Ogden and Richards, *Meaning*, 218.1)
79.25   general. This]   general; [. . .] This (Ogden and Richards,
          Meaning, 218.17–19)
79.26   relationships]   relations (Ogden and Richards, *Meaning*,
          218.22)
79.27–28 respect to]   respect of (Ogden and Richards, *Meaning*,
          218.24)
82.26   an]   the (Prall, "Value," 122.19)
82.27   *all*]   [*rom.*] (Prall, "Value," 122.19)
83.28   out]   forth (Prall, "Present Status," 100.30)
83.29   evaluations]   evaluation (Prall, "Present Status," 100.30–31)
83.36   the word]   this word (Ogden and Richards, *Meaning*,
          227.29)
84.1   have heard]   heard (Ogden and Richards, *Meaning*, 227.32)
84.9   no addition]   no difference (Ogden and Richards, *Meaning*,
          228.13)

87.1   toward]   towards (Perry, "Definition," 151.10)
87.1   interest]   the interest (Perry, "Definition," 151.10)
87.12   appears]   appears to be (Perry, "Definition," 150.34)
87.15   purely]   merely (Perry, "Definition," 150.37)
90.10   qualia]   [*ital.*] (Perry, "Definition," 153.20)
92.19   or]   and (Perry, "Definition," 160.22)
93.2   all of them]   them all (Santayana, *Life*, 5:201.15)
93.17   work]   work, life is in active operation, (Santayana, *Life*, 5:215.22)
93.18   situation]   the situation (Santayana, *Life*, 5:215.23–24)

Art in Education—and Education in Art

111.12   practical]   mere practical (Whitehead, *Science*, 279.10)
112.21   divorced]   which is divorced (Whitehead, *Science*, 276.3–4)

The "Socratic Dialogues" of Plato

135.2–3   of men . . . savages who]   of those who have been brought up in laws and humanities, would appear to be a just man and a master of justice if he were to be compared with men who (Plato, *Dialogues*, 1:127.12–14)
135.3   have]   had (Plato, *Dialogues*, 1:127.14)
135.3   nor courts and]   or courts of justice, or (Plato, *Dialogues*, 1:127.14–15)

Substance, Power and Quality in Locke

143n.2   Conceived . . . disbelieved]   [*ital.*] (James, *Psychology*, 2:301.26–27)
143n.5   upon]   on (James, *Psychology*, 2:301.29)
144.6   such]   and such (Locke, *Essay*, 169.14)
145.20   a body upon]   that body, on (Locke, *Essay*, 57.20–21)
145.23   the real]   that real (Locke, *Essay*, 61.17)
145.24   properties which]   properties that (Locke, *Essay*, 61.19)
145.24–25   found constantly]   constantly found (Locke, *Essay*, 61.19)
146.6   its essence]   the essence (Locke, *Essay*, 116.29)
146.8   all being]   being all (Locke, *Essay*, 116.30)
146.8   *depending on its real constitution*]   [*rom.*] (Locke, *Essay*, 116.31)

146.9   relation]   reference (Locke, *Essay*, 116.32)

146.12   as found]   to be found (Locke, *Essay*, 116.35)

146.15   the real]   real (Locke, *Essay*, 236.19)

146.15   of]   it is of (Locke, *Essay*, 236.19)

146.17   with one]   one with (Locke, *Essay*, 236.21)

146n.5   which]   whence (Locke, *Works*, 4:82.10)

146n.5   is]   to be (Locke, *Works*, 4:82.34)

146n.8   gives it]   gives (Locke, *Works*, 4:82.38)

147.9   relation]   [*ital.*] (Locke, *Essay*, 427.4)

147.10   respect]   [*ital.*] (Locke, *Essay*, 427.4)

147.11   thought]   thoughts (Locke, *Essay*, 427.6)

147.13   relatives]   [*ital.*] (Locke, *Essay*, 427.7)

147.14   related]   [*ital.*] (Locke, *Essay*, 427.8)

147.17   subject]   things related (Locke, *Essay*, 428.22–23)

147.34   of relation]   of *relation* (Locke, *Essay*, 310.13)

148.1   whatever]   what (Locke, *Essay*, 310.15)

148.8   upon]   on (Locke, *Essay*, 311.2)

148.9   All of]   All (Locke, *Essay*, 311.3)

148.11   simple ideas]   [*ital.*] (Locke, *Essay*, 311.5)

148.11   considered]   considered as (Locke, *Essay*, 311.5–6)

148.12   makes]   make (Locke, *Essay*, 311.6)

148.13   substance]   substances (Locke, *Essay*, 311.7)

148.37   jargon becomes sense]   This gives sense to jargon (Locke, *Essay*, 534.35–36)

148.37   is given to absurdity]   to absurdities (Locke, *Essay*, 534.36)

148.38   It is]   is (Locke, *Essay*, 534.37)

148.38–149.1   greatest errors]   greatest, I had almost said of all the errors (Locke, *Essay*, 534.37–535.1)

148n.2   nothing]   nothing else (Locke, *Essay*, 423.4)

149.4   of *reason*]   of our reason (Locke, *Essay*, 529.6–7)

149.6   being]   beings (Locke, *Essay*, 529.9)

149.14   seeing what]   seeing those objects which (Locke, *Essay*, 455.27)

149.14   upon]   on (Locke, *Essay*, 455.28)

149.16–17   by stopping our inquiry]   [*ital.*] (Locke, *Essay*, 455.33–34)

149n.1–2   mind puts]   mind, in making its complex ideas of substances, only follows nature; and puts (Locke, *Essay*, 79.5–6)

150.21   powers]   *Powers* therefore (Locke, *Essay*, 400.14)

150.21–22   substance]   substances (Locke, *Essay*, 400.15)

150.24   qualities]   qualities, which, depending on these, (Locke, *Essay*, 399.18)

150.27   *otherwise . . . cause*]   [*rom.*] (Locke, *Essay*, 399.21)
150.30   cohesion of solid]   [*ital.*] (Locke, *Essay*, 407.16)
150.30–31   and separable parts]   *and consequently separable, parts* (Locke, *Essay*, 407.16–17)
150.31–32   of . . . impulse]   [*ital.*] (Locke, *Essay*, 407.17–18)
151.9   their]   this their (Locke, *Essay*, 433.6)
151.11   thing]   thing, either simple idea, substance, or mode, (Locke, *Essay*, 434.19)
152.18   properties]   qualities (Locke, *Essay*, 401.5)
152.19   that they]   but they (Locke, *Essay*, 401.5)
153.16   those]   the (Locke, *Works*, 4:81.36)
153.22   a hundred]   an hundred (Locke, *Works*, 4:82.4)
153.25   upon]   on (Locke, *Works*, 4:82.7)
153n.6   the necessary]   a necessary (Locke, *Essay*, 259.25)
153n.10   all gold is malleable]   [*ital.*] (Locke, *Essay*, 259.30)
153n.10–11   three . . . ones]   [*ital.*] (Locke, *Essay*, 259.31–32)
154.2   *Connexion between most*]   Connexion between (Locke, *Essay*, 200.4–6)
154.2–3   *simple Ideas*]   simple Ideas in substances (Locke, *Essay*, 200.7–10)
154.3   is]   is for the most part (Locke, *Essay*, 200.10–12)
154.7   visible necessary]   [*ital.*] (Locke, *Essay*, 200.10)
154.11   that we]   we (Locke, *Essay*, 201.5)
154.12   other]   [*ital.*] (Locke, *Essay*, 201.5)
154.14   so]   so consequently (Locke, *Essay*, 201.7)
154.14   the complex]   that complex (Locke, *Essay*, 201.8)
154.28   *without trial*]   [*rom.*] (Locke, *Essay*, 216.20)
154.29   now know]   now (Locke, *Essay*, 216.21)
154.30–31   *beforehand*]   [*rom.*] (Locke, *Essay*, 216.27)
155.9   all]   aught (Locke, *Essay*, 260.26)
156.30   cause]   [*ital.*] (Berkeley, *Principles*, 67.29)
156.30   effect]   [*ital.*] (Berkeley, *Principles*, 67.30)
156.31   sign]   [*ital.*] (Berkeley, *Principles*, 67.30)
156.31   things]   thing (Berkeley, *Principles*, 67.30)
156.31   signified]   [*ital.*] (Berkeley, *Principles*, 67.31)

William James in Nineteen Twenty-Six

159.25   at]   in (James, *Philosophy*, 32.15)
159.29   all are]   are all (James, *Philosophy*, 32.20)
159.31   coincide]   so coincide (James, *Philosophy*, 34.2)

161.33   system,] system," as Henry Ford (certainly not an enemy of
business) declares, (Otto, *Natural Laws*, 87.12–14)

162.1   worse,] worse, from the cultural and humanitarian point of
view, (Otto, *Natural Laws*, 88.6–7)

We Should Deal with China as Nation to Nation

185.8   frankly] frankly that (Gannett, "Looking," 181.25)

Practical Democracy

215.29   a general] one general (Lippmann, *Phantom Public*, 47.13)

215.30   a Hegelian] an Hegelian (Lippmann, *Phantom Public*,
47.14)

215.30   mystery,] mystery, as so many social philosophers have
imagined, (Lippmann, *Phantom Public*, 47.15–16)

The Changing Intellectual Climate

222.8   the *union*] this union (Whitehead, *Science*, 3.33)

222.11   has] had (Whitehead, *Science*, 4.3)

222.30   opportunity. In] opportunity. [. . .] In (Whitehead,
Science, 259.4–260.22)

222.31   defeat] a defeat (Whitehead, *Science*, 260.22–23)

222.35–36   proclaims] proclaim (Whitehead, *Science*, 263.13)

222.37   there] that there (Whitehead, *Science*, 263.15)

223.33   sciences] science (Whitehead, *Science*, 150.14)

225.5   has aped] apes (Whitehead, *Science*, 144.33)

A Key to the New World

226.25   now tried] tried (Russell, *Education*, 316.24)

229.39   bad] these bad (Russell, *Education*, 83.20)

The Public and Its Problems

261.11   Each house has] Each had (Hudson, *Traveller*, 110.19)

261.22   each villager] every individual (Hudson, *Traveller*, 111.10)

261.28   though]   although (Hudson, *Traveller*, 111.18)

294.4   art]   to art (Mill, *Essays on Government*, 32.17)

294.4   legislation]   to legislation (Mill, *Essays on Government*, 32.17)

294.4   its]   their (Mill, *Essays on Government*, 32.18)

294.5   and which is the]   the (Mill, *Essays on Government*, 32.18)

294.5   that is]   that has (Mill, *Essays on Government*, 32.18)

294.6   refined and exalted]   exalted and refined (Mill, *Essays on Government*, 32.19)

294.6   in human]   human (Mill, *Essays on Government*, 32.19)

294.7   which the]   which, if the basis of Representation were ever so far extended, the (Mill, *Essays on Government*, 32.20)

294.7   influence]   opinion (Mill, *Essays on Government*, 32.21)

295.14   individuals]   individual men (Wallas, *Society*, 3.4)

295.15   new age]   new era (Wallas, *Society*, 3.7)

304.9   the printing press and]   writing, (Carlyle, *Works*, 1:156.10)

335.5   is]   is thus (James, *Psychology*, 1:121.12)

335.6   influence]   agent (James, *Psychology*, 1:121.13)

335.6   us]   us all (James, *Psychology*, 1:121.13)

335.8   uprisings]   envious uprisings (James, *Psychology*, 1:121.15)

Checklist of Dewey's References

This section gives full publication information for each work cited by Dewey. When Dewey gave page numbers for a reference, the edition he used was identified exactly by locating the citation. Similarly, the books in Dewey's personal library (John Dewey Papers, Special Collections, Morris Library, Southern Illinois University at Carbondale) have been used to verify his use of a particular edition. For other references, the edition listed here is the one from among the various editions possibly available to him that was his most likely source by reason of place or date of publication, or on the evidence from correspondence and other materials, and its general accessibility during the period.

Antisthenes. *Socratis, Antisthenis, et aliorum Socraticorum epistolae.* Translated by Leone Allacci. Paris, 1637.

Ayres, Clarence Edwin. *Science: The False Messiah.* Indianapolis: Bobbs-Merrill Co., 1927.

Barker, Ernest. "The 'Rule of Law.'" *Political Quarterly* 2 (1914): 117–40.

Barnes, Albert C. *The Art of Painting.* 2d ed., rev. New York: Harcourt, Brace and Co., 1928.

Barnes, Harry Elmer. *Sociology and Political Theory.* New York: Alfred A. Knopf, 1924.

Berkeley, George. *A Treatise concerning the Principles of Human Knowledge.* Chicago: Open Court Publishing Co., 1920.

Borchard, Edwin M. "Government Liability in Tort." *Yale Law Journal* 34 (November 1924): 1–45; (December 1924): 129–43; (January 1925): 229–58.

Broad, Charlie Dunbar. *Scientific Thought.* New York: Harcourt, Brace and Co., 1923.

Brown, Harold Chapman. "Value and Potentiality." *Journal of Philosophy, Psychology and Scientific Methods* 11 (1914): 29–37.

Brown, William Montgomery. *My Heresy.* New York: John Day Co., 1926.

Bush, Wendell T. "Value and Causality." *Journal of Philosophy, Psychology and Scientific Methods* 15 (1918): 85–96. [*The Middle Works of John Dewey, 1899–1924*, ed. Jo Ann Boydston, 11:375–87. Carbondale: Southern Illinois University Press, 1982.]

Carlyle, Thomas. *The Works of Thomas Carlyle.* Vols. 1 and 8. New York: John B. Alden, 1885.

Cooley, Charles Horton. *Social Organization: A Study of the Larger Mind.* New York: Charles Scribner's Sons, 1909.

Craies, William Feilden. *A Treatise on Statute Law, with Appendices Containing Words and Expressions Used in Statutes Which Have Been Judicially or Statutably Construed, the Popular and Short Titles of Certain Statutes, and the Interpretation Act, 1889.* London: Stevens and Haynes, 1907.

Dewey, John. *Studies in Logical Theory.* University of Chicago, The Decennial Publications, second series, vol. 11. Chicago: University of Chicago Press, 1903. [*Middle Works* 2:292–375.]

———. "The Logic of Judgments of Practice." In *Essays in Experimental Logic*, pp. 335–442. Chicago: University of Chicago Press, 1916. [*Middle Works* 8:14–82.]

———. "Valuation and Experimental Knowledge." *Philosophical Review* 31 (1922): 325–51. [*Middle Works* 13:3–28.]

———. "Values, Liking, and Thought." *Journal of Philosophy* 20 (1923): 617–22. [*Middle Works* 15:20–26.]

Dicey, Albert V. "The Combination Laws as Illustrating the Relation between Law and Opinion in England during the Nineteenth Century." *Harvard Law Review* 17 (1904): 511–32.

Drake, Durant. "What Kind of Realism?" *Journal of Philosophy, Psychology and Scientific Methods* 9 (1912): 149–54. [*Middle Works* 10:431–38.]

Duguit, Leon. *Law in the Modern State.* Translated by Frida and Harold Laski. New York: B. W. Huebsch, 1919.

Dunning, William Archibald. *A History of Political Theories, Ancient and Mediaeval.* New York: Macmillan Co., 1923.

Durant, William James. *The Story of Philosophy: The Lives and Opinions of the Greater Philosophers.* New York: Simon and Schuster, 1926.

Freund, Ernst. *Standards of American Legislation: An Estimate of Restrictive and Constructive Factors.* Chicago: University of Chicago Press, 1917.

Gaius. *The Institutes of Gaius.* Translated by John Graham Trapnell. New York: Macmillan Co., 1908.

Gannett, Lewis Stiles. "Looking at America—in China." *Survey* 56 (1926): 181–82, 216.

Geldart, W. M. "Legal Personality." *Law Quarterly Review* 27 (1911): 90–108.

Gierke, Otto Friedrich von. *Das deutsche genossenschaftsrecht*. Vol. 3. Berlin: Weidmann, 1881.

———. *Die genossenschaftstheorie und die deutsche rechtsprechung*. Vol. 2. Berlin: Weidmann, 1887.

Great Britain, *Law Reports* (Lords). "Amalgamated Society of Railway Servants *v*. Osborne," 1910, pp. 87–116.

Great Britain, *Law Reports* (Lords). "Free Church of Scotland *v*. Overtoun," 1904, pp. 515–764.

Great Britain, *Law Reports* (Lords). "Taff Vale Railway Company *v*. Amalgamated Society of Railway Servants," 1901, pp. 426–45.

Great Britain, *Statutes* (1833). 3 & 4 Will. 4, c. 74, pp. 691–722.

Green, Thomas Hill. *Works of Thomas Hill Green*. 2d ed. Vol. 1. Edited by R. L. Nettleship. New York: Longmans, Green, and Co., 1890.

Hayes, Carlton J. H. *Essays on Nationalism*. New York: Macmillan Co., 1926.

Henderson, Gerard Carl. *The Position of Foreign Corporations in American Constitutional Law*. Cambridge: Harvard University Press, 1918.

Hocking, William Ernest. *Man and the State*. New Haven: Yale University Press, 1926.

Höffding, Harald. *A History of Modern Philosophy: A Sketch of the History of Philosophy from the Close of the Renaissance to Our Own Day*. Vol. 1. Translated by B. E. Meyer. New York: Humanities Press, 1900.

Hudson, William Henry. *A Traveller in Little Things*. New York: E. P. Dutton and Co., 1921.

Hume, David. *A Treatise of Human Nature: Being an Attempt to Introduce the Experimental Method of Reasoning into Moral Subjects*. London: John Noon, 1739.

James, William. *Collected Essays and Reviews*. New York: Longmans, Green, and Co., 1920.

———. *The Letters of William James*. Vol. 2. Edited by Henry James. Boston: Atlantic Monthly Press, 1920.

———. *The Meaning of Truth: A Sequel to Pragmatism*. New York: Longmans, Green, and Co., 1909.

———. *The Philosophy of William James*. Introduction by Horace M. Kallen. New York: Modern Library, 1925.

———. *Pragmatism: A New Name for Some Old Ways of Thinking*. New York: Longmans, Green, and Co., 1907.

————. *The Principles of Psychology.* 2 vols. New York: Henry Holt and Co., 1893.

Joël, Karl. "Der λόγος Σωχρατιχός." *Archiv für Geschichte der Philosophie* 8 (1895): 466–83; 9 (1896): 50–66.

Jowett, Benjamin. Introductions to *The Dialogues of Plato* Vol. 1. New York: Jefferson Press, 1871.

Kallen, Horace M. "Value and Existence in Art and in Religion." *Journal of Philosophy, Psychology and Scientific Methods* 11 (1914): 264–76.

————. "Value and Existence in Philosophy, Art, and Religion." In *Creative Intelligence: Essays in the Pragmatic Attitude*, pp. 409–67. New York: Henry Holt and Co., 1917.

Kant, Immanuel. *The Metaphysic of Morals.* London: William Richardson, 1799.

Laski, Harold J. *The Foundations of Sovereignty and Other Essays.* New York: Harcourt, Brace and Co., 1921.

————. "The Personality of Associations." *Harvard Law Review* 29 (1916): 404–26.

Lindsay, Alexander Dunlop. "The State in Recent Political Theory." *Political Quarterly* 1 (1914): 128–45.

Lippmann, Walter. *The Phantom Public.* New York: Harcourt, Brace and Co., 1925.

————. *Public Opinion.* New York: Harcourt, Brace and Co., 1922.

Locke, John. *An Essay concerning Human Understanding.* 2 vols. Oxford: At the Clarendon Press, 1894.

————. *The Works of John Locke.* Vol. 4. London: Thomas Tegg, 1823.

Lovejoy, Arthur Oncken. "Pragmatism *versus* the Pragmatist." In *Essays in Critical Realism: A Co-operative Study of the Problem of Knowledge*, by Durant Drake et al., pp. 35–81. London: Macmillan and Co., 1920. [*Middle Works* 13:443–81.]

Macaulay, Thomas Babington. *Essays, Critical and Miscellaneous.* New York: D. Appleton and Co., 1879.

Machen, Arthur W. "Corporate Personality." *Harvard Law Review* 24 (February 1911): 253–67; (March 1911): 347–65.

Maitland, Frederic William. *The Collected Papers of Frederic William Maitland.* Vol. 3. Cambridge: At the University Press, 1911.

————. Introduction to *Political Theories of the Middle Age*, by Otto Gierke. Cambridge: At the University Press, 1900.

Marden, Orison Swett. *Peace, Power and Plenty.* New York: Thomas Y. Crowell Co., 1909.

Michoud, L. "La Notion de personnalité morale." *Revue du droit public* 11 (1899): 5–32.

Mill, James. *Essays on Government, Jurisprudence, Liberty of the Press, and Law of Nations.* London: J. Innes, 1825.

Mill, John Stuart. *A System of Logic, Ratiocinative and Inductive; Being a Connected View of the Principles of Evidence, and the Methods of Scientific Investigation.* New York: Harper and Bros., 1850.

Munro, Thomas. "Franz Cizek and the Free Expression Method." *Journal of the Barnes Foundation* 1 (1925): 36–40.

Ogden, Charles K., and Richards, Ivor Armstrong. *The Meaning of Meaning: A Study of the Influence of Language upon Thought and of the Science of Symbolism.* New York: Harcourt, Brace and Co., 1923.

Otto, Max Carl. *Natural Laws and Human Hopes.* New York: Henry Holt and Co., 1926.

Peirce, Charles S. *Chance, Love, and Logic.* New York: Harcourt, Brace and Co., 1923.

———. "How to Make Our Ideas Clear." *Popular Science Monthly* 12 (1878): 286–302.

———. "What Pragmatism Is." *Monist* 15 (1905): 161–81.

Perry, Ralph Barton. "The Definition of Value." *Journal of Philosophy, Psychology and Scientific Methods* 11 (1914): 141–62.

Picard, Maurice. *Values, Immediate and Contributory, and Their Interrelation.* New York: New York University Press, 1920.

———. "The Psychological Basis of Values." *Journal of Philosophy, Psychology and Scientific Methods* 17 (1920): 11–20.

Plato. *The Dialogues of Plato.* 4 vols. Translated by Benjamin Jowett. New York: Jefferson Press, 1871.

Pollock, Frederick. *Essays in the Law.* London: Macmillan and Co., 1922.

———. "Has the Common Law Received the Fiction Theory of Corporations?" *Law Quarterly Review* 27 (1911): 219–35.

Prall, David Wight. "In Defense of a *Worthless* Theory of Value." *Journal of Philosophy* 20 (1923): 128–37. [*Middle Works* 15:338–48.]

———. "The Present Status of the Theory of Value." *University of California Publications in Philosophy* 4 (1923): 77–103.

———. "A Study in the Theory of Value." *University of California Publications in Philosophy* 3 (1918–1921): 179–290.

———. "Value and Thought-Process." *Journal of Philosophy* 21 (1924): 117–25. [*The Later Works of John Dewey, 1925–1953*, edited by Jo Ann Boydston, 2:393–402. Carbondale: Southern Illinois University Press, 1983.]

Richards, Ivor Armstrong, and Ogden, Charles K. *The Meaning of*

Meaning: A Study of the Influence of Language upon Thought and of the Science of Symbolism. New York: Harcourt, Brace and Co., 1923.

Rignano, Eugenio. *The Psychology of Reasoning.* Translated by Winifred A. Holl. New York: Harcourt, Brace and Co., 1923.

Russell, Bertrand. *Education and the Good Life.* New York: Boni and Liveright, 1926.

Saleilles, Raymond. *De la personnalité juridique: histoire et théories.* Paris: Arthur Rousseau, 1910.

Santayana, George. *The Life of Reason; or, The Phases of Human Progress.* Vol. 5. New York: Charles Scribner's Sons, 1905.

———. *Winds of Doctrine: Studies in Contemporary Opinion.* New York: Charles Scribner's Sons, 1913.

Sheldon, Wilmon H. "An Empirical Definition of Value." *Journal of Philosophy, Psychology and Scientific Methods* 11 (1914): 113–24.

Smith, Adam. *The Wealth of Nations.* New York: P. F. Collier, 1902.

Smith, Thomas Vernor. *The Democratic Way of Life.* Chicago: University of Chicago Press, 1926.

Stein, Leo. "The Art in Painting." *New Republic* 45 (2 December 1925): 56–57.

Tocqueville, Alexis de. *Democracy in America.* Translated by Henry Reeve. New York: Adlard and Saunders, 1838.

U.S., *Reports of Cases Argued and Adjudged in the Supreme Court of the United States in February Term, 1809.* Bank of the U.S. *v.* Deveaux, 5 U.S. 61–92 (1809).

Vinogradoff, Paul. "Juridical Persons." *Columbia Law Review* 24 (1924): 594–604.

Wallas, Graham. *The Art of Thought.* New York: Harcourt, Brace and Co., 1926.

———. *The Great Society: A Psychological Analysis.* New York: Macmillan Co., 1914.

Weeks, Raymond. *Boys' Own Arithmetic.* New York: E. P. Dutton and Co., 1924.

Whitehead, Alfred North. *An Enquiry concerning the Principles of Natural Knowledge.* Cambridge: At the University Press, 1919.

———. *Science and the Modern World.* New York: Macmillan Co., 1925.

Wilson, Woodrow. *The New Freedom: A Call for the Emancipation of the Generous Energies of a People.* New York: Doubleday, Page and Co., 1913.

Index

Absolutism: in method, 357–61
Aesthetics, 107, 111–13, 115
"Affective Thought," xxi
Affectivity: and integration with environment, 105, 106
Althusius, Johannes, 39, 40
Amusements: rival political interests, 321–22
Anarchism, 252
Anarchy, State, and Utopia (Nozick), xxxv
Anfu party, 183
Angell, Norman, 33*n*
Animals: community responsibility toward, 98, 100–102; scientific experimentation with, 98–100
Anti-clerical legislation, 195. *See also* Mexico
Antisthenes, 125, 128–29
Apostles Creed, 165
Appreciation: aesthetic, 111–13, 115
Apprehension, 74*n*
Architecture: Byzantine and Turkish, 191
Aristippeans, 133
Aristotle, xxiv, 78–79, 86, 128, 241; on citizenship, 215, 321; and criticism of Plato, 131; on nature of "individual," 34; on state, 238–39
Art: African, 384; Barnes on, 108–10; of communication,

349–50; in education, xx–xxi, 111–15, 375–77; method in, 114–15; in Mexico, 202–5, 208–9; nature of, 107–8, 114; relationship of biological conceptions to, 109–10
"Art in Education—and Education in Art," xxi
Artisans: discipline of, 128, 130–31; tradition of, 57–58
Art of Thought, The (Wallas), xxii, 160, 231–34
Association: and democracy, 325; distinguished from community, 330–31; domination of one form of, 356; economic, 300–302; revolt against, 290, 296–97; territorial and functional, 468; traits of, 250–51; as universal fact, 249–50, 257, 330, 348. *See also* Community; Groups; Society
Athens, Greece, 125, 126
Atomists, 139
Attachment: political need of, 322, 368–69
Authority: and tradition, 58, 59
Ayres, Clarence Edwin, 272*n*

Bacon, Francis, 20, 389
Bain, Alexander, 7*n*
Bank of the United States v. Deveaux, 36*n*. *See also* "Person"

Barker, Ernest, 40, 42 and *n*
Barnes, Albert C., 114, 115; on the historic development of painting, 109; on the plastic arts as integration, 108–10
Barnes, Harry Elmer, 40*n*, 42
Barnes Foundation, 114, 115, 382–85. *See also* Art; Education
Beck, James Montgomery, 179, 403
Becoming: and the future, 65–66
Behaviorism, 15, 19
Being: insight into, 131
Benn, Gottfried, 124*n*
Bentham, Jeremy, 213, 293*n*
Berkeley, George, 7*n*, 156
Bias, 80, 81, 94
Biology: and the social, 243, 330–31, 357
Bolshevism, 117, 177, 199, 210
Borah, William Edgar, 171
Borchard, Edwin M., 42*n*
Bosanquet, Bernard, 14, 77
Bourdeau, M., 7*n*
Boxer indemnity, 174. *See also* China
Boyle, Robert, 142
Boys' Own Arithmetic (Weeks), 386
Bradley, Francis Herbert, 14
Broad, Charlie Dunbar, 29*n*; on event, 62–68
Brown, William Montgomery: spiritual development of, 163–66
Burlingame, Anson, 174
Business, 161–62; political control by, 349; private action in, 214–15; as rival to political interest, 321. *See also* Economics

Caird, Edward, 6
Calles, Plutarco Elías, 194, 196, 199

Capitalism, 161
Carlyle, Thomas, 217, 298, 304
Carranza, Venustiano, 195
Cartesian thinking, 142
Catholics, Roman. *See* Church, in Mexico
Causal forces: *vs.* the causal order, 361; and state, 242, 246–49, 251, 258, 259, 265, 269, 276
Causation, 50; as affected by relational theory of knowledge, 142–43, 146; Hume's theory of, 154
Chamber of Commerce, 161
Chance, Love, and Logic (Peirce), 28*n*
Charmides (Plato), 124, 127, 134, 138; discussion of *sophrosyne* in, 131; and knowledge of knowledge, 135
Child Labor amendment, 310
China: Bolshevism in, 177; compared with Turkey, 193; fears Japan and Russia, 176–78; interference of democratic nations with, 181–84; moves toward tariff autonomy, 181–84; seeks break with own past, 182–83; and U.S., 173–75, 176–80, 181–84
Church: autonomy of, 40–41; conflict between empire and, 32–33, 35; future of Christian, 163–66; in Mexico, 194–98, 200–202, 208
Cizek, Franz, 55, 58
Cohen, Morris R., 28*n*
Collected Essays and Reviews (James), 6–7
Collected Papers of Frederic William Maitland, The, 42*n*
Collectivism: and individualism, 351–56
Common interest: nature of, 246,

256–57. *See also* Conse-
quences; Public
Common law: and *filius nullius*,
23–25
Common sense: enlightened, empirical, 49, 53, 54, 228
Communication: as art, 348–50;
and knowledge, 345–46; as
public function, 253, 273; social necessity of, 330, 370–72.
See also Symbols
Community: communication in,
259–60; conditioning of,
300–301; effect of organization of, 214–16; importance of
local, 367–72; and society,
296, 333–34. *See also* Great
Society, The
Comparative method, 265
Conjoint behavior. *See*
Association
Conscience: origin of private,
266–67
Consequences: effect of, 271–74;
expansion of, 314, 333, 358;
importance of, for politics,
243–44, 245, 246–47, 250–
51, 255, 260, 262, 265, 276,
313, 333, 358; individual and
social, 356; irreparable, 274–
75; and relation to state and
government, 276–78; and
rules of law, 270–71
Constantinople, Turkey, 191
Continental law, 27*n*, 28
Control: of human nature, 358–
60; political, 243, 246
Cooley, Charles Horton, 295
Corporate legal personality: concession theory of, 34–36, 37
and *n*; defined by non-legal
theories, 22, 24–25, 31–34;
fiction theory of, 34–36, 37*n*,
41*n*, 43; nature of, 22–43
"Corporate Personality," viii

Corporations: illustrate relation
of individual and social, 354;
legal personality of, 22–43
Courage: connected with wisdom, 130
Critias: as affiliated with Cyrenaic humanism, 136–37, 138,
139; compared with Nicias,
140; and *sophrosyne* in
Charmides, 131–33
Criticism: and objective reference, 78, 87, 88–89, 90–91;
related to value, 78, 94–97
Culture: human, 32
Cynics, 134; as related to Plato,
125, 128–29, 130, 133; as represented by Laches, 130; as
school of philosophy, 124,
135, 136
Cyrenaics, 133, 138–39; as represented by Nicias, 131; as school
of philosophy, 124, 125, 134–
35, 136–37

Darwin, Charles, 222
De la personnalité juridique
(Saleilles), 30*n*
Democracy: alleged unity in,
286–87; American, 304–7;
and experts, 362–65; historic
genesis of, 287–90; inchoate,
303; and individualism, 289–
95; intelligence and, xxix,
465–66; Lippmann on,
213–20; and local community,
367–68; machinery of political, 283, 325–27; as moral
idea, 325–26; nature of ideal,
xxviii–xxix, 327–29; pessimism about, xxviii, 304; pure,
293; significance of, 287; in
Turkey, 190–91
Democritus, 136, 138, 140
Descartes, René, 290
Desire, 106

De Tocqueville, Alexander, 364
"Development of American Pragmatism, The," xii
Dialectic: Plato's, 128–29, 130
Díaz, Porfirio, 197–98, 199, 200
Dicey, Albert V., 42–43
Direct action, 255
Dissemination: and art, 349–50; means of, 347; and social knowledge, 345–46. *See also* Communication
Duguit, Leon, 39, 41 and *n*
Dunning, William Archibald, 33*n*
Durant, William, 387
Duration, 62; and the future, 63–64
Dynastic states, 290–91

Economics: determinism in, 309–54; forces and politics in, 290–93, 296, 297, 299–302, 306–7, 309–10, 315–17, 323–24, 325–26, 332, 344, 348–49, 378–79; Turkish struggle with, 191–93. *See also* Business
Education: absolutistic method in, 360; art in, 111–15, 382–85; of children, 116, 117, 118–22, 226–30; as Dewey's purpose in writing, x; faith in, 226; finances in, 117, 118–19, 120; immigrants and, 118; instrumentalism in, xvii–xviii, 55–61; means and ends in, 57, 58, 59, 60; mechanical control in, 55–61; in Mexico, 199–205; and political democracy, 364–65; quality of, 120–23; and social action, 358–59; tradition in, 56, 57, 58, 60; and women, 117, 118–19
Einstein, Albert, 222
Electoral college, 305

Emerson, Ralph Waldo, 207, 231, 372
Emotion: in word usage, 82–85
Empiricism, 11–12, 13
Ends, 106
English jurisprudence, 28, 41–42; and actions as a body corporate, 35–36; and statutory law, 29–30, 30*n*
English Parliament, 176–77
Enjoyment: aesthetic, 108–9, 115
Enlightenment: British and French, xiv, xxxiii
Epistemology, xv–xvi, xvii; and sense-perception, 45–49, 51, 54
Equality: nature of, 328–29
Essay concerning Human Understanding (Locke), xvii, 144–54
Essence: internal, 153; Locke on, 145–47, 149–51; as related to power, 150–52; Stillingfleet on, 146*n*
Europe: British Isles isolated from, 167; emigrants against, 167; Turkey's relationship to, 192–93; views U.S. investment in China, 173; World War I reflects strife in, 168–69
Euthydemus (Plato), 124
Event: and becoming, 65–66; and duration, 62, 64–65; as related to location, 53
Existence, 65–66, 74–75
Experience, ix, 11–12, 16; and individuality, 55–61; practical, 3–4, 6
Experience and Nature, xviii
Experimentalism, 2, 4–5, 20
Experimental method: defined, 362; in politics, 356–61
Experts: and democracy, 362–63; importance of, 312–13, 319–20

Factions, 309

Facts: and meanings, 238; physical and social, 240–41, 243–44; and theories, 246

Faraday, Michael, xxxii, 366

Farmers, 316

Federation, 377

Figgis, John Neville, 39, 40

Fission of the atom, 380–81

Ford, Henry, 161

Foundations of Sovereignty (Laski), 40*n*

Fourteenth Amendment, 36

Free Church of Scotland v. Overtoun, 41*n*

Freedom: in education, 58–59, 60

Freudianism, 229

Freund, Ernst, 36*n*

Futurity, 66–67

Gaius, 35*n*

Geldart, W. M., 22*n*

Genossenschaftslehre (Gierke), 39

Germany: law in, 26–27, 31*n*, 41 and *n*; modern philosophy in, 27; as related to China, 176. *See also* "Person"

Gerontocracy, 284

Gierke, Otto von, 25–26, 34*n*, 39, 41

Giotto di Bondone, 114

Good: knowledge of the, 136, 138; as related to value, 83–84, 92–94; science of the, 129, 132 and *n*

Government: dynastic, 285–86; economic control of, 301–2; fear of, 289, 291, 292–93; and opinion, 355–56; and the public, 216–20, 252–53, 255, 256, 259, 275–79; as representative, 282–83. *See also* State

"Government Liability in Tort" (Borchard), 42*n*

Great Society, The: and lack of community, 296, 314–15, 324, 327, 333, 350; Lippmann on, 218, 219, 404

Great Society, The (Wallas), 295

Greece, 191

Green, Thomas Hill, 6, 15, 147*n*

Groups: local, 261; and the state, 238–39, 252, 279–81. *See also* Community

Guadalajara, Mexico, 209

Habit: and individualism, 334–36; political effects of, 273, 341

Hay, John, 174

Hayes, Carlton J. H., 341*n*

Hedonists, 139

Hegel, Georg Wilhelm Friedrich, 279

Henderson, Gerard Carl, 31*n*, 36*n*

Hippias, 128, 129

History: contemporaneous, 347; continuity of, 336

Hobbes, Thomas, 40*n*

Hocking, William Ernest, 271

Hodgson, Shadworth, 7*n*

Homer, 128, 129

"How to Make Our Ideas Clear" (Peirce), 4

Hudson, William Henry, 261–62

Hume, David, 7*n*, 154, 270

Idealism: practical, 167, 171, 172

Ideas: in experience, 156; knowledge as related to, 152, 154; Locke on, 141–42

India, 177, 179

Indians, in Mexico: 201–2, 205; education among, 200–205

Individual: and acts, 247, 249; defined, 351–53; distinction

Individual (*continued*)
　between social and, xxx–xxxi,
　244–45, 250, 274, 290, 327–
　28, 330, 351–55; economic,
　292; as fiction, 299, 333–34;
　and invention, 271–72; and
　officials, 282, 286, 309. *See
　also* State
Individualism: and collectivism,
　351–56; economic, 256–57;
　and experience, 55–61; expla-
　nation of, 296–99; influence
　of, 307–8; and method, 357;
　origin of, 249, 389–94; and
　private property, 273–74
"Individuality and Experience,"
　xvii–xviii
Innocent IV, Pope, 37; on spiri-
　tual power, 33 and *n*
Inquiry, xii, xxi; epistemological,
　45–49, 51, 54; naturalistic, 44,
　45, 54; social, xxx–xxxiv,
　351–72
Instincts: and social theory,
　241–44
Instrumentalism, 3, 19, 21; in
　education, xvii–xviii, xxi,
　55–61; and James, 13–15; as
　theory of intelligent conduct,
　ix–xxi
Intellect, 105–6
Intelligence: in conduct of social
　life, 231–34; and democracy,
　365–66; embodied, 360–61;
　and method, 114–15; necessity
　of, 243, 250–51, 329–37,
　353. *See also* Consequences;
　Knowledge
Interdependence, 332
International Conference: in Pe-
　king, 181, 184
Isolationism, 168, 169, 375

James, William, ix, 3, 40 and *n*,
　126, 231; achievement of,

158–59; on knowledge, 143*n*;
　on habit, 335; on pragmatism,
　xiii–xv, 6–8, 9–11, 13–17,
　160–62
Japan: anti-American attitude in,
　179–80; relationship of, with
　China, 176–78, 183
Jowett, Benjamin, 127
Juárez, Mexico, 195
Judgment: theory of, 17–18
Judicial empiricism, 28
"Juridical Persons" (Vino-
　gradoff), 41*n*
Justice, 138; and property, 292

Kallen, Horace M., 159, 160
Kant, Immanuel, 3, 4, 7*n*, 15, 27,
　31*n*; and "synthetic" value,
　88–89
Kemal, Mustapha, 190
King's Peace, 265
Knowledge: and causation, 142–
　43; and communication, 282–
　84, 371–72; correlated with
　certainty, 149, 153; divided,
　344–45; epistemological prob-
　lem of, 141, 143, 151; of the
　good, 92–94; of knowledge,
　132, 133, 135–36, 137–38,
　139, 141–42, 146; as percep-
　tion of a *relation*, 141–42,
　156; political, 336–37; as re-
　lated to temperance and cour-
　age, 128–31, 134

Labor legislation, 277
Laches (Plato), 124, 134, 139*n*;
　illustrates divisive philosophies,
　130, 132*n*; Jowett on, 127. *See
　also* Socratic Dialogues
Laissez-faire, 281, 292
Language: effect of, 47–49, 50
"La Notion de personnalité
　morale" (Michoud), 26*n*
Laski, Harold J., 39, 41*n*; on

groups within the state, 40 and *n*

Lausanne, second conference of, 190

Law: "natural," 291, 294, 299, 332; nature of, 268–71; Roman, 31*n*, 35 and *n*, 41 and *n*; social and physical, 357–58

Law in the Modern State (Duguit), 41*n*

League of Nations, 177, 375; court of, 170

Learning: two principles of, 56

Legal institutions, 246, 265; history and status of, 32

"Legal Personality," 22

Leibniz, Gottfried Wilhelm, 70

Lesser Hippias (Plato), 124, 127

Levinson, Salmon O., 171

Liberalism, 319

Liberty: as end in itself, 289; and "individualism," 296–97, 355–57; nature of, 329; of thought, 277–79; and uniformity, 369–70

Liking: thoughtful and impulsive, 74–76, 77

Lindsay, Alexander Dunlop, 32

Lippmann, Walter, 308*n*; on methods for practical democracy, xxiii, 213–20; and the "omnicompetent" individual, 334

Locarno, Switzerland, 169

Location: relation of, to event, 53

Locke, John, ix, xvii, 7*n*, 15, 48*n*, 51, 228; and contrast between idea and object, 142; on knowledge, 141–42, 146–47, 149, 151, 153–57; on natural rights, 289; on power, 141, 146, 147–48, 150–52; and threefold distinction of qualities, 143–45

Locomotion, 53

Logic: The Theory of Inquiry, xiv, xxiv

Logical method: in defining "person," 31

Lotze, Rudolf Hermann, 14

Lucretius, 133

Lysis (Plato), 124, 127

Macaulay, Thomas B., 298

MacDonald, Ramsay, 176

Machen, Arthur W., 22, 37*n*

Maitland, Frederic W., 30*n*, 34*n*, 35*n*; on nature of corporate legal personality, 23, 26, 39, 41, 42

Majorities, 364–65

Marden, Orison Swett, 207

Marx, Karl, xxxv, 378

Materialism, 343–44; compared with theism, 9

Meaning of Truth, The (James), 7, 10

"Meaning of Value, The," xix

Means and ends: in independent thinking, 57–60

Mechanism, 223–25

Megarics, 124, 125, 128

Meno (Plato), 130

Metaphysic of Morals (Kant), 3

Method: in creativity, 114–15; problem of, 355–62

Mexico: anti-clerical legislation in, 194–96; art in, 203, 208–10; Bolshevism in, 199, 210; education in, 199–205; Indians in, 200, 201, 202–3, 205; labor unions in, 207; as land of contradictions, 207–8; public health in, 206–10; relationship of U.S. with, 201–2, 205, 209–10; religion in, 194–98, 200–201, 208

Mexico City, Mexico, 206, 207, 208

Michoud, L., 26, 30

Middle Ages, 112
Mill, James, 148; on democratic government, 293–94
Mill, John Stuart, 7n, 357 and n
Mind and body, 104
Mobility: social effect of, 322
Monism, xiii, 8–9, 10
Moore, George Edward, 71, 77
Moral responsibility: between nations, 376
Moslems, 178
Münsterberg, Hugo, 77
My Heresy (Brown), 164

Nationalism, 341
"Naturalistic Theory of Sense-Perception, A," xv
Nature: division of, 47
Neo-Kantian idealism, 14
"News": meaning of, 347–48. See also Inquiry, social
Newton, Isaac, xxxii, 20, 142, 366
Nicene Creed, 165
Nicias: compared with Critias, 139; as humanist in Socratic Dialogues, 130–31, 136. See also Plato
Nishihara loans, 183, 403–4
Nominalism, 7
Nozick, Robert, xxxv–xxxvi

Oaxaca, Mexico, 208
Object, 86, 87; of mind, 141–42; and value, 88, 89–91; well-being of, 81–82; word reference to, 83–84
Objective reference: as related to criticism, 78, 87, 88–89, 91, 94–97; as related to value, xx, 78, 82–85, 88–89
Officers: as agents of public, 246–47, 256, 257, 277–78, 282; dual capacity of, 283, 286; selection of, 283–86

Old and New Testament, 165
Open Door, 174
Opinion, 345, 347
Organism, 223–25; integration of, 105, 106, 107–8
Organization: of community, 214–15
Osborne case, 41n
Otto, Max C., 161 and n, 162
Ottoman Empire, 192
Outlawry of war system, 167–72

Party politics, 309–11
Paternalism, 274
Peirce, Charles S.: on pragmatism, xii–xiii, xiv, 3–6, 7, 28–29
Peking, China, 181, 184
Perception: epistemological problem of, 45, 51. See also Consequences; Intelligence
Perry, Ralph Barton, xx, 80; defines value, 86, 90, 92
"Person": church and, 34n; fiction theory of, 33, 37 and n, 41n, 43; as legal conception, 22–43; the state as, 32 and n, 33 and n, 38; as subject of rights-duties, 26–27
"Personality of Associations, The" (Laski), 40n
Phaedo (Plato), 133
Phantom Public, The (Lippmann), xxii, xxiii, 213
Philebus (Plato), 133n
Philosophers: rivalry of, 124–26
Philosophy: divorced from science, 224–25; totalitarian, 379
Phronesis, 132n, 135. See also Good
Physical sciences: use of, 443–44
Picard, Maurice, 80
Pioneer conditions, 304–5
Plato, ix, 70, 71, 165; Socratic Dialogues of, 124–40

Pluralism, xiii, 8–9; political, 280–81

Political Theories, Ancient and Mediaeval (Dunning), 33*n*

Political Theories of the Middle Age (Gierke), 26

Politics: and business, 321, 348–49; parties and, 309–10

Populus: defined, 246

Position of Foreign Corporations in American Constitutional Law, The (Henderson), 31*n*

Potentiality, 47–48

Power: as related to Locke, 141, 146, 147–48, 150–52

Pragmatism, 28–29; American, 3–21; James on, xiii–xiv, 6–8, 9–11, 13, 14–17, 160–62; Peirce on, xii–xiii, 6–8, 9; and success, 161

Pragmatism (James), 161

Prall, David Wight, xix–xx; defines "Value," 69–77, 82, 83, 85–86; and influence of value on thought-process, 393–402. *See also* Value

Press, 219

Principles of Psychology, The (James), xiii, 15–16

Private: defined, 245

Prodicus, 132

Prohibition, 317–18

Propaganda, 348–49

Property: and government, 292–93; and individualism, 274; and justice, 292. *See also* Economics

Protagoras, 135

Protagoras (Plato), 127, 130*n*, 133, 134

Protestantism, 163, 166

Psychological adaptation, 223–25

Psychology: of habit, 273, 334–36; of individualism, 290; of private consciousness, 297; social effects of, 458–59

Public: complexity of, 316–17; democracy and, 283; eclipse of, 307, 311, 316–17, 320, 351; education of, 305–6; as intellectual problem, 330; Lippmann on, 213–20; marks of, 260–75; and opinion, 345–46; and ownership, 273–74; and political agencies, 255, 257, 259–60, 277; and private, 243–47, 265–68; problem of, 313, 351, 365, 370; publicity and, 339–42, 371–72; welfare, 167

Public and Its Problems, The, ix, xxiii–xxxv

Qualities: Locke's distinction of, 143–46, 154, 156–57; related to power, 150; as states of consciousness, 156

Railways: and government, 318

Rationalism: "transcendental," 77

Rawls, John, xxxvi

Reason: and law, 270–72; and natural science, 221–25; and the state, 248

Reasoning: intellectual and affective, 105–7

Relation, 156–57; connexion as distinct from, 148, 149; knowledge as perception of, 141–43; qualities of substances in, 144–46

Religion: modernists and fundamentalists in, 163–66; resists change, 223; and social institutions, 261–62, 266, 340–42

Republic, The (Plato), 133; on the good, 129*n*, 132*n*; and practise of virtue, 131, 135, 137–38; on unity and plurality of virtues, 130

Right-and-duty-bearing unit: person as, 23, 25, 27; social consequences of, 27, 29
Rights: natural, 289, 294, 299
Rignano, Eugenio: on reasoning, 105–6
Robinson, James Harvey, 217
Roman law, 31*n*, 35 and *n*, 41
Rousseau, Jean Jacques, 31*n*, 332
Royce, Josiah, 19, 126
Rulers. *See* Government; Officers
Russell, Bertrand, 13*n*, 71, 77; on education, 226–30
Russo-Japanese treaty, 176

Saleilles, Raymond, 29*n*
Santayana, George, 19, 126, 367; on value, 70, 71, 72, 74, 80, 92, 94
Savigny, Friedrich Karl von, 41
Schneider, Herbert W., 31*n*
Scholasticism: attitudes toward, 388–89
Science: applied, 342–45; and art, 106–8, 111–13; distinct from knowledge, 337–38, 342–43; Locke influenced by, 142, 145, 150; and method, 361; and the press, 348–49; social and physical, 47–48, 51, 54, 342, 347, 359–60
Science and the Modern World (Whitehead), 221–25
Scientific inquiry, 49
Scientific Thought (Broad), 29 and *n*
Self-mastery, 138
Self-relation, 131, 133
Sense-organs, 47–48
Sense-perception: nature of, 44–54; theories of, 45–48, 51–54
Sense qualities, 45, 47, 54
Shaw, Bernard, 227

Singapore, 176
Situs: conception of, 52–53, 54. *See also* Location
Smith, Adam, 244, 291
Smith, Thomas Vernor, 327*n*
"Socialization," 279
Society: human, 251–52; and states, 252–54, 278–81, 327–29. *See also* Association; Public
Sociology and Political Theory (Barnes), 40 and *n*
Socrates, 128, 137; as centre of Dialogues, 124–26; and comparison of *Protagoras* and *Charmides*, 133–35, 138; and health of soul, 131–32, 137, 138, 139; and rational morality, 93; and science of the good, 132–33; subjects own views to criticism, 126–27; and teachability of virtue in *Protagoras*, 130*n*; and wisdom in *Laches*, 130
Socratic Dialogues, ix; define problems, 125; interpreted, 124–40; portray rival thinkers, 124–25; style of, 125–27
Sophists, 124*n*, 140
Sophrosyne: defined, 138, 139; discussed in *Charmides*, 131–32; as supreme virtue, 137
Soviet Russia, 177–78, 378, 379
Spencer, Herbert, 16, 275, 284
Spinoza, Benedict, 70
Stages of history, 64
Standards of American Legislation (Freund), 36 and *n*
State: Aristotelian-Hegelian adulation of, 39, 40; as ideal, 377; as person, 32*n*, 33*n*, 41–42; relationship between groups and, xxiv–xxviii, 40 and *n*; and supreme power, 35

State Department, 181; in Mexico, 210
"State in Recent Political Theory, The" (Lindsay), 33n
Stein, Leo, 113, 114–15
Stillingfleet, Edward, 146n, 153
Story of Philosophy, The (Durant), 387
Studies in Logical Theory, 15
Substance: Locke on, 144–46
"Substance, Power and Quality in Locke," xvii
Supreme Court, 179
Symbolization, 79; of words, 83–84
Symbols: social import of, 323–24, 330–31, 371

Taff Vale case, 41n
Tariff, 317
Taste: aesthetic, 76
Teachers: reflect social conditions, 115–23; women as, 117–19, 121–22, 204
Technological development, 378
Theaetetus (Plato), 124, 130, 133n
Theism, 9
Theocracy, 261–62, 266, 285
Theories: of knowledge, xv–xvii, 46–51; political, 238–39, 241, 288. See also Causal forces; Individualism; Utilitarianism
Theory of Justice, A (Rawls), xxxv
Thinking: Cartesian sense of, 141
Thomas Aquinas, Saint, 33, 34
Thought: epistemological and naturalistic, 45–51; scientific, 221–25; social, 231–34
Thrace, 139
Tilden, Samuel J., 365
Tlaxcala, Mexico, 203
Tocqueville, Alexander de, 364
Toleration, 266–67

Tradition: authority and, 58, 59; European, 172; piety to, 166; revolt against, 288–89
Transcendentalism: German, 7
Truth: absolute, 12; meaning of, 6, 7, 8, 11, 12, 16
Turkey: China compared with, 193; democracy in, 191; economics in, 191–93; foreigners in, 190; Greece and, 191; as military state, 190–91, 192; problems in governing, 189–93; war-psychology in, 190

United States: capitalism in, 161; and China, 173–74, 176–80, 181–84; debates control of atom, 452; democracy in, 304–7; educational theory in, 115; and Europe, 170; Great Britain's relationship with, 177; immigration policies of, 178–79; influence of environment on thought in, 18–21; jurisprudence in, 36; and Mexico, 198, 201, 205, 209–10; practical idealism of, 167, 170; reflected in James's writing, 158–62; refuses to join League, 375; supports outlawry of war, 167–72
Universe, 13
Universitas, 26, 33. See also Corporate legal personality
Utilitarianism, 292

Value: ambiguity of term, 69–71, 82; criticism and, 78–97; defined by liking, 70, 71, 80, 82, 83, 87, 89–91, 95–96; differentiation of, 85–87; as essence, 72; existential question of, 71, 73, 94, 95; fulfillment and, 87–88, 89, 91; ideational

Value (*continued*)
  factor in, 88–89, 92–96; Kant
    on, 88–89; meaning of, xviii–
    xx, 69–77, 78–97; and objec-
    tive reference, 82–85, 87, 88–
    89, 91; thought and occurrence
    of, 69, 71, 73, 74
"Value and Thought-Process"
    (Prall), xix
Value-judgments, 78–79, 91–92,
    96–97
"Value, Objective Reference and
    Criticism," xx
Vasconcelos, José, 203
Vinogradoff, Paul, 41*n*
Virgil, 165
"Vitalism," 224

Wallas, Graham, xxii, 160, 231–
    34, 295
Wants: individualistic theory of,
    299; socially conditioned,
    299–300

War: First World, 314–16; mod-
    ern, 376–77, 378; outlawry
    of, 167–72; and selection of
    rulers, 284–85
Watson, John, 15
Whitehead, Alfred North, 29*n*,
    111, 113, 114; on sciences,
    221–25
Whitman, Walt, 350
Will: as cause of state, 248,
    259–60; and command theory
    of law, 269; general, 331; and
    government, 278; Kant's the-
    ory of, 31*n*; nature of, 30–31
Wilson, Woodrow, 295–96
Women: as teachers, 115–19, 121,
    204
Workers: emancipation of, 296–
    97. *See also* Economics
World War I, 314–16; disillusion-
    ment following, 168